God at War raises the current discussion of spiritual warfare
to a new and unanticipated level of scholarly investigation.
I am ecstatic with the integrity with which
Gregory Boyd develops his convincing argument
for a biblical warfare worldview. This is an extremely
important work for all who wish to
advance God's kingdom today.
C. PETER WAGNER
Fuller Theological Seminary

the goal of this book, p. 22

Glenn Schwartz (WMA) introduces
this book to me, April 7, 2000.

pp. 231-236

1. the classical philosophical tradition coming from Augustine
   ~~I~~ makes "the problem of evil" abstract & intellectual

   Boyd says this leads to quiet resignation and attributing evil to God.

2. the rationalism coming from the Enlightenment:
   "there are no personal demons."

3. the warfare worldview

   (Boyd)
   There is a conflict between God & Satan. Through the cross & the empty tomb, Christ is victorious over the powers, and so are we.

   We look forward to the climax. Maranatha!

GOD AT WAR

THE BIBLE & SPIRITUAL CONFLICT

GREGORY A. BOYD

— openness theology (a variation of Arminianism)

InterVarsity Press
Downers Grove, Illinois

InterVarsity Press® is the book-publishing division of InterVarsity Christian Fellowship®, a student movement active on campus at hundreds of universities, colleges and schools of nursing in the United States of America, and a member movement of the International Fellowship of Evangelical Students. For information about local and regional activities, write Public Relations Dept., InterVarsity Christian Fellowship, 6400 Schroeder Rd., P.O. Box 7895, Madison, WI 53707-7895.

Scripture quotations, unless otherwise noted, are from the New Revised Standard Version of the Bible, copyright 1989 by the Division of Christian Education of the National Council of the Churches of Christ in the USA. Used by permission. All rights reserved.

Cover photograph: Erich Lessing/Art Resource, NY

ISBN 0-8308-1885-5

Printed in the United States of America ♾

Library of Congress Cataloging-in-Publication Data

Boyd, Gregory A., 1955-
   God at war: the Bible and spiritual conflict/Gregory A. Boyd.
     p.   cm.
   Includes bibliographical references (p.   ).
   ISBN 0-8308-1885-5 (alk. paper)
   1. Demonology in the Bible.   2. Powers (Christian theology)—
Biblical teaching.   3. Spiritual warfare—Biblical teaching.
   4. Good and evil—Biblical teaching.   5. Christian ethics.
   6. Theodicy.   7. Evangelicalism.   I. Title.
   BS680.D5B68   1997
   235'.4—dc21   96-29821
                                                  CIP

21 20 19 18 17 16 15 14 13 12 11 10 9 8 7 6 5 4

14 13 12 11 10 09 08 07 06 05 04 03 02 01 00 99

This book is dedicated to Denay, Alisha and Nathan,
the three beautiful children with whom the Lord
has blessed my wife, Shelley, and me. We love you each profoundly.
But this is only a glimmer of what your Creator,
Savior and Warrior thinks of you.
May you accept and walk in the light.

Abbreviations

AB	Anchor Bible
ABD	*Anchor Bible Dictionary*, ed. D. N. Freedman et al., 5 vols. (1972)
ALUOS	*Annual of Leeds University Oriental Society*
AnBib	Analecta Biblica
ANET	*Ancient Near Eastern Texts Relating to the Old Testament*, ed. J. B. Pritchard, 3d ed. (1969)
ANF	Ante-Nicene Fathers
ANRW	*Aufstieg und Niedergang der römischen Welt*
AOAT	Alter Orient und Altes Testament
AOS	American Oriental Society
BA	*Biblical Archaeologist*
BAGD	W. Bauer, *Greek-English Lexicon of the New Testament and Other Early Christian Literature,* trans. and ed. W. F. Arndt, F. W. Gingrich and F. W. Danker, 2d ed. (1979)
BASOR	*Bulletin of the American Schools of Oriental Research*
BHH	*Biblisch-Historisches Handwörterbuch*, ed. B. Reicke and L. Rost, 3 vols. (1962-1979)
Bib	*Biblica*
BIS	Biblical Interpretation Series
BJRL	*Bulletin of the John Rylands University Library of Manchester*
BJS	Brown Judaic Studies
BSac	*Bibliotheca Sacra*
BTB	*Biblical Theology Bulletin*
BWANT	Beiträge zur Wissenschaft vom Alten und Neuen Testament
BZNW	Beihefte zur *ZNW*
CBQ	*Catholic Biblical Quarterly*
ConBOT	Coniectanea Biblica, Old Testament
CRINT	Compendia rerum iudaicarum ad novum testamentum
CSR	*Christian Scholar's Review*
CTJ	*Calvin Theological Journal*
DDD	*Dictionary of Deities and Demons in the Bible*, ed. K. van der Toorn et al. (1995)
DJG	*Dictionary of Jesus and the Gospels*, ed. J. B. Green et al. (1992)
EBC	*Expositor's Bible Commentary*, ed. F. E. Gaebelein, 12 vols. (1976-1981)
EMQ	*Evangelical Missions Quarterly*
ERT	*Evangelical Review of Theology*
ETSMS	Evangelical Theological Society Monograph Series
EvQ	*Evangelical Quarterly*
ExpTim	*Expository Times*
GP	Gospel Perspectives

HDR	Harvard Dissertations in Religion
HeyJ	*Heythrop Journal*
HSM	Harvard Semitic Monographs
HTR	*Harvard Theological Review*
HUCA	*Hebrew Union College Annual*
IB	*Interpreter's Bible*, ed. G. Buttrick, 12 vols. (1951-1957)
ICC	International Critical Commentary
IDBSup	*Interpreter's Dictionary of the Bible, Supplement Volume*, ed. K. Crim
Int	*Interpretation*
IRT	Issues in Religion and Theology
JAAR	*Journal of the American Academy of Religion*
JAOS	*Journal of the American Oriental Society*
JBL	*Journal of Biblical Literature*
JETS	*Journal of the Evangelical Theological Society*
JJS	*Journal of Jewish Studies*
JNES	*Journal of Near Eastern Studies*
JQR	*Jewish Quarterly Review*
JSJ	*Journal for the Study of Judaism*
JSNTSup	*Journal for the Study of the New Testament* Supplement Series
JSOT	*Journal for the Study of the Old Testament*
JSOTSup	*Journal for the Study of the Old Testament* Supplement Series
JSPSup	*Journal for the Study of the Pseudepigrapha* Supplement Series
JSS	*Journal of Semitic Studies*
JTC	*Journal for Theology and the Church*
JTS	*Journal of Theological Studies*
LUÅ	Lunds Universitets Årsskrift
NEB	New English Bible
NICNT	New International Commentary on the New Testament
NICOT	New International Commentary on the Old Testament
NIDNTT	*New International Dictionary of New Testament Theology*, ed. C. Brown, 3 vols. (1986)
NIV	New International Version
NovT	*Novum Testamentum*
NovTSup	*Novum Testamentum* Supplements
NPNF	Nicene and Post-Nicene Fathers
NRSV	New Revised Standard Version
NTS	*New Testament Studies*
OBT	Overtures to Biblical Theology
Or	*Orientalia*
OTP	*Old Testament Pseudepigrapha*, ed. J. H. Charlesworth, 2 vols. (1983-1985)
OTS	*Oudtestamentische Studiën*
POS	Pretoria Oriental Series
RelS	*Religious Studies*
RHR	*Revue de l'histoire des religions*
RSV	Revised Standard Version
SBLDS	SBL Dissertation Series
SBLSP	SBL Seminar Papers
SBS	Stuttgarter Bibelstudien
SBT	Studies in Biblical Theology
SHR	Studies in the History of Religion (*Numen* Supplements)
SJT	*Scottish Journal of Theology*
SNTSMS	Society for New Testament Study Monograph Series
SR	*Studies in Religion/Science religieuses*

INTRODUCTION
THE NORMATIVITY OF EVIL WITHIN A WARFARE WORLDVIEW

---

*A*FTER PRAYING AND FASTING FOR THREE WEEKS, DANIEL WAS finally visited by an angel. The angel reassured Daniel that his prayer had been immediately heard by God, and that he had been instantly dispatched in response to this prayer (Dan 10:12). Unfortunately, God's intended quick response was significantly delayed by the activity of a certain evil cosmic power that the angel identified as "the prince of the kingdom of Persia."

In the words of the angel to Daniel:

From the first day that you set your mind to gain understanding and to humble yourself before your God, your words have been heard, and I have come because of your words. But the prince of the kingdom of Persia opposed me twenty-one days. So Michael, one of the chief princes, came to help me, and I left him there with the prince of the kingdom of Persia. . . . Now I must return to fight against the prince of Persia, and when I am through with him, the prince of Greece will come. (10:12-13, 20)

There is no doubt among scholars that the "princes" referred to here, among whom Michael is "chief," are spiritual beings who oversee various territories.[1] The account, therefore, depicts some sort of angelic battle that took place behind the scenes of physical reality. Were it not for the revelation given by the angel, neither Daniel nor anyone else would have had any knowledge of this unseen battle.

For the author this behind-the-scenes battle explained the twenty-one-day delay in Daniel's receiving a response to his petitions. According to this passage, God's messenger literally got caught up in a spiritual battle that seemed to center on the "prince of Persia" trying to prevent Daniel from getting this message.[2] Were it not for Michael, apparently, Daniel might have been waiting even longer to hear from God.

The whole account sounds unbelievably bizarre to most modern Westerners, who are culturally conditioned to dismiss talk about non-physical conscious beings (angels) as superstition. Such concepts seem to be on the same level as science fiction. Even for modern Christians, who on the authority of Scripture theoretically accept the existence of such invisible beings, this account, for other reasons, sounds incredible.

After all, how many of us believers would consider the possibility of angelic interference as an explanation for why *we* sometimes do not see an answer to our particular prayers? Or how many of us might seriously consider the possibility of a menacing presence of an evil "prince" over our region as a factor in whether a child is molested, a baby is born healthy or ill, or a group of people accept or reject the gospel?[3]

This passage and others like it raise some questions that do not fit easily with our traditional Western theology. Do certain evil invisible cosmic beings really possess the power to disrupt a plan of God to answer a prayer? Can transcendent evil beings negatively affect us in a way that is similar to the way people who have authority over us (earthly princes) affect us? Is it really the case that whether we hear from God might have to do not only with God's will and our faith, as we Western believers customarily assume, but with the will of various created invisible beings who exist "above" us but "below" God?

What is more, is it really possible that our lives can be affected for better or for worse by what such invisible beings do, whether God is for or against their behavior? If so, where does this land the "omnipotent sovereignty of God" the church has always believed in? Finally, and most importantly for our purposes, what implications does Daniel 10 have for our understanding of the problem of evil? For among other things, the problem of evil centrally concerns the question of why God does not more often, and more speedily, intervene in the world in response to suffering.

Obviously, a number of significant features of this passage of Scripture simply do not rest well either with the naturalistic worldview of our post-Enlightenment culture or with standard evangelical theology regarding God's sovereignty and angels. The post-Enlightenment naturalistic worldview rejects such beings outright, while modern evangelical theology, following the Augustinian tradition, has tended to view angels merely as agents who invariably carry out God's sovereign will.[4] Yet, if read in a simple straightforward manner, Daniel 10 clearly affirms not only the existence of powerful angelic beings but also their ability either to cooperate with or to resist God's will. This passage further implies that at least part of what may be in the balance, as these beings either cooperate with or resist God's will, is our welfare.

Now if this passage stood alone within the corpus of Scripture, we might be able to dismiss it as a piece of apocalyptic hyperbolic imagery. But it does not. While few passages are as explicit as Daniel 10, the Bible from beginning to end presupposes spiritual beings who exist "between" humanity and God and whose behavior significantly affects human existence, for better or for worse. Indeed, just such a conception, I argue in this work, lies at the center of the biblical worldview.

Furthermore, one is hard-pressed to find any culture, prior to or contemporary with our own, that does not assume something like this perspective. From a crosscultural perspective, the insight that the cosmos is teeming with spiritual beings whose behavior can and does benefit or harm us is simply common sense. It is we modern Westerners who are the oddballs for thinking that the only free agents who influence other people and things are humans. As a means of exposing the myopic nature of our modern Western worldview, consider the following representations of this nearly universal worldview.[5]

The Warfare Worldview: A Crosscultural Perspective

The Shuar Indians of eastern Ecuador believe that there are two levels of reality: the "ordinary" physical world, which we experience with our senses, and the "real" one, which is experienced only occasionally, and mostly in dreams or in shamanic journeys.[6] Not only is the former level of reality less real than the latter; for the Shuar it is, in a most significant sense, regarded as being an out-and-out lie. For example, the notion that certain things in the physical world can exercise a causal influence on other things in the physical world is, they believe, an utter illusion.

According to the Shuar, the genuine cause of events in our "unreal" physical world is found in the "real" spiritual world, a mostly invisible dimension of reality that is virtually saturated with spirits. Some of these spirits are "true souls" *(nekás wakani)* of deceased ancestors now living among their descendants. Others are "true demons" who wander the forest in rather ugly (but usually invisible) forms. Some ancestors in the "real" world temporarily materialize as animals (often with their spouse). Others, after being "true demons" for a time, are transformed into huge butterflies *(wampam)*. Still other spirits are malicious (e.g., the *iwanci*) and can appear as various life-threatening animals, or as trees that attempt to fall on a person.

This invisible society of spirits is behind everything that occurs in the physical world—though one has to see past "the lie" to discern this society. The Shuar understand almost all sickness, misfortune and death, for example, to be the result of the activity of various kinds of hostile spirits, often summoned by the tribe's enemies.

Most sinister among the numerous types of spirits the Shuar speak of are the above-mentioned *iwanci*, or demons. Violent "accidental" deaths are usually attributed to these demons, who are believed to derive from souls *(muisak)* of slain warriors among the enemies of the Shuar. These demons, then, seek to avenge the murdered warrior—a conception of demons that is very frequent among primordial peoples.[7] It is believed that this vengeance of the *muisak* can be prevented only by shrinking the head of the slain warrior and capturing the soul before its departure. Hence the practice of headhunting for which the Shuar have become famous.[8]

The primary business of shamans (medicine men) within Shuar culture, as in many other primitive cultures, is to engage in warfare with these spirits on behalf of the members of his tribe. There is no "natural" evil here; there are only victims of supernatural evil.[9] The shaman's business, therefore, is to enter into the "real" nonordinary world and fight against such supernatural attacks.

The shaman is not defenseless, however, nor is he alone. He has been given supernatural "darts" *(tsentsak)* by digesting the regurgitation of a superior shaman, abstaining from sex for a year, and ingesting various insects believed to contain certain magical qualities. He also has at his disposal a number of different "spirit helpers," such as the *pasuk,* which can appear as an insect and spit fatal venom at the shaman's enemy, and the *wakani,* which is in the form of a bird and can cause insanity and death by flying over his enemy. High-level shamans can also transform their darts into other supernatural creatures that can fight on the shaman's behalf.

The warfare worldview. The worldview of the Shuar is one in which everything on the physical plane is understood against the backdrop of a highly influential, intricate and remarkably detailed spiritual world in which forces are at war with each other and through which people wage war against each other; the Shuar do not clearly differentiate these two spheres. While this worldview, like the one behind Daniel 10, sounds bizarre to many modern Westerners, it is hardly exceptional by historical and global standards. To the contrary, it was apparently self-evident to the vast majority of ancient people, and still is to primitive people today, that the world is not all physical, not even primarily physical, and certainly not all right.[10] It was, rather, a world that was populated with influential spiritual beings, some of whom were evil, and most of whom were at war with one another.

I call this basic understanding of the cosmos a *warfare worldview.* Stated most broadly, this worldview is that perspective on reality which centers on the conviction that the good and evil, fortunate or unfortunate, aspects of life are to be interpreted largely as the result of good and evil, friendly or hostile, spirits warring against each other and against us.[11]

The central thesis of this work is that this warfare worldview is in one form or another the basic worldview of biblical authors, both in the Old Testament and even more so in the New. This is not to suggest that the biblical authors (or any ancient people-group for that matter) deny that evil is also a reality of the human heart and of human society. To the contrary, biblical authors consistently demonstrate a passionate concern for confronting evil in all the individual and societal forms it takes. Therefore no biblical author suggests that warfare prayers or exorcisms are cure-alls for all that is wrong in the world.

I do suggest that biblical authors generally understood all evil in the context of spiritual war, however. For biblical authors, to wage war against such things as injustice, oppression, greed and apathy toward the needy was to participate directly or indirectly in a cosmic war that had

engulfed the earth. The central task of this work is to demonstrate just
this claim. The ultimate canvas against which the unfolding drama of
world history is played out is, for biblical authors, a warfare worldview.
In this regard these authors share a great deal with most other ancient
peoples.

A universally shared intuition.[12] It will prove helpful in demonstrating
the near universality of the intuited reality of spiritual conflict, and thus in
proving the myopic nature of the Enlightenment Western worldview, if we
illustrate the warfare worldview with a few more crosscultural examples. The
Wemale of Ceram, Indonesia, are continually at war against *halita*, demonic
spirits whom they believe can abduct and eat human beings, especially
children. They also must, through their shamans, wage war against the spirits
of disease that inhabit the sky, spirits called *waitete*, who specialize in sexual
problems, and evil *weddu*, who are believed to incarnate themselves (usually
as members of other tribes) and must be fought physically. Killing *weddu* is
almost as dangerous as letting them live. For if proper precautions are not
taken, it is believed that a *weddu* corpse can sever its own head, then fly
through the night and avenge its death by slaying its killers (usually with
curses, diseases, etc.).[13]

The Kamwe of northeastern Nigeria hold similar convictions. They
believe in one supreme being, Hyalatamwe, who is perfectly just and
created the world "perfect with no sickness and no death."[14] Evil arises
neither from Hyalatamwe nor from good spirits, but from evil spirits
who are almost always associated with various trees, rivers, stones or
caves. Breaking various taboos or offending ancestral spirits also invites
sickness and misfortune.[15]

Something like this spiritualistic worldview can be seen throughout
the ancient world, among the Babylonians, Canaanites, Egyptians (to a
lesser extent), Sumerians and even among the ancient Greek philosophers. For example, Plato simply assumes that the cosmos is inhabited
by good and evil demons *(daimons)*.[16] He and his colleagues assume that
these "middle creatures," being free, were capable of benefiting or
harming human beings.[17] For instance, it is common knowledge that
Socrates credited his personal *daimon* with leading him and instructing
him throughout his life.[18]

Moreover, these ancient Greeks, like almost all ancient and contemporary primitive cultures, believed that a person could willingly or
unwillingly be possessed by beneficent or malevolent spirits. Hence both

ecstatic trances and exorcisms, or something like them, are common in ancient cultures. While these possessions and exorcisms look quite a bit alike, how they are understood and how they are to be carried out differ widely from culture to culture. But the assumption that good and evil spirits (whether seen as gods, angels or deceased ancestors) can and do possess people is present nonetheless.[19]

Warfare mythologies. The prevalence of the warfare worldview is revealed not only in the similar practices of ancient and contemporary primitive peoples but also in the similar mythologies these various cultures possess. Their mythologies reveal the nearly universal conviction that the battlefield appearance of the world is the result of a real battle that once took place, or is still taking place, in "nonordinary" reality. Among the Iroquois, for example, hazardous aspects of the natural world like cliffs and mountains are seen as creations by the evil god Flint, who designed them as a means of preventing effective communication between humans and Flint's beneficent divine brother.[20]

Similarly, among the Yanomamö of South America, humanity's propensity toward violence is explained by telling a story of how two deities slew the evil spirit Mon, who was devouring the souls of their children. The dripping blood of this vicious Mon turned into human beings when it hit the earth.[21] The ancient Sumerians account for the uncontrollable features of human beings, and of the cosmos in general, in much the same way. As we shall see more fully in chapter two, these people speak of a certain good god Marduk, who successfully fended off the onslaught of an evil god of chaos named Tiamat. Marduk celebrated his victory by carving up Tiamat's body and forming the cosmos from her body parts, and by carving up her evil cohort to form humans. Our less-than-ideal natures are thus explained by referring to our less-than-ideal origin. The world is created by a mostly good god, but out of mostly destructive material. No wonder it is characterized by perpetually conflicting good and evil features.

Another fascinating and insightful myth is told by the Maidu tribe of northern California. Like many primitive peoples (see chapter three), the Maidu believe in one supreme Creator god along with a multitude of lesser gods or spirits. This Creator, with the help of two assistants, the "World-Chief" and the "Turtle," made the first two human beings out of the clay of the ground. All would have been well except for the intrusion of the mysterious Coyote. His origin is unknown, for he came out of the ground while the Creator was preoccupied elsewhere. But, interestingly enough, he is at once the greatest of all beings aside from the Creator (for he alone can behold the face of the Creator) and the worst of all beings (for he is incapable of doing anything other than evil).[22] All the evil in the Creator's world is somehow connected with this evil, but incredibly powerful, Coyote.

Closely related (though located on the opposite side of the globe) is the mythology of the Bhils of central India. Though they have absorbed some of Hinduism's propensity to think about God in impersonal terms, they nevertheless preserve an ancient belief in a personal creator named Bhagwan. Bhagwan created some lesser gods who lived in the bliss of Bhagwan's house, until "the Evil Spirit" tempted them to cease from doing work in order to be like Bhagwan (who has no need of work). In anger Bhagwan cast down these rebellious gods to the earth, out of which Bhagwan fashioned people to replace the fallen gods.[23] The fallen gods, and the Evil Spirit, still menace Bhagwan and his creation. As in all these myths, this story evidences a clear awareness that something has gone wrong with the world, that the world is at war, and that this war largely concerns unseen beings whose behavior significantly affects our lives, for better or for worse. Judged by biblical standards, this awareness must be affirmed as valid.

Santeria warfare mythology. Some of the most colorful and fascinating legends of spiritual warfare, and some of the most interesting and apparently effective divining techniques for engaging in warfare, come from the Santeria religion.[24] Almost every particular feature of the physical world is directly or indirectly explained by reference to some interaction between the gods *(orichas)*. But all evil, according to the legends of Santeria, derives ultimately from a certain Olosi. Olosi was made by the creator, Oloddumare, in order to remedy his own loneliness. The creator graciously (but somewhat unwisely) gave Olosi a power that was almost equal to his own.

Olosi became arrogant and greedy, however, and decided to usurp Oloddumare as the ruler of the earth. Since Olosi was nearly equal in power to Oloddumare, Oloddumare could not destroy Olosi or revoke his power. What he could do, however, was create other divine beings who could themselves (through procreation) create other divine beings, all primarily as a means of raising up an army against Olosi. In this fashion an entire family of deities *(orishas)* was eventually created by Oloddumare, each one of these deities having certain strengths and certain weaknesses.

Humans also were created in this program of Oloddumare. He had assigned his first and best creation, Oddudúa, to make a race of people out of clay to help care for the earth. Unfortunately, the evil Olosi caused Oddudúa to get drunk during the creation, which explains why humans are imperfect, weak and prone to illness, and why deformities frequently occur. Moreover, Olosi, having a power nearly equal to that of Oloddumare, was able himself to create other *orishas,* sinister gods who do his evil bidding. Hence it is not surprising that the world is full of pain and woe. It is, after all, a perpetual war zone between good and evil *orishas,* with a weak and deformed race of people in the middle of it!

We see that for the followers of Santeria, as for most other primordial peoples, the unusual combination of amazingly good and unthinkably evil features in our world is explained, or intuited, to be the result of the world being caught in a cosmic war between powerful good and powerful evil spiritual beings. Similar warfare stories serving a similar purpose can be found throughout the oral and written traditions of ancient and contemporary primitive peoples: the Hottentots of South Africa; the Nahuatl of Mexico; the Apaches, Chiricahua, and Papagoes of the American Southwest; and the Vedic poets of early Hinduism, to name but a few.[25] For all the significant differences among these various traditions, the fundamental and nearly universally shared intuition seems to be quite similar: the world is a spiritual battle zone, which is why it looks that way!

The Truth of the Warfare Worldview
It is all too easy for modern Western people, Christian and non-Christian alike, to dismiss mythologies and religious practices such as those we have been examining as amounting to nothing more than ignorant, primitive superstition. The warfare worldview that comes through in these mythologies and practices simply does not square with either our modern Western materialistic view of the world or many traditional Christian assumptions about God.

Nevertheless, it is the central contention of this work, and of a forthcoming volume (entitled *Satan and the Problem of Evil*), that the basic warfare worldview exhibited in these primitive mythologies and practices of these otherwise widely diverse cultures must be taken seriously, especially by Christians. Three considerations form the basis of my conviction.[26]

The warfare worldview of Scripture. First, as mentioned above, the warfare worldview is not only shared by most biblical authors but is central to the whole New Testament. The way in which Scripture portrays this warfare worldview differs significantly from that of most other cultures. For the biblical worldview is predicated on the assumptions that there is only one eternal God whose character is perfect and who is the omnipotent Creator and sustainer of all that is.[27] It is nevertheless clear that the biblical authors do espouse a warfare worldview that demonstrates many similarities to the warfare worldviews of other cultures.

Hence for all their emphasis on the radical uniqueness, sole eternality and absolute sovereignty of Yahweh, biblical authors generally assume the existence of intermediary spiritual or cosmic beings. These beings, variously termed "gods," "angels," "principalities and powers," "demons," or, in the earliest strata, "Leviathan" or some other cosmic monster, can and do wage war against God, wreak havoc on his creation and bring all manner of ills upon humanity. Whether portraying Yahweh as warring against Rahab and other cosmic monsters of chaos or depicting Jesus as casting out a legion of demons from the possessed Gerasene, the Bible as well as the early postapostolic church assumes that the creation is caught up in the crossfire of an age-old cosmic battle between good and evil. As in other warfare worldviews, the Bible assumes that the course of this warfare greatly affects life on earth.

Now, the very prevalence of the warfare worldview among so many different people-groups, in such radically different times and unrelated locations, should itself be enough to inspire us to take this worldview seriously. If we modern Westerners cannot "see" what nearly everyone else outside the little oasis of Western rationalism the last several centuries has seen, then perhaps there is something amiss with our way of seeing. It is just possible that the intensely materialistic and rationalistic orientation of the Enlightenment has blinded us to certain otherwise obvious realities. It is just possible that our chronocentrism—our tendency to assume that the worldview we hold at the present time is the ultimately true worldview—is preventing us from seeing significant features of reality.[28]

But even if the nearly universal intuition of cosmic conflict is not enough to call our own naturalism into question, the fact that this warfare worldview constitutes a central component of Scripture's understanding of God and the cosmos should surely inspire us to do so. At least for those of us for whom this collection of canonical books is no mere collection but rather constitutes the inspired Word of God, not seriously considering the warfare worldview can hardly be said to be an option, however much such a view may conflict with our own naturalistic cultural presuppositions. For again, as I demonstrate in this work, the thematic unity of Christ's ministry (as well as that of his disciples and the early postapostolic church) becomes fully intelligible only against the backdrop of a warfare worldview.

Myth anticipates reality. Indeed, I would go still further and argue that, if we consider the variety of warfare worldviews throughout the world and throughout history from a perspective that is thoroughly committed to Scripture, the most plausible way of understanding them is to see them as approximating and anticipating the truth revealed in Scripture. If we arrive at a full appreciation of just how thoroughly a warfare perspective is woven into the fabric of Scripture, all the pagan warfare perspectives present themselves as intuitive confirmations of the truth revealed in Scripture.[29]

In Scripture, and especially in the person of Jesus Christ, myth becomes reality, as C. S. Lewis insightfully put it.[30] In this light, the nearly universal myth of our world being largely shaped by warfare among various cosmic forces and spirits is here incarnated as the one true God-man warrior of God enters our real war zone and wages war against God's real foes.

In sum, then, the truth to which all these mythologies point, and indeed the truth to which the mythological warfare dimensions of the Old Testament itself point (see chapter three), is the truth that God's good creation has in fact been seized by hostile, evil, cosmic forces that are seeking to destroy God's beneficent plan for the cosmos. God wages war against these forces, however, and through the person of Jesus Christ has now secured the overthrow of this evil cosmic army. The church as the body of Christ has been called to be a decisive means by which this final overthrow is to be carried out (see chapters six to ten).

This is the truth to which the nearly universal intuition of spiritual warfare points. Thus from the perspective of Scripture, all the so-called primitive stories of cosmic conflict, and all the supposedly primitive techniques for waging war against evil spirits, must be judged as being far more true to reality than the Western "enlightened" worldview, which presumptuously holds that the cosmos is strictly material, that noncorporeal beings do not exist, and that humans are the highest form of life in the cosmos. If we can free ourselves from our own chronocentrism, which is in reality another form of ethnocentrism, the heavily tinted nature of our Western Enlightenment spectacles will become apparent.

The warfare worldview and evil. A second reason why I believe that the warfare worldview needs to be taken seriously is that it provides a remarkably different, and a remarkably better, understanding of evil than does the classical-philosophical Christian (or any other) approach to this problem.[31] In a nutshell, the way in which classical-philosophical Christian theists have approached the problem of evil has generally been to frame evil as a problem of God's providence and thus of God's character. Assuming (rightly) that God is perfectly loving and good, and assuming (wrongly, I hold) that divine omnipotence entails meticulous control, the problem of evil has been formulated within the classical-philosophical theistic tradition as the problem of locating a loving and good purpose behind evil events.[32] This, I later argue, represents an impossible task, and hence the problem of evil becomes simply unsolvable within this framework.

By contrast, the warfare worldview is predicated on the assumption that divine goodness does not completely control or in any sense will evil; rather, good and evil are at war with one another. This assumption obviously entails that God is not now exercising exhaustive, meticulous control over the world. In this worldview, God must work with, and battle against, other created beings. While none of these beings can ever match God's own power, each has some degree of genuine influence within the cosmos.

In other words, a warfare worldview is inherently pluralistic. There is no single, all-determinative divine will that coercively steers all things, and hence there is here no supposition that evil agents and events have a secret divine motive behind them. Hence too, one need not agonize over what ultimately good, transcendent divine purpose might be served by any particular evil event.

If the world is indeed caught up in the middle of a real war between good and evil forces, evil is to be expected—including evil that serves no higher end. For in any state of war, gratuitous evil is normative. Only when it is assumed that the world is meticulously controlled by an all-loving God does each particular evil event need a higher, all-loving explanation. For only then is evil not expected, hence only then is it intellectually problematic at a concrete level. In other words, only when we reject the view that the cosmos is something like a society of free beings, most of whom are invisible, and all of whom have some small degree of influence on the whole—in short, only when we reject the warfare worldview in favor of a monistic one in which one sovereign will governs all—are we saddled with an understanding of God and his relationship with the world in which evil becomes impenetrably mysterious on a concrete level.

Now, on the biblical assumption that God is the sole Creator of all that is, there is still the ultimately metaphysical question of why God would create a world in which cosmic war could break out. In this sense the problem of theodicy remains, even within a warfare worldview. But unlike the futile quest for the elusive good divine motive for any particular evil within the world, this metaphysical question is answerable. Instead of futilely trying to locate a particular loving divine reason for a particular evil event, we are now attempting to conceptualize God's most general reason for creating a societal cosmos in which a multiplicity of creatures share power, and in which moral conflict (and thus suffering) can therefore occur. But as was said, in contrast to the problem of evil within the classical-philosophical tradition, this question is not impossible to address.

Resignation versus revolt. Once the intelligibility of the war itself is accepted, no other particular evils require explanation. Hence Scripture gives none. This shift away from the classical-philosophical monistic perspective is empowering in terms of confronting evil, and this represents the third reason why I believe that Christians today need to take Scripture's warfare worldview seriously.

Put succinctly, the classical-philosophical assumption that a mysterious, loving, sovereign, divine plan lies behind even evil events in our world encourages an approach to evil that defines it as an intellectual problem to be solved rather than a spiritual opponent to be overcome. If all evil is believed to serve a higher divine purpose, then clearly one's sense of urgency in fighting it is compromised, while one's ability to render it intelligible is diminished.

This is precisely what has tended to happen within the Christian tradition since at least the time of Augustine. I believe it largely explains the Western church's long-standing propensity to theologize so much *about* evil while being relatively impotent in waging war *against* it. Whereas the New Testament exhibits a church that is not intellectually baffled by evil but is spiritually empowered in vanquishing it, the Western tradition has more frequently exhibited a church that is perpetually baffled by evil but significantly ineffective in and largely apathetic toward combating it.

Within a warfare worldview, however, particular evils are their own ultimate explanation: they flow from the wills of creatures, hence there need be no higher "good" divine reason for their occurring. Thus evil must be understood as being what God is unequivocally against, and thus what God's people must also be unequivocally against. Whereas the classical-philosophical theology of sovereignty encourages a theology of resignation, a theology rooted in a warfare worldview inspires, and requires, a theology of revolt: revolt against all that God revolts against.[33]

This is the only understanding that squares with Jesus' ministry and the whole of the New Testament, on the one hand. On the other hand, it is the only theology that is going to reappropriate for the contemporary church the power of the New Testament church to confront and overcome the evils in our present world. It is, as such, a theology that the church today must take seriously, despite the significant difficulties such a theology may create with our culture's naturalistic assumptions and with some of the church's traditional theology.

About This Work

As mentioned, this volume will be followed by another, entitled *Satan and the Problem of Evil.* The objective of both volumes is to explore the significance of the biblical portrait of Satan for a contemporary theodicy. The goal of this first volume is to demonstrate the thesis that the biblical writers, like almost all ancient peoples, held what I call a warfare worldview. Indeed, I hope to demonstrate the centrality of this warfare worldview for the biblical writers, especially in the New Testament, a centrality that has rarely been given its due.

The goal of *Satan and the Problem of Evil* shall be to provide a critical history of how the early church compromised the warfare worldview, and then to attempt to render the warfare worldview biblically and logically self-consistent, ironing out difficulties and objections that can

be raised against it. I hope to demonstrate thereby that this warfare
perspective constitutes the foundation for a theodicy that is philosophically superior to all alternatives, Christian and non-Christian alike.

To demonstrate the centrality of the warfare worldview in Scripture,
I have divided this volume into two parts. Following an introductory
chapter, chapters two through five concern cosmic forces of evil in the
Old Testament, while the last five chapters concern themselves with the
warfare worldview of the New Testament.

To be more specific, in my introductory chapter I set the stage by
presenting as concretely as possible the central problem we shall grapple
with throughout this volume and the next—the problem of evil—and
by addressing the two most fundamental obstacles that immediately
present themselves in the face of my warfare thesis: the problem of
believing in free and influential spiritual beings ("angels" or "gods") in
our modern age, and the problem of affirming their autonomous power
in the light of traditional understandings of God's omnipotence.

Chapters two through five discuss the warfare worldview of the Old
Testament. Chapter two first explores the Old Testament's appropriation
of the ancient Near Eastern view that the earth is inhabited by demons
and enveloped by hostile raging waters. Chapter three then explores the
Old Testament's use of various Near Eastern mythological representations of cosmic evil (Leviathan, Rahab, etc.). Chapter four addresses
the Old Testament's remarkable reflections on the existence and function
of angels (usually termed "gods" at this stage of revelation) who operate
under, and sometimes against, Yahweh. Chapter five addresses the Old
Testament's reflection about one particular angel who, we begin to learn
at this early stage of revelation, tended to operate outside, and against,
Yahweh's purposes. Throughout all of this I am interested in drawing a
connection between this reflection and the Old Testament's understanding of evil and suffering in this world.

The next five chapters (part two) address the nature and centrality of
the warfare worldview in the New Testament. Chapters six, seven and
eight explore the way in which the Gospels portray almost everything
Jesus was about within a warfare framework. He had, as John later put
it, come "to destroy the works of the devil" (1 Jn 3:8). Chapters nine
and ten explore how this warfare motif is carried on and developed
throughout the rest of the New Testament. Chapter nine centers on the
New Testament's cosmic warfare understanding of Christ's death, while

chapter ten focuses on the New Testament's warfare understanding of the church's mission.

Method. The goal of this volume is by no means uncontroversial, if not because of the thesis I defend, then because of the methodological issues it invites. As has been said, I essentially devote this volume to developing a broad biblical theology of Satan, the demonic and the human experience of evil, and I do so with the ultimate aim of constructing a contemporary compelling theodicy that understands evil within a warfare worldview. From a historical-critical perspective, however, such a project is problematic, to say the least. Indeed, the very concept of developing a topic-specific, trans-testamental biblical theology is, according to many, simply impossible.[34]

Thus many scholars today argue that the very attempt to discover what any particular author originally meant is misguided. Meaning is to be found (if it is to be found at all) between the reader and the text, not behind the text. Moreover, even if one could discover the original meaning of an author, the goal of developing a single "biblical" teaching on the basis of what various individual authors teach is altogether impossible. According to this perspective, the idea that a unity underlies the rich diversity within Scripture on any given theme is nothing more than a myth spun out of an uncritical bygone era. It should, as such, be rejected at the outset by historical-critical scholarship.

Such a perspective would utterly rule out developing a biblical theology about Satan, demons and suffering. Indeed, it would render any attempt to arrive at the biblical perspective on any matter impossible. But I simply do not accept this perspective. I cannot here offer anything like a thorough refutation of this objection, or even enter into a discussion of the issues. But it may prove helpful to the reader for me simply to state what my position is in response to this objection.

First, I write as a committed evangelical Christian, and so make no pretense to conducting my study from some supposedly neutral vantage point with a merely "descriptive" purpose. Practically speaking, then, I approach my task in a manner similar to those who would espouse a "canonical approach" to Scripture.[35]

Unlike some within this broad camp, however, I would argue for an objective, author-centered hermeneutical approach (as opposed to a purely community-based, "fideistic" hermeneutic), rooted in a strong, unifying view of divine inspiration.[36] I hold this position for a number of reasons, but in the end it centers on my historical grounds for believing in Jesus Christ as the Son of God, in believing on historical grounds that he held to a high view of Scripture, and in believing in the perspicuity of divinely inspired literature.[37]

The end result is that I hold to a divinely inspired unity that underlies the rich diversity of the biblical texts and that serves as the foundation for this present project of biblical theology, as well as the more constructive philosophical theology volume *(Satan and the Problem of Evil)* to be published subsequently.[38]

Style. A word should also be said about the style of this work. My driving conviction is that this issue is far too important not to be discussed in accordance with the stringent expectations of biblical and theological scholarship, but too important as well not to be communicated in a way that opens it up for nonspecialists. Most of the works on Satan and spiritual warfare in the last several decades have had popular appeal but have lacked scholarship, while most sophisticated works on the problem of evil, in the present as well as in the past, have been intellectually inaccessible to lay readers. My hope is that this work can bridge these two worlds. I am aiming to provide a comprehensive scholarly work on Satan and the problem of evil that is, nevertheless, accessible to nonspecialist readers.

I have attempted to accomplish this task by writing the body of the text without presupposing any prior acquaintance with the relevant issues and by keeping the main text as free as possible from specialist jargon and specialist issues. I have attempted to maintain the academic integrity of the work by incorporating the specialist discussions and bibliographical information into the endnotes. The result may be that some scholars will find the main text at times to be too general, while some lay readers will find some of the endnotes to be too technical. Specialists are therefore advised to take the endnote discussions seriously, while nonspecialists are advised not to worry if they occasionally have difficulty with the endnotes.

Central objective. Throughout our investigations and deliberations, I trust that it will become increasingly apparent that the understanding of the world as being caught up in cosmic warfare constitutes one of the central threads that weave together the whole tapestry of the scriptural narrative. God's age-long (but not eternal) battle against Satan forms one major dimension of the ultimate canvas against which everything from creation to the eschaton within the biblical narrative is to be painted and therefore understood.

As I proceed with this endeavor, I trust that it will also become apparent that this warfare perspective produces a radically different way of framing evil than the way Christians today tend to frame it. We shall see that New Testament authors were inclined to attribute pain and suffering to the evil purposes of Satan and demons. By contrast, we (indebted as we are to Augustine) are inclined to attribute pain and suffering to the mysterious "good" purposes of God. New Testament authors were inclined to expect evil and fight against it. By contrast, for theological reasons we are inclined not to expect it, therefore to be baffled by it when it occurs, but (all too often, at least) nevertheless to strive to accept it as coming from the loving hand of Providence when it occurs. The problem of evil that New Testament authors grappled with was simply the problem of overcoming it. The problem of evil we Westerners usually grapple with is the problem of intellectually understanding what we unfortunately rarely seek to overcome.

If this work helps us move more toward a New Testament (viz., a warfare) perspective on the problem of evil, it will, from my vantage point, have been a success.

A Word of Appreciation

Finally, a number of individuals share the credit for whatever value this work has. My deepest gratitude and love goes out to my wife, Shelley, and my three children, Denay, Alisha and Nathan (to whom this book is dedicated), who patiently put up with a sometimes sleep-deprived and grouchy husband and father. I also appreciate so much their sharing in my enthusiasm over new findings and new ideas—even when they did not have a clue as to what I was talking about.

I wish to also express a word of gratitude to Bethel's new provost, Jay Barnes, who granted me course release time to complete this project; to my colleague David Clark, who offered critical insights into sections of this work; to Tyler and Chelsea DeArmond and Sandra Unger for their outstanding editorial work; and to my friend and the senior editor of this project, Rodney Clapp, whose critical insight has made this work much better than it would have otherwise been, and whose humor has made getting this book finished much more fun than it would have otherwise been.

I must also express my gratitude to the many passionate believers of Woodland Hills Church whom I have had the great privilege of serving as a preaching pastor for the past four years. They have helped fuel my passion for spiritual war, and have then put up with me when I have occasionally become perhaps a little obsessive in my preaching on this topic. Finally, I need to give a special word of appreciation to my friend, colleague and now fellow laborer in the church, Paul Eddy. His deep biblical and historical knowledge, combined with his spiritual insight, has proved invaluable in the many prolonged discussions and debates we have had on this topic. Though he by no means embraces all the views expressed in this book, much of its content has been crystallized by my interactions with him.

PART I

THE WARFARE WORLDVIEW OF THE OLD TESTAMENT

1

HEARING ZOSIA

THE PROBLEM WITH THE PROBLEM OF EVIL

*A*S I SAID IN THE INTRODUCTION, THE CULTURES OF THE OLD and New Testaments, like most ancient and primordial cultures, exemplify a warfare worldview: a fundamental view of the world as engulfed by spiritual beings who are, at least at times, in conflict with one another and whose behavior significantly affects our lives, for better or for worse. I maintain that this worldview accounts for the fact that biblical authors, unlike us, saw little need to wrestle with the intellectual problem of evil, while, again quite unlike us, they were passionately engaged and supernaturally empowered in confronting it. Generally speaking, these believers did not, for example, wonder why God allowed a person to be crippled with scoliosis; they simply attributed it to Satan and exercised spiritual authority in coming against the affliction (Lk 13:10-17; cf. Acts 10:38).

Three Fundamental Objections
For many, however, three fundamental considerations could disqualify this spiritual warfare perspective on evil at the outset. Therefore we need

to address them before we begin to flesh out the warfare thesis.

First, the apologetic need for a warfare perspective on suffering and evil will not be seen if there is an insufficient appreciation for the radicality of evil in our world and the radical nature of the problem this poses for the classical-philosophical understanding of divine sovereignty as meticulous control. Many times this radicality is not appreciated in contemporary discussions on the problem of evil, a fact that contributes to a pervasive willingness to accept shallow explanations for why evil occurs.

Second, this thesis requires a willingness to think about the power of God, the reality of evil and the influence of Satan in some rather untraditional ways. This point is disturbing to many more traditionally minded believers.

Third, the warfare thesis requires, as a central component, a belief in angels, Satan and demons as real, autonomous, free agents, as well as a belief that the activity of these beings intersects with human affairs, for better or for worse. Many modern people, including many Christian theists, find this belief inherently implausible.[1]

Before discussing the biblical material, therefore, we need to address these three obstacles. Hence in this chapter I first attempt to present the problem of evil in a concrete, as opposed to an abstract, form. Evil cannot be adequately conceptualized in the abstract. It can be experienced only in particular forms. The plausibility of a warfare worldview within our naturalistically inclined culture, however, hangs upon an ability to realize the full horror of evil, which means acknowledging it on a concrete level. Radical solutions are plausible only as solutions to radical problems. When considered concretely, the classical-philosophical problem of evil is a radical, indeed an unsolvable, problem for the understanding of God's power and providence that has prevailed within classical-philosophical theism. Though it may indeed appear radical to believers who are strongly influenced by the classical-philosophical perspective, I believe that the cosmic warfare perspective on evil constitutes the only orthodox theistic approach that avoids this unsolvable problem.

Following this discussion, in response to the second obstacle I attempt to lay the groundwork for a subsequent revision of the classical-philosophical approach to understanding evil by noting several peculiar features of its formulation of the problem of evil. These unusual features suggest that something is askew in the manner in which the problem of evil has been construed as a search for a divine reason behind each and every particular evil. This point further suggests that perhaps the understanding of providence which lies behind this formulation of the problem is mistaken.

Finally, in response to the third obstacle, I examine various features of our rapidly changing Western culture that suggest that, while many may still find a belief in angels, Satan, demons and the like to be implausible, our culture as a whole increasingly does not. The Western church, and the whole of Western culture, is now embarking on a postmodern age in which most of the features of the classical-philosophical theistic worldview, and certainly fundamental features of the rationalistic Enlightenment worldview, are being jettisoned. While this "new age" presents unique problems for the church to address, it also presents many unique positive opportunities—if the church is willing to seize them.

One of these opportunities is the chance to reappropriate and render intellectually viable a largely lost dimension of the biblical worldview: the dimension of spiritual warfare. This warfare worldview not only contributes to the resolution of the intellectual problem of evil by providing an ultimate context in which radical evil is not unexpected; it also, for this very reason, inspires believers to take on the problem of evil at a spiritual level—at the level of spiritual warfare—which is by New Testament standards where the real "problem" of evil lies.

The Concrete Problem of Evil

Historian Philip Friedman provides the following eyewitness account of what happened to a young Jewish girl living in the Warsaw ghetto during the Nazi occupation.

> Zosia was a little girl . . . the daughter of a physician. During an "action" one of the Germans became aware of her beautiful diamond-like dark eyes.
>
> "I could make two rings out of them," he said, "one for myself and one for my wife."
>
> His colleague is holding the girl.
>
> "Let's see whether they are really so beautiful. And better yet, let's examine them in our hands."
>
> Among the buddies exuberant gaiety breaks out. One of the wittiest proposes to take the eyes out. A shrill screaming and the noisy laughter of the soldier-pack. The screaming penetrates our brains,

pierces our heart, the laughter hurts like the edge of a knife plunged into our body. The screaming and the laughter are growing, mingling and soaring to heaven.

O God, whom will You hear first?

What happens next is that the fainting child is lying on the floor. Instead of eyes two bloody wounds are staring. The mother, driven mad, is held by the women.

This time they left Zosia to her mother. . . .

At one of the next "actions," little Zosia was taken away. It was, of course, necessary to annihilate the blind child.[2]

While philosophers argue endlessly about how precisely to define "evil" in abstract terms, none of us has difficulty recognizing this concrete nightmare as an example of it. At the very least, evil consists of the fact that for far too many people—as for Zosia and her mother, along with six million other Jews during the Holocaust—life becomes a horrifying nightmare from which they cannot awake, a nightmare as full of pain as it is devoid of meaning.

Radical evil of this sort cannot be captured in abstract definitions. Indeed, "abstractions . . . *distract* us from that immediate reality [of evil] and reduce evil to a statistic," as Jeffery Burton Russell suggests.[3] The essence of evil transcends words, for words are always one step removed from concrete reality. Evil cannot be adequately grasped in a detached, neutral, abstract way. It cannot be known through faceless, nameless statistics or abstract theorems. All approaches to the problem of evil that do not go beyond these will be in danger of offering cheap and trite solutions. Radical evil can be known only when incarnated and experienced concretely.

For our purposes, then, evil is the concrete picture of Zosia, her mother and a million other similarly unthinkable atrocities. We must entertain concrete pictures like this when we discuss the problem of evil, if our discussion is to be authentic. As Russell again observes: "Only when the abstractions are put aside can we see the face of the Devil gloating over suffering. The modern experience of evil is the reek of burning children. Every honest view of reality must confront the immediate, personal, physical reality of the burning child."[4]

Hence when I speak of "evil" throughout this work, I am not referring primarily to some abstract "absence of goodness" (Augustine) or any other merely theoretical definition of evil. I am, rather, referring to Zosia, her mother and the unheeded cries and unpunished laughter that rose

up to heaven on that day. By extension (but not abstraction!), I am
referring to every concrete horrifying experience that in various ways
looks and feels like this one.

The fact that real life is often demonically nightmarish is a problem
for all humans on at least emotional, psychological and practical levels.
It is the problem of staying sane in a world where little children can be
treated as Zosia was treated. It is the problem of understanding how
humans can sink to the level of the mindless Nazi pack that tortured her.
And it is the problem of devising ways of protecting the Zosias of the
world from the Nazis of the world.

But evil is a problem on a metaphysical level as well for people who
believe that God exists, at least as "God" has been defined in the
classical-philosophical tradition of the Christian church.[5] This philosophical and theological tradition, represented most forcefully by such
towering figures as Augustine and Aquinas, and in my view expressed
with the most logical consistency by Calvin and the Reformed tradition,
formally holds that God is among other things altogether above time,
change and passivity (viz., the capacity to be influenced by another).
Without usually intending to deny free will, this tradition also held that
God exercised absolute sovereignty over the world, which entailed that
he directly or indirectly exercised a meticulous control over things. Most
importantly for our purposes, this view at the very least held that all
things, even bad things, have a specific divine purpose for their existence.[6]

Now, when these divine attributes and this view of meticulous providence are combined with the biblical understanding that God is altogether loving, then a significant problem arises. For it seems that, within
this sort of divine providence, innocent little children should never have
to suffer as Zosia suffered. If God is all-loving and perfectly good, he
must *want* to protect Zosia. And if God exercises total control over the
world, he must *be able* to protect Zosia. Yet Zosia suffers an unspeakable
ordeal, then is murdered. This makes no sense and constitutes, in its
starkest form, the intellectual problem of evil.

The occurrence of one nightmare like Zosia's is thus an intense intellectual problem for classical-philosophical theists. But to fully grasp the
problem that evil poses to a theist, we must consider, as concretely as
possible, that history is awash with unimaginable nightmares like Zosia's.
Indeed, while we believers frequently wax eloquent in declaring how the

intricate design and grand beauty of the cosmos are evidence of an all-good Creator, in honesty we must also confess that the world is full of occurrences that evidence either the nonexistence of a good and all-powerful God, or the existence of a very powerful, competing, evil god.

Adrio König certainly expresses an impression shared by many: "Anyone who refuses to idealize or romanticize reality, but looks it straight in the eye, sees around him more signs of the demonic than of the true God. Indeed, there is more pain and misery, injustice and violence in this world than love, prosperity, justice and joy."[7]

Hence, the intensity and scope of radical evil in the world is a significant problem for classical-philosophical Christian theists. If we consider it concretely and do not retreat to romanticized abstractions and sheltered idealizations, the macabre dimension of reality seems to require some alteration in the classical-philosophical Western understanding of God. How can we intelligently and morally believe that an altogether loving God is altogether sovereign over the world when the world he is supposedly meticulously controlling is in so many ways an obvious abomination?

Hymns of praise and screams of terror. Even this statement of the problem of evil is too abstract, however. It does not yet capture the sharpness of the antinomy created by radical suffering for belief in an all-loving, meticulously sovereign God. Like the problem of evil itself, the antinomy must be made as concrete as possible to be adequately grasped.

Nothing expresses the faith and trust of the church in the controlling sovereignty of God more concretely than its traditional hymns. With a view to attaining a ruthlessly honest perception of the problem we are up against, consider the following very real possibility: While Zosia was being held down and tortured, while she was screaming and the guards were laughing and her mother was going mad, at that very moment, in other corners of the earth—and perhaps just around the block—Christians were gathered together and were singing traditional hymns of praise to the Lord, hymns that exalt the Creator for his faithfulness, his loving care for the world, and his providential tender protection of his children.

For all we know, a congregation just down the road from Zosia's hell was singing Sandell's famous hymn "Day by Day."

The protection of his child and treasure
Is a charge that on himself he laid;
"As thy days, thy strength shall be in measure,"
This the pledge to me he made. . . .

Help me, Lord, when toil and trouble meeting,
E'er to take, as from a father's hand,
One by one, the day, the moments fleeting,
Till I reach the promised Land.[8]

The hymn captures poignantly the church's traditional theology of God's character, his meticulous providential care, and thus the pious resignation that, according to the classical-philosophical teaching, should characterize believers who truly trust in their heavenly Father. Following the admonition of Augustine, we ought to consider all the harm inflicted on us by others, however painful, as coming from our Father's hand. For, the teaching goes, no one can do anything to us except as he "allows"—and allows for a good specific reason.[9]

Hymns like this one have provided peace and security to countless believers throughout the ages. But if we do not cover our ears, our singing must be haunted by Zosia's screams and the Nazis' laughter. Was Zosia not "God's treasure"? Why was she not protected?

What is more, can anyone really regard the "toil and trouble" she and her mother endured as coming from "a father's hand"? If so, what kind of father are we singing about? Or, some might even dare to wonder, was Zosia (and her six million kinfolk) perhaps not included in God's loving care because she was Jewish? Isn't such a suggestion—all too frequent in the church's history—as thoughtlessly shallow and non-Christian as it is demonically insensitive?[10] Didn't we all crucify Christ? Didn't he already pay the price for all sin? Don't Christian children sometimes suffer nightmarishly too?

In any event, we must wonder what sort of God would inflict, or "allow," anything like this hideous savagery on an innocent little girl for any reason—let alone for something her remote ancestors supposedly did. Such "explanations" simply express and exacerbate the problem in need of explanation. The childish screams and Nazi laughter of Zosia and her predators haunt whatever solace hymns like "Day by Day" bring us. To be sure, if we follow König's advice and refuse to "idealize or romanticize reality" but look it straight in the eye, it becomes questionable whether the lyrics of this hymn, and all hymns like it, continue to provide any real comfort. To some of us, it has become questionable whether they are even meaningful in light of nightmarish experiences like that of Zosia.

Another hymn that nicely captures the classical-philosophical theology of God's providence, a hymn that, for all we know, was being exuberantly proclaimed while Zosia's mother was being driven mad, is Lloyd's famous hymn "My Times Are in Thy Hand."

> My times are in thy hand
> Whatever they may be:
> Pleasing or painful, dark or bright,
> As best may seem to thee.
>
> My times are in thy hand:
> Why should I doubt or fear?
> My Father's hand will never cause
> His child a needless tear.[11]

Again, if we have the courage to allow the antinomy between the lyrics of this hymn and Zosia's tortured screams to engage us on a concrete level, the antinomy borders on the unbearable. What does it mean to assert that the hand of the all-powerful and all-loving Father "will never cause his child a needless tear" when asserted in the vicinity of a child who just had her eyes plucked out and of the screams of Zosia's terrorized mother? In this concrete context, does not suggesting that this event came from the hand of God, and that it came about "as best it seemed to thee," come close to depicting God in Hitlerian terms? What is more, would not such a conception significantly undermine the godly urgency one should have to confront such evil as something that God is unequivocally against?[12]

And so it is with a hundred other hymns that Christian congregations around the globe sing routinely, and indeed could have been singing at the moment of Zosia's torture. Ascending up to heaven alongside the screams and sinister laughter could have been the sung proclamation that "Behind a frowning providence [God] hides a smiling face," or "His purposes will ripen fast, Unfolding every hour. . . . The bud may have a bitter taste, But sweet will be the flow'r."[13] Zosia's torture, we are apparently to believe, was but the bitter-tasting bud of a beautiful, divinely ordained flower. Behind the apparent divine frown here (the Nazi guards) is, we are supposed to affirm, God's hidden, sovereign, smiling face.

Divinizing the nightmare. Such conceptions, I submit, simply add a divine dimension to, and thus infinitely intensify, the enormity of the barbarism under consideration. It is no longer simply the purpose of the Nazi guards we must struggle against—that is nightmarish enough. We must now intellectually struggle with the supposed purpose of a sovereign smiling God using them to achieve his own beautiful providential ends. The Nazis' agenda somehow here seems to receive divine approval. Yet while we are to view the Nazis' agenda as being diabolically evil, we are apparently supposed to accept that God's agenda in ordaining or allowing the Nazis' behavior is perfectly good.

Within the classical-philosophical theology expressed in many traditional hymns, such a conclusion seems unavoidable, however unpleasant it sounds, and however contradictory to our reason it seems. For the foundation of the classical-philosophical portrait of God's relationship to the world is the conviction that whatever happens must somehow fit into God's sovereign plan. All things must ultimately follow a divine blueprint that is, in detail, foreknown and willed by God. Thus whether we speak of God "ordaining" or "allowing" the evil to occur, there must always be a divine purpose for it occurring. It is all decreed by God because "all things work together for good" (according to one common interpretation of Rom 8:28). In classical theological thinking, events may occur "against" God's will, but paradoxically they can never occur outside God's will.[14]

R. C. Sproul well presents the classical-philosophical reasoning behind the understanding of omnipotence as omni-control:

> If there is one single molecule in this universe running around loose, totally free of God's sovereignty, then we have no guarantee that a single promise of God will ever be fulfilled. Perhaps that one maverick molecule will lay waste all the grand and glorious plans that God has made and promised to us. . . . Maybe that one molecule will be the thing that prevents Christ from returning.[15]

Among a host of other problems, this "all or nothing" line of reasoning seems oblivious to contemporary quantum theory, which successfully operates with a purely statistical understanding of natural regularity.[16]

But our present interest concerns the problem of evil. While this omni-control model of divine sovereignty may provide a sense of security to many believers, it functions as something of a cosmic megaphone for the macabre screams of the Zosias of the world—if we do not run from the concrete world into the realm of romanticized abstractions. When we do not flinch from gazing upon evil in its concrete manifestations, all such talk begins to ring hollow and borders on becoming meaningless if not positively immoral, as Ivan suggests in *The Brothers Karamazov*.[17]

Evil and faultfinding. Nevertheless, the theology of God's sovereign, all-controlling providence, expressed throughout the Western church's hymns, has permeated Christian theology and Western culture in general. With such a view, it is hardly surprising to find believers and nonbelievers alike, past as well as present, instinctively attributing various evils to the "mysterious will" of the all-holy God of the Bible.

To mention a few examples I am personally acquainted with, a local newspaper recently quoted a mother of a twelve-year-old girl who had years before been kidnapped, raped and killed by an evil person. In the course of speaking about the killer's soon release from prison (on good behavior!) the woman sorrowfully admitted that she had never forgiven God for taking her child the day she was murdered. She lost her faith, she confessed, when she lost her daughter.

But what, we must ask, could have led this poor woman instinctively to blame God for her daughter's diabolical death? What could have inspired her to implicate God for what a twisted, evil person freely chose to do? Was it not the widespread cultural assumption, derived from the classical-philosophical theology and traditional hymnody of the church, that believing in God means accepting all things as coming "from the Father's hand"? Was it not the entrenched belief that somehow all events, however horrifying, fit into God's plan, and thus that this young girl's vicious suffering must somehow serve a divine purpose? Indeed, if God the Father's hand oversees every event in world history, and if, as the hymn says, "the Father's hand will never cause his child a needless tear," was not this woman correct in thinking that it was ultimately God's will, not just the will of her daughter's killer, that caused her daughter to endure such an unthinkable ordeal?

Such thinking is widespread both inside and outside the church—outside often in the form of rage, as with this tormented mother; inside often in the form of clichés. It is expressed in the young man's rage against God for paralyzing him in a freak rugby accident as well as in the televangelist's shallow and insensitive assurance to the people of Oklahoma City, the day following the tragic bombing of their Federal Building in the spring of 1995, that God is "up to great things" in Oklahoma and that all the people of this good city should "expect a miracle!" (One wonders what consolation this "word of encouragement" ministered to the dozens of parents of the murdered children.) It is expressed in one man's indignation toward God for taking his loving young wife with leukemia, as well as in another man's assurances to this distraught husband that "God knows what he is doing," "God's ways are not our ways," "God is still on his throne," "There's a silver lining in every cloud," "All things work together for the good," and the like.

Christian orthodoxy, of course, has always taught that God is omnipotent, and for good reason. Scripture is unequivocal on this point. But the question that needs to be asked is this: Does this omnipotence necessarily entail that God is all-controlling, as the classical-philosophical tradition after Augustine has been inclined to assume? Does affirming that God is omnipotent commit one to the view that a good divine purpose lies behind all particular events, as the above hymns suggest? If it does, then it seems that we must consider both the rage of the unbeliever and the shallow, trite piety of the believer to be essentially correct. Zosia's torment, then, is indeed from her heavenly Father's loving hand.

In what follows, however, I propose an alternative understanding, one that I believe characterizes both the Bible and the early pre-Augustinian church, and one that avoids the unacceptable consequences of the Augustinian model.[18]

Perhaps even more disturbing, however, has been the church's tendency to go beyond merely supposing that God has a mysterious reason for allowing suffering to specifying what this reason is: God's desire to punish us for our sin. While the Bible certainly teaches that God sometimes uses suffering to punish or to discipline people, this motif did not attain the status of a universal explanation for evil until Augustine.[19] Since Augustine, it has constituted the most frequent explanation in the church, and in Western culture in general, for why people suffer. Though it directly opposes the standard Protestant understanding of the atonement (in which all sin has already been atoned for), and though an entire book of the Bible is devoted to its refutation (Job), and though Jesus himself teaches against it (Lk 13:1-5; Jn 9:1-5), it has nevertheless dominated the church's thinking on this subject throughout history and continues to exercise a strong influence today.[20]

Whenever we respond to misfortune with the question, "What did I do to deserve this?" we are echoing this traditional theodicy. Whenever we ask (as our culture incessantly asks), "Why do bad things happen to good people?" we are reflecting the widespread assumption that bad things are supposed to happen to bad people.[21] That is how God "gets even" and sinners learn their lesson.

When well-intentioned Christians sometimes attribute a person's sickness or failure to get healed to their supposed lack of faith, this assumption is also at work. When various people try to explain AIDS as God's punishment for homosexuality, or the Midwest's floodings or California's earthquakes and fires as God's retribution for sin, or when anti-Semitic believers follow the darkest tradition of the church in explaining Hitler's attempted genocide of the Jewish race by appealing to their complicity in crucifying Christ, this traditional Augustinian assumption is at work. People suffer, we are to believe, because they deserve it!

"Explanations" like this obviously accomplish something, otherwise they could not have survived so long. At the very least, they express a confidence in God's absolute sovereignty (defined here as "control") that seems to provide many believers with a great deal of security. However bad things may appear, this view says, everything is under God's control. Everything is proceeding as divinely planned. Everything somehow fits together. In the words of Boethius: "God, the author of all natures, directs and disposes . . . all things towards goodness. . . . Everyone thinks that evil is so prevalent on earth; but if you could truly see the plan of providence, you would perceive that evil has no place left for it at all."[22]

Undoubtedly most people would like to think that this belief is true—hence the mass appeal of the classical-philosophical Augustinian theodicy. Such "explanations" themselves become the problem in need of explanation, however, when it becomes painfully obvious that life is simply not okay. In the vicinity of Zosia's screams—that is, when it is our spouse who dies, or our child who is kidnapped, or our relatives who were gassed in Auschwitz—such explanations ring hollow at best. More probably, they sound positively abusive. How can God not see this as

evil? What could you (as opposed to someone else?) have done to deserve
this? What kind of God would even consider punishing you, for any
reason, by torturing your child? What good and wise divine purpose
could lie behind any child's kidnapping?

There comes a point when even suggesting such an overarching
"good" scheme becomes as cruel as it is ridiculous—if we continue to
think concretely about the reality of evil. If we do not flinch from the
concrete horror, there comes a point when the notions that God has a
purpose for everything, that things always go his way, and that nothing
can genuinely oppose him get stretched to the breaking point. Then we
are ready to consider abandoning the Augustinian divine blueprint
model of divine sovereignty and seriously reconsider the pre-
Augustinian, biblical understanding of the world as involved in cosmic
war. Aside from its biblical grounding, no other view of the world really
makes sense in the vicinity of Zosia's nightmare.

The Problem with the Problem of Evil
This intellectual problem of evil constitutes the single most difficult
challenge to classical-philosophical Christian theism. Not surprisingly, then, the church's theological tradition has often been obsessed
with this issue, at least since the time of Augustine. Volumes upon
volumes have been written with the express purpose of rationally
reconciling the belief in an all-good and all-powerful God with the
reality that life is frequently an inescapable nightmare. Indeed, it is
not overstating the case to claim that no single theological problem
has occupied more intellectual energy, time and ink than this one.

This way of formulating the problem of evil has, however, three rather
curious features that call into question the assumptions that give rise to
it. First, at least according to the thinking of many theists (including
some classical-philosophical theists), this way of posing the problem
seems to render it logically unsolvable. This is odd if the classical-philosophical theistic view that gives rise to this problem is indeed a true view
of God. Second, in sharp contrast to the history of Christian reflection
within the classical-philosophical tradition, Scripture shows no awareness
of this problem, a point that further suggests that Scripture reflects a
conception of God (and perhaps the cosmos in general) different from
that of the classical-philosophical tradition. Third, not only is the classi-
cally formulated problem of evil absent from Scripture, but the view of

evil that is found in Scripture runs directly counter to the view of evil presupposed in this formulation of the problem.

All of this suggests that there is a serious and fundamental problem with the problem of evil as it has been formulated in the classical-philosophical tradition. In what follows I shall flesh out each of these three features in their respective order.

The unresolvability of the problem of evil. Despite the enormous amount of intellectual energy poured into this problem by the church's most brilliant minds, as well as by people outside the church, the problem of evil, as it has been formulated within the Western classical-philosophical tradition, has not been solved. According to many thinkers, this is because this problem, as it is here formulated, is simply logically unsolvable.[23]

The core problem seems to lie in the classical-philosophical equation of power with control, and thus omnipotence with omnicontrol, an equation that forces the problem of evil to be seen as a problem of God's sovereignty. If it is accepted that God is all-loving and all-powerful, and if maximum power is defined as maximum control, then by definition there seems to be no place for evil. If goodness controls all things, all things must be good.

Yet Zosia and her mother experienced an unthinkable nightmare. How is this possible? The reality of our experience and the assumptions of our theology seem to contradict one another here. Though classical-philosophical theologians have valiantly, and at times ingeniously, attempted to resolve this contradiction, many believe that it has not been and cannot be removed.

I have already alluded to the possibility that one could remove the contradiction while retaining the view that God is all-loving and all-powerful by simply denying that the world is evil. Remarkably, this view has exercised a strong influence on the church's reflections on theodicy throughout history. Some of the church's most weighty authorities, such as Boethius and Augustine, explicitly embraced it.

This view in essence maintains that what looks like evil does so simply because of our limited perspective on "the universal good." If we could but view any "evil" event from God's transcendent, panoramic, timeless perspective, we would supposedly see how any given event "fits" in with the God-ordained harmonious cosmic whole. However horrifying the event may appear to our limited perspectives, from God's universal perspective, and in accordance with God's meticulous universally controlling will, the "evil" event actually contributes to the beauty of the whole.

Hence as both Augustine and Boethius admit explicitly, for God there is, quite literally, no evil. "Evil does not exist at all," Augustine says, "and not only for you [God], but for your created universe, because there is nothing outside it which could break in and destroy the order which you have imposed upon it. But in parts of the universe, there are certain elements which are thought evil because of a conflict of interest."[24]

What seems evil, because it conflicts with our finite interests, is actually a dimension of a higher harmony. For Augustine, therefore, we ought to regard everything as flowing from God's sovereign loving hand. Even when an innocent person suffers unjustly at the hands of another person, Augustine maintains, "he ought not to attribute [his suffering] to the will of men, or of angels, or of any created spirit, but rather to His will who gives power to wills."[25]

The Nazi guards, we are apparently to believe, could do to Zosia only what God explicitly empowered them to do to her. Thus she and her mother, together with the rest of us, are apparently supposed to attribute her tragedy not so much to the evil will of the diabolical Nazi guards as to the will of Zosia's Creator. Why would Zosia's Creator will such a thing? Again, Augustine declares,

> God would never have created any . . . whose wickedness He foreknew, unless He had equally known to what uses in behalf of the good He would turn him, thus embellishing the course of the ages, as it were an exquisite poem set off with antitheses. For what are called antitheses are among the most elegant of the ornaments of speech.
> . . . As, then, these oppositions of contraries lend beauty to the language, so the beauty of the course of this world is achieved by the opposition of contraries, arranged, as it were, by an eloquence not of words, but of things.[26]

Zosia's torture, and all the pain of the cosmos, is divinely "arranged" because the cosmos, like a poem, is more beautiful when it is "set off with antitheses." The "opposition of contraries" renders God's creation all the more "exquisite." In this sense, there is ultimately no evil.

Such an approach has some appeal when evil is considered merely at an abstract level, as "the absence of the good." As said above, it is certainly comforting to believe that there is a silver lining in every cloud.

But when evil is considered in all its dimensions at a concrete level, the supposition that there is a higher perspective that harmonizes all the conflicting parts of this sometimes nightmarish earthly existence simply becomes unacceptable. As Ivan cries out in *Brothers Karamazov*, "I renounce the higher harmony altogether. . . . It's not worth the tear of . . . one tortured child."[27]

Affirming that what happened to Zosia was, from any perspective, not utterly evil sounds not only shallow but also as if it partakes in the evil of the deed itself. However much theologians may protest, the affirmation, if thought through consistently, seems to make God out to be a Nazi, and the Nazis' butchering of Zosia to be in some mysterious way godly. Hitler and most Nazis believed that the extermination of the Jews was "good" only in the sense that it was a necessary step toward "the greatest good." If this classical-philosophical Augustinian approach is correct, the only mistake the Nazis made was in determining just what "the greatest good" was.

If we further consider that this divine panoramic view within which all evil is supposedly a "secret good" is held by a God who, according to Scripture, has a passionate hatred toward all evil, the "solution" becomes more problematic still. For it is certainly not clear how God could hate what he himself wills and sees as a contributing ingredient in the good of the whole. If all things ultimately play themselves out according to a prescripted divine plan, how can God genuinely hate anything?

Yet in scriptural terms God is all-holy at least in part precisely because of his holy hatred toward evil. Evil is evil precisely because God hates it. For example, we read:

You hate all evildoers. You destroy those who speak lies; the LORD abhors the bloodthirsty and deceitful. (Ps 5:5-6)

Pride and arrogance and the way of evil and perverted speech I hate. (Prov 8:13)

You love righteousness and hate wickedness. (Ps 45:7)

His soul hates the lover of violence. (Ps 11:5)[28]

Hence too, all who love the holy God are enjoined to hate evil with him (Ps 97:10; Amos 5:15). Indeed, "the fear of the LORD is hatred of evil" (Prov 8:13).

This central scriptural theme, however, presupposes that evil exists for God as well as for humans, that God does not will it, and thus that some beings (those who are evil) have the ability to act against God's will. It requires the understanding that it is possible for some beings (angels and humans at least) genuinely to resist, and even to thwart, whatever blueprint God might wish their lives to follow. It requires accepting the view that God, for whatever reasons, designed the cosmos such that he does not necessarily always get his way, and may in fact detest the way some things are turning out. It requires the view that God does not monopolize power, and hence that omnipotence cannot be equated with meticulous omnicontrol. It therefore requires that we do not find solace in any view that would try to reduce evil down to an aesthetic antithesis that secretly contributes to the higher harmony of the cosmic whole.

But it is precisely this view of omnipotence as omnicontrol that the classical-philosophical theistic perspective logically implies and has often explicitly affirmed. Hence it has always leaned strongly in the direction of affirming that evil ultimately fits into God's beautiful sovereign plan, even though he (paradoxically) hates it. As Augustine teaches, evil may go against God's will, but it does not occur outside it. The unresolvability of the classical-philosophical problem of evil lies precisely in the unintelligibility of this position.

Freedom and providence. This is not to say that the classical-philosophical tradition explicitly denied that humans, and even angels, have free will. To the contrary, except in a few extreme forms of Calvinism, the freedom of creatures has in some fashion always been affirmed. Therefore the ability of these creatures in some sense to go freely against God's will has always been affirmed as well.

Unfortunately, this trajectory of reflection that centered on the self-determination of angels and humans, a line of reflection implicit in the biblical narrative and explicit in the pre-Augustinian early church, was severely compromised with the increasing influence of Platonic and Aristotelian categories, climaxing in the Neo-Platonic/Christian synthesis of Augustine. For now, all things, including free actions, were subsumed within the sovereign divine will. This rendered the freedom of the actions in question ambiguous, to say the least.[29]

Hence while both Augustine and Boethius (not to mention Aquinas, Luther and indeed most theologians in the classical-philosophical tradition) affirmed that evil originated from the freedom of creatures, not from God, they nevertheless also held that there was a transcendent divine purpose behind the creaturely willing that, we have seen, meant that the evil performed by the creature ultimately contributed to some higher good. For these authors, the blame for evil attached to the creature, though the evil as a preordained constituent to a higher good was credited to God. For example, these theologians would generally want to affirm both that the Nazi guards were to blame for the evil they freely inflicted on Zosia and her mother, and that the event was nevertheless ordained by God for a greater good.

This approach, then, wanted to hold both to the freedom of creatures and to the absolute sovereignty (defined here as meticulous control) of God. They wanted to accept the morally responsible freedom of creatures, but also to retain the belief that all events, including morally responsible free actions, follow a divine blueprint and thus fit into God's ultimate will for his creation.

Unfortunately, however, the maneuver simply cannot be rendered logically coherent, despite the best efforts of some of the church's best minds to make it so. While it lies outside the scope of this present work to attempt to make this case, the postulation of a preordained divine blueprint logically undermines the force of seeing creatures as genuinely free, and vice versa. In the end, therefore, I would argue that the paradoxicality of this "solution" simply repositions the paradoxicality of the problem of evil it is designed to solve. Indeed, it is the problem of evil all over again, but restated from a different direction.

Some theologians within the classical-philosophical tradition, however, have been somewhat more logically consistent in working out the implications of the concept of freedom and have therefore significantly qualified the classical-philosophical understanding of God's omnipotence as entailing omnicontrol. Especially in the post-Reformation era many have explicitly rejected the Augustine assumption that the will of God can never be thwarted. These theologians (traditionally labeled Arminians) have seen that the affirmation of creaturely freedom entails that God might not always get his way.

This approach, if carried through consistently, removes the earlier mentioned contradiction between the experience of Zosia screaming and the classical-philosophical theology of God's power precisely because it removes the classical-philosophical equation of ideal power and maximum control that gave rise to it. Unfortunately, however, this view has rarely been carried through consistently. More specifically, four problems have tended to surround the traditional Arminian approach to understanding freedom and evil, all of which concern the fact that it has not removed itself far enough from classical-philosophical assumptions about God.

First, Arminian theologians have not generally followed through the logic of their insight into the nature of creaturely freedom to its logical (and biblical) conclusion. For example, despite their view of freedom, Arminian theologians have on the whole still accepted the classical-philosophical understanding of God's immutability, timelessness, impassibility and so on. These attributes, I have elsewhere argued, derive more from Hellenistic philosophy than from the Bible, and they render genuine freedom on the part of created beings impossible.[30]

Second, and closely related to the first point, even though they affirm that creatures have power to act over and against God, Arminian theologians have nevertheless usually rejected the possibility of strictly gratuitous evil. That is, despite their view of creaturely freedom, they have nevertheless usually wanted (inconsistently, in my view) to affirm that God allows specific evil events to transpire for a specific divine purpose.[31] They would, for example, still be inclined to say that "God had his reasons" for at least allowing Zosia's torture to transpire.

Traditional Arminian theologians, therefore, have actually had their own qualified "blueprint" understanding of providence, despite their emphasis on human freedom. In this respect they have remained within the classical-philosophical theistic tradition. But just this traditional understanding largely undermines the advantages their understanding of freedom has for a cogent theodicy. We are still left with the unsolvable theodicy question of what a specific "loving" reason might look like for God "allowing" Zosia's eyes to get plucked out.

Third, and again closely related to their classical-philosophical view of God, Arminian theologians have generally wanted to affirm that God possesses exhaustive, detailed knowledge of what shall occur in the future. This view may further call into question the integrity of creaturely freedom within their theological framework.[32] Affirming that what shall transpire is eternally known by God in exhaustive detail presupposes that the future is in some way eternally "there" in exhaustive detail. But this understanding of the future, I suspect, is unbiblical on the one hand, and perhaps undermines the openness to possibilities that is the sine qua non of morally responsible, free decision-making, on the other. Unless the future really consists (at least in part) in possibilities among which free creatures choose, and thus unless the future is known by God as being (at least in part) a realm of open possibilities (for God's knowledge always perfectly corresponds with reality), then self-determining free-dom, it seems, cannot be consistently maintained.[33]

Put otherwise, if God's knowledge of the future eternally consists exclusively in a knowledge of "this and not that" (viz., it is exhaustively definite) rather than including elements of "possibly this or that" (viz., it is indefinite), then it is difficult to understand how free creatures can have the genuine power to choose between "this and that." Nor is it easy to come to grips with the clear meaning of many passages of Scripture that speak of God changing his mind or that speak in hypotheticals ("perhaps") and conditionals ("if . . . then").[34]

It is this understanding of the future as eternally definite in God's mind that largely contributes to the assumption that there must be a divine reason for why God allowed, or explicitly ordained, a particular evil event to transpire. For if God has exhaustively definite knowledge of what shall transpire, then it seems that he, being all good, must have a particular good reason for choosing to create this particular world in which he knows that this particular evil will certainly occur. For example, we must wonder why God created Adolf Hitler when he supposedly knew with absolute certainty—and eternally—exactly what monstrosities Hitler would carry out. God, it seems, unleashed a rabid pit bull on humanity, knowing full well exactly what this pit bull would do, and to whom he would do it. Since God is all-good, it seems that he must have had a specific good reason for unleashing this (and every other) pit bull on his children. But this is obviously the classical-philosophical problem of evil all over again. We still must wonder, what might this higher good reason look like?[35]

In my estimation, classical-philosophical Arminian theologians have provided no adequate answer to this question. But the very way the question is posed requires that there must be some such higher reason, if indeed the future is there for God to exhaustively foreknow. As I have said, it is this supposition of a particular divine reason behind all particular evils in the world that generates the classical-philosophical unresolvable formulation of the problem of evil.

Finally, and for our purposes perhaps most importantly, the traditional Arminian theodicy has been significantly weakened because it has on the whole restricted its understanding of freedom to human freedom. At the very least, it has not made a robust appeal to angelic freedom in its theodicy reflections, and thus has attempted to wring an explanation of evil almost entirely out of the exercise of human freedom (and from an inconsistent view of this freedom at that). When measured against the vastness of the cosmos and the enormity of evil in need of explanation, however, human freedom seems remarkably small and quite incapable of bearing the cosmic weight that the classical Arminian approach has usually wanted to place on it.[36]

If, however, we are willing to suspend for a time the classical-philosophical conception of God as altogether above time, change, passivity, and as exhaustively controlling; and if we are willing to think through the implications of creaturely freedom in a consistent, logical and biblical manner; moreover, if we are willing to consider the possibility that spiritual forces exist, some of whom are perhaps major cosmic forces who possess morally responsible free will just as we do, then, I believe, we are on our way to a perspective of God and his relationship to the world in which evil does not constitute an unsolvable intellectual problem. We are, in short, on our way to embracing a warfare worldview.

The absence of the problem in the Bible. Thus far I have spoken of the peculiar unsolvability of the problem of evil as one indication that something is perhaps amiss in the way this problem has been formulated within the classical-philosophical tradition. A second peculiarity of this problem that further calls into question the classical-philosophical assumptions about God which generate it is that the problem seems to be wholly absent from the New Testament, and arguably from the whole Bible.

To be sure, individuals throughout the biblical narrative occasionally express convictions that come close to the classical-philosophical formulation of the problem of evil. Why do the righteous suffer and sometimes feel forsaken? David wonders (Ps 10:1; 22:1; 42:9). What wrong has Job done to deserve the suffering he is going through? his friends inquire. Why has God brought starvation and disaster on his people? Jeremiah cries out (Lam 2:20-22). Why was a certain man born blind? Jesus' disciples wonder (Jn 9:1-5). What divine purpose might have been served by a tower falling on a crowd of Gentiles? others ask (Lk 13:1-5).

What is interesting about all this, however, is that Scripture itself never teaches that these questions are based on an accurate understanding of God! To be sure, some narratives clearly teach that affliction is sometimes brought about as a punishment or as discipline from God, as mentioned earlier (e.g., Gen 18:20—19:29). Several passages are even sometimes misinterpreted to teach that Yahweh is himself the cause of evil (see chapter four). But never does Scripture teach that suffering is always, or even usually, a form of divine punishment.

Indeed, as mentioned earlier, in a number of places Scripture seems to directly refute this position. The book of Job, I later argue, is a prolonged assault on just this erroneous "moralistic accountant" conception of God (see chapter four). The false dichotomous assumption, reflected throughout this poetic dialogue, that Job's sufferings are either Job's fault or God's fault is refuted by both the prologue of this book, which ascribes the afflictions to Satan (Job 1—2), and the divine monologues in which Yahweh does not take responsibility for Job's afflictions but rather refers Job to the vastness and complexity of the creation, a creation that includes forces of chaos (such as Leviathan [chap. 41] and Behemoth [40:15-24]) which need to be tamed).

Similarly, Jesus undermines his disciples' erroneous assumption that the cause of blindness had anything to do with the ethics of the blind man or his parents (Jn 9:1-5; cf. chapter eight). He explicitly teaches that catastrophes are not necessarily indications of the victims' sinfulness or of God's judgment (Lk 13:1-5). Indeed, as we shall see in chapters six and seven, whenever Jesus does identify a spiritual agenda behind an evil in the world, he identifies it as Satan's, not God's.

What argues for the same point in a more general way is the simple observation that biblical authors on the whole seem largely unaware of any antinomy between their faith in an all-good and all-powerful God, on the one hand, and the reality of intense suffering in the world, on the other. As Walter Wink notes specifically about the New Testament: "The early Christians devoted a great deal of energy to discovering the meaning of Jesus' death, but nowhere do they offer a justification of God in the face of an evil world. They do not seem to be puzzled or even perturbed by evil as a theoretical problem."[37]

Indeed, following Wink, we may go even further: Whereas the later church's intellectual problem with evil consisted in the seemingly obvious fact that evil is not what one would expect in a world run by an all-good and meticulously sovereign Creator, the earliest disciples, including the earliest postapostolic fathers, seemed to think that evil was precisely what one should expect in this world. Nowhere is there the slightest hint in the New Testament or in the early postapostolic church of anyone asking the earlier mentioned question modern people instinctively ask: "Why do bad things happen to good people?"[38] To the contrary, these early Christians rather teach that suffering in this world is precisely what a person should expect, especially if they are "good."[39]

But why is there this radical difference between the view of evil held by the New Testament and early postapostolic church and the later post-Augustinian church, especially since the church is supposed to be doctrinally rooted in Scripture? How could the later church be so obsessed with something that the New Testament virtually ignores?

The answer is obviously not that Jesus or his disciples were unacquainted with real suffering. Nor is the answer that they lacked the intellectual astuteness to see that a belief in an all-good God who exercises exhaustive control over the world is inconsistent with the prevalence of unjust suffering in the world. As suggested earlier, the answer is rather that one works within a warfare worldview, which expects evil, whereas the other does not.

Put otherwise, in contrast to the later church, neither Jesus nor his disciples seemed to understand God's absolute power as absolute control. They prayed for God's will to be done on earth, but this assumes that they understand that God's will was not yet being done on earth (Mt 6:10). Hence neither Jesus nor his disciples assumed that there had to be a divine purpose behind all events in history. Rather, they understood the cosmos to be populated by a myriad of free agents, some human, some angelic, and many of them evil. The manner in which events unfold in history was understood to be as much a factor of what these agents individually and collectively willed as it was a matter of what God himself willed.

For example, Paul's inability to reach Thessalonica had nothing to do with either what he willed or what God willed: in his mind, it was simply the result of Satan hindering him (1 Thess 2:18). Similarly, a person's deafness or muteness had nothing to do with either what that person willed or what God willed: it was, for Jesus, at times at least the result of demons (Mk 9:25). Or, to cite an Old Testament example, the delay in heavenly assistance in response to Daniel's desperate prayer had nothing to do either with Daniel or with God: both wanted the prayer answered! According to this inspired work, it rather had to do with a menacing demonic power that interfered with the whole process (Dan 10; cf. Ps 82).

All of this brings us to the third and most important questionable feature of the classical-philosophical formulation of the problem of evil:

its failure to express the central role Satan and evil angels play in the New Testament's understanding of evil in the world.

Satan in the New Testament and later church. The central difference in perspectives between the New Testament and early postapostolic church on the one hand and Augustine and the later church on the other is that the former almost unanimously locates the ultimate reason for why there is evil in the world in the evil will of Satan, while the post-Augustine church and the whole of the classical-philosophical tradition following him tends paradoxically to locate the ultimate rationale for evil within the mysterious, omnibenevolent, all-encompassing will of the Creator. "Providence," writes Boethius, "is the unchangeable direct power that gives form to all things which are to come to pass." It is a "definite order [which] embraces all things," for "the Creator of all nature . . . directs and disposes all things for good." Thus, Boethius concludes, a believer should "reckon naught as bad of all the evils which are held to abound upon earth."[40]

Hence instead of combating an evil agent who is believed to inflict evil upon the earth, in Boethius's writings we are encouraged to accept all that is reckoned as bad as coming from an all-good agent—the "Creator of all nature . . . [who] disposes all things for good." Augustine argues in the same fashion. To put the contrast in its most terse form: the classical-philosophical problem of evil is constituted by the difficulty of conceptualizing God's reason for ordaining, or at least allowing, particular evils to occur, while the New Testament everywhere assumes that the ultimate reason behind all evil in the world is found in Satan, not God.

The later church thereby acquired an intellectual problem with evil that the New Testament simply does not have. For a variety of reasons, the later church attempted to understand evil as a function of God's all-good and all-controlling providence rather than as a function of Satan's evil, controlling rule over the world.[41] The former is problematic while the latter is not, assuming (as the New Testament does) that angelic free will is intelligible. If a self-determining, supremely evil being rules the world, then it is hardly surprising that it is deluged with nightmarish evil, despite having been created by an all-good, omnipotent Creator.

To be more specific, Satan is portrayed in the New Testament as being the "god of this world," "the ruler of the power of the air," and "the ruler [*archōn*] of this world" (2 Cor 4:4; Eph 2:2; Jn 12:31; 14:30;

16:11). He is portrayed as possessing all the kingdoms of the world, and is explicitly said to have control of the entire world (Lk 4:6; 1 Jn 5:19). He is portrayed as being ultimately the one behind murder, lying, persecution, and even physical sickness and disease (Jn 8:44; 1 Jn 3:12; Lk 13:16; Acts 10:38; Eph 6:12-13). Moreover, he and his fallen army are portrayed as having supernatural capabilities to obstruct kingdom work, manipulate crowds, choke faith, demonize people and even keep little children in spiritual bondage (2 Thess 2:9, 18; 1 Cor 2:8; Mt 13:19; Mk 7:25; 9:17-22).[42]

Indeed, the general assumption of both the Old and the New Testament is that the earth is virtually engulfed by cosmic forces of destruction, and that evil and suffering are ultimately due to this diabolical siege.[43] As we shall subsequently explore in depth (chapters six to eight), Jesus most centrally defined himself and his ministry in terms of aggressively warring against this Satanic kingdom. Both he and his disciples recognized that he had come to destroy the devil and his works, thereby redeeming his people from the realm of darkness and setting them free for the kingdom of God (Jn 3:8; Col 1:13; Heb 2:14; Col 2:13-15). Indeed, as I shall show, all the various aspects of Jesus' ministry—his healings, teachings, exorcisms, death and resurrection—attain a thematic unity only when viewed against the background of this cosmic warfare.

In the light of all this, it is quite peculiar that after Augustine, throughout the church's history up to the present, very few thinkers conceived of Satan as being in any way relevant to, let alone central to, the solution to the problem of evil.[44] It is remarkable that the one who in Scripture and in the earliest postapostolic fathers is depicted as the ultimate originator of evil and the one ultimately behind all the world's horrors has been thoroughly ignored in discussions on the problem of evil.

To be sure, the figure of Satan continues to permeate the thinking of the church in other respects throughout history, at least up until the time of the Enlightenment. As was said, the church retained at least an echo of the warfare worldview. But in terms of arriving at an ultimate explanation for evil, after Augustine the question always gets filed under the category of God's providence instead of under the category of spiritual warfare, that is, under the topic of what Satan, rebel angels and fallen humans freely choose to do against God's will.

With Augustine it becomes a problem of understanding evil as part of God's will.[45]

By contrast, the New Testament and early postapostolic church always thought of the problem of evil in the context of spiritual warfare. The world is caught up in a cosmic battle and thus is saturated with horrifying suffering and diabolical evil. *That* is the final explanation for evil. No one prior to Augustine (except, in a peculiar way, Origen) suspected that above this freely generated warfare there existed an even more fundamental explanation: an all-good and all-determinative blueprint in the mind and will of God.[46]

It is, I contend, this undermining of the explanatory ultimacy of the free agency of angelic and human beings, and thus this undermining of the explanatory ultimacy of the cosmic war for the sake of preserving a particular Hellenistic view of divine omnipotence and providence (viz., as meticulous control), that more than anything else generates the unsolvable intellectual problem of evil we have been wrestling with throughout the ages. For now we must wonder how we (and angels) are genuinely free while yet inevitably following God's will; how God somehow wills, or at least "allows" with a definite purpose, what he says in Scripture he positively hates; why we are called to actively resist what God himself ordains; how what appears to be grotesquely evil is actually a contributor to a greater good; and how there must ultimately be a good and holy reason for everything Satan does.[47] If one admits that angelic and human beings are ultimately free agents, however, and thus admits the ultimacy of the cosmic war that has resulted as a consequence of this freedom, then the contradictions disappear.

A warfare versus a providential blueprint worldview. To say that the New Testament and early postapostolic church regarded the appeal to the free will of angelic and human beings as an ultimate explanation for all the evil in the cosmos is not to suggest that these authors construed Satan, angels or humans as being metaphysically ultimate alongside God. They never approached the dualistic heresy of construing the forces of evil as coeternal and coequal competitors with God.

To the contrary, New Testament and early church fathers unequivocally taught that the Lord God alone is eternal, alone almighty, and alone the Creator of all things.[48] In this sense, God was seen as the final "why" as to the *existence* of all things and all beings. But no one before Augustine unequivocally assumed that God was the final "why" for *how* these things and beings existed.

While the early church never provided a detailed philosophical justification of this view (though they were moving in this direction), they assumed that free beings provide their own ultimate explanation for their behavior, and thus for why things they affect for better or for worse are affected the way they are.[49] In this view free beings can and do genuinely affect the flow of history. When they affect the flow of things, for better or for worse, there is no necessary higher reason than what can be located within their own self-determining free decision to explain why the flow of history was affected the way it was.

In this light, it still makes sense to attempt to render intelligible the concept of freedom as self-determination; it still makes sense to inquire why the Creator would have created a risky world with such radical freedom as opposed to a world without it; it still makes sense to probe what all this entails about God's control, or lack of it, in history; and it still makes sense to worry about how this openness to contingency squares with Scripture's guarantee that God's ultimate purposes for creation shall in the end be accomplished. Indeed, I shall apply myself to just these questions in my forthcoming volume (*Satan and the Problem of Evil*).

But if the reality of human and angelic freedom is granted, it does not make sense to look for a higher divine "why" to explain the particular actions of any one of these free agents. It therefore does not make sense to seek for a higher "why" in God's will to explain the occurrence of any particular evil in the world. From a warfare worldview perspective, this quest is misguided, and the unsolvable problem it generates is in fact a pseudoproblem. The only "why" that can be found is located in the free agent who freely does what it does.

In any event, the fact that the New Testament locates the ultimate "why" of evil actions in the angelic or human beings who bring about those actions, and the fact that it therefore directly or indirectly attributes the responsibility for the world's evils to the wills of free agents, and especially to Satan, should be strong indications that the Western preoccupation of wondering how evil fits into God's sovereign will is misguided. From a biblical and early church perspective, evil "fits" in the cosmos only by constituting that which God is unequivocally against, and that which God shall someday ultimately overcome.

Satan and Postmodernity

The above-mentioned curious difficulties with the classical problem of evil, when combined with the radical seriousness that the concrete experience of nightmarish evil creates for a belief in God, argue strongly for the conclusion that the classical-philosophical identification of divine power with divine control, and thus the classical-philosophical meticulous blueprint model of providence, is seriously mistaken. This conclusion, in turn, suggests that we need seriously to reexamine and reconsider the motif of spiritual warfare in Scripture and in the early postapostolic church as an alternative model for understanding evil.

In contrast to the classical-philosophical, post-Augustinian model of providence, the warfare worldview implicit in Scripture and the writings of the earliest church fathers presupposes that the power to affect things is not monopolized by God but is by God's own design a shared commodity throughout his creation. The cosmos is, by divine choice, more of a democracy than it is a monarchy. The warfare worldview thus presupposes the reality of relatively autonomous free creatures, human and angelic, who can and do act genuinely on their own, and who can and do sometimes go against God's will. It thus presupposes the reality of radical contingency and of genuine risk. It further presupposes that this risk has sometimes gone bad, even on a cosmic scale, and that this has turned the earth into a veritable war zone.

For just these reasons, the warfare worldview "fits" the perverse reality of concrete evil we experience in our sometimes horrifying world in a way the classical-philosophical blueprint model of providence does not. If the earth has indeed been besieged by a controlling diabolical force (Satan) who commands legions of hostile demons, as I argue the New Testament teaches, then, but only then, it is not surprising that we see around us "more signs of the demonic than of the true God," as König says. Then, and only then, are we not surprised to find that in this war-torn land, "there is more pain and misery, injustice and violence . . . than love, prosperity, justice and joy," as König further observed.[50]

For this is exactly what war looks like. If we grant the intelligibility of the war itself, there is simply no further problem in intellectually understanding why any particular atrocities occur. In a state of war, bullets fly, bombs explode, mines are stepped on, and children are maimed. War is hell. This is expected. The only real problem is in confronting the evil and in overcoming it. Hence this worldview at once frees us from futilely asking questions we cannot answer and empowers us and motivates us to fight battles we can win.

Despite these advantages, however, the warfare worldview is admittedly not a worldview that many modern people find easy to accept. To many contemporaries, the notion is preposterous that real, semi-autonomous, self-determining and invisible spirits exist that can and do influence our lives. The whole thing sounds to them more like something out of a Star Wars movie than like serious contemporary theology. This brings us to the third and final fundamental obstacle to accepting Scripture's warfare worldview.

Satan and mythology. We must take seriously the claim that one simply cannot ask modern people to entertain the possibility that angels might actually exist, let alone ask them to believe that the behavior of these supernatural beings might explain features of our physical and social world. For it is true that, until recently (see below), Western culture had been going down a track of increasing secularism. Our perspective of the world had been increasingly colored by materialistic presuppositions, and this had been leaving less and less room for a belief in such things as angels and demons.

Hence Walter Wink's diagnosis of our culture must be taken seriously (though not necessarily accepted) when he writes concerning angels and demons:

> We moderns cannot bring ourselves . . . to believe in the real existence of these mythological entities that traditionally have been lumped under the general category "principalities and powers." . . . It is as impossible for most of us to believe in the real existence of demonic or angelic powers as it is to believe in dragons or elves, or a flat world.[51]

For this reason, many modern theologians, following in the footsteps of Rudolf Bultmann, have thought that the New Testament needs to be to some extent "demythologized" if its existential significance is to be salvaged for modern people. At the very least, this means that the Bible's talk about angels and spiritual warfare and the like has to be translated into modern naturalistic categories. The principalities and powers perhaps referred to social institutions, as Schlier, Berkhof and many others have suggested.[52] Or, more recently, and less reductionistically, perhaps all the Bible's talk about angels and the like could be taken to refer to something like the corporate "interiority" of social groups, as Wink suggests.[53]

The intelligibility of the warfare worldview, however, requires us to reject all such attempts to render the New Testament's conceptions more palatable to modern people. Not that we can expect modern people to accept any literal view of the Old Testament's talk about cosmic monsters (see chapter two), and not that we can or should accept the Victorian portraits of cherubic angels or the traditional caricatures of the devil. As C. S. Lewis recognized concerning the demonic, and Barth saw concerning angels, such caricatures are more pagan than they are biblical, and actually lead to a trivialization of the spiritual world.[54] But insofar as any modern revisioning of the "powers" entails a denial that these beings are real beings who have an autonomous existence and free will, the warfare worldview requires their rejection. For the notion that angels can and do genuinely fight against God, against each other and especially against us presupposes at the very least that they have a real self-determining existence over against God, each other and us.

Nonetheless, there is a significant element of truth, judged by scriptural standards, to Wink's identification of "the powers" with the "interiority" of social wholes. Wink's trilogy is in many respects a masterful demonstration of just how closely both good and evil "powers" are linked with good and evil structures of human society, both in our experience and in Scripture. Thus combating the evil "powers," Wink and others have shown, is not just a matter of prayer but also a matter of social activism.[55]

But never does the New Testament strictly *identify* the powers with these social structures, or even with a spiritual dimension of these social structures. The social structures are under the power of these forces, and the structures are held together by these forces, but they are not themselves these forces. Rather, in New Testament thought the principalities and powers exercise a power over these structures precisely because they transcend these structures.

According to Wink and others, however, this latter affirmation is no longer possible for modern people. Against this, I argue below that it is rather the denial of the autonomous real existence of these cosmic powers that is quickly becoming an implausible belief, even for us "modern" people.

Other people may have little problem accepting the real autonomous existence of a spiritual society between humans and God, but may be inclined to reject the warfare thesis at the start on altogether different grounds. The warfare worldview, these people may argue, "robs" God of his sovereignty and grants angels and humans far too much power. For many of these people, influenced as they are by the classical-philosophical tradition, God's greatness and his control are correlative concepts: a maximally great deity entails a maximally controlling deity. Hence any view suggesting that creatures have enough autonomy to operate outside, and even against, God's universal and meticulous control must be rejected at the start. It leaves "no place for sovereignty."[56]

In some respects these two fundamental objections to the warfare thesis can only be answered at the end of a thorough development and defense of the warfare worldview on biblical and philosophical grounds. That is, such objections can only be thoroughly addressed by presenting the thesis as a completed whole and by then asking, "Isn't this credible to you modern people?" and "Isn't this view of God more, not less, praiseworthy than the view of God as all controlling?"

Still, I can say a few preliminary words to help assuage these objections somewhat at the start and to lay the foundation for what is to follow. In concluding this chapter, therefore, I offer four considerations which suggest that, despite these and other understandable criticisms, the church today and our culture as a whole are not only ready for a statement and defense of something like the warfare thesis but are in dire need of it.

The postmodern awakening. First, while Western culture as a whole, including the Western church, has certainly been under the strong influence of naturalistic assumptions the last three hundred years, it is doubtful that the oft-repeated objection that moderns are simply incapable of believing in the supernatural any longer is or was ever entirely accurate. In truth, this objection seems to be more a confession of secularized academic professionals, reflecting their own unbelief and perhaps the unbelief of their own academic circle, than an accurate description of Western culture as a whole.

Even if the claim was once largely accurate, however, it is certainly no longer so. As many cultural observers have noted, Western culture has recently, and with remarkable speed, moved out of the modernist period into what many are now calling a "postmodern" period. On the issue of what is and is not credible, this move is all-important.[57]

What this shift means, at the very least, is that the dominance of

Enlightenment rationalistic and naturalistic assumptions concerning the nature of reality and the means by which we know it is rapidly waning. There is now an increasing openness to, if not explicit awareness of, "nonordinary reality." Or, stated more accurately, there is an increasing awareness of how arbitrary the standard Enlightenment definition of "ordinary reality" was. All perspectives on reality, the postmodern perspective is saying, are jaundiced and relatively myopic, including (perhaps especially) the Western rationalistic perspective.

This observation can be, and often has been, pushed to the point of total relativism in which all truth claims are "deconstructed" in order to reveal their noncognitive dimensions (usually related to an assumed quest for power).[58] Beyond being philosophically problematic, such a position is disastrous for Christianity for a number of reasons, not least of which is the fact that Christianity is inextricably rooted in a number of objective historical and metaphysical truth claims.[59]

At the same time, however, this postmodern perspective has served to expose the narrowness and arbitrariness of the Enlightenment assumption that reality can be exhaustively defined and understood by empirical categories. Postmodernism has been helpful in revealing the arrogance involved in the modern, Western, chronocentric, elitist, intellectual tendency to dismiss every other worldview that has ever existed as "primitive" and "superstitious."

Along the same lines, it has been helpful in heightening our awareness that the Western materialistic worldview is (as all worldviews to some extent are) a social construct.[60] Indeed, it is a construct that seems to have in part been evolved precisely to censor out all aspects of reality that are not manageable by empirical techniques. It allowed us to live in a world we could "handle," and handle well. But it thereby blinded us to those dimensions of reality that were beyond our control but that were no less (and perhaps more) important for that reason. The reality of the spirit world is a perfect case in point.

Things are now changing, however. While the dismantling of this socially constructed vision of reality is creating new challenges for the church, it is also having the positive effect of opening up our cultural vision to include the supernatural, and this cannot be bad for Christianity. There is now an increasing appreciation for and validation of the "commonsense" assumption of nearly every culture outside our own that the world is not simply physical. There are now fresh attempts at giving nonreductionistic interpretations to the nearly universal conviction that reality is both physical and spiritual, visible and invisible, and that these two dimensions are two sides of the same coin. There is increasingly a new openness toward and appreciation for the nearly universal worldview that sees the cosmos as inhabited by spiritual beings whose behavior influences our lives, for better or for worse.[61]

In short, without rejecting the value of Western science and technology, Western culture is in many respects beginning to relearn what many primitive people have, in however a distorted form, never forgotten: The cosmos is a veritable society of intelligent interacting beings, some of whom are not physical.

In this light, taking Satan, angels, demons, supernatural interventions and the like seriously meets with significantly less intellectual resistance in our culture today than it did fifty, twenty or even ten years ago. Indeed, as is obvious from a casual visit to any bookstore, Western culture presently seems to be undergoing an obsession with just such concepts, especially (but not exclusively) at a popular level.[62] For this reason, I do not believe that asking contemporary people to consider the possibility that angels (and one fallen angel in particular!) might be centrally relevant to understanding evil in the world is either asking too much of them or is apologetically disastrous.

To the contrary, in this present climate such a postmodern (yet biblical) approach will, if anything, be prima facie judged by many as inherently compelling. Far from being a liability, the supernatural dimension within the warfare worldview may increasingly be one of its strongest apologetic features. Indeed, it is likely that future theologies and theodicies that persist in operating within the narrow structures of modern Western naturalistic categories will increasingly find themselves irrelevant to Western minds.

In my opinion, this is already becoming the case. The narrowness, arbitrariness, presumptuousness and inaccuracy of the Enlightenment worldview are increasingly being exposed. Christians should be the last ones to regard this exposure, with its resultant paradigm shift, as at all unfortunate. In my estimation, Christianity never had any business not taking the supernatural seriously!

Waking up to spiritual warfare. A second and closely related reason why I believe that a return to a New Testament warfare worldview with its Satan-centered understanding of evil is possible, and needed, concerns certain dramatic shifts that are occurring in the church today. Since the mid-1980s we have witnessed major segments of the Western church abandoning wholesale their previous modernist mindset, which held that spiritual warfare was at best peripheral to the life of the church. One has only to note the explosion of works published on spiritual warfare since that time to confirm this point.[63] I would go so far as to submit that no single topic in the last several years has received more press within evangelical circles than this one. Christian fiction dealing with the subject has become extremely popular as well, as evidenced by the sales of Frank Peretti's novels.[64] Conferences on the topic of spiritual warfare have also enjoyed unprecedented success.

Perhaps even more significant, however, is that we are now witnessing more and more churches actually getting involved in overt spiritual warfare. We are increasingly hearing reports, from a wide variety of ecclesiastical backgrounds, of Christians engaging in "power encounters," often with attendant demonic "manifestations" that look remarkably like what has for centuries been reported in other cultures, remarkably like what we read about throughout church history, and remarkably like what we find in the New Testament.[65]

Not all these cases are equally credible. Nor is all the attention that is now being paid to the topic of spiritual warfare and the deliverance ministry healthy, as some commentators have noted.[66] When cultural pendulums swing, excess is usually the order of the day, and repeated calls for balance are necessary. The only point I am making here is that, for better or for worse, the cultural pendulum has swung. Christians are now moving quite decisively (and perhaps at times somewhat excessively) toward something like what I have been calling a warfare worldview. This opens up the possibility of plausibly integrating the warfare motif into our reflections on theodicy.

One can discern a number of causes for the paradigm shift Western Christianity is going through. One is that, owing to the new postmodern atmosphere we are living in, as well as the explosive growth of Christianity in the Third World and the development and popularity of liberation theologies, Western theologians have (finally) begun paying more attention to the perspectives of their Third and Second World sisters and brothers. Western theology is, in a word, becoming globalized.[67] Indeed, whereas the Western church used to be generally regarded as the teacher of these other cultures—often to the spiritual detriment of these cultures[68]—we now understand that we are also, and perhaps even more so, the student of these other cultures. Among other things, we are learning from them how central the "world in between" (the world of spirits between humans and God) is for a vibrant Christianity.[69]

A second possible cause of this present paradigm shift, one that has been detected by multitudes of spiritually discerning believers but that obviously cannot be objectively demonstrated, is this: As our culture as a whole moves more and more in the direction of embracing a modified Third World perspective—as we move into "the New Age"—the reality of the spirit world, and more specifically of the demonic world, is simply becoming more and more evident.

It is no longer possible to dismiss, a priori, all the claims to supernatural phenomena being reported by people outside Christianity in our culture. From gardens supernaturally growing, to miraculous healings, to impressive "channellings," to a bizarre assortment of other paranormal phenomenon, we are, as a culture, being barraged with claims that we simply cannot ignore.[70] Nor is it possible any longer to dismiss as merely psychological the increasing number of cases of overt exorcism that Western Christians are involved in.[71] All this has had the advantage of gradually waking up the Western church from its naturalistic slumber to the reality of the spirit world, and to the need for the supernatural dimension of the work of the Holy Spirit if Christianity is going to continue to be viable in our postmodern world.

We might say that "the war" has started to "come out of the closet" after three centuries of taking place mostly behind the closed doors of the western, naturalistic worldview. As a result, we Western Christians increasingly find ourselves in situations similar to that of the New Testament, the early postapostolic church and much of the church in Third World environments. However much it may grate our naturalistic intellectual assumptions, we find ourselves more and more in situations in which the reality and power of Satan and demons is increasingly manifested before our eyes as this dark kingdom competes with the kingdom of God for the hearts and minds of people.[72] Where believers are open to it, we increasingly discover the Holy Spirit rising to the occasion and manifesting God's incomparable power in these situations.[73]

The overall result of this new spiritual climate is that the parameters of what many Western believers have previously regarded as being "normal" Christianity are being stretched. In my estimation, this is a very positive development. It means, among other things, that the climate is ripe for a restoration of a New Testament model of the church as the supernaturally empowered body of Christ that carries on the work which the Son began during his incarnate ministry. And it means that the time is ripe for a return to a biblical perspective on the problem of evil that defines it more as a spiritual problem to confront than an unsolvable intellectual problem to ponder futilely.

The present atmospheric change we are experiencing at a spiritual level in our culture contributes to my conviction that both the culture and the church are ready to seriously reconsider appropriating, or at least recentering, the warfare worldview of the Bible, especially as played out in the New Testament and early postapostolic, pre-Augustinian church. But this reconsideration of the warfare worldview is needed for another reason as well. Despite the incredible volume of literature that has been published in the area of spiritual warfare in recent years, there has to date been no serious in-depth theological or philosophical attempt to sympathetically think through the implications of what much of this literature is saying about spiritual warfare, and hence about God, the world, the devil and free will.

To be sure, much of this literature is of immense value on a practical level, and some of it does a fine job of providing an exposition of what the Bible teaches on various subjects related to spiritual war. But the spiritual warfare movement itself has offered little on the topic by way of either a comprehensive biblical treatment or a systematic theological/philosophical treatment. Next to nothing has been done systematically to integrate the warfare motif with a doctrine of God, theological anthropology, soteriology, angelology and, for our purposes most importantly, theodicy.

While I cannot begin to provide extensive coverage of all these topics, my goal in this present work is to provide a foundation for such a coverage by engaging in a comprehensive exegetical and theological treatment of all scriptural passages that concern spiritual warfare. Building on this, I shall provide a thorough treatment of the last topic—the problem of evil—in a forthcoming work.

The move away from classical categories. Yet a third feature of our present postmodern age which suggests that an intelligent defense of a warfare worldview may be possible today concerns the demise of classical philosophical categories in our postmodern culture. One of the main reasons why the warfare worldview was gradually compromised in the thinking of the early apologists, especially in Augustine's theology, and one of the central reasons why believers have to some extent resisted it since, is that this worldview runs counter to a particular model of divine perfection—a model that did not derive principally from Scripture, nor was it required by logic. It was, rather, derived mostly from Hellenistic philosophy.[74]

For example, from Plato, Aristotle and the subsequent Hellenistic tradition, the church arrived at the notion that God was altogether unmoved, impassible, immutable, nontemporal and purely actual. Yet it was precisely these features of the church's doctrine of God that logically undermined the integrity of the warfare worldview. On the basis of this model of God, a meticulous, sovereign, divine blueprint was postulated to encompass all temporal events, including the cosmic war.

This had the effect, however, of rendering the war a sham. For a war that meticulously follows a blueprint that has been drawn up by one of the parties involved in the war (God) is hardly a real war. It was principally for this reason that the problem of evil stopped being the New Testament problem of confronting and overthrowing the enemy and started being the intellectual problem of figuring out how this enemy (and all evil) fits into God's providential script.

We are now living in an age in which the classical Platonic and Aristotelian categories are becoming less and less persuasive, if not altogether unintelligible, to people in Western culture.[75] This gives further reason to believe that the church and the culture are set for a reappropriation of the biblical warfare worldview.

To speak in more detail, from the move to dynamic philosophical categories in Leibniz and Jonathan Edwards in the eighteenth century, to Einstein's relativity theory and the rather bizarre discoveries of quantum physics, to the thoroughly relation- and event-oriented philosophies of Laszlo's systems theory and Whitehead's process thought, we have been witnessing a gradual but decisive abandonment of classical Western categories.[76] For example, the classical Western assumptions about the nature of the physical world as consisting of enduring substances is now being replaced with an understanding of the world that places verbs over nouns and therefore understands events to be more fundamental than "substances."

Indeed, the very notion of an "individual thing" is coming to be seen as an abstraction from a substratum of dynamic events, as quantum physicist David Bohm has argued.[77] With this, then, the older mechanistic model of physical reality is being replaced with one which embodies spontaneity, contingency, interrelatedness and creativity at its center.[78]

What is for our purposes even more important, however, is that this demise of Hellenistic categories has been having an impact on the assumptions that have, since the early apologists, exercised such a decisive influence on Christian theology. As mentioned above, the notion that "divine perfection" necessarily implies changelessness, atemporality, pure actuality and impassibility is, at least in some quarters, no longer taken as self-evident. Indeed, it is now being radically called into question on biblical, philosophical and even sociopolitical grounds.[79]

This rethinking of the nature of God has been in process for some time within more liberal theological circles, but more often than not without any adequate biblical foundation. Recently, however, these Hellenistic assumptions have been subjected to critical scrutiny by conservative evangelical theologians as well. Most significantly, this scrutiny is being carried out principally on biblical grounds.

For example, the classical Western assumption that the Bible teaches that God is altogether unchanging, even in his experience, and that God therefore experiences the whole of reality as a completed "timeless block," has taken some very serious blows recently. In its place, we are seeing an increasing number of evangelical Bible scholars and theologians affirming a more open view of God, a view that stresses the contingent, creative, open nature of reality and therefore of God's experience of reality.[80] In contrast to process theology, these Christian scholars are by no means denying the truths that God alone is eternal, that God is self-sufficient within his own triune identity apart from the world, that God is altogether omnipotent and omniscient, and thus that God is sovereign over world history.[81] What they are saying, however, is that the way in which Augustine reinterpreted these concepts was more in line with Neo-Platonism and the broader Hellenistic philosophical tradition than it was with the Bible. Hence out of fidelity to Scripture, Augustine's framework for understanding these truths needs to be seriously reexamined.

At the very least, all this questioning means that the classical-philosophical conception of God as necessarily possessing the traditional

Hellenistic attributes of changelessness, timelessness, unrelatedness and so on are no longer regarded as self-evident. This, in turn, provides greater opportunities for theologians to openly investigate whether these attributes are really biblical. The more these attributes are questioned, the more theologians are moving toward an understanding of God and his relationship to the world that can include the sort of contingency, openness and risk that is essential to a genuine warfare perspective of the world. And the more they do this, the less the problem of evil will be perceived to be an intellectual problem, and the more it will be experienced as a spiritual, existential problem about which one is called to do something.

In any event, the fact that this classical-philosophical portrait of God and the traditional "timeless block" understanding of reality is now loosing its grip on thinkers today is certainly one more indication that we are now positioned to reconsider reappropriating Scripture's warfare worldview. Despite the serious reservations modern "enlightened" culture might have had, and might yet have, regarding the autonomous reality of angels and demons, and despite the reservations traditional Christians might have had, and might yet have, regarding the reality of spiritual beings and cosmic forces who can genuinely war against God, the time is ripe for a systematic reconsideration of this warfare worldview. The biblical and common cultural conviction that invisible beings exist who have power to effectively fight against God, each other and us is simply not as far-fetched as it once was. Indeed, for an increasing number of us, it is an inherently plausible concept.

The experience of the demonic. A fourth and final dimension of our contemporary age that leads me to believe that we are ready for, and in need of, a spiritual warfare approach to the problem of evil concerns the intense experience of evil in the past century. Arguably, never before has humanity as a whole experienced the amount, the depth and the intensity of evil that we experienced in the twentieth century. Not only has the amount of suffering and the madness inflicting it been unprecedented, but because we now live in the information age, within an ever-shrinking world, the opportunity for people to know about and empathetically experience this evil is unprecedented as well. The result of all this is that the corporate human experience of the demonic side of reality has been unprecedented in recent decades.

This experience obviously has to affect our understanding of evil.

Among other things, it makes simple answers and reassuring clichés harder to swallow. Consider, again, the Holocaust. If the sound of one innocent child screaming under torture calls into question all talk of a beautiful sovereign plan behind and above all events (and therefore this event), what does the ruthless slaughter of a million Zosias do?[82] According to many post-Holocaust authors, writing yet "within hearing distance" of the unanswered cries of these Jewish children, this depth of evil not only despoils the myth of a beautiful divine blueprint lying behind all events but also requires that we reconsider the possibility of a demonic master plan behind events such as the Holocaust.

This depth of horror, this scope of barbarism, these authors contend, cannot be explained on strictly naturalistic terms. It can be rendered intelligible—in the type of perverse intelligibility such events are capable of—only by the category of the demonic.[83] Just as certain experiences of the holy require that we postulate a transcendental category of "the holy," as Rudolf Otto has argued in his classic work, so certain experiences of evil, such as the Jews' experience of the Holocaust, require the postulation of a transcendental category of "the unholy," "the demonic" or "the tremendum" to be understood.[84] Hence some post-Holocaust theologians have judged the previous modernist assessment of Satan and demons as myth to itself be a modernist myth.

Emil Brunner, who was certainly no friend of theological conservatism, but who had himself witnessed the atrocities of World War II, expressed the fundamental basis for this reassessment well:

> A generation which has produced two world wars, and a totalitarian state with all its horrors, has very little cause to designate the Middle Ages "dark." . . . On the contrary, it is just because our generation has experienced such diabolical wickedness that many people have abandoned their former "enlightened" objection to the existence of a "power of darkness," and are now prepared to believe in Satan as represented in the Bible.[85]

Brunner is hardly alone in this assessment. Even before, and certainly during and after World War II, a number of otherwise quite progressive thinkers observed that something was transpiring, or had just transpired, that they could only describe as demonic. In 1936, for example, Carl Jung wrote of Hitler: "One man, who is obviously 'possessed,' has infected a whole nation. . . . A god has taken possession of the Germans. . . . A hurricane has broken loose in Germany while we still believe it is

fine weather."[86] It seems that Hitler and his Nazi regime incarnated the
demonic in such an intense fashion that almost anybody who did not fall
under his spell could see, and had to admit, the reality of a transcendent
force of evil in their activity—even when their own theological convictions did not require it, and perhaps even when their previous worldviews
did not even allow for it.[87]

What further confirms this is that shortly after the war some serious,
high-level discussions were carried out among some of the world's top
theologians (e.g., Barth, Brunner) over whether Germany had become
a nation possessed. A good number of these theologians were inclined
to answer this in the affirmative. In my estimation, the evidence suggests
they were right.

The point of all this is that the nightmarish experience of the demonic
in Nazi Germany seems to have served to break a "stronghold" (if I may
so speak, following 2 Cor 10:3-5) of Enlightenment rationalism which
had previously gripped much post-Enlightenment Western theology and
had caused it to dismiss the demonic as an outmoded piece of mythology.

The Holocaust was not alone in opening up modern people's eyes to
the reality of evil. The horror of World War I had already served for many
(such as Barth) to undermine the unrealistic, hopelessly optimistic
anthropology of nineteenth-century liberalism and to point in the
direction of a reappropriation of the biblical categories of sin and the
demonic.

Moreover, the experiences of Hiroshima, of Stalin, of the Korean and
Vietnam wars, and of a host of barbaric leaders such as Idi Amin and Pol
Pot (to say nothing of the more recent butcheries in Rwanda and Bosnia)
have all served to suggest to many contemporary people that perhaps
the Bible is not as altogether "primitive" as was once supposed in
describing this world as under the bondage of an evil cosmic force (e.g.,
1 Jn 5:19). Perhaps it is, after all, not the warfare worldview of "primitive" cultures that is unenlightened.

Not surprisingly, then, we see writers, and not just evangelicals, taking
the categories of the devil and the demonic in general far more seriously
than has been the case in the past.[88] It is, I believe, a "sign of the times."

Yet to date no one has attempted explicitly and consistently to
integrate this new interest with the theological problem of evil—the very
thing that, in the New Testament and early church, was most associated
with Satan. Hence while I hold no illusion that the majority of people,

and perhaps even the majority of Christians, are going to agree with every aspect of this work, I do not fear that it will be rejected on a widespread scale simply because it takes the Bible's talk about "gods," angels, demons and Satan seriously. On this score, I believe this work fits in well with the Zeitgeist that we are now as a culture and as a church entering into.

Conclusion

On the basis of these four considerations, I am convinced that our Western culture, and especially the Western church, is positioned to reconsider the warfare worldview of the New Testament and the early church—even though it runs contrary to certain fundamental aspects of both the Western church's classical theological assumptions as well as our culture's standard naturalistic orientation. As our culture acquires a more Third World perspective on reality, the naturalistic philosophical assumptions that supported the Enlightenment worldview and the Hellenistic philosophical assumptions that supported the classical theological worldview are both losing their dominance.

Having laid this foundation, I turn now to consider afresh the Bible's teaching on God's ongoing battle against spiritual forces—what constitutes what I call the Bible's warfare worldview. What we shall find is that the notion of spiritual warfare in Scripture is far more central, and far more radical, than most believers have been able to appreciate. The next four chapters cover the warfare worldview as expressed in the Old Testament.

2

LOCKING UP THE RAGING SEA

THE HOSTILE ENVIRONMENT OF THE EARTH

*T*HE MANNER IN WHICH A PERSON INTERPRETS APPARENTLY GRA-
tuitous suffering—the sort Zosia and her mother endured—depends
wholly on one's worldview. If one attempts to understand Zosia's
nightmare against a canvas that depicts the cosmos as meticulously
controlled by an all-loving God, one must question either the genuineness of God's love or the genuineness of the evil. But if a person views
such suffering against a canvas that depicts the world as a veritable
battlefield, ravaged by eons of conflict among powerful invisible forces,
such suffering begins in a perverse way to make sense, for this is what
war looks like.

While the church since Augustine has mostly followed the first
alternative, I contend that the Bible, the early postapostolic church,
reason and a nearly universally shared spiritual intuition strongly favor
the second. This work is concerned strictly with the first of these claims:
I seek to demonstrate that the Bible exhibits a warfare worldview. In this
chapter, more specifically, I demonstrate that Old Testament authors
understood the world to be inhabited by demons and engulfed by hostile

forces that perpetually sought to destroy it.

But before turning to scriptural exegesis, I must first say a word about the warfare motif in the belief systems of the cultures surrounding the Hebrews of the Old Testament period. For though the biblical authors were divinely inspired, they were nevertheless children of their own culture. We cannot, therefore, adequately understand their views until we have set them against their background or milieu.

Following this background, I discuss the extent to which Old Testament authors share the views of their neighbors that the world is inhabited by multitudes of evil spirits. I conclude with an overview of the Old Testament's teaching, also shared in various forms by its neighbors, that the world is surrounded by raging seas that seek to engulf it and that Yahweh must therefore defeat to preserve world order.

The Warfare Motif in Ancient Near Eastern Literature

As with the Shuar, the Welame, the Kamine and most other primitive peoples (see the introduction), the people of the ancient Near East lived with the assumption that the cosmos was populated with both good and evil spirits. Also, as with these other peoples, this belief was not simply a theoretical piece of information for the people of the ancient Near East. They believed that the activity of these spirits greatly affected their lives. When things went well on earth, it was an indication that things were going well in the unseen world. When things were going poorly, however, when sickness, disease and tragedy abounded, then sinister spirits were clearly getting the upper hand.

Indeed, in a series of exhaustive studies of the demonology of the cultures that form the background to the Bible, Otto Böcher has argued that the prevailing view which dominated the thinking of the people of the ancient Near East (including the Hebrews), and continuing on through the New Testament period, was that all evil was the direct result of demonic activity.[1] With some justification, some scholars have accused him of overstatement, since we do find instances where a distinction seems to be drawn between illnesses that are caused by demonic activity and those that are not.[2] But if Böcher is guilty of overstatement, the overstatement is not great, at least as it concerns those cultures closest to the Old Testament authors.

It is clear that both the ancient Greeks and the ancient Egyptians also shared the customary view that the world is populated with good and evil spirits that can strongly influence the lives of people, for better or for worse.[3] Their views of the spirit world, however, are toned down relative to that of Israel's Mesopotamian neighbors. The thousands of texts recovered from the peoples of ancient Mesopotamia reveal an obsession with the activity of various good and (especially) evil spirits. The welfare of each person was viewed as largely contingent upon how good and evil spirits interacted with them. If one's protective spirit (*šêdu*) abandoned one (for fear? carelessness?), one was immediately open to attack from demonic spirits.

Among the more prominent of the evil spirits in these texts are *ašakku*, a demon of diseases and burning fevers; *nantar*, a demon of plagues; *aḫḫazu*, whose name means "seizure," and *labāṣu*, whose name means "to throw down" (either or both perhaps referring to accidents, epileptic fits or demon-possessed states); *ilu lemnu*, an evil spirit who apparently brought misfortune; *alû*, a demon who hid in dark areas; *lamaštu*, who especially preyed on women in childbirth and on newborn babies (apparently when a *šêdu* was inclined to leave); *anu*, a vampirelike demon who drank the blood of children; *pazūzu*, a demon of the scorching north wind; and *lilītu* and *rabisu*, a night demon and a crouching demon, respectively, both of whom make appearances in the Old Testament, as we shall see. The list could easily be expanded.[4]

The Mesopotamians made every effort to ward off these many ever-threatening demons, and to expel them once they had afflicted a person. Various prayers, incantations and magical spells were used to avert such spirits, as were a variety of figurines and amulets that honored various gods or spirits.[5] When these failed, however, a demon might possess a person, who then required an exorcism. Signs of possession included a strong sense of condemnation by a god; outbursts of anger against a god or goddess; delusions, madness, inability to communicate, muscle paralysis with eyes turning (or seeing) different colors, and so on.[6]

The Old Testament has a much more optimistic understanding of Yahweh's control over spirits, though it shares more of this demon-infested worldview than is usually conceded.

Myths of cosmic conflict. The warfare worldview of ancient Near Eastern peoples is seen not only in their demonology but in their cosmologies as well. Like most cultures throughout history, the ancient cultures of Mesopotamia gave mythological expression to the conviction that the world is in an ongoing state of war between forces of good and forces of evil. Indeed, for these people, as for many other ancient and primitive peoples today who provide evidence of their views, the very creation of the world was understood to involve cosmic conflict.

The best-known warfare myth among the ancient Mesopotamians is the Babylonian *Enuma Elish,* probably dating back to the second millennium B.C.7 In the beginning, according to this story, Apsu and Tiamat lived peacefully in "the happy nothingness of the pristine abyss," as Russell puts it.[8] In time, they together engendered other gods who eventually made too much noise and irritated them. Apsu therefore decided to kill them, but the younger gods learned of Apsu's plan and beat him to the punch. Tiamat became enraged over this and therefore created a vast horde of demons, who were as frightful in appearance as they were in character, in order to exterminate this band of rebels.

In response, the rebels elected Marduk, god of Babylon and hero of this myth, to fight Tiamat and her evil cohorts. Marduk and Tiamat then engaged in a fierce battle until Marduk finally vanquished her by sending a storm wind into her as she opened her mouth to swallow him (cf. Gen 1:2, where Yahweh's *rûaḥ*—"wind" or "spirit"—hovers over *t*hôm*). The victorious Marduk then carved up "the monster" to do "artful works."[9] From her body parts Marduk created the orderly world. He assigned each god to play a role in preserving the order of this creation: the moon, the night, the sun and stars, and so on. He posted guards to keep "her waters," upon which the earth rests, from escaping. He imprisoned and set guards over the demonic followers of Tiamat. Then, out of Kingu, Tiamat's evil adviser, he created human beings for "the service of the gods."[10]

Among other things, this mythological poem clearly expresses the conviction that order must fight and overcome chaos. Tiamat is a chaos monster who tries to "swallow up" order (Marduk).[11] She must be slain and order imposed on her. The chaotic waters of her inner being must be perpetually kept at bay—a concern about the threatening waters that were believed to encompass the earth, a belief found throughout the ancient Near East, including the literature of the Old Testament, as we shall soon see.

As with all mythical texts, the conflict envisioned in this poem must be understood as expressing a perennial conflict, though the event itself is portrayed as taking place in the primordial past.[12] The poem is a story of the creation of the cosmos, but it is also a story about the reality of the cosmos *now.* Hence the poem was reenacted, and the victory of

Marduk celebrated, at every New Year's Festival. The victory of order over chaos, of fertility over infertility, of a helpful Nile over a flooding Nile, and so on, had to be won anew each year.

In this regard, it is also significant that humans and the world as a whole are created out of the body parts of these chaos monsters. Though we are created by Marduk (representing order), we are composed of Kingu (representing evil) and surrounded by chaos (represented by Tiamat). For this reason both humans and the world as a whole need constant divine supervision in order to keep evil and destruction at bay. The ancient poem recognizes that there is something sinister about the cosmos as a whole and humans in particular. As I said in the introduction, this theme is reflected in the majority of the world's myths of origin, and is certainly found throughout the literature of the Anciet Near East. As we shall see, it is also prevalent in many of the Bible's creation accounts, though it is, on the traditional reading, altogether absent from what has become the normative creation account, Genesis 1.

Moreover, it is important to note that the chaotic dimension of creation and of humans is the result of a conflict that did not need to arise. This point is frequently overlooked. For example, Walter Wink argues that the Babylonians had "no problem of evil" because for them, as expressed in *Enuma Elish*, evil "is simply a primordial fact." "Evil is an ineradicable constituent of ultimate reality and possesses ontological priority over good." Hence, he concludes, "the origin of evil precedes the origin of things."[13]

On the one hand it is certainly true that neither the Babylonians nor any other ancient people wrestled with the "problem of evil," for they did indeed see evil "as a primordial fact." For them the world was simply the kind of place in which evil, suffering, chaos and so on were expected. But it is not quite correct to go beyond this and claim that this poem portrays evil as a constituent of "ultimate reality." Evil is here certainly "primordial" in that it precedes the creation of the world. Indeed, as we have just seen, the creation of the world is itself the result of a war in this ancient myth, as in many others. But this is not to say that evil is either eternal or ultimate.

While none of the gods in *Enuma Elish*, or any of the other ancient combat myths, is morally perfect or even particularly admirable, they are nevertheless generally portrayed as being at least devoid of overt conflict until a rebellion breaks out that leads to war. In *Enuma Elish* and most other warfare myths of creation, the origin of overt evil is rooted in this act of rebellion.[14]

The reasons for this rebellion and warfare in *Enuma Elish* are, from a Christian perspective, comically trite, as they frequently are in such stories. This again does not speak well of the moral character of the victors in *Enuma Elish*. But this is not quite the same as saying that evil itself is a necessary and eternal feature of primordial reality. Rather, as in most warfare myths of origin, this poem reflects a dim awareness that actual evil goes back to decisions made by personal divine agents. In the Old Testament as well, argues Robert Murray, the origin of cosmic conflict is construed as the breaking of a "cosmic covenant."[15] Therefore, the biblical tradition generally construed evil as an interruption of the way the cosmos is supposed to obey God. It is not itself a natural feature of reality. This dim awareness becomes much more explicit, refined and expanded in the New Testament and early church.

The conflict-with-chaos motif (often referred to by the German term *Chaoskampf*) occurs in a wide variety of forms throughout the literature of the ancient world. According to Mary Wakeman, who examined the cosmic conflict lore of twelve civilizations, they are all essentially "about the same thing." A hostile monster threatens creation; a heroic god defeats the monster and releases forces necessary for life; and the god then controls or fashions these life forces to bring about the creation of the world, or at least significantly influence life in this world.[16]

In the well-known *Epic of Gilgamesh* from ancient Sumer, for example, we read about a dragonlike sea monster named Huwawa who has to be vanquished by the hero Enkidu. In other ancient stories we read of a certain Tishpack battling the dragon Labbu; of Ninurta (the warrior god) battling Azag (a water demon); or, in another version, of the Anzu-bird that stole "the tablets of destiny" (the fate of humankind). In still other stories Enki (god of subterranean waters) must wage war against the personified primal waters who threaten to engulf him, or (among ancient Greeks) Zeus must conquer the evil Titans or (in another version) the evil Typhon.

While a great deal could be said about the varying particular agendas of each of these stories, the fundamental theme that runs throughout each is the same: order and good must war against chaos and evil; and the explanation for the imperfect nature of the world, and the future destiny of an orderly world, is found in just this war.[17] Fortunately for the orderly world, the good (or at least the "better") god always ultimately ends up winning—another intuition that, from a biblical perspective, must be judged as accurate.

We must pay more attention to the warfare myth as it is found among the Canaanites since, on the reckoning of most scholars, this culture exercised the most direct influence on the thinking of the Israelites.[18] Here the *Chaoskampf* motif is prominent and occurs in a number of different versions.

One prominent combat story has Baal, the chief god in the Canaanite pantheon, battling the sea monster Yamm (*yām* means "sea"). Yamm initiates the conflict by taking Baal prisoner as a means of establishing his own lordship. With the help of a sympathetic craftsman who fashions a weapon, however, Baal is able to rise up and vanquish Yamm. He then proclaims, "Sea verily is dead, Baal rules."[19] Variations of this story represent Yamm as Lotan, a twisting serpent of the sea ("Leviathan" in the Old Testament). Or we read of the evil god Mot (*môt* in Hebrew and Canaanite means "death"), whom Baal can defeat only with the help of his sister Anat.

As with *Enuma Elish*, we see here that the order of the world is perpetually threatened and must be defended. In a cosmology that understands water to encircle the earth, and in a culture in which life itself hangs upon the behavior of rivers and rains, this threat is primarily portrayed as being the threat of the sea. The world is encompassed by an evil force that, unless tamed, will certainly overwhelm it.

This theme was appropriated by the ancient Hebrews and incorporated into their inspired tradition, though much of its explicit mythological trappings were left aside. It constitutes the most fundamental way Yahweh's battle against cosmic forces was expressed in the Old Testament.

Demons in the Old Testament

Having overviewed the perspectives of the cultural milieu of the Old Testament authors, we are now in a position to appreciate more fully their own perspectives on these matters. We shall therefore first consider their views of demons, then their views of hostile forces engulfing the earth and, in the next chapter, their views of cosmic monsters threatening to devour the world.

The first thing that must strike us as we compare the Old Testament with the surviving writings of the Israelites' neighbors is the radical differences in their attitudes toward the spirit world. The Old Testament has none of the obsession with evil spirits that we find in the surrounding cultures. The fear and superstition, as well as the preoccupation with methods of protection and exorcism, that characterize these other Near Eastern cultures are altogether absent from the Old Testament.

Indeed, given its cultural context, it is remarkable how little the Old Testament says about evil spirits.[20] Even where it does refer to evil spirits, it makes little of them. Nevertheless, the little we find here is important to our theme of God's cosmic conflict with hostile forces, if only because it paves the way for what will in New Testament times become a full-blown demonological worldview.

Evil spirits "from the Lord." A number of Old Testament passages refer to an "evil spirit" that Yahweh sends to perform various functions. Thus Judges 9:22-25 tells us that God "sent an evil spirit between Abimelech and the lords of Shechem" that stirred up civic unrest and apparently increased crime among the lords of Shechem (v. 25).[21] Similarly, Saul is several times said to have been "tormented" by an evil spirit sent from Yahweh (1 Sam 16:14, 22; 18:10-11; 19:9-10). It made him act in a violent and irrational manner and ultimately contributed to his downfall as king. 1 Kings 22:21-23 refers to a "lying spirit" that was sent by Yahweh's heavenly council (see chapter four below) to deceive the false prophets of Ahab into telling him he could safely war against Ramoth-gilead, a prophecy that led ultimately to his death (vv. 29-37).

Many scholars cite such passages as evidence that Yahweh was seen as being morally ambiguous at this early stage of Israelite thinking. In this view, all evil, as well as all good, issues from Yahweh's will. I argue against this view at some length in chapter five. For our present purposes it is enough simply to note that in none of these passages was the sending of the evil spirit an immoral or capricious act on Yahweh's part. Rather, in each passage the Lord sent the spirit as an act of judgment. There was nothing morally ambiguous about the deed.

Hence the author of Judges 9 states explicitly that the evil spirit was allowed to arouse civic tension and crime because Abimelech and the citizens of Shechem had helped murder Abimelech's brothers (9:23-24). Similarly, Saul's spiritual torment was a direct result of his disobedience, deceit and arrogance (1 Sam 16:14-16, 23; cf. chap. 15). And the deception of Ahab's prophets that led to his death was the direct result of his own apostasy (1 Kings 21:25) and his refusal to heed the advice of the true prophet of God (1 Kings 22:7-8, 23-28). Far from revealing an unrighteous dimension to Yahweh, then, the point of each passage is wholly predicated precisely on the righteousness of Yahweh, a righteousness that judges rebellion severely.

Nor do these passages require us to view these various evil spirits as simply obedient servants in Yahweh's heavenly council, as many scholars hold.[22] Each passage clearly stresses that the "evil" work of these spirits was in these instances carrying out Yahweh's retributive will. But this need only imply that the Lord can at times use the evil intentions of malicious spirits to his own end, as he used the evil intentions of Joseph's brothers to his own good end (Gen 50:20). The passages show how Yahweh can use evil spirits, but they do not in any way suggest that Yahweh himself wills evil.

Various other demonic spirits. The Old Testament also portrays several spirits as affecting the dispositions of people. Here too the operation of these spirits is understood to coincide with Yahweh's righteous plan to bring judgment on individuals or on nations. For example, Isaiah 19:14 mentions that the Lord sent a "spirit of confusion" as judgment upon the Egyptians. Similarly, as punishment Sennacherib received "a spirit" that led him to return to his own country and get killed (Is 37:7). Jeremiah reports that the Lord was going to "stir up the spirit of a destroyer against Babylon and the people of Leb Kamai" in response to their sin (Jer 51:1).

It is possible that the "spirit of confusion" and the spirit that led Sennacherib to his death are simply metaphorical references to a particular state of mind. It is also possible that the "spirit of a destroyer" in Jeremiah is simply a reference to a mighty wind, as Frederick Lindström has argued.[23] But given the Near Eastern context in which the authors were writing, a context in which a wide variety of dispositions as well as "natural" disasters were attributed to evil forces, it seems more probable that these phrases refer to actual hostile entities.

The Old Testament refers, always in an incidental manner, to a number of other demonic beings who were believed to inhabit the world. Two passages mention *šēdîm,* usually translated simply as "demons" (following the Septuagint, the Greek translation of the Old Testament; Deut 32:17; Ps 106:37). The Babylonians and Assyrians appear to have regarded *šēdîm* as protective spirits, but the Old Testament authors see them in strictly negative terms.[24]

Along the same lines, Isaiah 34:14 refers to Lilith, who will inhabit Edom after it is rendered desolate. Lilith was well known throughout Mesopotamia as a demon who was believed to attack people, especially children, at night. This same demon may be referred to in Psalm 91:5, which speaks of the "terror of the night."[25] Isaiah 34:14 and 13:21 also refer to *sᵉʿîrîm,* which many scholars take to be a reference to hairy demons or goat spirits, though the NIV translates it simply as "wild goats." The concept of certain hairy and goatlike spirits was common among Israel's neighbors, and it is likely that this conception lies behind the Old Testament prohibition against worshiping these *sᵉʿîrîm* (Lev 17:7; 2 Chron 11:15).[26]

Genesis 4:7 may refer to another demonic spirit. On the basis of Mesopotamian parallels, E. A. Speiser and others make a fairly strong case that this passage refers to sin as a crouching demon, waiting to seize its victim.[27] Also on the basis of such parallels, many scholars argue that references to "the pestilence that stalks" and "the destruction that wastes at noonday" in Psalm 91:6 are references to demons of pestilence and plagues commonly believed in throughout the Mesopotamian area.[28]

Finally, again on the basis of Mesopotamian parallels, many scholars argue that the Azazel *(ᵃzā'zēl)* referred to in Leviticus 16:8-26 is a vile desert demon.[29] In this view, the scapegoat of the Yom Kippur ritual was believed to be loaded with all of Israel's uncleanness, then banished from Israel and delivered over to the unclean demon. The act at once separated the people of Israel from their own sin and from the hostile demon who could seize this sin and use it against Israel. Whatever one makes of this theory, it is not insignificant to note that apocryphal literature later viewed Azazel (or Asael) as one of the most prominent leaders of the demonic army.[30]

Various scholars have attempted to find references to demonic spirits in other Old Testament passages, but they are all even more tentative than the references treated here.[31] In any event, the Old Testament view of demons is clearly quite restricted compared to that of Israel's neighbors. Although the Old Testament evidences that some spirits can torment, deceive and confuse people as well as bring about civic rebellion and national disasters—it has, in a word, something of a warfare worldview—it never treats these spirits as being anything more than of peripheral interest. Their reality is affirmed, but their autonomy from the will of Yahweh is minimized.

Such an emphasis was perhaps necessary at this early stage of biblical revelation in order to establish among God's people the singularity and sovereignty of the Lord in the face of a culture that absolutely denied it. As the cosmic warfare motif develops in Scripture, however, the autonomy of these demonic entities, and the reality of their opposition to the Lord, becomes much more central. The themes of Yahweh's battle with hostile cosmic forces (see below) as well as his ongoing struggle with other cosmic spiritual beings (sea monsters, see chapter three; and "gods," chapter four) and with Satan himself (chapter five) get fused together with the theme of the world as being inhabited by demons. The result is a worldview in the New Testament that sees the earth as having been thoroughly seized by demonic forces.

Yahweh's Conflict with the Raging Sea

As is the case with its view of demons, the first thing that must strike us as we compare the Old Testament's understanding of Yahweh's cosmic battles is how radically it differs from the views of all its neighbors. In place of the various songs that depict a multiplicity of imperfect gods fighting each other, in the Old Testament we find—polemicizing explicitly against such views—the proclamation that Yahweh is the one Lord God Almighty, and he is altogether "holy" (e.g., Lev 10:3; 11:44-45; Josh 24:19; 1 Sam 2:2; Ps 71:22; 89:18; 99:9; Is 41:14-16; 43:3, 14-15, etc.). In place of the variously construed myths of humanity being formed from the dismembered carcass of an evil deity, we here find the divinely revealed understanding that humanity is made in the image of the holy God and after his likeness (Gen 1:26-27). Like God, we are given a dominion of authority—the earth—not because God needs help, as in pagan mythology, but simply because having this sort of dominion is what being godlike means.[32]

What is more, while the notion that creation involved cosmic conflict is pervasive in the Old Testament, as it is in Mesopotamian myths, the emphasis on Yahweh's sovereignty over other gods is unprecedented. In place of the demon-infested paranoia that plagued other cultures, in the Old Testament we find a robust confidence that "the whole earth is the Lord's." The existence of demons is admitted, but their ability to afflict humans—at least God's people—is at this early stage of revelation strongly minimized.

To say that the inspired Old Testament view of God, humans and the world stands far above what we find in other ancient Near East literature, however, is not to suggest that it altogether lacks elements found in this literature. Like their neighbors and most other non-Western cultures, the Israelites held the conviction that the world is, at least to some extent, characterized by a state of cosmic war. The Hebrews' intense monotheism did not prevent them from adopting the belief that the world was under siege by forces that were hostile to it. Understandably, given the surrounding cultures, they too expressed this by talking about such things as the raging waters that they believed encircled the earth, or the ferocious sea monsters that waged war upon it.

This theme constitutes one of the oldest and (judged by later revelation) one of the most profound elements of the cosmic warfare motif found in the Old Testament, though modern Bible readers often minimize or overlook it altogether. We shall review the most prominent examples of this motif.

Like all ancient Near Eastern peoples, the Israelites believed that the earth rested upon waters. When the author of Genesis 1 begins his creation account by referring, without explanation, to "the surface of the deep" (*t'hôm*) and "the waters" (1:2), no ancient Near Eastern person would have had trouble understanding what he was speaking about. This was "the deep" or "the waters" on which everyone believed the earth had been founded (Ps 24:1-2). As a number of different creation accounts in the Old Testament make clear, Old Testament authors believed that, in some primordial chaotic form (see Gen 1:2), the earth was originally completely engulfed by water—"the deep"—but that Yahweh pushed back the waters to make dry land appear. He separated the waters below the earth (upon which its "foundations" rest) from the waters above the earth, holding up the latter with the stretched-out "expanse" (Gen 1:6-10; Ps 24:1-2; 104:2-9; Prov 8:27; Job 9:8; 38:6-12).

Now in the Genesis account, the "waters have been not only neutralized, but demythologized and even depersonalized."[33] Perhaps as a means of emphasizing God's complete sovereignty in creation (or complete victory over anticreation forces of chaos; see chapter three below), and perhaps in order to express unambiguously the altogether novel conviction that the physical world is in and of itself "good," the author presents the many "gods" of his Near Eastern neighbors as strictly natural phenomena.

Hence the "deep" that in *Enuma Elish* was represented as the evil Tiamat is here simply water. Far from battling it, Yahweh's "Spirit" (or "breath" or "wind") simply "sweeps" or "hovers" over it (1:2).[34] So too, the stars, moon and sun, which Babylonian and Canaanite literature viewed as enslaved rebel gods, are here simply things that Yahweh has created (1:14-19). The expanse, the earth and human beings, far from being carved out of the bodies of defeated gods, are simply spoken into existence by God with the rest of creation (1:6-10, 26-27). In creating the world, according to this author, Yahweh has no competitors.[35]

Yahweh and personified hostile waters. Not all Old Testament passages demythologize water in this fashion, however. Some texts follow the pagan Near Eastern traditions more closely and express the conviction that while the creation itself is good, something in the foundational structure of the cosmos exhibits hostility toward Yahweh. While God created the world under a "cosmic covenant" of peace, as Robert Murray puts it, this primordial covenant has been broken, and the creation itself has fallen into a state of war.[36] To express this breach of covenant and its ensuing war in the context of ancient Near Eastern culture meant talking about personified hostile waters.

From this perspective, the mythological Mesopotamian and Canaanite stories about Tiamat, Leviathan or Yamm could be seen as erroneous, but not altogether erroneous. Insofar as they express the conviction that something about the cosmic environment of the earth ("the waters") was, and still is, hostile toward Yahweh and toward humanity, the biblical authors could understand these stories to express a profound truth. Insofar as they expressed this truth, this dissolution of the cosmic covenant, they could be appropriated into the inspired canon, so long as it was made clear that Yahweh, not the divine heroes of the surrounding cultures, defeated these foes and restored order to the cosmos.

For example, the psalmist affirms Yahweh's sovereignty in creation in a way ancient Israelites could understand when he says of the Lord: "You stretch out the heavens like a tent, you set the beams of your chambers on the waters. . . . You set the earth on its foundations" (104:2-3, 5). But, precisely as part of his emphasis on Yahweh's sovereignty, the psalmist adds that it was at Yahweh's (not Baal's or Marduk's) "rebuke" that "[the waters] flee" and "at the sound of your thunder they take to flight" (v. 7). It was, moreover, the Lord and no other who gave these rebel waters their assigned place (v. 8) and who "set a boundary that they may not pass, so that they might not again cover the earth" (v. 9). Not only the general concepts, but even the very wording of this ancient revelatory poem correlates with Canaanite accounts of Baal's conflict with Yamm.[37]

Similarly, the author of Proverbs 8 states that Yahweh "established the fountains of the deep" *(tˁhôm)* and "assigned the sea *[yām]* its limit, so that the waters might not transgress his command" (vv. 27-29). The author here plainly understands God's act of creation to have involved some type of conflict with cosmic chaos, but also clearly portrays Yahweh as being more than up to the task.

Similarly, the author of Job, perhaps transforming another Canaanite hymn, records Yahweh inquiring of Job as follows:

> On what were [the earth's] bases sunk, or who laid its cornerstone? . . . Who shut in the sea *[yām]* with doors when it burst out from the womb?—when I . . . prescribed bounds for it, and set bars and doors, and said, "Thus far shall you come, and no farther, and here shall your proud waves be stopped"? (Job 38:6-11)[38]

As Jon Levenson notes, we have here

> a sense of the Sea as a somewhat sinister force that, left to its own, would submerge the world and forestall the ordered reality we call creation. What prevents this frightening possibility is the mastery of YHWH, whose blast and thunder . . . force the Sea into its proper place.[39]

Similarly, in another passage that many scholars believe directly echoes (but transforms) a Canaanite hymn, the psalmist writes:

> The voice of the LORD is over the waters; the God of glory thunders, the LORD, over mighty waters. The voice of the LORD is powerful; the voice of the Lord is full of majesty. . . . The LORD sits enthroned over the flood; the LORD sits enthroned as king forever. (Ps 29:3-4, 10)[40]

The point of these passages is clearly to stress that Yahweh (and no other god) reigns supreme over the "proud" chaotic waters that threaten the foundation of the earth. Indeed, unlike Baal, Tiamat, Enki or any other Near Eastern hero who is said to have controlled the chaos, Yahweh's sovereignty is such that he can master these destructive forces by his mighty voice alone. Unlike the pagan gods, Yahweh does not even need a weapon! The voice that simply speaks the world into existence simply speaks control over the forces that threaten the world.[41]

Nevertheless, it is important to note that these passages do not take Yahweh's supremacy over the waters to entail that the waters are not really hostile to God and do not pose a genuine threat to the earth. The supremacy of Yahweh in these passages is predicated on just the opposite conviction.[42] A very real battle took place when God created the world, and it is still taking place as Yahweh (not Baal or Marduk) preserves the world from chaos. As Levenson again expresses it, "Creation endures because God has pledged in an eternal covenant that it shall endure and because he has, also in an eternal covenant, compelled the obeisance of his great adversary."[43]

Yamm as God's opponent. The motif of raging waters occurs in a number of other Old Testament contexts as well. In a passage that many scholars believe mentions the Canaanite god Yamm by name, the psalmist writes: "How long, O God, is the foe to scoff? Is the enemy to revile your name forever? . . . You divided the sea *[yām]* by your might; you broke the heads of the dragons in the waters" (Ps 74:10, 13).

This passage, which is possibly echoing another Canaanite hymn, seems to identify *yām* with "the dragons in the sea," and the monster is clearly a mocking enemy of Yahweh. The author is affirming the Canaanite imagery of order fighting cosmic chaos, but crediting Yahweh rather than Baal with the victory.[44] In typical Near Eastern and biblical fashion, he is portraying this chaos as a hostile, rebellious sea monster.

As Levenson notes, the whole tenor of the passage testifies to the author's belief in the authenticity of Yahweh's struggles against the forces of chaos. Yahweh's cosmic victory over evil is "invoked here precisely when conditions have rendered belief in God's mastery most difficult."[45] Though the psalmist affirms God's "power to defeat even the primeval personifications of chaos," he refuses to "pretend that there is some higher or inner world in which . . . horrific events are not known."[46] In short, even though God is in an ultimate sense sovereign, for the psalmist his battles with evil are not on this account in any sense a sham. In contrast to Augustine, the psalmist sees that evil and thus warfare are absolutely real for God just as they are for his creation.

Yamm may also be referred to by name in Job's frank question to Yahweh about the way he had been treated: "Am I the Sea *[yām]*, or the Dragon, that you set a guard over me?" (Job 7:12). In other words, he is objecting to being treated like one of God's cosmic opponents, Yamm. The sea monster Yamm, he acknowledges, needs to be kept under guard, but why Job?[47] Similar references to Yamm may perhaps be found in Job 9:8, which speaks of Yahweh treading "the waves of the Sea" *[yām]*, and Habakkuk 3:8-15, which speaks of Yahweh's "rage against the sea *[yām]*" that "roared and lifted its waves on high" (3:8, 10). The author then proclaims, "You trampled the sea *[yām]* with your horses, churning the mighty waters" (3:15).[48]

This last reference seems to combine elements of the cosmic conflict motif with the historic deliverance of Israel out of Egypt (cf. vv. 12-13), a combination that occurs elsewhere. Thus Isaiah 51:9-11 also sees Yahweh's deliverance of the children of Israel through the Red Sea as a type of "Yahweh's cosmogonic battle with Yamm."[49] Isaiah first proclaims how Yahweh "cut Rahab in pieces" and "pierced the dragon" (v. 9). Rahab, we shall see, is one of the names for the sea monster(s) Israelites believed inhabited the waters surrounding the earth. Isaiah then continues by proclaiming that it was Yahweh who "dried up the sea *[yām]*, the waters of the great deep *[tʰhôm]*," and thus "made the depths of the sea a way for the redeemed to cross over" (v. 10). Isaiah sees in the parting of the Red Sea a reenactment of (and perhaps a renewed victory over) the great sea monster Rahab. The one victory is a microcosm of the other.

The same thing seems to occur in Psalm 77:16, where the psalmist speaks about Yahweh's parting of the Red Sea in terms that sound much like a Canaanite cosmic battle myth: "When the waters saw you, O God, when the waters saw you, they were afraid; the very deep trembled." He then concludes, "Your way was through the sea, your path, through the mighty waters; yet your footprints were unseen" (v. 19). Again, the Red Sea that would have held Israel in captivity is here seen as a type of the raging cosmic waters that, if not for Yahweh's power, would have held the very order of creation in captivity.

A similar phenomenon occurs in Psalm 74:10-17, where the psalmist cries out for Yahweh to silence his (and Israel's) enemies as he did when he split open Yamm and "crushed the heads of Leviathan" (vv. 13-14), Leviathan being yet another sea monster personifying cosmic chaos. So also the Lord's overthrow of Nineveh is celebrated as God's victory over Yamm (Nah 1:4).[50] Earthly battles against evil mirror and reenact cosmic battles against evil. When Israel's enemies "roar" against it, the roar of the raging primordial sea is heard. When Yahweh sets these enemies fleeing with his rebuke, his victory over this raging sea is accomplished once again (cf. Is 17:12-13).[51] When Israel is conquered, however, it is like being swallowed and then spewed out by the mighty sea serpent (Jer 51:34; cf. v. 55).

Given the general cultural context within which all this is being written, one cannot take these statements as mere metaphors. We have simply no reason to assume that the biblical authors did not believe that these cosmic monsters existed. To the contrary, such expressions make sense only on the assumption that the biblical authors did believe in the existence of these anticreation cosmic forces, and did believe that Yahweh had to genuinely battle them.

Leviathan is alive and well on planet earth. But the central point of such expressions was not simply to assert as a piece of theoretical information the sheer existence of these various cosmic chaos creatures. This much everyone at the time took for granted. Rather, these hymns express the authors' perception that the cosmos is besieged at a structural level with forces of evil that God himself must battle: evil is not a minor anomalous occurrence on the otherwise pristine stage of the world. They also express the deep biblical conviction that this same warfare is played out in the life of God's children as they confront their enemies.

In other words, this cosmic warfare is not a thing of the past, nor is it a war that occurs "in the heavenlies," nor is it a war that God fights alone. To the contrary, the thrust of this last group of passages is to proclaim that this war is a present struggle, it occurs in human history, and it very much involves the human race, especially those who know God. The insight is that all who name the name of the Lord are called to identify and resist, in the power of God, the structural forces of evil that work to thwart God's plan for the earth in general and for humanity in particular. When we fight, we do not do so on our own power, but God himself reenacts his primal victory over these destructive forces through us.

For the ancient Israelites, there was no bifurcation between what occurs "in heaven" and what occurs "on earth," and neither should there be with us, if our perspective is to be truly biblical. We might (and must) express and apply this ancient biblical conviction in our own times by identifying and then resisting "the cosmic serpent" in the structural evil that besieges our own culture and the church of God. For example, when we resist the spiritual complacency and empty religiosity that has deeply infected much of Western Christianity at a structural level, we participate in God's cosmic battle with Leviathan. When we fight the ongoing tendency to compromise the radicality of the gospel by identifying it with this or that political ideology, or by allowing it to be taken hostage by this or that cultural ideal or movement, we are resisting "the twisting serpent."

But Israel's battles with hostile waters were not always religious in nature, and neither are ours. When we "take up arms" against corporate greed, and when we follow the call of the Lord in feeding the hungry, clothing the naked, sheltering the homeless, befriending the guilty, embracing the socially repulsive, and siding with victims, we are participating in God's cosmic struggle against cosmic chaotic forces of destruction. Similarly, when we strive to be responsible stewards of the earth we were originally given responsibility over (Gen 1:28-29) and resist the fallen tendency to rape it for our own convenience, we are fighting anticreation forces that are attempting to thwart God's plan for the earth.

Moreover, when we refuse to benefit from another culture's (or our own) slave labor, and when we come against governments that systematically oppress the masses, we are taking up arms against Rahab. When we expose and confront the many subtle forms of structural hatred that presently choke our own culture, whether in the form of systematic prejudice, institutional injustice, or the demonization of other peoples in the name of nationalism, we participate with God in the same spiritual battle that has been going on since the dawn of history.

What occurs on earth, again, is a replica and a mirror of what occurs in heaven. Indeed, it is a microcosmic example of the macrocosmic spiritual struggle. In God's power, we are mandated to join in the fight.

The seas and individual struggles. The cosmic war is not only fought on a structural or corporate level, however. From a biblical perspective, evil affects everything at every level and therefore must be fought on every level as well. Thus individual struggles also reflect a dimension of this cosmic war.

Hence biblical authors occasionally express their personal woes in terms that are reminiscent of the ancient Near Eastern conflict myths. For example, the psalmist cries out to God, "Rescue me from sinking in the mire; let me be delivered from my enemies and from the deep waters. Do not let the flood sweep over me, or the deep swallow me up, or the Pit close its mouth over me" (Ps 69:14-15). And again, "Stretch out your hand from on high; set me free and rescue me from the mighty waters, from the hand of aliens" (144:7).

Given the original cultural context within which they were written, these statements cannot be taken as mere poetic flourishes. To the contrary, the very meaning of such expressions in ancient culture was predicated on the belief that such demonic realities actually existed. Hence in a manner that resembles Jesus' portrayal of Peter as a channel for Satan (whom Jesus certainly believed was real, Mt 16:23), David is portraying his enemies as conduits for the destructive cosmic forces he truly believes in. Indeed, like Jesus, David here actually identifies his enemies with these raging rebellious cosmic waters.

Elsewhere, David compares the proud and rebellious cosmic seas, which lifted themselves up against God at the time of creation, to the enemies who now rail against him (Ps 93:3-4). Just as the Lord defeated rebellious chaotic forces at the time of creation and throughout the ages past, so David now cries out for God once again to defeat these forces, as exhibited in his enemies.[52] All this is clearly predicated on the belief that these raging seas and cosmic monsters are real and can be confronted in individual struggles.

Such a motif should not be taken as giving us carte blanche to demonize all our personal enemies—a tendency that can itself certainly be demonic! But it does entail that individual believers are not to be "ignorant of [Satan's] designs" (2 Cor 2:11). When we wrestle individually with forces that seek to destroy us, whether it be literal physical enemies who seek our life, as with David, or emotional, psychological and spiritual forces that seek to incapacitate us, we are combating powers that oppose God's will for our life. In short, our personal struggles have a cosmic, spiritual dimension.

Not that prayer is the cure-all for such maladies; David certainly did not respond to all his battles with Yamm only in this fashion. Rather, prayer is only one form (albeit a crucial form) of spiritual warfare. We resist the anticreation forces that oppose God whenever we do anything that genuinely restores creation—including ourselves as central features of God's creation—to the place where God originally planned it to be. As the Israelites never bifurcated the heavenly from the earthly, so we should never bifurcate the spiritual from the earthly and the practical. For example, we have every biblical reason to assume that the discovery and use of medication, the development and use of Christ-centered counseling, and the committed tough love of friends walking beside us to keep us accountable, to help us overcome temptation, and to encourage us when we fall are all forms of spiritual warfare.

Conclusion

While believers today cannot affirm as literal the mythological portrayals of the cosmic forces that the biblical authors give us, we can and must affirm the reality to which these mythological portrayals point. There was and still is something hostile to God at a cosmic level, infecting the cosmos at a structural level, which he has battled and must continue to battle to establish and preserve his good creation. Moreover, this is a battle that all who side with God are called to participate in.

Put in a nutshell, the Old Testament assumes a type of warfare worldview and thus views the very creation and preservation of the earth as something that has to be fought for. There is, at this point of revelation, little reflection as to why these forces are hostile to God or how the continued existence of these forces squares with God's omnipotence. Later revelation will begin to address these questions. For now, simply note that the texts do not necessarily imply that the evil forces are either primordial (viz., not created) or willed by God (common positions argued sometimes by contemporary scholars). Rather, the nature of both the cosmic forces and the demonic spirits seem to be such that they *ought* to have been different than they are and hence are sometimes explicitly portrayed as *rebellious* (following Near Eastern parallels).

Later revelation, as well as church tradition, portrays these powers as having been involved in a freely chosen mutiny—the view that alone allows us to affirm the full reality of the evil these powers represent, while also holding to the omnipotence and utter uniqueness of the one eternal Creator.[53]

Far from holding to any view of the world as meticulously following a divinely ordained blueprint, the Old Testament operates with the assumption that Yahweh faces real opposition, and this opposition concerns forces that are foundational to creation. While the whole cosmos was originally created good, at some early point something went profoundly wrong at a structural level. Only God's fighting on our behalf preserves the order of the world.

As we shall now see, however, to have said this much is to have hardly begun to flesh out the full dimension of the Old Testament's understanding of God's cosmic opponents. We have yet to consider Leviathan, Rahab and Behemoth, to which we now turn.

3

SLAYING
LEVIATHAN

COSMIC WARFARE AND THE PRESERVATION AND RESTORATION OF CREATION

*I*N THE LAST CHAPTER WE EXAMINED THE OLD TESTAMENT'S TEACHing regarding malicious demons and rebellious raging waters that encompass the earth. While the point of this teaching is clearly to reinforce confidence in Yahweh's ability to handle such forces, never does the Old Testament question the genuineness of the battle he must engage in to emerge victorious over them. To the contrary, Yahweh's lordship is understood to be great precisely because his foes are understood to be formidable. This is no petty, all-too-human, monarchical manipulation of puppets that Old Testament authors are talking about. Rather, it is an admirable sovereignty of wisdom and power against genuine cosmic forces that oppose him. As we have seen, the manner in which this cosmic opposition, and thus Yahweh's sovereignty, is expressed in the Old Testament draws significantly on the warfare cosmologies of the cultures that surround Israel.

What captures this cosmic warfare motif even more poignantly, however, is the Old Testament's appropriation of the ancient Near

Eastern conception of the world as being surrounded by hostile monsters that forever seek to devour it. As we saw in the previous chapter, the likely allusions to Yamm in Psalm 74:10, Job 7:12, and Habakkuk 3:8 and 15 are references to one such monster. But we also read about Leviathan, Rahab and Behemoth, each of which represents "forces of chaos . . . which threaten man's existence."[1]

In this chapter, then, I first provide an overview of each of these cosmic beasts, then tentatively propose a way in which the creation-conflict dimension of the combat mythology that surrounds these cosmic monsters can be harmonized with the creation story of Genesis 1.[2] The latter task, while speculative, is important insofar as the conventional understanding that nothing in creation can really oppose God derives largely from a particular reading of Genesis 1, as Levenson has forcefully argued.[3] It is this particular reading of this text that I wish to challenge.

Yahweh and the Cosmic Monsters
As in Canaanite imagery, Leviathan was portrayed as a twisting serpent of the sea with seven heads (a notion picked up by the psalmist when he praises Yahweh for crushing "the heads of Leviathan," Ps 74:14).[4] In customary Near Eastern fashion, Job sees Leviathan as a dragon that periodically threatens to reverse creation by engulfing the moon (during an eclipse) when aroused by evil soothsayers (Job 3:8).[5] The very sight of this beast causes panic (41:9, 25), and no one is mighty enough even to wake him up when he is sleeping, let alone to catch, control or domesticate him (41:2-14).

Moreover, this cosmic beast mocks human weapons, for he can eat iron like straw and crush bronze like rotten wood (41:26-27). The mouth of this dragon is filled with sharp ferocious teeth, his back is filled with pointed shields, and his belly is rock hard and horned on the sides (41:14-17, 30). Even worse, he snorts out lightning and smoke and blows hot flames of fire out of his mouth (41:18-21).[6]

Leviathan, then, is a formidable, hostile, cosmic creature, difficult to control, as even Yahweh intimates in his speech to Job. What is for these authors most significant about Leviathan, however, is that Yahweh has succeeded in subduing him. Indeed, the central point of Yahweh's speech in Job 41 is to say that Yahweh can do what Job could never do: stand up to and subjugate Leviathan, as he did at the time of creation. The psalmist expresses the same point when he proclaims that Yahweh crushed Leviathan's many heads and "gave him as food for the creatures of the wilderness" (74:14).

Isaiah 27:1, however, portrays the defeat of Leviathan as a future event. Indeed, it is portrayed as an end-time event that would usher in an era of peace. "The LORD with his cruel and great and strong sword will punish Leviathan the fleeing serpent, Leviathan the twisting serpent, and he will kill the dragon that is in the sea." The reference to Leviathan as "the fleeing serpent . . . the twisting serpent" has an exact parallel in an Ugaritic text, demonstrating once again how culturally indebted the biblical authors are at times for the way they express their convictions about Yahweh's enemies.[7] But whereas other Near Eastern myths (including the one Isaiah cites) generally portrayed the great sea dragon being slain so the world would be created, Isaiah here portrays the cosmic dragon as being slain so the creation may be delivered.[8] "The ancient Canaanite and Mesopotamian combat myth of creation," Levenson notes, "has been projected onto the onset of the future era."[9] The effect of this, as it concerns the problem of evil, is that "we are left with the bittersweet impression that the travails of the present, indeed of all history, are owing to the fact that the present order of things stands before rather than after the triumph of God. Leviathan is still loose, and the absolute sovereignty of the absolutely just God lies ahead."[10]

This eschatological reworking of the *Chaoskampf* myth was to become a defining and dominant motif in apocalyptic literature. As we shall see more fully in chapter six, the Jews in the intertestamental period came increasingly to define Yahweh's sovereignty as an eschatological reality and to see the present world as under the control of Leviathan (or some similar cosmic figure).

We are not surprised, then, to find this same eschatological depiction of Leviathan in the New Testament as John writes about a "great red dragon, with seven heads and ten horns, and seven diadems on his heads" who is "the deceiver of the whole world" (Rev 12:3, 9; cf. 13:1). This "great dragon," who is, significantly, identified explicitly as "the Devil and Satan" (v. 9), rises up to devour the church but is defeated by Michael and his angels (v. 7). The devil and his evil angels are then cast out of heaven down to the earth where, in their fury, they continue to bring woe "to the earth and the sea" (vv. 9-12).[11]

As already stated, given the genre of literature we are dealing with here, we must not suppose that there is any contradiction between saying that Leviathan had already been crushed, dismembered and eaten (Ps 74:14) and saying that his defeat still lay in the future (Is 27:1). The central point of each passage, couched in terms that ancient Near Eastern people could readily understand, is simply to express the truth that a hostile cosmic force opposes Yahweh and threatens the earth at a foundational level. But Yahweh has defeated him, and will continue to do so.

Another hostile monster that was believed to inhabit the sea is Rahab. Indeed, in some passages Rahab appears to be simply another name for Yamm. The word "Rahab" means "boisterous one" or "storm." Like Leviathan, this monster is portrayed as a threatening dragon in the waters that surround the earth.[12] Still, while the genuineness of Rahab's opposition to Yahweh is never questioned, the thrust of what the biblical authors say about Rahab is to stress how Yahweh reigns supreme over it.

Thus when Yahweh was angry, the author of Job writes that "the helpers of Rahab bowed beneath him" (Job 9:13).[13] It was by Yahweh's power that he "churned up the sea *[yām]*," by his wisdom that "he cut Rahab to pieces," and by "his hand" that he "pierced the gliding serpent" (Job 26:12-13).[14] So too the psalmist proclaims Yahweh's sovereignty over "the raging of the sea *[yām]*" by announcing that he has "crushed Rahab like a carcass" and has "scattered your enemies with your mighty arm" (Ps 89:9-10). Warfare there certainly is, but it is clearly a war that Yahweh can readily handle.

As we saw was the case with the raging waters motif, sometimes Yahweh's creation battle with Rahab is understood as being illustrated, or reenacted, in Israel's own history. Indeed, the above-mentioned psalm connects God's vanquishing of Rahab at creation with David's enthronement and his hope of divine assistance in defending his governance (Ps 89:20ff.).[15] Similarly, Isaiah calls upon the Lord to "awake" and deliver the children of Israel out of captivity by reminding him that in primal history he "cut Rahab in pieces" and "pierced the dragon" (Is 51:9). Thus he is assured that Yahweh will do it again and deliver his people (v. 11).

Along the same lines, both Isaiah and the psalmist can personify the evil empire of Egypt as Rahab, for Rahab's hostile and chaotic character is revealed in, and channeled through, Egypt (Ps 87:4; Is 30:7; cf. Ezek. 29:3; 32:2; Jer 51:34). In the same way that the Shuar and other primitive tribes weave together their reflections on earthly and spiritual enemies, so too the Israelites could understand their political wars as microcosms of the cosmic wars Yahweh fights. Since God is on David's side, when David marches into battle against his enemies the Lord and his army are, on a parallel plane, marching into battle against his enemies (2 Sam 5:24). No bifurcation between "spiritual" and "physical" realities is envisaged.

Yet a third creature that appears to be some sort of cosmic monster in the Old Testament is Behemoth, mentioned in Job 40:15-24. Even more so than with Leviathan, many have attempted to argue that the author of Job is referring to a natural creature, perhaps a hippopotamus or an elephant, rather than to a mythological cosmic monster.[16] While certainly possible—the depiction of this beast is markedly "this worldly"—both his proximity to the mythological Leviathan in Job and his overall description seem to count against such a notion.[17] The descriptions of the powerful muscles in this creature's stomach (v. 16), of his tail as being like a cedar (v. 17), of the strong sinews of his thighs, of his bones as "tubes of bronze" and of his limbs "like bars of iron" (vv. 17-18)—none of these conclusively fits the description of a hippopotamus, elephant or any other known creature, even after due allowance is made for poetic hyperbole.

What is more, Behemoth is described as "first of the great acts of God" (v. 19) whom no one can catch (v. 24), though "his Maker can approach it with the sword" (v. 19). This description does not fit easily with any natural creature. To be sure, Yahweh at one point rhetorically asks Job if he is able to trap Behemoth and pierce his nose as Yahweh is able (40:24). As John Day observes, were Behemoth any form of natural creature, it seems Job could have easily answered, "yes, I am able."[18]

Thus it seems likely that we are dealing with another cosmic monster that, like Leviathan, according to Day, may have Canaanite roots.[19] The title *b⁺hēmôt* is "an extension of the plural of *b⁺hēmâ* (q.v.) akin to the superlative in the English." Hence, according to Elmer Martens, Behemoth refers to "the brute beast *par excellence*."[20] Later Jews, in any event, took this term to refer to a demonic entity that, alongside Leviathan and Rahab, Yahweh had to subdue.[21]

Evil at the foundation of the earth. When we piece together the Old Testament's teaching on Yahweh's battle with and victory over the hostile waters and anticreation monsters that surround the earth (to say nothing yet of its teaching on Yahweh's conflict with other gods; cf.

chapter four), we see that the authors of the Old Testament shared significant elements of the common Near Eastern perspective that the earth was part of a cosmic war zone. The chaotic waters and cosmic monsters were "demonic creatures," as Day puts it, against whom Yahweh had to fight.[22]

The supremacy of Yahweh over these cosmic forces was always emphasized, but in contrast to the later classical-philosophical tradition, this was never taken to mean that the opposition of these forces was not ultimately real. There were, in fact, genuine battles Yahweh had to fight! As several exegetes have noted, the whole of the Old Testament's strong monarchial theology presupposes this much. On what basis could one celebrate a victorious military ruler, as the Old Testament frequently speaks of Yahweh, if there were no genuine enemies for the ruler to conquer? "The concept of a military ruler," Lindström argues, "presupposes that there is someone to defeat."[23]

Indeed, far from undermining the genuineness of Yahweh's battle with foes, Levenson rightly argues that in this tradition Yahweh's "victory is only meaningful if his foe is formidable."[24] And again: "What makes this a confession of faith in YHWH's mastery rather than a shallow truism is the survival of those potent forces of chaos that were subjugated and domesticated at creation."[25]

This "survival of . . . potent forces of chaos" is what permits classifying the Old Testament view as a warfare worldview. Yahweh's battles are not simply apparent, nor are they simply in the past: they are, for these authors, very real, and they are present, and they are even yet future. While some conservative exegetes fear that acknowledging the ongoing reality of this cosmic opposition compromises Yahweh's "absolute sovereignty," the point of this early Old Testament tradition is to portray Yahweh's sovereignty as being all the greater precisely because he has engaged in such conflict and has been victorious. This gives them confidence that he shall do so again in the future.[26]

In other words, Yahweh's sovereignty is no easy manipulation of controlled puppets; it is, rather, an admirable sovereignty that is won in the face of genuine, powerful, opposing forces which we humans could never begin to resist in our own power. This divine ability, for these authors, is one of the characteristics that distinguish Yahweh from humans and make him praiseworthy. We cannot capture Behemoth or pierce his nose (Job 40:24). Nor can we "press down [Leviathan's] tongue with a cord" or "put a rope in its nose" (Job 41:1-2). Such monster-taming feats of valor are reserved for the one true God alone.

All of this also implies that these authors understand the cosmic battles Yahweh engages in to be provisional. God's cosmic foes, as real and formidable as they may be, are not ultimate. Levenson again expresses the view well (referring here to Psalm 74):

> the author . . . acknowledges the reality of militant, triumphant, and persistent evil, but he steadfastly and resolutely refuses to accept this reality as final and absolute. Instead he challenges YHWH to act like the hero of old, to conform to his magisterial nature.[27]

Hence (though Levenson himself disagrees with this conclusion) it seems that the understanding manifested in this *Chaoskampf* material is that the forces opposing Yahweh had a beginning, which is precisely why the Old Testament authors can be confident that, sometimes despite appearances, they shall also certainly have an end. In contrast to everything their neighbors were saying about the matter, the Old Testament assumes, even in its earliest combat material, that Yahweh is the sole Creator of all that is.

This insight, combined with the conviction that the Creator is all-holy and thus does not himself will evil, leads inexorably to the conclusion that these cosmic forces have *made themselves* evil. They have freely rebelled against their Creator, and thus ought not to be as they now are. This view is implicit in this material, but it becomes more explicit in later material, eventually arriving at the explanation that the origin of evil is rooted in "the fall" of various angels (2 Pet 2:4; Jude 6; cf. 1 Tim 3:6; Mt 25:41). Only this view can provide an adequate foundation for theodicy within a creational-monotheistic context.[28]

If we take the Old Testament's combat motif seriously, we must acknowledge that, at the very foundation of creation and in the cosmic environment of the earth, something has rebelled against God and is therefore both hostile toward God and threatening toward the world.[29] The manner in which this insight is expressed is highly mythological at this early stage of revelation. Given the cultural situation of the authors, it is hard to see how the point could have been communicated in any other way. To talk about structural cosmic forces of evil in this context is to talk about Yamm, Leviathan and other mythological monsters.

A later inspired writer will express a similar conviction with a different set of cosmological assumptions by referring to a "ruler of the power of the air" who is "the spirit that is now at work among those who are disobedient" (Eph 2:2). The teaching is essentially the same, though the cultural packaging clearly differs. The cosmic monsters of the Old Testament play some of the same roles Satan and "principalities and powers" do in the New Testament.

In any case, while the Old Testament certainly teaches that this cosmos was created good (Gen 1), it clearly does not take this to mean that everything about the cosmos now is good. To the contrary, the goodness of creation is portrayed as something to be fought for.[30] At a foundational level, the cosmos at present embodies destructive, hostile elements. For these authors, the world is certainly no Edenic paradise where the will of God is meticulously carried out and in which everything somehow contributes to a higher good. It is, rather, a veritable battle zone.

Considering Zosia's torture from within this framework, one would not be inclined to wonder about a secret providential design that was somehow being fulfilled by means of the Nazis. One would rather discern in the eyes of the Nazis something of an evil "twisting serpent" seeking once again to undo creation.

Warfare and Creation

It will prove helpful to conclude our examination of the Old Testament's conception of hostile cosmic forces by addressing an issue that is important to our understanding of the Bible's *Chaoskampf* material but that has, for various reasons, been almost completely ignored by recent scholarship. I have acknowledged the obvious when I said that the specific portrayals of the evil cosmic forces Yahweh contends with in the Old Testament are culturally dependent and mythological. Yet I have also suggested that the reality to which these portrayals point should be affirmed, at least by those who hold to a high view of Scripture.

The still unanswered question, however, is this: What is the reality to which these mythological figures and forces point? More specifically, is the depiction of a cosmic conflict in the primordial past, leading up to the creation of this world, wholly part of the culturally dependent myth? Or is this feature of this *Chaoskampf* material perhaps part of the reality to which the myth points?

The relationship of myth and history in Scripture's creation-conflict material. The earlier mentioned fact that the temporal location of the *Chaoskampf* passages of Scripture (and the parallel literature in the surrounding cultures) varies from passage to passage certainly suggests that we cannot press this mythological language too far. This language is primarily designed to express a feature of the cosmos now—its warfare dimension and Yahweh's supremacy, despite appearances, over his opponents. Too much, then, should not be made of the temporal language surrounding the Lord's battles.[31] Therefore it admittedly may be the case that we are now asking the wrong question in even wondering whether the creation-conflict accounts entail the view that an actual battle once took place that led up to the creation of this present world.

Nonetheless, the fact that later Scripture leans strongly in the direction of explicitly endorsing a belief in a literal prehistoric fall of angels and cosmic forces as well as endorsing a literal eschatological battle between these forces and God's forces, combined with the further fact that later church tradition unequivocally endorsed the notion of a primordial fall, lends some support to the possibility that an actual prehistoric conflict can be inferred from this *Chaoskampf* material.[32] In other words, if we have other grounds for believing that God was actually involved in a war before the creation of this world (as the tradition claims), then it seems natural to wonder whether, or to what extent, the various scriptural accounts of cosmic conflict before creation refer to this event.[33] Though the manner in which the conflict and the beasts involved are portrayed is admittedly mythological, need this entail that the prehistoric conflict itself is mythological?[34] I suspect not.

The association of the cosmic conflict with creation is prevalent throughout the Old Testament and intrinsic to the various passages in question, lending further support to this suggestion. The conceptualization of creation as involving conflict occurs in many more than one or two isolated passages. As we have seen, such creation accounts are numerous, and this must count heavily for any person who is committed to a high view of Scripture.

Finally, the creational monotheism of the Bible and of the church seems to logically require something like a prehistoric fall, regardless of how we interpret the *Chaoskampf* material of the Old Testament. Assuming that there is one eternal Creator God who is all-good and all-powerful, it is illogical to posit a foundational structural evil within the cosmos (which is the main point of the *Chaoskampf* passages) without postulating a significant rebellion at some previous point that has corrupted the cosmos (which is the subsidiary point of the

Chaoskampf passages). In short, if the all-powerful Creator is perfectly good but creation is largely evil, something must have interfered with the creation.

The general teaching of Scripture seems to agree with this point. Whatever else may be said about the issue, the Bible is certainly far from any dualistic worldview that would posit evil as a coeternal reality alongside God or attribute evil to the creative activity of God himself.[35] The fact that all the scriptural authors have a confidence that evil shall ultimately be defeated demonstrates that they did not view it as "primordial" in the sense of being an ultimate constituent in the nature of things. If evil will have an end, it must have had a beginning, hence it is not coeternal with God.

But this point requires that we understand evil as an intrusion into the cosmos—which is precisely how the Old Testament construes it. This consideration lends further prima facie plausibility to that reading of the various biblical conflict-creation accounts which sees them as teaching us, in an admittedly mythological form, something not only about the structural fact of evil in the cosmos but also about the origin of evil in the cosmos.[36]

Genesis 1 and the warfare model of creation. The main reason this warfare view of creation has not traditionally been affirmed, or even seriously considered, is not that it is absent from the Bible. As we have seen, it is in fact sprinkled throughout the Old Testament. The reason for its neglect is due to its apparent contradiction of the creation story of Genesis 1, which many assume provides the paradigm for understanding creation.

In Genesis 1 the author seems to go out of his way to stress that creation occurred without any conflict, by the sheer fiat of God, and that it is all good. In contrast to the Near Eastern creation stories of his day, this author seems to emphasize that Yahweh had no opponents in creating the world. Thus if one starts with the assumption that this account is normative, it is hard to see how one could take the warfare-creation accounts as being anything more than mythological. Though they express structural features of the cosmos now, they cannot add anything specifically to our understanding of the act of creation. As to how and when the creation became structurally flawed, we simply cannot say based on this reading.

If we can for a moment step back from the traditional reading of

Genesis 1, however, the force of this objection can be somewhat assuaged. For one thing, it is not apparent why Genesis 1 should be granted normative status over the other, more numerous, conflict-creation accounts in the Bible. Some have argued that only the Genesis 1 account is consistent with "pure" monotheism, and hence only it can be taken in any sense "literally."[37] But the notion that monotheism is threatened if God must engage in genuine warfare with cosmic (or human) opponents is, as already suggested, nothing more than an arbitrary assumption that simply does not square either with the biblical data or with the early postapostolic church, though it unfortunately came to form one of the foundational assumptions of the classical-philosophical theistic tradition.

Others may argue that the warfare creation accounts should be dismissed as normative because of their obvious mythological features, features that Genesis 1 avoids. But the fact that the descriptions of the cosmic forces which opposed God at creation are mythological no more necessitates that the creation-conflict itself is mythological than it necessitates that either the opposing forces or God himself is mythological in these passages. Arguing in this fashion would be like dismissing the historicity of the Fall because one comes to the conclusion that the talking serpent or the forbidden fruit in Genesis 3 is symbolic. Ancient literature simply does not operate with such clear-cut categories.[38]

Moreover, on most reckonings Genesis 1 itself is not altogether free from elements of mythological expression. The primitive cosmology that is presupposed throughout the chapter as well as the notion of God "resting" on the seventh day perhaps indicates that Genesis 1, while certainly not as myth-laden as other creation-conflict accounts, is nevertheless hardly a modern, scientific, literal documentary of creation. Further, it is likely that the author yet preserves something of the sinister nature of the "deep" (*t'hôm*), of the waters and of the darkness (Gen 1:2)—elements that, significantly enough, the author does not say the Lord God created.[39] Absolutizing this one section of Scripture as doctrinally normative over other, more numerous creation-conflict accounts seems quite arbitrary.

Original creation or restoration? Even more fundamental, however, is that one can make a fairly solid case for reading Genesis 1 that avoids this arbitrary normativity, for it does not conflict with the Bible's creation-conflict tradition, nor does it require dismissing the creation-conflict tradition as purely mythological. According to this view, the author of Genesis 1 is not attempting to give the exhaustive and definitive account of creation. Rather, the author is providing an account that is supplemental to other warfare accounts. More specifically, while the scriptural conflict-creation accounts parallel (and polemicize against) the other conflict-creation accounts of their day in speaking of God's conflict with an evil anticreational force, the Genesis 1 account parallels (and polemicizes against) these other accounts in terms of God's creation of this world *after* his battle with his cosmic foes, and *out of* the remains of the battle.

Stated differently, both ancient and modern exegetes have argued with some plausibility that the account in Genesis 1 is not so much an account of creation as it is an account of God's restoration of a world that had through a previous conflict become formless, futile, empty (*tōhû wābōhû*) and engulfed by chaos (*tᵉhôm*)—the world of Genesis 1:2, in other words. According to this view, sometimes called "the restitution theory" or "the gap theory," but which I prefer to call "the restoration theory," the cosmos that had been created in verse 1 had become embattled, corrupted, judged and brought to the nearly destroyed state we find it in verse 2.[40] The rest of the chapter then describes God's creation of this present cosmos out of the formless and empty chaos of the previously ravaged one.

While this interpretation has never enjoyed anything close to a majority opinion, it has found impressive ancient as well as modern exponents.[41] Despite some ongoing difficulties,[42] a number of things can be said in its favor. I will briefly mention six.

First, as already stated, this reading of the Genesis 1 creation account most easily harmonizes with all the conflict-creation accounts in Scripture, a consideration that has to carry weight for all who affirm the plenary inspiration of Scripture. If this reading is correct, Genesis 1:2 can be understood as describing the desecrated creation immediately after God's battle with and judgment of evil cosmic forces—the same battle described in mythological language in other biblical and nonbiblical creation accounts. The author's emphasis on the sovereignty of God over the (now largely depersonalized) cosmic forces can thus be understood as one way of emphasizing Yahweh's victory over opposing gods, in the same fashion as *Enuma Elish* emphasizes Marduk's victory over Tiamat in describing his fashioning the world out of her and her cohorts in six days.[43]

On this reading, the Genesis 1 account, beginning with verse 2, presupposes the battle and starts with the fashioning of this world out of the battlefield; in *Enuma Elish* this is Tiamat's body; in the Genesis account it is the impersonal abyss (*t'hôm*) covering the wasteland earth (*tōhû wābōhû*). Levenson, though by no means holding to anything like the restoration theory, is among the few scholars who have acknowledged this point. He argues that the Genesis account *"begins* near the point when the Babylonian poem *ends* its action, with the primordial waters neutralized and the victorious and unchallengeable deity about to undertake the work of cosmogony."[44]

Other Old Testament scholars have recognized this aspect of the Genesis 1 account and have concluded that there must have been an earlier version of the Genesis 1 account containing a battle scene similar to that of *Enuma Elish*. This section, they speculate, has been lopped off for theological or redactional reasons in the received version.[45] The naturalness of reading Genesis 1:2 as a "postbattle" summary, when read against the background of *Enuma Elish*, lends plausibility to this theory.

For our purposes, however, the speculation seems irrelevant. Whether or not a prior version of Genesis 1 possessed a battle scene, the author/redactor certainly seems to have known of the earlier creation-conflict accounts. The author also assumes that his readers know about the "abyss," the "waters," the "formless and void" earth, as well as about other "gods" (significantly enough, also not mentioned in this creation account) with whom God consults before making humans (Gen 1:26).

It seems reasonable, then, to read the author not as offering an account that corrects the earlier creation-conflict accounts but as presenting an account that supplements them. He is starting where they leave off, and he is doing so to stress just how victorious Yahweh was over his enemies by emphasizing just how easily he fashions this creation—with the mere word of his mouth!—out of the mess left over from his battle with Leviathan (or Rahab or Tiamat), the battle that all his readers are familiar with.

To this end, the Genesis 1 author does not even give Tiamat or any of the other defeated gods the dignity of a personality (though echoes of it can perhaps still be heard). He simply describes the war-torn "world" as *tōhû wābōhû*, covered by *t'hôm*, and then proceeds to proclaim Yahweh's ease in carving this present ordered creation out of this battle-raged chaos. Such a view allows us to give full due to the significant influence of the creation-conflict accounts of Israel's neighbors while also (and far more importantly) harmonizing Genesis 1 with the other conflict-creation accounts in Scripture. I do not see any other reading that can claim this.

Moreover, and somewhat ironically, this interpretation at once allows for the most culturally relevant reading and the most literal reading of Genesis 1 as well as all the other scriptural creation-conflict accounts. This certainly has to count further in its favor both from a scholarly perspective committed to reading Scripture in its original cultural context and from an evangelical faith perspective committed to affirming the infallibility of Scripture.[46]

Second, reading Genesis 1 in the light of Scripture's creation-conflict material, and thus as describing a re-creation rather than original creation, helps explain several otherwise puzzling features of this account. For example, this reading provides a context in which we can perhaps begin to understand the unusual command given by Yahweh to humanity to "subdue" (*kābaš*) the earth (Gen 1:28). This term usually suggests the suppression, the conquering or the enslavement of hostile forces (Num 32:22, 29; Josh 18:1).[47] If what we have in Genesis 1 is a pure and pristine creation of all things ex nihilo, this command is odd. If all is exactly as God intended, what is there to conquer?

If, however, what we have in Genesis 1 is a creation that is good, but that is, following *Enuma Elish* and other primitive accounts, fashioned out of a battle-torn chaotic abyss and that, as such, must continually be controlled (as in the nonbiblical creation-conflict material), then this command begins to make sense. Humans in this case are charged with carrying on God's creational work of bringing order to chaos. For just this reason, we are said to be in the image and likeness of God (Gen 1:26-28). As we shall see in what follows, we are in this view corulers with God over the earth and cowarriors with God against the forces of chaos for the earth. God's plan for human beings and the earth shall be accomplished when all anticreation forces are vanquished and his kingdom is set up on the earth with him and his human subjects enthroned (Rev 5:10).

This reading also makes the best sense of the Lord's command to Adam to guard Eden (Gen 2:15).[48] The command is a bit puzzling unless the author was assuming that there were at the time forces which the garden needed protection against. When the tempting serpent appears in the next chapter, we perhaps get a clearer idea of what it was that Adam was supposed to beware of. But the sudden and unexplained presence of Satan (according to the traditional interpretation) in the garden is likewise difficult to account for on the supposition that Genesis 1 is providing anything like an exhaustive account of the original creation.[49]

According to the restoration view, however, neither the commands to subdue the earth and protect the garden nor the sudden appearance of Satan is puzzling. In this view the earth (this present earth) is birthed, as it were, in an infected incubator. It is fashioned in a warfare context. It is itself altogether good, but it is made and preserved over and against forces that are perpetually hostile to it, just as the other creation-conflict passages of Scripture suggest.

In this view, moreover, humans are made in the image of God and placed on the earth precisely so that they might gradually vanquish this chaos and establish—or better, reestablish—God's all-good plan for it. As God's earthly agents, we are "to effect the conquest of an evil being who had penetrated into creation."[50] Or, as Erich Sauer puts it, our "appointed vocation in Paradise consisted in the winning back of the earth for God . . . [and] to restore the whole earth to an abode of the presence and revelation of God."[51] The otherwise puzzling features of the Genesis narrative fit perfectly with this perspective.

This reading also makes sense of the unexplained and unexpected use of the first-person plural in Genesis 1:26. The standard Jewish interpretation—and it still remains the best (see chapter five)—is that the Lord is here consulting with angels prior to creating what is to be the pinnacle of his creation (or re-creation). That the narrative up to this point had not mentioned the creation of angels suggests that it simply presupposes their preexistence—which is enough to demonstrate that we are not here dealing with an exhaustive account of creation ex nihilo. According to the restoration view, such beings, usually termed "gods" as we shall see in the next chapter, were present eons before this creation was ever brought about. Indeed, it was Yahweh's battle against a rebellious faction of these "gods" that brought the creation to the dismal condition described in Genesis 1:2. It is, then, not surprising that Yahweh consults with them, as he apparently does with some frequency (see Gen 3:22; 11:7; 1 Kings 22:20; Is 6:1-8; cf. Jer 23:18; Ps 82:1; 89:7), when he comes to the climaxing act of his warfare against anticreational forces: the creation of humans to subdue the earth.

Third, this view is consistent with linguistic evidence. For example, Genesis 1:2 can be translated, "Now [or 'But'] the earth became [or 'had become,' *hāy^etāh*] formless and empty."[52] The terms "formless" and "empty" are usually pejorative in Scripture, denoting something gone wrong, laid waste or judged.[53] In the only other cases in Scripture where the terms are combined as they are in Genesis 1:2, they refer explicitly to a desperate state of being that results from God's judgment (Jer 4:23; Is 34:11).[54]

It is, then, easy to read the second verse of the Genesis account as referring to a judged and largely destroyed earth—"a chaos that . . . resembled the morning after a battle."[55] It is the kind of wasteland Jeremiah warns will result again after God's eschatological judgment (Jer 4:21-24; see also Is 24:10). Conversely, it would seem odd if the author was suggesting that God originally created the earth in these wasted, futile and chaotic conditions, and even more odd if he believed this but did not bother to tell his readers.

As the text stands, the formless and futile chaos of verse 2, together with the "deep," are the only things in this chapter that the author does not say God created or fashioned. Other passages of Scripture seem to go yet further and suggest that this state of being is something God explicitly did not and would not create (see esp. Is 45:18).[56] What is more, with the exception of the creation of animals and humans (vv. 21, 26-27), the passage does not use the word "create" (*bārā*) but "make" (*^eāśāh*), which means to fashion out of preexisting material—again suggesting that we are dealing not with an original creation but with a re-creation.[57]

Fourth, this reading of Genesis 1 provides the most flexible, and perhaps the most fruitful, paradigm within which the Bible's creation accounts can be unqualifiedly affirmed without any possibility of running into problems with modern scientific theories concerning the antiquity of the earth. This theory postulates a prehumanoid world of indefinite duration, about which we know nothing more than that it somehow became a battlefield between good and evil and was consequently made into a total wasteland.

This very indefiniteness allows for a remarkably wide range of possible ways of squaring biblical theology with contemporary scientific theories, though unfortunately these ways have hardly begun to be explored, owing to the traditional normativity of Genesis 1 as the definitive creation account. Indeed, though it lies outside the purview of this work, a case can be made that the supposition of a worldwide instantaneous catastrophe alone accounts for much of the geological and paleontological evidence discovered.[58]

Further, and perhaps most important for the purposes of this project, this understanding provides us with one plausible way of beginning to make sense of what appears to be millions of years of prehumanoid suffering on the earth. It provides a context in which we can perhaps begin to take seriously and develop C. S. Lewis's speculation that the earth might have become demonized long before humans ever arrived on it.[59] It begins to provide some biblical context in which we can perhaps make sense of the fact that most of the fossils we find in the paleontological record are of animals that do not now exist. Long before humans ever came on the scene—or fell—nature was already "red with tooth and claw."

Fifth, this approach to Genesis 1 allows us to construe an ultimate warfare canvas against which we can begin to make some sense out of cosmic evil. This reading, if accepted, begins to make sense of the fact that both Scripture and our own experience tell us that the whole cosmos is, at a most profound level, corrupted. I take this to be the most fundamental point of the earlier discussed creation-conflict material. Despite valiant attempts to the contrary, there is simply no way to approach an explanation for this cosmic catastrophe by appealing to puny human wills. Our fall cannot explain the cosmic fall, but the fall of cosmic wills can help explain our fall, and with it, the fall of the world we were put in charge of. It is, as C. S. Lewis noted, significant in this regard that the Bible talks much more about "powers of darkness" than it does about the human fall, a point that ought to (but thus far has not) factor significantly in our explanations for why there is evil. This reading of Genesis 1 confirms this observation and thus encourages a more cosmic approach to the problem of evil.[60]

Sixth, and finally, the understanding that Genesis 1 is about restoring a world that had been ruined by hostile forces is consistent with the otherwise puzzling cosmic dimension of the Bible's portrayal of humanity's role on the earth and of Christ's role as savior.

Immediately after declaring that we have been made in "the image of God," the Lord tells humans to "subdue" and "have dominion" over the whole of creation (Gen 1:26-30). "I have given you every plant yielding seed that is upon the face of all the earth," the Lord says, and everything else, plant and animal, that is upon it (1:29-30). As Sauer notes, "These words plainly declare the vocation of the human race to rule."[61] We were made in "the image of God" precisely because we are created for the purpose of reigning with God over the earth.[62]

This theme, in a variety of ways, runs throughout the biblical narrative. For example, after the psalmist declares that Yahweh rules "the raging of the sea" and that he "crushed Rahab like a carcass" (Ps 89:9-10), he records the Lord's promise to his earthly servant: "I will set his hand on the sea, and his right hand on the rivers" (v. 25). As Levenson notes, this text portrays a sort of diarchy, as do a number of other psalms. God rules, but his desire is to rule through his earthly coregents.[63]

For this reason, as Sauer again notes, the redemption of the earth is intrinsically connected with the redemption of humanity. Indeed, the whole creation, according to Paul, "waits with eager longing for the revealing of the children of God" (Rom 8:19). For this reason also the redemption of the cosmos is intrinsically connected to defeating the evil force that now holds humanity, and thus the whole earth, in bondage (see chapters nine and ten below).

Humanity as the restorative viceroy over the earth. The restoration theory provides an ultimate background against which the themes of human coregency with God over creation and the liberation of the earth and humanity from evil forces can be rendered most coherent and plausible, and through which their unity can be seen. For according to this reading, the creation of humans and their placement in the garden can be seen as God's means of completing his "conquest of an evil being who had penetrated into creation," as the great Old Testament scholar Franz Delitzsch put it.[64]

As a little seed of yeast leavens a whole lump of dough (Lk 13:21; 1 Cor 5:6), so too, we might suppose, God planned on using humans, beginning in Eden, to restore his lordship over the earth by themselves establishing their dominion over the earth, a dominion that would, in every respect, be under the authority of the Lord.[65] Or, as suggested earlier, the creation (in Genesis 1) was birthed in an infected incubator, and humanity was given leadership over this earth as the means of killing the infection.

Sauer expresses this view in these terms:

Man's appointed vocation in Paradise consisted in the winning back of the earth for God, and this again was based upon the sovereignty of God over man and the sovereignty of man over the creation. . . .

Man's calling was to "destroy the works of the devil" and to renew the earth, thus transforming it into an abode of light and life. . . . The first man . . . received the task, beginning from Paradise, to restore the whole earth to an abode of the presence and revelation of God. His service as ruler consisted in bringing the whole of creation through his mediation into relation with the glory of God and in making the "fullness of him that filleth all in all" accessible to it.[66]

For this reason, when humans voluntarily rebelled against God's sovereignty, the whole of creation once again suffered. God had, as the ancient Israelites would say, "shut up Yamm behind closed doors" in order to re-create the world and turn it over to a new viceroy. According to the restoration view, this is what Genesis 1 is all about. But since God's supremacy is of a moral character, it must be freely chosen.[67] Hence the key that could either unleash Yamm once again upon the earth or keep him at bay was placed into the hands of the new viceroy.

When humanity rejected Yahweh's lordship, we accepted (by unleashing) a new "god of this world." We compromised our assigned task to have dominion over the world and thus subjected ourselves and all of nature once again to the destructive influence of the forces that oppose God. The guardians of the world, and therefore the world itself, were thus taken hostage by an illegitimate hostile power. Satan now seizes "control of the entire world" and becomes "the prince of this age" and "the ruler of the kingdom of the air" (1 Jn 5:19; Jn 12:31; Eph 2:2; cf. 6:12). Through Christ, however, the key has been given back to those originally intended as landlords, and we are once again commissioned to shut up Yamm on the Lord's authority (Mt 16:17-19; see part two).

This reacquired demonic lordship has already led to a partial return to the judged state of affairs in Genesis 1:2, when the Lord allowed the chaotic waters to burst upon the earth with the flood (Gen 6—8). The intended viceroys of the earth had become so corrupt that they apparently cohabited with sinister angelic beings (6:1-4), and the Lord was grieved to the point of wishing he had never created humanity (6:5-6). Hence he allowed the "deep" (1:2) once again to cover the earth, as he sought to start over the project of recovering the earth for his glory.

Moreover, according to Jeremiah and Isaiah, the earth shall at some point be brought one more time under this sort of judgment and returned to a state of *tōhû wābōhû* (Jer 4:23; Is 34:11), the very state it was in, according to the restoration theory, prior to this present creation. The "dragon, that ancient serpent, who is the Devil and Satan," who has been locked up in "the bottomless pit," shall "be released from his prison" (Rev 20:1-2, 7). However, as in the Genesis 1 account, the Lord shall vanquish his foe and re-create "a new heaven and a new earth" (21:1).

In this final form, however, the hostile powers shall be permanently defeated and locked up. In the eschaton, "the sea was no more" (Rev 21:1). Satan, death, the beast, *t'hôm*, all rebels and even Hades itself shall be cast into the lake of fire (20:13-15). Hence Scripture assures us that there shall be no more threat to the creation in this its third restoration.

God's kingdom shall be established on earth, and his children shall be its rulers as he originally intended. Humanity's prehistoric failure as guardians did not cause the Creator to abandon us in his plan to restore and reclaim the embattled world of Genesis 1:2. To the contrary, and quite remarkably, the Lord's goal throughout has been to reestablish his lordship upon the earth through the viceregency of humans, and to ultimately vanquish his cosmic foes in the process.

Now, however, and even more remarkably, this goal was to be achieved by the Lord himself freeing humanity—and thus creation—from the dominion of Satan, and to do so by becoming a human himself. This little plot of land in the cosmos apparently became a sort of "Normandy beach" on which creation's D-Day was waged. As we shall later see, Jesus' incarnation, his teaching, his healing and deliverance ministry, and especially his death and resurrection are all about vanquishing Leviathan (Satan) and restoring the reign of God on earth over against the illegitimate tyranny of Satan. He will do so by rescuing humans from Satan's domain and restoring them as God's viceroys on the earth.[68]

Conclusion

The restoration theory is part of a cosmic warfare background against which the cosmic dimension of humanity's purpose, the cosmic dimension of nightmarish evil, and the cosmic purpose of Christ's coming, death and resurrection begin to make sense. It completes the pattern of creation to chaos to restoration that runs throughout the biblical narrative and thereby brings a thematic unity to the Bible it would otherwise lack. From start to finish, this inspired literary collection is about God restoring his creation through humanity (and by himself becoming a human) and destroying his cosmic opponents in the process.

This reading of Genesis 1 has the fringe benefit of fitting with any estimation of the earth's age that science might arrive at. It also has the advantage of making the most sense (Custance would argue the only possible sense) out of all the linguistic evidence. Moreover, it fits best with Scripture's later teaching regarding the fall of Satan and his angels, and makes sense out of otherwise puzzling features of the Genesis narrative (e.g., "subduing" the earth, "guarding" the garden, the unexplained sinister serpent, the presence of angels). It also allows for the most literal reading of the creation-conflict accounts in Scripture. Perhaps most significantly, it at once squares Genesis 1 with these other creation accounts in the Bible, while also allowing for the most use of nonbiblical creation accounts, especially *Enuma Elish*, in understanding this creation account.

A good deal can be said in favor of the restoration theory. However, I am by no means claiming that this handling of the creation-conflict stories in Scripture is the only way to handle them. Nor would I want to invest too much weight in such a speculative matter. While the case for the restoration view is defensible and compelling, the evidence is nevertheless admittedly tentative and controversial and should not be raised to the level of a doctrine.

Nor would I want the credibility of the warfare worldview to depend on this tentative theory alone. The Bible's warfare understanding of evil remains intact even if the restoration understanding of Genesis 1 is rejected and the creation-conflict passages of Scripture are taken to be completely mythological (viz., lacking a temporal reference to an actual primordial battle). Still, if this reading of Genesis 1 is accepted as persuasive, it cannot help but further enhance our appreciation for the warfare worldview of the Bible.

4

JUDGING
"THE GODS"

YAHWEH'S CONFLICT WITH ANGELIC BEINGS IN THE OLD TESTAMENT

*T*HUS FAR WE HAVE SEEN THAT THE BELIEF IN YAHWEH'S ULTIMATE sovereignty and the goodness of his creation did not prevent Old Testament authors from appropriating fundamental features of the Near Eastern cosmic battle motif and, to a lesser extent, its demonology. As in other Near Eastern literature, the Old Testament affirms the reality of hostile seas, cosmic monsters and evil spirits in the world, though it also affirms Yahweh's ability to vanquish them and preserve order in his creation. Indeed, Yahweh's supremacy over these evil forces of chaos and demons has no parallel in the literature of Israel's neighbors. Nonetheless, the Old Testament does express the belief that the creation is at a foundational level threatened by evil forces, though at this stage of biblical revelation the expression is highly mythical and somewhat ambiguous.

This limited demonology and these creation-conflict accounts, however, by no means exhaust the Old Testament teaching on Yahweh's battle with hostile forces. As we shall see in this and the following chapter, the warfare worldview of the Old Testament also includes the understanding that Yahweh must contend with a sometimes disobedient and incompetent council of spiritual beings (usually called "gods"), and must in fact contend with one particularly malicious god entitled "the adversary" (*haśśāṭān*). As with the motifs of hostile cosmic forces and demons, the reality of this struggle with other gods is never taken to compromise the supremacy and sovereignty of Yahweh. Rather it is taken to express the way Yahweh is supreme and sovereign.

In this chapter I first consider in general terms the relationship that Old Testament authors understand Yahweh to have with other gods, then survey the hotly contested and important debate concerning the nature and origin of "true monotheism." This is followed by an examination of the Old Testament's concept of Yahweh being surrounded by a heavenly council of gods. I conclude with some examples of what happens when these gods rebel against their Creator.

Yahweh and Lesser "Gods"

In explicit opposition to the cultures around them, the Israelites believed that there was only one true God. Unlike everything these surrounding cultures believed, the Old Testament unanimously portrays Yahweh as being the sole Creator of all that is, and thus as being alone eternal and sovereign. What is more, the Old Testament everywhere assumes that Yahweh has this sovereignty by nature. Unlike the powerful gods of Near Eastern pantheons, Yahweh did not have to seize his power by force.

This is not to suggest, however, that the Israelites denied the existence of angelic or spiritual beings. In fact, they often referred to these beings as "gods." What is more, while many today understand angels to be rather innocuous creatures, mere extensions of God's will, lacking a mind and volition of their own, the Old Testament authors everywhere assume that these gods have a good deal of autonomous power. Appreciating this autonomy is crucial for an understanding of the Old Testament's view of evil, and for an adequate understanding of how Old Testament thought evolved into what we find in the New Testament.

For this reason, as well as out of simple fidelity to Scripture, it seems advisable to retain the word "god," over the word "angel," when discussing the views of authors who use that term. While the term "gods" may sit uncomfortably with some contemporary evangelical readers, it has a strong biblical foundation, even in the New Testament (1 Cor 8:6; 2 Cor 4:4), and is free from much of the unbiblical cultural baggage associated with the term "angels." But neither I nor any Old Testament author means by the term "god" a being who is in any sense coeternal, cocreator or coruler with the one true God. The gods are very powerful beings, but they all have their power on loan from the Creator God.

Old Testament authors do not deny the existence of lesser gods alongside Yahweh, though several passages are sometimes taken to imply this. For example, speaking to God's people at a time when they were being led astray by idols, Isaiah emphatically repeated the refrain that Yahweh alone is God and there is no other: "Before me no god was formed, nor shall there be any after me. I, I am the LORD, and besides me there is no savior" (Is 43:10-11).[1]

A similar refrain is used by Jeremiah, writing in the midst of a similarly idolatrous situation. Through him the Lord says to Israel, "How can I pardon you? Your children have forsaken me, and have sworn by those who are no gods" (Jer 5:7; cf. 10:2-16).

Do such passages imply that these authors believe that there are literally no gods besides Yahweh? I think not. Elsewhere both Jeremiah and Isaiah depict a heavenly council of gods who surround Yahweh (Jer 23:18, 22; Is 6:2-8).[2] Moreover, as Ulrich Mauser has argued, Isaiah speaks in this same hyperbolic fashion about nations, princes and armies being nothing before God (Is 40:17, 23; 41:12).[3] Yet Isaiah was clearly not literally denying the existence of these realities.

The existence of other gods seems to have been an assumption shared by all Hebrews before as well as after these two prophets. If Isaiah and Jeremiah were categorically denying the existence of other gods, they would be unique in the history of Israel. A better approach is to understand Isaiah and Jeremiah as expressing an exaggerated form of mockery in denying the reality of pagan gods, as Adrio König, among others, has argued.[4] These gods and idols, they are sarcastically saying, are so puny in comparison with Yahweh that they do not even warrant the title "god." In so arguing, Isaiah and Jeremiah are expressing the radical uniqueness of Yahweh as the sole true God, the radical subordination of all other spiritual beings to him, and the radical sinfulness of worshiping idols as God. But they cannot be taken as categorical denials of the existence of other spiritual beings.

Ulrich Mauser sums up the general Old Testament perspective well:
The Old Testament speaks freely, without any hesitation or embarrassment, about the existence of gods other than the God of Israel.

... To be sure, the supremacy of Israel's God over all other gods is everywhere asserted. But the assertion always drives home the dominion of Yahweh over other gods, not the denial of their existence.[5]
In any case, the remainder of the Old Testament exhibits no reservation in acknowledging the existence of gods outside Yahweh and of the gods who form his heavenly council. But even here Yahweh's supremacy is always at the forefront of their thoughts. Hence the first commandment reads, "You shall have no other gods before me" (Ex 20:3). The existence of other gods is presupposed, but they are subordinate to the one who alone is the Lord God Almighty.

A refrain occurs throughout the Old Testament, especially in the Psalms: "There is none like you among the gods, O Lord" (Ps 86:8); "great is the LORD, and greatly to be praised; he is to be revered above all gods" (96:4); "our Lord is above all gods" (135:5). Similarly, all the gods are commanded to worship Yahweh (29:1; 97:7), for he is "exalted far above all gods" (97:9) and is, in fact, their King (95:3). Similarly, Moses pleads for God's mercy to let him go over to the Promised Land: "What god in heaven or on earth can perform deeds and mighty acts like yours! Let me cross over to see the good land" (Deut 3:24-25). The divine realm is envisaged as a veritable society of gods, though Yahweh is clearly understood to be incomparably greater than all others, for he alone is Creator.[6]

While later Jewish-Christian tradition will back off somewhat from the term "god," it never backs away from this conception of spiritual beings populating the cosmos. Thus, to cite one remarkable example, against the Corinthian's misuse of the Shema, the teaching that "there is no God but one" (1 Cor 8:4), Paul argues that there are, in fact, "many gods and many lords" (8:5). But, he adds, "for us there is one God, the Father . . . and one Lord, Jesus Christ" (8:6). As Mauser again notes, his admission of "many gods" and "many lords," as well as this clear distinction between God the Father and the Lord Jesus Christ, is "most uncomfortable for a clean monotheism."[7]

As mentioned earlier, while the Old Testament never questions the ultimate sovereignty of the Creator, this sovereignty is nowhere taken to imply that the other gods of heaven possess no autonomous power. To the contrary, the Old Testament assumes that they have power to think and act on their own.

For example, it is difficult to escape the clear import of Jephthah's question to the Ammonite king: "Should you not possess what your god Chemosh gives you to possess? And should we not be the ones to possess everything that the LORD our God has conquered for our benefit?" (Judg 11:24). Like all people of his time, Jephthah believed that spiritual forces—the gods of various nations—were deeply involved in human battles and played a crucial role in whether they won or lost a battle.[8] Thus if Yahweh defeats the god Chemosh and gives "Sihon and all his people into the hand of Israel" (v. 21), then Israel wins the battle and the land of the Amorites is rightfully theirs.

It can, however, apparently also work the other way, as when the king of Moab inspired the wrath of Chemosh to burn against Israel by sacrificing his son to him. Though Israel had been routing the Moabites up to this point, they then had to retreat quickly (2 Kings 3:26-27). If we allow the text to stand on its own terms, if we do not demythologize it according to our modern Western assumptions, this text certainly seems to assume the reality of the god Chemosh. Indeed, the text also seems to assume the ability of the Moabite king to influence, and perhaps even empower, this demonic being through sacrificing his child; the text also seems to assume the ability of Chemosh in this case to rout Israel in battle.[9]

The power of gods to assist or resist Yahweh in war, to hinder his answers to prayers, to influence "natural" disasters, to inflict diseases on people, to deceive people and the like is assumed throughout the Bible. Yahweh is unquestionably understood to reign supreme over the whole cosmic society of spiritual and earthly beings, but this sovereignty is never—even in Isaiah and Jeremiah—taken to imply either that he is the only divine being or that the other divine beings are mere extensions of his will.

This dimension of significant self-determination and power, shared by the angelic and human society, opens up the possibility of conflict in the spiritual and earthly realms. This quasi-democratic view of the cosmos, this freedom to influence others for better or for worse, is the sine qua non of a warfare worldview. For just this reason, when Augustine and the later church undermine the genuine self-determination of angels and people by identifying divine sovereignty with meticulous control, the warfare worldview itself is logically compromised. Again, for just this reason, the intellectual problem of evil is necessarily placed center stage in Christian theology. If the cosmos is not something of a free democracy (under the ultimate rulership of God), it has to be something of a tyrannical monarchy. Either some power is shared or it is not. If not, all the blame for all the evil in the cosmos has ultimately to rest squarely on the lap of the monarch whose will is (purportedly) never thwarted.

The Nature and Origin of Ancient Jewish Monotheism

In the minds of many scholars and laypeople alike, this affirmation of the reality and influence of other gods next to Yahweh seems incompatible with "true monotheism." Rooted in the misreading of Isaiah and Jeremiah is the common assumption that monotheism means denying that other gods exist alongside the one true God, at least gods who could exercise any sort of autonomous power (such as Chemosh). To the extent that we admit the existence of other gods, it has often been assumed, we compromise true monotheism and degenerate to some form of "henotheism" or "monolatry."[10] It is because of this arbitrary but pervasive assumption about the exclusive nature of true monotheism that so many have difficulty accepting the warfare worldview of Scripture at face value.[11]

Biblical scholarship is increasingly recognizing that the assumption that monotheism is necessarily exclusive is false, at least if we are operating with a phenomenological definition of monotheism, not an idealistic philosophical one. Hence N. T. Wright argues that "the postulation of supernatural beings other than the one God has nothing to do with a declining away from 'pure' monotheism." He adds, "if it does, we must say that we have very few examples of 'pure' monotheism anywhere, including in the Hebrew Bible."[12]

Peter Hayman agrees and goes so far as to contend that if monotheism is defined as a belief that denies the existence of all gods save one, then one is hard-pressed to find any true monotheist in the history of Israel up to the Middle Ages, and even then it is doubtful.[13] Given this exclusivistic definition, he argues, "it is hardly ever appropriate to use the term monotheism to describe the Jewish idea of God."[14] For, in a wide variety of ways, people in both biblical and postbiblical times assumed that Yahweh must work with or confront other friendly or hostile divine powers (whether called "angels" or "gods"). Presumably to capture this notion of shared power, Hayman offers the unusual label "cooperative dualism" to replace "monotheism" as a descriptive phrase for the Jewish perspective on Yahweh and his relationship with the world.[15]

While I agree with Hayman's thesis that the general scholarly definition of monotheism as exclusive is arbitrary and inaccurate for the phenomena it is supposed to describe, he seems to overstate his case. Most importantly, Hayman gives insufficient weight to the nearly universal Jewish and Christian affirmations that <u>among all the gods, angels or spiritual forces, Yahweh alone is the Creator of all that is, and therefore Yahweh alone is to be worshiped.</u>

To be more specific, while the doctrine of creation ex nihilo is perhaps not explicit in Genesis 1:1, it is (pace Hayman) implicit in many other passages of Scripture (see, e.g., Neh 9:6; Ps 90:2; 102:45; 148:5-6; Rom 11:36; 1 Cor 8:6; 2 Cor 5:5; Eph 3:9; Heb 2:10; 5:4; 11:3; Rev 4:11). It is also explicit and implicit throughout most of the Judeo-Christian traditions. Jews and Christians have rarely endorsed the pagan idea that some eternal beings or impersonal cosmic realities exist alongside the one true God. They have generally resisted any suggestion that the Creator is limited by anything outside himself.[16]

For just this reason, never have believers within the parameters of the orthodox Judeo-Christian tradition endorsed the worship of spiritual beings other than the Creator. Reverence and requests for assistance have on occasion been admitted; indeed, at times they are even encouraged. But never has worship in the sense of ultimate adoration been permitted.[17] The biblical teaching that the Lord is a "jealous" God has generally been understood to apply to just this point (e.g., Ex 20:5; 34:14; Deut 4:24). It is the defining characteristic of monotheistic praxis.

For these reasons, while I concede Hayman's and Wright's observation that the Jewish conception of one God has almost always included a conception of a number of other spiritual powers surrounding God, some of which are outside his direct control, Hayman's proposal to replace the term "monotheism" with "cooperative dualism" to describe traditional Jewish faith seems overreactive and ill advised. In orthodox Judeo-Christian terms, whatever general state of affairs exists—for example, whether there is a multiplicity of gods and whether this multiplicity embodies the possibility of warfare—it is a state of affairs the Creator, in his wisdom, has himself chosen.

In this light, Wright's term "creational monotheism" seems more appropriate. Unlike philosophical monotheism with its speculative conjecture about what "pure" monotheism entails, creational monotheism does not rule out the acknowledgment of the existence of lesser gods.

But neither does it say that one among all the gods happens to be above the rest, or that one among all the gods happens to be preferred by us (henotheism, monolatry). Arising out of the biblical revelation, creational monotheism affirms that there are indeed a multiplicity of gods, but only one is eternal, only one is Creator, only one is Lord, and only one is omnipotent, while all others have their being and their power only by virtue of being given it by their Creator. Hence the Creator is in a class all by himself, and for this reason he and he alone is to be worshiped.

Creational monotheism maintains that while Yahweh must genuinely battle with spiritual cosmic rivals, this "must" is itself something Yahweh himself has brought into being. It need not imply that Yahweh secretly controls his rivals, only that the very power of his rivals to resist him is given by him.[18]

Nevertheless, Hayman's polemic against the standard philosophical exclusivistic definition of monotheism is both insightful and necessary. With the proviso that Yahweh is the primordial Creator of all (hence, by implication, the sole eternal being) and the one appropriate object of worship, Hayman is correct in noting the significance of the fact that the Bible and later Jewish tradition are largely free from the standard exclusive view of "pure monotheism." By both biblical and traditional standards, so long as Yahweh is confessed to be Creator and is alone worshiped as the Creator, there is simply no incompatibility between affirming that Yahweh is the one true God and affirming that a multiplicity of other gods exists.

Abandoning the exclusive philosophical definition of monotheism has important implications for several other issues that surround Judaism's and Christianity's views of God and other gods. For one thing, the birth and rapid growth of Christianity on Jewish soil become intelligible only when we free ourselves from the standard caricature of "pure monotheism" as entailing the belief that no other gods exist. That Jesus could from the start be portrayed in terms of deity and worshiped in some sense alongside God the Father demonstrates how flexible the Jewish monotheism of the time was. It was hardly a monotheism that was stuck on a mathematical understanding of God's "oneness."[19]

Nor was this Jesus devotion the result of excessive Hellenization through which "pure monotheism" was supposedly compromised, as Wilhelm Bousset and others have argued.[20] So far as can be determined, the Jewish concept of the "oneness" of God was never primarily a numerical concept; rather, the confession that "the Lord our God is one Lord" (Deut 6:4; Mk 12:29, 32) was intended to refer to the uniqueness of Yahweh (among all gods) and Israel's singular devotion to him. The early Jewish Christians' acceptance of Jesus as the divine Son of God, while still remarkable, is far more intelligible in this light than if they had previously been holding to anything like the philosophical exclusivistic definition of monotheism discussed above.

Evolution or devolution? The adaptation of a more flexible definition of monotheism also contributes to the long-standing but important debate over whether monotheism or polytheism is the primordial faith. Stated most generally, the issue is this: Does monotheism represent an evolution out of polytheism (as most critical scholars over the last century have argued),[21] or does polytheism represent a devolution from original monotheism (as a minority of scholars, but a majority of conservatives, have argued)?

Among the number of things that hang upon this question is the integrity of the biblical account of prehistory that clearly implies that the earliest humans were monotheists (creational, not exclusive, monotheists). Equally important, however, is that our understanding of the relation between monotheism and polytheism is at stake here. If, for example, one evolved or devolved out of the other, then it seems we must view the Old Testament's tendency to affirm the supremacy of the one true God while also conceding the existence of many other influential gods as either an imperfectly evolved or a partially devolved form of monotheism.

I contend, however, that both schools of thought have tended to skew the available evidence because of an a priori assumption about the mutually exclusive nature of "pure" monotheism and "pure" polytheism. One school has generally tried to locate the first occurrence of pure (viz., exclusive) monotheism at some point in Israel's history (Abraham, Moses, Elijah, Isaiah, Ezra and Hosea are proposed candidates) and has then conjectured a long line of evolution leading up to this point. In contrast, the other school has generally postulated the existence of a pure form of monotheism at the beginning of human history and has then conjectured a long line of devolution leading to full-blown polytheism.

But what if these pure forms of monotheism and polytheism are simply theoretical constructs that do not actually describe what monotheists, and perhaps what polytheists, have generally believed, as Hayman suggested? What if we did not decide a priori that monotheism and polytheism were necessarily exclusive? We might find that the supposed evidence to argue that one evolved or devolved from the other simply does not exist.

Rather, the primordial faith (if we can speak of *the* primordial faith) was constituted by a devotion to one true God and a belief that a multitude of other powerful gods either serve him or oppose him. In short, we might find evidence suggesting that neither monotheism nor polytheism is, as such, more ancient than the other, and hence that neither necessarily evolved or devolved out of the other.

I would argue in just this direction. It is my conviction that these two schools both read the available evidence as signifying either an evolution or a devolution only because they start with an arbitrary philosophical definition of "true monotheism" as exclusive. They then postulate this "true monotheism" either at the beginning of history, from which polytheism devolves, or late in history, to which polytheism evolves.

All the evidence used to support each position, however, can be adequately accounted for, with none of the concomitant pitfalls, simply by allowing for the possibility that a devotion to one supreme Creator God and a belief in many lesser gods can fruitfully exist side by side. Indeed, if we simply look at what most monotheists and most polytheists actually believe instead of theorizing on the basis of what we suppose they ought to believe, we quickly see that this possibility has in fact usually characterized both belief systems.

The case for a primal creational monotheism. Those who hold that monotheism evolved out of polytheism have justifiably observed that no concrete evidence suggests there ever was a time when people did not believe in a multiplicity of gods. There simply is no conclusive evidence of a primordial faith in one God to the exclusion of the existence of other gods. As far back as we can go (and this is still reflected in primitive cultures today), believing in a multiplicity of gods, and living in the tension that sometimes exists among these gods and between these gods and humans (viz., the warfare worldview), seems to have been a staple of human culture throughout history.

Thus far the evolutionist camp seems on solid ground. This does not, however, come close to proving that monotheism evolved out of polytheism. For one thing, the evidence suggesting that deities tend to be conflated over time is sparse. Indeed, some archaeological evidence suggests the opposite (as the devolution camp is quick to point out).[22] For another thing, no one has yet succeeded in providing a convincing account of when, why and how Israel went from a (supposed) primordial polytheism to a Yahweh-centered monotheism. The sheer multitude of contradictory theories offered over the last century is enough to demonstrate how conjectural each position is.[23]

Although a "pure" form of primordial monotheism hasn't been discovered, a far stronger case than is usually conceded can be made for the view that prehistoric humanity tended to be monotheistic in the sense of believing in one supreme God who was qualitatively above all others.[24] A number of reputable scholars have argued in this direction on the basis of archeological evidence.

For example, the famous Assyriologist and Sumerologist Stephen Langdon has argued that, generally speaking, the older an inscription is, the more monotheistic it tends to be.[25] Concerning the Sumerians, Langdon maintains that the evidence suggests that the Sumerians originally had a belief in a supreme "personal god with the name *An* Heaven, Sky."[26] Similarly, Leopold von Schroeder and others have claimed that archeology suggests that behind all forms of Indo-Germanic polytheism is a faith in the supremacy of one unique Sky-God.[27] Others have argued the same for ancient Egyptian polytheism, as well as for the polytheism of ancient Greece, India and even China.[28]

More compelling than this, however, is the strong evidence of a type of monotheistic faith among primitive peoples today, peoples whose cultures by all accounts provide us with some of the clearest windows into what prehistoric humanity was like. Evidence along these lines is forthcoming from a wide variety of sources (only a few of which can be mentioned here).[29]

The Halakwulups of Tierra del Fuego have a belief in a single, spiritual, all-good God who, though he is too remote to be prayed to, still rewards and punishes people on the basis of their behavior.[30] Similarly, though the aborigines of southeast Australia believe that the world is populated with various grades of spirits, they nevertheless believe in a single, morally superior, omniscient deity named Darmulun.[31] Significantly enough, while these tribes believe that all spirits are to be reverenced, only the high god is to be worshiped.

Among the Bambuti pygmies of Central Africa and Andaman Islanders in the Gulf of Bengal—two tribes that had not yet learned how to make fire when first discovered—there is, in the midst of their animistic polytheism, a belief in a single god who is above the rest, alone immortal, creator and omniscient.[32] Such a perspective is almost universal among African tribes. As Ninian Smart argues, studies done on virtually thousands of African tribes reveal that "in most, if not all . . . there is belief in a supreme Spirit ruling over or informing the lesser spirits and gods."[33] And again: "ruling over the world which teems with divinities and sacred forces, there is—high above in the sky, but not of the sky—some kind of supreme Being. . . . He governs natural forces, dwells on high, is inexplicable, creates souls, men, and all things."[34] We see that, among those peoples who we would most suspect to preserve echoes of humanity's prehistoric past, we find that a form of monotheism is present, and that it seems to go hand in hand with a form of polytheism.

This phenomenon is not limited to African tribes. It is found in various forms around the globe in other primordial traditions. For example, the Lenape-Delaware Indians, an ancient eastern branch of the Algonquin tribe, express a strong faith in a single creator god, despite their otherwise vibrant polytheism. Indeed, their view of the creator and even many of the details of their creation account closely parallel the view and details of Genesis 1. Respect and invocations are given to a variety of lesser deities, but worship is reserved for the one supreme Creator.[35]

The list of primal tribes who combine a clear form of monotheism with a form of polytheism could be expanded greatly. The Selknam have from time immemorial offered up their first fruits to a high God who they know does not need nourishment.[36] The Yamana tribe believe in Watauinaiwa, who is "the Ancient One," ever watchful, rewarding good and punishing evil.[37] The Bhils of central India profess a faith in a personal creator Bhagwan, who created humans after all the gods he had earlier created rebelled against him because of "the Evil Spirit."[38]

How are we to account for this global phenomenon? If the possibilities of sheer coincidence and of "Christian contamination" are ruled out[39]—as they assuredly must be—we need to wonder along with David Rooney whether the common conceptions and stories serve "as eloquent reminders of an original common store of knowledge before the human diaspora over the face of the earth." Rooney continues: "Most anthropologists tend to accept diffusion of technology rather than simultaneous invention, as a likely explanation for the appearance of similar objects in different locations. Presumably the same should hold for myths as well."[40] In other words, the simplest explanation for this global presence of monotheism among primitive peoples is to trace it back to a shared tradition and a shared stock of knowledge.[41]

Even more forceful in arguing in this direction, however, is the widespread phenomenon in primitive tribes around the globe of a belief in a highest god who now plays no role in the spirituality of the people, a *deus otiosus* as it has been labeled. As N. A. Snaith observes,

> In . . . primitive strata of human development there . . . exist notions of Supreme Beings, vague, shadowy, often otiose, not worshipped. . . . Such are Koevasi of Florida, Kahausbwe of San Cristoval and Utikxo of the Amazulu. To these we would add Altjira of the Australian Aruna, and the Man-never-known-on-earth of the Wichitta Indians of Texas.[42]

The "high God" in each of these instances is conceptualized as being too far removed to be of practical value. He or she (Koevasi is female) is thought to be too exalted to be concerned with human affairs and to care about human worship.[43] If ever there was a time when the high God interacted with the people (and, curiously, often such a time before a "fall" is vaguely recalled) this time is now long past. Now, the high God is "gone away," as many of their myths say, and the only gods with whom the people have to do are the "low gods": the gods in charge of rain, vegetation, health, war and the like.[44]

What is most intriguing about this, as Snaith himself elsewhere points out, is that there is no way to account for how these singular hypertranscendent deities evolved, since they are altogether irrelevant to the everyday faith of the people. They make sense only as echoes of a once vibrant belief in a relevant supreme God.[45]

Primal monotheism and polytheism. Thus the evidence for a primal monotheism that acknowledged and worshiped a single Creator while nevertheless also acknowledging the existence of other lesser gods is quite compelling. Attempts to discredit this evidence have not been successful. Indeed, as a number of commentators have noted, the attempts have been largely circular and frequently ad hominem. They are often based primarily on the presupposition that monotheism reflects a sophisticated form of abstract reasoning that primordial peoples simply were not capable of. Hence the evidence must somehow be skewed. It has been suggested that since many of these tribes were initially investigated by Catholic missionaries and scholars, perhaps the documentation on each tribe's beliefs was prejudiced.[46] Subsequent research, however, has largely substantiated the original Catholic assessment and has shown the detractors to be the ones involved in circular reasoning.[47]

The case for a primal creational monotheism is quite strong, although largely ignored. Against most of the defenders of the primal monotheism theory, however, the evidence for some form of a primal polytheism is quite strong as well. While there is, as some archaeologists have argued, in some instances a discernible trend toward the multiplication of gods, the postulation of a time in which these gods were altogether absent carries us far beyond the available evidence.

The conclusion that seems most warranted by the available data is well expressed by Snaith:

> Those who think in terms of a necessary evolutionary development . . . upwards to monotheism are mistaken. We think that the theory of an original primitive monotheism is also mistaken. . . . We do not suppose that there ever was a so-called animistic people who had not also some kind of a Supreme Being. Equally we do not suppose that there ever was a people who believed only in a Supreme Being. . . . They had a belief in a Supreme Being, a High God, and at the same time a belief in all the "low gods," those who control the near-by elements by which man lives, food, rain, etc.[48]

We have no reason to suspect that there was ever a time when people did not believe in one supreme God and in a multiplicity of lesser gods. This view is found throughout the Old and New Testaments. There is one true God and a multiplicity of lesser gods.[49]

However, what is also found in both the Old and New Testaments is the strong belief that the supreme God, Yahweh, is the Creator of all other gods and of the whole world. Further, we find here the uncompromising conviction that only Yahweh, the Creator, is to be worshiped. These twin convictions phenomenologically define the creational monotheism of the Bible.[50]

It is not the acknowledgment of the existence of other gods that is the problem from a scriptural perspective. This much is assumed. Problems with other gods arise only when people begin to forget that these gods were themselves made, and hence that these gods are not to be worshiped. If a degeneration of religious views can be traced from the primordial faith, it is not a degeneration from a supposedly pure belief in one God to a corrupted belief in many gods. It is, rather, a degenera-

tion from a pure worship of one supreme Creator God to the corrupt
worship of many lesser gods. In other words, monotheism conflicts with
polytheism only when monotheistic worship and living (monotheopraxis) degenerates into polytheistic worship and living (polytheopraxis).

How might this degeneration have occurred? While we can only
conjecture an answer, the process is not hard to envisage if one accepts
the biblical account of a historical Fall. If one accepts the reality of a
primordial spiritual catastrophe at the fountainhead of the human race,
then it becomes easy to understand how the various traditions about the
high God "going away" originated.

Put simply, sin separates people from their Creator (Gen 3:8). We are
all born in a sin-infected environment, hence we all experience this
separation. Experiencing this distancing from God, we have no difficulty
understanding how primordial humanity could begin to seek assistance
on various matters from the "lower gods," who were deemed to be
nearer, perhaps less holy and thus less threatening.

The suggestion becomes more plausible when we consider that
throughout the biblical tradition, as throughout almost all primordial
cultures, we find the understanding that lesser gods were put in charge
of various aspects of creation. As we shall see below and throughout the
following chapters, much of the biblical tradition as well as church
history has assumed that everything in creation is directly or indirectly
under the authority of some angel.[51] The soil, wind, rain, sun, animals,
vegetation and so on each has its own guardian angel.

Many primordial peoples seem to have preserved this insight, by either
spiritual intuition or oral tradition.[52] Hence if the Creator himself is
judged to have withdrawn (because of the experience of sin), it is easy
to understand how more focus, hope and religious reverence began to
be placed on the mediating spiritual beings who were put in charge of
various aspects of creation. Instead of praying to the Creator God for
rain, one prayed to the closer god who was supposed to be in charge of
rain. In this fashion, perhaps, monotheopraxis gradually degenerated
into polytheopraxis.[53] Israel's ongoing tendency toward idolatry can
perhaps be seen as a microcosm of an ongoing tendency among humans
in general.

We may conclude that the monotheism of the Bible is not about
conflating various gods into a new monotheistic view of the cosmos, as
the evolutionists have argued. Rather, it is about reestablishing the

supremacy of the Creator, who alone is deserving of worship amid the gods. What lies behind the Bible's ongoing polemic against other gods, then, is not the issue of whether these other gods exist. It is the issue of who is the Creator, and thus the issue of who is the appropriate object of worship. If we are to recapture the biblical warfare perspective of the cosmos, it is imperative that we give full credit to the Bible's robust affirmation of a divine society that exists between humans and the supreme God.

So long as we see monotheism as threatened by the acknowledgment of other relatively autonomous and powerful gods, we simply cannot accept the central scriptural and primordial understanding that our world is caught in the crossfire of a tremendous spiritual cosmic struggle. Thus our ability to make headway in understanding evil is correspondingly impoverished. For it is precisely in the acknowledgment of the society of free spiritual beings in between humans and the Creator that the primary explanation for evil on a cosmic scale is to be found. When one possesses a vital awareness that in between God and humanity there exists a vast society of spiritual beings who are quite like humans in possessing intelligence and free will, there is simply no difficulty in reconciling the reality of evil with the goodness of the supreme God.

For example, it has been noted that African people routinely blame various gods, nature spirits or ancestors for ills that befall them and for prayers that go unanswered. But they never blame the Supreme Being, who is envisaged as being all-good.[54] This position is quite congruent with the scriptural position (minus, of course, the inclusion of ancestors in the divine society), and it virtually sidesteps the problem of evil. One is inclined to blame the Supreme Being for the ills that befall us only when we do not accept the existence of lesser gods or do not accept that these gods are, like human beings, free moral agents.

We now turn to the robust affirmation of the significance of gods in between the Supreme God and humanity within the Old Testament.

The Council of Yahweh

While the supremacy of Yahweh among the gods is never qualified in the Old Testament, this supremacy is not generally interpreted in a strictly autocratic fashion. That is, the gods are never portrayed as mere puppets of Yahweh. Rather, they appear to be personal beings who not only take orders but also are invited to give input to their Sovereign (1 Kings

22:20; Is 6:8). They collectively constitute a "heavenly council" that, in the Old Testament, is similar to many portraits of a heavenly council in prebiblical Near Eastern texts. In the Old Testament, as elsewhere, the heavenly hosts surround the captain to discuss the issues and affairs at hand and help make decisions on important matters.

These gods never rival the Creator's authority. Thus they are never construed as major competing deities. Herein lies the central difference between the Old Testament and pagan conceptions of the heavenly council. But it is important to note that the Old Testament certainly accepts that some such council exists, and that the members of this council have some say in how things are done.[55] In sharp contrast to the later Augustinian monopolizing view of divine sovereignty, the sovereign One in this concept invites and responds to input from both his divine and human subjects. The supplications and decisions of his creatures genuinely affect him, to the point where he may even alter previous plans in response to his creatures' requests and behavior (e.g., Ex 32:14-15; Jon 3:4-10; Is 38:1-5; Jer 18:6-11).

The classical-philosophical theistic tradition has judged all of this scriptural talk to be anthropomorphic. It has had to, not because anything in Scripture suggests this but because of a nonbiblical philosophical presupposition. At the heart of this concept of God is the Hellenistic philosophical assumption that divine perfection means changelessness, impassibility, immutability, pure actuality and so on. Such a concept rules out the idea that God could ever be affected by, let alone receive advice from, angelic or human beings.

Omnipotence, in this view, means omnicontrol, which further entails divine impassibility and immutability. But if God exercises total control, what power does anyone outside God have to affect, influence or move God in any way? If then some passages of Scripture portray a different view (are there passages that do *not*?), we must understand them to be anthropomorphic.

This hermeneutic amounts to an illegitimate exaltation of what is taken to be general revelation over special revelation. In essence it says: since we know (from Hellenistic philosophy!) that God is immutable, timeless, impassible, purely actual, devoid of contingency and so on, these passages cannot mean what they seem to mean. In contrast, if we stick with the text, we cannot avoid the conclusion that biblical authors understood God to be genuinely open to and affected by the input of his creatures, both angelic and human. Nothing in the texts suggests that Scripture is in these instances speaking nonliterally.[56]

The centrality of this concept of the Lord as being surrounded by a council of gods is seen in the fact that one of the most frequent ascriptions of Yahweh is "the LORD of hosts."[57] He is described as being revered by the multitudes of "holy ones" who "are around him" in his heavenly council (Ps 89:7), for it is he who "has taken his place in the divine council" and "in the midst of the gods . . . holds judgment" (82:1). While these hosts are themselves "mighty ones," their primary job is to "do his bidding, obedient to his spoken word," as well as give him praise (103:20-21; 148:2). Paralleling other Near Eastern conceptions, this heavenly council is also seen as including the sun, moon and stars (Deut 4:19-20; 17:13; Job 38:7; Judg 5:20; Ps 148:1-6; Is 14:13; Hab 3:11), as well as the winds and thunder (Ps 104:4; cf. Heb 1:7).[58]

This conception of a heavenly council lies behind the prologue to the book of Job. All the *b'nê hā"lōhîm* (sons of God) present themselves before the Lord (Job 1:6; 2:1), probably to give a report on their various duties such as Satan gives (1:7-8; 2:2-3).[59] These are the "holy ones" to whom Job's "friend" Eliphaz later chides him to turn (5:1; cf. 15:5).

This conception also lies behind Micaiah's vision in 1 Kings 22: "I saw the LORD sitting on his throne, with all the host of heaven standing beside him to the right and to the left of him. And the LORD said, 'Who will entice Ahab, so that he may go up and fall at Ramoth-gilead?' " (vv. 19-20). Micaiah is allowed to be privy to the otherwise concealed "great assembly" where crucial decisions "among the gods" are made (Ps 82:1). Interestingly enough, one possible qualification of a legitimate prophet, Jeremiah tells us, is that they have "stood in the council of the LORD so as to see and to hear his word" (Jer 23:18; see Is 6:1). The prophet is one who has been granted access into the inner chambers of the Lord's assembly. This is precisely what Micaiah did.[60]

This understanding of the divine council also perhaps explains the first-person plural used by God when crucial decisions are being made in Old Testament history. The most famous of these is Genesis 1:26. In creating or fashioning every previous feature of the cosmos and all that is in it, the Lord had simply used his word (1:3, 6, 9, 14, 20). But in creating humankind, the pinnacle of his creation, the Lord says, "Let *us* make humankind in *our* image, according to *our* likeness" (v. 26).

Attempts have been made to explain this as a "plural of majesty" or as a reference to the Trinity.[61] While these are possibilities, the standard interpretation among the Jews has been to understand this plural as a reference to the heavenly council. In light of subsequent revelation, this plurality within the divine council can be understood in terms of the triune divine society. But in fidelity to the original meaning of the text, we must also admit that the original author or his audience would not have understood the text in this way, and thus it should not be taken as the primary meaning of the text.

The heavenly-council interpretation also seems to make the most sense of the Lord's statement made just prior to casting Adam and Eve out of the garden: "The man has become like one of *us*, knowing good and evil" (Gen 3:22).[62] There is obviously a connection between the first-person plurals of these verses, but in this later verse a plural of neither majesty nor the Trinity is possible. The author (or redactor) is certainly aware of other divine beings (6:1-4), and it is most likely that these references in the first-person plural in both passages are to these beings.

So too in Genesis 11, when the Lord makes the monumental decision to scatter the people throughout the world in response to their attempt to build a tower to heaven, he says, "Let *us* go down, and confuse their language" (Gen 11:7).[63] In Isaiah 6, which is explicitly a scene of the heavenly council, the Lord seeks to turn Israel around from its wayward ways by asking his heavenly court (which Isaiah, being a prophet, is privy to), "Who will go for *us*?" (v. 8).

If we interpret all this in the way it was originally intended and do not simply dismiss it as anthropomorphic because our theology does not allow for it, a picture begins to emerge in which the Lord shares power and decisions both with his council and with human beings. This conception is as pervasive in the Bible as it is absent in the Western Christian philosophical tradition, which in part accounts for the fact that the academic problem of evil is intractable for us but nonexistent in Scripture.

The army of the Lord. Closely related to the conception of the gods as Yahweh's council is the frequent Old Testament portrayal of these gods as Yahweh's warriors. As Elijah's servant was allowed to see, the Lord possesses a vast army of mighty angelic warriors who fight on his behalf (2 Kings 2:11). These warriors surround Elijah and his servant, as they protectively surround all who fear the Lord (Ps 34:7). The vastness of this army is beyond imagination. "With mighty chariotry, twice ten thousand, thousands upon thousands," the psalmist writes (68:17).[64]

Daniel prophetically sees "the Ancient of Days" going into battle with "a thousand thousands" attending him and "ten thousand times ten thousand" standing before him (Dan 7:10).

It is these "heavenly beings" (Ps 29:1) or "mighty ones" (103:20) to whom Joel refers when he prays, "Bring down your warriors, O LORD" (Joel 3:11), and Deborah when she proclaims, "The stars fought from heaven, from their courses they fought against Sisera" (Judg 5:20). According to some scholars, these same warriors, again depicted as the "starry host," are called into military file "one by one" in Isaiah 40:26 (cf. Is 45:12).[65] This spiritual army is also referred to in an otherwise cryptic piece of military instruction the Lord gives to David as he is about to attack the Philistines:

> You shall not go up; go around to their rear, and come upon them opposite the balsam trees. When you hear the sound of marching in the tops of the balsam trees, then be on the alert; for then the LORD has gone out before you to strike the army of the Philistines. (2 Sam 5:23-24)

The battle between the Israelites and the Philistines was more than a physical battle. "Marching in the tops of the balsam trees" was "an army of God" (1 Chron 12:22), his legions of "mighty ones," fighting on David's behalf. The passage also suggests that evil spiritual warriors were fighting on the side of the Philistines. As Wink notes, "What occurs on earth has its corollary in the heavens."[66] The earthly battle, involving God's people against a people who were opposing God's will, corresponds to a heavenly, and perhaps far more important, battle being carried out by God's army, a view also suggested by Judges 5:20 and 2 Kings 3:26-27.

Just as biblical authors could see Israel's battles, or their own personal battles, as partaking in God's battle against cosmic forces of chaos (e.g., Rahab), so too they could envisage their earthly battles as participating in God's battle against evil armies. Indeed, these two conceptions are based on the same conviction.

As we shall see more fully in the next chapter, this conception of the Lord and his army engaging in battles that parallel on a spiritual level the battles of the righteous on earth became more developed and explicit in later Jewish thought. And in this developed form it exercised a significant influence on the New Testament authors, though in distinctly modified form. This motif is clearly seen, for example, in the Qumran

War Scroll (1 QM), which describes a final battle in which God's angels and human servants ("sons of light") will wage war against Belial, his evil angels and human forces of wickedness ("sons of darkness"). One illustrative passage reads as follows:

> On this [day], the assembly of the gods and the congregation of men shall confront each other for great destruction. The sons of light and the lot of darkness shall battle together for God's might, between the roar of a huge multitude and the shout of gods and of men, on the day of the calamity. . . . The King of glory is with us together with his holy ones. The heroes of the army of his angels are enlisted with us; the war hero is in our congregation; the army of his spirits, with our infantry and our cavalry.[67]

Like 2 Samuel 5:24 (in a less developed form), this passage clearly assumes that physical and spiritual realities interpenetrate. It assumes that battles on earth can reflect battles in the heavenlies, and that armies align themselves with one side or the other in these earthly/cosmic battles. Passages such as these assume that humans are part of a much more vast, invisible, cosmic society, and that this society, on both a spiritual and a physical plane, is in a state of war.

A note on Israel's "Holy War" tradition. It is, I maintain, in the light of this intimate connection between the spiritual and physical planes of warfare that the Old Testament's "holy war" tradition must be understood.[68] That is, Yahweh's various commands that the Israelites go to war against other nations must be understood against the backdrop of Yahweh's own cosmic warfare. What is at stake in such wars is not simply earthly territories or the dominion of earthly governments: from the perspective of the Old Testament, what is at stake is the kingly rule of the one true God. The struggle of nations to dominate, or at least to resist, Israel is also, and even more fundamentally, a struggle of other gods, with whom these nations are in league, to resist Yahweh.

Nowhere is this inextricable connection between earthly and spiritual battles more evident in the Old Testament than in the paradigmatic military deliverance of Israel by the power of God—the exodus. Here, in describing the purpose of the plagues, Yahweh proclaims, "On all the gods of Egypt I will execute judgments: I am the LORD" (Ex 12:12, cf. 2 Sam 7:23). And so each of the ten plagues affects some aspect of the Egyptians' false religious system.

For this reason, when the Israelites break covenant with Yahweh and align themselves with other gods, Yahweh goes to battle against them! There are apparently no boundaries of immunity: wherever and whenever a people turn from the Creator God to serve other gods, they and their gods become inextricably linked together as Yahweh enacts judgment against this type of concrete actualization of earthly/cosmic rebellion and chaos.[69]

This close connection between cosmic and earthly battles is also exhibited in the way the Israelites were to engage in holy war. As M. C. Lind has carefully argued, the earliest discernible Israelite war tradition emphasized the notion that Yahweh's people "were not called to do battle in the usual sense of the word, but to respond to and trust in Yahweh as their sole warrior against the military might of Egypt." In the celebration hymn of the exodus deliverance—the Son of the Sea (Ex 15)—victory is accomplished "not through human fighting, but through a nature miracle of Yahweh."[70] This vision serves as a unifying undercurrent for Israel's theology of warfare. As a nation, they are constantly reminded, through events such as the exodus, the Jericho conquest (Josh 6), the timing of Gideon's troops (Judg 7), David's match with Goliath (1 Sam 17) and his eventual sin of counting Israel's troops (2 Sam 24), that Yahweh alone—not their own military might—is the source of their deliverance and protection. In the end, their earthly battles were not really theirs at all: the battle, rather, belonged to the Lord.[71]

The gods of the nations. One aspect of the Old Testament's teaching on Yahweh's council that was to have a profound impact on subsequent Jewish and Christian thinking was the teaching that the Lord assigns a god to each nation upon the face of the earth. The principal text for this teaching is Deuteronomy 32:7-9, which in the Septuagint (the Greek version of the Old Testament relied on by the New Testament and early church authors) reads:

> Remember the days of old, consider the years for past ages. . . . When the Most High divided the nations, when he separated the sons of Adam, he set the bounds of the nations according to the number of the angels of God. And the people Jacob became the portion of the Lord.[72]

As D. S. Russell argues, the point of the passage seems to be that the "nations of the earth are given over into the control of angelic powers," though Yahweh keeps Israel as his own "portion."[73] The members of his heavenly council rule other nations, but it is ultimately Yahweh who rules the whole earth through them.[74] Indeed, the passage teaches explicitly that it was with this delegated authority in view that the nations were divided (perhaps recalling Gen 11:7-8: "Let *us* go down. . . . So the LORD scattered them").[75]

This understanding of the gods of other nations probably lies behind the Old Testament prohibition against the Israelites following other gods, "gods whom they had not known and whom he had not allotted to them" (Deut 29:26; cf. 6:13-17; 32:17). These gods were never intended to become objects of worship, and when they become such objects (perhaps through their own fallen initiative; see below), they are no longer regarded as legitimate "sons of God" but as "demons" (Deut 32:17; cf. Ps 106:37; also 95:5 LXX).[76] Their role was to oversee the welfare of the nation assigned to them, not to become surrogate objects of devotion for the Lord himself. When they fail in this duty, they become evil and are judged.

In this light also we are to understand Psalm 82. Here the Lord passes judgment "in the divine council . . . in the midst of the gods" by saying to these gods:

"How long will you [plural] judge unjustly and show partiality to the wicked? Give justice to the weak and the orphan; maintain the right of the lowly and the destitute. Rescue the weak and the needy; deliver them from the hand of the wicked." . . . I say, "You are gods, children of the Most High, all of you; nevertheless, you shall die like mortals, and fall like any prince." (vv. 2-4, 6-7)

We see here, as Russell notes, that "the Lord judges the members of his heavenly court and causes them to fall for their sin."[77] As Wink notes, "Those gods who obeyed their Sovereign's will were members in good standing (Ps 103:21; 148:1-6). Those gods who failed to do justice among their people were judged and sentenced to die like mortals."[78] The gods here are clearly no mere puppets who are simply extensions of Yahweh himself. They apparently have a mind and will of their own (Gen 6:2-3 also implies this). Although they can never threaten Yahweh's supremacy, they can fail to carry out his will to administer justice in their assigned land.

Rebellion Among the Gods
The understanding that Yahweh rules through the administration of lesser gods, and that these gods are capable of rebelling against Yahweh's

.order, sheds light on another fascinating passage of Scripture. In Daniel 10 Daniel prays, fasts and mourns for three weeks on behalf of Israel's state of captivity (v. 2). Finally, through a vision, he is visited by an angel who tells him:

> From the first day that you set your mind to gain understanding and to humble yourself before your God, your words have been heard, and I have come because of your words. But the prince of the kingdom of Persia opposed me twenty-one days. So Michael, one of the chief princes, came to help me, and I left him there with the prince of the kingdom of Persia. (vv. 12-13)

Later he concludes:

> Now I must return to fight against the prince of Persia, and when I am through with him, the prince of Greece will come. But I am to tell you what is inscribed in the book of truth. (vv. 20-21)

The scholarly consensus is that the "prince of Persia" is a divine figure who in this instance is opposing God's plan to work with Daniel.[79] As with the Moabite god Chemosh (1 Kings 11:35; 2 Kings 23:13; cf. 2 Kings 3:26-27) this "prince" is probably to be understood as being the "god" assigned to this nation (if not, where was its guardian "god"?). But in the light of Psalm 82, this national prince seems to have grossly failed in his duties. He is, as Wink notes, still contending for the best interests of the Persian Empire, narrowly defined. For this reason he has a stake in censoring a message that foretells the destruction of the Persian Empire.[80]

But his national guardianship is now at odds with the One who ultimately "rules over the nations" (Ps 22:28; 47:8; Jer 10:7; cf. Ps 113:4). It has, in fact, become demonic. Hence Michael, who has been assigned special care over Israel (see Dan 10:21; 12:1), is dispatched by the Lord to assist this angel in fighting this "prince," and all indications from the text are that the battle will continue and will now include the "prince of Greece" as well.[81]

It is clear that "the angels of the nations have a will of their own, and are capable of resisting the will of God."[82] In this regard they are similar to humans. They have a delegated moral and spiritual authority that is a gift from God. But, if they choose, this delegated authority can become demonic authority. When it becomes demonic, the passage shows, God must contend with it. The possibility of warfare seems to be a necessary concomitant to Yahweh's plan to rule the cosmos through intermediary beings, human and divine, who are free to some extent.

Another important passage that has traditionally been taken to refer to the ungodly behavior of certain "gods" is Genesis 6. Here, as a prelude to the flood narrative, the author states that "the sons of God saw that the daughters of men were beautiful, and they married any of them they chose" (v. 2 NIV), a situation that grieved the Lord greatly (v. 3). The progeny of such marriages were Nephilim (giants), who, the author notes, "were the heroes that were of old, warriors of renown" (v. 4)—a likely reference to some of the widespread tales of giant beings who were great warriors in the past.[83] The point of the passage is clearly to depict just how bad things had gotten on the earth so as to explain the Lord's regret over ever having made humans (v. 6) and then his radical decision to destroy the world by a flood (vv. 11-13).

Later Jewish thought understood these "sons of God" to be divine beings. Indeed, during the intertestamental period, as we shall later see, this interbreeding of divine beings with human women was often identified as the first fall of the angels. According to this tradition, these "sons of God" were angels who were charged with caring for humans (they were sometimes called "the Watchers"). But, like the god of Persia in Daniel 10, they forsook their duties and abused their divine authority.[84] Their progeny were thus giant, hybrid, evil beings who furthered the corruption of the earth.

In some traditions, demons in the world were not identified as fallen angels but as spiritually mutated beings that resulted from the interbreeding of these Nephilim.[85] This identification of the "sons of God" with divine beings (without its attendant explanation of demons) is perhaps present in the New Testament and is certainly the dominant view of the early church.[86]

Other interpretations of this passage, however, have been offered both in ancient and in modern times. One alternative interpretation is to identify the "sons of God" with the righteous lineage of Seth who married sinful women who descended from Cain.[87] Another possibility is to identify the "sons of God" with mighty rulers who married commoners and perhaps acquired large harems of women as a sign of their power.[88]

Both of these interpretations have the advantage of not requiring us to accept the rather difficult idea that divine beings copulated with human beings. This "advantage," however, renders them suspect. And both interpretations are beset with other significant difficulties. Perhaps most significant, neither interpretation explains the Nephilim. The passage assumes that these giants were unnatural, and it explains this by referring to the unnatural union that brought them about—the union of the "sons of God" with the "daughters of men." Interpreting the "sons of God" as either righteous men or mighty rulers does not explain why their offspring were unnaturally huge and identified with the giants of various mythological traditions.[89]

Further, while there is clear evidence that gods or angels were called "sons of God" (Job 1:6; 2:1; 38:7; Ps 82:6), there is no clear precedent for calling a lineage of male descendants, or a class of mighty rulers, "sons of God." In a few instances rulers are called "gods" (Ex 21:6; 22:8; 1 Sam 2:25), and David, as an anointed king, was referred to as "God's son" (Ps 2:7), but these are not solid precedents for understanding this passage. Nor do we have any biblical or extrabiblical precedent for speculating that certain mighty rulers were acquiring large harems for themselves, and that this is what lies behind this passage. Hence all presuppositions about what angels can and cannot do aside, the most probable interpretation of "sons of God" is in reference to divine beings.

What strengthens this interpretation even more is that the "sons of God" are explicitly contrasted with the "daughters of men." It is precisely this contrast that expresses the unnaturalness of their union, and hence the unnaturalness of their progeny. This contrast is not between the righteous and unrighteous, or between the mighty and the lowly. Rather, it is explicitly a contrast between sons associated with God and the females born from humans. The starkness of this contrast explains why their unnatural union produces mutant progeny.

While conceding that this is the most natural interpretation of this passage, some Christian exegetes nevertheless reject it on the basis of Jesus' teaching that in the resurrection there will be no marriage, for we will be "like angels in heaven" (Mt 22:30). The implication, it is argued, is that angels are sexless and thus could not copulate with human women as the divine beings interpretation of Genesis 6 requires.[90]

Two considerations quickly dismiss this objection, however. First, Jesus is clearly speaking about unfallen angels in their natural state ("heaven"), whereas Genesis 6 (if this interpretation is correct) is speaking about angels "who did not keep their positions" (Jude 6). The point of Genesis 6 seems to be that what the "sons of God" did was rebellious and unnatural for them, so it can hardly be argued that these "sons of God" could not be angels because sexual activity is unnatural for them.

Second, the point of Jesus' instruction in Matthew 22 is not about the sexuality or asexuality of people or angels in heaven at all; it is about the social institution of marriage (see vv. 23-32). Jesus' point in this passage is to say that marriage covenants do not carry over into the next life. It may be that angels in their natural state of heaven (and people in heaven?) are asexual, but we cannot arrive at this conclusion from this passage.

It seems that the traditional Jewish and Christian understanding of Genesis 6 is best, however difficult it is for modern Western people to accept.[91] This being the case, this passage can justifiably be seen as yet another Old Testament example of gods who did not carry out their God-given duties within the council of heaven (Ps 82:2-4). Rather, they rebelled and thereby contributed to the moral decay of the antediluvian human society.

Modern Westerners and the free beings of the "society in between." This notion that there exists a council, or a society, of divine beings between humans and God who, like us, have free wills and can therefore influence the flow of history for better or for worse is obviously jarring to a number of Western worldview assumptions. Indeed, for many believers it is foreign to their Western Christian assumptions as well. For a variety of reasons, Westerners have trouble taking seriously the "world in between" us and God, what one missiologist appropriately called "the flaw of the excluded middle."[92] Even when Westerners do theoretically acknowledge the existence of "angels," we tend to view them as mindless, volitionless, wholly innocuous winged marionettes completely controlled by the will of their Creator.

If we take the Old Testament teaching on the gods seriously, however, we must confess that our Western assumptions about "the world in between" are erroneous. For these writers—and it shall prove even more obvious and pervasive for New Testament authors—the "heavenly" world was not much different or distant from our "earthly" world. Indeed, the two worlds largely overlap and can hardly be said to form two worlds at all. The "world in between" is, from a scriptural perspective, simply part of the cosmos.

We are light-years removed from the Greek metaphysical assumption that the "heavenly" is composed of timeless "forms" that lack all contingency, a notion that would exercise a profound influence on later Christian theology and contribute to the church's eventual abandonment of the warfare worldview.[93] For the biblical authors, the freedom and moral authority of created divine beings were just as commonsensible as the freedom and moral authority of created nondivine (viz., human) beings were. The cosmos was constituted by a vast society of free, intelligent, morally responsible agents governed by (but not dictated by) God at the top, with humans at the bottom. In this view, contingency characterized the whole domain.

In Scripture, therefore, as opposed to the dominant Hellenistic philosophical tradition that so influenced the apologists and especially Augustine, there was nothing "heavenly" about being timeless, immutable, purely actual and devoid of contingency. There was nothing "perfect" about being an "Unmoved Mover" (Aristotle), and no sense could be made of saying that "time is the moving image of eternity" (Plato).[94] Though it forms the cornerstone of the classical-philosophical tradition of the Western church, no biblical author ever dreamed of such a notion. The "heavenly" world paralleled the earthly world, but for this reason it was not conceptualized as a radically otherworldly blueprint of this world. Rather, for biblical authors, the reality of human freedom and contingency in this world had its counterparts in the reality of divine freedom and contingency in the council of heaven. These "two" worlds overlapped and therefore influenced one another.

Because of our indebtedness to Greek thought through the classical-philosophical theistic tradition as well as our indebtedness to Enlightenment naturalism, modern Westerners have difficulty affirming the existence of—let alone the significant freedom and power of—this "world in between." For these reasons many conservative theologians have difficulty positing genuine contingency in God himself. But it is precisely this unbiblical philosophical tradition more than anything else that creates the intractable intellectual problem of evil.

In biblical terms, then, the cause of Zosia's torment might be the result of evil human intentions. Or it might be due to a malicious "prince" of Germany, or even a cosmic Leviathan. But on biblical terms it could not be an ordained feature of a secret blueprint Yahweh has for the whole of world history, and for Zosia and her mother in particular.

In the end, the character of God can remain untarnished in the face of the terrifying dimensions of our experience only to the degree that our view of the free, contingent world in between us and God is robust. Only to the extent that we unambiguously affirm that angels and humans have significant power to thwart God's will and inflict suffering on others can we unambiguously affirm the goodness of God in the face of Zosia's torture. The Bible, I maintain, provides just such a conception. The Western philosophical-theological tradition, however, does not. This is why it has an intellectual problem with evil that the Bible does not have, while biblical authors have a revolting activism and power in the face of evil that the church has lacked.

5

REBUKING
THE ADVERSARY
THE ACTIVITY AND
ORIGIN OF SATAN
IN THE OLD TESTAMENT

W E HAVE THUS FAR SEEN THAT, ALONGSIDE ITS UNDERSTANDING that the world is surrounded by hostile cosmic forces, the Old Testament assumes the presence of an invisible society of created gods existing beneath Yahweh and above humankind. This divine society is construed as being like human society in many respects. These spiritual beings, like human beings, clearly have a mind and a will of their own. They can choose to work for God or against him. They are, like human beings, morally responsible. Hence their decisions affect others, for better or for worse; for example, the answer to Daniel's prayer is delayed (Daniel 10), the poor and the weak are oppressed (Psalm 82), a boy is sacrificed and Israel looses a battle (2 Kings 3:26-27), and the world becomes hopelessly corrupt because of their activity (Gen 6:1-4).

The most powerful and rebellious of these gods was (and is) one who came to bear the name Satan. While this figure does not play a central role in the thinking of Old Testament authors, the raging cosmic sea and threatening sea monsters demonstrate an awareness, however dim, that one of the gods is particularly opposed to Yahweh's rule. On the basis of this opposition toward God and his consequent opposition toward God's special creation, human beings, this god is called "an adversary" (Hebrew *śāṭān*).[1]

This *satan* is portrayed as a force that Yahweh must reckon with, and thus falls under the warfare motif of the Old Testament. Therefore, especially in the light of his later infamy, it is important that we note what the Old Testament has to say about the one who came to bear the name Satan. The goal of this chapter shall be to analyze the Old Testament's references to this being and to discuss the issues surrounding these texts.

We begin with Job 1, which constitutes the most extensive reference to Satan in the Old Testament. This text provides the opportunity to enter into what is, for our purposes, a crucial issue: the Old Testament's understanding of God's relationship to evil in general and to Satan in particular. We shall attempt to offer a refutation of the theory that has for the last half century held center stage in critical scholarship, the theory often referred to as the "demonic-in-Yahweh" theory. This theory proposes that Yahweh was thought of as the originator of evil, and Satan as his alter ego, throughout much of the Old Testament narrative. Following this discussion, I examine each passage that refers explicitly to Satan, as well as several passages that have traditionally been considered opaque references to this figure.

Is God the Author of Evil?

The most extensive reference to the *satan* is also likely the oldest. In the prologue to the book of Job the *satan* appears when the *b'nê hā'ĕlōhîm* ("sons of god") gather for their council meeting with the Lord (1:6; 2:1). This *satan* questions God's conviction that Job is serving God out of a pure heart. Rather, he suggests that Job reveres God because of all the "fringe benefits" (1:9-11; 2:4). In response, Yahweh allows the *satan* to test Job by destroying everything he possesses, including his children and his own health (1:12-22; 2:6-8). This sets the stage for the dramatic epic poem that follows.

While many exegetical and theological issues surround this famous prologue, one in particular concerns us presently. Many exegetes contend that the adversary in this prologue is that member of the heavenly council of gods who serves as Yahweh's "public prosecutor," "legal arm" or the one in charge of "quality control and testing."[2] According to this interpretation, the *satan* is merely performing the duties assigned to him by Yahweh when he puts Job through his nightmarish testing.

This understanding makes God the ultimate author of Job's evil, something most of these theorists are willing to grant. According to this "demonic-in-Yahweh" theory, Yahweh was not considered perfectly good in the early stages of Israelite religion.[3] At this stage, God was understood to be morally ambivalent. "In pre-exilic Hebrew religion," says Russell, "Yahweh made all that was in heaven and earth, both of good and of evil."[4] On the strength of Isaiah 45:7, Forsyth concludes straightforwardly, "Yahweh creates evil."[5] Satan, in this scheme, is therefore viewed as "the shadow, the dark side of God, the destructive power wielded by God."[6]

This understanding of the "development of Yahweh" is often combined with a Jungian understanding of the development of the self as a process of objectifying, and then integrating, evil within oneself.[7] Attempts are made to support it by citing passages such as Isaiah 45:7, Lamentations 3:38 and Amos 3:6 (to be discussed below).[8]

We cannot here enter into a comprehensive discussion of this prevalent line of argumentation. But given the relevance of this issue to our understanding of the warfare motif of Scripture, at least a summary refutation of this theory is in order. Six considerations can be briefly made that seriously call this theory into question.

Six arguments against the "demonic-in-Yahweh" theory. First, whatever grounds there are for holding to the divine inspiration of the Bible are grounds against this position.[9] For if there is anything that is clear from Scripture considered as a whole, it is that Yahweh is perfect: he is, among other things, perfectly holy, righteous, loving and just (e.g., Deut 32:4, 35; 2 Sam 22:31; Ps 48:1, 10; 89:1; 92:10; Mt 5:48; see 2 Chron 19:7; Ps 18:30; 33:5; 1 Sam 2:2; 1 Chron 16:10). While we must make liberal allowances for later revelation to augment earlier revelation, postulating that evil had its origin in Yahweh blatantly contradicts the central teaching of Scripture concerning Yahweh's character. In the "progress of revelation," later inspired material may reveal that aspects of earlier revelation were incomplete. But it surely cannot reveal that they were blasphemous!

The "demonic-in-Yahweh" position, therefore, is not an option for one who holds to a high view of Scripture. All historical and philosophical arguments that favor the inspiration of Scripture must be regarded as indirect refutations of this position.

Second, the Jungian model for understanding the conception of Yahweh as having gone through different stages of development presupposes a historical-critical understanding of the Old Testament that is, for many, highly questionable. In this view, the Old Testament material must be organized according to a chronology which postulates that all of the material portraying evil as something that God opposes comes late, after the exile, when the Israelites (per hypothesis) had come under the strong influence of Persian Zoroastrianism. Many scholars question this whole scheme, and they have good grounds for doing so.[10]

Third, even if one accepts the standard historical-critical chronology for the Old Testament literature, there are still difficulties with the "demonic-in-Yahweh" theory. It is undeniable that the cosmic warfare motif as well as the "Yahweh as warrior" motif that we examined in the last two chapters appears within the oldest material we have in the Old Testament.[11] It is difficult to see how these motifs could coexist, and could in any sense be harmonized, with the view that Yahweh causes all things, good and evil. Are we to imagine that these authors conceptualized Yahweh fighting against the evil he himself had caused?

While it would be anachronistic to expect these ancient authors to have systematically thought through and rendered self-consistent all the implications of their theologies, it is certainly not too much to suppose that they would have noticed this blatant contradiction. "What sense would there be," Lindström rightly asks, "in God's punishing an evil action which he was himself in the last instance the cause of?"[12] Whatever else one may say about these motifs, it is clear that the Old Testament authors never questioned that Yahweh was really fighting (not meticulously controlling) his various enemies. This point argues strongly against the "demonic-in-Yahweh" theory.

Fourth, turning specifically to the book of Job, it is not at all clear that this work portrays the *satan* as a "member in good standing" of Yahweh's heavenly council. Job 1:6 says that on the day "the heavenly beings [lit. 'sons of God'] came to present themselves before the LORD . . . Satan *also* came *among them*" (cf. 2:1). Some distinction between the "sons of God" who regularly form God's council and the *satan* seems to be implied here.

Moreover, Yahweh asks the *satan*, "Where have *you* come from?" (1:7; 2:2), to which the adversary replies, "From going to and fro on the earth, and from walking up and down on it." While the text does not require this explanation, it is natural to read in this an element of surprise on Yahweh's part, and an uncontrolled dimension to the *satan's* activity. The members of God's council, we have seen, carry out their delegated duties in battling for Yahweh and watching over nations. The adversary, however, is simply roaming about, and God's question, "Where have you come from?" implies that that was not a duty God had assigned him (see 1 Pet 5:8).

Fifth, it is not clear that the *satan* in this prologue is as innocuous as the defenders of the "demonic-in-Yahweh" theory suggest. It is important to note that his questions to Yahweh about Job (1:9-11; 2:4-5) reflect no concern for the genuineness of Job's piety. Rather, the *satan* is calling into question Yahweh's wisdom in the way he orders his creation. It is not Job who is on trial here, but God "for his conduct of world order, from the very beginning."[13] Job is the unfortunate victim of the unjust "accuser" who has raised his hand against the Almighty.

There is also something sinister about the eagerness of the *satan* to destroy Job. "Stretch out your hand now, and touch all that he has" (1:11), he cries. After his first assault fails, he again challenges God: "Skin for skin! All that people have they will give to save their lives. But stretch out your hand now and touch his bone and his flesh, and he will curse you to your face" (2:4-5).

This does not appear to be an angel who is simply intent on following God's orders. When he carries out his own destructive desires, he clearly does it with excessive thoroughness (1:13-19; 2:7-8). Hence James Morgenstern concedes that Satan in this prologue "has become semi-independent of God, a true, creative power and source of evil in the world and the inveterate, malicious enemy of man."[14] Even E. Langton, who otherwise agrees that Satan in Job is simply a servant of Yahweh's court, admits that "there appears to be an element in the character of Satan which is contrary to the will of God. . . . If not yet a malignant being, he is tending to become so."[15] In my estimation, the malignancy is already present.

Sixth and finally, it is also important to note that Yahweh, when he finally appears to Job (chaps. 38—41), does not defend his (supposed) right to inflict evil on people indiscriminately, as the "demonic-in-Yahweh" theory would suggest. The thrust of his speeches to Job is rather to drive home the point—the point of the entire epic poem—that neither Job nor his "friends" are in a position to understand the goings-on of the vast cosmos Yahweh has created. Hence neither Job, who accuses God, nor his friends, who accuse Job, are correct.[16]

In these majestic speeches the Lord emphasizes how far beyond human comprehension are his works in creation. But he does not stress how far beyond human comprehension is his character. Nor does he suggest that he has the right to do whatever he wants on whoever he wants. To the contrary, the divine speeches in this book make clear that, far from containing evil, Yahweh's character is set against evil. In particular, the speeches reveal that one aspect of Yahweh's incomprehensible task in creating and preserving order in the world is to contend against the cosmic forces that perpetually threaten it, as we saw in the last chapter.

For example, we read in Job that it is the Lord who "shut in the sea [*yām*] with doors when it burst out from the womb [of Tiamat?]" (38:8). It is the Lord (not Marduk) who "prescribed bounds for it [*yām*], and set bars and doors, and said, 'Thus far shall you come, and no farther, and here shall your proud waves be stopped' " (38:10-11). It is the Lord who, unlike Job or any other human, has journeyed to the abysmal and chaotic "springs of the sea" (*yām*) and "walked in the recesses of the deep" (*t°hôm*; 38:16), and who binds up and loosens the gods of the skies to set up his dominion upon the earth (38:31-32). It is the Lord who alone can capture and tame the mighty Behemoth and the ferocious Leviathan, whose "snorting throws out flashes of light" and whose "eyes are like the rays of dawn" (40:15-24; 41:1-24). "On earth," the Lord says, "it has no equal, a creature without fear" who "is king over all that are proud" (41:33-34).

Running the cosmos, in short, is no easy matter, even for the Creator. There are forces of chaos (to say nothing of the *satan*) to contend with. Unless Job can do it himself, the poem suggests, he ought to refrain from arrogant accusations (38:1—41:34).

Whatever else may be said about these cosmic conflict passages, it is certainly clear that Yahweh, as portrayed in the book of Job, is not himself the creator of destruction. Rather, he is the One who fights against cosmic forces of destruction. If Job and his "friends" (as well as the readers) understood this better, the poem is saying, they would not be so quick to lay the blame for evil either on God or on each other. As we also learn from Daniel's delayed answer to prayer (Dan 10) and Israel's unexpected defeat by the fury of Chemosh (2 Kings 3:26-27), things go on behind the scenes of the human drama, sometimes thwarting the will of God, about which we know next to nothing—unless, of course, there is a prophet who is privy to the Lord's council meetings (Jer 23:18-22), or unless one is told about them by an angel or in the prologue of an inspired book (Dan 10:4ff.; Job 1—2). The evil of the sort that Job experienced had its origin there.[17]

If any book of Scripture addresses the problem of evil, it is this book. The answer it gives as to why evil happens is decisively not that it is the will of God. Evil is a mystery, but it is not a mystery concerning Yahweh's character. It is rather the mystery of what goes on among the gods in "the great assembly" and in an incomprehensibly vast cosmos threatened by cosmic forces. In other words, the mystery of evil is located not in the heart of God but in the heart of humanity and in the hidden world between humans and God.[18]

The questionable exegesis of the "demonic-in-Yahweh" theory. There are, we see, some good arguments against the prevalent scholarly view that the early Israelites viewed Yahweh as morally ambiguous. But we have not yet examined the scriptural exegesis that is used to defend this theory. Again, we cannot enter into a comprehensive discussion of this issue here, but a brief consideration of three foundational texts used by supporters of this view is in order.[19]

Isaiah 45:7 records the Lord as saying, "I form light and create darkness, I make weal and create woe; I the LORD do all these things." The "demonic-in-Yahweh" theorists have made this one of their *loci classici.* From this text, for example, Westermann argues that

each and every thing created, each and every event that happens, light and darkness, weal and woe, are attributed to him, and to him alone. . . . This shuts the door firmly on any dualism—if the creator of evil and woe is God, there is no room left for a devil.[20]

Such an interpretation, however, misses the explicitly historical and soteriological (hence noncosmological) intent of the passage. The context of this passage (see 45:1-6) is specifically about the future deliverance of the children of Israel out of Babylon; it is not concerned with God's cosmic creative activity. Hence the "light" and "darkness" of this passage, Lindström argues, denote "liberation" and "captivity" (as in Is 9:1; Lam 3:2) and thus refer to "YHWH's impending salvific intervention on behalf of his people."[21] The "prosperity and disaster" refer to Yahweh's plans to bless Israel and to curse Babylon.

Creating "light and darkness" and bringing "weal and woe," then, are not arbitrary activities, but rather flow from the moral character of God in direct response to the unjust captivity of his people in Babylon. The Lord creates light and darkness, prosperity and disaster, in just response to human behavior. The implication of this verse, then, is precisely the opposite of what the "demonic-in-Yahweh" theorists suggest.

In Lamentations 3:38 Jeremiah the prophet asks: "Is it not from the mouth of the Most High that good and bad come?" Taken out of context, and made into a general statement, the verse could support the view that evil originates from God. But if read in its proper context, it says nothing of the sort.[22]

The preceding verse (v. 37) indicates that the subject matter of this verse concerns inspired prophecy. Israel had been warned that calamity was going to come upon them. Why was this calamity going to come? The three verses preceding verse 37 tell us: "When all the prisoners of the land are crushed under foot, when human rights are perverted in the presence of the Most High, when one's case is subverted—does the LORD not see it?" (vv. 34-36).

In other words, the Lord had seen the injustice of Israel and had prophetically warned them. Most ignored this prophecy, wanting to believe only prophecies that announced "good things." When calamity did strike, they blamed it on God! In response, Jeremiah reminds them of their sin and of the warning that had come "from the mouth of the Most High." Their present dire situation was not God's fault—precisely the opposite point that the "demonic-in-Yahweh" theorists want to make with this verse.[23]

A third verse that is cited in support of the "demonic-in-Yahweh" theory is Amos 3:6: "Is a trumpet blown in a city, and the people are not afraid? Does disaster befall a city, unless the LORD has done it?" Again, this verse can be understood to imply that God causes all disasters only if it is taken out of its original context. As with Lamentations 3, when it is read in its context it becomes clear that the verse is addressing the subject of prophecy.

The central point of this chapter, and really of the whole book of Amos, is to warn the people in the northern kingdom that their materialism, greed and practices of injustice would ultimately lead to their downfall, though at the present time they were experiencing prosperity.

In chapter 3 Amos communicates this warning by posing a series of rhetorical questions. After announcing God's promise to punish the sins of the people he has chosen (v. 2), Amos asks, "Does a lion roar in the forest, when it has no prey? Does a young lion cry out from its den, if it has caught nothing? Does a bird fall into a snare on the earth, when there is no trap for it? Does a snare spring up from the ground, when it has taken nothing?" (vv. 4-5).

After he climaxes his series of questions with verse 6, he then applies the point of his rhetorical teaching in verses 7-8: "Surely the Lord GOD does nothing, without revealing his secret to his servants the prophets. The lion has roared; who will not fear? The Lord GOD has spoken; who can but prophesy?"

In the light of this context, two things about this passage mitigate against the "demonic-in-Yahweh" understanding of verse 6. Amos's argument here is designed to make the point that disaster does not arbitrarily come from the hand of God. Lions do not roar unless there is something to roar about. If this were the case, if Yahweh's supposed disastrous activity were arbitrary, what good would it do to try to warn the people (under the prophetic inspiration of God!) to change their ways in order to avert disaster? Rather, God's punishment comes as a result of the sins of his people.

But even as such it does not come without warning, and this is the second point that needs to be made. God had been trying to turn the people of the northern kingdom around by sending prophets who "roared" out against their injustices, who warned them that their behavior was going to lead to disaster (3:7-9), and who pointed out that the disasters they and others (e.g., the southern kingdom) had already experienced were themselves the direct consequence of sin (4:6-11). But the people foolishly missed this connection and rather insisted, "Evil shall not overtake or meet us" (9:10).

It is to reinforce this connection between their national misfortune and their sin that Amos proclaims that the disaster that has befallen them and the southern kingdom is caused by God. His (and God's) hope is that the people will see this connection and turn from their wicked ways. As such, this verse can hardly be made to support any view that would suggest that all disasters on any cities are caused by God, or that any Old Testament author ever thought this. In Amos this verse has a particular and precise application.[24]

An analysis of other major texts used to support the "demonic-in-Yah-weh" theory would bear similar results.[25] Neither the textual evidence in general nor the prologue of Job in particular supports it. If we further consider other grounds for regarding the Bible as being inspired and thus as being at least reasonably self-consistent, the case against this theory must be regarded as very strong.

The adversary in the prologue of Job, then, is not to be taken as just one of the many servants in Yahweh's council or as an (evil) extension of Yahweh himself. While at this early stage of revelation he has not yet acquired the proper name "Satan," the uncontrolled dimension of his being (roaming about), his arrogance toward God and his zealous malice toward Job reveal him to be a being who is not on God's side. While the main forces God is explicitly against in Job (and elsewhere) are the common cosmic forces of the Near Eastern warfare myths (Leviathan, Behemoth), the later Jewish and Christian traditions were certainly justified in eventually relating these forces with Satan: Satan was himself Leviathan.[26]

The fallen morning star. Beyond the book of Job, Satan is explicitly mentioned in only two other passages in the Old Testament.[27] One is Zechariah 3:1-10, which portrays "the high priest Joshua standing before the angel of the LORD, and Satan standing at his right hand to accuse him."[28] Either in response to the adversary's accusation or in response to the prospect of the *satan* accusing Joshua, the Lord twice cries out, "The LORD rebuke you!" (v. 2). The Lord then takes off Joshua's "filthy clothes" and places on him "festal apparel" (vv. 3-4).

As one might expect, there is a great deal of discussion about what Zechariah is getting at in this passage. For our present purposes, how-ever, only one issue need concern us: the nature of the *satan* spoken of here. Once again many scholars have assumed that the *satan* here is simply a member of Yahweh's court who is in charge of legal affairs and who is carrying out his assigned duties in pointing out the shortcomings of Joshua as a high priest.[29]

While nothing about this text rules out such an interpretation, neither does it explicitly support this. It may just as well be that the *satan* is present in this scene simply because Joshua is an extremely prominent person whom the *satan* wishes to condemn. As some commentators suggest, in coming against Joshua the *satan* would be coming against the whole priesthood of Israel and against the nation of Israel itself. In any case, nothing requires us to suppose that this *satan* was supposed to be present or that he was simply a "member in good standing" of Yahweh's heavenly council.

Even more significantly, Yahweh rebukes the adversary twice, then takes measures to invalidate his accusations (vv. 3-5). Indeed, through Joshua, Yahweh promises that there will come a time in which "I will remove the guilt of this land in a single day" (v. 9). In other words, there will come a time when "the accuser" will have nothing to accuse the people of God of. Christians throughout the ages have justifiably found in these verses a prophetic reference to the work of Christ on the cross and a beautiful prophetic illustration of how believers are freed from the accuser and "robed" in Christ's righteousness. It is clear that, once again, God and the *satan* are not on the same side. God is for mercy, and for Joshua's high priesthood; Satan wants only condemnation.[30]

The only other explicit reference to Satan—and the one time where *satan* is apparently used as a proper name—is in 1 Chronicles 21:1: "Satan stood up against Israel, and incited David to count the people of Israel."[31] The point seems to be that Satan was motivating King David to place more trust in his military power than in the Lord. Given the fear and guilt of David and his court after they gave in to Satan (see 2 Sam 24:3, 10), it seems clear that David knew that the deed was wrong.[32] In *cf 30:11-16* any event, Satan is clearly portrayed here as a malicious being who is "against Israel" and against God's plans.

This analysis is complicated by a parallel passage in 2 Samuel 24 which says that it was God, rather than Satan, who incited David to take the census because "the anger of the LORD was kindled against Israel" (24:1). The standard explanation given in historical-critical commentaries for the discrepancy is that the author of 2 Samuel had a morally ambiguous view of Yahweh (in accord with the "demonic-in-Yahweh" theory) while the author of 2 Chronicles held to a loftier and purer view of God. Hence the author of 2 Samuel could attribute to God the activity of inspiring David to sin, but the author of 2 Chronicles found this offensive and hence changed the reference to Satan.[33]

It is obvious that the author of 1 Chronicles edited the passage in 2 Samuel to fit his own theology and purpose for writing, something he does in a number of places. But it is less obvious that this scenario entails that the author of 2 Samuel held to a morally ambiguous view of God, or even that there is here an irreconcilable contradiction between the two accounts. It may just be that the two authors are approaching the same event from significantly different perspectives.[34]

Unlike what we find in Zechariah 3, it is possible to suppose that God's plan and Satan's desire came into surprising alignment with one another. The Lord was burning with anger toward Israel on a number of counts, and Satan was (as usual?) looking for any opportunity he could to incite David to rebel against God and thereby bring the nation of Israel under God's judgment. God wants to judge Israel; Satan wants Israel judged. Thus God allows Satan to motivate David to carry out an act that is going to result in Israel's judgment. From one perspective it was Satan who incited judgment, but from a broader perspective it was God himself.

It is in this context that we are to understand the several references to Yahweh "sending forth an evil spirit," or to an evil spirit "coming forth from the Lord" that we looked at in chapter two (Judg 9:23; 1 Sam 16:14ff.; 18:10-11; 19:9-10; 1 Kings 22:19-23; Is 29:10). As the Lord did with Joseph's evil brothers, and as Christ did with Paul's "thorn in the flesh" that originated from Satan, God can sometimes use the evil wills of personal beings, human or divine, to his own ends (Gen 50:20; 2 Cor 12:7-10).

This by no means entails that there is a divine will behind every activity of an evil spirit—for usually we find that God and evil spirits (whether called angels, gods or demons) are in real conflict with each other. It certainly does not entail, as the "demonic-in-Yahweh" theorists (and, ironically, conservative Calvinists) hold, that the evil spirits are nothing more than extensions of Yahweh's own will. But it does entail that Yahweh is the sovereign Lord of all history and can therefore at times employ evil divine beings in his service—even Satan himself.

Other Possible References to the Devil

While neither the role of the *satan* nor Satan as a proper name is elsewhere mentioned in the Old Testament, three other passages have traditionally been interpreted as referring to him and thus warrant brief consideration. The first of these is the notorious narrative of the Fall in Genesis 3:1-6.

Genesis 3: The deceptive serpent. The serpent in this passage is identified simply as being "more crafty than any other wild animal that the LORD God had made" (v. 1). It deceives Eve about God's character, her own potential, and the promise of the forbidden fruit (vv. 2-4), and thereby influences her to disobey the Lord (vv. 6-13). As a result, the serpent is cursed "among all animals and among all wild creatures," and is made to slither on its stomach and eat dust all the days of its life (vv. 14-15). The consequences for Adam and Eve and their descendants were not much better.

Many critical scholars regard this story as simply providing a primitive explanation for why human life is "cursed" and an etiological tale for why snakes crawl on the ground and are so repulsive to humans.[35] This view is similar to how later rabbinic thought sometimes interpreted the passage. The serpent, some rabbis thought, was originally a beast created by Yahweh that was beautiful, stood upright (two feet tall), had arms and legs, and had the ability to speak.[36] Because of his deception, however, he lost these limbs and his capacity to reason and speak. He must now crawl on the ground and "eat dust."

Other scholars, however, have argued that the serpent in this passage does not symbolize evil; rather, it symbolizes life, wisdom and fertility.[37] This positive estimation of the serpent, while utterly foreign to orthodox Christianity, was quite common in early Christian Gnostic circles.[38]

In the intertestamental apocryphal literature and in early Christian thought, however, the serpent in this passage most frequently came to be identified with a cosmic evil figure, and often explicitly with Satan himself (e.g., Wisdom of Solomon 2:24; *Psalms of Solomon* 4:9; 1 Tim 3:13ff.; Rom 16:20; Rev 12:9; 20:2). Satan's designations as "the Tempter" (Mt 4:3; 1 Thess 3:5) and "the old serpent" (Rev 12:9) presumably refer back to this passage as well, though the context of the last passage also unmistakably includes images of the cosmic serpent Leviathan. Thus, throughout church history, the serpent of Genesis 3 has been taken to refer to Satan, or at least to a beast that was at this time possessed by Satan.[39]

Is this reading justified? From the evangelical hermeneutical circle within which I read Scripture and out of which I write, the explicit designation of the serpent as Satan by later inspired New Testament authors is enough to settle the question on a theological level, however one interprets the author's original intent. In this case, the theological import of the passage is to teach that Satan deceived Adam and Eve and thereby brought about the fall of humankind. But there are other grounds as well for taking even the original meaning of this passage to refer to a demonic type of creature.

First, it is significant that demons and other anticreation beings were frequently pictured in the form of serpents throughout Near Eastern cultures. For example, according to R. S. Hendel:

> The symbol of the underworld deity Ningishzida . . . is a venomous horned snake, which is depicted rising from his shoulders. Ningishzida is named in incantations as a guardian of underworld demons, and in the Adapa myth is a guardian of the gates of heaven. The female demon Lamashtu is depicted grasping snakes in both hands, while the male demon Pazuzu can be depicted with the exposed phallus as a snake.[40]

Further, the close literary connection we sometimes find between serpents and chaos, evil, and destruction throughout these cultures is also highly significant, as K. J. Joines, F. Landy and several other scholars have convincingly argued.[41] So too is the association sometimes made between serpents and human mortality. In this light, Joines seems justified in concluding that "the underlying purpose of this serpent is to deceive and to destroy mankind; consequently, it basically symbolizes chaos."[42]

Closely related to this is the argument of Flemming Hvidberg in his exploration of the Canaanite background to Genesis 1—3. Against those scholars who argue that the story is either an etiological tale about snakes or is portraying the serpent in a positive light, he concludes:

> The old Jewish-Christian belief that the serpent is the devil is far more historically true than late Judaism and early Christianity could conceive.
>
> The serpent is Zbl Baal (Prince Baal), Bel Zebul, Jahweh's great adversary in the ancient struggle for the soul of Israel which is the theme of the whole of the Old Testament.
>
> There is a profound connection between the Canaanite Baal-deity and the devil of Judaism. . . . It is possible that a line can be traced from the powers of chaos down to the devil of late Judaism.[43]

In sum, the background of Genesis 3 thus lends credence to the traditional Christian identification of the serpent with Satan.

A close reading of the text itself lends further weight to this interpretation. For one thing, while the author twice compares the serpent to wild animals (viz., it is more crafty, and more cursed, than the animals, 3:1, 14), he does not explicitly identify the serpent as a natural animal.

For another, the author seems to set this creature apart from the other creatures insofar as he has previously concluded that all the creatures that the Lord made were good (1:24-25), whereas the serpent is clearly not good.[44] That the serpent can talk, reason and deceive also seems to set it apart from the animal kingdom. Significantly, these abilities are not taken away with its curse, a point that further indicates that the author was not simply identifying the cursed serpent with a natural snake. He presumably would have known that snakes do not talk!

The references to the cursed serpent crawling on his belly, eating dust, striking at the heels of people but ultimately having his head crushed by them (3:14-15) do not necessarily refute this view. Crawling on one's belly and "eating dust" (something snakes do not do) were idiomatic ways of referring to defeat and humiliation in ancient Semitic culture (e.g., Mic 7:17). Such references clearly refer to the loathsome behavior of snakes, but they do so metaphorically. So too with the picture of the serpent striking at people's heels but having his head crushed. They are most easily taken as metaphorically depicting the animosity between humans and "the serpent" by referring to the natural enmity between people and snakes. They strike out at us, but we crush their heads.

Concerning the serpent in this passage, I would argue that the author is neither trying to explain why snakes crawl on the ground nor portraying the serpent as a symbol of goodness and fertility. He is rather seeking to illustrate the cursed nature of a demonic serpent (later identified as Satan) by referring to ground-crawling snakes. The author is saying that the serpent, the master of "seditious chaos" (F. Landy), now faces certain defeat and humiliation (like a snake), though he can yet inflict wounds on us (strike our heel). In this light, the later Jewish and Christian traditions were justified in linking this demonic creature with the prince of all demons, Satan.

Isaiah 14:1-23. This passage contains a prophecy against Sennacherib, who after conquering Babylon proclaimed himself as its king (v. 4). Verses 4-11 address his humiliating end. Though he is mighty now and able to inflict suffering and turmoil on his subjects (v. 3), he shall be brought down to the grave and mocked (vv. 9-11). Then follows a passage that has traditionally been taken to apply more profoundly to Satan than it does to the king of Babylon.

How you have fallen from heaven, O morning star, son of the dawn! You have been cast down to the earth, you who once laid low the nations! You said in your heart, "I will ascend to heaven; I will raise my throne above the stars of God [El]; I will sit enthroned on the mount of assembly, on the utmost heights of the sacred mountain [Zaphon]. I will ascend above the tops of the clouds; I will make myself like the Most High [Elyon]." But you are brought down to the grave [Sheol], to the depths of the pit. (vv. 12-15 NIV)

The traditional argument has been that the wording of this passage goes beyond what can be appropriately applied to any human being, even to the king of Babylon. What human could ever "fall from heaven" and "be brought down to the earth?" Who would ever think they could ascend to heaven, rise above the stars of God (viz., the gods, here seen as stars), and ascend above the clouds? Hence the church has traditionally tended to see this passage as extending beyond Sennacherib and applying ultimately to Satan, the evil cosmic force working through Sennacherib.[45] Is this interpretation valid? Two things may be briefly said.

First, the traditional exegesis is certainly not required by the text as it stands, which is why the majority of modern critical exegetes dismiss it outright. While the language of Isaiah goes beyond what could be literally intended of any human being, nothing in the text itself suggests that Isaiah is here talking literally. Isaiah is simply comparing the king of Babylon to the planet Venus, the morning star (*hêlēl* = shining one; *ben-šāḥar* = son of dawn). It rises bright at dawn and climbs to the highest point in the sky, only to be quickly extinguished by the brightness of the rising sun. Thus, Isaiah says, shall be the career of the presently shining king of Babylon. He appears on the stage of world history as the brightest star, ascending higher and higher. But in the end he shall quickly disappear in the light of the sun.

Hence nothing in the text requires that we take Isaiah's poetic language as referring to anyone other than the man Sennacherib. The fact that every verse following this passage speaks about this fallen star as a mere mortal further confirms this point: "You are brought down to Sheol. . . . 'Is this the man who made the earth tremble, . . . who made the world like a desert?' . . . You are cast out, away from your grave, like loathsome carrion, . . . like a corpse trampled underfoot" (vv. 15-19). Such language, obviously, could hardly apply to a spiritual, cosmic force like Satan. But this is not to say that the central insight of the traditional teaching was misguided, and this is my second point.

Read in the context of other Near Eastern conflict myths, Isaiah's use of Venus as a metaphor for a rebellious and arrogant king does not seem simply to draw attention to something that shines, rises and then diminishes. The curious association of the God-created natural behavior of this bright morning star with something rebellious is significant. One of the recurring themes we find in the Near Eastern cosmic conflict myths is that of a young god who aspires to advance himself beyond his powers and appropriate domain, and who is thereby vanquished. In several contexts this god is associated with Venus.

For example, we know of one Canaanite story of a god named Athtar the Rebel, who wanted to rule on the throne of Baal. Unfortunately, he was too small for the throne. "His feet did not reach the footstool, his head did not reach the top." Apparently in frustration, he says, "I will not reign on the reaches of Zaphon" (the sacred mountain). Thus he is instead given rulership over the earth (or underworld), a much smaller affair that he can presumably handle.[46]

What is most interesting about this for our purposes is that Athtar's name means "Shining One, Son of Dawn."[47] Indeed, in another story about Athtar, his aspirations to reign with the god El by disclosing Yamm's plans on building a palace for himself are thwarted by none other than the sun-goddess Shapash.[48] The morning star, again, is vanquished by the sun! Variations on this theme seem to have found their way onto Greek soil as well, where stories of rebels (such as Phaeton, whose name means "shining") being defeated by rising too close to the sun were not uncommon.[49]

Understood against this background, Isaiah's poetry takes on new significance. The very fact that Isaiah associates the rising morning star with an act of rebellion suggests that he is tapping into some dimension of the Near Eastern cosmic conflict motif. That Isaiah further specifies that this rising star wanted to rise above "the stars of El," to sit enthroned on "the recesses of Zaphon" and "become like Elyon"—all of which play a role in the Canaanite stories of Athtar—strengthens the conviction that Isaiah is intentionally drawing on familiar Canaanite themes to make a point to his audience.[50] As Forsyth argues, the point seems to be the identification of "the king of Babylon, the power responsible for the fall of Jerusalem . . . with the figure of the cosmic rebel."[51]

In this light, we can interpret Isaiah as reworking the cultural stories about the rebellious rising star in the same way as other Old Testament authors reworked the cultural myths of Baal's battle with the raging

Yamm, or Marduk's battle with Tiamat. Isaiah portrays the arrogant activity of the king of Babylon as representing and reenacting the arrogant activity of a cosmic rebel, just as other authors had seen Yahweh's parting of the Red Sea as a reenactment of Yahweh's primordial defeat of Yamm or Rahab (Ps 77:16; 89:9-10; Is 51:9-11).

Isaiah is not thereby endorsing any particular story about Athtar. But he is using this known story to reveal a truth that the Athtar story illustrates: there is a cosmic rebellion, and the rebellious and arrogant extension of Sennacherib's kingdom beyond its legitimate domain is both a participant and a prototype of it.

We can therefore concede that Isaiah's prophecy is from beginning to end about none other than the man Sennacherib while also affirming that this prophecy has a cosmic dimension to it. Earthly battles correspond to heavenly battles. Hence we may consider the drama of Sennacherib's illegitimate kingship as a participant in and a prototype of a much vaster drama of another oppressive conqueror who attempted to set up an illegitimate kingship on a cosmic scale.

As such, in the words of Bertoluci, this passage about one particular hostile king also points toward "an archetype of the political and religious powers which through the ages are hostile to God and His people, and is, as well, the impellant force behind every evil activity."[52] Or, in the words of K. L. Schmidt, both a "heavenly and earthly . . . demonic and human" event is being alluded to in this passage. Schmidt continues, "Such a myth applies to a finally enigmatic incident, to a demonic . . . event, which illuminates the foreground and background of the history of the doings of mankind."[53]

When we consider the cosmic dimension of the mythological motifs Isaiah was alluding to in this passage, the later church tradition seems quite justified in identifying Helel ben-Shahar (translated as "Lucifer" in the Vulgate) with Satan. In its own fashion, the story of the rebellious king of Babylon illumines the story of the rebellious king of the whole world, and thus provides a cosmic backdrop for a warfare understanding of "the history of the doings of mankind."

Ezekiel 28: The fall of the perfect one. The case for the traditional Christian reading of Ezekiel 28 as referring to the fall of Satan is similar to that of Isaiah 14. Here too we find a person, in this case the king of Tyre, about whom things are said that do not seem applicable to a mere human being. He is said to be "wiser than Daniel"; indeed, no secret is

hidden from him (v. 3).[54] He sees himself as having "the mind of a god" (v. 6) and even refers to himself as "a god" (v. 2).

Far more significant, however, is what the Lord himself says of this king:

> You were the model of perfection, full of wisdom and perfect in beauty. You were in Eden, the garden of God; every precious stone adorned you . . . You were anointed as a guardian cherub, for so I ordained you. You were on the holy mount of God; you walked among the fiery stones. You were blameless in your ways from the day you were created till wickedness was found in you. (vv. 12-15 NIV)

But because this guardian cherub's "heart was proud because of [his] beauty" and because he became "filled with violence," the Lord "cast [him] from the mountain of God" (vv. 16-17).

It is not difficult to see why the church quickly hit upon the interpretation that this prophecy was at once speaking about the fall of the king of Tyre and the fall of Satan. When Ezekiel speaks of the Garden of Eden, the holy mount of God and a guardian cherub walking among the fiery stones, he seems to have moved beyond the realm of "this-worldly" history, even after an allowance is made for Semitic hyperbole. When he speaks of this pagan king as being "the model of perfection, full of wisdom and perfect in beauty," someone other than the king of Tyre seems to be intended.

As with Isaiah, it is likely that Ezekiel is here appropriating aspects of the Near Eastern cosmic battle motif as a way of communicating the cosmic significance of the fall of the king of Tyre. The portrayal of the garden of God as the holy mountain surrounded by precious stones (sometimes conceived of as the stars) fits with various aspects of some Canaanite cosmic conflict stories. The theme of the rebel who possesses secrets is very common, and the notion that he is bright and beautiful fits well with other aspects of these myths (such as the rebellious Shining Son of Dawn stories mentioned above).[55] The mention of Eden and the cherub, however, suggests that features of these cosmic conflict stories have been combined with elements of the Genesis account of the fall of humans as well (Genesis 2—3). Such would be an understandable, and indeed clever, literary device if indeed the author is depicting the fall of a cosmic being.[56]

In any event, while little can be said with certainty about the exact background to this passage, it seems probable that Ezekiel, like Isaiah, is making both a historical and a cosmic point within this passage. The fall of the king of Tyre illustrates and reenacts the cosmic fall of some unnamed "guardian cherub" (one of the gods of the nations?) who was, among other things, the model of perfection before his fall.

What lends further credence to the interpretation of this passage as a fusion of cosmic and historical themes is that, in the passages that follow, Ezekiel appears to do the same thing with other kings and with other cosmic figures. Thus he portrays Pharaoh as the great monster of the sea (Ezek 29:3; 32:2) and then applies a version of the Babylonian and Canaanite battles between Marduk (or Baal) and Tiamat (or Yamm) to him—except, of course, that Yahweh is the vanquisher. In Ezekiel 29 the monster will be captured with a hook and fed to the beasts (vv. 4-6).[57] Chapter 32 says it will be captured with a net and left on dry land, where God "will cause all the birds of the air to settle on you, and I [God] will let the wild animals of the whole earth gorge themselves with you" (v. 4).

The cosmic dimensions of Pharaoh's (viz., the sea monster's) demise are then brought full circle when the Lord says, "When I blot you out, I will cover the heavens, and make their stars dark; I will cover the sun with a cloud, and the moon shall not give its light. All the shining lights of the heavens I will darken above you" (vv. 7-8).

It seems, then, that throughout this section Ezekiel portrays historical events as illustrating and intersecting with cosmic events. More specifically, he envisages Yahweh's overthrow of his present historical enemies as examples of his overthrowing his cosmic enemies. In this light, the Christian understanding, derived from later revelation that clearly depicts Satan as God's archenemy, can be considered justified in sensing that the fall of Satan himself is intimated in the fall of the king of Tyre (and we might add, the pharaoh of Egypt) as portrayed in this book.

Conclusion

We may summarize our investigation of the warfare motif in the Old Testament throughout the last four chapters by reviewing six conclusions.

First, while all the Old Testament authors are intent on expressing the sovereignty of Yahweh, they understand this sovereignty to entail that Yahweh does genuinely battle cosmic foes. In the only terms that they, in their ancient Near Eastern culture, could understand, it was revealed that hostile, proud, raging, destructive forces of chaos oppose God's will and threaten the very foundations of the earth. In short, Yahweh must battle the hostile waters, Yamm, Leviathan, Rahab and Behemoth.

While Yahweh has unquestionably already vanquished these monsters and will continue to do so on a cosmic scale, this victory never undermines the genuineness of Yahweh's present and future battles in the eyes of Old Testament authors. As in other Near Eastern myths, some authors understood Yahweh to have battled and defeated these forces prior to creation, a fact that I tentatively tried to square with the Genesis 1 creation account by entertaining a form of the restoration theory. Yet through the voluntary forfeiture by humans of their rightful rule, these anticreation forces continue to engulf and threaten the earth.

Indeed, so authentic is the ongoing cosmic spiritual battle that in a few instances Old Testament authors suggest that these forces successfully resisted God's will in opposing nations or individual persons. For three weeks the "prince of Persia" successfully blocks God's answer to Daniel's prayer (Dan 10); the demonlike Chemosh, feeding on a king's sacrificed son, successfully routs Israel (2 Kings 3:26-27); and Yamm at times successfully mocks God by engulfing Israel as he earlier (Gen 1:2?) engulfed the earth (Ps 74:10-13). Hence, as Levenson notes, the psalmist has to continually remind himself—in the face of evidence to the contrary—of Yahweh's primordial victory.[58] We shall shortly see that this conception of the power of hostile forces to thwart God's will becomes much more intensified in the apocalyptic period and in the New Testament.

Second, while only a small amount of attention is given to evil spirits ("demons") in the world, a significant amount of attention is given to the existence of gods who form a council of Yahweh and collectively constitute his army. While every Old Testament author unequivocally affirms that there is only one Creator and one Supreme God, they also assume the existence of other created gods. In so doing, they reestablish (not originate) a primal form of creational monotheism.

What is more, the Old Testament assumes that a significant amount of authority has been given to these gods to oversee the welfare of various nations (Deut 32; Ps 82). Others seem to be identified, or at least closely associated, with "natural" phenomena such as the sun, stars, moon, wind and thunder (Deut 4:19-20; 17:13; Judg 5:20; Job 38:7; Is 14:13; 40:26; 45:12; 104:4; 148:1-6; Hab 3:11). These gods, then, like humans (but on a larger scale), are in a position to carry out Yahweh's will for the good of others. But if they choose, they are also in a position to temporarily thwart Yahweh's will to the detriment of others, particularly those under their authority (Dan 10; Ps 82). If they choose the latter, they are, or at least shall be, judged accordingly (Ps 82). They shall eventually die "like mortals" and "fall like any prince" (v. 7).

Third, while Satan will later become the example par excellence of a god who went wrong (and the greatest of the gods beneath Yahweh at that!), in the Old Testament he remains a relatively minor figure, being mentioned by name only once (1 Chron 21:1). Nonetheless, against the views of many contemporary scholars, I have argued that he is, in the Old Testament, not seen as being a legitimate member of Yahweh's assembly, nor is he portrayed as simply carrying out Yahweh's orders. Rather, he is an adversary against God even more than he is an adversary against humans. His character is consistently seen as malicious.

It is this malicious element in his character at this early stage of revelation that lays the foundation for later perspectives. Here, we shall find, the figure of Satan comes to absorb within himself the chaotic cosmic characteristics previously attributable to Leviathan and other anticreation beasts.

Fourth, with some justification (in the light of subsequent revelation), the serpent of Genesis 3 can be interpreted as either symbolizing or embodying Satan. Isaiah 14 and Ezekiel 28 can also be understood as referring not only to the fall of human kings but also to the fall of Satan. While we are told virtually nothing about the time and circumstances of this cosmic fall, we are told enough to infer that it should not have happened.

These two prophetic passages are both spoken as lamentations for someone gone wrong. Drawing on familiar Near Eastern images, both passages depict someone created great who became prideful in his heart and rebellious in his spirit, and who then was cast down. Something similar can perhaps be inferred about the pride of Yamm, the waters, Rahab and Leviathan, as exemplified in other passages. These cosmic forces, it seems, ought not to be forces of chaos and destruction, and God ought not to have to oppose them.

All of this has significant repercussions for our understanding of the problem of evil. While an unambiguous "free will defense" is obviously not provided here, the Old Testament is laying the foundation for seeing evil as originating in the heart of free creatures—human and divine. It is, at the very least, certainly disallowing any understanding of evil as an eternal feature of the cosmos or of God. Evil is from the start construed as a tragic intrusion into God's otherwise good creation.

Fifth, the only place where anything like the problem of evil is explicitly addressed at length in the Old Testament is the book of Job. The central point of the entire epic is that neither Job's friends nor Job himself are correct in their explanations of his misfortunes. Job's sorry plight was neither punishment for his (supposed) sin nor part of some wise, righteous and judgmental divine plan, as his friends insisted. But it was also not the result of an arbitrary irrational streak in God, as Job (and contemporary "demonic-in-Yahweh" theorists) suspected.

Rather, the point of the book is to say that these are not the only two options, a point that the post-Augustinian philosophical tradition lost and has yet to regain consistently. Both the prologue to Job and Yahweh's speeches in Job leave us with the acute awareness that there is much more to this cosmos than just us and God. As almost all primordial peoples have realized, and as the New Testament makes even more explicit, there is also an incredibly vast, magnificent, complex and often-times warring and hostile "world in between" that we must factor in. Without undermining the sovereignty of God, the Bible generally portrays the cosmos as more like a divinely governed democracy than a divinely controlled dictatorship, and this democracy encompasses, but greatly transcends, free human beings.

But the book of Job and the entire Bible also assume that we know next to nothing about the goings on of this "world in between." For example, in the whole of Scripture, and in direct contrast to much other literature in the ancient world and throughout history, we are given the names of only two angels.[59] It is only through direct revelation that one gains a perspective like Daniel's on warring cosmic "princes," or the prophetic perspective Jeremiah speaks of as one who is privileged to listen in on the assembly of Yahweh's council of gods (Jer 23:18; see 1 Kings 22:19-20; Is 6:8; Ps 82:1; 89:7; 103:20-21; 148:2; Job 1:6; 2:1). It is because of our near total ignorance—not on the basis of his sheer divine authority—that Yahweh instructs Job and his friends to remain silent in the face of evil.[60] It is, in the end, neither God's fault nor Job's fault.

One of the primary reasons why the problem of evil is so intellectually intractable for us is precisely that we have not learned the lesson of Job, or of other primordial peoples. We have not moved beyond the false dichotomy of Job and his friends: evil in our culture is still generally seen as being either our fault or God's will, or both. We are yet caught in an Augustinian, classical-philosophical model of God's providence and an Enlightenment model of our aloneness in the cosmos.

This is, in a less direct way, also a lesson we can learn through the Old Testament motifs of Yahweh's battle with the sea monsters, Yahweh's struggle to control the gods, and even from the multitude of nonbiblical conflict myths that are found in most cultures throughout history. There is a "world in between"; it is largely characterized by warfare; and, for better or for worse, it significantly affects the world as a whole, and therefore each of our lives. It is my conviction that, until this "world in between" is factored into the equation, no attempts to render evil intelligible within a monotheistic context will significantly advance beyond where Job and his friends were (mistakenly) some thirty-five hundred years ago.

There are, of course, a multitude of questions this "world in between" poses for us Western Christians that need addressing, issues that we shall address later.[61] For example, how is this view of things compatible with a belief in God's omnipotence? Why would God create a world in which his will is not necessarily carried out? Why would God create beings who have the power to hurt so many others? How are we to conceptualize God being influenced by our prayer? Can God guarantee ultimate victory over his rebellious foes and our spiritual cosmic nemeses? If so, why does he not simply destroy these rebel forces now? Why does he tarry while the innocent suffer?

For now, however, it is enough to demonstrate the too frequently minimized truth that the Bible does hold to this warfare worldview, and thus to this understanding of evil. It is enough to demonstrate that the Bible does not assume that every particular evil has a particular godly purpose behind it. It is presently enough to show that the Bible attributes the responsibility for evil to forces that are hostile to God—especially to Satan—not to God himself. These are the primary data that any Christian theoretical understanding of God and evil must be founded on, and it is this foundation that this study seeks to establish.

If the material that composes this foundation creates tensions with our standard Western assumptions about reality, and perhaps even with some of our Western Christian assumptions about God and his control of the world, we must at this point simply let those tensions remain. In no case should we allow ourselves to revise the data merely because they cause us discomfort.

If all this is true of the Old Testament, it is, we shall now see, much more apparent in the New Testament. The relatively marginal concept of Yahweh battling cosmic forces here takes center stage. The awareness of and appreciation for the existence, influence and significance of "the world in between" intensify significantly. With it, the understanding of evil as not coming from God's hand but directly or indirectly originating in forces that oppose God gains greater clarity.

To this understanding of God, angels and evil in the New Testament, then, we now turn.

PART II

THE WARFARE
WORLDVIEW
OF THE
NEW TESTAMENT

6

TYING UP
THE STRONG MAN
THE KINGDOM OF GOD
AS A WARFARE
CONCEPT

*T*HOUGH THE COSMIC WARFARE MOTIF OCCURS THROUGHOUT the Old Testament, it never takes center stage. This foundational stage of written revelation affirms that there is a "world in between," that there is genuine conflict within this "world," and that this spiritual conflict affects affairs within our earthly domain. From Old Testament accounts it is clear that there is, at a fundamental level, something askew in creation.

Whether it be portrayed as Leviathan, Rahab, Yamm, Behemoth, hostile waters or a wayward rebellious god (e.g., "prince of Persia," Chemosh, *satan*), and whether it is portrayed as a battle that took place before the creation of this world or as something that is taking place in the present, the Old Testament clearly assumes that something profoundly sinister has entered God's good creation and now perpetually threatens the world. Not all is well in creation.

To this extent the Old Testament worldview overlaps with the general Near Eastern worldview. But the way the cosmic warfare dimension of the Old Testament worldview is played out is radically unique among

Near Eastern peoples, and this uniqueness has center stage throughout the Old Testament. Unlike all other warfare worldviews, the Old Testament repeatedly stresses the absolute supremacy of one God over all others, and therefore unequivocally maintains that this one God is never threatened by his enemies. Such an emphasis was needed as the solid foundation for everything else the Lord wanted to reveal subsequently to humankind.

Biblical authors never abandon this foundational monotheistic conviction, but its relation to the warfare motif significantly changes as we enter the New Testament. For here, alongside the supremacy of God, the reality of the warfare itself shares center stage. As an increasing number of New Testament scholars now recognize, almost everything that Jesus and the early church were about is decisively colored by the central conviction that the world is caught in the crossfire of a cosmic battle between the Lord and his angelic army and Satan and his demonic army. The most fundamental goal of the next five chapters is to defend this thesis.[1]

To this end, in this chapter I first provide an overview of the cultural background to the New Testament by looking at how the warfare motifs of the Old Testament were expanded upon and intensified during the intertestamental period. I then examine Jesus' view of Satan and his army, followed by an explication of his all-important understanding of the kingdom of God as a warfare concept.

Intertestamental Developments

The Jewish worldview underwent a significant transformation during the period between the Old and the New Testaments. Since the time of the exodus, the Jews had closely associated the truthfulness of their belief in Yahweh's supremacy with their political successes. Yahweh's lordship over Israel and over the world was, for them, most clearly evidenced by the fact that they had won, and preserved, an independent status as a nation. When they were taken into captivity and oppressed by heathen kings, therefore, this caused a crisis of faith for them. It seemed to imply that Yahweh was not, in fact, the sovereign Lord over the earth.

Still, so long as there was hope that Israel would someday regain its independence, Israel's national misfortunes could be explained as being the result of their own temporary infidelity to Yahweh. Their misfortunes were not, therefore, an indictment of their belief in Yahweh's supremacy so much as they were an indictment of themselves. The people believed that as soon as they as a nation repented of their sin and turned back to the Lord, the Lord would prove faithful and give them back the Promised Land.[2]

After several hundred years of painful oppression under pagan authorities, however, this chastisement theology began to wear thin. When this oppression turned to overt bloody persecution under Antiochus IV, many Jews abandoned this theology. An increasing number of Jews in the third and second centuries B.C. began to believe that what was happening to them could not be all their fault, and thus it could not all be Yahweh's disciplining will.

But if it was not God's will that was bringing about the disasters they were experiencing, whose will was it? To answer this question, some Jews of this period turned with fresh urgency to the warfare motifs found throughout their Scriptures.

If ever there was a time when it seemed that the raging seas, Leviathan, Satan and demons were having their way with Israel, and with the entire world, this was the time. Not surprisingly, then, we find in this oppressive, painful environment an intensification of the warfare themes of the Hebrew Bible. The conviction that the cosmos is populated with good and evil spiritual beings and that the earth is caught in the crossfire of their conflict became centrally important for many Jews during this intertestamental period. So too, the apocalyptic hope that Yahweh would soon vanquish Leviathan (or some parallel cosmic figure) and all its cohorts grew in intensity during this period.

This intensification of Old Testament themes, this incredible expansion of and centralization of the Old Testament ideas about the lesser gods and Yahweh's conflicts with them, constitutes what has come to be called the apocalyptic worldview. It is against the backdrop of this worldview that we must read the New Testament if we are to understand it properly.

Apocalyptic thought and Zoroastrianism. Admittedly, the above claim that it was principally to the Old Testament that the Jews of this period turned to answer the crisis created by their oppression, and thus that it is primarily the Old Testament that lies behind apocalyptic thought, is by no means undisputed. To the contrary, the issues surrounding the origin and development of apocalypticism are many, and many of them are hotly contested. Before proceeding further, then, we do well to pause briefly to address several of the more important of these issues.[3]

The problems associated with the study of Jewish apocalyptic thought begin with the controversy surrounding the very definition of "apocalyptic."[4] While attempts to arrive at a generally accepted definition have proved notoriously futile, it is at least widely agreed that it is important to distinguish among three distinct but frequently confused categories: "apocalypse" as a literary category, "apocalyptic eschatology" as a theological category, and "apocalypticism" as a comprehensive worldview.[5] The apocalyptic worldview includes the literary and theological apocalyptic elements, but the converse is not always true. It is principally the worldview that presently concerns us.

While articulating precisely what constitutes this worldview has proved difficult, scholars agree widely on several general characteristics. Among these are the use of pseudepigraphy; the dividing up of history into distinct periods (ages), often in a loosely deterministic fashion; an intensified interest in angels and demons; a concentration on heavenly journeys or visions; a belief in an ultimate resurrection and final judgment, often construed as impending; and perhaps most fundamentally, and for our purposes most importantly, an intense conviction that the world is engulfed in a cosmic struggle between good and evil. Apocalyptic thought considers evil more a structural characteristic of a war-torn cosmos than a feature of human decision-making.

Gabriele Boccaccini expresses the centrality of this last feature well when he writes concerning the Jewish apocalyptic tradition:

> In spite of all the differences, it is possible to identify its core in a peculiar conception of evil, understood as an autonomous reality, antecedent even to humankind's ability to choose. This conception of evil is not simply one of so many "apocalyptic" ideas; it is the generative idea of a distinct ideological tradition of thought, the corner-stone on which and out of which the whole "apocalyptic" tradition is built.[6]

As we shall see shortly, this "generative idea" lies at the foundation of the New Testament's own conception of the world.

A second set of issues surrounds the question of the extent to which the Jewish apocalyptic worldview of the intertestamental period is an outgrowth of Persian Zoroastrianism (and perhaps other pagan influences), or the extent to which it is an outgrowth of the Old Testament's own warfare worldview.[7] Since the time of Julius Wellhausen (mid-nineteenth century) up to the recent past, critical scholars have tended strongly toward the former. Indeed, until relatively recent times, it was common to find Jewish apocalyptic thought characterized in a decidedly negative fashion as a sort of hybrid compromise between the supposed "pure" (viz., exclusivistic) monotheism of the prophetic period on the one hand and Zoroastrian dualism on the other.[8]

In the last several decades, however, scholars have been increasingly emphasizing the Old Testament as the primary background for Jewish apocalypticism. Gerhard von Rad and others have attempted to argue that the Jewish wisdom tradition supplied the original soil on which apocalyptic thought was eventually to flourish.[9] Even more influentially, however, scholars such as F. M. Cross, H. H. Rowley and especially P. D. Hanson have made strong cases for seeing apocalyptic thought as firmly rooted in the Old Testament's prophetic tradition.[10] The key to understanding the development of apocalyptic thought, in this view, is found in the proto-apocalyptic passages of the Old Testament prophets, such as Isaiah 24—27, Ezekiel 38—39, and Zechariah 5—6 and 9—14.[11]

While conceding that the question of Persian (Zoroastrian) influence upon Jewish apocalyptic thought remains open, a majority of scholars today concur that it is, at best, merely one of a number of possible influences, all of which must be viewed as secondary to the Old Testament traditions themselves. Even those who continue to defend the primacy of a Zoroastrian influence agree widely that the claims of earlier proponents of wholesale borrowing were excessive and untenable.[12]

At least three factors have led to the demise of the strong Zoroastrian influence position. First, as was the case generally with the history-of-religions school, the supposed parallels between Zoroastrianism and Judeo-Christian thought were inconclusive upon further analysis. Indeed, as Edwin Yamauchi and others have demonstrated, each of the "parallels" can be more easily accounted for by reference to the Old Testament itself.[13]

Even worse for this once-dominant thesis, however, is that those Zoroastrian texts most frequently appealed to as providing strong parallels with Judaism and Christianity were demonstrably written or redacted after the period of Persian rule over Israel.[14] Further, a fairly strong case can be made for the contention that at least some of those texts (such as Job) that are supposedly most indebted to Persian influence were written before the period of Persian rule over Israel.[15]

(3)   Finally, and perhaps most decisively, despite shared features, the perspectives on God and Satan found in Zoroastrianism and the Judeo-Christian tradition are, on closer examination, actually significantly different from one another. Most fundamentally, while it is debated whether Zoroastrianism was thoroughly dualistic at the time of Israel's captivity, it was certainly tending in this direction.[16] But Judaism, even in its most extreme apocalyptic versions, remained within the parameters of "creational monotheism." While Satan (or, outside the canon, sometimes a parallel figure) was certainly acknowledged to have a great deal of control over this present fallen world, the power he wielded was always unambiguously understood to be a power that was given him by God, his Creator. In this sense, as Yamauchi argues, Satan differs significantly from "the primordial Ahriman, who was equal in power to Ohrmazd."[17]

In other words, the dualism of the Bible is a free will dualism, not a metaphysical dualism. It is there only because of how various free beings have exercised their free will. More precisely, it is there because (1) God chose to create a quasi-democratic cosmos in which dualism could result; and (2) some of these free beings whom God created (both human and angelic) have chosen to misuse their divine gift and are thus now freely existing in a state of rebellion.

In any event, the great difference of perspectives here makes it reasonable to conclude that if Zoroastrianism influenced Judaism at all, it was only in a very general, "atmospheric" way. Theologically speaking, perhaps in the progress of revelation the Lord providentially used Israel's captivity, and thus used Persian Zoroastrianism, to heighten their awareness of the scope of Satan's power and activity in the world. But any claim to a more significant influence than this is simply unwarranted.

The fall of the Watcher angels. Hence it was primarily from the Old Testament that the Jews of the intertestamental period developed their particular intensified convictions concerning cosmic spiritual warfare. This is not to minimize the radical newness of apocalyptic thought, however, for this intensification was by no means insignificant. To the contrary, the radical ideas about cosmic conflict that grew out of the intense, prolonged experience of evil these Jews were suffering went far beyond anything depicted in the Old Testament.[18]

In apocalyptic thought, the relatively opaque ideas about free gods (angels) we find in the Old Testament erupt in an explosion of speculations about the vast numbers, particular names, individual natures,

personal histories and the particular battles of all these various intermediary beings.[19] Undoubtedly, the most important example of this sort of
speculative development is the use Jews made of the story of the fallen
"sons of God" in Genesis 6 during this time.

This story, usually referred to as "the Watcher tradition," occurs in a
number of different forms, but in outline it runs as follows.[20] The Lord
had originally entrusted various angels with the responsibility of watching over humans, who in turn were assigned the task of watching over
the earth. These angels, the original "sons of God," were to be guardians
and educators of humankind, instructing them in the ways of God and
giving them useful advice in making tools, working the land, building
structures and so on.[21]

Unfortunately, however, many of these exalted spiritual beings suc-
cumbed to lust for beautiful earthly women (or, in some accounts, to
pride or envy) and then abused the divine authority they had originally
been given. For example, instead of providing moral instruction, these
(now rebel) angels instructed humankind in demonic magic; instead of
teaching useful crafts, they taught humans how to fashion weapons of
war to be used against each another.

Moreover, according to the Watcher tradition (as in the Genesis
account), these rebel angelic beings attained the pinnacle of evil (or, in
some accounts, the original act of evil) when they took human form and
copulated with human women ("the daughters of men," Gen 6:4; see
chapter four above). As in Genesis, the offspring of these hybrid unions
were believed to be mutant giants (Nephilim) whose own offspring,
according to some Watcher accounts, were mutant spiritual beings
(demons).[22] While the Watcher angels and Nephilim were generally
believed to have been defeated by Yahweh's angels, according to many
sources, their demon offspring still populate the earth. They possess
people, incite others to violence and deceit, and generally afflict the
world with famines and disease.

The central thrust of the whole Watcher story line is clearly that when
heavenly beings pervert their God-given authority, everything under
them (including the rest of creation) begins to grow perverse as well.[23]
This is one of the driving themes of the apocalyptic literature written just
prior to the time of Christ, and if we give it any credence (such as Jesus
and the disciples seem to give it), it has the potential to revolutionize
our understanding of evil.

The precarious role of guardian angels. In more specific terms, apocalyptic writers greatly expanded the relatively minor Old Testament portrayal of gods who are given assignments over nations and who are associated with certain natural phenomena. Indeed, the general thrust of this literature is to paint a picture of Yahweh's authority as being, in almost every respect, mediated by morally responsible angels.

For example, the book of *Jubilees* catalogs the "spirits which serve before [God]" by referring to angels who are variously given authority over fire, winds, clouds, darkness, snow, hail, frost, thunder and lightning, cold and heat. Others are put in charge of autumn, summer, winter and spring, while still others are charged with guarding over "all of the spirits of [God's] creatures which are in the heavens and on the earth."[24] The *Testament of Adam* adds to this list angels who are variously given authority over creeping animals, birds, fish, the atmosphere, rain, and even over the sun, moon and stars.[25]

The list could easily be expanded,[26] but the point is already clear: Everything under God's authority is also under some other "god's" authority. As Wink notes, in this worldview "every species and thing has its angel."[27] For apocalyptic writers, this meant that the divine governance of the universe was more precarious than had been previously thought. For if and when these guardian angels decide to turn evil, the authority and responsibility given to them is not (cannot be?) immediately retracted. As is the case with human parents and their children, when these angels fall, everything they are guardians of suffers accordingly. For these writers, the explanation for how God's good creation could be perverted on a cosmic scale is found in this "angelic variable." The blame for the evil within the cosmos is understood to land squarely on these intermediary beings and on the humans who align themselves with them.

This is not to suggest that apocalyptic writers held to anything like a uniform and consistently worked out view of angelic and human freedom as a means of accounting for this creaturely moral responsibility. To the contrary, while some of these writings are certainly explicit and emphatic in their understanding of creaturely freedom, others are decidedly deterministic.[28] The deterministic strand in apocalyptic thought has tended to receive the greater emphasis in the scholarly literature, but there are some indications that this is changing. For example, according to A. E. Sekki strict determinism is relatively rare even in the Qumran literature, which scholars frequently regard as displaying the most intense determinism of any writings of the period. The assumption that the Qumran community was deterministic in its outlook, Sekki has convincingly argued, is based on a mistaken identification of the "two spirits" with the "two angels" tradition found in the Manual of Discipline (1QS 3.13—4.26).[29]

If Sekki is correct, it is likely that the strand of intertestamental literature that emphasized free will has not been given its due. As E. H. Merrill and a number of other scholars have argued, it is clear that there was a wide variety of opinions on the matter of free will and determinism in this period, and thus a wide variety of expressions to this effect in the literature.[30] In my opinion, the ferment generated by the intensified warfare paradigm produced a variety of tensive perspectives that were just beginning to be worked out in this transitional period. This point must caution us in trying to draw too much out of this literature as background for the New Testament.

However these various authors landed on the free will-determinism issue, they all share the general perception that something has gone seriously wrong with the cosmos. Indeed, to put it in this fashion significantly understates their general view. Here we come to perhaps the most important modification these authors made to Old Testament themes.

These authors intensified the relatively minor Old Testament concept of Yahweh engaging in battle against opposing forces to preserve order in the world to the point that now Yahweh must do battle against these forces in order to *rescue* the world. In other words, if Old Testament authors saw Leviathan as threatening the earth, these authors sometimes saw this cosmic beast as having already devoured it. In their view, therefore, what was now needed was not so much protection from Leviathan but deliverance out of the belly of Leviathan itself.

These Jews, writing out of their own intense experience of evil, came to the remarkable conclusion that in a significant sense the battle between Yahweh and opposing hostile forces for the world had been, at least temporarily, lost by Yahweh. They were certain that Yahweh would ultimately (and soon) reclaim his cosmos, vanquish his foes and reinstate himself on his rightful throne. In this ultimate eschatological sense, Yahweh could yet be considered Lord over the creation. But in this "present age," their conviction was that "Satan had stolen the world," as James Kallas describes it, and thus that the creation had gone "ber-serk."[31]

In this "modified dualism," as William F. Albright appropriately labels it,[32] the highest mediating agent of Yahweh had gone bad, abused his incredible God-given authority, taken the entire world hostage, and therefore set himself up as the illegitimate god of the present age. This spelled disaster for the cosmos.[33]

Fundamentally, it meant that the mediating angelic authority struc-ture that Yahweh had set up at creation had gone bad at the very top. Hence everything underneath this highest authority, everything both in the heavens and on earth, had been adversely affected. Vast multitudes of powerful angels, having been given authority over various aspects of creation (or lesser angels), could now use this authority to wage war against God and against his people. Not all the angels fell, but in the minds of these writers, a great many of them did. Demons, sometimes portrayed as mutant offspring of the Nephilim but other times portrayed as fallen angels themselves, could now freely infest this satanically gov-erned world and work all manner of evil in it. What was to have been a godly council of heaven and a godly army for the Lord had turned itself into a fierce rebel battalion that fought against God, and did so in large part by terrorizing the earth and holding its inhabitants captive.

For these apocalypticists, then, it was no wonder that Yahweh's lordship was not manifested in Israel's political fortune. Nor was it any great mystery why God's people were now undergoing such vicious persecution. Indeed, to these writers it was no wonder that the entire creation looked like a diabolical war zone. In their view, that was precisely what it was.

Jesus' View of the Satanic Army

On the reckoning of the majority of contemporary New Testament scholars, it is primarily against this apocalyptic background that we are to understand the ministry of Jesus and the early church.[34] Jesus' teaching, his exorcisms, his healings and other miracles, as well as his work on the cross, all remain somewhat incoherent and unrelated to one another until we interpret them within this apocalyptic context: in other words, until we interpret them as acts of war. When this hermeneutical step is made, however, Jesus' ministry forms a coherent whole. The remainder of this chapter, as well as the following two chapters, seeks to demonstrate this coherence.

Satan's rule. As in apocalyptic thought, the assumption that undergirds Jesus' entire ministry is the view that Satan has illegitimately seized the world and thus now exercises a controlling influence over it. Three times the Jesus of John's Gospel refers to Satan as "the prince of this world" (Jn 12:31; 14:30; 16:11). He here uses the word *archōn,* which was customarily used to denote "the highest official in a city or a region in the Greco-Roman world."[35] Hence Jesus is saying that, concerning ruling powers over the cosmos, this evil ruler is highest.

Thus when Satan claimed that he could give all the "authority" and "glory" of "all the kingdoms of the world" to whomever he wanted—for they all belonged to him—Jesus did not dispute him (Lk 4:5-6). That much Jesus assumed to be true.[36] With the apocalyptic worldview of his day, and in agreement with John, Paul and the rest of the New Testament, Jesus assumes that the entire world is "under the power of the evil one" (1 Jn 5:19) and that Satan is "the god of this world" (2 Cor 4:4) and "the ruler of the power of the air" (Eph 2:2). Jesus therefore concedes Satan's rulership of the earth. What Jesus would not do, however, was to give in to Satan's temptation and worship this illegitimate tyrant as a way of getting (back) this worldwide kingdom (Lk 4:7-8).[37]

Also in keeping with the apocalyptic thought of his day, Jesus sees this evil tyrant as mediating and expanding his authority over the world through multitudes of demons that form a vast army under him. Indeed, Jesus intensifies this conviction somewhat in comparison to the apocalyptic views of his day. When Jesus is accused of casting demons out of people by the power of Beelzebul (another name for Satan), he responds by telling his hostile audience, "If a kingdom is divided against itself, that kingdom cannot stand" (Mk 3:24).[38] His response builds upon their shared assumption that the demonic kingdom is unified under one "prince" *(archōn),* who is Satan (Mk 3:22; Mt 9:34; 12:24; Lk 11:15). His point is that this kingdom of evil, like any kingdom, cannot be working at cross-purposes with itself.

Indeed, Jesus adds that one cannot make significant headway in taking back the "property" of this "kingdom" unless one first "ties up the strong man" who oversees the whole operation (Mk 3:27). This, Luke adds, can only be done when "one stronger than he attacks him and overpowers him" and thus "takes away his armor in which he trusted" and then "divides his plunder" (Lk 11:22). This is what Jesus came to do. His whole ministry was about overpowering the "fully armed" strong man who guarded "his property" (Lk 11:21), namely, God's people and ultimately the entire earth.

Far from illustrating how (per impossible) Satan's kingdom works against itself, Jesus' success in casting out demons reveals that his whole ministry was about "tying up the strong man."[39] The whole episode clearly illustrates Jesus' assumption that Satan and demons form a unified kingdom. They are, as John Newport puts it, a "tight-knit lethal organization" that has a singular focus under a single general, Satan.[40]

Because of this assumption Jesus can refer to the "devil and his angels," implying that fallen angels belong to Satan (Mt 25:41). For the same reason Jesus sees demonic activity as being, by extension, the activity of Satan himself (e.g., Lk 13:11-16; cf. Acts 10:38; 2 Cor 12:7), and he therefore judges that everything done against demons is also done against Satan himself.[41]

For example, when his seventy disciples returned to him after a successful ministry of driving out demons, Jesus proclaims that he saw "Satan fall from heaven like a flash of lightning" (Lk 10:17-18).[42] The "strong man" and his household clearly stand or fall together. They together form a single, relatively organized army, unified in its singular purpose of hindering God's work and bringing evil and misery to his people. The head of this army, and thus the ultimate principle of all evil, is Satan.[43]

The pervasive influence of Satan's army. As the Gospels portray it, this demonic alien army is vast in number and global in influence.[44] The sheer number of possessions recorded in the Gospels, the large number of multiple possessions recorded, and the many allusions to vast numbers of people who were possessed reveal the belief that "the number of evil spirits [was] . . . indefinitely large."[45] The world was understood to be saturated with demons, whose destructive influence was all-pervasive. Everything about Jesus' ministry informs us that he judged every feature of the world that was not in keeping with the Creator's all-good design as being directly or indirectly the result of this invading presence.

Jesus never once appealed to a mysterious divine will to explain why a person was sick, maimed or deceased, as many Christians today are inclined to do.[46] Rather, in every instance, he came against such things as being the byproducts of a creation gone berserk through the evil

influence of this Satanic army. Indeed, many times he attributed sicknesses to direct demonic involvement.[47]

For example, Jesus diagnosed a woman "with a spirit that had crippled
her for eighteen years" as one whom "Satan bound" (Lk 13:11, 16). Far
from trying to discern some secret, sovereign, divine blueprint behind
her grotesque deformity, Jesus treated her as a casualty of war. The one
ultimately responsible for her affliction, Jesus claimed, was the captain
of the opposing battalion himself. James Kallas poignantly expresses
Jesus' approach to such matters, in sharp contrast to our typical modern
Western approach:

> We see polio or crippling and we piously shake our heads and cluck
> all the trite absurdities of a non-thinking people by saying "it is the
> will of God . . . hard to understand . . . providence writes a long
> sentence, we have to wait to get to heaven to read the answer." . . .
> Jesus looked at this and in crystal clear terms called it the work of the
> devil, and not the will of God.[48]

As difficult as Kallas's assessment may be to accept, from a strictly
scriptural perspective he is surely correct. In the minds of the disciples,
such things as back deformities and diseases were, as Raymond Brown
argues, "directly inflicted by Satan." So for them, to be "saved" was not
simply about "spiritual regeneration" but also about being delivered
"from the evil grasp of sickness, from the dominion of Satan."[49]

Further, as Brown and others also make clear, Jesus and the Gospel
authors sometimes referred to the diseases people had as "scourgings"
or "whippings" (*mastix*; Mk 3:10; 5:29, 34; Lk 7:21).[50] The only other
times ancient authors used this term to describe physical maladies were
to refer to afflictions sent by God upon people.[51] In these particular
instances, God was punishing people with a scourging. But this clearly
cannot be its meaning here, since Jesus sets people free from this
scourging.

For example, after the woman who had been bleeding for twelve years
touched his cloak, Jesus says to her, "Daughter, your faith has healed
you. Go in peace and be freed from your scourging *[mastix]*" (Mk
5:34).[52] Jesus was certainly not freeing this woman from a God-intended
twelve-year whipping. But whose whipping is Jesus freeing her from? In
the total context of Jesus' ministry, the only other possibility is that he
understood himself to be setting this woman (and all like her) free from
the whippings of "the strong man," Satan.

Along the same lines, though Jesus never endorsed the apocalyptic tendency to speculate about the names, ranks and functions of various fallen angels, he does go so far as to rebuke a deaf and mute spirit (Mk 9:25), and Luke describes another exorcism as the driving out of "a demon that was mute" (Lk 11:14).[53] There are apparently various kinds of demons within Satan's army who have differing particular functions in afflicting people.

Elsewhere Jesus does not specify that a demon is causing an infirmity, but his exorcisms have the effect of freeing the person from a physical ailment, clearly showing that it was demonically induced (Mt 9:32-33). Other times the Gospels state that a person is demonized, but then note that Jesus heals the person, without mentioning exorcism (Mt 12:22; cf. 4:24; Lk 7:21). Clearly, the line between healing and exorcism in the Gospels is a fine one.[54]

Still other times a demon is not specifically mentioned, but Jesus treats the illness as though it were a demon. For example, Jesus rebukes Peter's mother-in-law's fever as though it were a demon, or at least demonically induced (Lk 4:39). Indeed, Jesus rebukes a threatening storm in a similar fashion (Lk 8:42; Mk 4:39). Finally, Jesus' general response to people when they came to him with their ailments was a response of compassion, revealing his conviction that what was afflicting them ought not to be there (Mk 1:41; Mt 9:36; 14:14; 20:34). There was no thought here of pious resignation or of seeking to discover what perfect plan God might have behind the illness. To the contrary, so far as we can discern from the Gospels, Jesus simply viewed these unfortunate people as casualties of war.

Thus the Peter of Luke's history of the early church can be understood to be reflecting Jesus' own attitude when he later summarizes Jesus' ministry by saying that Jesus "went about doing good and healing all who were oppressed by the devil, for God was with him" (Acts 10:38). When Jesus healed people, he saw himself as setting them free from the power, and the whippings, of the devil.[55]

Jesus and the Kingdom of God

It is crucial for us to recognize that Jesus' view about the rule of Satan and the pervasive influence of his army was not simply a marginal piece of first-century apocalyptic thought that he happened to embrace. It is, rather, the driving force behind everything Jesus says and does. Indeed,

Jesus' concept of "the kingdom of God" is centered on these views. For Jesus, the kingdom of God means abolishing the kingdom of Satan. As Kallas argues:

> This world [in Jesus' view] was a demon-infested world in need of liberation, and the advance of God's sovereignty was in direct proportion to the rout of the demons. . . . Exorcisms of demons was the central thrust of the message and activity of Jesus.[56]

So too Gustaf Wingren writes:

> When Jesus heals the sick and drives out evil spirits, Satan's dominion is departing and God's kingdom is coming (Matt. 12.22-29). All Christ's activity is therefore a conflict with the Devil (Acts 10.38). God's Son took flesh and became man that he might overthrow the power of the Devil, and bring his works to nought (Heb. 2.14f.; I John 3.8).[57]

The "kingdom of God," as Jesus uses the term, refers to nothing other than his ministry, and the ministry he gave to his disciples, of setting up God's rule where previously there had been Satan's rule. If "the kingdom of God" was the central concept of Jesus' ministry and teaching, as all scholars recognize, then the "kingdom of Satan" was, as a correlary concept, central as well. An increasing number of scholars are also coming to recognize this.[58]

The kingdom as a warfare concept. While no orthodox first-century Jew or Christian ever doubted that there existed only one Creator, or that this Creator would reign supreme in the eschaton, it seems equally clear that the New Testament authors also never doubted that in this present world the Creator's will was not the only will that was being carried out. Wills, human and angelic, oppose God, and he must fight against them. The kingdom of God, therefore, was something the New Testament authors prayed for, not something they considered already accomplished (Mt 6:10; Lk 11:2).[59] The only way it would be brought about, they understood, was by overthrowing the illegitimate kingdom that was now in place. In this sense, one might say along with John Newport that the New Testament authors, like the apocalyptic authors of their day, held to a "limited dualism."[60]

In any event, in New Testament terms the kingdom of God and the kingdom of Satan are correlative concepts. The former can be understood to be expanding only as the latter is diminishing. This is precisely why healings and exorcisms played such a central role in Jesus' ministry.

"If it is by the finger of God that I cast out the demons," Jesus says, "then the kingdom of God has come to you" (Lk 11:20). To accomplish the one was to accomplish the other.

Susan Garrett correctly summarizes this point: "Every healing, exorcism, or raising of the dead is a loss for Satan and a gain for God."[61] Or, as James Kallas again puts it, "The arrival of the kingdom is simultaneous with, dependent upon, and manifested in the routing of demons."[62] For Jesus, healings and exorcisms clearly did not merely symbolize the kingdom of God—they *were* the kingdom of God.[63] They were not byproducts of the message he proclaimed—they were the message. Warring against Satan and building the kingdom of God are, for Jesus, one and the same activity.[64]

Among the many ways Jesus' warfare conception of the kingdom of God is illustrated is the Gospels' association of Jesus' pronouncements about the kingdom and his demonstrations of the kingdom. This is a recurring phenomenon throughout the Gospels, but two examples pertaining to the thematic beginnings of Jesus' ministry in Mark and Luke make the point clear.

In the opening of Mark's Gospel, Jesus begins his ministry by announcing: "The kingdom of God has come near; repent, and believe in the good news" (Mk 1:15). This is the total content of what Mark tells us Jesus preached. But everything that follows informs us what this kingdom preaching means, and it does so by illustration.

After calling his disciples (vv. 16-20), Jesus amazes the people with the authority of his teaching (vv. 21-22). Immediately, however, a man demonized by an unclean spirit cries out, "What have you to do with us, Jesus of Nazareth? Have you come to destroy us?" The first-person plural here perhaps indicates that the demon is speaking on behalf of the entire army he is a part of. But he continues in the singular, "I know who you are, the Holy One of God" (vv. 23-24). In contrast to all earthly players in Mark's narrative, those in the demonic kingdom know who Jesus is and have suspicions about what he has come to earth to do (see v. 34; 3:11).[65] He has come to "destroy the works of the devil" (1 Jn 3:8), and the demons know this means their destruction.

Jesus rebukes the demon, telling him to "be silent" (Mk 1:25), literally, "be strangled" *(phimoō)*. After Jesus strangles the demon with his divine authority, the demon throws the man to the ground and leaves him with a shriek (v. 26). This is what the kingdom of God means! Mark then notes that the people were again "amazed" at this "new teaching" and new "authority" (v. 27). The two, we see, go hand in hand.[66]

Mark then records Jesus' healing of Peter's mother-in-law's fever (vv. 30-31), which Jesus assumed to be demonically induced in the Lukan parallel (Lk 4:38-39). That very evening "the whole city" brought "all who were sick or possessed with demons" to Jesus, and he "cured many" and "cast out many demons" (Mk 1:32-34). The kingdom of God was indeed near.

Next in Mark's account, Jesus tells his disciples that he wants to go into other villages and "proclaim the message there also" (v. 38). This he proceeds to do, and Mark summarizes his activity by noting, "He went throughout Galilee, proclaiming the message in their synagogues and casting out demons" (v. 39). Jesus then heals a man of leprosy (vv. 40-45), followed immediately by an account of Jesus healing a paralytic on the sabbath (2:1-12). After a brief interlude, we find Jesus again healing people, setting crowds of people free from the "scourges" of the enemy (3:10) and driving out evil spirits (3:11-12).[67] Several verses later we have Mark's account of the Beelzebul controversy, in which Jesus presents himself as the one who has come to tie up "the strong man" by the power of God (3:20-30). And we are not yet out of Mark's third chapter!

This is what the kingdom of God means. The point is hard to miss. Whatever else the rule of God is about, it is about vanquishing the rule of Satan, and thus about setting people free from demons and from the ungodly infirmities they inflict on people.

Luke's (and Matthew's) account of Jesus' ministry begins, quite appropriately, with Jesus confronting the devil in the desert. The cosmic war that has raged throughout the ages has now come to center on one person: Jesus.[68] Jesus withstands each temptation, including Satan's offer of all the kingdoms of the world he had authority over; and the devil, defeated, finally leaves him (Lk 4:1-13).

Unlike all other humans, Jesus did not come under Satan's power by becoming "a slave to sin" (Jn 8:34). As Jesus states in John, "The ruler of this world . . . has no power over me; but I do as the Father has commanded me" (14:30-31; cf. 8:29). Rather, it is Jesus who has gotten hold of the devil. One stronger than "the strong man" has finally arrived. Having now defeated him in his own life, Jesus could set out to defeat him for the entire cosmos.

In Luke, Jesus launches his mission from his hometown. As in Mark, but in a slightly expanded manner, he begins by announcing that the kingdom of God has arrived in his own person. Standing up in the synagogue, Jesus reads from Isaiah:

> The Spirit of the Lord is upon me, because he has anointed me to bring good news to the poor. He has sent me to proclaim release to the captives and recovery of sight to the blind, to let the oppressed go free, to proclaim the year of the Lord's favor. (Lk 4:18-19)

After a moment of awkward silence, Jesus adds, "Today this scripture has been fulfilled in your hearing" (v. 21). After some dispute, he is driven out of town (vv. 22-30); then, as Luke organizes his material, we begin to see what this proclamation of the kingdom means concretely. As in Mark, Jesus immediately confronts a demon-possessed man in a Capernaum synagogue who cries out, "What have you to do with us, Jesus of Nazareth?" (v. 34). As in Mark, Jesus strangles the demon and sets the "prisoner" of Satan free (v. 35). Jesus' exorcism, clearly, demonstrates his application of the Isaiah passage to himself. This is the kind of freedom Jesus is talking about.

Jesus then proceeds to "rebuke" a demonic fever (v. 39), heal multitudes of sick people (v. 40) and cast out multitudes of shrieking demons (v. 41). Shortly thereafter he heals a man of leprosy (5:12-16), a paralytic (5:17-26) and a man with a withered hand (6:1-10). As Clinton Arnold argues, the point is that the prisoners who are to be set free are "trapped in the bondage and oppression of Satan's kingdom."[69] What the kingdom of God means, therefore, is that the hostile alien kingdom of demonic captivity, oppression, poverty and blindness (physical and spiritual) is coming to an end through the ministry of Jesus. He is the bringer of the kingdom of God, for he is the vanquisher of the kingdom of Satan.

Jesus the healing exorcist. The centrality of warfare for the Gospels' understanding of Jesus' preaching of the kingdom of God is also clearly illustrated in the summary statements of Jesus' ministry that are sprinkled throughout the Gospels. In almost every instance, teaching (or preaching) about the kingdom is mentioned in the same breath as healing or casting out demons, activities that demonstrate the kingdom.[70] Consider the following verses:

> Jesus went throughout Galilee, teaching in their synagogues and proclaiming the good news of the kingdom and curing every disease

and every sickness among the people. So his fame spread throughout all Syria, and they brought to him all the sick, those who were afflicted with various diseases and pains, demoniacs, epileptics, and paralytics, and he cured them. (Mt 4:23-24)

For he had cured many, so that all who had diseases pressed upon him to touch him. Whenever the unclean spirits saw him, they fell down before him and shouted, "You are the Son of God!" (Mk 3:10-11)

He came down . . . with a great crowd of his disciples and a great multitude of people from all Judea, Jerusalem, and the coast of Tyre and Sidon. They had come to hear him and to be healed of their diseases; and those who were troubled with unclean spirits were cured. And all in the crowd were trying to touch him, for power came out from him and healed all of them. (Lk 6:17-19)

Jesus had just then cured many people of diseases, plagues, and evil spirits, and had given sight to many who were blind. (Lk 7:21)

That evening they brought to him many who were possessed with demons; and he cast out the spirits with a word, and cured all who were sick. This was to fulfill what had been spoken through the prophet Isaiah: "He took our infirmities and bore our diseases." (Mt 8:16-17; cf. Is 53:4)

Jesus went about all the cities and villages, teaching in their synagogues, and proclaiming the good news of the kingdom, and curing every disease and every sickness. (Mt 9:35)

People at once recognized [Jesus], and rushed about that whole region and began to bring back the sick on mats to wherever they heard he was. And wherever he went, into villages or cities or farms, they laid the sick in the marketplaces, and begged him that they might touch even the fringe of his cloak; and all who touched it were healed. (Mk 6:54-56)

Many crowds followed him, and he cured all of them. (Mt 12:15)

He left Galilee and went to the region of Judea beyond the Jordan. Large crowds followed him, and he cured them there. (Mt 19:1-2)

Such summary statements make clear that, in the mind of each Synoptic author, Jesus was first and foremost an exorcist and a healer. His preaching the good news had unprecedented "authority" (e.g., Mk 1:22, 27; Lk 4:32, 36) precisely because it was preached in deed as well as in word. Jesus not only talked about the kingdom but embodied it. Hence wherever he went, he was about freeing people from the scourges of the ruler of darkness (Acts 10:38).

What also illustrates the centrality of exorcism and healing in Jesus' conception of the kingdom of God is that Jesus never commissions his disciples to proclaim the latter without also commissioning them to perform the former.[71] Mark notes that he designated his twelve disciples as apostles "to be sent out to proclaim the message, and to have authority to cast out demons" (3:14-15). Word and deed go hand in hand.

Before Jesus sends out his twelve apostles on a particular mission, he tells them to "proclaim the good news, 'The kingdom of heaven has come near.' Cure the sick, raise the dead, cleanse the lepers, cast out demons. You received without payment; give without payment" (Mt 10:7-8).

Tell people "the kingdom has come near," Jesus is saying, with words and with action. Thus Jesus "gave them authority over the unclean spirits" (Mk 6:7; cf. Lk 9:1-2), and they "went out and proclaimed that all should repent," while they also "cast out many demons, and anointed with oil many who were sick and cured them" (Mk 6:12-13; cf. Lk 9:6). To proclaim that the kingdom is near is virtually synonymous with pushing back the kingdom of Satan by freeing people from their sin as well as from demons and disease.

In similar fashion, when Jesus at another time prepares to send out 72 disciples, he simply instructs them: "Whenever you enter a town and its people welcome you, eat what is set before you; cure the sick who are there, and say to them, 'The kingdom of God has come near to you' " (Lk 10:8-9).

Nothing more is needed to carry out Christ's ministry. Demonstrate the reality of the kingdom, and then interpret the demonstration for the people.[72] When the 72 return they are overjoyed with their success: "Lord, in your name even the demons submit to us" (Lk 10:17). In the light of Jesus' commission to them to heal, their response is somewhat puzzling—unless we understand that, for Jesus and his followers, healing the sick was centrally about having authority over demons (Acts 10:38). As such, it was about defeating the kingdom of Satan.

Jesus himself immediately exclaims, "I watched Satan fall from heaven like a flash of lightning" (Lk 10:18).[73] As one chasing a scared enemy on the run, he reiterates to his disciples, "I have given you authority to tread on snakes and scorpions [demons?], and over all the power of the enemy [viz., Satan and demons]" (v. 19). This is what his disciples are to preach.

Conclusion

In the light of all this, it must strike us as highly peculiar that many New Testament scholars over the last several hundred years have concluded that the historical Jesus was, in one way or another, simply a moral teacher. This can only testify to how thoroughly naturalistic presuppositions can filter one's reading of the evidence.[74] But it is hardly less puzzling that so many believing Christians today can read these same Gospels, while committing themselves to following this Lord, yet never seriously consider treating sickness and disease (to say nothing of demonized people) the way Jesus treated them. Far from considering such things as scourges of the devil, as Jesus did, we modern Christians are likely to attribute them to God's "mysterious providence." Rather than revolting against such things as scourges of the enemy, we are likely to ask God to help us accept such things "as from a father's hand."

This undoubtedly testifies to the strength of the post-Augustinian classical-philosophical theistic tradition as well as to the Western Enlightenment presuppositions that, until recently, have tended to dominate the thinking of everyone in the West, believer and nonbeliever alike. It also goes a long way toward explaining why our "problem of evil" is not the "problem of evil" Jesus and his disciples confronted.

If, in contrast to Jesus' approach, one believes that a good and wise divine purpose ultimately lies behind sickness, disease and all the atrocities that make the world a nightmarish place, then one subtly shifts the problem of evil from something one has to war against to something one has to think through. Rather than being a problem of overcoming the evil deeds of the devil and his army, our problem of evil has become a problem of intellectually explaining how an all-good and all-powerful God could will what certainly are evil deeds of the devil.

Perhaps most tragically, in trading problems in this fashion, we have surrendered a spiritual conflict we are commissioned to fight and will (despite ourselves) ultimately win for an intellectual puzzle we can never resolve. It is an exceedingly poor trade, whether considered on philosophical, biblical or practical grounds. If we were to follow the example of our Savior instead, our basic stance toward evil in the world would be characterized by revolt, holy rage, social activism and aggressive warfare—not pious resignation.

7

WAR OF THE WORLDS
THE WARFARE THEME OF JESUS' EXORCISMS AND MIRACLES

T HUS FAR WE HAVE ATTEMPTED TO DEMONSTRATE THE GENERAL truth that a warfare worldview is at the center of Jesus' understanding of his mission, and therefore of his understanding of the kingdom of God. What remains is for us to more closely examine Jesus' exorcistic, miracle-working and teaching ministries in order to fully ascertain what Jesus and the early church believed about this cosmic conflict. This is the focus of this chapter and the next. A number of vital principles may be gleaned from a closer inspection of Jesus' exorcisms, nature miracles and teachings that have a direct bearing on our understanding of Satan and the problem of evil.

In this chapter, therefore, I first examine in some detail two representative examples of Jesus' exorcistic ministry[1] and then follow with an investigation of the cosmic warfare significance of two representative miracles performed by Jesus that involve a supernatural control over nature. Then, in chapter eight, I consider the various ways in which the warfare theme plays out in a number of Jesus' teachings.

Exorcisms in Jesus' Ministry

The first of the two exorcism accounts I wish to look at is Jesus' exorcism of a multitude of demons out of a man at Gerasa (Mk 5:1-27; Mt 8:28-34; Lk 8:27-39).[2] This account is the most developed, dramatic and detailed exorcism narrative in the Gospels.

Casting out Legion. Here we find Jesus confronted by a demonized man who lived amid the tombs of this town (Mk 5:3; Mt 8:28; Lk 8:27).[3] Mark's account depicts the man as possessing a terrorizing supernatural strength, to the point where

> no one could restrain him any more, even with a chain; for he had often been restrained with shackles and chains, but the chains he wrenched apart, and the shackles he broke in pieces; and no one had the strength to subdue him. Night and day among the tombs and on the mountains he was always howling and bruising himself with stones. (Mk 5:3-5; cf. Lk 8:29)

Now, however, someone "strong enough"—stronger than the "strong man" (Mk 3:27; Mt 12:29; Lk 11:21-22)—had arrived to subdue him. As in many other accounts, the demons knew who Jesus was and what he had come to do, for they caused the man to run up to Jesus and to shout "at the top of his voice, 'What have you to do with me, Jesus, Son of the Most High God? I adjure you by God, do not torment me' " (Mk 5:7). Interestingly enough, Mark and Luke both note that this was said *after* Jesus had commanded the unclean spirit to come out of the man (Mk 5:8; Lk 8:29), making this the only account in which it seems that Jesus' word *did not* immediately effect an exorcism.[4] Some demons, Jesus elsewhere teaches, are harder to cast out than others (Mk 9:14-29), and it may be that the sheer numerical force of the demons that challenged Jesus prolonged this exorcism.

His first command having apparently failed, Jesus investigates further (perhaps to find out more precisely what he is up against).[5] So he asks the demon what his name was, to which the demon replied, "My name is Legion; for we are many" (Mk 5:9; Lk 8:30).[6] Knowing they cannot ultimately withstand the Son of God, the demons then beg Jesus not to be sent "out of the country" (Mk 5:10; Luke has "into the abyss," 8:31). Instead, they ask to be sent into a local herd of swine. Surprisingly, Jesus acquiesces to their request.

The plan seems to backfire on the demons, however, for instead of finding a permanent abode that would allow them to stay in the region, the pigs immediately rush headlong over a cliff and drown (Mk 5:11-13; Mt 8:32-33; Lk 8:33-34). Where they went after that—whether to another area or to the "abyss"—is not clear. But it *is* clear that they did not get what they wanted, which seems to have been Jesus' plan all along.

The result is that the man is returned to his "right mind" (Mk 5:15; Lk 8:36), but the townspeople are filled with fear, apparently at the realization that one even stronger than the demons who afflicted this man is in their midst. Perhaps assuming, as many others had done, that Jesus was driving out demons by the power of the strong man himself (Mt 12:24), they beg Jesus and his disciples to leave, which they do (Mk 5:16-17; Lk 8:36-37).

This account has a number of noteworthy features. First, the shift from the singular to the plural on the part of the demons is interesting and quite puzzling to most Western readers, though it is not at all unfamiliar to either ancient or modern exorcists. It may mean that one dominant demon initially spoke, or that the collective identity of demons is such that they can speak in either the singular or the plural.

In any case, what is far more significant is their collective name, "Legion." This is a military term denoting a large army unit. Jesus used the term (in the plural) to refer to a vast army of heavenly warriors (Mt 26:53), and in the Roman army (which, significantly, occupied the whole area) it customarily referred to a unit of six thousand soldiers. This term as a name for the demons afflicting this man, then, reveals how thoroughly demonized he was.[7]

Indeed, given their name "Legion," we should not be too surprised when Mark tells us that the number of pigs the demons entered when they left the man was two thousand (Mk 5:13). The Gospels include several other references to multiple demonization (e.g., Mk 1:22-23; Lk 4:24; 11:26; Mt 12:45), but the next highest number we read of is seven, the number of demons cast out of Mary Magdalene (Lk 8:2; Mk 16:9).[8] In any event, the passage reveals that Jesus and the Gospel authors assumed that the world was virtually infested with demons, that the number of these demons was indefinitely large, and that people and animals were capable of being demonized by any number of these unclean invaders.[9]

The military term "Legion" is also significant in that it designates this multitude of demons as being a subgroup of a much larger army. Like the Romans in the eyes of Jews, Jesus saw the kingdom as an army which had invaded territory (the earth) that did not rightfully belong to it. And in this particular passage, a "Legion" of soldiers within this Satanic army had illegitimately captured a person. Jesus comes, however, to reclaim territory that belongs to his Father and bring it under his rightful rule. Hence when Jesus shows up, the legion of demons must leave.[10]

The demons' desperate plea to remain in the area by entering a local herd of swine is also significant. Ancient people generally associated particular demons with particular regions (especially around tombs and desert regions, Lk 8:27, 29; 11:21), and this seems to be reflected in this passage.[11] The desperation of their cry makes it appear that these degenerate spirits somehow needed to remain in this region, as though (perhaps) this were some sort of geographical assignment they had received from their chief and had to obey.[12]

Ancient people often believed that certain kinds of demons needed to reside in something, and this belief is also consistent with this account.[13] Why the need to go into swine as opposed to just existing on their own? The demons' existence appears to be parasitic. They seem to be like spiritual viruses that cannot survive long on their own; they need to infect someone or something.[14]

This belief may be reflected in Jesus' teaching in Luke 11:24-26 (cf. Mt 12:24-25):

> When the unclean spirit has gone out of a person, it wanders through waterless regions looking for a resting place, but not finding any, it says, "I will return to my house from which I came." When it comes, it finds it swept and put in order. Then it goes and brings seven other spirits more evil than itself, and they enter and live there; and the last state of that person is worse than the first.

This passage presents the reverse principle of the teaching just before it, namely, that Jesus was stronger than the "strong man" who guards his house, and that his ministry was about overpowering this tyrant and "dividing his plunder" (Lk 11:21-22). In other words, what applies to the kingdom of God also applies to the kingdom of Satan. The teaching states that when a demon has been cast out of a "house," one can expect it to return with stronger reinforcements to attempt to reclaim what it regards to be its territory. It needs "rest," and it will do whatever it needs to do to find it.

In the context in which these words are spoken, it is clear that this principle applies not only to individuals but to whole generations.

Hence, after giving this teaching, Jesus adds, "So will it be also with this evil generation" (Mt 12:45), implying that it is possible for an entire generation to be demonized by multitudes of demons.[15] An apocalyptic conception of demonic national gods is perhaps implied here.[16] As much as such a notion may clash with our modern Western individualistic assumptions, in the light of our modern experience of Nazi Germany, we should perhaps not reject it too quickly.[17]

It is dangerous to have Jesus simply cast out a demon; one needs to follow him, to have the kingdom of God present in one's "house" as well. Hence he prefaces his teaching by saying, "Whoever is not with me is against me, and whoever does not gather with me scatters" (Lk 11:23). He concludes by saying, "Blessed . . . are those who hear the word of God and obey it" (v. 28). The only protection against the kingdom of darkness is to belong to the kingdom of God. When an individual, or an entire generation, resists the kingdom, they open themselves up to significant demonic activity.

Finally, the whole teaching is based on the premise that demons are "restless," like one traveling in a desert without water, until they locate a "house," whether this be a person, a region, a nation or a generation. Having "abandoned their own home" by rebelling against their Creator (Jude 6), these spiritual parasites perpetually seek to make another being their host. Reading in this light, we can perhaps better understand why "Legion" begged Jesus to let them remain in the "house" of their "country," by entering the "house" of the swine.

Delivering a demonized child. The second account concerns Jesus' exorcism of a young boy (Mk 9:14-30; Mt 17:14-21; Lk 9:37-45).[18] Coming down from the mountain upon which Jesus had been transfigured before Peter, James and John (Mk 9:2-12), Jesus finds his other disciples arguing with certain "scribes" or "teachers of the law" in the midst of a great crowd of people (Mk 9:14-16). The issue, it turns out, concerns a man's demonized son and why Jesus' disciples could not exorcise the demon from him. In some detail, Mark recounts the distraught father's predicament as well as his plea to Jesus.

> Teacher, I brought you my son; he has a spirit that makes him unable to speak; and whenever it seizes him, it dashes him down; and he foams and grinds his teeth and becomes rigid; and I asked your disciples to cast it out, but they could not do so. (Mk 9:17-18; see Mt 17:15-16; Lk 9:38-41)

Jesus expresses his frustration with this "faithless generation," implying that it was in part a lack of faith that prohibited the exorcism, and then quickly moves to help the young boy (Mk 9:19; Mt 17:17; Lk 9:41). As soon as the demon in the boy sees Jesus, he throws the boy down on the ground in a fit or convulsion (Mk 9:20). Jesus is apparently impressed by the severity of this case of possession, for he then asks the father, "How long has this been happening to him?" (Mk 9:21), to which the father replies, "From childhood. It has often cast him into the fire and into the water, to destroy him; but if you are able to do anything, have pity on us and help us" (Mk 9:21-22; Mt 17:15).

In Mark's narrative the need for faith is then reiterated as Jesus tells the man, "All things can be done for the one who believes." The father responds with a tentative but honest confession of faith: "I believe; help my unbelief!" (Mk 9:23-24). This is apparently enough for Jesus, for he proceeds to "rebuke the unclean spirit" saying, "You spirit that keeps this boy from speaking and hearing, I command you, come out of him, and never enter him again!" (Mk 9:25; Mt 17:18; Lk 9:42). The exorcism is successful, but (according to Mark) only after the demon "shrieked" and "convulsed him violently," leaving the boy so lifeless that the crowd thought he was dead (Mk 9:26).

Following this scene, Mark and Matthew include a conversation Jesus has with his disciples concerning why they had been unsuccessful in driving the demon out of the boy. In Mark, Jesus' response is that "this kind can come out only through prayer" (Mk 9:29), while in Matthew Jesus attributes their inability to a lack of faith (Mt 17:20).[19]

Three things about this account are especially noteworthy. First, the terrorizing characteristics exhibited by this child and by the Gerasene demoniac are typical of demonizations and exorcisms as they were understood throughout the ancient world. For that matter, they are typical of cases of demonizations and exorcisms reported throughout the world today. Experiences of radically demonized people having sporadic supernatural strength, becoming mouthpieces for demons, convulsing on the ground, foaming at the mouth, becoming stiff and rigid, and so on, were frequent in ancient times and are common on the missions field yet today. Indeed, the relative absence of such phenomena in our culture over the last several hundred years has been something of a historical anomaly, though even our culture seems to be experiencing more of these phenomena in recent years.[20]

Operating from within this naturalistic cultural anomaly, many liberal New Testament scholars have attempted to explain cases of demonization and exorcism such as the one recorded in Mark 9 as merely primitive ways of describing and dealing with epilepsy or similar disorders. Hence the boy that Jesus treated, they would hold, was probably an epileptic.[21] But if one grants that this account in the Gospels is at least minimally rooted in actual history—and few today deny it—this explanation must be judged as inadequate, for it does not fully explain what transpired.[22]

This exclusively naturalistic explanation fails to account either for why the boy fell into convulsions when he saw Jesus or for why the seizures involved suicidal behavior. Nor does it account for why Jesus' exorcism worked, why the demon "shrieked" when it left (though the boy had been mute), or how Jesus, the Son of God, could have misdiagnosed the boy's condition (while still getting the cure right). Finally, it does not account for why some today still exhibit these characteristics when a demon is being exorcised, though they are not epileptic.

In any case, in the context in which the Gospels were written, the physically violent and grotesque behaviors sometimes exhibited by demonized people appear to be simply the physical byproducts of an evil, parasitic force living its life through that person. When these behaviors occur during exorcism, they are perhaps the physical manifestations of a spirit who is fighting for its life to stay in its "house." Why this occurs sometimes and not others we are not told, though one guess, based on this passage, is that it has something to do with how long the demon has been there, and thus how thoroughly entrenched the demon is in the "house." Hence Jesus responds to the boy's convulsing behavior by asking, "How long has this been happening to him?" (Mk 9:21). However, it may also have something to do with the kind of demon that was occupying the "house" (viz., how strong it is), as evidenced by Jesus' statement: "This kind can come out only through prayer" (Mk 9:29).[23]

A second significant feature of this story concerns the simple fact that we here find a young boy being demonized. Indeed, not only does the exorcism involve a young person, but we learn from his father that he had been in this condition since "childhood" *(paidiskē),* an expression that suggests he was like this from infancy. This point is highly significant, for it tells us that demonization, as it is understood by Jesus and the Gospel authors, was not something for which the demonized person was responsible.

Nowhere does Jesus imply that the demonization of a person is his or her fault, even in the case of Mary Magdalene, out of whom Jesus cast seven demons (Lk 8:2).[24] As Raymond Brown notes, for Jesus and the Gospel authors, "demoniacal possession is not so much the result of a league with Satan as an expression of bondage under Satan's dominion."[25] Deliverance was a sign of the coming kingdom of God, not a sign of various individuals' moral improvement. The kingdom of God advances as victims of the kingdom of Satan are freed.

Jesus expressed intense anger toward those who were immoral, such as the self-righteous Pharisees, but he never suggested that they were demonized. Toward the demonized, however, he never expressed anger; rather, he exhibited only compassion. As Langton notes, "Pity rather than anger characterizes the attitude of Jesus toward the possessed. . . . He treats them as if they were the victims of an involuntary possession."[26] Indeed, he treats them as though they are casualties of war. For, in his view, this is precisely what they are.

This observation strongly contradicts an assumption that many Western Christians hold: that matters in the spiritual realm are supposed to be fair. The assumption is that God would not allow a person to be demonized unless they deserved it. If a person is demonized (and we actually recognize this as a possibility, which is rare), it is held that the person must have willed the evil spirit to occupy them, or must have done something (e.g., dabbled in the occult) that opened them up to becoming demonized. Demonized people, the assumption therefore goes, must be (or at least must have been) fundamentally bad people.[27]

This assumption is another version of the simplistic theology that Job's three friends endorsed in their cruel attack on Job. The only two variables in any spiritual equation, it assumes, are God and the human individual. Since God is all-good, if a bad spirit has invaded someone, it must be the person's fault. But both the Gospels and the book of Job resist this simplistic way of thinking.

These works assume that there is a very real "world in between" in which reside conscious, free beings who, like human beings, possess power to influence others, for better or for worse. They are, in short, morally responsible. They can therefore fight with each other and victimize human beings, quite apart from (indeed, quite against) the will of God.

In other words, just as evil adults can and do sometimes victimize children against their will and God's will, just as rapists victimize women against their will and against God's will, and just as despotic political powers victimize their subjects against their will and against God's will, so demonic spirits can apparently sometimes victimize people against their will—and against God's will. As we have already seen, the biblical assumption is that the spiritual realm is not all that different from the physical realm. Indeed, the one is simply a continuation of the other.

This means that life on all levels can be and often is profoundly unfair. This should not surprise us, for we experience life on earth as profoundly unfair. This is the price we pay, or at least the price we risk paying, for a cosmos composed of a vast multiplicity of free, morally responsible agents. People can and do misuse their freedom and power and thereby victimize others. For this reason, life on earth is often full of conflict, deep pain and gross injustice. But why should we think things would be different in the "world in between"? If history flows forward in a quasi-democratic fashion here below, for better or for worse, why think that the "world in between" is run as a strict dictatorship? Scripture, we have seen, certainly does not support such a notion.

If we have difficulty accepting that things are sometimes grotesquely unfair on a spiritual level, it is likely because we have trouble really believing in the "world in between" (i.e., physical rapists are "more real" to us than demons) and really believing that this world could be in a genuine state of spiritual war. It is also likely because we have a great deal of trouble believing that these spiritual beings are free. We are, to some extent, influenced by a pagan, unbiblical and narrow definition of God's power as control. Following Augustine, and after him the central tendency of the classical-philosophical theistic tradition, we are often inclined to postulate a secret "divine blueprint" behind everything, making everything, good or evil, somehow an extension of God's good (but very mysterious) will. Thus we have trouble accepting the relevance of the "world in between" for the good and evil of the world we experience. For if the "world in between" is not constituted by free beings such as ours is, it is not relevant to the problem of evil at all.

It is clear from Jesus' warfare ministry, however, that the common modern assumption that life in the spiritual realm is fair is simply wrong. God's will is not the only will, on earth or in the "world in between," and thus there is no guarantee that either of these spheres will exhibit more justice than injustice. In Jesus' view, as in apocalyptic thought (and, to some extent, as in the Old Testament), the "world in between" is characterized by warfare, and the earth is part of its battleground. Hence people, even innocent children (as in the passage under discussion), can sometimes become casualties of this war.

There is no suggestion in the Gospels that Jesus believed that demons or evil angels were carrying out a secret providential plan of God, despite themselves. Rather, Jesus treated each case of demonization as an instance of spiritual rape: an alien force had illegitimately and cruelly invaded a person's being. In the passage we are considering, the invading force had "robbed" this child of his speech and hearing and had attempted to rob him of his life as well. The enemy, Jesus elsewhere tells us, always comes to steal, kill and destroy (Jn 10:10). Judging from Jesus' ministry, one would have to say that nothing could be farther from the will of his loving Father than this.

For this reason, Jesus devoted his ministry to getting these "spiritual rapists" off their victims, by exorcism, by healing or by both. He didn't waste time searching for a hidden divine will behind evil, asking "How could God do this?" or "Why would God allow this?" Nor did he ever try to get people to piously resign themselves to God's supposed "secret plan for their lives" in the face of evil. Jesus' ministry was a ministry not of resignation but of revolt. He was about revolting against the cruel tyranny of a world ruler that was oppressing God's people. He was about seeking to give back to people, and to win back for his Father, what the enemy had stolen and destroyed. He was about restoring humanity to its rightful place of dominion over the earth, and thus about empowering humans to rise up against the cosmic thief who had stolen this from them.

Indeed, we are not going too far if we claim that Jesus' very existence as the God-man on earth was an act of revolt. As we shall see more fully in chapters eight and nine, the ultimate reason why Jesus became a man, carried out his ministry, died a God-forsaken death on the cross, and rose again from the dead was to destroy the devil and place under his foot all his cosmic enemies (e.g., 1 Jn 3:8; Heb 2:14). The incarnation, then, was an ultimate act of war, as the early church saw consistently.

Far from teaching any sort of pious resignation, Jesus' whole being, his very God-man identity, was God's ultimate revolt against the devil's tyranny. Rather than teaching us to see the hand of God in all circumstances, Jesus' very being, and certainly his deeds and his teachings, were about teaching us to revolt against the enemy in all circumstances in

order to make our circumstance a place where we can discern the hand
of God. From this perspective, one ought never to pray to accept "as
from a father's loving hand" an event like Zosia's torture. We ought
rather to pray only that we and others will be empowered to rise up
against the human and angelic evil forces that bring such nightmares
about.

This whole scenario, however, obviously raises significant questions
concerning traditional assumptions Christians have made about the
exercise of God's omnipotence, as we saw in chapter one. For example,
what does it mean to affirm that "God is in control of the world" in the
light of the fact that throughout the Gospels Jesus assumes that Satan
and his army are significantly in control of certain people's lives and,
indeed, of the entire world?[28] How is it possible to live in peace, content
with one's situation, if one is also called to live a life of revolt against evil?

We need to address such questions at a later time. Presently a more
fundamental task occupies us, the task of simply letting Scripture speak
to us and perhaps confront some of our traditional Western assumptions.
For Christians who affirm the authority of the Word over their own
presuppositions, this is always the first and most important task in any
theological endeavor.

The third and final interesting feature of this narrative concerns the
fact that the disciples were unable to cast this demon out of the boy. As
Mark and Matthew tell the story, the point of the narrative is to drive
home the need for faith in God if the kingdom of God is going to expand
against the kingdom of Satan. We are told that the disciples lacked faith
and had not prayed enough in treating the boy (Mk 9:29); all the people
involved lacked faith (Mk 9:19); even the boy's father had only a
wavering faith (9:24). Hence the attempted exorcism had been unsuccessful.

In contrast to this, Jesus says, all things are possible to one who
believes and is willing to pray, including exorcising tenacious demons
like the one possessing this young child (Mk 9:23; cf. Jn 11:40). This
reliance on the power of God alone and this emphasis on simple faith
and prayer as the means by which God's power is manifested and the
kingdom of God is established set Jesus' exorcism and healing ministry
apart from the exorcistic and healing activities of his contemporaries. It
was customary for various exorcists and healers of this time to employ a
wide variety of magical devices, lengthy incantations and power names

(e.g., deities) in the attempt to exorcise demons, protect people from evil spirits and heal various diseases.[29] But a number of recent studies have demonstrated that such techniques played little or no role within the exorcistic methods of Jesus and his disciples.

John Rousseau sums up the contrast well:

> While [Jesus'] predecessors, contemporaries and successors used complex, lengthy procedures involving ingredients, herbs, magical objects, oral formulas, amulets and other methods, he came empty-handed, uttered simple irresistible commands immediately obeyed by the demons. . . . Jesus did not use any of the "powerful names" which were stock-in-trade of the profession. . . . He operated, as it seems, directly from the power which was in him and which his followers called the Holy Spirit.[30]

It was Jesus' reliance on the Holy Spirit, activated through faith and prayer, that more than anything else set his ministry apart. Indeed, the only weapons we ever see employed by Jesus in his deliverance ministry are faith and prayer. When faith is strong and (therefore) prayer is persistent, this passage teaches, the enemy is ultimately powerless against the onslaught of the kingdom of God. When faith is weak and prayer is lacking, however, demons that are strong and deeply entrenched in a person can apparently succeed in resisting exorcism.

It is also significant that the faith Jesus is talking about is not the faith of the person who is demonized. Unlike many of his healings, in none of Jesus' exorcisms does he ask the demonized person to have faith. It is, rather, on the faith and prayers of others that their deliverance depends. In the same way that demonization is the result of what free agents (viz., unclean spirits) do to persons in victimizing them, their deliverance seems to be contingent upon what other free agents (people of faith) do for these victimized persons.

Understandably, this inspired perspective also may not rest easy with some of us, conditioned as we are by both an Augustinian and an Enlightenment heritage. Not only does it presuppose that spiritual beings like demons are real, free and have power to influence others—all of which, we have said, we Westerners generally have difficulty accepting. It also presupposes that a person's deliverance from these spirits may be contingent upon what others do for the person. While we take such contingency as obvious on a physical level, it goes against the Augustinian, classical-philosophical, blueprint model of providence to

suppose that it characterizes the spiritual level as well. But from a
scriptural perspective this is the case.

In the same way that a person's deliverance from a potential rapist
may completely hang upon whether others hear her call and respond, so
too events in the spiritual realm seem at times genuinely contingent upon
what people do or do not do. This passage presupposes that, at least at
times, whether prisoners are set free from demonizing oppressors is
genuinely contingent upon whether others exercise faith and pray for
them. The general principle seems to be that we are, to a large degree,
morally responsible for one another. Hence the destiny of each one of
us is contingent not only on decisions we make but also on decisions
made by others regarding us.

Besides grating against our modern acute sense of individualism, the
understanding that an individual's fate might be significantly contingent
on the free decisions of others obviously stands in tension with both the
Augustinian blueprint model of providence and the teaching on prayer
that often accompanies it. The view that the purpose of prayer is not to
change God or change things but only to change *us* is a pious-sounding
teaching many evangelical Christians instinctively accept as true.[31] This
is, after all, the only understanding of prayer that is logically compatible
with the Augustinian understanding of God as omni-determinative,
impassible and altogether timeless. The only trouble with it is that it is
altogether unscriptural.

The primary purpose of prayer, as illustrated throughout Scripture, is
precisely to change the way things are. Crucial matters, including much
of God's own activity, are contingent upon our prayer. Consider the
following small sampling of passages relevant to prayer:

Ask, and it will be given you. (Mt 7:7)

If you have faith and do not doubt, . . . if you say to this mountain,
"Be lifted up and thrown into the sea," it will be done. Whatever you
ask for in prayer with faith, you will receive. (Mt 21:21-22)

If my people who are called by my name humble themselves, pray,
seek my face, and turn from their wicked ways, then will I hear from
heaven, and will forgive their sin and heal their land. (2 Chron 7:14)

The prayer of faith will save the sick, and the Lord will raise them
up. . . . Therefore . . . pray for one other, so that you may be healed.
The prayer of the righteous is powerful and effective. (Jas 5:15-16)

It seems that whether we pray, how faith-filled our prayer is, how persistent it is and even how many people agree together in prayer are all factors that have a real effect in getting God to move and thus in changing the world (cf. also Jas 1:6-8; Mt 18:18-19). So it is not surprising to find Jesus attaching a real urgency to prayer (e.g., Lk 11:5-13; 18:1-8), and believers are therefore to strive to be involved in it on a nonstop basis (1 Thess 5:17).[32]

This is, in fact, the general teaching of Scripture, if only we read it in a straightforward manner. According to Scripture, prayer can save a nation (Ex 32:10-14), and the lack of prayer can destroy it (Ezek 22:30). Faith-filled prayer moves God to bless, and the lack of prayer moves God to curse (2 Chron 30:18-20; Lk 18:1-8). Prayer can cause God to change his mind, saving cities that he had previously prophesied would be destroyed (Jer 18:6-10; Jon 3:7-10) and adding years to a person he had previously said would soon die (Is 38:1-8). Also, as we have seen in the Gospel passage under consideration, faith-filled prayer empowers one to free other people from demons, while the lack of faith-filled prayer leaves these very people enslaved.

In a warfare worldview, things genuinely hang upon what free, morally responsible beings do or do not do. What this view may lose by way of providing believers with security it gains by way of inspiring believers to take responsibility. In terms of building the kingdom, the main thing we do, as Jesus both teaches and demonstrates, is to exercise prayer and faith. When disciples do this, no demonic obstacle to the kingdom, however formidable, can stand in their way (Mt 21:21-22).

Jesus' Mastery over Rebellious Nature

As we saw in chapters two and three, the Old Testament reveals some awareness that nature, while created good, has somehow gone awry. The cosmic monsters and hostile sea, which (on the restoration view) had to be contained for the present world order to be established, still surround the earth and perpetually threaten its order. Hence both Yahweh and his earthly viceroys must continually fight back the forces of evil that plague the world.

We have further seen that this awareness that something in nature has "gone bad" is significantly elaborated and transformed in the apocalyptic tradition. Here it is no longer Leviathan, Rahab or Yamm that are the key players, but angels who were given charge over various aspects of nature and who rebelled. They function in much the same way as the sea monsters in the Old Testament, except in a more intensified form. They threaten the order of God's good creation. Under the leadership of Satan (or some corresponding figure), these angels work to afflict the world with earthquakes, famines, hailstorms, diseases, temptations and many other things that are not part of God's design for his creation.

Though Jesus occasionally referred to "deaf and mute" demons as well as to different "kinds" of demons, and though Paul (we shall see) speaks about various levels of spiritual beings, the New Testament as a whole says little about these matters. Still, there are suggestions that Jesus and Paul accepted the apocalyptic view that demonic powers could adversely affect nature. More specifically, some of Jesus' nature miracles, if interpreted against this apocalyptic background, seem to suggest that he saw himself as battling demonic "nature" strongholds. I shall examine two such miracles in detail, and make several general observations about several others.[33]

Muzzling a rebellious sea. The most significant of Jesus' miracles over nature for our purposes is undoubtedly Jesus' calming of the raging sea (Mt 8:18-27; Mk 4:36-41; Lk 8:22-25). While crossing the Sea of Galilee one evening, Jesus and his disciples got caught in a fierce storm. The boat looked like it was going to go under, and the disciples were thrown into a state of panic. Jesus, however, was sleeping(!). When they woke him, he "rebuked the wind, and said to the sea, 'Peace! Be still!'" (Mk 4:39). It immediately obeyed. He then chastised his disciples for lacking faith, and they marveled at his power to command even the winds and sea (v. 42).

What is most significant about this passage is that the description of Jesus "rebuking" the wind (found in all three Synoptic Gospels) and his commanding the waves to be "quiet" sounds remarkably like other exorcism narratives in the Gospels. Indeed, as we noted in the last chapter, the root meaning of *phimoō*, translated here as "quiet," means to "muzzle" or "strangle." Both Mark and Luke thematically open up their accounts of Jesus' ministry with accounts of him "muzzling" a demon (Mk 1:25; Lk 4:35). It therefore appears that this theme is being carried over into Jesus' nature miracle. That the account is followed in all three Gospels by the episode of Jesus casting out "Legion" strengthens this impression. It thus appears that, in "muzzling" this storm, Jesus is muzzling yet another demon. As James Kallas puts it: "If language means anything at all, it appears that Jesus looked upon this ordinary storm at sea, this ordinary event of nature, as a demonic force, and he strangled it."[34]

What is more, all the Gospels portray Jesus as frequently exorcising demons by "rebuking" *(epitimaō)* them (e.g., Mk 9:25; Mt 17:18; Lk 4:41; 9:42). The term, as used in these contexts, denotes more than a mere reprimand. In keeping with the Old Testament and apocalyptic traditions of Yahweh "rebuking" his enemies, the term denotes an authoritative exercise of God's power in subduing his enemies. It accomplishes what it speaks.[35]

Hence it appears that Jesus is speaking an authoritative word against an enemy in order to subdue him. Indeed, as some have argued, the identical language of Jesus rebuking and subduing hostile waves and Yahweh's rebuking and subduing hostile waves in the Old Testament can hardly be coincidental (see Ps 18:15; 104:7; 106:9).[36] It is as though Yahweh is, in the person of Jesus Christ, once again confronting his archenemy Yamm in the chaotic and threatening waves of the Sea of Galilee.[37]

I would therefore argue that we have good reason for supposing that the Gospels are not just being poetic in saying that Jesus "rebuked" the sea, nor was Jesus speaking poetically when he "muzzled" it. Understood in an apocalyptic context, these terms should be taken literally. Behind this storm Jesus perceived a demonic power, perhaps here strategizing to kill him and his disciples. To cite Kallas again: "Rain may be normal, but to Jesus, when nature goes berserk and tries to drown men and wipe them off the earth sucking them down to a watery grave, this is demonic and he treats it like a demon."[38]

Thus, as he always did in confronting the demonic, Jesus rebuked it, strangled it and thereby returned the sea back to the state God created it to be in. One stronger than the strong man who had hitherto controlled the seas had arrived and bound him up. As usual, those who beheld this feat were amazed.

This understanding of a "natural phenomenon" and potential "natural disaster" as manifesting a demonic power inevitably strikes those of us who have had our thinking shaped by the scientific and Enlightenment revolutions as exceedingly strange, if not absurd. It is perhaps appropriate, however, to remind ourselves that we are among the few people-groups in world history for whom this would be the case. Unless we are to be guilty of a chronocentric, Eurocentric, myopic prejudice, this awareness of how out of sync our own worldview is by global standards must cultivate in us a certain humility, especially those of us who already have reasons for accepting the Gospel perspective as authoritative.

The barren fig tree. Another of Jesus' nature miracles may help illustrate the warfare motif of Jesus' ministry and its impact on his view of nature. It is the unusual account of Jesus cursing the barren fig tree, and it constitutes the only destructive miracle of the Gospels (Mk 11:12-14; Mt 21:18-19). Here a hungry Jesus goes to eat from a fig tree only to find it barren. He therefore curses it: "May no one ever eat fruit from you again" (Mk 11:14). It consequently "withered away to its roots" (v. 20). This is a rather bizarre account, if for no other reason than because Mark explicitly states in his narrative that the reason why the fig tree had no figs was because "it was not the season for figs" (v. 13).

Many scholars have tried to make sense of the text by arguing that the tree is meant to symbolize the religious leadership of Jesus' day.[39] The fact that Mark sandwiches the account of Jesus' cleansing the temple into the middle of his narrative lends some credibility to this thesis (Mk 11:15-19). But if this were the main point of the narrative, one would not have expected Mark to add that "it was not the season for figs." This seems to undermine the culpability of the tree, and hence of unfruitful religious leaders—if this is the central point Jesus was trying to make. One might also have expected Jesus to have made some explicit statement to this effect to drive home the point, but he did not. Instead, both Matthew and Mark have Jesus draw a lesson about the power of faith and prayer from his cursing of the fig tree (Mk 11:20-26; Mt 21:19-22). Thus, while I certainly believe there is a reference here to the rejection of the Messiah on the part of Jewish leadership, I cannot see this as the central point of the story.

Another possible dimension is added to our reading of this account if we analyze it against the background of the apocalyptic thought of Jesus' day. In the apocalyptic worldview, the entire world is understood to be under a demonic curse, which affects even the "natural" order of the world. The angels-turned-demons in charge of various natural functions are now bent on wreaking havoc with the creation. Everything from plagues to earthquakes to famines to rain storms could therefore be attributed to demonic activity. It is, we shall later see, an understanding that is not foreign to the New Testament.

In this light, the expectation for the kingdom of God included an expectation for a restoration of the natural order to the state God originally created it to be in. As throughout the New Testament, apocalyptic thought envisaged a time when the whole cosmos would be restored (Acts 3:21; Rom 8:19-22; Col 1:18-20; 2 Pet 3:13).[40] When God is finally victorious over all his enemies, they believed, there would be no more famines, floods, plagues, war, tears, sin or death. There would, as Revelation 21:1 puts it, be "a new heaven and a new earth." The demonic curse on the cosmos would itself be cursed, and the rule of God, with the viceroyalty of humanity, would be reestablished.

Read in this light, Jesus' cursing of the fig tree perhaps takes on new meaning. In apocalyptic thought, fruit trees that failed to give fruit, or whose fruit was infected, were considered objects of Satan's curse.[41] In other words, barren trees and famines were understood to be the result of Satan's dominion, and when God's rule is reestablished, these curses shall themselves be cursed. Hence we may in this passage perhaps understand Jesus to be cursing the demonically cursed fig tree as a means of demonstrating that he has come to restore creation to its proper order and vanquish the work of Satan. In symbolically "cursing the curse," his ministry spells the beginning of the fulfillment of the apocalyptic hope.

Moreover, as R. H. Hiers and J. D. M. Derrett have argued, in some quarters of apocalyptic thought fig trees in particular had taken on a symbolic messianic function. The fruitfulness of fig trees became a prototype of the blossoming of creation when the Messiah comes and God's rule is reestablished.[42] In this light, the cursing of the fig tree can perhaps be understood as illustrating not only the "cursing of the curse" but also the fallen creation's resistance to the Messiah. When God sets out to restore his creation through his Messiah, creation had better respond! In line with the first and more conventional interpretation considered above, we may perhaps also read in this a reference to the refusal of Israel's religious leaders to acknowledge their Messiah.

Mark's note that the cause of this barrenness was the climate may, in this apocalyptic context, simply once more illustrate the apocalyptic belief that even the climate has been adversely affected by the angelic fall. While we may deem fruit-killing winters to be the result of "normal" and "natural" weather patterns, it is possible that when God's reign is restored, we will see just how unnatural many of these "natural patterns" are.

In any event, the main point of Jesus' demonstration seems to be that he is bringing about a new kingdom in which every tinge of Satan's work, every aspect of creation that does not bring forth fruit as God intended, shall someday be "withered to the root." This is as true of fig trees and the whole "natural" order as it is of human beings. It is why in the eternal kingdom of God there shall be no famine and no hunger; neither shall there be unredeemed sinners. Everything that does not bear fruit, in harmony with God's design, shall be cut down (cf. Lk 13:7). Under the rule of God, things shall be as they were always intended to be.

Only in this light does Jesus' teaching about prayer and faith that he associates with this nature miracle begin to make sense. If Jesus' whole ministry was about reversing the work of Satan by bringing about the kingdom of God and restoring humanity to its proper place of dominion over the earth, and if this was the ministry he was passing on to his disciples, then it makes sense for him to draw a lesson about faith and prayer from the cursing of the fig tree. As we have seen, these were their primary weapons against the occupying army they were now opposing.

If they too are to be about "cursing the curse," about rebuking demons and healing people, about reclaiming the entire cosmos for the Father and restoring humanity to its proper place of dominion over nature, then they too must have faith. Faith, Jesus adds, has the power to do this. It can not only curse a cursed tree, he says; it can move mountains into the sea, and it brings answers to prayer (Mk 11:20-24; Mt 21:19-22). This is the power that alone shall bring about the kingdom of God.

This teaching on faith, however, becomes less intelligible in connection with Jesus' cursing of the tree if we attempt to read his actions merely as a symbol for the fate of barren leadership. Indeed, if this was the only point Jesus was trying to make, then both his action and his teaching must be judged as exceedingly opaque.

Other nature miracles of Jesus. If read in the light of apocalyptic thought, other miracles of Jesus take on a warfare significance as well, though we need not discuss them at length now. Consider, for example, Jesus' miraculous feeding of the multitudes (Mk 6:30-44; 8:1-10; and parallels). If, as apocalyptic writers believed, and as Jesus and Paul elsewhere suggest, famine is a work of the devil (Mk 13:8; Rom 8:35); and if Jesus came principally "to destroy the devil's work" (1 Jn 3:8); and if hunger shall be absent from the kingdom of God when the creation is restored back to God (Rev 7:16), then should we not perhaps understand Jesus' miraculous feeding of the multitude as in some sense an act of war against the famine-inciting devil?

Read in this light, Jesus can here be understood as demonstrating the reality of the kingdom of God, mediated through the viceroyalty of restored humanity, by countering the curse of hunger and the curse on the earth and sea, which do not readily yield up wheat and fish as God designed them to. Thus we can see him as providing an eschatological lesson about what creation will be like when the kingdom of God is fully realized, when the oppression of Satan is fully ended and hence when humanity's power of dominion is fully restored.⁴³ Food will no longer come by "the sweat of your face" (Gen 3:19).

Something similar could perhaps be said of Jesus' power to make the sea produce fish when previously none had been caught (Lk 5:3-10; cf. Jn 21:1-8). God's original design was to bless nature by having humans rule it, and to bless humans by having nature sustain them (Gen 1:20-31). When Satan became "ruler of the world," however, humans and nature turned against each other. Instead of humans having dominion over the sea, the sea often has dominion over humans. Nature becomes a weapon in the hands of a hostile army. Under a demonic influence, the seas try to harm humans by force (as in Mk 4:36-41), by flooding (hence the Leviathan, Rahab, Yamm imagery), and by refusing to give up its produce. The God-man warrior for the kingdom, however, restores to his disciples, and wins back for his Father, both of their dominions over the sea. He subdues Yamm, and he thereby manifests kingdom authority over forces of darkness that pervert the natural order of God's creation. Once again humans have the dominion over the fish of the sea that God's earthly viceroys were always intended to possess and enjoy (Gen 1:26).

Finally, we should mention in this regard the several accounts of Jesus raising people from the dead, and that of Jesus himself rising from the dead. We may regard death as "a natural part of life," but for Jesus and other apocalypticists it was not so. Indeed, throughout the New Testament, death is treated as "the last enemy to be destroyed" (1 Cor 15:26). It reigns as a foreign invader, given access to God's children by their sin (Rom 5:12-17; 1 Cor 15:21; Jas 1:15; cf. Gen 2:16-17; 3:19-23). The one who holds "the power of death" is "the devil" (Heb 2:14), the one who has been "a murderer from the beginning" (Jn 8:44). Hence there is in this worldview nothing "natural" about death. At least as we presently experience it, death was never part of God's design for creation.[44] It is, rather, the ultimate "scourge" of the evil one.

In bringing the kingdom of God, therefore, Jesus came to destroy death by destroying "the one who has the power of death, that is, the devil" (Heb 2:14; 1 Cor 15:56-57; 2 Tim 1:10). Indeed, according to the New Testament and the early postapostolic church, this was the central significance of Jesus' atoning work on the cross and of the resurrection. Jesus' exorcism and healing ministry finds its climax in this event.[45] Hence when Jesus was told that Herod was trying to kill him, he responded, "Go and tell that fox for me, 'Listen, I am casting out demons and performing cures today and tomorrow, and on the third day I finish my work' " (Lk 13:32).

Jesus refers to his coming death and resurrection here as the consummation (teleioō) of his ministry. Satan and his legions would rise up against him (1 Cor 2:8), and demonic darkness would in fact momentarily reign (Lk 22:53; Jn 9:4).[46] But through the very act of being crucified by the hostile cosmic powers, Jesus would ultimately overthrow them.

Indeed, as Jesus expresses it here, his preliminary victories over the evil one in his ministry all lead up to and find their ultimate meaning and fulfillment in this one event.[47] For through his death and resurrection, "the ruler of this world will be driven out" (Jn 12:31). What is more, having robbed Satan of his chief weapon of condemnation (Col 2:14-15) and chief "scourge" of death (Heb 2:14), Jesus made Satan and all his cohorts into a "public spectacle" (Col 2:15), while Christ himself is exalted and enthroned at the right hand of God (Acts 2:32-36; Phil 2:9-11). When death itself is conquered, the one who is a "murderer from the beginning" (Jn 8:44) and who holds "the power of death" (Heb 2:14) will be utterly defeated, subjected, humiliated and destroyed.

In any event, it is clear that death as we now experience it is seen in the New Testament as an evil consequence of Satan's tyranny over the earth. Hence it is not surprising to find that freedom from death (immortality) was seen as being one of the central aspects of the early church's vision for the eternal kingdom. When the kingdom is fully realized, when the created order shall be restored back to the Father, death shall itself be destroyed (2 Tim 1:10), thrown into the lake of fire (Rev 20:14), so that in heaven there will "be no more death or mourning" (Rev 21:4). What Christ achieved on the cross will finally be manifested throughout his creation. Thus Paul can proclaim that even now, for those who believe, "Death has been swallowed up in victory" (1 Cor 15:54).[48]

Viewed in this light, the various accounts of Jesus' raising people from the dead come to mean a lot more than simply nice miracles that Jesus did for people. Like his exorcisms, healings and other miracles over nature, they reveal yet another dimension of his war on Satan. As when he saw the sick and hungry, Jesus was moved by compassion toward those who had died and those who mourned, for he knew that these things were never intended to be part of God's creation (e.g., Jn 11:33-35). They were, rather, the work of the devil, and it grieved and angered him to see it.

Hence the God-man warrior and bearer of the kingdom demonstrated kingdom power in overturning this enemy and anticipated his own consummate victory over Satan in raising Jairus's daughter (Mk 5:41-43; Mt 9:18-26; Lk 8:40-56), the widow's son at Nain (Lk 7:11-17) and Lazarus (Jn 11:1-44).[49] All such resuscitations must be viewed as acts of war against a cosmic foe who had been mastering mortality for far too long.

The "inaugurated eschatology" of Jesus' ministry. Yet, with the exception of Jesus, death still reigns over humanity. All whom Jesus resuscitated eventually died once again. This observation leads to the final point that needs to be made concerning Jesus' miracles over nature. While Jesus proclaimed by word and deed that the kingdom had come with his arrival, and while the New Testament unequivocally proclaims that Jesus was victorious over the enemy in his ministry, death and resurrection (Col 2:14-15), both Jesus and other New Testament authors see the ultimate realization of this kingdom victory to be in the future. This constitutes the well-known "inaugurated eschatology," or the "already-but-not-yet" paradoxical dynamism of New Testament thought.[50] The kingdom has already come, but it has not yet been fully manifested in world history.

What this means is this: Jesus' miracles over nature, as well as his healings, exorcisms and especially his resurrection, were definite acts of war that accomplished and demonstrated his victory over Satan. These acts routed demonic forces and thereby established the kingdom of God in people's lives and in nature. But their primary significance was eschatological. People are still obviously being demonized; all people still get sick and die; storms still rage and destroy lives; famines are yet prevalent and starve thousands daily. But Jesus' ministry, and especially his death and resurrection, in principle tied up "the strong man" and

established the kingdom of God and the restoration of a new humanity
in the midst of this war zone. In doing this, Jesus set in motion forces
that will eventually overthrow the whole of this already fatally damaged
Satanic assault upon God's earth and upon humanity.[51]

Gustaf Wingren expresses this "already/not yet" dynamic well when
he argues that with Christ's resurrection

> The war of the Lord is finished and the great blow is struck. Never
> again can Satan tempt Christ, as in the desert. Jesus is now Lord,
> Conqueror. But a war is not finished, a conflict does not cease with
> the striking of the decisive blow. The enemy remains with the scattered
> remnants of his army, and in pockets here and there a strong resistance
> may continue. That is the position of the church.[52]

Jesus' miraculous ministry, therefore, was not simply symbolic of the
eschaton—in principle it achieved the eschaton. He in principle won the
war, struck the decisive deathblow, vanquished Satan, restored humanity,
established the kingdom; yet some battles must still be fought before this
ultimate victory is fully manifested. Hence Jesus did not just carry out
his warfare ministry; he commissioned, equipped and empowered his
disciples, and the whole of the later church, to do the same. He set in
motion the creation of a new humanity, one that again exercises dominion over the earth, by giving us his power and authority to proclaim and
demonstrate the kingdom just as he did (e.g., 2 Cor 5:17-21; Mt
16:15-19; Lk 19:17-19; cf. Jn 14:12; 20:21).

Jesus thus gives to all who will in faith receive it his authority to break
down the gates of hell and take back for the Father what the enemy had
stolen, just as he himself had done (Mt 16:18). Now that the strong man
has been bound, it is a task we can and must successfully carry out. In doing
all this, we the church are further expanding the kingdom of God against
the kingdom of Satan, and laying the basis for the Lord's return when the
full manifestation of Christ's victory, and of Satan's defeat, will occur.

We could spend our time and spiritual energy striving graciously to
accept all this "apparent" evil as coming from the Father's hand, supposedly in strict accordance with his omnipotent and unthwartable will, and
supposedly in perfect conformity to his meticulous blueprint for world
history. But it is difficult to conceive of any activity that would be further
removed from the mandate we have received from our Lord. We are
called to *revolt!*

8

STORMING THE
GATES OF HELL

KINGDOM CONFLICT
IN THE TEACHINGS
OF JESUS

*W*E HAVE THUS FAR SEEN THAT JESUS' TEACHING ON THE KING-
dom of God and his healing and exorcism ministry, as well as his miracles
over nature, are fully intelligible only within a warfare worldview. What
remains is to consider the way this worldview is exhibited in the rest of
Jesus' teachings. In this chapter, then, I seek to demonstrate that Jesus'
teachings were not first and foremost about high ethical ideals or
profound religious insights, though they are frequently that as well.
Rather, most fundamentally they are about what Jesus himself was most
fundamentally about: engaging in mortal combat with the enemy of all
that is godly, good and true.[1] In his teachings we find many valuable
insights into the nature of the war that ravages the earth, insights that
should influence our understanding of the problem of evil.

In what follows, then, I simply highlight the warfare dimension of a
selection of Jesus' teaching. I first consider several of Jesus' teachings in
the Synoptics, then several of Jesus' teachings in the Gospel of John.

Jesus' Warfare Teaching in the Synoptic Gospels

Jesus asked his disciples, "Who do people say that the Son of Man is?" They offered a few of the opinions that were floating around at the time. Then Jesus asked, "But who do you say that I am?" Peter, never known for his shyness, quickly shot back, "You are the Messiah, the Son of the living God" (Mt 16:13-16). Jesus was delighted with Peter's correct response and told Peter that he was "blessed," for "flesh and blood has not revealed this to you, but my Father in heaven" (v. 17).

When Peter later (only five verses later) tried to thwart the Father's kingdom plan to have Jesus crucified and raised, however, Jesus sternly told him that this was of "Satan" (vv. 22-23). Everything that opposes God's will, in Jesus' view, derives from "the evil one." Indeed, in the same way that David identified his enemies with Leviathan or Yamm (see chapter two), Jesus goes so far as to call Peter "Satan," saying, "You are a stumbling block to me; for you are setting your mind not on divine things but on human things" (v. 23). But when Peter confessed Jesus as the Son of God, he was operating under the opposite influence. His confession was then inspired by the Father.[2]

Storming the gates of hell. Jesus then used Peter's confession of faith to give his disciples an important lesson about the future church. Using Peter's name as a springboard, Jesus says:

> And I tell you, you are Peter [*petros* = rock], and on this rock I will build my church, and the gates of Hades will not prevail against it. I will give you the keys of the kingdom of heaven, and whatever you bind on earth will be bound in heaven, and whatever you loose on earth will be loosed in heaven. (Mt 16:18-19)

Several points are crucial to note in this important teaching. First, "Hades" was the standard term for the underworld, the realm of darkness and death, in Hellenistic culture. As is generally recognized, in using it here Jesus was probably referring to the whole of the Satanic kingdom.[3] Second, the phrase "*gates* of Hades" is clearly a metaphorical reference to the fortified walls of the Satanic fortress. They are closed to keep opposing forces out. Hence they need to be overcome. Jesus may also be referring to the center of power of the Satanic kingdom with this phrase, inasmuch as the gates of a city in the ancient world were usually where the officials resided and important military decisions were made.

Third, Jesus says that these gates will not be able to "prevail against" the church. This translation of *katischyō* is preferable to the NIV's "overcome," for "gates" are defensive structures that keep an enemy out, not offensive weapons used to "overcome" an enemy. Jesus is here portraying the church as being on the offensive and Satan's kingdom as being on the defensive. In the "conflict motif between Satan and the kingdom of God," George Ladd rightly observes, "God is the aggressor; Satan is on the defensive." Again, "it is the kingdom of God which attacks the kingdom of Satan."[4]

Jesus is saying that he is going to build his church on the rock of his divinity—the confession that he is "the Son of the living God"—and the way this church is going to be built will be by bashing down the gates of Satan's fortress. In other words, the church is to be involved in the very same warfare work that Jesus himself was involved in throughout his ministry. Based squarely on the "rock," ministering in his authority and his accomplished victory, the church is to storm the fortress of Hades and bash down its gates.

Jesus also gives to all who confess his divine sonship "the keys of the kingdom of heaven" so that whatever they bind and loose on earth will be (or will have been) bound and loosed in heaven.[5] While the exact meaning of this phrase is disputed, it is clear that it is an essential part of the kingdom-building activity the church is to be part of.[6] Having been given "the keys" to the kingdom, Jesus is saying, whatever the church locks up when it bashes down the gates of Hades will be locked up in heaven, and whatever it unlocks and sets free will be set free in heaven. Understood in the light of Jesus' overall healing and exorcism ministry, I can only read this as referring to the church's authority to bind up demonic forces and to set people free. According to Hiers, "In the NT the terms 'binding' and 'loosing' refer to the binding of Satan or satanic beings (e.g., demons) and the loosing of such beings or their erstwhile victims."[7]

This teaching provides a blueprint of what the body of Christ is to be about. It is to be about what Jesus was about: aggressively breaking down Satanic fortresses wherever we find them. In people's lives, in families, in churches and in society at large, the church is to expand the rule of God on the authority of Christ by binding evil and setting people free. In a word, our charter is to live out a theology of revolt, throwing all we are and all we have into guerrilla warfare against the occupying army, the tyrannizing powers of darkness. When the church opts instead for a theology of resignation and thus attempts to accept as from God

what Jesus fought as coming from Satan, the church exists in radical contradiction to its defining vocation.

The Lord's Prayer. Without question the most famous of all Jesus' teaching is the prayer he taught to his disciples, usually called "the Lord's Prayer."[8] As often as this prayer is invoked, however, its eschatological and warfare emphasis is rarely acknowledged. If read in the context of the apocalyptic framework Jesus operated within, however, this dimension of the prayer becomes evident.

Jesus begins this instruction in prayer by telling his disciples to pray for the Father's name to be "hallowed," for his kingdom to come, and for his will to be established on earth as it is in heaven (Mt 6:9-10).[9] He is, in effect, telling them to pray for the fulfillment of everything his ministry, and their ministry, is about—glorifying the Father by bringing about the rule and will of God on earth. Such a prayer assumes, however, that the will of God is not being carried out in this present world. As John Meier argues, "If . . . Jesus makes a major object of his prayer the petition that God come to rule as king, this naturally means that in some sense, according to Jesus, God is not yet fully ruling as king."[10]

This prayer, then, is a prayer for change, and the change involves moving from a world in which the Father's name is not honored, his will is not done, and his rule not established, into a world in which these things are as they should be. "Out of a world which is enslaved under the rule of evil," Jeremias writes, "and in which Christ and Antichrist are locked in conflict, Jesus' disciples, seemingly a prey of evil and death and Satan, lift their eyes to the Father and cry out for the revelation of God's glory."[11]

As Jeremias, Brown, Meier and others have argued, then, this petition is in essence a petition for the arrival of the eschaton, and it has decisive warfare overtones.[12] Jesus is telling his disciples to pray that God's eschatological reign, effected by the final overthrowing of his cosmic foes, the present world rulers, will be accomplished now.

The same eschatological and warfare significance is found in the petition of the Father to "give us this day our daily bread" (Mt 6:11). The passage may be implying that the disciples are to rely utterly upon the Father and to trust him for their daily bread as they work to bring about his eschatological rule (cf. Mk 6:8-9; Mt 10:9-10; Lk 9:3). More likely, however, is the solid case being made by a host of scholars that the word "daily" here (*epiousios*) should be translated "tomorrow."[13] In this case, the disciples are being told to pray for the "bread of tomorrow," referring to the banquet feast planned for the eschaton (see Mt 22:2-3: Rev 19:9, 17). It is another way of asking for God's rule to be established now.[14]

Two points need to be made concerning the next clause, the teaching that we are to ask the Father: "Forgive us our debts, as we also have forgiven our debtors" (Mt 6:12). First, in its original Aramaic, Jeremias argues, this phrase would not be understood as a type of quid pro quo declaration.[15] Rather, Jesus is reminding the disciples of their need to forgive in the light of the Father's forgiveness, especially the forgiveness that will characterize the final judgment (cf. Mt 5:23-24). He is certainly not teaching the disciples to ask God to condition and proportion his forgiveness on theirs.

Second, as already intimated, in its original context the petition for forgiveness is best understood as a "request [which] . . . looks toward the great reckoning which the world is approaching . . . the final judgment."[16] Throughout the Synoptics the fatherhood of God is associated with his willingness to forgive (e.g., Lk 15:11-32; 18:35), and the full manifestation of this fatherhood, and thus of God's forgiveness, is understood eschatologically.[17] Hence as Brown says, "it is by anticipation of his eschatological state that the Christian can confidently beseech God for the final pardon of debts."[18]

The eschatological warfare theme comes out in an especially strong way in the final petition of the prayer: "do not bring us to the time of trial, but rescue us from the evil one." The word "trial" (*peirasmos*) speaks not of moral "temptation" (cf. NIV) but of trials and hardships (as in Gal 4:14; Jas 1:12; 1 Pet 1:6; 4:12; 2 Pet 2:9; Rev 3:10). The disciples are not, therefore, asking God not to play the role of "the tempter" (Mt 4:13; 1 Thess 3:5; cf. 1 Cor 7:5), something God could never be suspected of doing (Jas 1:13). They are, rather, asking God to protect them from hardships that accompany their kingdom work as they approach the end of the age.

From whom would they expect such hardships? The closing line of the prayer makes it explicit: "rescue us from the evil one." Jesus knew that carrying out the Father's kingdom work would evoke attacks from Satan and his army. Thus he frequently warned his disciples of this, and here taught them to pray for divine deliverance (Lk 22:31; Mt 10:17-31; 26:41; Jn 15:18-20; 16:31-33; cf. 2 Cor 2:10-11; Eph 6:10-17).

It is likely, then, that the final clause of this prayer is requesting divine aid for the coming trials facing the disciples. This view has received a good deal of scholarly support, but it can be given an even sharper eschatological focus. Some New Testament scholars have argued that in ancient Judaism and apocalyptic thought, *peirasmos* (and related terms) was often used as a technical term in the context of God's covenant relationship with humans. Against this background, its use in the Lord's prayer implies "primarily a testing of the partner in the covenant to see whether he is keeping his side of the agreement."[19]

Even more significantly, it has now been demonstrated that in apocalyptic thought, Satan (or some parallel figure) had come to be identified as the primary instigator of such "testings." Further, it has also been shown that the final period before God's ultimate victory over Satan had generally come to be identified as the ultimate period of testing (or tribulation; see, e.g., Mt 24:4-13; 2 Thess 2).[20] What all this means for our understanding of this final clause of the Lord's Prayer is this: if true, we must here understand Jesus to be teaching his disciples to pray not just for protection from satanically inspired trials and hardships in general, but even more fundamentally for deliverance from the fiery end-time trial, or at least for aid in remaining faithful during its terror.[21]

It is clear that the whole of the Lord's Prayer, if read in its original context, is thoroughly eschatological and thoroughly entrenched in a warfare worldview. It is in various ways ushering in with prayer the eschatological rule of God over and against this present age, which is under the rule of Satan.

Oaths from "the evil one." Throughout the Gospels we find Jesus prescribing a radical countercultural ethical system for those who participate in the kingdom of God. In contrast to all other ethical systems that focus on external behavior, the ethics of the kingdom focuses on the inner disposition of people. For example, Jesus teaches that it is not whether one murders someone that is the crucial ethical issue; in the context of the kingdom, the real issue is whether one has unforgiveness and hostility in one's heart (Mt 5:21-26). It is not whether one commits adultery or engages in divorce that is the crucial ethical issue in the kingdom; it is whether one harbors such things in one's heart (Mt 5:27-32). Living under the rule of God means having one's heart, as well as one's behavior, unconditionally submitted to the Lord.

For the same reason, Jesus forbids his followers to participate in the cultural convention of making ostentatious oaths as a way of buttressing

STORMING THE GATES OF HELL   *221*

their promises (Mt 5:33-37). They are not to make pledges on the basis of heaven, God's throne, the earth, Jerusalem or their head. Nothing external to oneself is to be leveraged as a way of securing one's words. One's integrity, Jesus is saying, is to stand on its own. Hence kingdom people are to let their "word be 'Yes, Yes,' or 'No, No.' " Then, most significantly, Jesus adds, "anything more than this comes from the evil one" (v. 37; cf. Mt 6:13; 13:19, 38).[22]

We here see manifested an important assumption of Jesus that is all the more noteworthy because it comes through in such an incidental manner. His assumption is that any impulse to go outside the parameters of kingdom ethics (viz., to define righteousness externally rather than internally, and to base one's credibility on external matters rather than internal character) derives ultimately from Satan. He also assumes, obviously, that persons who violate this teaching are morally responsible for what they do. Why else give them this instruction? The New Testament never takes the ascription of responsibility to Satan in any way to qualify the moral responsibility of the person who carried out the act under Satan's inspiration. By the same token, however, the assumption of a person's moral responsibility is never taken to imply that Satan could not also, and even more fundamentally, be responsible for a particular evil. As with Adam and Eve in the garden, Jesus and the New Testament authors assume that both Satan and those who are influenced by him are responsible for the evil they freely bring about.

In any event, Jesus sees Satan as ultimately behind the temptation to attempt to buttress up our character with oaths. One is reminded of Paul's later teaching that doctrinal systems that focus on legislating external behaviors derive from demons (1 Tim 4:1-3). The central point is that for Jesus (and Paul), walking in the kingdom means resisting the temptations of the one who at every turn opposes the kingdom. In other words, practicing kingdom ethics is not so much a matter of simply endorsing high ethical ideals as it is of engaging in spiritual war.

Sowing seeds and collecting weeds. The kingdom of God, Jesus taught, is like a farmer sowing seeds (Mk 4:1-12; Mt 13:1-9; Lk 8:4-10). Some seed falls on the path and is devoured by birds. Some falls on rocky ground and burns up in the sun. Some falls among thorns and is choked. And some falls on good ground and produces a healthy crop, up to a hundred times what has been sown.

The thorns, Jesus then explains, are the cares of this life and "the deceitfulness of wealth" (Mt 13:22 NIV; cf. Mk 4:19; Lk 8:14). The seed on rocky ground represents those who initially receive the good news but have no root. They therefore fall away when persecution comes. Reminiscent of other apocalyptic parables, the birds represent "the evil one" who "comes and snatches away what is sown in the heart" (Mt 13:19; cf. Mk 4:15; Lk 8:12).[23] The portrait of Satan here is that of an ever-present predator seeking to undermine kingdom work by devouring whatever fledgling faith he can (1 Pet 5:8).

A similar theme is found in Jesus' parable about the weeds sown among the wheat (Mt 13:24-30). Here the kingdom of heaven is likened to a man who sows "good seed" in his field. But while he was sleeping "an enemy came and sowed weeds among the wheat" (v. 25). When his servant asked where the weeds came from, the owner of the field correctly responds, "An enemy has done this" (v. 28). But, so as not to disturb the growing wheat, he decides to postpone pulling the weeds till harvest time. Then the wheat and the weeds will be separated, the wheat being put into the barn, while the weeds are tied up in bundles and burned (v. 30).

Lest there be any ambiguity, Jesus explains to his disciples that the weeds are "the children of the evil one" (v. 38) and the enemy, of course, is the devil (v. 39). The harvest is the end of the age, and the harvesters are, interestingly enough, the angels (v. 40). In close alignment with a number of teachings found in John's Gospel (as we shall see shortly), Jesus is expressing a limited dualistic worldview in which all that does not come from the hand of God is seen as coming from the hand of Satan, who is at every turn working to thwart the kingdom of God.

In this light, Beasley-Murray's summary of the parables of Matthew 13 seem quite appropriate.

> Along with the powers of the kingdom of God among men there is a contrary force, and it is apparently formidable enough to threaten the promise of the future. . . . The prominent element in this parable—the "enemy action" as it were—is deeply significant for Jesus' ministry.[24]

Violence and the kingdom. The apocalyptic background of Jesus' ministry helps shed light on several Synoptic teachings of Jesus that have proved notoriously difficult to interpret. For example, while Jesus' kingdom ethics included an intense pacifism—his followers were to use no violence, not even to defend themselves (Mt 5:38-42; 26:31ff.; Jn 18:10-

11)—Jesus elsewhere said: "Do not think that I have come to bring peace to the earth; I have not come to bring peace, but a sword" (Mt 10:34; Lk 12:51).

The context of the saying, especially in Matthew, renders its apocalyptic orientation explicit, and helps us reconcile it with Jesus' otherwise pacifistic orientation. Jesus had just sent out the twelve disciples to preach that "the kingdom of heaven has come near" and to demonstrate the reality of this kingdom by overcoming the "works of the devil" (1 Jn 3:8): to "cure the sick, raise the dead, cleanse the lepers, cast out demons" (Mt 10:8). But he warned them that not everyone was going to appreciate their proclamation and demonstration of the good news (10:11-15). Indeed, he told them that he was sending them "like sheep into the midst of wolves" (v. 16) and that they must therefore expect all forms of hideous persecution, even from their friends and family (vv. 17-31).

It is in this context that Jesus announces that he has come to bring bloodshed on the earth. It is not that his followers are to practice violence, but that they should expect violence to be done to them. Spreading the kingdom of God invites retaliation from the evil one, who owns all the kingdoms of this world (Lk 4:6; Jn 12:31; 1 Jn 5:19); they should not think that the "powers that be" will remain neutral toward them. If the spiritual powers of this world incite violence against the Master, they will most certainly do so against the Master's servants (Mt 10:24-25; cf. 1 Cor 2:8). Hence they are always to pray for protection "from the evil one" (Mt 6:13).[25]

Protection from Satan, however, is not guaranteed. In a significantly democratic cosmos, populated by billions of free human beings and countless free spiritual beings, and ripped asunder by a violent cosmic war, the Creator's will and any individual human will are not the only variables. Thus Jesus tells his disciples that when they do come under persecution, they are not to fear "those who kill the body but cannot kill the soul"; only God can kill "both soul and body in hell," and he is on their side (Mt 10:28). Hence if they lose their life, they will find it (10:39). They should rejoice over the fact that their names have been "written in heaven" even more than they rejoice over the fact that "the spirits submit" to them (Lk 10:20-21; cf. 6:23). In this war zone, Jesus is saying, bearers of the good news may in fact die by the sword. But nothing can touch their status as children of the kingdom (cf. Rom 8:35-39).

The violence Jesus was speaking of, then, is the violence that this demonically hostile world will bring against those who spread the kingdom of God. What strengthens this reading even further is that Matthew immediately follows it with an account of John the Baptist questioning Jesus' messiahship from prison. Living in prison conditions and facing likely execution, Jesus' forerunner was apparently having second thoughts about Jesus being the promised bringer of the kingdom. He asks, "Are you the one who is to come, or are we to wait for another?" (Mt 11:3).

Given the thrust of Jesus' ministry to demonstrate the kingdom by overcoming the scourges of the enemy, we are hardly surprised when we hear Jesus respond by telling John's messengers: "Go and tell John what you hear and see: the blind receive their sight, the lame walk, the lepers are cleansed, the deaf hear, the dead are raised, and the poor have good news brought to them" (Mt 11:4-5). Then Jesus adds the central point he was making in his previous teaching: "Blessed is anyone who takes no offense at me" (v. 6). Those who push back the work of the enemy by carrying out Jesus' ministry must expect violence, and blessed is the one who does not fall because of this (cf. 24:13).

Finally, Jesus gives a bit of teaching on the stature of John the Baptist. This man was no mere prophet, he insists; rather, John was nothing less than the forerunner of the King of Glory himself (Mt 11:10, quoting Mal 3:1). In this sense he was greater than any preceding person of God. Yet, Jesus cryptically adds, "the least in the kingdom of heaven is greater than he" (Mt 11:11). Then Jesus explains himself: "From the days of John the Baptist until now the kingdom of heaven has suffered violence, and the violent take it by force" (Mt 11:12).

A number of issues surround this difficult passage, only a few of which we can presently address. The first is whether the verb *biazetai* is to be translated in the middle or the passive voice. The middle voice leads to a positive reading of the verse (e.g., "forcefully advancing"), whereas the passive voice has a negative connotation (e.g., "suffered violence"). The issue is grammatically unresolvable, but a slight majority of scholars favor the second reading for a variety of reasons.[26]

Closely related to this issue is a second one. While the NIV and a number of other translations render the noun *biastai* as "violent men," the word means literally "violent ones." This leaves open the issue of whether Jesus is speaking about people or spiritual forces, or both.

Now, if *biazetai* is taken in the middle voice, *biastai* must be taken as a reference to godly people violently advancing the kingdom. If *biazetai* is taken in the passive voice, however, *biastai* must be taken as a reference to some ungodly, hostile group of beings, spiritual or human.

While I do not pretend to be able to conclusively resolve this issue, several arguments against the first alternative and several arguments in favor of the second, when combined with the overall portrait of Jesus' ministry as warfare, convince me, as well as an increasing number of scholars, that Jesus is referring to "Satan and his forces, including or excluding their human manifestations."[27]

Against the first interpretation, consider four things. First, construing the "violent ones" in a positive light does not explain why John is less than those after Jesus who spread "the kingdom of heaven." Yet explaining this is the point of the verse. Second, this interpretation is inconsistent with Jesus' teaching that the kingdom is to spread without the use of violence. Third, this interpretation does not give sufficient strength to the verb *harpazō*, which has the connotation of violently or suddenly seizing something (e.g., Jn 10:28-29; Acts 8:39; 23:10). Indeed, I find it very significant that the only other two times Matthew uses this verb in his Gospel, it refers explicitly to the activity of Satan (Mt 12:29; 13:19). At the very least, it is quite unclear what Jesus could mean and who he could be referring to in saying that godly violent people violently seize the kingdom of heaven.

Finally, this interpretation is also inconsistent with the fact that John the Baptist, at this time, is in no position to be violent in any positive sense. He is, rather, the victim of violence done to him. How this verse, interpreted in a positive way, relates to the preceding verses on John the Baptist is unclear. But it fits the context perfectly to understand Jesus to be referring to hostile demonic forces, and perhaps the people they inspire (especially religious leaders), trying to violently seize the kingdom of God.[28] According to this reading, Jesus is saying that his bringing of the kingdom of God has activated the kingdom of darkness into violent warfare on an unprecedented scale. What John is now experiencing, he is saying, is one small fallout of this violent activity from the demonic kingdom against the kingdom of God. Those who choose to fight for the kingdom of God from now on must expect even worse, as Jesus had just been teaching them. Concerning the assault of the "violent ones" against the kingdom of heaven, John is the least among those in the kingdom.[29]

The kingdom of darkness would eventually experience momentary success in violently seizing the kingdom, for Jesus would be crucified (1 Cor 2:8).[30] But that victory would be very short indeed. For, as we shall see in the next chapter, according to the New Testament and the early postapostolic church, the very act by which this violent kingdom sought to achieve final victory resulted in its final defeat.

This second interpretation avoids the shortcomings of the first and fits in well with the general apocalyptic, warfare orientation of Jesus' ministry. It also fits in better with the heavily apocalyptic context of this specific passage (see Mt 11:20-24). As such, it strikes me as the better option. Jesus is once again warning his disciples to expect strong opposition from the violent kingdom he, and they, are opposing.

An apocalyptic discourse. While we could discuss a number of other passages, one final sampling from Jesus' teachings in the Synoptic Gospels must suffice to highlight the warfare dimension of his teaching ministry. All three Synoptic Gospels record a discourse that Jesus gave concerning the end of the world (Mk 13:1-17; Mt 24:1-51; Lk 21:5-36). In response to the disciples' question about how they will know that the end is near, Jesus described a number of "signs" that were common in the apocalyptic thought of his day.

To follow Mark's account, Jesus says that many deceivers will perform "signs and omens" to lead astray multitudes (Mk 13:5-6, 21-22). There will also be a violent widespread persecution of believers such that the level of "suffering" will go beyond anything previously witnessed on earth (vv. 9-20). Indeed, unless God "cut short those days," no one, Jesus says, would survive (v. 20). Then, Jesus adds, the "sun will be darkened, and the moon will not give its light, and the stars will be falling from heaven, and the powers in the heavens will be shaken" (vv. 24-25).

The entire account speaks of a time of unparalleled demonic activity and warfare upon the earth, a time when deceiving and violent spirits will possess a "wicked generation" and bring unprecedented havoc upon the earth (cf. Rev 16:13-14; Mt 12:43-45). The references to "wars, earthquakes, and famines" are, as Beasley-Murray notes, "standing elements in prophetic and apocalyptic descriptions of the end and of the times leading up to it."[31] They are cataclysmic features of the final *peirasmos* ("tribulation") when all the forces of heaven and hell are unleashed against each other.

The references to deceptive "signs and omens" and to the persecution of the saints refers to the assault that the people of God shall experience at the hands of the enemies during this time of "suffering." These cataclysmic events are not initiated by God in judgment of the earth, though they are perhaps used by God to test and develop his people. But far from being God's design, the passage says that the Lord will (apparently supernaturally) shorten the days during this period precisely in order to protect his elect (Mk 13:20).

In the end, the passage seems to be teaching that the "violent ones," who were throughout Jesus' ministry trying to violently seize the kingdom, shall at the end of time erupt in one final blast of violence. The fallen powers that (in the apocalyptic view) can afflict the world with all sorts of ills will intensify their demonic activity. Hence, Jesus says, famines, earthquakes, wars and the persecution of the righteous shall abound.

But, Jesus emphatically adds, these violent ones shall certainly be defeated. Indeed, as a number of scholars have suggested, read in the light of the broader apocalyptic tradition, "the stars" falling from heaven and "the powers in the heavens" being shaken (v. 25) may refer to rebel cosmic powers being defeated in battle.[32] In the end, Jesus concludes, the Son of Man will reign victorious, seen by all as exalted "with great power and glory" (v. 26) as "he will send out the angels, and gather his elect from the four winds" (v. 27). The kingdom that he in principle established throughout his ministry will then be perfectly manifested, and the kingdom that he in principle defeated during his ministry will finally be utterly vanquished. He and all who belong to his kingdom shall reign over the earth (Rev 5:10)—God ruling through his vice-regents—just as God had intended from the start.

Jesus' Teaching in the Gospel of John

In radical distinction from the Synoptic Gospels, John records no exorcisms by Jesus in his Gospel. The only case of demonization he speaks of is that of Judas being possessed by Satan, and this has a very different character from those instances of demonization related in the Synoptic Gospels (Jn 6:70; 13:27; cf. Lk 22:3).[33] John's precise reasons for omitting Jesus' exorcisms are disputed, but for our purposes they are irrelevant, for this omission certainly does not lessen in the least John's understanding of Jesus' ministry as an act of war.[34]

Indeed, if anything, John's Gospel is even more emphatic about the

warfare nature of Jesus' ministry than are the Synoptics. His entire
portrait of Jesus is depicted in "strikingly dualistic" terms, which center
around Jesus as the Son of God entering into "the world" and overthrowing its "ruler."[35] As Coetzee observes, "for St. John the confrontation between Satan and Jesus (and his church) belongs to the very heart
of the redemptive history which finds its fulfillment in Jesus Christ."[36]

In what follows, I briefly overview three interrelated themes in this
work that highlight the centrality of the warfare dimension of John's
portrayal of Jesus' ministry.[37] I conclude by examining one passage that
has frequently been used to support the classical-philosophical theistic
understanding of God's sovereignty as encompassing even evil events in
the world.

Light and darkness. John introduces the theme of the drama he is
about to tell by providing the reader with a proleptic summary statement
of Jesus' ministry: "in him [the Word] was life, and the life was the light
of all people. The light shines in the darkness, and the darkness did not
overcome it" (Jn 1:4-5). As is well known, John heavily employs the
apocalyptic use of light as a metaphor for God or God's kingdom and
darkness as a metaphor for Satan or Satan's kingdom.[38] John is setting
up the theme of Jesus' ministry by stating that it most fundamentally
constituted a conflict between the kingdom of light and the kingdom of
darkness.[39] As in Genesis 1 (which a majority of scholars believe is in the
background here), the light shines against the darkness, and the darkness
cannot overtake it.[40] John is summarizing Jesus' ministry as an ongoing
warfare between light and darkness (a depiction that agrees perfectly with
what we have found in the Synoptics).[41]

These same metaphors are used, with the same limited dualistic
connotations, throughout John's Gospel. In 3:19-21, for example, John
again summarizes Jesus' ministry:

This is the judgment, that the light has come into the world, and
people loved darkness rather than light because their deeds were evil.
For all who do evil hate the light and do not come to the light, so
that their deeds may not be exposed. But those who do what is true
come to the light.

So it is throughout John's Gospel: Jesus is consistently depicted as "the
light of the world" (8:12; 9:5; 12:35, 46), and all who put their trust
"in the light" are "children of light" (12:36). Indeed, for John "God is
light and in him there is no darkness at all" (1 Jn 1:5), and all believers

must "walk in the light as he himself is in the light" (1 Jn 1:7; cf. 2:9-10). By contrast, those who resist the light stumble in the darkness (Jn 11:9-10; cf. 1 Jn 2:10-11). The conflict between light and darkness, we see, ultimately divides humanity between those who knowingly participate in the kingdom of God and those who knowingly or unknowingly are under "the ruler of this world" (Jn 12:31; 14:30; 16:11). The life and ministry of Jesus, according to John, simply make this distinction explicit.

The "archōn" of this world. The Johannine manner of referring to Satan as "the ruler *[archōn]* of this world" leads us to a second distinctive feature of Jesus' warfare teaching in John. The term *archōn* clearly denotes a being who possesses "great power and authority."[42] Indeed, in terms of denoting power, the word is second only to *basileus* (used of Jesus in an ironic sense in Jn 18:37). While Satan is not king of creation, for John he is the present evil controller of "the whole world" (1 Jn 5:19). As Paul puts it, he is "the god of this world" (2 Cor 4:4) and "the ruler of the power of the air" (Eph 2:2).[43]

For John, clearly, God created the world through his Son (Jn 1:3, 10), and he will ultimately rule it, again through his glorified Son (17:5, 24). But in "this world," in this present evil age, the "evil one" (17:15) exercises an illegitimate tyranny over the King's creation. Thus it is no surprise to discover that, according to John, the central reason why the Son of God appeared was to "destroy," "drive out" and "condemn" this evil ruler (1 Jn 3:8; Jn 12:31; 16:11). Jesus has come quite literally to exorcise Satan out of the world, to restore God as the rightful ruler over humanity and humanity as the rightful ruler of the world. Judith Kovacs is certainly correct (yet unfortunately exceptional) in recognizing in John 12:31 and 16:11 a theme that is fundamental to John's whole Gospel.[44]

Nevertheless, while John's language is indeed "strikingly dualistic" (Kovacs), and while John clearly sees Satan as possessing incredible power over the world, it is also clear that John is miles away from any form of Gnostic or Manichaean dualism.[45] The fact that each of the three passages that call Satan the "ruler of the world" does so in a context where Jesus' victory over him is in view is enough to demonstrate the provisional nature of John's dualism. But there are many other indications of this as well.

For example, while Satan is construed as the ultimate, powerful, evil force inspiring murders, and while he is said to have been a murderer "from the beginning" (Jn 8:44), he is not said to have been this murdering spirit "from eternity." In John, only God with the Word and Spirit is understood to be eternal.[46] What is more, though Satan indeed has control of "the whole world," he does not and cannot exercise control over Jesus. "He has no power over me," John's Jesus teaches, for "I do as the Father has commanded me" (14:30-31; cf. 10:18).[47] Most important, the oppressive tyranny of this evil "god" (2 Cor 4:4) shall come to an end, and indeed has in principle already been "driven out" and "condemned" through the obedient life as well as the death and resurrection of Christ (Jn 12:31, 42-45; 16:11; cf. Rev 12:5, 8-10).[48]

John's dualism, therefore, is a "transitory dualism," not a metaphysical dualism.[49] Still, it is no less intense for this reason. In John's view God must genuinely fight his evil cosmic foe; he is not playing charades. Jesus Christ, through his work on the cross, is the principle means by which this battle is being fought and won.[50]

"From God" and "from the devil." This brings us to the third distinctive feature of Jesus' warfare teaching in John. Unlike the Synoptic Gospels, one of the primary ways John expresses Jesus' divinity is to describe him in terms of his origin: he comes "from above" (Jn 3:31; 8:23; cf. 6:33, 38, 41-42, 50-51, 58). Also, those that believe in Jesus are said to be born "from above" (3:3). Indeed, believers are consistently portrayed as being birthed by the Father and given to Jesus as a gift (1:12-13; 6:38-39; 10:28-29; 17:2, 9, 24).

By contrast, those who choose not to put their trust in Christ are said to be "from below" (8:23).[51] They do not belong to the Father, but to "the world," John's term for this present fallen world order that is under the "ruler of this world" (12:31; 14:30; 16:11; cf. 1:10; 8:23; 14:17, 27; 15:18-19; 16:33; 17:9; cf. 1 Jn 2:15-17; 4:4-5; 5:4-5).[52]

With the same meaning, the Jesus of John's Gospel describes those who believe in him as "children of God" (1:12-13; cf. 12:36; 13:33), while those who do not believe are portrayed as children of the devil (8:44).[53] As in Paul, the view here seems to be that the "god of this world" had blinded the minds of unbelievers "to keep them from seeing the light of the gospel of the glory of Christ" (2 Cor 4:4; cf. Eph 2:2). Hence they cannot "know the truth" and be set free by the truth (Jn 8:32). They are, rather, "slaves to sin" (8:34), and only the Son of God can free them from this slavery (v. 36). But it is precisely this Son whom these people will not receive.

Indeed, as was said above, the only one in the world whom the devil does not have a hold of is Jesus himself, for he alone has not sinned but has consistently loved the Father and kept his commands (Jn 14:30). The rest of the world, however, is "under the power of the evil one" (1 Jn 5:19). Because of our sin, we are all part of the "kingdom of this world," and will become part of Jesus' kingdom, which is "not of this world," only when we believe in him (Jn 8:12, 23; 15:18-19; 17:6-16). Getting us to this point, John tells us, was precisely why he wrote his Gospel (20:31).

The Jesus of John's Gospel, we see, is a Jesus who has entered into a war zone between light and darkness, between the "ruler of this world" and the King of the earth, between what is "from above" and what is "from below," between what is "of this world" and what is "not of this world"—in short, between God and Satan. Everything Jesus is depicted as saying and doing in John intersects with this central thematic point. In this respect, John's depiction of Jesus is very much in line with that of the Synoptics.

John 9:1-3: The man born blind. We have seen that the assumption that runs throughout the Gospels is that sickness and disease are the works of the devil, not God, and hence that Jesus opposes them as he works to establish God's kingdom. When we adopt this same attitude, I submit, we are motivated to do something about the evil we confront, rather than resigning ourselves to it as though it came from the mysterious providential hand of God.

One passage from John's Gospel, however, has frequently been used to overturn this pervasive teaching and to argue the traditional theological position that even the devil's work is ultimately in line with God's sovereign plan. There may be war going on, this view says, but it is ultimately God who controls even what his enemies do.

In answer to the disciples' misguided question about who sinned to cause a particular man to be born blind (Jn 9:1ff.), Jesus said, "Neither this man nor his parents sinned; he was born blind so that God's works might be revealed in him." This translation seems to suggest that it was God's will for this man to be born blind. He was blind "so that" God could be glorified. A number of interpreters have seized this verse to support the classical-philosophical theistic position that God's good will lies behind even apparently evil events in this world.

For example, in his commentary on the Gospel of John, D. A. Carson draws the following conclusion from this verse: "John certainly does not think that the occurrence of blindness from birth was outside the sweep of God's control, and therefore of his purpose."[54] Carson's view, however, is exceedingly reserved compared to Calvin's. Calvin insists that the plural "works" (v. 3) is used by Jesus to emphasize explicitly that this man's blindness is as much a work of God as is his miraculously receiving sight.

> For so long as he was blind, there was exhibited in him an example of the divine severity, from which others might learn to fear and to humble themselves. It was followed by the benefit of his deliverance, in which the wonderful goodness of God was reflected. . . . He reminds them in general that this cause [of God] must be abundantly seen as true and lawful in the theater of the world when God glorifies his name. Nor have men any right to argue with God when he makes them the instruments of his glory in both ways, whether he appears as merciful or severe.[55]

James Boice develops the classical-philosophical line of reasoning even more fully as he explains this verse with the help of his interpretation of the book of Job. He argues, in good Augustinian fashion, that all suffering is either to punish sin, to build character or to glorify God. Both Job and the blind man in John 9 are examples of the latter. Then he asks rhetorically:

> Would God Almighty permit a man to be stripped of his family and all his possessions, to be struck with such illness that he would find himself sitting in ashes bemoaning that he had ever been born, just so that God himself might be vindicated? Would God permit a man to be struck with total blindness throughout the better part of his life so that in God's own time he might become the object of a miracle performed by the Lord Jesus Christ? . . . In the light of the Word of God we answer not only that God would do such things but that he has done them and, indeed, continues to do them.[56]

What are we to make of this? Does this verse require that we conclude that when Zosia was getting her eyes plucked out, God was glorifying himself, or, according to Boice, punishing her or building her character? Thankfully, the verse implies nothing of the sort. I offer five points in brief response to the above translation and interpretation.

First, even if this verse did imply that God willed for this man to be born blind, it would be the one exception to what we have seen is the general Gospel understanding of afflictions as the work of the devil.[57] As such, it should not be used to overturn the general teaching of the Gospels on the matter. It would simply mean that, in this one instance, God had a particular purpose in creating a man blind, or in allowing the devil to blind him.[58]

Second, it is significant that Jesus explicitly tells what this "higher purpose" is: God wants to display his power over blindness in *healing* the man. Hence this verse is particularly ill suited to serve as an example of how blindness as such fits into God's providence.

But the verse should not be interpreted as suggesting that God's will is behind this man's blindness in the first place, and this is my third point. The original verse does not say that "he was born blind so that God's works might be revealed." The Greek simply has *hina* with the aorist subjunctive passive of *phaneroō* ("to manifest") and can readily be translated as, "But let the works of God be manifested." As is certainly the case in Mark 5:23, Ephesians 5:33, 2 Corinthians 8:7; as is likely the case in Mark 2:10, 5:12, 10:51 and a host of other passages; and as is frequently the case in the Septuagint and later postapostolic writings, the *hina* here should be taken as forming an imperative, not a purposive, clause.[59]

In this light, Jesus is simply saying that, in contrast to the misguided moralistic speculations of the disciples, the only thing that matters concerning this man's blindness is that God can overcome it and thus be glorified through it. In the satanically ruled world in which he and his disciples ministered, and in which we ourselves still live, there is no discernible particular reason why this man was born blind. The disciples' questions, like the many assertions of Job's "friends," were based on the false assumption that God is behind all things, and thus that there must be a good reason for such things as blindness and the demonic torturing of a little girl—punishing sin, building character or glorifying God, for example.

In this reading, however, Jesus is simply refuting (not modifying) this assumption. He is, in effect, saying that the only response to this man's sorry condition is, "Let the works of God be manifested!" This obviously has monumental theological implications. As Nigel Turner notes,

> The hypothesis of the imperatival *hina* . . . releases the text from the fatalism which had obsessed it, and dissolves the picture which had become familiar through all our English versions, a man destined from

birth to suffer for the sole purpose of glorifying God when he was healed.[60]

Fourth, this reading is also consistent with what we find elsewhere in the Gospels concerning Jesus' view of evil. Not only does Jesus attribute all evil to the work of Satan, as we have seen, but he also explicitly rejects the assumption that God's will is behind evil events. In Luke 13:1-5 Jesus refutes the popular moralistic view that certain Galileans were slain by Pilate, and eighteen people were killed by the collapsing tower of Siloam, because they were being punished for their sins. "Do you think that they were worse offenders than all the others living in Jerusalem?" Jesus asks (13:4). His answer is an unequivocal no (13:3). All sin will ultimately be punished, Jesus then adds (13:5), but his response flatly denies that one can interpret tragic events or "natural" disasters as being this sort of punishment—the very assumption the disciples were expressing in John 9:1.

If Jesus had any inclination to endorse the common view that God's mysterious providence is ultimately behind the evils in the world, the context of Luke 13:1-5 would have been the perfect place for him to express it. Instead, we get an unequivocal denial. In my view, Jesus is doing much the same thing in John 9:2-3.[61]

Finally, this reading of John 9:1-3 fits in with the context in which it is given. In typical Johannine fashion, the miracle is immediately spoken of as a "work of day" and "light" staving off the "night" (9:4-5). The miracle once again illustrates the Johannine perspective that the one who is the "light" brings divine light to one who had previously been in demonic darkness.[62] It also squares best with 10:20-21, which strongly suggests that this man's blindness was a demonic work, which is why Jesus could not have healed him (as the Pharisees claimed) by demonic power (recall the Beelzebub controversy, Mk 3:20-30 and parallels). As throughout the Gospels, then, it seems best to see this miracle as an example of Jesus manifesting the work of God against the power of darkness that "scourges" people with such things as blindness.

Conclusion

From the last three chapters it should be clear that Jesus and the earliest disciples operated within an intense warfare worldview. They were as certain about the reality of Satan and demons as they were about the reality of God and good angels. They were certain that these two kingdoms were now engaged in mortal combat with each other. And they were certain that Jesus was the decisive player in this war.

This present *kosmos* was not in any sense seen by them as an Edenic garden in which God's will was already being sovereignly carried out, sometimes bringing blessings and sometimes bringing curses to its inhabitants. Rather, in good apocalyptic fashion, this *kosmos* was understood to be a veritable war zone in which the sovereignty of God had to be established over against formidable forces of evil by faith and prayer.

As we have seen, Jesus and his disciples understood all the evil in the world—from barren trees to threatening storms to sicknesses and diseases, to demonized little children and sinful behavior—as being ultimately (and sometimes directly) due to the work of the all-pervasive Satanic kingdom. They therefore understood that their central mission was to oppose such things and overthrow them.

There is never any suggestion, John 9:1-3 included, that God has some "higher" good purpose behind or above this cosmic evil, as though Satan and his legions were secretly carrying out God's will. From the Gospels' perspective, all talk about finding "the sovereign will of God" above or behind the atrocities of the world is utterly misguided. Their view was, in the words of Karl Heim, that "the satanic power is God's mortal enemy, that is to say not merely an intermediate stage on the way to the divine end of the world but the radical evil against which a total war must be waged."[63]

Satan, therefore, was not for them an agent of God, but the enemy against God. Despite volumes of learned classical-philosophical theistic writings attempting to argue the contrary, these two offices are simply not compatible. As Howard Pendley inquires, "If Satan's activity is part of God's plan, how can it be said that Satan is God's enemy?"[64] Yet the assumption that he is God's enemy runs throughout the whole New Testament.[65] Hence all who hold this inspired library to be authoritative ought to abandon the impossible claim that he is also God's "secret" agent, or (what is the same thing) that God is his "secret" controller.

Finally, in the last three chapters we have seen that this warfare is intrinsically connected to everything Jesus was about, centered on his teaching about and demonstrations of the kingdom of God. The kingdom of God is set up only as the kingdom of evil is torn down. The rule of God, the carrying out of God's purposes, is not found in evil, behind evil or above evil, for, it is assumed, all evil ultimately comes from Satan, pure and simple. Rather, the rule of God is found in opposing evil. And just this ministry of coming against the "god" of all evil is what ultimately defines and unites all the various activities and teachings of Jesus.

In this light, the problem of evil in the New Testament is not the classical-philosophical theistic problem of finding a particular transcendent divine purpose behind every particular evil: Jesus and his disciples assume that there is none. The "buck stops" with the evil beings, human or otherwise, who perpetrate the evil. For Jesus and his disciples, the "problem of evil" is simply the problem of overcoming evil by the power of God. It is the task of setting up the kingdom of the Father in a war zone where it is resisted.

By contrast, as we have already said, the problem of evil for classical-philosophical theologians has been the problem of locating and explaining a mysterious, all-good, divine purpose behind all particular evils. Hence they search for the particular reason God must have had in decreeing (according to Calvinists), or at least in allowing (according to Arminians), children like Zosia to be ruthlessly tortured. This is not, I submit, the question Jesus or his disciples (when they were thinking in accordance with their Master) would have asked.

It is the question Job's "friends" would perhaps have asked. It is the question multitudes of people in Jesus' time asked in the face of various tragedies (Lk 13:1-6). It is the question Jesus' disciples asked when they were not thinking straight, before he corrected them (Jn 9:1). But it is not the question Jesus or any inspired New Testament author would have asked. The only question they asked was, How can this diabolical work of the enemy be overthrown? How can "the works of God" be manifested here?

The fact that our construing of the problem of evil tends to have more in common with Job's friends and those Jesus opposed than it has in common with Jesus and the New Testament is very significant for all of us who claim Christ as Lord. At the very least, it means that we need to seriously reconsider some of our classical-philosophical assumptions about God and the world. Perhaps the reason for our differences with the New Testament—and the reason for the traditional befuddlement over the problem of evil—is our unwittingly adopted assumptions that are not consistent with theirs.

Exploring this question will be my task in *Satan and the Problem of Evil* (forthcoming). But we have not yet completed the more fundamental task of assessing exactly what Scripture says about God's battles with his foes. We have yet to examine what Paul and other New Testament writers have to say on the matter (chapters nine and ten). What we shall find is that the warfare theme is not diminished. If anything, it becomes even more intensified.

9

CHRISTUS VICTOR

THE WARFARE SIGNIFICANCE OF CHRIST'S DEATH AND RESURRECTION

*I*N KEEPING WITH THE OLD TESTAMENT AND ESPECIALLY THE APOCA-lyptic worldview of the time, we have seen that Jesus and his earliest disciples operated within a warfare worldview. In direct contrast to the "enlightened" worldview that has characterized Western culture for the last several hundred years, but in essential agreement with the worldview of almost all other cultures throughout history (and increasingly that of Western culture as well, as it heads into the "postmodern" age), Jesus and his earliest disciples believed that the universe was inhabited by a myriad of spiritual beings, some good and some evil, which were at war with one another. And they believed that Jesus was the decisive player in this warfare.

The most fundamental unifying theme throughout Jesus' ministry is that he was setting up the kingdom of God over against the kingdom of Satan. Jesus' exorcistic and healing ministry constitutes preliminary victories over this enemy, while his death and resurrection spell Satan's ultimate demise.

Yet even Jesus' victory over death was eschatological. It pointed beyond itself into the future, a future in which his accomplishment would be manifested. Though Jesus' death in principle "drove out" the cosmic murderer (Jn 12:31; 8:44), this victory has not yet been manifested in the world, for people continue to die. Though Satan's fortress has in principle been toppled and the strong man himself "tied up," his fortress has not yet toppled to the ground. Though the power to set people free from the scourges of this enemy has in principle been established and distributed to all who follow Christ, the world continues to be held hostage by this (now mortally wounded and bound) strong man (1 Jn 5:19).

As the New Testament authors realize, this means there is still work to be done, and the church is the means by which it is to be done. In the time between the "already" of Christ's work and the "not yet" of the eschaton, the church is to be about what Jesus was about. It is, in a real sense, his "body" here on earth. As such, the church is to be an extension of the ministry he himself carried out in his incarnate body while here on earth (2 Cor 5:18-19).

The church is to manifest the truth that God's kingdom has come and that Satan's kingdom is defeated. Thus in its own way, under the victorious authority of Christ, the church is to engage and overthrow evil powers, just as Jesus himself has done. Indeed, when the church does this through the Spirit, it is Jesus himself who is still doing it. This is why, despite his disciples' exuberant confidence in the accomplished work of the cross, we do not find the warfare worldview of Jesus lessened one iota among them.

For our purposes, we need to investigate five themes related to warfare in these New Testament writings outside the Gospels. The first two are explored in this chapter, and the following three in the next chapter. In this chapter, I examine in more detail the New Testament's understanding of Christ's death and resurrection as accomplishing a cosmic victory over God's enemies, followed by an overview of how this understanding is present in various New Testament authors' views of salvation as deliverance from bondage to the devil. In the following chapter, I examine the various ways Acts and the Epistles portray the demonic realm, followed by an investigation of what they say about the ongoing activity of this kingdom. I conclude with a brief overview of what this literature says about both the origin and destiny of Satan and his rebel kingdom.

The Victory of the Cross

The New Testament speaks about the significance of the cross in a variety of ways: it was an atoning sacrifice for our sins (Heb 10:10-14); it satisfied God's justice (Rom 3:25); it provided an example for believers (Phil 2:5-11; 1 Pet 2:21); and it conquered Satan (Jn 12:31; Col 2:14-15; 1 Jn 3:8). The cross accomplished all of this. The "wisdom of God in its rich variety" (Eph 3:10) is displayed in God's ability to use this one central event of history to accomplish a number of different things at the same time. But this "variety" raises the question of how these various aspects of the cross are related to one another.

The cosmic significance of the cross. Since at least the time of Anselm in the eleventh century A.D., and especially since the Reformation in the sixteenth century, the tendency of the Western church has been to focus almost all its attention on the anthropological dimension of the atonement, usually to the neglect of the cosmic dimension that is central to the New Testament. In the standard Protestant view, the chief thing God was accomplishing when he had Jesus die on the cross was satisfying his perfect justice and thereby atoning for our sins. The work of the cross is centered on us. Other aspects of the cross, to the extent that they are acknowledged, are seen as subsidiary to this anthropocentric dimension of Christ's work.

I by no means want to minimize this aspect of Christ's work, for it is a profound source of freedom and joy for the believer, and is certainly deeply rooted in Scripture.[1] At the same time, however, I cannot agree that the primary significance of the cross is found here. From the perspective of the New Testament, I maintain, the anthropological significance of Christ's death and resurrection is rooted in something more fundamental and broad that God was aiming at: to defeat once and for all his cosmic archenemy, Satan, along with the other evil powers under his dominion, and thereby to establish Christ as the legitimate ruler of the cosmos, and human beings as his legitimate viceroys upon the earth.

To state it otherwise, whereas since Anselm the dominant way of thinking about the atonement focused on what it accomplished for humanity (reconciliation to God), and thus viewed what it accomplished against Satan and the evil powers as a byproduct, the view I am espousing in this chapter is that the New Testament construes the relation between these two aspects of the cross in the converse order.[2] Christ's achievement on the cross is first and foremost a cosmic event—it defeats Satan. In the words of G. H. C. MacGregor: "for Paul, just as . . . [the] demonic spirits are essentially cosmic powers, so is the redemption which Christ wins a cosmic redemption. Not only is the individual saved from bondage to sin and death. . . . the entire creation is affected by the redemptive event."[3]

Thus as Scripture portrays the matter, the foundational reason Christ appeared was "to destroy the works of the devil" (1 Jn 3:8), to disarm "the rulers and authorities" (Col 2:15), and to "destroy the one who has the power of death, that is, the devil" (Heb 2:14). The consequence of this victory is that he is seated on his rightful throne, the whole cosmos is liberated from a tyrannical and destructive ruler, humanity is delivered "from the power of darkness and transferred . . . into the kingdom of his beloved Son" (Col 1:13), and all who accept it are thereby reinstated to the original position and responsibility of stewards of the creation that God had always intended for us.[4]

While Christ's substitutionary death for sinful humans is central for understanding what Christ did for us, therefore, this dimension of Christ's work is possible only because of the broader cosmic victory Christ won on the cross. This is what I mean by referring to the warfare dimension of Christ's work on the cross as primary. I believe that regaining a proper emphasis on it is theologically crucial.

Among other things, regaining this New Testament cosmic warfare emphasis on the cross is important if we are to arrive at a biblical understanding of the problem of evil. One of the features of Western thought that has most handicapped our efforts to reconcile the existence of evil with a belief in an omnipotent and omnibenevolent God is that we have tended to understand evil, and therefore Christ's solution to evil, anthropocentrically and individualistically. For example, many theologians have traditionally attempted to explain cosmic evil by appealing to human wills alone, and have attempted to understand the central significance of the cross by appealing to human salvation alone.

From a New Testament perspective, however, as well as from the perspective of our own experience of evil, the existence of evil far outruns what any appeal to human willing is capable of explaining. Further, the significance of Christ's work on the cross far outruns what it accomplishes for human beings.

Regaining a biblical emphasis on the cosmic dimension of the cross will broaden our perspective and appreciation of the cure for evil, and thereby broaden our perspective on the nature of evil. Within a full-fledged warfare worldview, neither evil nor its cure is first and foremost about human beings at all. Rather, it is, we shall see, primarily about free willing agents ("the powers") whose cosmic power and influence dwarf the free agency of human beings. Only when this is understood can we arrive at a worldview—a biblical worldview—in which evil is not unexpected, is not about God's planning and activity, and hence is not in any given instance an unsolvable intellectual problem.

Subjugating the enemy. Something of the centrality of the warfare theme in Scripture, and especially of the warfare dimension of Christ's death, is signified by the fact that the first messianic prophecy given to us in the Bible proclaims that Christ will crush the head of Satan. Symbolically building on the natural antagonism between people and snakes (see chapter four above), the Lord says to the serpent who had just deceived Eve: "I will put enmity between you and the woman, and between your offspring and hers; he will strike your head, and you will strike his heel" (Gen 3:15).

As traditionally interpreted, this verse proclaims that the Messiah will ultimately end the age-long struggle between God and the serpent by crushing its head. According to Ralph Martin, this understanding dates back at least to the translation of the Septuagint and is found in many rabbinic writings as well.[5] A similar understanding of this passage also seems to lie behind a number of New Testament texts (e.g., Rom 16:19-20; Heb 2:14; Rev 12) and, according to some scholars, is even behind the designation of Jesus as "the Son of Man" and of Mary as "woman."[6]

However much the understanding is or is not tied to Genesis 3:15, it is clear that in the understanding of the New Testament, Christ came to earth primarily to accomplish what this interpretation of Genesis 3:15 proclaims: "to destroy the works of the devil" (1 Jn 3:8). The misery and bondage that the serpent first brought about in Eden in principle came to an end when the prophecy given in Eden was fulfilled. On the cross the serpent struck the "heel" of Christ (more on this below), but it was Christ who ultimately crushed the head of the serpent.[7]

A related warfare passage that has been traditionally interpreted as messianic is Psalm 110:1. Here David says: "The LORD says to my lord, 'Sit at my right hand until I make your enemies your footstool.' "

In David's day it was common for a king to symbolize his conquest of another kingdom by using the defeated ruler's neck as a footstool (e.g., Josh 10:24). This prophecy is proclaiming that the Messiah would rule at the "right hand" (viz., the power) of God until he did just that to his enemies. The rulership of the Messiah, clearly, is about subjugating enemies.

The importance of this passage for the New Testament is reflected by the fact that no other Old Testament passage is quoted so often.[8] In a saying found in all three Synoptic Gospels, Jesus indirectly applies this verse to himself (Mt 12:44; Mk 12:36; Lk 20:43), and it is explicitly applied to Christ a number of other times throughout the rest of the New Testament. In almost every instance, it is associated with Christ's death and resurrection.

Hence in the first sermon preached by the newly birthed church, Peter proclaims:

This Jesus God raised up, and of that all of us are witnesses. Being therefore exalted at the right hand of God, and having received from the Father the promise of the Holy Spirit, he has poured out this that you both see and hear. For David did not ascend into the heavens, but he himself says, "The Lord said to my Lord: 'Sit at my right hand, until I make your enemies your footstool.'" (Acts 2:32-35)

Peter concludes by saying,

Therefore let the entire house of Israel know with certainty that God has made him both Lord and Messiah, this Jesus whom you crucified. (Acts 2:36)

Peter is clearly depicting the significance of Christ's death and resurrection as centering on the way it fulfills Psalm 110:1. By raising Christ from the dead, the Father has made his Son "both Lord and Messiah," and has now set him at "his right hand" so he can reign over his enemies, until they all are made his footstool.[9] In this sense the death and resurrection of Jesus was, for Peter, first and foremost an act of war.

Paul expresses the same conviction. In a passage that is talking about the resurrection, Paul writes:

For as all die in Adam, so all will be made alive in Christ. But each in his own order: Christ the first fruits, then at his coming those who belong to Christ. Then comes the end, when he hands over the kingdom to God the Father, after he has destroyed every ruler and every authority and power. For he must reign until he has put all his enemies under his feet. (1 Cor 15:22-25)

As David Hay notes, "the kingdom of Christ is here represented exclusively in terms of a subjugation of powers to him." He adds, "The powers chiefly in view seem to be supernatural ones."[10] The resurrection enthroned Christ over every "ruler, authority, and power," and when they are finally "destroyed" (*katargeō*), the goal of the incarnation, death and resurrection of the Son of God will be achieved.[11]

As with Peter, the death and resurrection of Christ was, for Paul, most fundamentally a decisive act of war initiated by God against everything that opposes him. It put Christ in a position above all demonic powers, and he shall continue to battle from this exalted position until every one of these powers has been destroyed—until what he accomplished in principle through his death and resurrection is realized as a completed act.

In a similar fashion, the author of Hebrews notes that Jesus is superior to all angelic powers because it was to him, not them, that the Father offered to "sit at my right hand until I make your enemies a footstool for your feet" (1:13). Later, fusing the theme of the cross as the means by which atonement is made for sinners and the theme of the cross as the means by which Jesus comes to reign over his enemies, this author notes that this enthronement occurred only because of Jesus' sacrifice on the cross (Heb 10:12-13; cf. 1:3). We again see that Jesus' death and resurrection were the means by which he gained the decisive upper hand over the enemies of God.

In the light of the foregoing, the assessment of the central significance of Psalm 110 for the New Testament given by Oscar Cullmann must surely be judged as warranted:

> Nothing shows more clearly how the concept of the present Lordship of Christ and also of his consequent victory over the angel powers stands at the very center of early Christian thought than the frequent citation of Ps. 110:1, not only in isolated books, but in the entire NT.[12]

Seated at the right hand of God. The theme of the resurrected Messiah reigning victorious over his enemies, based on Psalm 110:1, also lies behind many of the references throughout the New Testament to Christ being seated "at the right hand of God." Each of them refers to Christ's being enthroned in a position of strength ("right hand") and hence in a position over his enemies.

For example, "Peter and the other apostles" proclaim that because Jesus was raised from the dead, "God exalted him at his right hand as Leader and Savior that he might give repentance to Israel and forgiveness of sins" (Acts 5:31).

Through Jesus' death and resurrection, the former "ruler of the world" has been "driven out" (Jn 12:31) and a new "Leader," a legitimate ruler, has been enthroned in his place.[13] Whereas the former ruler held humanity in misery, sin and bondage, this Leader offers "repentance and forgiveness of sins" at no cost. Christ becomes our "Savior" because he has become our "Leader" by ousting the old "ruler of the world" through his death and resurrection.

Paul has something similar in mind when he writes that no one can condemn the believer because Jesus, who now justifies us, died and was raised to life and is now seated "at the right hand of God" (Rom 8:34), the very place from whence Satan used to accuse us (Zech 3:1). Because he now rules from this exalted position, Paul says, nothing can separate us from the love of Christ: "neither angels nor demons . . . nor any powers, neither height nor depth, nor anything else in all creation" (Rom 8:38-39 NIV).

As has been generally recognized in the secondary literature, the point of this last passage is to say in effect that every possible form of demonic power has been subjugated to Christ.[14] Thus while these demonic spirits can perhaps still bring persecution, famine, danger and death (Rom 8:35-36)—they have not yet been utterly "destroyed" (1 Cor 15:24)—they cannot separate the believer from the love of God. Christ's reigning in the power of God secures the believers' standing in him (cf. Lk 10:18-20).

In just the same way, Peter notes that baptism now saves believers "through the resurrection of Jesus Christ, who has gone into heaven and is at the right hand of God, with angels, authorities, and powers made subject to him" (1 Pet 3:21-22).

The ordinance of baptism has meaning, Peter says, not because it is a literal washing (v. 21), but because it connects the believer with the death and resurrection of Christ. The foremost thing that the death and resurrection of Christ accomplished, we again see, was the subjugation of all other cosmic powers under him. In baptism, therefore, believers express and participate in Christ's cosmic victory.[15]

Hence too, Peter notes in this same context how Jesus, after his crucifixion, preached to "spirits" who had been imprisoned since the days of Noah (3:18-19). The old rulers held people in bondage; the new ruler sets them free—apparently even those who were imprisoned before he arrived.[16]

Along similar lines, Paul prays that the Christians at Ephesus will come to an understanding of "the immeasurable greatness of his power for us who believe," to which he adds: "according to the working of his great power. God put this power to work in Christ when he raised him from the dead and seated him at his right hand in the heavenly places" (Eph 1:19-20).

It was, again, through Christ's death and resurrection that Jesus came to be seated in the power position ("right hand") of the Father. As Karl Heim puts it, the cross was "God's final settlement of the Satanic opposing power which has arisen against God."[17] Hence Christ is now exalted "in the heavenly places."

Where are these "heavenly places"? They are, Paul continues, "far above all rule and authority and power and dominion, and above every name that is named. . . . And he has put all things under his feet and has made him the head over all things for the church" (1:21-22).

The point is unmistakably clear. Through the death and resurrection of Jesus Christ, God stripped Satan and all levels of demons of all their power (Col 2:15). Therefore Christ now reigns in the power of God far above all such demonic powers. Expressing the tension of the "already/not yet" that characterizes the entire New Testament, Paul can here say that "all things" are already "under his feet," though the actual manifestation of this truth is yet in the future. But the central point remains: the work of the cross was about dethroning a cruel, illegitimate ruler and reinstating a loving, legitimate one: Jesus Christ. When Jesus Christ is reinstated, all who are aligned with his rule, all who are "in Christ," all who are his "bride" and part of his "body," are reinstated to their appropriate position of authority as well. In a word, we are saved because he is victorious.

From glory to glory. Several key passages in the New Testament express this warfare understanding of the cross and resurrection by tying in Christ's postresurrection glory with his preexistent glory as the Son of God. Perhaps the clearest example of this is found in Philippians 2. Here, as a means of encouraging humility among the Christians at Philippi, Paul tells his congregation to follow the example of Christ, who, though he was "in very nature God," did not grasp after "equality with God."

Rather, he emptied himself and took on "the very nature of a servant."
Indeed, in contrast to Adam, Christ became obedient to the Father to
the point of death, "even death on a cross" (Phil 2:6-9 NIV). For this
reason, Paul concludes,

> God also highly exalted him and gave him the name that is above
> every name, so that at the name of Jesus every knee should bend, in
> heaven and on earth and under the earth, and every tongue should
> confess that Jesus Christ is Lord, to the glory of God the Father. (Phil
> 2:9-11)

According to this passage, the primary thing that Jesus' death and
resurrection accomplished was to enthrone Christ in the place where he
rightfully belongs. Jesus has always been "by very nature God," according to Paul. As the divine Son and Creator of the cosmos (Jn 1:1-3; 1
Cor 8:6; Col 1:15-17), he is deserving of the highest honor that can be
given. But not everything "in heaven," "on earth" and "under the earth"
acknowledges this. Indeed, as we have seen, much in these realms has
been explicitly fighting against Christ's lordship. This rebellion, however, is coming to an end, writes Paul, because of Christ's incarnation,
death and resurrection. Through these means Christ has now won back
his lordship, and it is simply a matter of time before every creature in
heaven, on earth and even in hell acknowledges this fact. Every knee shall
bow.[18]

The same theme is expressed in Colossians 1:15-20. Here Paul
expresses Christ's rightful rule over all of creation by saying that Christ

> is the image of the invisible God, the firstborn of all creation; for in
> him all things in heaven and on earth were created, things visible and
> invisible, whether thrones or dominions or rulers or powers—all
> things have been created through him and for him. He himself is
> before all things, and in him all things hold together. (1:15-17)

As the Creator of all, the Son of God is the rightful ruler of all. But some
of the "thrones," "dominions," "rulers" and "powers" Christ created
have apparently chosen to fight against this lordship rather than to carry
out their functions in harmony with it. For now, Paul continues, these
powers need to be "reconciled." Paul immediately follows up this hymn
of creation with a hymn of redemption.

> He is the head of the body, the church; he is the beginning, the
> firstborn from the dead, so that he might come to have first place in
> everything. For in him all the fullness of God was pleased to dwell,

and through him God was pleased to reconcile to himself all things, whether on earth or in heaven, by making peace through the blood of his cross. (Col 1:18-20)

The logic of the passage is clear enough. The One who created all things is seeking again to have supremacy over all things by being "the head of the body, the church." He is the head of this body by virtue of the fact that he became incarnate, shed his blood and rose from the dead. Through his death, and by means of this body, he is ultimately going to "reconcile to himself all things," including, apparently, the demonic powers that have thus far opposed him.

Several things are noteworthy about this passage. First, it once again stresses that the focal point of Jesus' death and resurrection was ending the cosmic war between himself and his enemies. As throughout the New Testament, this is the primary purpose of Christ's death and resurrection. Second, this passage stresses the role of the church, his "body," in bringing about this eschatological reality. The church is called to carry on Jesus' ministry and to manifest the victory of the cross to a world that is still under bondage to hostile forces. Third, Paul here portrays the end of Christ's exaltation as reconciliation. Through his death on the cross Christ "makes peace" where once there was war.

How we are to square this cosmic reconciliation with Paul's teaching elsewhere that the hostile cosmic enemies of God shall be "destroyed" (1 Cor 15:24), and with the general New Testament teaching that Christ's enemies shall be made into his footstool, is a difficult question. Some use this passage to support a form of universalism, and simply decide that other passages which appear to teach something else are either provisional (viz., speaking about a time prior to the ultimate end) or are simply less inspired. Such a position attributes to Paul a rather serious inconsistency and undermines a strong view of biblical inspiration.

Here we cannot and need not embark on the difficult subject of the New Testament's eschatological perspective. Simply note that it is not self-evident that "reconciliation," as Paul uses it here, and "redemption," as it is used by Paul and other New Testament authors, are equivalent concepts.[19] Rather, it may be that in saying all things shall be ultimately reconciled to the lordship of Christ, Paul is simply saying that nothing will ultimately be able to effectively oppose this lordship. There is "peace" throughout Christ's cosmos because everything is put in its proper place. In the case of the unredeemable hostile powers of darkness, this place is under Christ's feet.

In any event, it is again clear that the central means by which the Creator has regained supremacy in his creation was by dying on the cross and rising from the dead. As the postapostolic church almost universally conceded, this is the primary significance of Christ's sacrifice. The cross was a cosmic event that defeated the enemies of God, enthroned the Son of God, and thereby in principle liberated the whole cosmos from its bondage to an illegitimate evil ruler. As expressed by Robert Roth: "Atonement between the creator God and his rebellious creatures includes first of all a victory over the adversary and then liberating, adopting, cleansing, renewing, justifying, sanctifying, and finally raising from the dead."[20]

Contrary to the dominant way in which it has been interpreted since Anselm, then, Jesus' death and resurrection was not simply, or even primarily, about God reconciling humanity to himself, though it certainly accomplished this too. Rather, it was, as Heim puts it, primarily about "the overcoming of the diabolical power, the mortal enmity to God."[21] It is also about everything else that pertains to salvation because it is first and foremost about this.

Deliverance from the Devil

While the understanding that the central significance of the cross was to "destroy the works of the devil" (1 Jn 3:8) may be unconventional, at least since Anselm, it should surprise us if this were not the case, given the centrality of the warfare theme that we have already observed running throughout Jesus' ministry (chapters six through eight). The one motif that unifies all the other aspects of Jesus' ministry is his mission to spread the kingdom of God by pushing back the kingdom of darkness. It should strike us as peculiar if Jesus' death and resurrection were not most fundamentally understood in this light as well. Indeed, as we have seen, Jesus himself anticipated this warfare interpretation when he spoke of his death as a "ransom" (Mt 20:28; Mk 10:45) and portrayed it as the "goal" of his exorcising and healing ministry (Lk 13:32 NIV).

When the rest of the New Testament outside the Gospels depicts Christ's death as disarming and destroying the devil and as thereby restoring to Christ his rightful throne as Creator and Savior of the world, above all powers and authorities that oppose him, it is simply speaking in a manner that is consistent with what we have learned about Jesus' ministry in the Gospels. Also consistent with the Gospels, we must now add, is the New Testament's portrayal of our salvation as being primarily the result of Christ having successfully carried out this cosmic warfare feat. Christ drove out demons and healed the sick in order to establish God's kingdom against the kingdom of darkness, and people who received it were the benefactors of this mission. So it is throughout the New Testament: Salvation is most fundamentally construed as being the direct result of Jesus having overcome the powers of darkness through his work on the cross. In other words, Christ's cosmic victory results in our personal salvation.

Christ's victory applied to us. The basic pattern found throughout the New Testament when it speaks of our salvation in Christ is first to state what Christ accomplished on a cosmic level, then to present what this means to us. This pattern reemphasizes the point that the central significance of the cross is found in the fact that through it Christ won a cosmic battle against Satan. Its anthropological significance is a consequence of this.

To give a few examples, we saw above how Paul, in writing to the Colossians, portrayed Christ's death and resurrection as the means by which the one who by nature should reign supreme comes to actually reign supreme—over and against all cosmic forces that might resist him. The whole of the creation comes from Christ and exists for Christ, and now, because of his death and resurrection, it is just a matter of time before he ultimately reconciles his creation—including his opponents—to himself (Col 1:15-20).

Only after this cosmic dimension of the cross is stressed does Paul then turn to talk about what this means for believers. Immediately after stating that Christ has accomplished cosmic peace "through the blood of his cross" (v. 20), Paul adds:

> And you who were once estranged and hostile in mind, doing evil deeds, he has now reconciled in his fleshly body through death, so as to present you holy and blameless and irreproachable before him. (vv. 21-22)

This passage clearly presents our reconciliation to God as one aspect of the cosmic reconciliation to God accomplished through the cross. The cosmic conquest, one might say, logically precedes the anthropological application. The implication of the cosmic conquest for us is that we are rendered "irreproachable" or "free from accusation" (NIV). Since our sins are atoned for, "the accuser" has no more claim on us, and hence we are set free (Rom 8:1, 31, 33; Col 2:13-15). But it is crucial to note that this freedom is a function of a victorious enthronement, the significance of which far outruns what it does for us. The cross and resurrection are anthropologically significant only because they are first of all cosmologically significant.

We simply cannot grasp the depth of the significance of the cross and resurrection so long as we restrict our perspective to what they accomplish for us, any more than we can make sense of the evil the cross and resurrection in principle overcame so long as we restrict our perspective to human evil. An impoverished understanding of evil and a deficient understanding of the work of Christ go hand in hand. Both are fully intelligible only as cosmological realities, and only as related to spiritual war.

The same pattern is found in Ephesians 1:22—2:8. Paul first praises God for his display of the "immeasurable greatness of his power" (1:19) in raising Jesus from the dead (1:19-20). This act is what seated Christ at his "right hand" and enthroned him "in the heavenly places, far above all rule and authority and power and dominion" (1:21). Hence this act brought about God's ultimate victory, for through it God "has put all things under his feet" (1:22).

Having spoken of the cosmic dimension of Christ's resurrection, Paul then turns to apply it to the status of believers: "You were dead through the trespasses and sins in which you once lived, following the course of this world, following the ruler of the power of the air, the spirit that is now at work among those who are disobedient" (Eph 2:1-2).

Whether we knew it or not, we believers used to be "dead" in our sin and enslaved by "the ruler of the power of the air," as are all nonbelievers even now, according to Paul. We therefore indulged "the desires of flesh and senses, and we were by nature children of wrath, like everyone else" (2:3). We were part of a damned kingdom, under a diabolical ruler, and were ourselves headed for destruction.

But through the resurrection, Paul is saying, Christ has overthrown this kingdom with its diabolical ruler, and hence we are slaves no longer. Indeed, we are not only no longer under Satan's authority, but in Christ we are far above it. For God has "raised us up with [Christ] and seated us with him in the heavenly places in Christ Jesus" (2:4-6).[22] Because of God's "great love" and "grace," every believer has been "saved" from "the ruler of the power of the air" and has been given all the inheritance that belongs to Christ (Eph 2:7-9; cf. 1:7, 14). Our fundamental status has changed. We are each "a new creation; everything old has passed away; see, everything has become new" (2 Cor 5:17).[23]

For our purposes, most important to note here is that everything said about the believer on an anthropological level is said on the basis of what has already been said about Christ on a cosmic level. Our salvation is a function of Christ's exalted lordship, and his lordship is a function of his victory over, and now enthronement above, all "rule and authority and power and dominion, and above every name that is named" (Eph 1:21). We are allowed by God's grace to share in the cosmic victory Christ has accomplished through the cross. There is quite literally a new King on the throne. And all who will simply acknowledge this kingship have a share in his gracious kingdom, and even in his powerful authority over opposing forces. We shall reign with Christ over all the earth (Rev 5:10; cf. Mt 19:28; Lk 22:28-30; 2 Tim 2:12; Rev 3:21; 20:4-6; 22:5). Our creation-covenant commission to rule the earth (Gen 1:26-31) shall at last be fulfilled.

We may go further still. Elsewhere in Ephesians Paul tells us that our sharing in Christ's victory is itself part of the cosmic purpose God was aiming at through the cross. Concerning the preaching of the Gospel, Paul writes that God's intent was "that through the church the wisdom of God in its rich variety might now be made known to the rulers and authorities in the heavenly places. . . . in accordance with the eternal purpose that he has carried out in Christ Jesus our Lord" (Eph 3:10-11).

The point seems to be that the Lord is using us earthly benefactors of his cosmic victory (the church) to display to the angelic society of the heavenly realms, including the now defeated powers, the greatness of the Creator's wisdom in defeating his foes.[24] We who used to be captives of the Satanic kingdom are now the very ones who proclaim its demise. The church is, as it were, God's eternal "trophy case" of grace—we eternally exist "to the praise of his glorious grace" (Eph 1:6; cf. v. 12)—and we are this because we evidence God's brilliance and power in bringing about the destruction of his foes, and thus the liberation of his people.[25]

On a strictly natural level this plan appears absurd. For it is painfully obvious that the church is, and has always been, full of a great deal that does not in any way glorify God. Let us be honest: the church has always been a very human and a very fallen institution, exhibiting all the carnality, pettiness, narrowness, self-centeredness and abusive power tendencies that characterize all other fallen human institutions. On the surface we hardly look like trophies God would want to showcase.

What we must understand, however, is that far from disqualifying us from this divine service, this radical incongruity between what the church looks like and what God nevertheless uses it for is precisely the reason why God uses it. The church unambiguously proclaims the glory of God to the angelic society, and especially to the defeated principalities and powers, precisely by obviously lacking any "glory" of its own to proclaim. The church's very weakness and vulnerability is what displays the strength of God in freeing us and in using us to finish up his battles (2 Cor 12:7-10). The enemies of God are mocked (Col 2:15) by his employment of their own former slaves to finish up the war.

This is consistent with how God has operated throughout history. He has always chosen to use the foolish and weak things of the world to overthrow the "wise" and "strong" in the world who resist him (1 Cor 1:18-30). Thus for the same reason that God chose to slay a multitude of Philistines with the "foolishness" of a jawbone wielded by a man of questionable character (Judg 15:15), for the same reason that God chose to slay Goliath by the "foolishness" of a stone slung by a young shepherd boy (1 Sam 17:45-52), and for the same reason that God chose to save the world through the "foolishness" of preaching about a crucified first-century Jewish carpenter (1 Cor 1:18), so the Lord now chooses to carry out his coup de grâce of the enemy by the foolishness of his church, these weak, struggling, imperfect people whose only qualification for warfare is that they have said yes to the Lord's gracious invitation to be set free.

The church not only is a benefactor of Christ's cosmic victory but is also called to play a vital cosmic function in Christ's victory. We the church, in all our foolishness, are called to manifest on earth and in heaven Christ's kingdom-building ministry, taking what is already true in principle because of what he has done and manifesting it as accomplished reality by what we do. In this way "the wisdom of God in its rich variety" is declared to the principalities and powers.

This wisdom we are to manifest obviously includes the deliverance of humans from Satan's kingdom (Col 1:13), hence we are to be vitally interested in saving individual souls. But in contrast to far too much modern conservative Christian thinking, the saving of individuals does not exhaust the content of what the church should be about as we proclaim God's manifold wisdom. To the contrary, as we have seen, the wisdom revealed in Christ Jesus, the very wisdom we are to proclaim, was cosmic before it was anthropological.

Just as our redemption is a feature of Christ's broader cosmic accomplishments, so too the church's passion to save individuals should be a feature of our burden to manifest Christ's victory over his cosmic foes in all areas of life. For example, since part of God's goal all along has been to restore humans to their rightful place as caring (not tyrannizing) stewards of the earth, since Christ has in principle accomplished this by freeing us from the lordship of Satan, and since the restoration of nature is throughout Scripture understood to be one dimension of God's eschatological vision, the church can hardly dismiss ecological concerns as being outside the parameters of its "spiritual" interests. Quite the contrary, through prayer and activism we are called to "curse the curse" and to free the earth from all forms of spiritual and physical destructive oppression, or rather to manifest the truth that the earth is in principle already freed from such oppression. The corrupted angelic guardians of nature have been defeated, and it is time for the church to proclaim it.

So too, since Christ has in principle defeated the fallen "gods" (principalities and powers) who have for ages inspired injustice, cruelty and apathy toward the weak, the poor, the oppressed and the needy (Ps 82), the church can hardly carry out its role in manifesting, on earth and in heaven, Christ's victory over these gods without taking up as a central part of its mission just these causes. We can, in truth, no more bifurcate social concerns and individual salvation than we can bifurcate the cosmic and anthropocentric dimensions of Christ's work on the cross.

To cite one more example, if Christ on the cross has in fact torn down the racial wall of separation that divided people-groups (Eph 2:11-22), and if his Spirit now seeks to manifest this by reversing the effects of the catastrophe at the tower of Babel (Acts 2:5-12), then the church has no choice but to seek to manifest this reality as intensely as we have sought to manifest the reality that the forgiveness for our individual sins was purchased on the cross. In other words, that racism has ended ought to be as demonstrable in the church—to our culture and in the face of the (now defeated) spiritual powers of racism—as is the gospel truth that personal condemnation has ended.

This is our part in spiritual war. We proclaim Christ's truth by praying it, speaking it and (undoubtedly most importantly) by demonstrating it. We are not to accept with serene pious resignation the evil aspects of our world as "coming from a father's hand." Rather, following the example of our Lord and Savior, and going forth with the confidence that he has in principle already defeated his (and our) foes, we are to revolt against the evil aspects of our world as coming from the devil's hand. Our revolt is to be broad—as broad as the evil we seek to confront, and as broad as the work of the cross we seek to proclaim. Wherever there is destruction, hatred, apathy, injustice, pain or hopelessness, whether it concerns God's creation, a structural feature of society, or the physical, psychological or spiritual aspect of an individual, we are in word and deed to proclaim to the evil powers that be, "You are defeated." As Jesus did, we proclaim this by demonstrating it.

The divine comedy. Another dimension of "the wisdom of God in its rich variety" we have not yet considered is a dimension of the gospel that is rarely seriously discussed in Christian circles today (especially among Protestants). But it was a significant feature of the New Testament's proclamation, and it played a vital role in the theology of the early postapostolic church. Our own appreciation for the rich variety of God's wisdom is increased by recovering it.

I am referring to the prevalent early church view that in the death and resurrection of Christ, God actually outsmarted Satan and his legions with the result that they ultimately brought about their own demise. "None of the rulers of this age understood [God's secret wisdom]," Paul writes, "for if they had, they would not have crucified the Lord of glory" (1 Cor 2:8).

Perhaps blinded by their inability to understand love, even those demons who seemed to know who Jesus was could not understand why he had come to earth (Mk 1:24; 5:7; Lk 8:21), an ignorance apparently shared by higher demonic powers ("rulers of this age") as well. Since his early attempt in the desert to tempt Jesus into collaboration with his evil kingdom had failed miserably, Satan, along with his rulers, apparently set about to seize what they thought was a moment of vulnerability (viz., the Son is now human) and had Jesus crucified. Indeed, according to John, Satan possessed Judas for the express purpose of inciting him to betray Jesus and bring about the crucifixion (Jn 13:27).

The greatest irony in all of history, however, is that Satan and his minions were all the while playing right into God's hands, precisely when they thought they were striking a decisive blow against him. In a genius stroke of military planning, God seems to have tricked Satan into signing his own death warrant. The cross was God's plan, but it was carried out by "the rulers," and thanks to these foiled rulers, it brought about Christ's—not Satan's—victory.

It seems that God used Satan's insatiable lust for more (viz., his desire to capture the Son) to take away what Satan had already acquired (his captives). The "foolishness" of the cross thus made fools of God's opponents and demonstrated God's wisdom in liberating his children from their captivity. As we saw above, throughout eternity these liberated children will declare to all the "powers" the manifold wisdom of God that made a mockery of God's opponents, that freed them from their sins, that employed them in all their frailty to finish up his warfare work, and that made these former slaves into coheirs on the throne of God over all the earth.

This reading was by far the most popular way in which the warfare significance of the cross and resurrection was thought through in the early postapostolic church. Sometimes called "the fishhook theory," it portrayed Christ as "bait" that God used to "hook" Satan. The theory at times became remarkably extravagant, as when God was portrayed as deceptively giving Christ to Satan as a "ransom" for his children, only to take him back again. However, though a fair amount of fantasy was often interwoven into the conception, and though the way in which this "outsmarting" was articulated at times expressed a less-than-ideal view of God (viz., God was deceptive), the core of the concept is biblical. God used Satan's evil to bring about Satan's own demise. Just this constitutes a central dimension of "God's wisdom, secret and hidden."

This reading of 1 Corinthians 2:8 is not unanimous, however. A minority of scholars argue that the term *archontōn* in this passage refers to human rulers.[26] Their case is usually argued along one or more of three lines, which we do well to address briefly.

First, many point out that the plural *archontōn* is nowhere else used of demonic beings in the New Testament. Second, some argue that the immediate context fits better with human rather than demonic rulers. Third, others argue that the interpretation of *archontōn* as human rulers is more consistent with the New Testament teaching as a whole, since elsewhere demons are portrayed as knowing who Jesus was.

None of these arguments is strong, in my estimation.[27] Concerning the first argument that the plural of *archōn* is not elsewhere used of demonic beings in the New Testament, we must consider four refutations.

☐ The singular *archōn* is certainly used to refer to a demonic being (Satan) numerous times (e.g., Mk 3:22; Jn 12:31; 14:30; 16:11; Eph 2:2), which is enough to show that a plural use of this term referring to demonic powers would be entirely possible.

☐ A plural form of *archē* is used several times to refer to demonic beings (Eph 3:10; 6:12; Col 1:16; 2:15), and no one has yet demonstrated that *archē* and *archōn* differ precisely in that the plural form of the latter, but not the former, can refer only to human rulers. Moreover, the plural use of *archē* in the New Testament is enough to show that the New Testament has no theological reservation about referring to a plurality of demonic powers as "rulers." This clearly opens up the possibility of understanding *archontōn* as referring to, or at least as including, just such supernatural "rulers."

☐ The word sampling in the New Testament is so small that it is always dangerous to make too much of the absence of a particular form of a particular word within this literary collection. The same logic that would prohibit *archontōn* from referring to demonic rulers in 1 Corinthians 2:6-8 might also rule out understanding Matthew 8:31 to be referring to "demons" simply because it is the only place where the plural of *daimōn* (as opposed to the more usual *daimonion*) is used. But for obvious reasons no one argues in this fashion concerning this use of the singular form.

☐ Finally, a precedent for reading 1 Corinthians 2:6-8 as referring to demonic beings is found in the Septuagint translation of Daniel 10:13. Here Michael is said to be the chief angel among the "rulers" *(archontōn)*. What is more, a precedent for understanding *archontōn* in this fashion is found in later church fathers.[28] Indeed, it is difficult to understand how the "fishhook" and "deception" theories of the atonement came about, let alone became dominant, unless *archontōn* in 1 Corinthians 2:8 was taken as referring to demonic principalities and powers by the earliest church fathers.

The second and third arguments against reading *archontōn* as referring to demonic rulers are even weaker. The immediate literary context, the wider Pauline theological context and the general teaching of the New Testament favor reading *archontōn* as referring to demonic powers.

Consider the following five arguments.

□ It is true that following Paul's reference to the *archontōn*, he proceeds quickly to contrast "those who are spiritual," who understand the wisdom of God, with "those who are unspiritual," for whom the wisdom of God is "foolishness" (1 Cor 2:14-15). But this does not itself imply that he has only human rulers in mind in 2:6-8. The more fundamental contrast being made throughout this passage is between "the spirit of the world" and "the Spirit that is from God" (2:12). As in John, for Paul human divisions exemplify more fundamental spiritual divisions. Satan is, for Paul, "the spirit that is now at work among those who are disobedient" (Eph 2:2) and "the god of this world" who has "blinded the minds of the unbelievers" (2 Cor 4:4). Given this perspective, it is difficult not to suppose that Paul has both ungodly human and demonic beings in mind when he speaks of "the rulers of this age."

□ The reading of *archontōn* as including demonic rulers fits in best with the apocalyptic orientation of Paul's thought. The political state that is at war with God—demonstrated in the crucifixion of his Son—is a state that is significantly controlled by powers that are at war with God. As a number of commentators have noted, such a reading of 1 Corinthians 2:6-8 is thoroughly at home in an apocalyptic context.[29]

□ Conversely, reading *archontōn* as referring only to human rulers seems a bit awkward, especially when read in this apocalyptic context. Such a reading, while in sync with modern sensibilities, grants more significance and autonomy to political powers than Jewish apocalyptic thought was usually inclined to grant. But even beyond this, the connection between earthly powers and God's wisdom seems stretched on this reading. As Conzelmann succinctly poses the question, "What should earthly powers have to do with supernatural wisdom?"[30] If *archontōn* here refers merely to earthly rulers, it seems we are comparing apples with oranges. Posed otherwise, why would Paul or anyone expect that pagan earthly rulers would know the wisdom of God? Why would he think that if they had known this wisdom, they would not have crucified Jesus?

□ Further, it is difficult to understand how the "rulers of this age" are "coming to nothing" (1 Cor 2:6 NIV), and are doing so because they ignorantly crucified the Lord of glory, if these rulers are mere humans. In the light of Paul's strong teaching about how Jesus' death and resurrection is the means by which the spiritual opponents of God are ultimately to be destroyed, it is much easier to read *archontōn* as referring primarily to demonic powers (and to human authorities only as expressions of this demonic kingdom).

☐ Finally, the fact that the Synoptic Gospels portray demons as sometimes knowing who Jesus is hardly counts against understanding 1 Corinthians 2:6-8 as including demonic powers. After all, it was not "the Lord of glory" whom the "rulers" did not know, according to Paul. It was rather "God's wisdom, secret and hidden" (2:6). As in the Synoptic Gospels, the demonic powers know very well who Jesus is. What they are unable to understand is the secret wisdom of God in sending him to earth. Hence demons in the Synoptic Gospels ask continually, "Why have you come?" Thus we can imagine that it was precisely because of this ignorance that they unwittingly played into God's master plan, a plan that apparently wisely anticipated their ignorance. This reading of 1 Corinthians 2:6 and 8 thus squares perfectly with, and even sheds further light on, the Gospels.

I thus conclude that we have every reason to interpret Paul in this passage as teaching that it was the demonic powers who were ultimately behind the crucifixion of Jesus, and that in doing this these powers unwittingly played into God's hand. For in crucifying the Lord of glory Satan and his legions sealed their own doom (cf. Col 2:14-15).

Tying up the strong man and releasing the captives. We see, then, that part of the wisdom which the church is to proclaim—and perhaps part of what Christ himself proclaimed (*kēryssō*) when, according to the dominant tradition, he descended into "prison" to announce his victory to the rebellious spirits (1 Pet 3:19-20)—is that God orchestrated the destruction of Satan's empire by having it devour itself through its own evil. The cross and resurrection were the central means of this downfall, and God used Satan himself to bring it about.

This brilliant victory over the rebel powers through the foolishness of the cross stands at the center of everything the New Testament is about. It certainly is the presupposition of every feature of the anthropological significance of the cross. We now add that it is the presupposition of every aspect of Christian living, for Christian life is, in the end, simply life lived to manifest the truth of what Christ accomplished.

For example, John writes that because Christ has already overcome Satan, the one who is ultimately behind all sin (1 Jn 3:8,12; 4:3, etc.), believers too can "overcome the evil one" (1 Jn 2:13-14) and live free from sin (Jn 3:6, 9; 5:18). We can now overcome "that ancient serpent, who is called the Devil and Satan, the deceiver of the whole world," for we war against him "by the blood of the Lamb and by the word of [our] testimony" (Rev 12:9, 11). Our freedom and our victory, we again see, are predicated on Christ's shed blood and hence his victory over our former ruler, Satan.

The author of Hebrews expresses the same prioritization when he writes that Christ shared in our humanity "so that through death he might destroy the one who has the power of death, that is, the devil" (2:14). The consequence of this, he adds, is to "free those who all their lives were held in slavery by the fear of death" (2:15). Before the chains of death could be broken, the "strong man" who tyrannized us with them had to be "tied up" (Mt 12:29) or "destroyed." Before those imprisoned in his kingdom could be released, he had to be bound. This is precisely what Christ's death accomplished. To state it in Johannine terms, the cross "drove out" the "ruler of this world" (Jn 12:31) and condemned him (16:11). The result, for all who will receive it, is freedom.[31]

This conception of salvation as deliverance from Satan is clearly expressed in the Lord's commissioning to the newly converted Saul of Tarsus:

> I am sending you [to the Gentiles] to open their eyes so that they may turn from darkness to light and from the power of Satan to God, so that they may receive forgiveness of sins and a place among those who are sanctified by faith in me. (Acts 26:17-18)

In the light of Satan's defeat because of the cross, proclaiming the good news means offering people a chance to "escape from the snare of the devil, having been held captive by him to do his will" (2 Tim 2:26).[32] When they receive the liberating life of Christ into their life, they are "set free from this present evil age" (Gal 1:4), forgiven their sins, and made righteous by the blood of Jesus Christ.

So too Paul can encourage the Christians at Colosse to give thanks "to the Father, who has enabled you to share in the inheritance of the saints in the light" (Col 1:12). He then tells them what this qualification consists of: "He has rescued us from the power of darkness and transferred us into the kingdom of his beloved Son, in whom we have redemption, the forgiveness of sins" (1:13-14).

What "enables" us to participate in the inheritance of the saints is the fact that our former slavery to the strong man has been abolished. Satan has been defeated, and the sin that gave him authority over us has been canceled. Hence we have been "rescued" from one kingdom and transported (*methistēmi*) into another.[33] We have, in a word, been literally "saved" (Eph 2:5, 8).[34]

This is the same thought that lies behind another passage in Colossians, one of the most victorious passages found in the whole Bible:

> He forgave us all our trespasses, erasing the record that stood against us with its legal demands. He set this aside, nailing it to the cross. He disarmed the rulers and authorities and made a public example of them, triumphing over them in it. (Col 2:13-15)

"Record" (*cheirographon*) most probably refers to an official certificate of indebtedness.[35] For Paul, it here stands for everything believers ever did, or did not do, which sold them into slavery to the enemy and set them at war with God. This metaphorical document, Paul then says, Christ "erased" (*exaleiphō*, literally "wiped clean") by removing it from us and nailing it to the cross. This last phrase is likely an allusion to the tablet fixed over a criminal's head describing the crimes for which the criminal is crucified.[36] Paul is graphically saying that Christ was crucified "for our transgressions" (Is 53:5). As he elsewhere puts it, God made Christ "to be sin . . . so that in him we might become the righteousness of God" (2 Cor 5:21).

In doing all this, Paul then says, Christ "disarmed" or "stripped away" (*apekdyomai*) the weapons of the demonic powers (Col 2:15).[37] He seems to have specifically in mind the power of these spiritual rulers to condemn believers. They have, quite literally, nothing more on the believer who stands righteous and holy in Jesus Christ (Rom 8:1, 31-34). The certificate of indebtedness has been canceled. Thus the tyrants who once ruled over us are now made into a "public example" or "public spectacle" (NIV), a likely reference to a military general leading his captives through the streets of his kingdom to display his victory over the vanquished army.[38]

The passage is clearly speaking about the significance of the cross for us by weaving together its anthropocentric and cosmic dimensions. The cross triumphed over God's enemies. The war that had been waged for eons was here, in principle, brought to a close. What this means for us is total and unconditional freedom. We are no longer slaves to demonic condemnation, for everything Satan and his legions could ever condemn us for was destroyed in the same act that destroyed them.

Indeed, Paul can go so far in expressing our freedom from demonic powers as to say that we "with Christ died to the elemental spirits of the universe" (Col 2:20). Even more, Paul insists that we "have come to fullness in [Christ], who is the head of every ruler and authority" (2:10). Not only are we dead to demonic powers, but we have within us, according to Paul, the very same power over them that Christ himself has.[39]

The descent into prison. Closely related to this theme is the earlier mentioned depiction of Christ's descent into prison, a theme that vividly captured the imagination of the early church. Two passages in particular address this theme.

The first passage that addresses this theme is the earlier cited 1 Peter 3:18-20.

> For Christ also suffered for sins once for all, the righteous for the unrighteous, in order to bring you to God. He was put to death in the flesh, but made alive in the spirit, in which also he went and made a proclamation to the spirits in prison, who in former times did not obey, when God waited patiently in the days of Noah, during the building of the ark.

Three basic interpretations have been offered regarding the identity of the "spirits in prison" referred to in this passage.[40] Calvin suggested that the "spirits" here are the souls of faithful Old Testament saints.[41] Few have followed him. A number of scholars have argued that the "spirits" are the souls of people killed in the flood.[42] But the majority of scholars, past and present, have argued that these "spirits" are the fallen angels or the demonic offspring of their hybrid union with women referred to (according to the Watcher tradition; see chapter six above) in Genesis 6:1-4.[43]

The majority view seems the most compelling. While I cannot fully enter into the issues presently, three basic considerations are worth mentioning. First, the New Testament never elsewhere refers to deceased human beings as "spirits" in an unqualified way, as Peter does here. Rather, it uses the term *psychē* (soul). "Spirits," unless qualified, always refers to nonhuman spiritual beings.[44]

Second, only the third interpretation gives adequate weight to the unusual fact that the spirits here are distinctly associated with the Noachian judgment. If the Lord is here preaching to deceased humans, why limit his audience to those involved in the flood?

The reference to the Genesis 6 rebellion unmistakably brings to mind the Watcher tradition, which in turn makes highly unlikely any suggestion that Peter does not have in mind here fallen angels (or the demons that sprang from them). In fact, and most significantly, this tradition had already spoken of the fallen angels ("stars of heaven") who transgressed their assigned places in Genesis 6 as being bound in prison.[45] Given the prevalence of this tradition in the culture within which Peter is writing (see chapter six above), it seems quite improbable that he is not here appropriating something like this conception.

Finally, the third interpretation fits best with the verses that immediately follow this passage. Peter ties in the flood with Christian baptism (vv. 20-21), which, as is well known, was associated primarily with deliverance from evil spirits in the early church.[46] Then, in typical New Testament fashion, he associates the significance of baptism with Christ's resurrection (v. 21), and Christ's resurrection with his exaltation to "the right hand of God, with angels, authorities, and powers made subject to him" (v. 22).

It is difficult to avoid linking Christ's proclamation to the spirits in prison with this angelic submission to him. In my view, Christ announced (*kēryssō*, not "evangelized" [*euangelizō*], as in 1 Pet 1:12, 25; 4:6) the victory he had accomplished on the cross (Col 2:15) to spirits that had been put in "chains of deepest darkness to be kept until the judgment" (2 Pet 2:4).[47] It was his first official act as the new ruler of this once enslaved planet, and the act whereby their submission to him became explicit.

The second passage is only slightly less controversial regarding the theme of Christ's "descent." It is found in Ephesians 4:7-10.

> But each of us was given grace according to the measure of Christ's gift. Therefore it is said:
> "When he ascended on high he made captivity itself a captive;
> he gave gifts to his people."
> (When it says, "He ascended," what does it mean but that he also descended into the lower parts of the earth? He who descended is the same one who ascended far above all the heavens, so that he might fill all things.)

What is indisputable about this passage is that Paul is illustrating Christ's victory over his enemies at the resurrection and ascension by drawing an illustration from Psalm 68. The fundamental point of the passage is to liken Christ's ascension after he conquered his enemies on the cross to David's ascent on Mount Zion after he conquered his enemies (see Ps

68:11-18). The reasoning of the passage is that Christ's victorious ascension, like David's, presupposes a warring "descension." Christ descended into battle, and he ascended victorious, "leading captives in [his] train" (Ps 68:18). Like a victorious king, he divided the spoils of his conquest among those in his kingdom—"he gave gifts to his people" (Eph 4:8).

This much is not disputed, and it is itself enough to demonstrate that this passage provides one more illustration of the centrality of the warfare motif for the New Testament's understanding of the significance of the cross and resurrection.[48] There is, however, a good amount of scholarly debate concerning what exactly Christ's "descent" refers to, and what "the lower parts of the earth" refers to. Again, to speak most generally, three interpretations have been offered.[49]

First, some take "the lower parts of the earth" to be simply a reference to the earth, and hence interpret the descent Paul is speaking of as Christ's incarnation.[50] But an increasing number of noteworthy scholars have argued that the "descent" refers to the descent of the Holy Spirit after Christ's victorious ascension.[51] The view most rooted in the church tradition, however, is that the descent refers to Christ's descent into Hades.[52] It is, in my estimation, also the view most rooted in the evidence. While I again cannot begin to explore all the issues surrounding these different interpretations, five considerations are worth briefly mentioning.

First, in the context of Hellenistic thought, Paul's phrase *katōtera merē tēs gēs* ("lower earthly realms") is most easily taken as a reference to the "underworld."[53] Second, that this phrase stands in contrast to the place where Christ ascended, "far above all the heavens," suggests that he is referring to a place which is antithetical to this (viz., the lowest regions).[54] Third, as Dunn notes, the genitive following *merē* ("realms") "most naturally denotes the whole to which the parts belong—parts of the earth, rather than parts which are the earth."[55] This again argues against the descent being simply to earth, whether as incarnate Son or as Spirit.

Fourth, and more decisively, this reading closely parallels Romans 10:6-7, which explicitly contrasts the ascent with Christ's descent "into the abyss" *(abyssos)*, a term that elsewhere always refers to hell (Lk 8:31; Rev 9:1-2, 11; 11:7; 17:8; 20:1, 3). This parallel renders it extremely likely that this is what is intended by the descent and ascent pattern in

Ephesians, especially if one grants the Pauline authorship of Ephesians. That this reading also parallels 1 Peter 3:18-19 quite closely (on the reading I have argued for) adds a bit more weight to reading Ephesians 4:8-9 as referring to a descent into Hades.

Finally, and perhaps most significantly, the Hades interpretation alone parallels what we have seen is the common New Testament pattern of intimately linking the death and resurrection of Christ with the subjection of God's foes. Just as the resurrection carries with it the prior thought of his death, so here, according to Dunn, "the assertion of his ascension (a formulation determined by the quotation from Ps. 68.18) carries with it the thought of his (prior) descent into the place of the dead."[56]

All of this links perfectly, according to the New Testament pattern, with seeing Christ as taking principalities and powers captive. Following the pattern of Colossians 2:15, the death and resurrection of Christ are understood to bring about the subjection of all powers that formerly enslaved people, a view that, incidentally, is strongly supported by the fact that Paul had previously talked of Christ's exaltation over the enslaving powers (1:21-22; cf. 2:2).[57] While no systematic account can be deduced from such vague references as we have in Ephesians and 1 Peter, it seems that after his death Christ somehow descended into hell and enslaved all his enemies, viz., all who had formerly enslaved humanity.

Hugo Odeberg summarizes this interpretation well in a manner that discloses its continuity with both the cosmic warfare and cosmic redemption motifs of the New Testament:

> Christ's descent has a cosmical, universal import. To save mankind he must grapple with and become victor over, vanquish, the cosmical powers and the evil agencies in their totality and he must pursue them into the farthest recesses of their activity. He must, hence, go beyond the surface-world, in which fallen mankind dwells, to the depths of Darkness, the utmost sphere of the authority of evil.[58]

Redeemed from slavery. Finally, one of the most frequent and fundamental ways in which the New Testament depicts our salvation as a freeing consequence of Christ's cosmic victory over Satan is by referring to it as "redemption" (Rom 3:24; 8:23; 1 Cor 1:30; Eph 1:7, 14; 4:30; Col 1:12; Heb 9:12; Tit 2:14; 1 Pet 1:18-19; Rev 14:3).[59] The root of this term *lytron* means a "ransom" or "price of release," and the term "redemption" (*apolytrōsis*) was "almost a technical term in the ancient world for the purchase or manumission of a slave."[60] As applied to believers in the New Testament, it implies that our salvation consists fundamentally in being freed from a form of slavery.

According to the New Testament, we are set free from slavery to sin and guilt (Rom 6:7, 18-20; Col 1:22; Heb 9:15; Rev 1:5) as well as from the law as a way of trying to acquire righteousness before God (Rom 3:20-21; Gal 2:16, 19-21; 5:1). But the most fundamental reality we are set free from is the devil.[61] We were slaves to sin and condemnation primarily because we were slaves to Satan. In "redeeming us" out of this slavery, in rescuing us out of this kingdom (Col 1:13; Gal 1:4), Christ in principle bought us out of every other form of slavery as well. The price of this redemption, Peter tells us, was "not . . . perishable things like silver or gold, but . . . the precious blood of Christ" (1 Pet 1:18). For this reason as well, Jesus himself describes his life as a "ransom" (*lytros*, Mk 10:45; Mt 20:28; cf. 1 Tim 2:6; Heb 9:15).

Of course, we need not accept all, or any, of the extravagant and sometimes crude ways the postapostolic church attempted to explain how, and to whom, this ransom was paid.[62] We need not, for example, construe this redemption as God literally "buying off" Satan with Christ's life (and then taking it back?). The thrust of Scripture is only to say this much: Christ was willing to do whatever it took—to pay whatever "price" was necessary—in order to defeat the tyrant who had enslaved us and thereby to set us free. What it took, the New Testament teaches, was nothing less than the Son of God becoming a man and dying a hellish death upon the cross.

In some mysterious way, this event "disarmed," "drove out," "tied up," "condemned" and "destroyed" the "god of this age" who had held us in slavery (Col 2:15; Jn 12:31; 16:11; 2 Cor 4:4; Heb 2:14). It thereby enthroned the Son of God as rightful king of his Father's universe, which is where he was eternally destined to be. And it therefore spelled freedom, liberation, redemption and complete salvation for all those previously enslaved subjects who were willing to receive it. Indeed, it shall ultimately reestablish us as the lords over the earth we were always meant to be.

 The cross and resurrection, then, were not first and foremost about us. They were about overcoming evil. From a New Testament perspective, evil is something much greater, much more powerful and much more pervasive than what transpires in our relatively small lives, on our relatively small segment of the cosmos, by means of our relatively small wills. This is not to suggest that we are ourselves not evil, for the New Testament unequivocally concludes that, apart from Christ, we are. We were, indeed, "dead through [our] trespasses" (Eph 2:1). Hence we were in desperate need for a high priest to enter into the sanctuary and offer up a perfect sacrifice to atone for our sins (Rom 8:34; Heb 7:25; 10:10-14; 1 Jn 2:2). Christ made this offering, effecting our salvation to the glory of God the Father.

But Christ did this only because he did something even more fundamental, as we have seen: he dealt a death blow to Satan and recaptured his rightful rule over the whole creation. This is, first and foremost, what Jesus' ministry, death and resurrection are all about. Evil can be overcome in our life only because the "evil one" who previously ruled the cosmos has himself in principle been overcome. We are set free only because the entire cosmos has in principle been set free from the one who had previously enslaved it. And we are reconciled to God only because the entire cosmos, and the whole of the spiritual realm, has in principle been reconciled to God.

What pertains to us most is that we are forgiven. Thus it is natural that Scripture, and therefore our preaching, focuses a great deal on this crucial dimension of Christ's work. But to try to make this the primary, let alone exhaustive, significance of Jesus' death and resurrection is to miss the cosmic dimension of God's solution to the problem of evil; it is to miss the cosmic dimension of the problem of evil itself; and it is to miss the cosmic dimension of the church's calling to revolt against all forms of evil in order to demonstrably proclaim Jesus' victory over them.

Concerning the New Testament's view of "salvation" James Kallas concludes:

since the cosmos itself is in bondage, depressed under evil forces, the essential content of the word "salvation" is that the world itself will be rescued, or renewed, or set free. Salvation is a cosmic event affecting the whole of creation. It is not simply the internal renewal of man's religious attitude. . . . Salvation is not simply the overcoming of my rebellion and the forgiveness of my guilt, but salvation is the liberation of the whole world process of which I am only a small part.[63]

When this cosmic dimension is lost, Kallas continues, salvation comes "to be seen as a personal affair, an individual thing." It is, he insists, an "egocentric" interpretation. "In the deepest sense," Kallas continues,

"God is [here] denied any independent existence—he exists only to serve and to save man, a celestial errand runner."[64] This is precisely what he believes has happened with the classic Protestant substitutionary understanding of the atonement.

When we view redemption theocentrically rather than anthropocentrically, however, and when we therefore see human salvation as an aspect of a universal cosmic restoration, we see both God's glory and humanity's redemption in the most exalted terms imaginable.

10

ENGAGING
THE POWERS

THE CHRISTIAN
LIFE AS SPIRITUAL
WARFARE

*A*S THE LAST CHAPTER MADE CLEAR, THE SINGLE MOST FREQUENT, and important, thing the canonical epistles say about the devil and his kingdom of powers and demons is that they have been defeated by the death and resurrection of Christ. The confident proclamation of Christ's victory resounds throughout the whole of the New Testament. But this is not the only thing these writings have to say about the demonic realm. Since we live in the dynamic tension between the "already/not yet" of Christ's victory, these defeated forces yet have to be reckoned with. Between the D-day of the cross and the V-day of the eschaton, there are battles yet to be fought.[1] Though Satan is in principle defeated, we still need to be rescued "from the present evil age" (Gal 1:4) and to "struggle . . . against the rulers, against the authorities, against the cosmic powers of this present darkness, against the spiritual forces of evil in the heavenly places" (Eph 6:12). The New Testament has a good deal to say about what this struggle looks like, how it is to be fought, and how it shall be won. This is what this final chapter concerns.

In what follows, then, I first examine the various ways Paul and other

New Testament writers refer to Satan and demonic powers, followed by an overview of how they understand the ongoing activity of this realm in the world and against the church. I conclude with a brief discussion of what these authors say about the origin and ultimate destiny of these powers.

The New Testament's Conception of the Demonic Realm

In most respects Acts and the Epistles follow quite closely the terminology of the apocalyptic thought of their time in referring to the demonic realm.[2] But they identify the head of this realm as Satan much more consistently than apocalyptic writings do, though Paul also refers to him as Belial (2 Cor 6:15).[3] In most other respects the identification of this chief evil ruler (Eph 2:2) is thoroughly in keeping with apocalyptic thought.

The variety of apocalyptic terms. Satan is also referred to throughout these writings as "the devil" (Acts 10:38; 13:10; Eph 4:27; 6:11; 1 Tim 3:6-7; 2 Tim 2:26; Heb 2:14; Jas 3:15; 4:7; 1 Jn 3:8, 10), the "god of this world" (2 Cor 4:4), the "evil one" (Eph 6:16; 2 Thess 3:3) and "the enemy" (1 Tim 5:14). He is further identified as "the tempter" and "the serpent" of Genesis 3 (2 Cor 11:3; 1 Thess 3:5; Rev 12:9; 20:2). Paul also identifies him as an "angel of light" (2 Cor 11:14), while John taps into the Old Testament traditions of Leviathan and identifies him as "the great dragon" (Rev 12:9; 20:2). None of this terminology is unique to the New Testament.

The many references to lesser demonic figures follow the same pattern. As in the Gospels, they are often referred to simply as demons (Rom 8:38; 1 Cor 10:20-21; 1 Tim 4:1; Jas 2:19; Rev 9:20; 16:14; 18:2). Other times they are referred to as messengers or angels (Rom 8:38; 1 Cor 6:3; 11:10?; 2 Cor 12:7; Gal 1:8; Col 2:18; 1 Pet 3:22; Jude 6; Rev 12:7, 9).

Still other times, especially in Paul, we find suprahuman beings, some good and some evil, referred to in more esoteric apocalyptic terminology. Hence Paul sometimes refers to what appear to be high-level angelic beings as *archai* or *archontes* ("rulers" or "principalities," Rom 8:38; 1 Cor 2:6, 8; 15:24; Eph 1:21; 3:10; 6:12; Col 1:16; 2:10, 15). He seems to be referring to other high-level classes of beings with the terms *exousiai* and *dynameis* ("powers" or "authorities," Rom 8:38; 13:1?; 1 Cor 15:24; Eph 1:21; 2:2; 3:10; 6:12; Col 1:16; 2:10, 15), and to still other classes of heavenly beings with the terms *kyriotētos* ("dominion," Eph 1:21; Col 1:16), *kosmokratores* ("cosmic powers," Eph 6:12), *thronoi* ("thrones," Col 1:16) and *pneumatika* ("spiritual forces," Eph 6:12).[4] Finally, he is in all probability referring to something akin to "angels of nature" with his phrase *stoicheia tou kosmou* ("elemental spirits of the universe," Col 2:8, 20; Gal 4:3, 8-9).[5]

It is more than likely that these terms overlap with one another in some instances, but in general it seems clear that some sort of hierarchical distinction is being made.[6] In this regard, neither Paul nor any other New Testament author is unique. These various ways of referring to different classes or types of good or evil divine beings were already in place in the apocalyptic thought of Paul's day. For example, *2 Enoch* relates a vision in which the seer saw,

> an exceptionally great light, and all the fiery armies of the great archangels, and the incorporeal forces [*dynameis*] and the dominions [*kyriotētes*] and the origins [*archai*] and the authorities [*exousiai*], the cherubim and the seraphim and the many-eyed thrones [*thronoi*]. (20:1)[7]

Similarly, *1 Enoch* contains a prophecy of the end times that states that God will summon

> all the forces [*dynameis*] of the heavens and all the holy ones above, and the forces of the Lord—the cherubim, seraphim, ophanim, all the angels of governance [*archai*], the Elect One, and the other forces [*exousiai*] on earth and over the water. (61:10)[8]

Indeed, not only were concepts circulating in Jewish culture, but as Arnold argues, they are found in Gentile texts as well.[9] Thus while these terms may indeed be somewhat opaque to us, in all likelihood they were not so to Paul's original audience.

The opaqueness of this terminology to us, however, means that we are clueless as to exactly how Paul thought the demonic realm was structured. That the "world in between" was hierarchically structured is as clear for Paul as it was for Jesus.[10] But like Jesus, and quite unlike many apocalyptic writers of his day, Paul never speculates on the details of the ranks and functions of the various levels of demonic beings.

The significance of the powers. A number of studies in relatively recent times have elucidated the cosmological and societal dimension of these concepts as used in Paul and in apocalyptic thought in general. To summarize the trend in a general fashion, since the publication of two short monographs by Heinrich Schlier and Hendrikus Berkhof, a number of scholars have argued in the direction that the "powers" and "authorities" in Paul's terminology refer principally to "structures" created by God to preserve order within creation in general and within human society in particular.[11] Paul, it is argued, saw these structural forces as originally (and hence inherently) good, but as having become corrupt through the Fall. Hence, as they are now, they are hostile to God and stand in need of redemption.[12] Polluted with human sin, these forces become ends in themselves, and hence have become destructive idols. Indeed, they now form the skeleton of "the present evil age" (Gal 1:4). They thus need to be subjugated to the authority of Christ and made to serve his lordship.

Christ's crucifixion, it is sometimes added, was carried out under the authority of these powers. But it is this very crucifixion that in principle liberated these forces from their diabolic dimensions. The church, ministering within the interval between "the victory achieved" and "the victory manifested," is therefore called to bear witness against the diabolical corruption of these forces, and thereby to work to restore them to their original God-created place. Quite understandably, this line of interpretation has been strongly advocated by certain Anabaptist and liberation theologians who have become keenly aware of structural evil.[13]

There is, I believe, a great deal that is profoundly correct with this analysis of Paul's thought. The abstractness of Paul's language and the terms he employs suggest that he has in mind general rather than particular phenomena. His use of such phrases as "rulers," "powers," "dominions," "thrones" and "elemental spirits" depicts these forces as exercising a great deal of influence over general regions, realms or aspects of creation and society. As such, they are qualitatively different from the many references to particular demons that we find throughout the New Testament.

These "powers" seem not to hassle individuals so much as foundational structures of the whole cosmos and therefore of society. At the very least, then, there seems to be something more general, more powerful and more sinister (because less obvious) about the operation of the "powers" than there is about the work of particular demons. Paul's terminology seems to suggest this much, especially when read against an apocalyptic background.

Hence it seems appropriate to follow this scholarship and diagnose, say, idolatrous nationalism, or systematic political corruption, or societal racism, or Western materialism and so on as falling under the category of the "powers" Paul is referring to. It also seems appropriate, therefore, to understand part of the church's mission as its call to rise up against these powers. We are, in this understanding, called to take back for the Father all aspects of creation that do not conform to the lordship of Christ. Hence we are to fight systematic evil as forcefully as we are to fight individual evil.[14] Through prayer and social activism we are to labor toward exorcising the corrupted powers that structure fallen society as earnestly as we are to labor in exorcising individual demons out of individuals. This is a message that the church has needed, and still needs, to hear. This whole line of interpretation concerning Paul's terminology has served to remind us of this fact.

There is a downside to this approach, however, at least as some have carried it out. Following a tendency found in Schlier and Berkhof, a number of influential scholars have suggested that Paul altogether identified these "powers" with the "structures of earthly existence."[15] Paul "demythologized" the personal demonic apocalyptic understanding of these terms and construed them as impersonal aspects of God's good creation.[16] In other words, this view contends that the "powers" were not transcendent personal beings for Paul. Hence the only volition these "powers" have, according to this view, is the volition people who are under them give them.

For example, in discussing Colossians 1:16, Wink argues that "thrones" refers to "the institutionalizing of power in a set of symbols that guarantee its continuity over time," "dominions" refers to "the 'sphere of influence' the 'throne' possesses," and "principality" refers to "the incumbent in office . . . the investiture of power in a person." "Power" refers to "the legitimations and sanctions by which authority is maintained."[17] These "powers," Wink adds, are not simply human structures; Wink is not, strictly speaking, anthropologically reductionistic. But neither are the powers distinct from human structures, according to Wink. Rather, they are "the inner aspect of material or tangible manifestations of power," or "the inner or spiritual essence, or gestalt, of an institution or state or system."[18] Hence while these "Powers do not . . . have a separate spiritual existence," for Wink, they nevertheless are not "simply a 'personification' of institutional qualities." Rather, they exist "as a real aspect of the institution even when it is not perceived as such."[19]

One can easily understand why this reading of Paul would be attractive in our contemporary setting. It at once both squares with the modern proclivity to deny the actual autonomous existence of "the world in between" while also squaring with our post-World War II experience of the destructive potential of structural evil. Nevertheless, there are several problems with it.

First, it is difficult to deny that Paul had personal agents in mind when we read him in the light of the apocalyptic literature of this day. The parallels with Paul's terminology in apocalyptic and magical literature strongly suggest that Paul had personal beings in mind. For example, it is easy to see how moderns such as Schlier and Wink could take Paul's reference to "the ruler of the power of the air" (Eph 2:2) as a demythologized reference roughly equivalent to, say, "spiritual atmosphere."[20] But, as Clinton Arnold has demonstrated, it is difficult to maintain that Paul himself was demythologizing anything, for in his culture "air was regarded as the dwelling place of evil spirits in antiquity."[21]

Indeed, references to various "spirits of the air" abound at this time, and none of them can easily be taken as a metaphor for "spiritual atmosphere." For example, Beliar is called "an aerial spirit" (Testament of Benjamin 3:4), and in various magical texts people are protected from "every demon in the air" by calling on "the one who is in charge of the air."[22] In this light, the "ruler . . . of the air" Paul speaks of can hardly be understood as an impersonal atmospheric force. Rather, the expression refers to a personal god who controls the world by controlling "the air" (cf. 2 Cor 4:4).

Second, Paul clearly attributes to these "powers" something like personal activity, implying again that he sees them as personal agents. Hence immediately after calling Satan "the ruler of the power of the air," he adds that he is "the spirit that is now at work among those who are disobedient" (Eph 2:2). The "ruler" is clearly a personal agent, and Paul's portrayal of him as intentionally inspiring disobedience is strictly in keeping with similar portrayals of Satan in apocalyptic literature (cf. 1 Cor 5:4-5; 2 Cor 2:11; 11:14; 6:15).[23] So too, Paul's portrayal of demons as personal agents is completely in keeping with the apocalyptic thought of his day (1 Cor 10:19-21; 2 Cor 12:7).

Along the same lines, "our struggle" (palē) as believers is "against the rulers, against the authorities" (Eph 6:12), who are intentionally set against us as they carry out "the wiles of the devil" (6:11). This seems to go well beyond any demythologized conception of them as the "gestalt of institutions." So too, Colossians 2:14-15 implies that the powers are "armed" (and hence can be "disarmed") and can be humiliated, while still other passages imply that they can be subjugated, they can worship, they can rebel, they can be destroyed, and they can be reconciled. Such characterizations are not easy to square with the view that Paul is merely speaking about impersonal cosmic structures. It seems, rather, that Paul placed the "powers" on the same personalistic, transcendent, ontological level as he did Satan, demons and angels.[24]

In this respect, Paul's characterization of the "powers" differs from the way he speaks when he is clearly talking about structural aspects of creation. This is my third point. Paul and other New Testament authors frequently refer to such things as "the world," "the flesh" and "sin" as structural realities of this fallen existence from which people need to be freed.[25] While these realities are frequently personified, they are never portrayed as having any autonomous existence over against the people who constitute them.[26] Hence they are never portrayed as independently fighting against God or as ultimately submitting to God. In this respect, they differ from the "powers" Paul refers to, and this difference is one more indication that the "powers" are more than structural aspects of the cosmos.[27]

Finally, it is important to note that Paul explicitly distinguishes between "powers" in heaven and "powers" on the earth. Christ, Paul says, created all things "in heaven and on earth, things visible and invisible, whether thrones or dominions or rulers or powers" (Col 1:16). Through his victory on the cross, he shall reconcile to himself all these things, "whether on earth or in heaven" (Col 1:20; cf. Phil 2:9-11; Eph 1:10). Paul is clearly differentiating between powers on earth and powers in heaven, and hence the latter "powers" cannot be exhaustively reduced to the former.

The contrast between these two spheres of power is also brought out by Paul in Ephesians 6:12: "For our struggle is not against enemies of blood and flesh, but against the rulers, against the authorities, against the cosmic powers of this present darkness, against the spiritual forces of evil in the heavenly places." To be sure, earthly structures of power can exercise much destructive influence over God's creation, but these are not what the Christian's struggle is primarily against. These earthly "powers" are, for Paul, simply tools used by far more significant powers "in the heavenly places." It is, therefore, against these that we must principally struggle. The point is, as much as Paul might see demonic activity in structural societal evil, he clearly does not equate the demonic powers with structural societal evil.

➤In sum, Paul viewed the various cosmic "powers" as transcendent personal beings, created by God and ordered in a hierarchical fashion. At least some of these powers have now become evil and thus have to be fought against by the church and overthrown by Christ.

The Activity of the Demonic Realm

As we have seen, Satan, demons and the hostile cosmic powers were understood in the New Testament to be in principle defeated through Christ's ministry, death and resurrection. It was, however, further understood that Christ's victory had not yet been fully applied to the world at large, and for this reason the non-Gospel New Testament authors generally did not understand demonic activity to have lessened since the time of Christ.[28] This "in-between time" is the time in which we live, and hence understanding this literature's teaching on the ongoing activity of the Satanic kingdom during this time is important for our assessment of the problem of evil, at both an intellectual and a spiritual level. Thus we do well to conclude our overview of the New Testament's teaching on the demonic realm by briefly surveying what Acts and the Epistles have to say about the Christian life as warfare, and what they have to say about how this warfare will end.

The "god of this world." Though it was understood that Jesus dealt a fatal blow to the Satanic kingdom, the authors of Acts and the Epistles affirm the rule and influence of this kingdom no less strongly than did Jesus. Satan is still viewed as "the god of this world" (2 Cor 4:4), "the ruler of the power of the air" (Eph 2:2) who heads up a rebel kingdom (Rev 9:7-11) and through whom he still controls "the whole world" (1 Jn 5:19).[29] He is the "adversary" who "like a roaring lion . . . prowls around, looking for someone to devour" (1 Pet 5:8). Thus, as in Jesus' view, this literature continues to see the world as being fundamentally evil (Gal 1:4; Eph 5:16). Indeed, because the world is yet saturated with a diabolical influence, putting people outside the church as a form of chastisement is seen as turning them over to Satan (1 Cor 5:1-5; 1 Tim 1:20; cf. 1 Tim 5:15).

As in the Gospels, and as in apocalyptic thought generally, Acts and the Epistles portray this demonic kingdom as being directly or indirectly behind much of the evil in the world. In Romans 8:34-39, for example, Paul implies that demonic powers can bring about "hardship, or distress, or persecution, or famine, or nakedness, or peril, or sword" (death), though he insists that none of these things, and none of the demonic powers, "will be able to separate us from the love of God in Christ Jesus our Lord" (8:39). Further, Paul identifies a certain tormenting "thorn in the flesh" as resulting from "a messenger of Satan" (2 Cor 12:7), and he encourages the Corinthians to turn an unrepentant person "over to Satan for the destruction of the flesh" (1 Cor 5:5).[30] Clearly, for Paul, Satan is an ever-present reality ready to inflict physical suffering whenever able to do so.

Finally, in the apocalyptic vision of Revelation, Satan is named "Abaddon" and "Apollyon" (Rev 9:11)—the "destroyer"—who in the last days is permitted to head up a vicious attack of demonic forces (symbolized as locusts) upon the earth, using plagues, fire, "natural" catastrophes and death as their weapons (Rev 9; 6:12-17). Hence the "loud voice in heaven" proclaims, "woe to the earth and the sea, because the devil has come down to you with great wrath, because he knows that his time is short" (Rev 12:10, 12).[31]

Further, the "god of this world" is understood to be a primary influence behind all sin. He is portrayed as "the tempter" (1 Thess 3:5; 2 Cor 11:3; 1 Cor 7:5), and all who surrender themselves to his influence are "children of the devil" (1 Jn 3:8, 10; cf. Acts 13:20). Hence Peter asks Ananias, "why has Satan filled your heart to lie to the Holy Spirit?" (Acts 5:3).

Satan is also the master deceiver according to this literature. According to Paul, Satan blinds the minds of all unbelievers so they cannot receive the truth (2 Cor 4:4). He, along with his lesser cohorts, is ultimately behind all false teaching (1 Jn 4:1-4; 2 Jn 7), enslaving people in legalism, astrological superstitions, false doctrines and false philosophies (Gal 4:8-10; Col 2:8; 1 Tim 4:1-5). So too, according to Paul, sacrifices offered to idols are really "offered to demons," and those who offer such sacrifices are "partners with demons" (1 Cor 10:20). Demons seem to be the driving force behind idolatrous religious practices.

Satan's power to deceive is further illustrated by the fact that he, or his messengers, can appear as "an angel of light" or "an angel from heaven" teaching false doctrine (2 Cor 11:13; Gal 1:8). He and his legions can, and will, perform "counterfeit miracles, signs and wonders" as a means of deceiving "those who are perishing" (2 Thess 2:9 NIV; cf. Rev 13:2). Indeed, so powerful is Satan's ability to deceive that he is even portrayed as deceiving entire nations (Rev 20:3, 8, 10) and is called "the deceiver of the whole world" (Rev 12:9).

Satan's war against the church. The demonic kingdom is still prevalent in the world according to the New Testament. But following its pattern with Jesus in the Gospels, this kingdom focuses most of its activity on hindering the ministry of the church. Where the kingdom of God is being spread, there the kingdom of darkness will be most at work.

Hence Paul tells the Thessalonians that he and his companions wanted to come to them "again and again—but Satan blocked our way" (1 Thess 2:18). Just as Paul understood the "rulers of this world" to be at work provoking the crowds and authorities to crucify Jesus (1 Cor 2:8), so too, it seems, he saw the activity of Satan behind the crowds who prevented him from fellowship with the Thessalonians (cf. Acts 17:1-9). The contrasting of Paul's earnest desire with Satan's obstruction also says something about Paul's view of just how powerful and successful Satan could be in his opposition to the ministry.[32] There is here no hint of the later Augustinian assumption that God is truly sovereign only if his will can never be thwarted.

The strong opposition of the kingdom of darkness against the church is also seen in that Satan is portrayed as continually at work to bring trials to Christians in order to discourage them (1 Thess 3:5; cf. Rom 8:35-39). He is also at work to entrap church leaders, apparently by slandering their reputations, according to Paul (1 Tim 3:7). For this reason Paul, following the advice of Jesus, prays that leaders would be protected "from the evil one" (2 Thess 3:2-3; cf. Mt 6:13). What is more, in Paul's understanding, Satan is prowling to devour young Christian widows (1 Tim 5:11-15) as well as young churches by inciting divisions among them. Hence as he encourages them to preserve unity in the body (Rom 16:17-19), Paul reassures the Roman Christians that "the God of peace will shortly crush Satan under your feet" (Rom 16:20).[33]

The Satanic kingdom is also heavily at work in trying to deceive believers (1 Tim 4:1-7) and to pollute their minds with falsehood. Indeed, one of the primary areas of spiritual warfare, according to Paul, is the believer's mind:

Indeed, we live as human beings, but we do not wage war according to human standards; for the weapons of our warfare are not merely human, but they have divine power to destroy strongholds. We destroy arguments and every proud obstacle raised up against the knowledge of God, and we take every thought captive to obey Christ. (2 Cor 10:3-5)

Elsewhere Paul urges believers: "Do not be conformed to this world"—the world governed by Satan's regime—"but be transformed by the renewing of your minds" (Rom 12:2). The Christian's mind, for Paul, is a battlefield between the evil one who blinds and the Savior who brings light (2 Cor 4:4-6).

The heart of the believer is a battlefield as well, according to Paul. Hence he encourages Ephesian believers: "do not let the sun go down on your anger," and do not "make room for the devil" (Eph 4:26-27). The proximity of these verses may suggest that suppressing legitimate anger is one of the ways people give the devil a region in their life ("room," *topos*) out of which he can operate to further pollute their heart. In any event, the teaching presupposes that the enemy is constantly present, seeking to gain an entrance into the believer's life.

This conception is also presupposed in Paul's instruction to young widows "to give the adversary no occasion to revile us" (1 Tim 5:14), as well as in his instruction to all believers to "put on the whole armor of God, so that you may be able to stand against the wiles of the devil" (Eph 6:11). In Paul's view, the devil and his kingdom are as pervasive in this fallen world as the air we breath (cf. Eph 2:2; 1 Pet 5:8). The atmosphere of the world is diabolical, with the enemy persistently seeking to find an entrance into the believer's heart.

The notion that the believer's heart is a battlefield also lies behind Paul's encouragement to the Corinthians to follow his example in forgiving others "so that we may might not be outwitted by Satan; for we are not ignorant of his designs" (2 Cor 2:10-11). One of Satan's "designs" is apparently to cause believers to harbor unforgiveness. This again gives the devil a "room" in the believer's heart; it can drive the repentant person in need of forgiveness into despair (2 Cor 2:7); and it can bring about divisions within the body of Christ as well.[34] When any of this occurs, Paul is saying, we have been "outwitted." The teaching presupposes not only that Satan is ever present, seeking "an occasion" to work destruction, but that he is very crafty in the way he works.

The Christian Life as Warfare

In the light of all this, it comes as no surprise that one of the most frequent ways the Christian life is portrayed throughout the New Testament is that <u>it is the life of a soldier.</u> While many contemporary Western readers of the Bible instinctively take this to be nothing more than a catchy metaphor for the Christian life, in the context of the New Testament <u>it is meant quite literally.</u>[35] To follow Jesus is to do battle with the ever-present prince of darkness.

Exorcisms in Acts. As in Jesus' ministry, this warfare can sometimes involve actual exorcisms, according to Acts. <u>While there are only four references in Acts to exorcisms</u>, the way they are recorded, combined with <u>the numerous references to exorcism in the postapostolic church,</u> indicates that <u>exorcism was a standard part of early Christian life.</u>[36]

The first reference in Acts comes by way of a summary statement of Luke: "Many signs and wonders were done among the people through the apostles. . . . A great number of people would also gather from the towns around Jerusalem, bringing the sick and those tormented by unclean spirits, and they were all cured" (Acts 5:12, 16). The passage mentions, as a matter of course, that freeing people from evil spirits was a standard aspect of the ministry of the apostles. We are not surprised, then, when we read that Philip exorcised many shrieking evil spirits out of people while evangelizing Samaria (Acts 8:7), or that Paul exorcised <u>a spirit of divination (literally "spirit of python"</u>) out of a "slave girl" who was apparently hindering his ministry by undermining his credibility (Acts 16:16-18).[37] As in the ministry of Jesus, <u>exorcisms seemed to be an assumed aspect of the early church's ministry.</u>

Finally, <u>the regularity of exorcisms</u> in the early church is perhaps also revealed in Luke's unusual account of the seven sons of Sceva. They, along with other Jewish exorcists, were unsuccessfully trying to exorcise demons "by the Jesus whom Paul proclaims" (Acts 19:13-14).[38] At one point an evil spirit whom they were trying to exorcise said to them, "Jesus I know, and Paul I know; but who are you?" Through the man, the demon then "mastered them all, and so overpowered them that they fled out of the house naked and wounded" (16:15-16).

Though this particular account is unusual in some respects, it nevertheless confirms what we know from other sources: practicing exorcism was quite common in first-century culture, both among Jews and Greeks.[39] In this light it would be odd if the early church had not regularly practiced exorcisms. What set the early church and Jesus apart from these other exorcists was not that they practiced exorcism but that they were so successful at it.[40] Hence the Jewish exorcists were trying to borrow their power by using their "formula."

But the regularity of exorcism in Paul's ministry, as in Jesus', is perhaps further revealed by the fact that the demon knew very well who they were, but did not know who the Jewish exorcists were. As in the Gospels, demons seem to know who their real opponents are, and they fear them. Other exorcists, however, they can apparently at times intimidate and physically abuse.

Putting on spiritual armor. There is no question but that Jesus' successful exorcism ministry was carried over into the early apostolic and postapostolic church. But this was not the only, or even the primary, way that the Christian life as warfare is portrayed. For Paul, the whole of the Christian life is an act of warring against the enemy. As a matter of course, Christians are to "be strong in the Lord and in the strength of his power," which means putting on "the whole armor of God, so that you may be able to stand against the wiles of the devil, . . . against the rulers, against the authorities, against the cosmic powers of this present darkness, against the spiritual forces of evil in the heavenly places" (Eph 6:10-12).

For this reason, "truth," "righteousness," "the gospel of peace," "salvation" and "the word of God" are all portrayed as various aspects of "the whole armor of God" used by the Christian to ward off demonic attacks (Eph 6:14-17). Moreover, faith itself is portrayed as a "shield" by which we "quench all the flaming arrows of the evil one" (6:16).[41] With all this armor, Christians are to "stand firm" and to "keep alert and always persevere in supplication for all the saints" (6:13-14, 18). The first charge (*histēmi*) is to "hold your ground against" an assailing force,[42] while the second is to be ever watchful of an ever present enemy. The battle motif here is thick, and this is not some rare battle Paul is talking about. He is talking about the whole of the Christian life.

Finally, while Paul does not specifically mention prayer as part of the Christian's "armor," in this context it is most certainly seen as a warfare strategy, just as it was in the teaching of Jesus. Immediately after mentioning "the word of God" as "the sword of the Spirit" Paul adds, "Pray in the Spirit at all times in every prayer and supplication" (6:18). As if this were not enough, he adds further, "To that end keep alert and always persevere in supplication for all the saints." The injunction to "keep alert" while we pray is yet another clear indication that prayer is here portrayed as something a soldier does. It is, in short, an act of war.[43]

The same theme is found elsewhere. Using similar terminology, Paul reminds the Thessalonians to put on "the breastplate of faith and love, and for a helmet the hope of salvation" (1 Thess 5:8), for they are "children of light and children of the day" and "are not of the night or of the darkness" (5:5). Paul tells the Roman Christians to "lay aside the works of darkness and put on the armor of light" (Rom 13:12), the Ephesians to "take no part in the unfruitful works of darkness, but instead expose them . . . by the light" (Eph 5:11, 13), and the Corinthians not to participate in evil, for "what fellowship is there between light and darkness? What agreement does Christ have with Beliar?" (2 Cor 6:14-15).[44]

Paul's language of "light" and "darkness" in these three passages is reminiscent not only of John but also of the Qumran community, which (in good apocalyptic fashion) perceived the entire world as caught up in a cosmic struggle between light and darkness.[45] Paul's use of this terminology, then, as well as his explicit identification of darkness with Belial and his further reference to military armor, are more indications of just how thoroughly his view of the Christian life was colored by the warfare motif.

Reflecting the same outlook, Paul tells Timothy to "share in suffering like a good soldier of Christ Jesus" and reminds him that "no one serving in the army gets entangled in everyday affairs; the soldier's aim is to please the enlisting officer" (2 Tim 2:3-4). So too he refers, quite incidentally, to Epaphroditus and to Archippus as "fellow soldier" (Phil 2:25; Philem 2; cf. 1 Cor 9:7).

Thus the Christian life is for Paul a life of spiritual military service. It is about being a good soldier (2 Tim 2:4), about "fighting the good fight" (1 Tim 1:18; 6:12), about "waging war" (2 Cor 10:3), and about "struggling" with a cosmic enemy (Eph 6:12). Given his view of the ever-present reality of Satan and his kingdom, and given his understanding of what Christ was about and what the church is supposed to be about, it is hard to see how he could have viewed the Christian life differently.[46]

At the very least, it should be evident that any perspective which would construe the spiritual warfare motif as being incidental to the New Testament is seriously mistaken. Whether the motivation be to minimize the "mythological" elements of the New Testament or to maximize the classical-philosophical model of the sovereignty of God by downplaying indications of a genuine and pervasive battle, the attempt to sidestep the centrality of the warfare motif fails. As was the case with the life and teachings of Jesus, God's conflict and victory over Satan lies at the heart of the proclamation that the early Christians brought to the world.

The reality of the battle. The ongoing war that the early Christians understood they still had to participate in constituted the only "problem of evil" they knew or cared about. It was the problem of living out the kingdom of God in a world under siege from the kingdom of Satan. It was not an intellectual problem but an existential and spiritual problem. It was a problem to resolve by spiritual activism, not by intellectual contemplation and pious resignation.

These authors never pondered "why bad things happen to good people," for they lived with a warfare worldview that expected bad things to happen to good people. If the world is as thoroughly saturated with evil forces as they envisaged, then nightmarish suffering would not come as a great surprise. They understood (because Jesus taught) that, if the Lord of all creation suffered at the hands of these evil forces, they could hardly expect to fare better (Jn 15:20-21; cf. 1 Cor 2:8). The New Testament tells "good people" to *expect* bad things!

We must once again note that all of this presupposes that the war between God and Satan, the war in which humanity itself is centrally caught up, is a very real war. That is, it presupposes, at the very least, that God genuinely has to fight Satan. To suggest, as the classical-philosophical tradition tends to argue, that the forces of evil always play into the hand of God, that God is secretly in control of the activity of Satan and demons, and thus that these evil forces always end up carrying out God's sovereign purposes is to undermine completely the reality of this war and render wholly unintelligible the driving motif of the entire New Testament. What is more, it is to generate an unsolvable problem, for now we cannot rationally avoid the heinous conclusion that God is ultimately responsible for what Satan, his demons and evil people do.

The Origin and End of Satan and Fallen Angels
But how do these rebel creatures get their power to rebel? And if God does not control them, what guarantee is there that God shall ultimately defeat them? We have hovered around the New Testament's answer to this question several times in the last few chapters, but we do well to

conclude this study by examining in more detail what the New Testament says regarding the origin and ultimate demise of Satan and his rebel kingdom.

The catastrophic fall. From what has been said, one cannot deny that the warfare motif of the New Testament presupposes a dualistic world-view of sorts. At the very least, there is clearly a God/non-God duality of power. In other words, significant powers exist with some measure of autonomy over against God, with whom God must therefore work or against whom God must genuinely fight.

But this dualism, as intense as it is, never crosses over into metaphysical dualism in the New Testament. That is, never does the New Testament come close to affirming that the forces that oppose God are metaphysically ultimate, such as later Zoroastrianism and Manichaeism affirmed. Rather, the powers that oppose God are uniformly understood to be created by God. They are not eternal, and they are not infinite. Hence while they can and do genuinely oppose God and wreak destruction throughout his cosmos, they never pose a threat of overthrowing God.

But if the cosmic powers were all created by God, and if God is perfectly good, how is it that these created powers now are evil? Unlike much of the apocalyptic literature of their day, the New Testament authors never offer extravagant speculations to answer this question. Indeed, these authors reflect almost no concern about this question at all. In my view, their relative silence on this matter is not due to their thinking that an answer to this question was irrelevant, or to their thinking that there was no answer. Rather, it is due to the fact that they considered the answer to this question *obvious.*

While the apocalyptic literature offers no agreed upon answer to when and why evil forces "fell," all the apocalyptic authors who deal with the issue agree that the evil forces did fall. These powers chose to rebel against their Creator and to throw off his plans and his lordship.[47] The Old Testament view that sin is the result of free decisions of human beings to rebel against their Creator is applied to cosmic beings to explain their sinfulness. Indeed, as we have seen, the Old Testament itself occasionally approaches this insight (Gen 6:1-4; Ps 82; Is 14:12-14; Ezek 28:1-19; cf. chapter five). Like human beings, cosmic beings are free; thus for these authors, the sinfulness of cosmic beings is in principle no more inexplicable than is human sinfulness. For Jews who believed that God was both perfectly holy while also being the Creator of all that exists, it is hard to see how they could have reached any other conclusion.

This is, I submit, a fundamental assumption of the New Testament. The origin of evil among the cosmic powers is much like the origin of evil among human beings. Neither they nor their apocalyptic counterparts ever saw the need to explain freedom itself any further. For them, freedom itself was an "ultimate explanation." These Jews possessed no metaphysical proclivity to investigate the matter further (even if such an investigation were metaphysically possible).[48] They knew only that they and all humans were free to choose to obey or to disobey God, and that if they disobeyed God this was not God's fault. They understood cosmic powers in the same fashion.

In the New Testament we therefore find no discourses on the freedom of cosmic powers, any more than we find discourses on the freedom of human beings. But we do find much that presupposes that humans are free, and some passages that presuppose that cosmic powers are free. For example, Jude 6 refers to "the angels who did not keep their own position, but left their proper dwelling." These, the author says, are now "kept in eternal chains in deepest darkness for the judgment of the great Day." Then, Jude adds,

> Likewise, Sodom and Gomorrah and the surrounding cities, which, in the same manner as they, indulged in sexual immorality and pursued unnatural lust, serve as an example by undergoing a punishment of eternal fire. Yet in the same way these dreamers [viz., godless people] also defile the flesh, reject authority, and slander the glorious ones. (Jude 7-8)

It is impossible to determine whether Jude is tapping into some strand of the Watcher tradition—hence referring to the "fall" of Genesis 6—or whether he has some other angelic rebellion in mind. At the very least, his reference to these angels not keeping "their own position" and abandoning "their proper dwelling" suggests that he has in mind something like the Old Testament view of gods given authority over nations, or the apocalyptic conception of angels given charge over various aspects of nature.

In any event, what is important for us to note is that Jude assumes that the fall and punishment of these angels is directly parallel to the fall and punishment of sinners in Sodom and Gomorrah and with ungodly people in Jude's own day. Like these latter examples, the angels freely rebelled against God and were morally responsible for their evil decisions. As we have seen a number of times, for ancient Jewish authors in general, things "in the heavenlies" were not seen as being all that different from things here on earth. Hence the freedom and moral responsibility that characterized humans were also seen as characterizing angels.

This same understanding is reflected in 2 Peter 2. Here Peter is arguing that ungodly people (specifically, teachers of heresy) will certainly be punished, while godly people shall certainly be rescued from condemnation. To make this point he says:

> For if God did not spare the angels when they sinned, but cast them into hell [*Tartarus*] and committed them to chains of deepest darkness to be kept until the judgment; and if he did not spare the ancient world . . . when he brought a flood on a world of the ungodly; . . . and if by turning the cities of Sodom and Gomorrah to ashes he condemned them to extinction; . . . and if he rescued Lot, a righteous man greatly distressed by the licentiousness of the lawless . . . then the Lord knows how to rescue the godly from trial, and to keep the unrighteous under punishment until the day of judgment. (2 Pet 2:4-9)

Again, we cannot say with any confidence what specific event Peter has in mind when he speaks of the condemnation of sinning angels. He may be tapping into the Watcher tradition, or perhaps he has in mind a precreation fall. In any case, this issue is irrelevant to the more fundamental point we are making: Peter reflects the New Testament assumption that angels can and do sin, just as people can and do sin; and angels, like people, are morally responsible for their sinning. They are therefore punished, just as rebellious people are. When they sin, in other words, they are not carrying out some preordained plan of God. Rather, they are rebelling *against* God's preordained plan.

A similar conception lies behind Paul's instruction to Timothy not to make a recent convert an overseer "or he may be puffed up with conceit and fall into the condemnation of the devil" (1 Tim 3:6). The implication seems to be that conceit had something to do with the devil's fall (perhaps recalling Is 14:13-14) and that those who become conceited as the devil did can fall into a similar condemnation.[49] The willful fall of Satan and his angels is also assumed in Jesus' teaching that those whom he does not know on the judgment day are "cursed" and will depart "into the eternal fire prepared for the devil and his angels" (Mt 25:41).

This passage not only assumes that Satan and his angels are, like people, morally responsible for their fall, but also, interestingly enough, that hell was intended for ("prepared for") them, not for humans.

Thus hell is first and foremost the destiny of God's cosmic enemies, not us. If humans go there, it is because they have willfully aligned themselves with the ones for whom it was prepared. As was the case in examining Christ's work on the cross, we once again get the distinct impression that humans have been caught up in cosmic events that are far beyond the domain of human history. We are blessed or cursed by how we align ourselves in the fight between two cosmic kingdoms. We either share in Christ's victory, or we share in Satan's defeat. But we are, in either case, always only the secondary participants, never the main players.

Behind the whole conception is the understanding that these two kingdoms are divided for moral (not metaphysical) reasons. Their separation and their subsequent warring are not "in the eternal nature of things." The war is not coeternal with God, nor was it created by God. Rather, it is the result of a catastrophic misuse of freedom given to Satan "and his angels." Because it was a moral decision, Jesus is implying, it shall be punished. This is what hell is for.

The ultimate victory of God. From the perspective of the New Testament, there is no possibility that the enemies of God shall escape this destiny. God has ordained *temporal* parameters around the freedom of angelic and human creatures, just as God has ordained parameters around the *scope* of this freedom. Hence the ability of any within the angelic or human society of God's creation to rebel freely against God shall someday come to an end. Apparently out of integrity for the gift of freedom he has given, God endures for a time the wrath of these destructive rebels. To do otherwise would undoubtedly render the gift of freedom disingenuous.[50] While the gift of life God gives to those who choose him is eternal, the gift of freedom to choose against him is apparently not. Hence there shall come a time, Scripture declares, when God shall conclude this cosmic epoch by fully manifesting throughout his cosmos the victory that he has already won through his Son.

This declaration is at the same time a proclamation of heaven to the elect and a warning of hell to the reprobate. To those who have used their freedom to enter into a covenantal relationship with their Creator, the New Testament's eschatology is rapturous joy. The nightmare of the war shall finally be over. Love shall finally reign throughout God's creation. There shall be no more sin, no more pain, no more tears, hunger or death. The creation shall be all that God created it to be, all that he has fought for it to be, and all that he died for it to be. All who suffered life as a nightmare, such as the young Zosia, shall be vindicated. In a way we can scarcely begin to imagine, the sufferings of this nightmare, the Lord promises, will be dwarfed by the joy of creation's fulfillment when he in all his love and glory shall reign (Rom 8:18-25; 2 Cor 4:17-18; 1 Pet 1:6-9).

But we must not think that God's victory concerns only human welfare. To the contrary, as Christ's work was cosmic before it was anthropological, so too the biblical proclamation of God's ultimate victory concerns the cosmos as a whole before it centers on us. The whole creation now travails under the curse of the illegitimate tyrant who has seized it, and the whole creation shall ultimately benefit when this "god of the world" is toppled and creation is freed.

Hence when the Lord has finally destroyed this anticreation tyrannical Leviathan, he shall "restore everything, as he promised long ago through his holy prophets" (Acts 3:21 NIV). When he finally vanquishes his cosmic nemesis Yamm, there shall be "no longer any sea" in the kingdom (Rev 21:1 NIV). In sharp contrast to the war that has been raging for eons, God shall at this time "gather up all things in [Christ], things in heaven and things on earth" (Eph 1:10), so that his presence may fill "all in all" (Eph 1:23; cf. 4:10). Again, among the benefactors of this cosmic restoration are all those humans who have simply said "yes" to the gracious invitation to accept his love and fight on his side.

But what then is to become of those angelic hosts who have fought against God's plan from the start, and of all those humans who have willingly been co-opted in this futile attempt at a cosmic mutiny? The manifestation of Christ's victory shall at the same time be the manifestation of their defeat. When light shall be fully manifested, darkness must thereby be brought to nothing. When love shall reign universal, there shall be no longer any place among the living for hatred, apathy, greed, jealousy or any such disposition. When divine justice shall rule, all that is wrong, all that will not be reconciled, shall be punished. In short, when God's presence and glory shall fill "all in all," there simply shall be no place in the kingdom for anything or anyone that continues to resist him.

This is the central point of Scripture's teaching on hell. Scripture's teaching does not seek to satisfy some morbid curiosity we might have about the details of this "place" by giving us a literal snapshot of it, though many church fathers and leading figures in the church (e.g., Tertullian, Aquinas) unfortunately took at least some of the remarkably wide variety of graphic apocalyptic images literally. The point of the New Testament's teaching is rather to express the certainty, universality, severity and finality of God's victory over the evil one, and in the strongest possible terms to warn those of us who can yet do something about it that aligning with the evil one will have nightmarish consequences. In rejecting God, one is rejecting all that is love, life, joy, goodness and peace. How could existence without these be anything less than a nightmare? Indeed, as some of the images of damnation in Scripture make clear, it is a stretch even to call it "existence."

One set of warnings in the Bible describes hell as almost the complete absence of being. For example, Scripture describes the fate of Satan, his legions and all those humans who have aligned themselves with him as being cast into a cosmic version of the dump outside Jerusalem in the valley of Hinnom (Gehenna).[51] These are now unsalvageable broken vessels who do not and will not do what they were created to do. They are, therefore, total waste, refuse. Whereas they once had the possibility of sharing in God's triune life throughout eternity, they are tragically now good for nothing, fit only for destruction.

All such rebels, therefore, shall be brought to nothing (Mt 10:28; Mk 1:24; 1 Cor 1:19; 3:17; 6:13; 15:24-26; 2 Thess 2:8; Phil 1:28; Heb 2:14; 10:39; Jas 4:12; 2 Pet 2:12; 3:10-11; Jude 10). Under the weight of God's justice, they shall all "perish" (*apollymi*, Lk 13:3; Jn 3:16; 10:28; 1 Cor 1:18; 2 Cor 2:15; 4:3; Rom 2:12; 2 Thess 2:10; 2 Pet 3:9). They are like chaff that is burned up in a fire that cannot be quenched (Mt 3:12; 13:30; cf. Is 1:31). Similarly, in the light of God's universal rule, Scripture declares that these rebels shall "be no more. . . . like smoke they vanish away. . . . the posterity of the wicked shall be cut off" (Ps 37:10, 20, 38). They "shall be as though they had never been" (Obad 16) and "like a dream when one awakes" (Ps 73:20).[52]

Along slightly different lines, having rejected the Author of life itself, these defeated rebels can now be compared to dead, rotting, worm-infested corpses (Rom 6:21, 23; Jas 1:15; Is 66:24; Mk 9:48). From yet a slightly different angle, these raging rebels can be compared to people who are thrown out of the banquet, cast "into the outer darkness"(Mt 8:12; 22:13; 25:30).

The central point of all such graphic images is clear: there is no place for the wicked, angelic or human, in the kingdom of God. When the light and life of God's triune love and life shines sovereignly over the whole of creation, all that is darkness, all that is against love and all that is against life must (to mix metaphors) be vanquished, extinguished, destroyed, burned up and relegated to the garbage dump "in the outer darkness." Again, this is not said to satisfy all our questions about the "topography" or "temperature" of *Gehenna* (hell) but to warn all who can still change to do so if they need to. The message is: all enemies of God, angelic and human, shall certainly be defeated, they shall certainly be justly judged; and this judgment shall certainly be nightmarish for them. To describe it as endless fiery torment is not to exaggerate its terror (Rev 14:9-11; 20:10; cf. Mt 25:41, 46; Lk 16:24).[53] In choosing against God, Satan and all who follow him are forever choosing against life and love. Nothing could possibly be worse.

Conclusion: The Centrality of the Warfare Perspective

The most fundamental point in the last five chapters is that the New Testament is thoroughly conditioned by a warfare worldview. In this view the whole of the cosmos is understood to be caught up in a fierce battle between two rival kingdoms. This view entails that the earth has, quite literally, become a fierce war zone and a desecrated battlefield.

In chapters six through eight we saw that Jesus entered this war zone to set up the rightful rule of God over against the illegitimate rule of Satan. Jesus' healings, miracles, exorcisms, resurrection, as well as much of his teaching, make sense only as various aspects of a unified ministry within the context of this worldview.[54] In chapter nine we saw that within this apocalyptic context the early church understood the central significance of Christ's death and resurrection. The cross and resurrection were, above all else, the act by which God vanquished his archenemy. Our salvation is at once the liberating result of this conquest and one further means by which God is reclaiming the earth for his glory.

There are, however, still battles to fight. As we have seen in this present chapter, what has in principle been achieved has not yet in fact been manifested, for the fatally wounded kingdom of darkness still reigns upon the earth. Despite Christ's victory, the New Testament continues to define the Christian life in warfare terms. The outcome of the war is settled, but there are still important battles to be fought. Fighting them is what the Christian life is all about. As Wingren puts it, "It is impossible for man in the days of . . . the Church, to have to do with God without at the same time, in some way, having to do with the Devil. These two . . . fill all existence."[55] The confidence and hope of the believer in all of this is that Christ has once and for all time vanquished the enemy, and that someday this victory over Satan and the cessation of all the evil that flows from him shall be perfectly manifested.

The warfare worldview and the problem of evil. The centrality of this warfare motif is the single most important observation to be made as one approaches "the problem of evil." How one tries to resolve this problem depends entirely upon how one frames the problem. And how one frames the problem is decisively colored by the kind of world, the kind of God and the kind of evil that one thinks needs explaining. A young Jewish girl being tortured by a group of men means something completely different in a worldview in which it is believed that God's will is always perfectly carried out than it does in a worldview in which it is believed that God's will is often thwarted by evil cosmic forces.

It is all a matter of where one starts: do we start with a view of God as being at war with evil or with a view of God as controlling evil? Do we start with a view of the world as a hostage to an evil cosmic force or with a view of the world as one in which God's will is perfectly carried out? Do we start with a view of evil as a hostile alien intrusion into God's cosmos or with a view of evil as always and everywhere secretly fulfilling God's sovereign, always beneficent, purposes?

The central thrust of this work has been to argue that if we model our approach to the problem of evil after the New Testament, we must in every instance opt for the former, not the latter, starting points. When we do this, we find that we are freed from ceaselessly inquiring into supposed divine reasons behind the world's nightmares, and freed and empowered to rise up and combat these nightmarish features of existence as what God is unequivocally against. In other words, when we accept the warfare worldview of Scripture, the intellectual problem of evil is transformed into the practical problem of evil, just as it was in the New Testament.

In this worldview, the only "reason" why Zosia is tortured is because free beings, human and angelic, can will such atrocities. While the sovereign God can and will strive to bring some good out of the horrifying demonic event (Rom 8:28), the evil event itself exists only because free beings who are against God have willed it. The "ultimate reason" for this ghoulish torment lies there. If the words "good" and "loving" mean anything as applied to God, if Scripture's testimony regarding the perfect character of God and the antidemonic ministry of Jesus mean anything, and if God's power is to be construed as supremely admirable, as truly transcendent, not simply as coercive after the impoverished image of fallen human ideals of power, then we simply cannot suppose that it is ultimately God himself who is secretly willing Zosia's nightmare for some supposed "higher" reason.

Coping with evil. Where does all this leave us in terms of our coping with the atrocities of our world? Whatever else may be said about the classical-philosophical blueprint model of God's providence, it does provide the believer with a certain kind of security that the warfare worldview seems to lack—so long as one steers clear of concrete atrocities. A certain peace comes, for many at least, in resigning oneself to whatever (one believes) the hand of God might bring to one. Herein lies the appeal of the sort of traditional hymns spoken of in chapter one.

If, however, we can no longer find solace in the conviction that a mysterious providential plan governs every event in world history, in what can our hearts find hope? If Zosia's torment is truly as gratuitous and barbaric as it appears, must we not despair?

It is, I think, undeniable that the warfare worldview on one level depicts a scarier world than the providential blueprint worldview, for the simple reason that opening one's eyes to the reality of war is indeed scary. At the same time, this prospect strikes some of us as less scary than the prospect of living in an actual spiritual war but being ignorant of this fact. It certainly seems less scary than living in a cosmos that is being coercively run by a supreme being who secretly wills the torture of little girls —"for his glory."

Yet even if we were to concede that the genuine contingency and real battles of the warfare worldview present a world that is scarier than the divine blueprint worldview, it would not follow that this worldview is less hopeful than the blueprint model. Precisely the opposite is the case, I would argue. The warfare worldview of the New Testament offers more hope, precisely because it unabashedly acknowledges the dismal and demonic state of the world in its present war-torn condition.

The hope that the New Testament offers is not the hope that God has a higher, all-encompassing plan that secretly governs every event, including the evil intentions of malicious angelic and human beings, and that somehow renders these evil wills "good" at a higher level. To my way of thinking, at least, that supposition generates a truly hopeless position. For if God's will is already being done as Zosia's eye sockets are bleeding, what have we to look forward to? If justice is, on some secret transcendental plane, already being served, what do we have to look forward to? If God is already vindicated because "the big picture" justifies Zosia's torment "for the good of the whole," then we really have no reason to hope that things will fare better for Zosia or ourselves in the world to come.

In direct contrast to all this, the ultimate hope that the New Testament offers is eschatological. As sure as the Lord came the first time to defeat his cosmic enemy and our oppressor in principle, just as certainly he shall return again to defeat him in fact. Because sickness, disease, war, death, sorrow and tears are not God's will, and because God is ultimately sovereign, we can have a confident assurance that someday, when his foes are ultimately vanquished, God will end all sorrow, and every evil which causes such sorrow, and will wipe away every tear from our eyes (Rev 20:4). Precisely because our present suffering is not God's will—however much he can now use it for our ultimate good—we can have an assurance that it shall not always be this way.

Indeed, Paul has the inspired audacity to proclaim that, when the kingdom has finally fully come, the glory and joy that we shall know will render all the sufferings of this present world insignificant. Whatever else this may mean, it means that God will somehow make it up to Zosia, and to her mother.

With such a promise, given in the vicinity of Zosia's childhood screams, I close with the simple prayer that characterized the faith communities of New Testament times:

Maranatha: Our Lord, come! (1 Cor 16:22)

Notes

Introduction

[1]See, e.g., G. L. Archer, "Daniel," in *EBC*, 7:124-25; J. J. Collins, *Daniel*, Herme-neia (Minneapolis: Fortress, 1993), pp. 374-76; J. E. Goldingay, *Daniel*, WBC 30 (Dallas, Tex.: Word, 1989), pp. 291-92, 312-14; L. F. Hartman and A. A. Di Lella, *The Book of Daniel*, AB 23 (Garden City, N.Y.: Doubleday, 1978), pp. 282-84; R. Wallace, *The Lord Is King: The Message of Daniel* (Downers Grove, Ill.: InterVarsity Press, 1979), p. 179.

[2]W. Wink suggests plausibly that this territorial spirit was protecting his territorial interests in trying to block this divine messenger. See *Unmasking the Powers: The Invisible Forces that Determine Human Existence* (Philadelphia: Fortress, 1986), pp. 89-90. I discuss this passage more fully in chapter four.

[3]A growing number of missions-minded evangelicals are taking the possibility of menacing "territorial spirits" seriously. Daniel 10, along with the wider notion of the "angels of the nations" to which it is connected, plays a central role in this perspective. See, e.g., J. Dawson, *Taking Our Cities for God: How to Break Spiritual Strongholds* (Altamonte Springs, Fla.: Creation House, 1989); G. Otis Jr., *The Last of the Giants* (Tarrytown, N.Y.: Chosen, 1991); C. P. Wagner, ed., *Breaking Strongholds in Your City* (Ventura, Calif.: Regal/Gospel Light, 1993); idem, ed., *Engaging the Enemy: How to Fight and Defeat Territorial Spirits* (Ventura, Calif.: Regal, 1991). For further background on the "angels of the nations" theme in Scripture and the early church, see J. Daniélou's excellent little work *The Angels and Their Mission, According to the Fathers of the Church*, trans. D. Heimann (Westminster, Md.: Newman, 1957), esp. pp. 22ff.; and W. Wink, *Naming the Powers: The Language of Power in the New Testament* (Philadelphia: Fortress, 1984), pp. 26-35.

[4]I must nevertheless add that as we make the transition out of modernity into postmodernity, the Western naturalistic tendency to dismiss the existence, or at least the importance, of angelic beings is rapidly and dramatically changing, a fact that is of some consequence in the next chapter.

[5]Although many issues surround the question of what exactly constitutes a "world-view," we need not enter into them here. But it is helpful to clarify what I mean by this term. I mean to refer to a dominant feature of the ultimate gestalt within which individuals or a people-group interpret their experience. By a "warfare worldview," therefore, I refer in a most general fashion to a dominant feature of that ultimate gestalt, shared in different ways by almost all primordial cultures, within which people understand their experience as being to some significant extent affected by a spiritual conflict that is believed to be going on in an invisible (but sometimes

visible) realm. It is true that the worldview of these people-groups can in no instance be exhaustively defined as "warfare." But this much is true of any label about any worldview, which is why labeled worldviews frequently overlap with one another. Worldviews are highly complex matters, and no single label can ever exhaustively describe them. Hence it is true to say that the warfare worldview is (or at least originally was) a dimension of the Christian worldview, while it is just as true to say that the Christian worldview is (or at least originally was) one instance of the more general "warfare worldview." On the concept of a "worldview," see P. Hiebert, *Anthropological Insights for Missionaries* (Grand Rapids, Mich.: Baker, 1985), p. 46; C. Kraft, *Christianity with Power: Your Worldview and Your Experience of the Supernatural* (Ann Arbor, Mich.: Vine Books, 1989), passim, but esp. p. 20; and M. Kraft, "Spiritual Power and Worldview," in her *Understanding Spiritual Power: A Forgotten Dimension of Cross-Cultural Mission and Ministry* (Maryknoll, N.Y.: Orbis, 1995), pp. 20-36.

[6]The name Shuar has largely replaced the earlier name Jívaro, which acquired a pejorative connotation in Ecuadorian usage. See M. Harner, *The Jívaro* (Berkeley: University of California Press, 1972), pp. v-xvi. The following information on the Shuar derives largely from this work, esp. pp. 134-66.

[7]See A. E. Jensen, *Myth and Cult Among Primitive People*, trans. M. T. Choldin and W. Weissleder (Chicago: University of Chicago Press, rpt. 1963), pp. 307-12.

[8]Facilitated by several early influential works on this tribe, most notably F. W. Up de Graff, *Head Hunters of the Amazon: Seven Years of Exploration and Adventure* (Garden City, N.Y.: Garden City Publishing, 1923); and R. Karsten, *The Headhunters of Western Amazons: The Life and Culture of the Jibaro Indians of Eastern Ecuador and Peru*, Commentationes Humanarum Litterarum 7/1 (Helsinki: Societas Scientarum Fennica, 1935).

[9]In speaking of the invisible world as "supernatural," I am importing a Western category and partially distorting a Shuarian category. For them, it is not so much that the invisible world is "supernatural" as it is that the physical world is less than natural. Perhaps a more accurate manner of speech is to distinguish between "ordinary" and "nonordinary" (rather than "natural" and "supernatural") reality. See C. Castaneda, *The Teachings of Don Juan: A Yaqui Way of Knowledge* (New York: Simon & Schuster, rpt. 1974); idem, *Journey to Ixtlan: The Lessons of Don Juan* (New York: Simon & Schuster, 1972); idem, *A Separate Reality: Further Conversations with Don Juan* (New York: Simon & Schuster, 1971). In general, however, since I am talking primarily to Westerners, I follow Marguerite Kraft and refer to this perspective on the world that affirms the reality of spiritual beings as a central feature as "supernaturalism." See Kraft, "Investigating Supernaturalism," in *Understanding Spiritual Power*, pp. 79-87; as well as J. Henninger, "The Adversary of God in Primitive Religions," in *Satan: Essays Collected and Translated from "Etudes Carmelitaines,"* ed. B. de Jésus-Marie, trans. M. Carroll, et al. (New York: Sheed & Ward, 1951), pp. 105-20.

[10]Some schools of Buddhism, such as Zen, and certain segments of Hinduism and Taoism provide notable exceptions to this view. The world, as it is, is seen as being absolutely one and in perfect harmony with itself. Indeed, such a monistic teaching is found in Neo-Platonism, which, through Augustine, strongly influenced Christian theology. Still, it is also true to say that even in Buddhist cultures the masses have rarely followed this monistic teaching in anything like a pure form. The teaching is invariably fused to some extent with widely shared spiritual intuitions

and popular folk traditions that revolve around good and evil spirits. Hence, for example, Hinduism is at once the most intensely monistic and polytheistic major religion in the world, for while all of reality is understood on a philosophical level to be Brahman, on a popular level more than thirty million different gods are adored, while multitudes of demon-type spirits are frequently feared. In the case of Christianity, Augustine's monistic teaching could not overturn not only popular folk traditions about good and evil angels, but the scriptural teaching on the matter. As I shall argue in a forthcoming volume entitled *Satan and the Problem of Evil,* the result is that traditional Christianity has usually operated with a quasi-warfare worldview. For a collection of conflict myths within Hinduism, see S. Husain, *Demons, Gods and Holy Men* (New York: Schocken; Vancouver: Douglas & McIntyre, 1987); and W. D. O'Flaherty, *Hindu Myths* (London: Harmondsworth, 1975). On the demonic in folk traditions in India, see G. H. Sutherland, *The Disguises of the Demon* (Albany: SUNY, 1991); and J. Varenne, "Anges, démons et génies dans l'Inde," in *Génies, anges et démons* (Paris: Editions du Seuil, 1971), pp. 257-94.

[11]As is well known, ancient or primitive perceptions of the spirit world usually do not break down along clear-cut "good" and "evil" categories. Most of their deities are somewhat morally ambivalent (though, as we shall see in chapter four, primordial peoples often have a vague conception of an all-good highest God). The more fundamental categories among primitive peoples are usually "friendly" and "hostile."

[12]By "intuition" here I mean to refer to the spiritual sense humans have, by virtue of their being made in the image of God, by which they access general revelation. We need not enter into the thorny issues regarding what can and cannot be known from general revelation or how reliable this general intuition is or is not. It will suffice to simply note my working assumption that an intuition of spiritual realities is valid to the extent that it agrees with Scripture and invalid to the extent that it does not.

[13]Jensen, *Myth and Cult,* pp. 314-18. See also Jensen, *Die drei Ströme: Züge aus dem geistigen Leben der Wemale* (Leipzig, 1948), pp. 192ff.

[14]Kraft, *Understanding Spiritual Power,* p. 77.

[15]Ibid., pp. 77-78.

[16]The word *daimon* was used to denote any incorporeal spirit at this time, much like the word "angel" is used today. It was not necessarily pejorative. On the early history and development of the notion of *daimon,* see F. F. Brenk, "In the Light of the Moon: Demonology in the Early Imperial Period," in *ANRW* (1986), ed. H. Temporini and W. Haase, 2/16.3:2068-2145; also H. W. M. de Jong, *Demonische ziekten in Babylon en Bijbel* (Leiden: Brill, 1959). On Plato's demonology, see especially S. S. Jensen, *Dualism and Demonology: The Function of Demonology in Pythagorean and Platonic Thought* (Copenhagen: Munksgaard, 1966).

[17]See Plato, *Symposium* 202D-203A. For an excellent discussion of the conception, see Jensen, *Dualism and Demonology,* pp. 77-101; and Brenk, "In the Light of the Moon," pp. 2085-88. As Jensen (ibid., p. 65) notes, *daimons* were at this point simply regarded as "beings intermediate between the gods and man." For the demonologies of the Pythagoreans and Xenocrates, see Jensen, ibid., pp. 640-76 and 102-7. On perceptions of the *daimonic* in the Greco-Roman world at large, see Brenk, "In the Light of the Moon"; E. R. Dodds, "Man and the Daemonic World," in his *Pagan and Christian in an Age of Anxiety: Some Aspects of Religious*

Experience from Marcus Aurelius to Constantine (Cambridge: Cambridge University Press, 1965), pp. 37-68; E. Ferguson, *Demonology of the Early Christian World* (New York: Mellen, 1984), chap. 2, pp. 33-67; and J. Z. Smith, "Towards Interpreting Demonic Powers in Hellenistic and Roman Antiquity," *ANRW* (1978), 2/16.1:425-39.

[18] Some early sources suggest that Socrates' claim of dependence upon his personal *daimon* was used in the charges that eventually led to his death. See Plato *Euthyphro* 3B; and Xenophon *Memorabilia* 1.1-3.

[19] On the understanding of demonic influence upon humans in the Hellenistic world, see E. A. Leeper, "Exorcism in Early Christianity" (Ph.D. diss., Duke University, 1991), pp. 26-38. While most Greek philosophical writers regarded the notion of demon possession as superstition (see Brenk, "In the Light of the Moon," p. 2108), the evidence suggests that the masses did not share their perspective. A. Tripolitis (*"Daemons/*Spirits in Hellenistic Literature" [paper presented to the Jesus Seminar, Rutgers University, Oct. 22-25, 1992]) presents evidence of exorcisms in the ancient Hellenistic world where invasive *daimons* are cast out through spells and even by quoting verses from Homer! For a superb study of demon possession and of spiritual warfare in general from a rather naturalistic anthropological perspective, see F. D. Goodman, *How About Demons? Possession and Exorcism in the Modern World* (Bloomington: Indiana University Press, 1988), as well as her earlier work *The Exorcism of Anneliese Michel* (New York: Doubleday, 1981). Other works I have found informative have been W. Davis, *Dojo: Magic and Exorcism in Modern Japan* (Stanford: Stanford University Press, 1980); and E. Colson, "Spirit Possession Among the Tonga of Zambia," in *Spirit Mediumship and Society in Africa*, ed. J. Beattie and J. Middleton (New York: Africana, 1969).

[20] J. B. Russell, *The Devil: Perceptions of Evil from Antiquity to Primitive Christianity* (Ithaca: Cornell University Press, 1977), p. 60.

[21] See S. Mansfield, *The Gestalts of War* (New York: Dial, 1982), p. 56. See N. A. Chagnon, *Yanomamö: The Fierce People*, 2d ed. (New York: Holt, Rinehart and Winston, 1977).

[22] See W. Schmidt, *High Gods in North America* (Oxford: Oxford University Press, 1933), pp. 34-39.

[23] W. Koppers, *Primitive Man and His World Picture*, trans. E. Raybould (London: Sheed & Ward, 1952), pp. 75-94.

[24] For a collection of *patakis* (legends of the gods), see M. González-Wippler, *Legends of Santeria* (St. Paul: Llewellyn, 1994).

[25] See, e.g., Kraft, *Understanding Spiritual Power*, pp. 67-78; Russell, *Devil*, p. 67; Mansfield, *Gestalts of War*, p. 58. On Satanlike and demonic figures, or elements and structures that suggest a general "warfare" view of the cosmos in other religious perspectives, see E. A. A. Adegbola, ed., *Traditional Religion in West Africa* (Ibadan: Daystar, 1983), pp. 215ff.; P. J. Awn, *Satan's Tragedy and Redemption: Iblis in Sufi Psychology*, SHR 44 (Leiden: Brill, 1983); J. W. Boyd, *Satan and Mara: Christian and Buddhist Symbols of Evil*, SHR 27 (Leiden: Brill, 1975); Henninger, "Adversary of God"; E. C. Krupp, *Echoes of the Ancient Skies: The Astronomy of Lost Civilizations* (New York: Harper & Row, 1983), pp. 14-19, 212-13; L. Massingnon, "The Yezids of Mount Sindjar," in *Satan: Essays*, pp. 158-62; S. P. Rao and M. P. Reddy, "Job and His Satan: Parallels in Indian Scripture," *ZAW* 91 (1979): 416-22; M. E. Spiro, *Burmese Supernaturalism* (Englewood Cliffs, N.J.: Prentice-Hall, 1967), pp. 47-54; Sutherland, *Disguises of the Demon*; M. Taussig, *The Devil*

and Commodity Fetishism in South America (Chapel Hill: University of North Carolina Press, 1980); A. T. Welch, "Allah and Other Supernatural Beings: The Emergence of the Qur'anic Doctrine of Tawd," in *Studies in Qur'an and Tafsir,* ed. A. T. Welch, (Chico, Calif.: Scholars Press, 1979), pp. 733-58.

One of the most remarkable ancient examples of the warfare worldview is that of Zoroastrianism. While the later Sassanid period (represented by the Pahlavi texts) reveals a strong cosmic dualism, the evidence suggests that Zoroaster's original faith was monotheistic, but with a strong emphasis on the power of one of God's creation who turned evil, Ahriman. See J. P. Asmussen, "Some Remarks on Sassanian Demonology," in *Commémoration Cyrus, hommage universel,* 3 vols., ed. A. Pagiliaro et al., Acta Iranica 2 (Leiden: Brill, 1974), 1:236-41; D. Bishop, "When Gods Become Demons," in *Monsters and Demons in the Ancient and Medieval Worlds: Papers Presented in Honor of Edith Porada,* ed. A. E. Farkus et al. (Mainz on Rhine: Verlag Philipp von Zabern, 1987), pp. 95-100; J. W. Boyd and D. A. Crosby, "Is Zoroastrianism Dualistic or Monotheistic?" *JAAR* 47 (1979): 557-88; E. R. Hay, "God and Evil: Zoroaster and Barth," *Dalhousie Review* 49 (1969): 369-76. I shall discuss Zoroastrianism further as concerns its influence on the Jewish conception of Satan in chapter five.

[26]This volume attempts to demonstrate that the Bible clearly espouses a warfare view of the world, and that this worldview decisively conditions its understanding of suffering and evil. In the volume that is to follow *(Satan and the Problem of Evil)* I shall attempt to provide a philosophical defense of this warfare worldview, especially as it was being developed in the early postapostolic church, over against the more monistic-tending perspective that came to dominate Christian theology after Augustine.

[27]Although at least an echo of creational monotheism (a belief in one Creator God) is found among many primordial peoples—a fact that must be accounted for (see chapter four)—the insight that this Creator God is altogether perfect and omnipotent seems quite rare.

[28]The term "chronocentrism" is from J. B. Russell, *The Prince of Darkness* (Ithaca, N.Y.: Cornell University Press, 1988), p. 260. On the myopic nature of the Western worldview, see M. Kraft, "The Problem with a Western Worldview," in her *Understanding Spiritual Power,* pp. 31-36.

[29]See note 12. Affirming this point does not in any way imply an endorsement of any specific features of any particular warfare worldview. From a scriptural perspective, many aspects of each pagan mythology must be judged as being themselves more erroneous, if not demonic, than correct and God-inspired. My only claim is that the basic insight that the world makes sense only against a backdrop of invisible, spiritual, cosmic conflict should, so far as it goes, be regarded as correct from the vantage point of Scripture.

[30]See Lewis's essay, "Myth Becomes Reality," in *God in the Dock: Essays on Theology and Ethics,* ed. W. Hooper (Grand Rapids, Mich.: Eerdmans, 1970), esp. pp. 65-67.

[31]See my forthcoming *Satan and the Problem of Evil.*

[32]By "classical-philosophical Christian theism" I mean that philosophical view of God that arose chiefly from Hellenistic philosophical sources and that tended to define God as essentially atemporal, immutable, impassible, *actus purus,* perfectly simple and (most importantly for our purposes) meticulously sovereign over the world. I distinguish it from simple "classical theism" or "traditional theism" in that these latter terms are more general and include not only what theologians have theorized

about God but also what lay Christians have tended to affirm about God (whether consistent with the official theology of the church or not). While I agree with most aspects of the classical and traditional views of God, and even many aspects of the classical-philosophical view of God (e.g., the belief that God exists necessarily and is self-sufficient apart from the world), and while I thus strongly side with both the traditional and classical-philosophical theistic traditions over against any form of process theism or dualism, I nevertheless maintain that some of the central attributes ascribed to God in the classical-philosophical theistic tradition are unbiblical, philosophically untenable and ultimately destructive to the warfare worldview because they logically undermine it. For an excellent collection of representative primary texts (with commentary) of classical-philosophical theologians (ranging from Philo to Augustine to Aquinas up to modern times), see C. Hartshorne and W. L. Reese, *Philosophers Speak of God* (Chicago: University of Chicago Press, 1953), pp. 76-164. For my own attempt to interact critically with both the classical-philosophical and process theistic traditions in order to produce a synthesis, see my *Trinity and Process: A Critical Evaluation and Reconstruction of Hartshorne's Di-Polar Theism Towards a Trinitarian Metaphysics* (New York: Peter Lang, 1992). I shall provide a thorough biblical and philosophical critique of various classical-philosophical theistic assumptions in my forthcoming *Satan and the Problem of Evil*.

[33]A warfare theistic worldview also inspires a revolt against any view of God that does not see him as revolting against evil and suffering. In this sense I agree with Jüngel, Kaspers and Küng, among others, who have argued that Christian theism has much to learn from the modern atheistic critique of (the classical-philosophical view of) God. The classical-philosophical omnicontrolling view of God that modern atheism rejects is neither biblically nor philosophically defensible, and hence *should* be rejected. For arguments along these lines, see E. Jüngel, *God as the Mystery of the World: On the Foundation of the Theology of the Crucified One in the Dispute Between Theism and Atheism*, trans. D. L. Gruder (Grand Rapids, Mich.: Eerdmans, 1983); W. Kaspar, *The God of Jesus Christ*, trans. M. O'Connell (New York: Crossroad, 1986), pp. 3-64; H. Küng, *Does God Exist? An Answer For Today*, trans. E. Quinn (Garden City, N.Y.: Doubleday, 1980), pp. 405-10.

[34]On the hazards, difficulties and possibilities regarding the task of biblical theology, discussed from various perspectives, see J. Barr, "The Theological Case Against Biblical Theology," in *Canon, Theology and Old Testament Interpretation*, ed. G. M. Tucker et al. (Philadelphia: Fortress, 1988), pp. 3-19; B. Childs, *Biblical Theology in Crisis* (Philadelphia: Westminster, 1970); and J. J. Collins, "Is a Critical Biblical Theology Possible?" in *The Hebrew Bible and Its Interpreters*, ed. W. H. Propp et al. (Winona Lake, Ind.: Eisenbrauns, 1990), pp. 1-17. For several excellent conservative assessments, see C. H. H. Scobie, "The Challenge of Biblical Theology," *TynBul* 42, no. 1 (1991): 30-61; idem, "New Directions in Biblical Theology," *Themelios* 17 (1991-92): 5-6; G. R. Osborne, "Can We Get Theology from the Bible?" in his *Three Crucial Questions About the Bible* (Grand Rapids, Mich.: Baker, 1995), pp. 120-79.

[35]For a recent discussion of the various approaches to biblical theology, along with a detailed exposition of the "canonical approach" (often termed "canonical criticism") from one of its foremost proponents, see B. S. Childs, *Biblical Theology of the Old and New Testaments: Theological Reflections on the Christian Bible* (Minneapolis: Fortress, 1993).

[36]In this regard, I am intrigued with, and initially hopeful about, P. R. Noble's

methodological and hermeneutical reconstruction of Childs's program in his *The Canonical Approach: A Critical Reconstruction of the Hermeneutics of Brevard S. Childs*, BIS 16 (Leiden: Brill, 1995), esp. pp. 187-218, 340-50. On the "author-centered" camp of textual interpretation, see E. D. Hirsch's seminal work *Validity in Interpretation* (New Haven: Yale University Press, 1967).

[37]My basic position is that we have it on Christ's authority, which itself can be established on solid historical grounds, *that* Scripture is divinely inspired, but next to nothing as to *how* Scripture is divinely inspired. Hence, though I defend the inspiration and infallibility of Scripture, I am in principle completely open to the historical-critical investigation of the particular historical processes by which various segments of Scripture came about. In my view, an unequivocal affirmation of scriptural inspiration does not entail anything in the direction of the "divine dictation theory" espoused by some American fundamentalists. On the defense of the historical Jesus as the Son of God (as opposed to various modern revisionist perspectives), see my *Cynic, Sage or Son of God? Recovering the Real Jesus in an Age of Revisionist Replies* (Wheaton, Ill.: Bridgepoint, 1995), chapters 5—13. For a classical defense of biblical inspiration on the foundation of the historical Jesus as well as a discussion of various surrounding issues, see B. B. Warfield, *The Inspiration and Authority of the Bible*, ed. S. G. Craig (Philadelphia: Presbyterian and Reformed, 1970). For several other helpful discussions, see P. J. Achtemeier, *The Inspiration of Scripture: Problems and Proposals* (Philadelphia: Westminster, 1980); S. T. Davis, *The Debate About the Bible* (Philadelphia: Westminster, 1977); M. J. Erickson, *Christian Theology*, 3 vols. (Grand Rapids, Mich.: Baker, 1983-85), 1:199-220; B. Vawter, *Biblical Inspiration* (Philadelphia: Westminster, 1972); C. Pinnock, *The Scripture Principle* (San Francisco: Harper & Row, 1984).

[38]On the issue of the normative unity underlying the diversity of Scripture, see my *Cynic, Sage*, pp. 129-32; D. A. Carson, "Unity and Diversity in the New Testament: The Possibility of Systematic Theology," in *Scripture and Truth*, ed. Carson and J. D. Woodbridge (Grand Rapids, Mich.: Baker, rpt. 1992), pp. 65-95; A. J. Hultgren, *The Rise of Normative Christianity* (Minneapolis: Fortress, 1994); I. H. Marshall, "Jesus, Paul and John," *Aberdeen University Review* 173 (1985): 18-36; idem, "An Evangelical Approach to 'Theological Criticism,' " *Themelios* 13 (April-May 1988): 79-85; B. L. Martin, "Some Reflections on the Unity of the New Testament," *SR* 8, no. 2 (1979): 143-52; and J. I. Packer, "Upholding the Unity of Scripture Today," *JETS* 25, no. 4 (1982): 409-14.

Chapter 1: Hearing Zosia

[1]Walter Wink has recently attempted to render a belief in good and evil "Powers" more credible to modern ears in the three volumes of his series *The Powers:* vol. 1, *Naming the Powers: The Language of Power in the New Testament* (Philadelphia: Fortress, 1984); vol. 2, *Unmasking the Powers: The Invisible Forces That Determine Human Existence* (Philadelphia: Fortress, 1986); vol. 3, *Engaging the Powers: Discernment and Resistance in a World of Domination* (Minneapolis: Fortress, 1992). Wink achieves this credibility, however, by denying that the Powers are autonomous and free agents. To this extent he "demythologizes" them. For Wink the Powers are most fundamentally the "spiritual interiority" of human social units—something like Jungian archetypes. The Powers, then, have no mind or will of their own, but are rather constituted by the collective mind and will of human groups (institutions, social groups, corporations, nations, etc.). For all the creativity,

and often the insight, of Wink's articulation and defense of this thesis, however, the thesis undermines at least one central aspect of the Powers in Scripture: their ability to wage war against humanity. It is for this reason that Wink's analysis of the Powers offers no advantage for a theodicy. (On this score, Wink favors process thought. See *Engaging the Powers*, p. 401, note 23.) It is also because the autonomous free agency of the Powers has been undermined that Wink ultimately embraces a universalistic and a pacifistic perspective of the Powers. In contrast, we shall see that Scripture offers the view that good and evil cosmic and angelic forces are in some sense personal, autonomous and free, and hence sometimes spiritual warfare must be carried out against the evil Powers in order that they might be eternally defeated. As C. S. Lewis argued, when free will is consistently embraced, universalism cannot be. See *Problem of Pain* (New York: Macmillan, 1962), pp. 121-28; idem, *The Great Divorce* (New York: Macmillan, 1946), pp. 120-21.

[2]P. Friedman, ed., *Martyrs and Fighters: The Epic of the Warsaw Ghetto* (New York: Praeger, 1954), pp. 166-67. Quoted in D. Rausch, *A Legacy of Hatred: Why Christians Must Not Forget the Holocaust* (Chicago: Moody Press, 1984), p. 122.

[3]J. B. Russell, *The Prince of Darkness* (Ithaca, N.Y.: Cornell University Press, 1988), p. 257. So argues K. Surin: "It is imperative . . . that the theodicist ask himself: Am I operating with a conception of evil that, because of its abstract nature, effectively reduces evil to banality?" See his "Theodicy?" *HTR* 76, no. 2 (1983): 230-32. Just this "abstractness," argues Hannah Arendt, is what allowed "decent" people to participate in the Holocaust. See her *Eichmann in Jerusalem: A Report on the Banality of Evil* (Harmondsworth, U.K.: Penguin, rpt. 1977).

[4]Russell, *Prince of Darkness*, p. 256. So too Surin, following Irving Greenberg, argues that after the Holocaust no theodicy can be taken seriously that does not itself "take burning children seriously." See his *Theology and the Problem of Evil* (New York: Blackwell, 1986), p. 151.

[5]See note 32 in the introduction regarding classical-philosophical theism. For a critical overview of the classical-philosophical definition of God, see the discussion (with references) in my *Trinity and Process: A Critical Evaluation and Reconstruction of Hartshorne's Di-Polar Theism Towards a Trinitarian Metaphysics* (New York: Peter Lang, 1992), pp. 196ff., 253ff., 296ff. For a trenchant critique of the classical-philosophical view of God as it concerns the problem of creaturely free will and the problem of evil, see D. Griffin, *Power and Evil: A Process Theodicy* (Philadelphia: Westminster, 1976). Unfortunately, Griffin thinks that only the process view of God, being necessarily related to a nondivine world that by metaphysical necessity has power over and against God, avoids the theodicy problems created by the classical-philosophical view of God. Something similar must be said of Langdon Gilkey's forceful critique of classical-philosophical theism in his *Reaping the Whirlwind: A Christian Interpretation of History* (New York: Seabury, 1976).

[6]This much is true even if we choose to speak of God "permitting" certain events as opposed to God "willing" certain events. As H. Blocher (following Calvin) argues, if God exercises meticulous control over the world, then even what he "allows" *must serve a particular divine purpose*. Thus the classic distinction between what God "wills" and what God "permits" amounts to very little. See Blocher, *Evil and the Cross*, trans. D. G. Preston (Downers Grove, Ill.: InterVarsity Press, 1994), pp. 96-97.

[7]A. König, *Here Am I: A Believer's Reflection on God* (Grand Rapids, Mich.:

Eerdmans, 1982), p. 20. As an expression of a *subjective impression* König's statement is certainly valid, though as a report about objective reality it is epistemologically dubious. How would one measure the balance between good and evil to gain such knowledge? For a painful representative selection of modern illustrations of the radicality of the problem of evil, see P. Schilling, *God and Human Anguish* (Nashville: Abingdon, 1977), pp. 14-24.

[8]L. Sandell, "Day by Day and with Each Passing Moment," trans. A. L. Skoog.

[9]See Augustine *City of God* 5.10.

[10]For a succinct but penetrating history of Christian anti-Semitism, see Rausch, *Legacy of Hatred.*

[11]W. F. Lloyd, "My Times Are in Thy Hand," adapted by W. H. Havergal.

[12]Schelling (*God and Human Anguish*, pp. 59-72) speaks against a "theology of resignation," which results from the sort of implicit theological determinism reflected in many of the traditional hymns of the church. We resign ourselves to accept as from the hand of God what we ought to revolt against as from the hand of Satan. We thereby trade in biblical spiritual activism for a nonbiblical form of passivity and pseudosecurity.

[13]William Cowper, 1731-1800, "God Moves in a Mysterious Way."

[14]For issues surrounding Augustine's classic statement of this position, see C. Kirwan, *Augustine* (London: Routledge, 1989), pp. 119-24.

[15]R. C. Sproul, *Chosen By God* (Wheaton, Ill.: Tyndale, 1986), pp. 26-27. Sproul has more recently expanded this argument in *Not a Chance: The Myth of Chance in Modern Science and Cosmology* (Grand Rapids, Mich.: Baker, 1994).

[16]For a fascinating exposition on the mathematical foundation of the conception of randomness in the sciences, especially as it functions in modern chaos theory, see I. Steward, *Does God Play Dice? The Mathematics of Chaos* (Cambridge, Mass.: Blackwell, rpt. 1995). Also relevant, and more theologically sophisticated, is D. J. Bartholomew, *God of Chance* (London: SCM, 1984).

[17]See F. Dostoyevsky, *The Brothers Karamazov*, trans. C. Garrett (New York: Modern Library, 1950), pp. 286-92.

[18]Regarding the term "Augustinian model/theodicy," a word of clarification is perhaps in order. Since John Hick's important work on the problem of evil (*Evil and the God of Love* [London: Fontana, 1968]) the term "Augustinian theodicy" has frequently come to be juxtaposed to Hick's "Irenaean theodicy," the crucial difference being that Augustine supposedly conceives of evil as a free intrusion into an originally perfect state (of angels, then of humans), while Irenaeus, according to Hick, conceived of the original state (of humans anyway) as innocent but not perfect. For Hick, then, the Augustinian model represents the classical version of the free will defense. My objection against the Augustinian theodicy is precisely the opposite of this. I hold that Augustine's view of the free Fall (of angels and humans) is biblical and can (contra Hick) be made philosophically intelligible. Augustine himself did not do this, however, because on top of his free will defense he posited a divine purpose preceding all events, including free actions. This all-encompassing divine blueprint undermines the explanatory value of his free will defense. For Hick's argument against the notion that originally perfect, finite, free beings could "fall," see "The Problem of Evil in the First and Last Things," *JTS* 19 (1968): 592. Similar objections are raised by B. Calvert, "Dualism and the Problem of Evil," *Sophia* 22, no. 3 (1983): 15-28, who uses this critique to argue for a necessary evil being. I shall address these objections to the free will defense in my forthcoming

Satan and the Problem of Evil.

[19]Many biblical scholars maintain that this is a dominant, if not *the* dominant, view of evil found throughout the Old Testament (and, it is sometimes argued, even in the New), especially in the Psalms. For a collection of references, see B. Whitney, *Evil and the Process God* (New York: Mellen, 1985), pp. 25-28, 182; E. S. Gerstenberger and W. Schrage, *Suffering* (Nashville: Abingdon, 1977), pp. 107, 227-331; and Schilling, *God and Human Anguish*, pp. 119-45. Without denying that this theme is found in the Old Testament, and thus without dismissing the truth that God can and does sometimes use evil to discipline people, many scholars question that this motif is dominant in Old Testament thinking. For a solid critique of this interpretation of many of the so-called complaint Psalms, see F. Lindström's outstanding work, *Suffering and Sin: Interpretations of Illness in the Individual Complaint Psalms*, trans. M. McLamb, ConBOT 37 (Stockholm: Almqvist & Wiksell, 1994). For a more general response to this reading of the Old Testament, see T. Fretheim, *The Suffering of God: An Old Testament Perspective*, OBT (Philadelphia: Fortress, 1984); K. Koch, "Is There a Doctrine of Retribution in the Old Testament?" in *Theodicy in the Old Testament,* ed. J. Crenshaw, IRT (Philadelphia: Fortress, 1983), pp. 57-87; as well as J. Crenshaw, "The Shift from Theodicy to Anthropodicy," in ibid., pp. 1-16. Also relevant to this and other supposed theodicy themes found in Scripture is J. Crenshaw, *A Whirlpool of Torment*, OBT (Philadelphia: Fortress, 1984).

[20]John 9:1-5 is often translated in such a way that it seems to support the view that God caused the person to be born blind. I argue against this translation in chapter eight.

[21]Hence the title of H. S. Kushner's popular book, *When Bad Things Happen to Good People* (New York: Schocken, 1981). That Rabbi Kushner's book (in which he simply denies that God is omnipotent) was a bestseller perhaps indicates that the hold which the classical-philosophical view of God had on Western people is waning.

[22]Boethius, *The Consolation of Philosophy* (New York: Random House, 1943), 4.74-100.

[23]So argues Kenneth Surin, for example: "despite the efforts of . . . theologians, the thought persists in many quarters that theodicy is perhaps one of the least satisfying areas of the theological enterprise" ("Theodicy?" *HTR* 76, no. 2 [1983]: 223). See also idem. *Theology and the Problem of Evil* (Oxford: Blackwell, 1986); T. W. Tilley, *The Evils of Theodicy* (Washington, D.C.: Georgetown University Press, 1990); and M. Scott, "The Morality of Theodicies," *RelS* 32, no. 1 (1996): 1-13. Similar pessimistic sentiments regarding theodicy as it has been understood within the classical-philosophical tradition are expressed in R. Worsely, *Human Freedom and the Logic of Evil: Prolegomenon to a Theology of Evil* (London: Macmillan, 1996), and W. C. Placher, *The Domestication of Transcendence: How Modern Thinking About God Went Wrong* (Louisville, Ky.: Westminister John Knox Press, 1996), pp. 201-15.

[24]Augustine, *Confessions,* trans. H. Chadwick (New York: Oxford University Press, 1991), p. 125. See Boethius *Consolation* 4.74-100.

[25]Augustine *City of God* 5.10; NPNF 2:93.

[26]Ibid., 11.18, pp. 214-15.

[27]*Brothers Karamazov*, p. 290.

[28]Cf., e.g., Deuteronomy 12:31; 16:22; Proverbs 6:16; 11:1; Isaiah 61:8; Zechariah 8:17; Malachi 2:16.

[29]Among the vast array of theologians and philosophers who have contended that the classical-philosophical view of God is incompatible with free will, understood as self-determination, Charles Hartshorne has arguably been the most forceful, and is undoubtedly the most prolific. For his two most succinct statements against the classical view of God and for his dipolar view of God, see *The Divine Relativity: A Social Conception of God* (New Haven: Yale University Press, 1948); and *Omnipotence and Other Theological Mistakes* (Albany: SUNY, 1984).

[30]See Boyd, *Trinity and Process*, as well as *Satan and the Problem of Evil*, chapters 3-8 (forthcoming). For several examples of Arminian theologians who are nevertheless significantly (and to some extent inconsistently) classical in their views of God, see T. Oden, *Systematic Theology*, vol. 1, *The Living God* (San Francisco: Harper & Row, 1987), pp. 53-82; H. O. Wiley, *Christian Theology*, 3 vols. (Kansas City, Mo.: Beacon Hill, rpt. 1963), 1:336-44, 349-60; T. O. Summers, *Systematic Theology*, 2 vols. (Nashville: Methodist Episcopal Church Publishing House, 1896), 1:75-109; W. B. Pope, *A Compendium of Christian Theology*, 3 vols. (London: Wesleyan Conference Office, 1880), 1:248-358.

[31]See, e.g., Summers, *Systematic Theology*, 1:122-46. For a more balanced but yet quite classical Arminian theodicy, see Ogden, *Living God*, 1:296-315. For an excellent philosophical defense of the possibility of gratuitous evil (and thus a rejection of the concept of providence as meticulous control), see M. Peterson, *Evil and the Christian God* (Grand Rapids, Mich.: Baker, 1982).

[32]See my forthcoming *Satan and Problem of Evil*, chapter 10.

[33]It is crucial to note that the issue I raise here is over the ontological status of the future in the present; it is not over whether God is omniscient. Orthodox Christianity has always rightly assumed that God is omniscient. Indeed, I have myself elsewhere argued that God's knowledge is, by metaphysical necessity, coterminous with reality (*Trinity and Process*, pp. 242-52). Reality—including the total reality of the future—is, in my view, by definition "that which is known by God." The issue being raised here concerns whether the future at the present time is wholly definite. Or is it, at the present time, partially indefinite, consisting at least in part of possibilities? Does the future consist only in "what *shall* transpire," or does it also include "what *may* transpire"? Put otherwise, does the content of God's perfect knowledge include the knowledge of possibilities, or is it (or must it be) exhaustively definite? Is the knowledge of possibilities defective? Does reality really include possibilities? If it does, then God's knowledge of them is certainly not defective.

Though many theologians presently argue that denying that God has exhaustive definite knowledge of what shall transpire limits God's knowledge, in truth this view limits God's knowledge no more than denying that God has exhaustive knowledge of the future as a realm of possibilities. Both views affirm in the same manner that God knows perfectly what is real, and deny that God knows what is not. Hence it is simply the content of the reality God perfectly knows, not the fact that this knowledge is omniscient, which the two views disagree over. David Basinger is among the few who properly locates the issue. See his "Can an Evangelical Christian Justifiably Deny God's Exhaustive Knowledge of the Future?" *CSR* 25, no. 2 (1995): 133-45. For an in-depth discussion, see my *Trinity and Process*, pp. 296-342. As mentioned in note 32 above, I shall again address this issue as it intersects with theodicy concerns in my forthcoming *Satan and the Problem of Evil*.

[34]See, e.g., Genesis 6:5-7, 22:12ff.; Exodus 3:18—4:9; 32:12-14; 1 Samuel 15:11,

35; 1 Kings 2:1-4; 1 Chronicles 21:15; Isaiah 38:1-5; Jonah 3:4-10; 4:2; Jeremiah 3:6-7, 19-20; 18:6-11; 26:3, 19; 38:17-18; Hosea 11:8-9; Joel 2:12-14; Revelation 3:5. The most extensive recent review of the biblical basis for an "open" view of God is J. Sanders, "Divine Providence as Risk-Taking" (Ph.D. diss., University of South Africa, 1996). Even more exhaustive, however, is the work of L. D. McCabe in the nineteenth century: *Divine Nescience of Future Contingencies a Necessity* (New York: Phillips and Hunt, 1882), and esp. *The Foreknowledge of God* (Cincinnati: Granston and Stowe, 1887). Other more recent works on the topic include C. Pinnock, ed., *The Openness of God* (Downers Grove, Ill.: InterVarsity Press, 1994), and R. Rice, *God's Foreknowledge and Man's Free Will* (Minneapolis: Bethany House, 1985).

[35]One might argue that God foreknows what shall transpire but can do nothing about it. He has what is sometimes called "simple foreknowledge." (For a fine discussion of different models of foreknowledge, see Sanders, "Divine Providence as Risk-Taking," pp. 212-29.) The view has the significant advantage of avoiding the question of why God did not do something about Hitler (or any given evil) if he knew about it ahead of time. But it is problematic in other respects. First, as a point of fact, it is not the traditional Arminian position, and indeed runs counter to the basic thrust of the Arminian position, which wanted to affirm foreknowledge as a means of asserting God's control over the world without denying freedom. Second, the simple foreknowledge view does not explain the passages where God changes his mind or expresses surprise at the way events transpire. Third, this view does not explain those passages where God is said to know (to some extent at least) the future, for the thrust of these passages is to assert that God is (to this extent) in control (e.g., Is 42:9; 44:7; 45:11; 46:9-10; Rom 8:29; 1 Pet 1:2). Fourth, this view still renders freedom philosophically problematic, for it assumes that the future as definite is in some sense eternally "there." (See W. Hasker, "A Philosophical Perspective," in *Openness of God*, pp. 126-54. I shall address this topic in my forthcoming *Satan and the Problem of Evil*.) Fifth, this view is in practice no different from the "open" view. It certainly does not in the least increase God's control over future events. It simply asserts that God knows what will happen. But this view has the disadvantage (in comparison to the open view) of reducing God to the level of the fabled Cassandra, the prophetess who was cursed to know the future without being able to do anything about it. Yet God is in this view even more unfortunate than Cassandra, for his foreknowledge is supposedly eternal. Foreknowledge, in this scenario, is hardly an advantageous attribute for God to have. It doesn't help him rule the world, but only ensures that there will never be any novelty or adventure in his experience of the world. So concludes H. H. Framer (*The World and God: A Study of Prayer, Providence and Miracle* [London: Nisbet & Co., 1935], p.35): "All that is left is the unspeakably sterile and depressing spectacle of omniscience playing an everlasting game of patience with itself, all possible combination of the cards being already known by heart."

Despite my misgivings regarding exhaustively definite foreknowledge, however, I am in general agreement with John Sanders and David Basinger in maintaining that free will theism does not require a denial of exhaustively definite foreknowledge. Similarly, the warfare worldview does not strictly require the view that the future is in part open, though I shall subsequently argue (*Satan and the Problem of Evil*) that affirming that the future is exhaustively and eternally definite, and thus of course known by God as such, is problematic from the perspective of the warfare worldview.

[36] For several discussions from various perspectives on the inadequacy of the free will defense as traditionally employed by Arminians, see H. Blocher, *Evil and the Cross*, trans. D. G. Preston (Downers Grove, Ill.: InterVarsity Press, 1994), pp. 36-94; J. Feinberg, *Theologies of Evil* (Washington, D.C.: University Press of America, 1979), pp. 49-83; M. Martin, *Atheism: A Philosophical Justification* (Philadelphia: Temple University Press, 1990), pp. 362-91; F. Tupper, *A Scandalous Providence: The Jesus Story of the Compassion of God* (Macon, Ga.: Mercer University Press, 1995), p. 427; W. Robinson, *The Devil and God* (New York: Abingdon-Cokesbury Press, n.d.), p. 123.

[37] Wink, *Engaging the Powers*, p. 314.

[38] Ibid., pp. 314-15.

[39] See, e.g., Matthew 5:10-12, 44; 10:16-18; 23:34-35; 24:8-10; Mark 13:9-13; John 15:18-19; 16:1-2; Romans 8:17-23; 1 Corinthians 4:12-13; 2 Corinthians 4:11-18; Colossians 1:24; 2 Timothy 2:12; 1 Peter 5:10.

[40] Boethius *Consolation* 91, 96.

[41] See my forthcoming *Satan and the Problem of Evil*, chapters 1—4.

[42] The Greek term *daimonizomai* means "to be acted on by a demon." For three reasons I have in most cases chosen to transliterate it "demonize" rather than to follow the majority of translations that render it "possess": (1) The term does not mean "to possess." This term is too strong, for it denotes total control and even ownership, while "demonize" admits of a wide variety of degrees. (2) The term "possess" has generated a good deal of wholly unnecessary controversy, especially around whether Christians can be "demonized." (3) The term "possessed" has, largely through Hollywood, acquired some unbiblical connotations that I wish to avoid. For a thorough review of the issues surrounding demonization and Christians, see F. Dickason, *Demon Possession and the Christian* (Westchester, Ill.: Crossway Books, 1989).

[43] I argue in chapters two and three that the Old Testament appropriation of ancient Near Eastern monster myths—its portraits of Leviathan, Yamm, Rahab and Behemoth as threatening the earth—are the rough equivalents of the New Testament's view of Satan as the principality and power of the air as well as the ruler of this world. It also anticipates the thinking of various early church fathers, such as Athenagoras, who view Satan as the ruler of all matter. In this view, Satan is "the spirit which is about matter who was created by God, just as the other angels were . . . and entrusted with the control of matter and the forms of matter" (*A Plea for the Christians*, ANF 2, ed. A. Roberts and J. Donaldson (Grand Rapids, Mich.: Eerdmans, rpt. 1979), chapter 24 (p. 142).

[44] Within the boundaries of orthodoxy there are exceptions, of course. But even among these exceptions the thesis is never fully developed. The most noteworthy contemporary orthodox apologists who make *some* use of Satan as at least relevant to the problem of evil are L. Hodgson, *For Faith and Freedom: The Gifford Lectures, 1955-57*, 2 vols. (Oxford: Blackwell, 1956-1957), 1:213-14; C. S. Lewis, *The Problem of Pain* (New York: Macmillan, 1945), pp. 121-23; E. L. Mascall, *Christian Theology and Natural Science: Some Questions on Their Relations* (London: Longmans, Green, 1956), pp. 301-3; W. Robinson, *The Devil and God*, pp. 18-23, 119-23; T. Penelhum, *Religion and Rationality: An Introduction to the Philosophy of Religion* (New York: Random, 1971), pp. 246-47; A. Plantinga, *God, Freedom and Evil* (Grand Rapids, Mich.: Eerdmans, 1974), p. 58; idem, *The Nature of*

Necessity (Oxford: Clarendon, 1974), pp. 191-93; S. Davis, *Logic and the Nature of God* (Grand Rapids, Mich.: Eerdmans, 1983), pp. 112-14; J. B. Russell, *The Devil: Perceptions of Evil From Antiquity to Primitive Christianity* (Ithaca: Cornell University Press, 1977), pp. 221-49; D. I. Trethowan, *An Essay in Christian Philosophy* (London: Longmans, Green, 1954), p. 128; C. C. J. Webb, *Problems in the Relations of God and Man* (London: Nisbet, 1911), pp. 36-37; J. W. Wenham, *The Enigma of Evil: Can We Believe in the Goodness of God* (Grand Rapids, Mich.: Zondervan, rpt. 1985), pp. 48, 86, 198; J. Kallas, *The Significance of the Synoptic Miracles* (Greenwich, Conn.: Seabury, 1961); idem, *Jesus and the Power of Satan* (Philadelphia: Westminster, 1968); idem, *The Satanward View: A Study of Pauline Theology* (Philadelphia: Westminster, 1966).

Though her thinking lies somewhat outside the parameters of traditional orthodox Christianity, and though her method is highly subjectivistic and unscholarly, it should be noted that Ellen White, the founder of the Seventh-day Adventist movement, integrated a warfare perspective into the problem of evil and the doctrine of God perhaps more thoroughly than anyone else in church history. See E. G. White, *Conflict of the Ages Series*, vols. 1-5 (Mountain View, Calif.: Pacific Press Publishing Association, 1890-1917).

[45]Throughout this volume and the forthcoming *Satan and the Problem of Evil*, I identify Augustine as the turning point in church history from a warfare to a providential blueprint worldview. There were, however, significant harbingers of such a move prior to Augustine, and the warfare view was not entirely lost after Augustine. But one can arguably trace the greatest impetus for this general move to the influence of Augustine's thought. This argument, with the requisite historical nuances, will be made in detail in *Satan and the Problem of Evil*.

[46]Origen anticipates Augustine "in a peculiar way" in that like Augustine he believes that all events, including free actions, meticulously follow a divine blueprint. But for Origen this divine blueprint is itself created by God in response to the free decisions made by his creatures in a preexistent state. Hence, as with other pre-Augustinian fathers, the ultimate explanation for evil in the world is free will. I shall thoroughly discuss Origen's views, as well as views of the postapostolic church in general regarding evil and free will, in chapters 1-4 of my forthcoming *Satan and the Problem of Evil*.

[47]This is not to suggest that all responsibility for all evil attaches to Satan, something Scripture clearly denies. But inasmuch as the origin of evil attaches to Satan, he shares in the responsibility for all evil.

[48]This point has rarely been disputed, but see E. Lewis, *The Creator and the Adversary* (New York: Abingdon-Cokesbury, 1948), who attempts to argue that the narrative of Scripture presupposes a full-fledged dualism. Also relevant here is Calvert, "Dualism and the Problem of Evil."

[49]Developing a philosophical and theological defense for this view, rooted in the thinking of the pre-Augustinian church, shall be my task in the forthcoming *Satan and the Problem of Evil*.

[50]König, *Here Am I*, p. 20.

[51]Wink, *Naming the Powers*, p. 4.

[52]H. Schlier, *Principalities and Powers in the New Testament* (Freiburg: Herder, 1961); H. Berkhof, *Christ and the Powers* (Scottdale, Penn.: Herald, 1977). This position will be critically discussed in chapter ten.

[53]See note 1 above.

[54]Hence Screwtape says to Wormwood, "If any faint suspicion of your existence begins to arise in his mind, suggest to him a picture of something in red tights, and persuade him that since he cannot believe in that . . . he therefore cannot believe in you" (C. S. Lewis, *The Screwtape Letters* [New York: Macmillan, 1982], p. 33).

[55]See, e.g., R. E. Webber's excellent and balanced work *The Church in the World: Opposition, Tension or Transformation?* (Grand Rapids, Mich.: Zondervan, 1986). See also P. O'Brien, "Principalities and Powers: Opponents of the Church," *ERT* 16, no. 4 (1992): 353-84, esp. 378; V. Eller, *Christian Anarchy: Jesus' Primacy over the Powers* (Grand Rapids, Mich.: Eerdmans, 1987); A. H. van den Heuvel, *Those Rebellious Powers* (New York: Friendship, 1965); and R. Sider, *Christ and Violence* (Scottdale, Penn.: Herald, 1979), who takes Ephesians 3:10 to be a mandate of the church to preach against the "powers" (p. 51), as does Wink, *Naming the Powers*, p. 89.

[56]R. K. McGregor Wright, *No Place for Sovereignty: What's Wrong with Freewill Theism* (Downers Grove, Ill.: InterVarsity Press, 1996). As an important aside, it should be noted that the argument that angelic and human free will undermines divine sovereignty works only on the assumption that "sovereignty" and "exhaustive control" are synonymous and that this is the model of rule that is most praiseworthy (worthy of God). To some free will theists, however, this type of rule seems least worthy of God. It strikes some of us as reflecting an insecure, petty and impersonal deity rather than the gloriously sovereign God of the Bible who is secure enough in his transcendence to grant personhood and self-determination to his creatures. True divine sovereignty, in the thinking of free will theists, is only affirmed when it is construed in relational, interpersonal terms. Against McGregor and other Reformed thinkers, then this view argues that it is the Calvinist perspective, not the free will theist perspective, that in truth leaves "no place for sovereignty."

[57]On the move from "modernism" to "postmodernism," especially as it concerns the new perspectives that define the latter, see S. Grenz, *A Primer on Postmodernism* (Grand Rapids, Mich.: Eerdmans, 1996); J. W. Bertens, *The Idea of the Postmodern: A History* (London: Routledge, 1995); R. J. Berstein, *Beyond Objectivism and Relativism: Science, Hermeneutics and Praxis* (Philadelphia: University of Pennsylvania Press, 1988); T. Docherty, ed., *Postmodernism: A Reader* (New York: Columbia University Press, 1993); C. Norris, *The Truth About Postmodernism* (Oxford: Blackwell, 1993); idem, *What's Wrong with Postmodernism: Critical Theory and the Ends of Philosophy* (Baltimore: Johns Hopkins University Press, 1990); F. B. Burnham, *Postmodern Theology: Christian Faith in a Pluralist World* (San Francisco: Harper & Row, 1989); N. Murphy and J. W. McClendon Jr., "Distinguishing Modern and Postmodern Theologies," *Modern Theology* 5, no. 3 (1989): 191-214; C. Walhout and L. Ryken, eds., *Contemporary Literary Theory: A Christian Appraisal* (Grand Rapids, Mich.: Eerdmans, 1991). For a helpful map of the rough terrain of postmodern theology, see D. R. Griffin, "Introduction: Varieties of Postmodern Theology," in D. Griffin, W. A. Beardslee and J. Holland, *Varieties of Postmodern Theology* (Albany: SUNY, 1989), pp. 1-7; as well as (from a very different perspective) G. E. Veith, *Postmodern Times: A Christian Guide to Contemporary Thought and Culture* (Wheaton, Ill.: Crossway, 1994).

[58]Interestingly enough, however, the truth claims of the deconstructionists themselves seem to be strangely exempt from this criticism. For solid critical reviews of deconstructionism, see G. Steiner, *Real Presences* (Chicago: University of Chicago Press, 1989); A. Jacobs, "The Values of Literary Study: Deconstruction and Other Developments," *CSR* 16 (1987): 373-83; D. L. Jeffrey, "*Caveat lector:* Structural-

ism, Deconstructionism and Ideology," *CSR* 18 (1988): 436-48; and G. P. Shaw, "The Rise and Fall of Deconstructionism," *Commentary* 92 (Dec. 1991): 50-53.
[59]For several evangelical assessments of postmodernism and deconstructionism, see D. S. Dockery, *The Challenge of Postmodernism: An Evangelical Engagement* (Wheaton, Ill.: Victor, 1995); T. C. Oden, *After Modernity—What? Agenda for Theology* (Grand Rapids, Mich.: Zondervan, 1990); T. R. Phillips and D. L. Okholm, eds., *Christian Apologetics in the Postmodern World* (Downers Grove, Ill.: InterVarsity Press, 1995); Veith, *Postmodern Times;* Grenz, *Postmodern Primer.*
[60]The classic text regarding the sociology of knowledge is P. Berger and T. Luckmann, *The Social Construction of Reality* (Garden City, N.Y.: Doubleday, 1966). Berger uses his sociological approach to critique Western naturalism in *A Rumor of Angels: Modern Society and the Rediscovery of the Supernatural* (Garden City, N.Y.: Doubleday, 1969).
[61]One outstanding example of a contemporary evangelical who has insightfully integrated non-Western perspectives into a Western Christian vision of reality is M. Kraft, *Understanding Spiritual Power: A Forgotten Dimension of Cross-Cultural Mission and Ministry* (Maryknoll, N.Y.: Orbis, 1995). For several anthropological studies that led the "Western"-minded investigators to take seriously various "supernatural" phenomena, see E. Turner, *Experiencing Ritual: A New Interpretation of African Healing* (Philadelphia: University of Pennsylvania Press, 1992); idem, "The Reality of Spirits," *ReVision* 15, no. 1 (1992): 28-32; J. Fauret-Saada, *Deadly Words: Witchcraft in the Bocage,* trans. C. Cullen (New York: Cambridge University Press, 1980); idem, *Corps pour corps: Enquête sur la sorcellerie dans le bocage* (Paris: Gallimard, 1981); P. Stoller, "Eye, Mind and Word in Anthropology," *L'Homme* 24 (1984): 91-114; M. Harner, *The Way of the Shaman* (San Francisco: HarperSanFrancisco, rpt. 1990), esp. pp. 1-19; L. Peters, *Ecstasy and Healing in Nepal: An Ethnopsychiatric Study of Tamang Shamanism* (Malibu: Undena, 1981), pp. 45-54. For several other anthropological studies of such things as the role of spirits and exorcism in various cultures, see I. M. Lewis, *Ecstatic Religion: An Anthropological Study of Spirit Possession and Shamanism* (Baltimore: Penguin, 1971); J. Beattie and J. Middleton, eds., *Spirit Mediumship and Society in Africa* (London: Routledge & Kegan Paul, 1969); E. Bourguignon, *Possession* (San Francisco: Chandler and Sharp, 1976); idem, ed., *Religion, Altered States of Consciousness and Social Change* (Columbus: Ohio State University Press, 1973); B. P. Levack, *Witchcraft, Magic and Demonology,* vol. 9: *Possession and Exorcism* (Hamden, Conn.: Garland, 1992); and esp. F. D. Goodman, *How About Demons? Possession and Exorcism in the Modern World* (Bloomington: Indiana University Press, 1988).
[62]M. Adler (*The Angels and Us* [New York: Macmillan, 1982]) anticipated the contemporary obsession. The phenomenon has been reported in a wide variety of venues; see K. L. Woodward, "Angels," *Newsweek,* Dec. 27, 1993, pp. 56-57; N. Gibbs, "Angels Among Us," *Time,* Dec. 27, 1993, pp. 56-65; E. Stone, "Are There Angels Among Us?" *New Age Journal* (March-April 1994): 88-93, 148-51; T. Jones, "Rumors of Angels," *Christianity Today* 37 (April 5, 1993): 18-22. I recently visited a major bookstore in the Twin Cities and counted no fewer than twenty-four newly published books on angels. Only six were written from a discernibly orthodox Christian perspective.
[63]Among the earlier noteworthy books on this topic are D. Basham, *Deliver Us from Evil* (Old Tappan, N.J.: Revell, rpt. 1980); M. Bubeck, *The Adversary: The Christian Versus Demon Activity* (Chicago: Moody Press, 1975); K. Koch, *Occult Bondage*

and Deliverance (Grand Rapids, Mich.: Kregel, 1970). Several of the most popular recent expositions are N. T. Anderson, *The Bondage Breaker* (Eugene, Ore.: Harvest House, 1990); E. Christenson, *Battling the Prince of Darkness: Rescuing Captives from Satan's Kingdom* (Wheaton, Ill.: Victor, 1990); G. Mallone, *Arming for Spiritual Warfare* (Downers Grove, Ill.: InterVarsity Press, 1991); E. Murphy, *The Handbook for Spiritual Warfare* (Nashville: Nelson, 1992); D. Sherman, *Spiritual Warfare for Every Believer* (Seattle: YWAM Books, 1990); and T. B. White, *The Believer's Guide to Spiritual Warfare: Wising Up to Satan's Influence in Your World* (Ann Arbor, Mich.: Servant, 1990). At the 1989 Lausanne II conference on world missions held in Manila, the three best attended tracks (sets of workshops) all had to do with spiritual warfare. A number of the papers presented there have been reproduced in C. H. Kraft and M. White, eds., *Behind Enemy Lines: An Advanced Guide to Spiritual Warfare* (Ann Arbor, Mich.: Servant, 1994).

[64]F. Peretti, *This Present Darkness* (Wheaton, Ill.: Crossway, 1986); idem, *Piercing the Darkness* (Wheaton, Ill.: Crossway, 1989).

[65]For several comparatively reliable contemporary accounts of exorcism, see T. K. Osterreich, *Possession and Exorcism* (New York: Causeway, 1974); M. Kelsey, *Discernment* (New York: Paulist, 1978); A. Rodwyk, *Possessed by Satan*, trans. M. Ebon (New York: Doubleday, 1975); M. Martin, *Hostage to the Devil: The Possession and Exorcism of Five Living Americans* (New York: Reader's Digest, 1976); M. S. Peck, *People of the Lie* (New York: Simon & Schuster, 1983); R. Curran, *The Haunted: One Family's Nightmare* (New York: St. Martin's, 1988); R. Duetch, *Exorcism: Possession or Obsession?* (London: Backman and Turner, 1975); E. Fiore, *The Unquiet Dead: A Psychologist Treats Spirit Possession—Detecting and Removing Earthbound Spirits* (Garden City, N.Y.: Doubleday, 1987); J. Lhermitte, *Diabolical Possession: True or False?* trans. P. J. Hepburne-Scott (London: Burnes & Oates, 1963); V. Stacey, "Christ Cleanses Buildings and Delivers People: Four Case Studies," *ERT* 16, no. 4 (1992): 342-52. The phenomenon of possession and deliverance can be traced throughout church history, as has been done by Paul Eddy in an unpublished manuscript entitled "The Deliverance Ministry Through Church History" (1983). Other discussions on deliverance in the early church include E. Ferguson, *Demonology of the Early Christian World* (New York: Mellen, 1984); E. A. Leeper, "Exorcism in Early Christianity" (Ph.D. diss., Duke University, 1991); F. X. Goeky, *The Terminology for the Devil and Evil Spirits in the Apostolic Fathers*, PS 93 (Washington, D.C.: Catholic University of America Press, 1961); H. A. Kelly, *The Devil, Demonology and Witchcraft: The Development of Christian Beliefs in Evil Spirits*, 2d ed. (Garden City, N.Y.: Doubleday, 1974); J. B. Russell, *Satan: The Early Christian Tradition* (Ithaca: Cornell University Press, 1981). I shall consider in depth the warfare worldview of the early church in part 1 of *Satan and the Problem of Evil*. Other works that consider deliverance and exorcism throughout church history include E. Langton, *Supernatural: The Doctrine of Spirits, Angels and Demons from the Middle Ages to the Present Time* (London: Rider, n.d.); D. P. Walker, *Unclean Spirits, Possession and Exorcism in France and England in the Late Sixteenth and Early Seventeenth Centuries* (Philadelphia: University of Pennsylvania Press, 1981); J. B. Russell, *Lucifer: The Devil in the Middle Ages* (Ithaca: Cornell University Press, 1984).

[66]Perhaps the most recent forceful attack on the "spiritual warfare movement" from a biblical perspective is that of R. Guelich, "Spiritual Warfare: Jesus, Paul and Peretti" *Pneuma* 13, no. 1 (1991): 33-64. Other critical assessments include T. Ice

and R. Dean Jr., *Overrun with Demons: The Church's New Preoccupation with the Demonic* (Eugene, Ore.: Harvest House, 1990); A. Konya, *Demons: A Biblically Based Perspective* (Schaumburg, Ill.: Regular Baptist Press, 1990); P. M. Miller, *The Devil Did Not Make Me Do It* (Scottdale, Penn.: Herald, 1977); C. Breuninger, "Where Angels Fear to Tread: Appraising the Current Fascination with Spiritual Warfare," *Covenant Quarterly* 53 (May 1995): 37-43; G. Corwin, "This Present Nervousness," *EMQ* 31, no. 2 (1995): 148-49; and M. Wakely, "A Critical Look at a New 'Key' to Evangelization," *EMQ* 31, no. 2 (1995): 152-62.

[67]Several of the most influential or fascinating works that arise from a Third World perspective are E. Milingo, *The World in Between: Christian Healing and the Struggle for Spiritual Revival* (Maryknoll, N.Y.: Orbis, 1984); J. Sobrino, *Christology at the Crossroads: A Latin American Approach* (Maryknoll, N.Y.: Orbis, 1978); and G. Gutiérrez, *A Theology of Liberation*, rev. ed. (Maryknoll, N.Y.: Orbis, 1988). On issues surrounding the influence of Third and Second World perspectives on Western theology, see W. Dyrness, ed., *Emerging Voices in Global Christian Theology* (Grand Rapids, Mich.: Zondervan, 1994); and idem, *Learning About Theology from the Third World* (Grand Rapids, Mich.: Zondervan, 1990).

[68]P. G. Hiebert ("The Flaw of the Excluded Middle," *Missiology* 10, no. 1 [1982]: 35-47) argues effectively that Western missionaries have been one of the chief global forces of secularization over the last two centuries chiefly because they imported their Western worldview, in which nothing significant occurs in the world between God and humanity, when they imported the gospel to other cultures. See also C. Kraft, *Christianity and Culture* (Maryknoll, N.Y.: Orbis, 1979); idem, "The Problem of 'What We Think We Know,'" *Faith & Renewal*, 16:2 (Sept.-Oct. 1991): 10-16; idem, *Christianity with Power: Your Worldview and Your Experience of the Supernatural* (Ann Arbor, Mich.: Servant, 1989).

[69]I have adopted the phrase "world in between" from Milingo's fascinating book by that title. This work does an excellent job of illustrating why Western Christianity needs to be open to learn from (as well as to preach to) other cultures.

[70]For example, the notorious Findhorn Community was purportedly able to produce luxurious gardens of vegetables and flowers in relatively barren sand dunes, much to the amazement of various biologists and horticulturalists who visited the community. Their secret, they claimed, was getting the "nature spirits" to cooperate with them. For a complete account, see *The Findhorn Garden* (New York: Harper & Row, 1975). (Incidentally, Walter Wink acknowledges his indebtedness to Dorothy Maclean, one of the founders of this community, for his own thinking on "the angels of nature." See *Unmasking the Powers*, pp. 156-57.) Perhaps the most popular modern testimony of the presence of supernatural elements in a non-Christian religious/philosophical setting is Shirley MacLaine's *Out on a Limb* (New York: Bantam, 1983). Others include B. Siegel, *Love, Medicine and Miracles* (New York: Harper & Row, 1974); T. Moss, *The Probability of the Impossible* (New York: New American Library, 1974); Harner, *Way of the Shaman*.

[71]See, e.g., the cases cited in notes 63 and 65 above. As a personal aside, my own waking up to the reality of Satan and the demonic realm, as well as their centrality for understanding the problem of evil and the call of the church, began in 1992, when I for the first time, and entirely unwittingly, confronted several overt cases of demonization in a short span of time and hence became involved in several exorcisms.

[72]I am not here suggesting that all miracles that take place outside Christianity are

necessarily demonic. The Spirit blows where he wills, not necessarily where we expect him to blow (Jn 3:2, 8). Hence Christians cannot preclude the possibility that God might in some instances be at work among non-Christian groups to bring about supernatural healing and deliverance (Mt 9:40ff. as well as 12:25-30 may be relevant here). My only point presently is that some miracles outside Christianity may be demonically inspired, as the Bible itself suggests (Mt 24:24; 2 Thess 2:9). At the same time, however, one cannot deny that some miracles even within Christianity might be demonically inspired (Mt 7:21-23).

[73]The "Third Wave" revival (following the earlier "Pentecostal" and "charismatic" revivals) has been a powerful impetus behind the recent rise in Christian conscious-ness regarding such matters. For works representative of this movement, see especially J. Wimber and K. Springer, *Power Evangelism* (San Francisco: Harper & Row, 1986); idem, *Power Healing* (San Francisco: Harper & Row, 1987); C. P. Wagner, *The Third Wave of the Holy Spirit* (Ann Arbor, Mich.: Servant/Vine, 1988); and J. White, *When the Spirit Comes with Power* (Downers Grove, Ill.: InterVarsity Press, 1988).

[74]As I shall argue in the forthcoming *Satan and the Problem of Evil*, chapters 3—7.

[75]For a fuller discussion of this shift, see my *Trinity and Process*, pp. 3-11, 108-21.

[76]For a discussion on this increasing dynamism leading up to, and including, the pivotal philosophical theology of Jonathan Edwards, see S. Lee, *The Philosophical Theology of Jonathan Edwards* (Princeton: Princeton University Press, 1988), pp. 10-14, 25-34, 97-106. For several good expressions of this shift as well as general discussions on what brought about this monumental shift, what it consists of and where it is going, see H. Oliver, *A Relational Metaphysics* (Boston: Marinus Nijhoff, n.d.), pp. 40ff.; J. Cushing and E. McMullin, eds., *Philosophical Consequences of Quantum Theory: Reflections on Bell's Theorem* (Notre Dame: University of Notre Dame Press, 1989); Ernst Cassirer, "Einstein's Theory of Relativity," in *Substance and Function in Einstein's Theory of Relativity* (New York: Dover, 1953); M. Apek, *The Philosophical Impact of Contemporary Physics* (Princeton: Van Nostrand, 1961); and E. Laszlo's now classic *The Systems View of the World: The Natural Philosophy of the New Developments in the Sciences* (New York: Braziller, 1972); as well as J. Buchler's classic *Metaphysics of Natural Complexes*, ed. K. Wallace, A. Marsoobian and R. Corrington (New York: SUNY, rpt. 1990).

[77]D. Bohm, *Causality and Chance in Modern Physics* (London: Routledge and Kegan Paul, 1957), p. 147. For Bohm's definitive attempt to work out the implications of quantum physics into a coherent metaphysics, see his fascinating *Wholeness and the Implicate Order* (London: ARK, rpt. 1983). Among other things, Bohm here attempts (unsuccessfully I believe) to construct a language that captures the primacy of verbs over nouns (pp. 27-47). See also the interview with Bohm in *The Holographic Paradigm and Other Paradoxes: Exploring the Leading Edge of Science*, ed. K. Wilber (Boulder: Shambhala, 1982), pp. 44-104. While many who hold to a so-called New Age worldview have co-opted such observations about reality as supporting a pantheistic understanding of God and the world, this is hardly the only way one can interpret such observations.

[78]The metaphysical system that has most thoroughly and insightfully worked through this new perspective on reality is process thought. The originator of this movement is A. N. Whitehead with his monumental work *Process and Reality: An Essay in Cosmology*, ed. D. R. Griffin and D. W. Sherburne (New York: Free Press, rpt. 1978 [1929]). While metaphysically ingenious, the system has radically heretical impli-

cations, owing to several misconstrued (and unnecessary) assumptions. See my *Trinity and Process,* passim, for a general critical assessment. For other orthodox critiques, see R. Nash, ed., *Process Theology* (Grand Rapids, Mich.: Baker, 1987); D. Basinger, *Divine Power in Process Theism: A Philosophical Critique* (Albany: SUNY, 1988); R. G. Gruenler, *The Inexhaustible God: Biblical Faith and the Challenge of Process Theism* (Grand Rapids, Mich.: Baker, 1983).

[79]See, e.g., L. Boff, *Trinity and Society,* trans. P. Burns (Maryknoll, N.Y.: Orbis, 1988); V. Brümmer, *Speaking of a Personal God: An Essay in Philosophical Thinking* (Cambridge: Cambridge University Press, 1992); idem, *The Model of Love: A Study in Philosophical Theology* (Cambridge: Cambridge University Press, 1993); J. Moltmann, *The Trinity and the Kingdom,* trans. M. Kohl (San Francisco: Harper & Row, 1981); A. O. Ogbonnaya, *On Communitarian Divinity: An African Interpretation of the Trinity* (New York: Paragon, 1994); and C. Pinnock and R. C. Brow, *Unbounded Love* (Downers Grove, Ill.: InterVarsity Press, 1994). E. Pagels offers a penetrating critique of Augustine's denial of genuine human self-determination on the basis of its sociopolitical consequences in "The Politics of Paradise: Augustine's Exegesis of Genesis 1-3 Versus That of John Chrysostom," *HTR* 78, no. 1 (1985): 67-99. I shall myself engage in a critique of the early apologists' appropriation of elements of the Hellenistic philosophical view of God in the forthcoming *Satan and the Problem of Evil.*

[80]See C. Pinnock, R. Rice, J. Sanders, W. Hasker and D. Basinger, *The Openness of God: A Biblical Challenge to the Traditional Understanding of God* (Downers Grove, Ill.: InterVarsity Press, 1994). See also my *Letters from a Skeptic* (Wheaton, Ill.: Victor, 1994), pp. 29-51; and *Trinity and Process,* pp. 296-327. Other evangelicals who espouse some form of the open view of God include W. A. Pratney, *The Nature and Character of God* (Minneapolis: Bethany, 1988); R. Rice, *God's Foreknowledge and Man's Free Will* (Minneapolis: Bethany, 1985); H. R. Elseth, *Did God Know?* (St. Paul: Calvary United Church, 1977); W. Hasker, *God, Time and Knowledge* (Ithaca: Cornell University Press, 1989). For a still unsurpassed survey of the biblical basis for the open view of God, see L. D. McCabe, *Divine Nescience of Future Contingencies a Necessity* (New York: Phillips and Hunt, 1882).

[81]A point frequently missed by the critics of this view. For example, three of the four reviewers of *The Openness of God* (ed. C. Pinnock) in *Christianity Today* in one way or another accused the open view of denying God's transcendence or of limiting God in some fashion. See R. Olson, D. Kelley, T. George and A. McGrath, "Has God Been Held Hostage by Philosophy?" *Christianity Today,* Jan. 9, 1995. Only Olson discerned that the authors of *Openness of God* were arguing for a different model of transcendence, not for a less transcendent view of God.

[82]Approximately one out of six of the Jews killed in the Holocaust was under the age of seven.

[83]For a recent assessment of how our culture has suffered by the loss of the category of evil, see A. Delbanco, *The Death of Satan* (New York: Farrar, Straus & Giroux, 1995). On the need for the recovery of the category of evil in psychotherapy, see Peck, *People of the Lie.* For a collection of essays arguing along these lines on different fronts, see P. Woodruff and H. A. Wiler, eds., *Facing Evil: Light at the Core of Darkness* (LaSalle, Ill.: Open Court, 1988).

[84]This use of the phrase "the tremendum" comes from Arthur Cohen's masterful work *The Tremendum: A Theological Interpretation of the Holocaust* (New York: Crossroad, 1981). See R. Otto, *The Idea of the Holy,* trans. J. W. Harvey (London:

Oxford University Press, 1923). For a comparison of Otto and Cohen, see J. K. Roth, *Approaches to Auschwitz: The Holocaust and Its Legacy* (Atlanta: John Knox, 1987), pp. 329-36. See also D. J. Fasching, *Narrative Theology After Auschwitz: From Alienation to Ethics* (Minneapolis: Fortress, 1992), pp. 143-48.
[85]E. Brunner, *The Christian Doctrine of Creation and Redemption,* trans. O. Wyon (Philadelphia: Westminster, 1952), p. 135.
[86]C. Jung, "Wotan," in *Civilization in Transition,* Collected Works 10, ed. H. Read, M. Fordham and G. Adler, trans. R. F. C. Hull (New York: Pantheon, 1970), pp. 185-87.
[87]See Wink, *Unmasking the Powers,* p. 54. On this theme of Germany being possessed, see H. G. Baynes, *Germany Possessed* (London: Jonathan Cape, 1941). A number of works attempt to disclose the Satanic, or at least occult, origins of Nazism. One of the most balanced is Nicholas Goodrick-Clarke, *The Occult Roots of Nazism: Secret Aryan Cults and Their Influence on Nazi Ideology* (New York: New York University Press, 1985).
[88]Some of the more interesting examples are D. R. Griffin (a postmodern process theologian), "Why Demonic Power Exists: Understanding the Church's Enemy," *Lexington Theological Quarterly* 28 (1993): 223-39; E. Pagels, *The Origin of Satan* (New York: Random House, 1995); T. J. J. Altizer, "Satan as the Messiah of Nature?" in *The Whirlwind in Culture: Frontiers in Theology, in Honor of Langdon Gilkey,* ed. D. Musser and J. Price (Bloomington, Ind.: Meyer-Stone, 1988), pp. 119-34; C. Nugent, *Masks of Satan: The Demonic in History* (London: Sheed & Ward, 1983); H. K. Bloom, *The Lucifer Principle: A Scientific Expedition into the Forces of History* (New York: Atlantic Monthly Press, 1995); L. S. Cunningham, "Satan: A Theological Meditation," *Theology Today* 51, no. 3 (1994): 359-66; A. R. Eckardt, *How to Tell God from the Devil: On the Way to Comedy* (New Brunswick, N.J.: Transaction, 1995). For excellent general assessments of the concept of Satan in the modern world from various perspectives, see J. B. Russell, *Mephistopheles: The Devil in the Modern World* (Ithaca: Cornell University Press, 1986); R. N. Ashen, *The Reality of the Devil: Evil in Man* (New York: Harper & Row, 1972); A. M. Olson, ed., *Disguises of the Demonic: Contemporary Perspectives on the Power of Evil* (New York: Association, 1975); P. Oppenheimer, *Evil and the Demonic* (New York: New York University Press, 1996).

Chapter 2: Locking Up the Raging Seas
[1]O. Böcher, *Dämonenfurcht und Dämonebabwehr* (Stuttgart: Kohlhammer, 1970); *Das Neue Testament und die dämonischen Mächte* (Stuttgart: Katholisches Bibelwerk, 1972); and *Christus Exorcista* (Stuttgart: Kohlhammer, 1972). This work has been lauded as the most complete work on demonology ever written. See P. Hollenbach, "Jesus, Demoniacs and Public Authorities," *JAAR* 49 (1981): 584.
[2]For a critique of Böcher's "pan-demonological" thesis, see Edwin Yamauchi, "Magic or Miracle? Diseases, Demons and Exorcisms," in *The Miracles of Jesus,* GP 6, ed. D. Wenham and C. Blomberg (Sheffield: JSOT Press, 1986), pp. 89-183.
[3]On ancient Greek and Egyptian demonology, see Böcher, *Dämonenfurcht und Dämonebabwehr;* F. E. Brenk, "In the Light of the Moon: Demonology in the Early Imperial Period," in *ANRW* (1986), ed. H. Temporini and W. Haase, 2/16.3:2068-2145; E. Ferguson, *Demonology of the Early Christian World* (New York: Mellen, 1984), pp. 33-67; A. E. Farkus, P. O. Harper and E. B. Harrison, eds., *Monsters and Demons in the Ancient and Medieval Worlds: Papers Presented in*

Honor of Edith Porada (Mainz on Rhine: Verlag Philipp von Zabern, 1987); S. K. Jensen, *Dualism and Demonology: The Function of Demonology in Pythagorean and Platonic Thought* (Copenhagen: Munksgaard, 1966); D. Meeks, "Génies, anges, démons en Égypt," in *Génies, anges, démons* (Paris: Editions du Seuil, 1971), pp. 17-84; Russell, *The Devil*, 122-73; Jonathan Z. Smith, "Towards Interpreting Demonic Powers in Hellenistic and Roman Antiquity," in *ANRW* (1978), 2/16.1:425-39; Yamauchi, "Magic or Miracle?" pp. 104-15.

[4]For discussions on the demonology of ancient Mesopotamia, see A. Green, "Beneficent Spirits and Malevolent Demons: The Iconography of Good and Evil in Ancient Assyria and Babylonia," in *Popular Religion*, ed. H. Kippenberg, L. Bosch et al. (Leiden: Brill, 1984), pp. 80-105; R. C. Thompson, *The Devils and Evil Spirits of Babylonia* (London: Luzac, 1903-4); P. Weber, *Dämonenbeschwörung bei den Babyloniern und Assyriern* (Leipzig: Hinrichs, 1906); E. Langton, The *Essentials of Demonology: A Study of the Jewish and Christian Doctrine, Its Origin and Development* (London: Epworth, 1949), pp. 12-15; J. Black and A. Green, *Gods, Demons and Symbols of Ancient Mesopotamia: An Illustrated Dictionary* (Austin: University of Texas Press, 1992); O. Böcher and W. Culican, "Phoenician Demons," *JNES* 35 (1976): 21-24; W. T. Davies, *Magic, Divination and Demonology Among the Hebrews and Their Neighbors* (London: Clarke, 1898; rpt. New York: KTAV, 1969); T. Jacobsen, *The Treasures of Darkness: A History of Mesopotamian Religion* (New Haven, Conn.: Yale University Press, 1976), pp. 12-13; S. N. Kramer, "Mythology of Sumer and Akkad," in *Mythologies of the Ancient World*, ed. Kramer (New York: Doubleday, 1961), pp. 108-15; Yamauchi, "Magic or Miracle?" pp. 99-103.

[5]For collections of some of the most ancient Mesopotamian incantation and magical texts available, see M. J. Geller, *Forerunners to UDUG-HUL: Sumerian Exorcistic Incantations*, FAS 12 (Stuttgart: Franz Steiner, 1985); M. Krebernik, *Die Beschwörungen aus Fara und Ebla* (Hildesheim: Olms, 1984). On incantations, spells, amulets, etc., from the ancient world, see H. Dieter Betz, ed., *The Greek Magical Papyri in Translation Including the Demotic Spells* (Chicago: University of Chicago Press, 1986); J. G. Gager, ed., *Curse Tablets and Binding Spells from the Ancient World* (Oxford: Oxford University Press, 1992); P. Gignoux, *Incantations magiques Syriaques* (Louvain: Peeters, 1987); C. Isbell, *Corpus of Aramaic Incantation Bowls*, SBLDS 17 (Missoula, Mont.: Scholars Press, 1975); idem, *Magic Spells and Formulae: Aramaic Incantations of Late Antiquity* (Jerusalem: Magnes and Hebrew University Press, 1993); E. Yamauchi, *Mandaic Incantation Texts*, AOS 49 (New Haven: American Oriental Society, 1967).

[6]See J. V. Kinnier Wilson, "An Introduction to Babylonian Psychiatry," in *Studies in Honor of Benno Landsberger*, ed. H. G. Güterbock and T. Jacobsen (Chicago: University of Chicago Press, 1965), p. 291.

[7]The text of *Enuma Elish* is found, with commentary, in A. Heidel, *The Babylonian Genesis* (Chicago: University of Chicago Press, 1951), as well as in *ANET*, pp. 60-72. My discussion of this and other ancient warfare myths of origin shall be relatively general since I am presently concerned only with demonstrating in broad outline the motif of cosmic conflict among the literature of Israel's neighbors. For a variety of helpful studies on the cosmic conflict motif in both the Near East and the wider Mediterranean world, see P. Amiet, "Les Combats mythologiques dan l'art mésopotamien du troisième et du début du second millénaire," *Revue archéologique* 42 (1953): 129-64; G. Barton, "Tiamat," *JAOS* 15 (1893): 1-27; J. Day,

God's Conflict with the Dragon and the Sea: Echoes of a Canaanite Myth in the Old Testament, UCOP 35 (Cambridge: Cambridge University Press, 1985); J. C. L. Gibson, "The Theology of the Ugaritic Baal Cycle," *Or* 53 (1984): 202-19; E. L. Greenstein, "The Snaring of the Sea in the Baal Epic," *Maarav* 3 (1982): 195-216; J. G. Griffiths, *The Conflict of Horus and Seth, from Egyptian and Classical Sources: A Study in Ancient Mythology* (Liverpool: Liverpool University Press, 1960); J. H. Gronbaek, "Baal's Battle with Yam—A Canaanite Creation Fight," *JSOT* 33 (1985): 27-44; H. Gunkel, *Schöpfung und Chaos in Urzeit und Endzeit: Eine religionsgeschichtliche Untersuchung über Gen 1 und Ap Joh 12* (Göttingen: Vandenhoeck & Ruprecht, 1895); Heidel, *Babylonian Genesis*; Jacobsen, *Treasures of Darkness*; C. Kloos, *Yhwh's Combat with the Sea: A Canaanite Tradition in the Region of Ancient Israel* (Leiden: Brill, 1986); S. E. Loewenstamm, "The Killing of Mot in Ugaritic Myth," *Or* 41 (1972): 378-82; J. A. Montgomery, "Ras Shamra Notes IV: The Conflict of Baal and the Waters," *JAOS* 55 (1935): 268-77; M. Wakeman, *God's Battle with the Monster: A Study in Biblical Imagery* (Leiden: Brill, 1973); A. Yarbro Collins, *The Combat Myth in the Book of Revelation,* HDR 9 (Missoula, Mont.: Scholars Press, 1976); P. J. van Zijl, *Baal: A Study of Texts in Connection with Baal in the Ugaritic Epics* (Neukirchen-Vluyn: Neukirchener, 1972). A few of the more helpful *general* overviews of the warfare motif in ancient Near Eastern literature are N. Forsyth, *The Old Enemy: Satan and the Combat Myth* (Princeton: Princeton University Press, 1987), pp. 21-89; J. B. Russell, *The Devil: Perceptions of Evil from Antiquity to Primitive Christianity* (Ithaca: Cornell University Press, 1977), pp. 85-98; T. Longman III and D. Reid, *God Is a Warrior* (Grand Rapids, Mich.: Zondervan, 1995), pp. 13-60.

[8]Russell, *Devil,* p. 88.
[9]*ANET,* p. 67.
[10]Ibid., p. 68.
[11]See Barton, "Tiamat."
[12]See F. M. Cross, *Canaanite Myth and Hebrew Epic: Essays in the History of the Religion of Israel* (Cambridge: Harvard University Press, 1973), p. 120; and Collins, *Combat Myth,* who adds that "the timeless and repeatable aspect of the combat myth is emphasized in a number of psalms of the royal cult" (p. 117).
[13]W. Wink, *Engaging the Powers* (Minneapolis: Fortress, 1992), p. 14. Wink attempts to trace the historical proclivity for achieving order through violence to this "myth of redemptive violence" (pp. 17-31). Prior to this violent myth, he speculates, people were more pacifistic in their approaches to resolving conflict (pp. 33-43). This myth, in its many different forms, creates a pessimistic perspective on human beings and the cosmos that buttresses social systems of domination and aggression, according to Wink. His evaluation of the conflict myth as necessitating evil lies behind his view that the "powers" are to be engaged not by conquering them but by transforming them through nonviolent means. See esp. pp. 171-257. Whatever else may be said for and against Wink's analysis, it is difficult to argue that his view is that of the apostle Paul. See the discussion in chapter ten below.
[14]On the theme of rebellion in warfare myths of origin, see Forsyth, *Old Enemy,* pp. 124-46. My central disagreement with Jon Levenson (*Creation and the Persistence of Evil: The Jewish Drama of Divine Omnipotence* [San Francisco: Harper & Row, 1988]) is that he understands the rebellion motif to arise only after Genesis 1, as a means of qualifying the combat myth of the early traditions in the light of a new understanding of God's absolute sovereignty. "The theology of the first chapter of

the Bible surely relativized the old combat myth and eventually required that it be seen as a revolt—primordial, eschatological, or both—but the optimistic theology failed to uproot the older and more pessimistic myth altogether" (p. 49). In my view, the notion that overt evil arises with rebellion is present, however tacitly, in all the traditions incorporated in Scripture as well as in the Mesopotamian and Canaanite hymns that form the background to Scripture's *Chaoskampf* (conflict-with-chaos) material.

[15]See R. Murray, *Cosmic Covenant: Biblical Themes of Justice, Peace and the Integrity of Creation* (London: Sheed & Ward, 1992). See also B. F. Battu, "The Covenant of Peace: A Neglected Ancient Near Eastern Motif," *CBQ* 49 (1987): 187-211.

[16]Wakeman, *God's Battle*, pp. 4-6.

[17]In many ways these combat stories reflect the degree to which the world is adversely affected when order is not conquering chaos. For example, when Ishtar is slain by Ereshkigal, the queen of the underworld, there is famine upon the earth until she is revived. "Hell," says Russell, "is here not only a region of death but a power that, when it imprisons the goddess of love and fertility, can cause blight and sterility on the earth" (*Devil*, p. 92). So too, the earth is said to suffer greatly when Baal is killed by Mot, and it does not revive until he does. The assumption is that what goes on "in the heavenlies" very much affects what goes on in the world, for better or for worse. Robert Murray argues that the Old Testament has a similar conviction, though it is expressed in a radically different fashion. Here, he argues, calamities come upon the earth because a cosmic covenant has been broken by now-hostile powers between God and the earth. See Murray, *Cosmic Covenant*, passim, but esp. pp. 44-67. I shall subsequently argue that this widespread spiritual intuition concerning the relationship between "spiritual" conflict and "natural" evils is shared by the New Testament and early church, and that this intuition can be made into an important component of a contemporary theodicy, especially as it concerns the problem of so-called natural evil.

[18]This is in contrast to the view of scholars in the past who generally identified Babylon as the backdrop for the combat motif in the Old Testament. See J. Day, *God's Conflict*, p. 4. The shift in opinion has largely been due to the discovery of the Ugaritic tablets in Ras Shamra in 1929. On the discovery and dating of Ugarit, see P. Craigie, *Ugarit and the Old Testament* (Grand Rapids, Mich.: Eerdmans, 1983); C. Gordon, *Before the Bible: The Common Background of Greek and Hebrew Civilization* (London: Collins, 1962), pp. 128ff.; G. R. Driver, *Canaanite Myths and Legends*, 3d ed., ed. J. C. L. Gibson (Edinburgh: T & T Clark, 1978 [1956]), pp. 1-2.

[19]There are a number of problematic issues in the reconstruction of this account, but the outline of the story is clear enough. See Forsyth, *Old Enemy*, pp. 46-48.

[20]This point of view is not undisputed. As mentioned earlier, Böcher attempts to argue that the Israelites attributed all sickness and disease to demonic influence, just as their Mesopotamian neighbors had done. See *Dämonenfurcht und Dämonen-abwehr*, p. 154. Hence he argues that many of the rituals in the Old Testament had an antidemonic function (pp. 162, 274-78, 288, etc.). J. Plöger argues along similar lines (*ʾᵃdhāmāh*," *TDOT*, 1:90), as does B. Levine (*In the Presence of the Lord* [Leiden: Brill, 1974], pp. 55-59). Such interpretations, however, are based more on an assumption that the Israelites adopted the demonological perspective of their neighbors than they are on any clear evidence in the Old Testament itself. If we let the Old Testament speak for itself, it becomes clear that the Israelites' perspective

was quite distinctive. For helpful overviews and discussions of the topic, see A. Caquot, "Anges et démons en Israël," in *Génies, anges et démons*, pp. 113-52; idem, "Sur quelques démons de l'Ancien Testament (Reshep, Qeteb, Deber)," *Semitica* 6 (1956): 53-68; H. Kaupel, *Die Dämonen im Alten Testament* (Augsburg: B. Filser, 1930); J. K. Kuemmerlin-McLean, "Demons: Old Testament," *ABD*, 2:138-40; Langton, *Essentials*, pp. 35-52; M. Gruenthaner, "The Demonology of the Old Testament," *CBQ* 6 (1944): 6-27; Davies, *Magic, Divination and Demonology*, pp. 95-130; H. Gunkel, *Folktale in the Old Testament*, trans. M. D. Rutter (Sheffield: Almond, 1987), chap. 6, pp. 83-106; N. S. Alexander, *Occultism in the Old Testament* (Philadelphia and Armore, Penn.: Dorrance, 1978), pp. 31-40; K. J. Cathcart, "The 'Demons' in Judges 5:8a," *Biblishe Zeitschrift* 21 (1977): 111-12; J. G. Gammie, "The Angelology and Demonology in the Septuagint and the Book of Job," *HUCA* 56 (1985): 1-19; J. Lust, "Devils and Angels in the Old Testament," *Louvain Studies* 5 (1974): 115-20; R. de Vaux, *Ancient Israel: Its Life and Institutions* (New York: McGraw-Hill, 1961), pp. 34, 463, 509; Yamauchi, "Magic or Miracle?" pp. 115-20.

[21]A similar understanding of demonic spirits being able to incite crowds may be behind 1 Corinthians 2:8, which attributes Jesus' crucifixion to evil powers, though the means by which they carried it out was willing, evil, human hands (Acts 2:23). So too Paul attributes his inability to reach Thessalonica to Satan (1 Thess 2:18), though Luke explains the same situation as resulting from social unrest (Acts 17:5-15).

[22]For example, Forsyth argues that the evil spirit in these passages was simply "a servant of the divine king, a shady but necessary member of the Politburo" (*Old Enemy*, p. 112).

[23]F. Lindström, *God and the Origin of Evil: A Contextual Analysis of Alleged Monistic Evidence in the Old Testament*, trans. F. H. Cryer, ConBOT 21 (Lund: Gleerup, 1983), pp. 112-14. See pp. 94-103 for his explication of Isaiah 19:14; 29:9-10; and 37:7.

[24]Yamauchi, "Magic or Miracle?" p. 16. For further discussion, see V. Hamilton, "*shēd*," *TWOT*, 2:905-6; Langton, *Essentials*, pp. 16-17, 51; Kuemmerlin-McLean, "Demons: Old Testament," p. 139.

[25]Langton, *Essentials*, p. 47. This creature factored significantly in the developed demonology of later Jewish writers. See the discussion on "Lilith" in J. D. W. Watts, *Isaiah 34—66*, WBC 25 (Waco, Tex.: Word, 1987), pp. 13-14; D. Aune, "Night Hag," *International Standard Bible Encyclopedia*, 4 vols., ed. G. W. Bromiley et al. (Grand Rapids, Mich.: Eerdmans, 1979-1988), 3:536; Langton, *Essentials*, pp. 16, 47; M. Gaster, "Lilith und die drei Engel," *Monatsschrift für Geschichte und Wissenschaft des Judentums* 29 (1880): 553-65; C. H. Gordon, "A World of Demons and Liliths," in his *Adventures in the Near East* (London: Phoenix, 1957), pp. 160-74; L. Handy, "Lilith," *ABD*, 4:324-25; Kuemmerlin-McLean, "Demons: Old Testament," p. 139; B. B. Koltuv, *The Book of Lilith* (York Beach, Maine: Nicolas-Hays, 1986); Russell, *Devil*, p. 215; C. Arnold, *Powers of Darkness: Principalities and Powers in Paul's Letters* (Downers Grove, Ill.: InterVarsity Press, 1992), p. 57; and H. Torczyner, "A Hebrew Incantation Against Night-Demons from Biblical Times," *JNES* 6 (1947): 18-29. Kinlaw ("Demythologization," p. 33) argues that Lilith was a natural creature on the basis of the fact that it is listed with other natural creatures. His case is weak, however, and in any event it is certainly not clear that all the other creatures in this passage are natural creatures. On this issue, see also

G. R. Driver, "Birds in the Old Testament, II. Birds in Life," *Palestine Exploration Quarterly* 87 (1955): 134-36.

[26]See Driver, "Birds in the Old Testament," pp. 135-36; Kuemmerlin-McLean, "Demons: Old Testament," p. 139; Langton, *Essentials*, pp. 40-41; Arnold, *Powers of Darkness*, pp. 57-58; König, *Here Am I*, p. 15. R. L. Harris ("ś*ā ir*," *TWOT*, 2:881) provides an example of those who dismiss any demonic connotations in regard to this term.

[27]E. A. Speiser, *Genesis*, 2d ed., AB 1 (Garden City, N.Y.: Doubleday, rpt. 1978), pp. 29, 33. See also Wakeman, *God's Battle*, p. 88.

[28]See the excellent articles by M. Malul, "Terror of the Night," *DDD*, pp. 1604-8; and N. Wyatt, "Qeteb," *DDD*, pp. 1269-72. See also Caquot, "Sur quelques démons de l'Ancien Testament," pp. 53-68; Kuemmerlin-McLean, "Demons: Old Testament," p. 139; Langton, *Essentials*, pp. 49-50; and esp. R. Arbesmann, "The 'Daemonium Meridianum' and Greek and Latin Patristic Exegesis," *Traditio* 14 (1958): 17-31, who demonstrates how later Jewish and Christian thought saw the "plague that destroys at noonday" as a demon, and argues persuasively that this reading is rooted in the original.

[29]E.g., R. de Vaux, *Ancient Israel*, p. 509; B. Mazar, *The Mountain of the Lord* (Garden City, N.Y.: Doubleday, 1975), p. 110; Langton, *Essentials*, pp. 43-45; M. Delcor, "Le mythe de la chute des anges," *RHR* 190 (1976): 35-37; O. Loretz, *Leberschau, Sündenbock, Asasel in Ugarit und Israel*, Ugaritisch-Biblische Literatur 3 (Soest: Altenberge, 1985), pp. 50-57; D. P. Wright, "Azazel," *ABD*, 1:536-37; idem, *The Disposal of Impurity: Elimination Rites in the Bible and in Hittite and Mesopotamian Literature*, SBLDS 101 (Atlanta: Scholars Press, 1987), pp. 21-25; König, *Here Am I*, p. 15; H. Tawil, "Azazel, Prince of the Steppe," *ZAW* 92 (1980): 43-49, who attempts to demonstrate that the name Azazel derives from the Canaanite god Mot, the god of the underworld. For an opposing view, however, see H. Kaupel, *Die Dämonen im Alten Testament* (Augsburg: B. Filser, 1930), p. 91. It is important to note that the scapegoat ritual found in the Old Testament (Lev 16) portrays a very different picture from that of other ancient Near Eastern rites of elimination that involve demonic beings. For a comparison, see Wright, *Disposal of Impurity*, pp. 21-74.

[30]See P. D. Hanson, "Rebellion in Heaven, Azazel, and Euhemeristic Heroes in *1 Enoch* 6—11," *JBL* 96 (1977): 195-233; L. L. Grabbe, "The Scapegoat: A Study in Early Jewish Interpretation," *Journal for the Study of Judaism* 18 (1987): 153-55; G. W. E. Nickelsburg, "Apocalyptic and Myth in *1 Enoch* 6—11," *JBL* 96 (1977): 397-404. R. A. Helm argues that *1 Enoch* and other intertestamental Jewish literature demonstrate an early strand of tradition holding that Azael was a demonic being to whom some type of sacrifice was given. See "Azazel in Early Jewish Tradition," *Andrews University Seminary Studies* 32 (Autumn 1994): 217-26.

[31]For example, as noted above, both Böcher and Levine read aspects of the Levitical law as being antidemonic in nature (e.g., Böcher, *Dämonenfurcht und Dämonenabwehr*, pp. 118, 162, 274-78, 288; Levine, *Presence of the Lord*, pp. 55-59). In similar fashion, Langton argues that all the animals referred to in Isaiah 13:21ff. are diabolical entities (*Essentials*, pp. 41-43). Such positions, while not impossible, are not widely received owing to their speculative nature. By contrast, Lindström's sustained case for reading many of the psalms that depict Yahweh as a warrior as containing references not to particular demons but to a suprahuman, supraindividual, demonic type of being (or "reality") is quite compelling (see his *Suffering*

and Sin, pp. 439-41).

[32]See the discussion in Levenson, *Persistence of Evil,* pp. 112-13. Drawing parallels from such passages as Psalm 2:8-9; 8:4-9; 72:8-11; 89:26-28; 110:2, Levenson rightly concludes that "the status of humanity as . . . just a bit less than a god is realized in their sovereignty over the rest of creation." We shall later see that a central component in the warfare theme of redemption in the New Testament concerns restoring humanity as God's viceroy upon the earth. With the Fall, we had surrendered it to Satan, who thus became the new (but illegitimate) "ruler of this world" (Jn 12:31).

[33]Levenson, *Persistence of Evil,* p. 122.

[34]König, Levenson, Barth and others have argued, however, that the "waters" and the "darkness" in the Genesis 1 account yet preserve some of the "menacing character" (König) they have in Ancient Near Eastern creation accounts. Yahweh separates the light from darkness and the dry land from the waters to protect his creation from chaos. See A. König, *New and Greater Things: Re-evaluating the Biblical Message on Creation* (Pretoria: University of South Africa, 1988), pp. 15-18; Levenson, *Persistence of Evil,* pp. 5, 122-23; K. Barth, *Church Dogmatics,* 3/1, *The Doctrine of Creation,* ed. G. W. Bromiley and T. F. Torrance (Edinburgh: T & T Clark, 1961), pp. 102-3. Cf. vol. 3/3:74-78. In favor of this view, it is significant that the author does not say that God created the darkness, the deep or the waters. This does not necessarily imply that the author thought of these as eternal realities, only that it did not suit his purposes in composing this account to state this at this point. See König, *New and Greater Things,* p. 72. Indeed, in the next chapter I suggest that it is possible that the author here does not say that God created the formless and futile *(tōhû wābōhû)* world engulfed in the deep because the author is suggesting that God did not create the world *this way,* but that it somehow became this way as a result of a prehistoric spiritual battle. Genesis 1, in this case, depicts God re-creating an already corrupted earth. For a sustained defense of this view, sometimes called "the gap theory" or "the restitution theory," see A. C. Custance, *Without Form and Void* (Brockville, Canada: Custance, 1970). Very different from both this view and that of Barth and König is the view of D. T. Tsumura, *The Earth and the Waters in Genesis 1 and 2: A Linguistic Investigation,* JSOTSup 83 (Sheffield: Sheffield Academic Press, 1989). Tsumura goes so far as to argue that *tʰôm* here does not even represent a demythologized version of the Canaanite *Chaoskampf* mythology. It is, rather, wholly unrelated to this tradition and simply derives from the term *tihâm,* meaning "ocean" (see esp. pp. 62-65, 141-58, 165-68).

[35]Critical Old Testament scholars most frequently regard the author of this account to be the Priestly redactor(s) in contrast to the J redactor(s) of other creation account(s). There is, in principle, no irreconcilable contradiction between some versions of the documentary hypothesis and a high view of scriptural inspiration so long as not too much is read into Christ's endorsement of the Mosaic authorship of the Pentateuch (cf., e.g., Mk 1:44; 7:10; 10:3-5; 12:19, 26). When, however, absolute contradictions are posited between the different strands of the biblical traditions (which, remarkably enough, supposed later redactors did not detect but modern critics have amazingly "discovered"), a Christlike view of the divine inspiration of the canon is no longer possible. In any event, I am in general inclined to think that the standard versions of the documentary hypothesis are not solidly rooted in historical evidence, especially as it concerns some of their fundamental conclusions regarding the dating, and therefore the cultural context, of different

traditions. The standard documentary approach thus plays no role in my own exegesis of Old Testament texts. For several fine assessments of the documentary hypothesis, see U. Cassuto, *The Documentary Hypothesis and the Composition of the Pentateuch: Eight Lectures*, trans. I. Abrahams (Jerusalem: Magnes, 1961); R. Alter, *The Art of Biblical Narrative* (New York: Basic Books, 1981); D. Garrett, *Rethinking Genesis: The Sources and Authorship of the First Book of the Pentateuch* (Grand Rapids, Mich.: Baker, 1991); G. Maier, "How Did Moses Compose the Pentateuch?" *Stulos Theological Journal* 1, no. 2 (1993): 157-61; A. F. Campbell and M. A. O'Brien, *Sources of the Pentateuch: Texts, Introductions, Annotations* (Minneapolis: Fortress, 1993), pp. 10-15.

[36]Murray, *Cosmic Covenant*, passim, but esp. pp. 1-67. Levenson argues that the most primitive *Chaoskampf* passages portray forces opposing Yahweh not as rebellious but as primordial (precreational). They follow "the Marduk pattern" rather than "the Baal pattern," for in the Marduk saga, creation is a result of the conflict. See *Persistence of Evil*, p. 11, but also pp. 3-46. I am inclined to agree, except that even holding that this creation is the result of a cosmic conflict is not yet to admit that the evil forces Yahweh has conflict with are uncreated. Even Genesis 1, I tentatively suggest in the next chapter, may presuppose creation and a prior conflict.

[37]See Day, *God's Conflict*, p. 53. Day argues that the Old Testament's *Chaoskampf* motif was centrally associated with the Feast of Tabernacles and with Yahweh's kingship (p. 19). See also König, *New and Greater Things*, pp. 43-47; and, for a different perspective, Levenson, *Persistence of Evil*, pp. 53-65. Levenson's work is, in general, among the most helpful in capturing the full force and extent of the *Chaoskampf* motif in the Old Testament. On the prevalence of the sea as a hostile force among ancient peoples and in the Old Testament, see F. Stolz, "Sea," *DDD*, pp. 1390-1402. Other helpful but more general studies that correlate the wider ancient Near Eastern pattern of *Chaoskampf* with various Old Testament texts, and do so from a conservative perspective, are T. Longman III and D. G. Reid, *God Is a Warrior* (Grand Rapids, Mich.: Zondervan, 1995), pp. 83-88; J. J. Niehaus, *God at Sinai: Covenant and Theophany in the Bible and Ancient Near East* (Grand Rapids, Mich.: Zondervan, 1995), pp. 111-16. For a variety of other approaches to the issue that I have drawn upon in my own presentation, see B. W. Anderson, *Creation Versus Chaos: The Reinterpretation of Mythical Symbolism in the Bible* (New York: Association, 1967); B. S. Childs, "The Enemy from the North and the Chaos Tradition," *JBL* 78 (1959): 187-98; A. H. W. Curtis, "The 'Subjugation of the Waters' Motif in the Psalms: Imagery or Polemic?" *JSS* 23 (1978): 245-56; Gunkel, *Schöpfung und Chaos*; J. G. Janzen, "On the Moral Nature of God's Power: Yahweh and the Sea in Job and Deutero-Isaiah," *CBQ* 56 (1994): 458-78; C. Kloos, "The Flood on Speaking Terms with God," *ZAW* 94 (1982): 639-42; idem, *Yhwh's Combat with the Sea: A Canaanite Tradition in the Religion of Ancient Israel* (Leiden: Brill, 1986); S. E. Loewenstamm, "The Ugaritic Myth of the Sea," in *Comparative Studies in Biblical and Ancient Oriental Literatures*, AOAT 204 (Neukirchen-Vluyn: Neukirchener, 1980), pp. 346-61; R. Luyster, "Wind and Water: Cosmological Symbolism in the Old Testament," *ZAW* 93 (1981): 1-10; M. R. Wright, *Cosmology in Antiquity* (London: Routledge, 1995), esp. pp. 75-92; Wakeman, *God's Battle*. I might also briefly note here the treatment of the issue by E. Pagels in her recent and highly acclaimed book *The Origin of Satan* (New York: Random House, 1995). Pagels argues that while sea monsters in Scripture symbolize cosmic evil, Satan symbolizes "the intimate enemy," viz., the evil in one's own

race, nation or religion (see esp. pp. 38-62).

[38]On the possible Canaanite background to this passage, see Day, *God's Conflict,* p. 43. See also König, *New and Greater Things,* pp. 63, 73.

[39]Levenson, *Persistence of Evil,* p. 15; see p. 122.

[40]On the Canaanite background to this passage, see P. C. Craigie, "Psalm XXIX in the Hebrew Poetic Tradition," *VT* 22 (1972): 143-51; T. H. Gaster, "Psalm 29," *JQR* 37 (1946): 55-65; Day, *God's Conflict,* pp. 59-60; Forsyth, *Old Enemy,* p. 65; Levenson, *Persistence of Evil,* p. 133.

[41]Forsyth, *Old Enemy,* p. 64. On the "rebuke" or "roar" of Yahweh, see Day, *God's Conflict,* p. 29, note 82. J. M. Kennedy argues that the best translation would be "blast." See "The Root *g'r* in the Light of Semantic Analysis," *JBL* 106 (1987): 47-64.

[42]Wakeman argues that the metaphor of Yahweh as "a rock" was the most frequently used metaphor precisely because his stability and safety contrasted so powerfully with the chaotic and threatening raging waters believed to encircle the earth. See *God's Battle,* p. 138. On the reality of the threat of chaos, see Levenson, *Persistence of Evil,* pp. 14-25. Here I should note that these various conflict-creation accounts "were not intended primarily to answer the theoretical question, 'Where does everything originate?' but the existential questions of people who are under threat: 'Are we safe?' and 'Shall we survive?'" (König, *New and Greater Things,* p. 45). Hence they make no attempt to explain when and how these hostile forces became inimical (p. 72). This is not to say that the question is inappropriate; it is, for all creational monotheists, absolutely necessary. It is only to say that it is not possible to answer these questions on the basis of these texts. As we shall later see, other texts are slightly more helpful in answering this question.

[43]Levenson, *Persistence of Evil,* p. 16.

[44]Forsyth, *Old Enemy,* pp. 144-45; Levenson, *Persistence of Evil,* pp. 18-19; König, *New and Greater Things,* pp. 47-49; Longman and Reid, *God Is a Warrior,* p. 77.

[45]Levenson, *Persistence of Evil,* p. 18. In Levenson's view, we have here a Canaanite creation-conflict hymn interpolated into a hymn of lament.

[46]Ibid., p. 19.

[47]A similar objection, invoking a similar parallel, is voiced by the psalmist in Psalm 44:19-20 according to Day, *God's Conflict,* p. 43.

[48]See the discussion in Wakeman, *God's Battle,* pp. 91-94, 118; Levenson, *Persistence of Evil,* pp. 11-12.

[49]Yarbro Collins, *Combat Myth,* p. 117. See Levenson, *Persistence of Evil,* pp. 20-21.

[50]Yarbro Collins, *Combat Myth,* p. 118.

[51]See Day, *God's Conflict,* pp. 88-112. See also Levenson, *Persistence of Evil,* p. 44, who notes that Israel's enemies are here no longer just earthly enemies but have become "cosmic forces of the utmost malignancy." The interconnectedness of creation and salvation is a theme brought out insightfully throughout König's *New and Greater Things.* See esp. pp. 34, 60-61, 104-5, 118. So too, Gustaf Wingren probes deeply the cosmic warfare significance of Israel's battles in his fascinating but largely unknown work on the theology of preaching, *The Living Word: A Theological Study of Preaching and the Church,* trans. T. V. Pague (Philadelphia: Muhlenberg, 1960 [1949]).

[52]Psalm 68:22, which speaks of the Lord bringing his enemies "from the depths of the sea" (*yām*), may be making a similar point with an explicit reference to Yamm.

[53]I shall attempt to render this position philosophically defensible in my forthcoming *Satan and the Problem of Evil.*

Chapter 3: Slaying Leviathan

[1]F. Lindström, *God and the Origin of Evil: A Contextual Analysis of Alleged Monistic Evidence in the Old Testament*, trans. F. H. Cryer, ConBOT 21 (Lund: Gleerup, 1983), p. 155. Mary Wakeman attempts to argue that the Old Testament also speaks of an "earth monster" (*'ere*) that is associated with the Canaanite god Mot (*God's Battle with the Monster: A Study in Biblical Imagery* [Leiden: Brill, 1973], pp. 106-17). She finds such references in Exodus 15:12, Numbers 16:32, Psalm 97:4-5, Micah 1:3-4, Amos 9:5-6, and Psalm 46:7 and 114:7. Her case, while not impossible, seems stretched and has not received widespread scholarly support. See the critique in J. Day, *God's Conflict with the Dragon and the Sea: Echoes of a Canaanite Myth in the Old Testament*, UCOP 35 (Cambridge: Cambridge University Press, 1985), pp. 84-86.

[2]For other overviews on the influence of the Near Eastern conceptions of sea monsters on the biblical tradition, see G. R. Driver, "Mythical Monsters in the Old Testament," in *Studi Orientalistici in onore di Giorgio Levi Della Vida*, 2 vols. (Rome: Instituto per l'Oriente, 1956), 1:234-49; T. Fawcett, "The Satanic Serpent," in *Hebrew Myth and Christian Gospel* (London: SCM, 1973), pp. 96-109; B. W. Anderson, "The Slaying of the Fleeing, Twisting Serpent: Isaiah 21:1 in Context," in *Uncovering Ancient Stones: Essays in Memory of H. Neil Richardson*, ed. L. Hopfe (Winona Lake, Ind.: Eisenbrauns, 1994), pp. 3-15.

[3]J. Levenson, *Creation and the Persistence of Evil: The Jewish Drama of Divine Omnipotence* (San Francisco: Harper & Row, 1988), passim, but esp. part 2, "The Alternation of Chaos and Order: Genesis 1:1—2:3," pp. 53-127.

[4]The root meaning of Leviathan *(lwh)* is "to twist. " See J. B. Payne, *"liwyātān,"* *TWOT*, 1:471-72. On Leviathan, see also C. Uehlinger, "Leviathan," *DDD*, pp. 956-64; J. Day, "Leviathan," *ABD*, 4:295-96; J. A. Emerton, "Leviathan and *ltn:* The Vocalization of the Ugaritic Word for the Dragon," *VT* 32 (1982): 327-31; C. H. Gordon, "Leviathan: A Symbol of Evil," in *Biblical Motifs*, ed. A. Altmann, Studies and Texts 3 (Cambridge: Harvard University Press, 1966), pp. 1-9; M.-H. Henry, "Leviathan," *BHH*, 2:1076-77; Wakeman, *God's Battle*, pp. 62-67.

[5]See S. R. Driver and G. B. Gray, *A Critical and Exegetical Commentary on the Book of Job*, ICC (Edinburgh: T & T Clark, 1921), pp. 33-34; M. Fishbane, "Jeremiah IV 23-26 and Job III 3-13: A Recovered Use of the Creation Pattern," *VT* 21 (1971): 153; T. H. Gaster, *Thespis* (Garden City, N.Y.: Doubleday, 1961), pp. 228-29; Day, *God's Conflict*, pp. 44-46. Job 26:13, which parallels Yahweh's clearing of the skies with his piercing "the fleeing serpent," may reflect a similar conception.

[6]Some conservative scholars have attempted to argue that Leviathan in the Old Testament was simply a crocodile or a whale. See, e.g., A. Heidel, *The Babylonian Genesis*, 2d ed. (Chicago: University of Chicago Press, 1951), pp. 105-7. Psalm 104:25-29 perhaps allows for such a view, but the remaining references to Leviathan strongly suggest otherwise. Such a naturalistic understanding does not do justice either to the description of Leviathan in Job 41, Psalm 74 or Isaiah 27 (e.g., many heads and breathing fire!) or to the Canaanite context in which this description occurs, for here Leviathan was certainly a mythological sea dragon. See B. Zucker-

man, "Job, Book of," *IDBSup*, p. 479; Day, *God's Conflict*, pp. 65-69. Other conservative scholars, unable to disregard the mythological element in these references but not wanting to concede that the biblical authors believed in anything mythological, attempt to dismiss such language as poetry. See, e.g., B. K. Waltke, "The Creation Account in Genesis 1:1-3: Part I, Introduction to Biblical Cosmogony," *BSac* 132 (Jan.-Mar. 1975): 25-36. In my estimation, such attempts are as futile as they are unnecessary. There is no antithesis between the concepts of divine inspiration and of myth, nor is there between truth and myth, nor is there between God's sovereignty and his conflict against formidable cosmic forces of evil.

[7]See Longman and Reid, *God Is a Warrior*, p. 78.

[8]While speaking about a cosmic event, it is likely that Isaiah has in mind a particular empire, though it is not clear whether this empire is Egypt, Babylon or Persia. See Day, *God's Conflict*, p. 177. We again see that Old Testament authors could tightly weave together cosmic and historical realities, as well as creation and salvation themes. On the chaos motif of this passage, as well as for helpful discussions of other interpretive approaches and issues surrounding this text, see D. G. Johnson, *From Chaos to Restoration: An Integrative Reading of Isaiah 24—27*, JSOTSup 61 (Sheffield: Sheffield Academic Press, 1988); Anderson, "Slaying of the Fleeing, Twisting Serpent"; B. C. Ollenburger, "Isaiah's Creation Theology," *Ex Auditu 3* (1987): 54-71, esp. 54-59.

[9]Levenson, *Persistence of Evil*, p. 27.

[10]Ibid., p. 48.

[11]For an excellent discussion of the combat myths behind Revelation 12, see A. Yarbro Collins, *The Combat Myth in the Book of Revelation*, HDR 9 (Missoula, Mont.: Scholars Press, 1976), pp. 57-85; as well as H. Wallace, "Leviathan and the Beast in Revelation," *BA* 11 (1948): 61-68. Day argues that a reformed and historicized vision of Leviathan also lies behind Daniel 7, in which we find four beasts rising out of a chaotic turbulent sea. The four empires, in this view, are playing the destructive role of Leviathan. See Day, *God's Conflict*, pp. 153-57.

[12]See Day, *God's Conflict*, p. 6. For an excellent overview of Rahab in the Old Testament, against its Canaanite background, see Wakeman, *God's Battle*, pp. 56-82; G. Schmitt, "Rahab," *BHH*, 3:1547-48; J. Day, "Rahab," *ABD*, 5:610-11.

[13]Another possible allusion to the Enuma Elish tradition. See *ANET*, p. 67.

[14]The parallelism between "churning up the sea" and "cutting Rahab to pieces" suggests that one event is being referred to here. Rahab is identified with Yamm, and Yahweh's vanquishing it signifies Yahweh's "continuous power over creation" (Day, *God's Conflict*, p. 40). So also argues Wakeman, *God's Battle*, pp. 118, 121. Forsyth sees a number of Canaanite deity figures represented in this passage, including "Shades" and "Mot," as well as the hero of the Labbu myth who clears the dragon from the sky while restraining the primeval waters (*Old Enemy*, p. 65).

[15]The unity of this psalm has been frequently questioned but is convincingly defended by J. M. Ward, "The Literary Form and Liturgical Background of Psalm LXXXIX," *VT* 11 (1961): 321-39; and R. J. Clifford, "Psalm 89: A Lament over the Davidic Ruler's Continued Failure," *HTR* 73, no. 1 (1980): 38-47.

[16]See, e.g., G. S. Cansdale, "Behemoth," *ZPEB*, 1:511.

[17]See M. Pope, *Job*, 3d ed., AB 15 (Garden City, N.Y.: Doubleday, 1973), pp. 320-21; Day, *God's Conflict*, pp. 76-77; Wakeman, *God's Battle*, p. 114; B. F. Batto, "Behemoth," *DDD*, pp. 316-22. The references to Behemoth's feeding on grass (v. 15), playing by wild animals (v. 20), lying in a marsh (vv. 21-22) and standing

in the Jordan River (v. 23) all seem to support seeing Behemoth as a natural creature. The issue is, is this a natural creature spoken of in hyperbolic language or a mythological creature spoken of in markedly natural language (as is Leviathan in Ps 104)? The case is open, but for reasons to be given, I support the latter.

18Day, *God's Conflict*, pp. 76-77.

19Ibid., pp. 80-82.

20E. A. Martens, *"b'hēmôt,"* *TWOT,* 1:93. See also G. S. Cansdale, "Behemoth," *ZPEB,* 1:511.

21Cf., e.g., *1 Enoch* 60:7-9; *2 Apocalypse of Baruch* 29:4; 2 Esdras 6:49-52. It is also likely that these two beasts lie behind Rev 13:1-8.

22Day, *God's Conflict*, p. 83. With König, Levenson and others, Day argues that the fact that Old Testament authors took these conflict myths literally does not compromise their monotheism. For these authors did not (like their pagan neighbors) take these sea monsters to be gods, at least not in any sense that would compete with the one true God. Rather, they saw them as "demonic forces, which we often find portrayed in animal form in the ancient world" (p. 189). Murray, however, argues that later Old Testament authors (the P tradition) did believe that the postulation of such evil cosmic forces overly compromised Yahweh's supremacy, and thus sought to demythologize the conflict motif. See *Cosmic Covenant,* pp. xviii-xix, 1-2, passim. In my view, Murray is influenced by a frequently held scholarly view that monotheism is pure to the extent that it is exclusivistic—hence the P tradition is more "purely" monotheistic than J if it affirms one God to the exclusion of all others. As I argue in chapter four, however, monotheists have rarely if ever assumed this. König and Levenson have the preferable analysis in my view.

23F. Lindström, *Suffering and Sin: Interpretation of the Individual Complaint Psalms,* trans. M. McLamb, ConBOT 37 (Stockholm: Almqvist & Wiksell, 1994), p. 178. Lindström convincingly demonstrates that even when the Psalms do not make explicit reference to demonic-type beings (viz., Leviathan, Yamm), they nevertheless sometimes depict "a general experience of a suprahuman and irrational evil, i.e., an affliction which cannot be reduced to moral evil or be connected to the individual's experience of the nature and activity of his God" (p. 17). These unspecified enemies, whose description in the Psalms "often has a supraindividual, metaphysical dimension . . . [and] can have demonic overtones," all coalesce around what Lindström describes as "the kingdom of Death" (p. 440). Similarly, J. D. Levenson demonstrates throughout his *Persistence of Evil* that God's sovereignty is "often fragile, in continual need of reactivation and reassertion" (p. 47). Levenson, unfortunately, concludes that this entails that Yahweh did not create the forces of chaos he must combat, a view that flies in the face of the strong canonical motif depicting Yahweh as "the Creator" (e.g., Gen 1:1-2; 14:19, 22; Deut 32:6; Ps 89:12; 104:30; 148:15; Is 27:11; 40:26-28; 41:20; 42:5; 43:1, 7, etc.) and the world as "the creation" (e.g., Gen 1:1; Hab 2:18; Rom 8:19-22; Col 1:15; Heb 4:13; Rev 3:14).

24Levenson, *Persistence of Evil,* p. 27.

25Ibid., p. 47. Cf. pp. 16-17. So also p. 48: "the continuation of the hostile forces is sometimes articulated as the survival of Leviathan (under whatever name) in captivity."

26Rather than "casting a shadow over God," A. König argues, the point of biblical authors who appropriate a creation-conflict theme is that it "all the more wonderfully expresses God's glory" (*New and Greater Things: Re-evaluating the Biblical*

Message on Creation [Pretoria: University of South Africa, 1988], p. 46). Hence biblical authors frequently speak of how God uses his victory over the chaos monsters for the benefit of creation (as in Ps 104:10-18) or for his own sport (as in Job 40:25-32). From this perspective Bruce Waltke must be judged as having missed the point when he argues that we cannot maintain that the biblical authors really believed in these monsters, for this would run against their stringent mono-theism. See "Creation Account, Part I," pp. 34-35. Here exegesis seems to be controlled by a theological assumption (a mistaken one, I believe) about what "strict monotheism" supposedly implies. The end result for Waltke is that Leviathan and the other cosmic monsters are mere poetic flourishes used to proclaim that "Yahweh will triumph over all His enemies in the establishment of His rule of righteousness. . . . As the Creator of the cosmos, He triumphed at the time of creation; as Creator of history, He triumphs in the historic present; and as Creator of the new heavens and the new earth, He will triumph in the future" (p. 36). The only question is, if having genuine opponents is inconsistent with strict monotheism, as Waltke argues, how can one meaningfully speak of Yahweh triumphing at all? König's (and Levenson's) point is that the Old Testament sees Yahweh as having genuine opponents, and as being all the more exalted because he ultimately vanquishes them. The arbitrariness of the common assumption that monotheism is "strict" or "pure" to the extent that it denies the existence of lesser gods is argued in the next chapter.

[27]Levenson, *Persistence of Evil,* p. 19.

[28]Developing and defending a theodicy that is rooted in this notion of a cosmic fall among spiritual free agents who exercise cosmic power shall be the goal of part 3 of my forthcoming work *Satan and the Problem of Evil.*

[29]Indeed, as Murray insightfully argues, according to some traditions at some level the creation itself seems to be involved in the rebellion (*Cosmic Covenant,* chaps. 1—4).

[30]If my reading of Genesis 1 is correct (see below), the goodness of *this* creation (or, better, re-creation) was always something Yahweh had to fight for.

[31]On the nontemporal nature of this language, see Day, *God's Conflict,* pp. 23ff.; König, *New and Greater Things,* pp. 45, 71-72.

[32]I refer to the cosmic fall as prehistoric because it lies outside what we can by ordinary means know about history, and thus outside our ordinary definition of "history." But in my view this event is not ahistorical, hence not "mythological." For while it lies outside our "history," it does not lie outside the sequence of events that bracket our history.

[33]As I make clear in what follows, affirming that a conflict occurred before the creation of this world is not to say that the players in this battle are uncreated. In my view, the only uncreated reality is God (all else is created ex nihilo). But created beings rebelled against God before the creation of Genesis 1 took place, and this creation was affected by their rebellion. In my view, Genesis 1:2 onward most probably concerns the re-creation of this present cosmos, not the creation ex nihilo of all things.

[34]The presence of the serpent, which has traditionally been identified with Satan, in the garden was always regarded as one of the surest pieces of evidence that Satan fell before humans fell. This figure shall be discussed in chapter four.

[35]Edwin Lewis is among the few explicit dualists in our age who denies this. See *The Creator and the Adversary* (New York: Abingdon-Cokesbury, 1949). Throughout *Persistence of Evil,* Levenson argues that "the assumption that the monstrous

adversary of YHWH was not primordial, but had been created by him, so that the challenge was only an act of rebellion, derives ultimately from Genesis 1" (p. 53). In other words, the biblical *Chaoskampf* material assumes that the adversary of YHWH is primordial, according to Levenson. Trying to harmonize Genesis 1 with the *Chaoskampf* passages "does violence to the plain sense of the text" (ibid.). I argue, on the one hand, that it is not clear that the intent of Genesis 1 is to rule out the *Chaoskampf* motif, but, on the other hand, that none of these passages requires that the adversary be understood as primordial (in the sense of being uncreated). I agree with Levenson, however, that the traditional interpretation of Genesis 1 (at least) has exercised far too much exegetical control over interpretations of other Old Testament creation accounts, with the result that most have significantly underappreciated the warfare motif that runs throughout the Old Testament.

[36]If this is correct, then we may read the nearly universal creation-conflict myths of various cultures just as we read (or, at least in my view, should read) the nearly universal myths of a worldwide flood, of giants stalking the earth, of the fall of humans, of a giant tower built out of rebellion, etc. They represent echoes of actual past events. All the details of such stories have been altered, expanded and distorted by being passed on orally from generation to generation. But we have reason to believe that the story itself is based on fact. The classic (if somewhat exaggerated) collection of such stories is James George Frazer's *Folklore in the Old Testament: Studies in Comparative Religion, Legend and Law* (New York: Hart, rpt. 1975). See also R. Graves and R. Patai, *Hebrew Myths: The Book of Genesis* (New York: McGraw-Hill, 1963). From a conservative perspective, see A. Heidel, *The Babylonian Genesis: The Story of Creation*, 2d ed. (Chicago: University of Chicago Press, 1951); and idem, *The Gilgamesh Epic and Old Testament Parallels*, 2d ed. (Chicago: University of Chicago Press, 1949).

[37]Waltke, "Creation Account, Part I," pp. 34-36.

[38]See, e.g., Ezekiel 19, where literal history and allegory are obviously interwoven with one another. On this see J. J. Davis, "Genesis, Inerrancy and the Antiquity of Man," in *Inerrancy and Common Sense*, ed. R. R. Nicole and J. Ramsey Michaels (Grand Rapids, Mich.: Baker, 1980), pp. 137-59.

[39]So notes Levenson, *Persistence of Evil*, pp. 121ff. See also chapter two, note 34.

[40]Alternatively, some have argued that verse 1 is a summary introduction and verse 2 begins to detail the actual account. Others have argued that verse 1 should be translated "when God *began* to create . . ." Both of these variations (and there are others) strengthen the restoration theory, though the theory hardly requires them. Arthur Custance argues, with some force, for the translation "In a former state God created the heavens and the earth." See his discussion in "Analysis of Genesis 1:1," in *Time and Eternity and Other Biblical Studies*, Doorway Papers 6 (Grand Rapids, Mich.: Zondervan, 1977), pp. 78-85. On this see also Levenson, *Persistence of Evil*, p. 121. Speiser makes a solid case that taking verse 1 as a temporal clause ("when God began to create") fits best with the parallel reading in *Enuma Elish* (E. A. Speiser, *Genesis*, 2d ed., AB 1 [Garden City, N.Y.: Doubleday, rpt. 1978], pp. 9-10). It must be noted that the restoration view need not deny the doctrine of creation ex nihilo, even if verse 1 is taken as a temporal clause, for this doctrine can arguably derive from other explicit verses as well as from the general depiction of Yahweh as Creator and the cosmos as a creation.

[41]By far the most thorough, learned and forceful defense of the gap theory has been Custance's unjustifiably neglected work *Without Form and Void* (Brockville, Can-

ada: Custance, 1970). See also idem, *Time and Eternity*, pp. 77-120. For other expositions, see D. G. Barnhouse, "The Great Interval," in his *The Invisible War* (Grand Rapids, Mich.: Zondervan, 1965), pp. 9-20; M. Unger, "Rethinking the Genesis Account of Creation," *BSac* 115 (Jan.-Mar. 1958): 27-35; E. Sauer, *The King of the Earth* (Palm Springs: Ronald N. Hayes Publishers, rpt. 1981), pp. 195-96, 230-42; idem, *The Dawn of Redemption* (Grand Rapids, Mich.: Eerdmans, 1953), pp. 35-36. Other notable scholars since 1850 who have in varying degrees endorsed this reading are Jamieson, Fausset and Brown (in their famous *Commentary on the Whole Bible*) and Thomas Chalmers, Johann H. Kurtz, William Buckland, Franz Delitzsch, George Pember and Dean Keerl. According to Sauer and Custance, among those who find some sort of "gap" between Genesis 1:1 and 1:2 in premodern times are a significant number of ancient Jewish commentators, Origen, perhaps Augustine, Hugo of St. Victor and Jacob Böhme. See Custance, *Without Form and Void*, pp. 10-40, 117-27.

[42]For attempts to refute this perspective, see W. W. Fields, *Unformed and Unfilled: A Critique of the Gap Theory of Genesis 1:1, 2* (Winona Lake, Ind.: Light and Life Press, 1973); B. Waltke, "The Creation Account in Genesis 1:1-3: Part II, The Restitution Theory," *BSac* 132 (Apr.-June 1975): 136-44.

[43]Levenson notes that "Genesis 1:2 . . . describes the 'world,' if we may call it that, just before the cosmogony began: 'unformed and void, with darkness over the surface of the deep *[tᵉhôm]* and a wind from God sweeping over the water.' Here again, a parallel with the *Enuma elish* readily offers itself. Marduk, having utilized the winds to overcome Tiamat, 'rested, examining her dead body' just before he split her in half to form the sky and the Earth" (*Persistence of Evil*, p. 121).

[44]Ibid., p. 122.

[45]See the discussion in W. G. Lambert, "A New Look at the Babylonian Background of Genesis," *JTS* 16 (1965): 287-300.

[46]This is not to suggest that recognizing mythological elements in Scripture amounts to a denial of scriptural infallibility, for myths can be as infallible in ways appropriate to them as can be literal propositions, poems, gospels or any other genre of literature. But the conservative evangelical faith perspective holds that whatever appears to be historical and literal should be taken as such, unless we have very good reason to think otherwise. This view contrasts, for example, with the usual modern historical-critical perspective, which holds that those apparently historical accounts involving features that do not fit our modern worldview (e.g., supernatural beings, miracles) are to be considered mythological, despite their obvious historical appearance. The creation-conflict passages seem to be talking about an actual battle in space and time, though their particular portrayals of the cosmic forces involved in this battle are indisputably, and I think inevitably, mythological. The point here is simply that the conservative position should try to affirm the temporal and factual dimension of the *Chaoskampf* passages, even while conceding the mythological and culturally conditioned nature of how it is expressed. A good case can be made for understanding the narrative of humanity's fall in Genesis 3 along similar lines. The account is certainly describing a temporal event, but it may at points be using mythological and culturally dependent elements to do it, as a number of orthodox commentators, past and present, have argued. See the discussion in Davis, "Genesis, Inerrancy."

[47]Hence the NIV translated some form of *kābaš* as "subdue" (enemies) in Numbers 32:22, "enslave" in Nehemiah 5:5 (cf. 2 Chron 28:10), "overcome" in Zechariah 9:15, "forced" in Jeremiah 34:16, "tread underfoot" in Micah 7:19, and to bring

an enemy "under control" in Joshua 18:1.

[48]The verb for "guard" here, *šāmar*, is used in Genesis 3:24, where the cherubim are placed by the entrance to the garden "to guard the way to the tree of life." See also, e.g., Exodus 23:20; Joshua 10:18; 1 Samuel 2:9; 7:1; 19:2; 26:15-16; 2 Samuel 20:10; 1 Kings 20:39; 2 Kings 6:10; 2 Chronicles 23:6; Nehemiah 3:29; 13:22; Psalm 25:20; 86:2; 91:11; Ecclesiastes 5:1.

[49]The issues surrounding the traditional interpretation of the serpent as the devil shall be addressed in chapter five.

[50]Franz Delitzsch, quoted in Sauer, *King*, p. 93.

[51]Ibid., pp. 92-93.

[52]See Custance, *Without Form and Void*, pp. 41-59; idem, "Analysis of Genesis 1:2," in *Time and Eternity*, pp. 86-105; idem, "A Translation of Genesis 1:1 to 2:4 with Notes," in *Hidden Things of God's Revelation*, Doorway Papers 7 (Grand Rapids, Mich.: Zondervan, 1977), pp. 273-99; M. Anstey, *The Romance of the Bible Chronology* (London: Marshall, 1913), p. 62. Custance argues that even verse 1 should be translated "In a former state God perfected the heaven and the earth, but the creation had become . . ." See his "Analysis of Genesis 1:2," pp. 86-92. Waltke, though opposed to the restoration theory, admits the possibility of reading Genesis 1:2 as "the earth had *become*," largely on the strength of the parallel in Genesis 3:20, which clearly must be translated to read that Eve "*became* . . . the mother of all living." See Waltke, "The Creation Account in Genesis 1:3: Part II, The Restitution Theory," *BSac* 132 (Apr.-June 1975): 139.

[53]For *tōhû*, see Isaiah 24:10; 34:11; Jeremiah 4:23; Deuteronomy 32:10 ("become a desert"); Isaiah 49:4; for *bōhû*, see Jeremiah 4:23; Isaiah 34:11. See the discussion in Custance, *Without Form and Void*, appendix 16, pp. 166-68.

[54]See D. Kidner, *Genesis*, Tyndale Old Testament Commentaries (Chicago: InterVarsity Press, 1967), p. 44. Similar to this is Barth's understanding of the chaos of Genesis 1:2 as the "No" over and against God's creative "Yes." See his discussion in *Church Dogmatics*, 3/1, *The Doctrine of Creation*, ed. G. W. Bromiley and T. F. Torrance (Edinburgh: T & T Clark, 1958), pp. 101-11.

[55]Sauer, *King*, p. 93.

[56]Some have argued that 1 Corinthians 14:33 expresses a principle that would be violated if the *tōhû wābōhû* of Genesis 1:2 were created by God. The argument carries little weight, as the context of the Corinthian letter is completely unrelated to the creation issue.

[57]Custance, "The Meaning of the Verb 'Make' by Contrast with the Verb 'Create,' " in *Time and Eternity*, pp. 115-17. If Genesis 1:1-2 (on this reading) is based on an archaic oral tradition, an explanation arises as to how it is that myths concerning a "world before this world" that was destroyed by a catastrophic war, and out of which this present world was created, are found around the globe. See Custance, *Without Form and Void*, pp. 182-85.

[58]It has been argued that the widely acknowledged paleontological evidence of a primordial catastrophe that is so often taken to support the reading of a universal flood in Genesis 6—8 better fits a reading of Genesis 1:2 as referring to a judged world. The issue, however, is highly controversial. See the balanced comments in Sauer, *King*, pp. 199-202, 238-42.

[59]Lewis, *Problem of Pain*, pp. 133-35.

[60]This issue of explaining cosmic evil in general, and animal suffering in particular, shall be explored further in *Satan and the Problem of Evil*.

[61]Sauer, *King,* p. 80. Sauer's whole book, but especially part 2, "Man as the King of the Earth" (pp. 72-100), is a most insightful treatment of this theme.

[62]See Levenson, *Persistence of Evil,* pp. 111ff.

[63]Ibid., pp. 117-18.

[64]Quoted in Sauer, *King,* p. 93.

[65]Sauer's suggestion that the four rivers flowing out of Eden in Genesis 2:10-14 symbolize the global function of Eden has some merit. See ibid., p. 94.

[66]Ibid., pp. 92, 94.

[67]"He, sole Deity, obviously had the power to wrest this area of the universe from Satan, the rebel, simply by force. But this would have contradicted His own moral principles of government. His fundamental nature is innately moral, and so the laws governing His cosmic world-order must also be of a purely moral character" (Sauer, *King,* p. 73).

[68]On this, see D. G. McCartney, "*Ecce Homo:* The Coming of the Kingdom as the Restoration of Human Vicegerency," *WTJ* 56 (1994): 1-21.

Chapter 4: Judging "the Gods"

[1]See also Isaiah 40:12-28; 41:21-29; 44:6-20; 45:14-17, 20-23; 46:9.

[2]See also Isaiah 63:9, mg, which speaks of "the angel of his presence." P. D. Miller argues that Isaiah 40:26 and 45:12 are to be understood as God calling stars, here portrayed as part of his heavenly council, into military file. See Miller, *The Divine Warrior in Early Israel,* HSM 5 (Cambridge: Harvard University Press, 1973), p. 139. See also James Muilenburg, "The Book of Isaiah, Chapters 40—66, Introduction and Exegesis," in *IB,* 5:442. Many scholars regard the strongly monotheistic section of Isaiah (chaps. 40—45) as deriving from a later scribe whose views do not necessarily reflect those of Isaiah himself. While little rides on the issue, I have never found the arguments for seeing Isaiah as a composite work compelling. See the defenses made for the unity of Isaiah by G. W. Grogan, "Isaiah," in *EBC,* 6:6-11; J. N. Oswalt, *The Book of Isaiah: Chapters 1—39,* NICOT (Grand Rapids, Mich.: Eerdmans, 1986), pp. 17-28.

[3]U. Mauser, "One God Alone: A Pillar of Biblical Theology," *Princeton Seminary Bulletin,* n.s. 12, no. 3 (1991): 259.

[4]See A. König, *Here Am I: A Believer's Reflection on God* (Grand Rapids, Mich.: Eerdmans, 1982), pp. 1-57. See H. D. Preuss, *Verspottung fremder Religionen im Alten Testament,* BWANT 92 (Stuttgart: Kohlhammer, 1971).

[5]Mauser, "One God Alone," pp. 255-65. James Kallas argues concerning the "no other gods" theme of Isaiah: "the emphasis is not on the soleness of Yahweh but rather on the supremacy" (*The Significance of the Synoptic Miracles* [Greenwich, Conn.: Seabury, 1961], p. 40). See also E. Langton, *The Essentials of Demonology* (London: Epworth, 1949), pp. 51-52; H. Ringgren, "*'elōhîm,*" *TDOT,* 1:276-77; R. K. Eaton, "The Nature of the Non-human Opposition to the Church in the New Testament" (Ph.D. diss., Fuller Theological Seminary, 1985), pp. 34-38. For an insightful discussion on the incomparability of Yahweh in relation to other gods (both in the Old Testament and today), see J. Labuschagne, *The Incomparability of Yahweh in the Old Testament,* POS 5 (Leiden: Brill, 1966); König, *Here Am I,* pp. 1-57. Also helpful in discussing the compatibility of creational monotheism with the acceptance of other gods is N. T. Wright, *The New Testament and the People of God* (Minneapolis: Fortress, 1992), pp. 248-59. The incomparability of Yahweh comes out in "power encounters" between Yahweh and other gods. Elijah's battle

with the priests of Baal is one such encounter, according to C. H. Pinnock, *A Wideness in God's Mercy: The Finality of Jesus Christ in a World of Religions* (Grand Rapids, Mich.: Zondervan, 1992), pp. 115-33. For Louise Holbert, Yahweh's assailing the Egyptians with the plagues is another example. Each of the ten plagues, she argues, is tailored against a particular Egyptian deity. See her "Extrinsic Evil Powers in the Old Testament" (Th.M. thesis, Fuller Theological Seminary, 1985), pp. 57-72; also J. J. Davis, "When the Gods Were Silent," in his *Moses and the Gods of Egypt* (Grand Rapids, Mich.: Baker, 1971), pp. 110-29.

[6]For a small sampling of Old Testament passages that unequivocally affirm the reality of other gods, see Exodus 12:12; 20:3; 23:32-33; Numbers 33:4; Deuteronomy 6:14; 29:25-26; 31:16; Joshua 24:15; Judges 2:12; 6:10; 10:6; 1 Kings 8:23; 11:33; 2 Kings 1:2-3, 6, 16; Psalm 89:6; 95:3; Jeremiah 5:19. In regard to such verses, Ringgren notes, "No question is raised as to whether these gods existed; their existence is simply accepted as a fact" (*TDOT,* 1:277).

[7]Mauser, "One God Alone," pp. 259-61. Mauser here notes that 1 Corinthians 8 is structured by Paul's responding to three Corinthian slogans: "all of us possess knowledge (8:1), "no idol in the world really exists," and "there is no God but one" (8:4). Paul rejects the Corinthians' interpretation of all three. Mauser seems to assume that a "clean monotheism" is somehow threatened by the acknowledgment that lesser gods exist. This is a common assumption among scholars, and one that I shall shortly call into question.

[8]See also 2 Samuel 5:24, to be discussed below, as well as Exodus 12:12; Numbers 33:4.

[9]Mauser argues along these lines in "One God Alone," p. 258.

[10]The good deal of difference among the various definitions of monotheism, henotheism, monolatry and polytheism has resulted in a good amount of confusion surrounding these terms. For example, the strong tendency among laypersons and scholars alike is to define monotheism such that it is necessarily exclusivistic—it denies the existence of other "gods." I shall soon argue that this is an arbitrary and phenomenologically inaccurate description of what monotheists believe. But once this definition is granted, henotheism and monolatry become defined as the worship of one god while admitting the existence of other gods, and polytheism becomes the worship of many gods. For reasons to be discussed shortly, I define monotheism as the worship of one supreme God who is seen as being the originator of all others, while affirming that other (created) gods exist. Given the absolute uniqueness of this creator God, it might be best to call this (following N. T. Wright) "creational monotheism." Henotheism and monolatry I take to be the worship of one god, while admitting the existence of other gods and while not drawing a qualitative distinction between the god worshiped and these other gods. Polytheism I take to mean a belief in and worship of a multitude of gods. I would call the belief that affirming one God excludes acknowledging other gods "philosophical monotheism," for it has been spun out on the basis of a philosophical ideal and does not correspond to what monotheists have actually believed.

[11]Recall, for example, Waltke's dismissal of Leviathan and Rahab as mere metaphors because of his assumption that believing in their existence runs into conflict with monotheism. See chapter three, note 37.

[12]Wright, *People of God,* p. 258. The opinion is anticipated much earlier by John Baillie: "Historically speaking, monotheism has never stood for the belief that there exists in the universe only one being of a supernatural kind. If we so define it, we

shall be faced with the necessity of admitting that it has never existed in the world. What monotheism has really stood for is rather the conviction that there is only one supernatural Being who counts *as far as religion is concerned*—one Being, that is to say, who is worthy of the name of God" (*The Interpretation of Religion* [New York: Scribner's, 1928], p. 430).

[13]P. Hayman, "Monotheism—A Misused Word in Jewish Studies?" *JJS* 42 (1991): 1-15.

[14]Ibid., p. 2.

[15]Ibid., p. 11.

[16]See Wright's clear discussion in *People of God*, pp. 248-56.

[17]For a comprehensive discussion concerning objects of worship and veneration within Judaism and Christianity (especially as it impacts the development of Jesus worship in the early church), see L. T. Stuckenbruck, *Angel Veneration and Christology: A Study in Early Judaism and in the Christology of the Apocalypse of John*, WUNT 2/70 (Tübingen: Mohr/Siebeck, 1995).

[18]This of course raises the question of why the Creator does not revoke the power he gives when his creatures choose to misuse it. As I shall argue more extensively in *Satan and the Problem of Evil*, if the Lord revoked self-determining power whenever it had been or was going to be misused, it could not be said that he genuinely *gave* self-determining power in the first place. In other words, the freedom to choose for or against God and his plans must, within limits, be *irrevocable*.

[19]So Mauser, "One God Alone," pp. 259-60. Wright argues, "Within the most fiercely monotheistic of Jewish circles throughout our period—from the Maccabean revolt to Bar-Kochba—there is no suggestion that 'monotheism,' or praying the Shema, had anything to do with the numerical analysis of the inner being of Israel's god himself" (*People of God*, p. 259). On the flexibility of monotheism and the phenomenon of Jesus devotion, see L. Hurtado, *One God, One Lord: Early Christian Devotion and Ancient Jewish Monotheism* (Philadelphia: Fortress, 1988).

[20]See W. Bousset, *Kyrios Christos*, trans. J. E. Steely (Nashville: Abingdon, 1970). The thesis has been given a new (and slightly different) lease on life by recent post-Bultmannians. For a refutation of this approach and a historical defense of the claim that the Gospel and epistolary portraits of Jesus as divine essentially reflect the perspective of Jesus' earliest disciples, see my *Cynic, Sage or Son of God? Recovering the Real Jesus in an Age of Revisionist Replies* (Wheaton, Ill.: Bridgepoint, 1995); and D. Wenham, *Paul: Follower of Jesus or Founder of Christianity?* (Grand Rapids, Mich.: Eerdmans, 1995), esp. chapter three.

[21]Most scholars who advocate this view also argue that polytheism itself represents an evolution of an even more primitive animism or totemism. Two classic statements are E. H. Tyler, *Primitive Culture* (New York: Harper & Brothers, rpt. 1958); and J. Wellhausen, *Prolegomena to the History of Ancient Israel*, trans. A. Menzies and J. Black (rpt. Cleveland, Ohio: World, 1957). The position has been largely discredited but is in any event irrelevant to the position I will shortly advocate. For a critique of the position, see S. H. Langdon, "Monotheism as the Predecessor of Polytheism in Sumerian Religion," *EvQ* 9 (April 1937): 136-46.

[22]For a thorough discussion of the evidence, see A. Custance, "From Monotheism to Polytheism," in *Evolution or Creation?* Doorway Papers 4 (Grand Rapids, Mich.: Zondervan, 1976), pp. 113-31.

[23]For example, Albrecht Alt argued that monotheism begins in pre-Yahwist cults that can be associated with the patriarchs (*Essays on Old Testament History and Religion*, trans. R. A. Wilson [New York: Doubleday, 1967], pp. 3-86). Yehezkel Kaufmann argued that monotheism originated with Moses (*The Religion of Israel: From the Beginnings to the Babylonian Captivity*, trans. and abridged by Moshe Greenberg [New York: Schocken, rpt. 1972]). Wellhausen, now followed by a major strand of critical Old Testament scholarship, held that true monotheism does not originate until the period of the classical prophets (Amos and Hosea). See also the strong statement of this position by B. Lang, *Monotheism and the Prophetic Minority: An Essay in Biblical History and Sociology* (Sheffield: Almond, 1983). More recent scholarship, operating with a thoroughly redactional approach to the Old Testament, has argued that monotheism does not become a characteristic of Israel until the formation of the Second Commonwealth under Ezra. See, e.g., F. M. Cross, *Canaanite Myth and Hebrew Epic: Essays in the History of the Religion of Israel* (Cambridge, Mass.: Harvard University Press, 1973). Each of the theories (and many variations of them could be elucidated) hangs upon rather tenuous pieces of evidence, conjectures, dating assumptions—to say nothing of their starting definition of monotheism and their assumptions about what characterizes it. For a most helpful discussion of the field today, see D. L. Petersen, "Israel and Monotheism: The Unfinished Agenda," in *Canon, Theology and Old Testament Interpretation*, ed. G. Tucker et al. (Philadelphia: Fortress, 1988), pp. 92-107.

[24]Defenders of the primordial monotheism theory have often argued that we do find instances of pure monotheism ("pure" being defined by exclusivity), but this claim really goes beyond the evidence (as argued, for example, by N. A. Snaith, "The Advent of Monotheism in Israel," *ALUOS* 5 [1963-1965]: 100-113, esp. 104ff.). Even Andrew Lang, one of the earliest and most capable defenders of the primitive monotheism position, admits that while there is solid evidence for a primordial supreme being, "we almost always find ghosts and a Supreme Being together," and hence "we have no historical ground for asserting that either is prior to the other." See Lang, *The Making of Religion*, rev. ed. (New York: AMS, rpt. 1968), p. 220.

[25]Langdon, "Monotheism as the Predecessor." For a more extensive discussion, see his *Semitic Mythology*, vol. 5 of *Mythology of All Races* (Boston: Archeological Institute of America, 1938).

[26]Langdon, "Monotheism as the Predecessor," p. 138.

[27]G. Foucart, "Sky and Sky-Gods," *Encyclopaedia of Religion and Ethics*, 12 vols., ed. J. Hastings (New York: Scribner, 1955), 11:580-85.

[28]For an overview of the evidence and citation of sources, see A. Custance, *Evolution or Creation?* pp. 113-24.

[29]Undoubtedly, the most comprehensive work done in defense of this position is by the Roman Catholic ethnologist W. Schmidt in his monumental work *Der Ursprung der Gottesidee: Eine historische-kristische und positive Studie*, 12 vols. (Münster in Westfalen: Aschendorffsche, 1926-1955). For an abridged translation (from which my knowledge of Schmidt derives) see *The Origin and Growth of Religion: Facts and Theories*, trans. H. J. Rose (New York: Cooper Square, rpt. 1972). For a sympathetic overview of Schmidt and his work, see E. Brandewie, *Wilhelm Schmidt and the Origin of the Idea of God* (Lanham, Md.: University Press of America, 1983). Other noteworthy scholars who argue along these lines are Lang, *Making of Religion*; Langdon, "Monotheism as Predecessor" and *Semitic Mythology*; Custance, "Monotheism to Polytheism."

[30]D. Rooney, "The First Religion of Mankind," *Faith and Reason* 19, nos. 2-3 (1993): 207.

[31]Ibid., p. 199.

[32]Ibid., p. 206.

[33]N. Smart, *The Religious Experience of Mankind*, 3d ed. (Santa Barbara: University of California Press, 1983), p. 33.

[34]Ibid. For more detailed discussions, see E. Smith, ed., *African Ideas of God: A Symposium* (London: Edinburgh House Press, 1950); R. Cameron Mitchell, *African Primal Religions* (Niles, Ill.: Argus Communications, 1977), pp. 23-29; G. Parrinder, *Africa's Three Religions*, 2d ed. (London: Sheldon, 1976), pp. 39-48. For a discussion on the important implications of this spirituality for Christian missions, see Gailyor Van Rheener, *Communicating Christ in Animistic Context* (Grand Rapids, Mich.: Baker, 1990), pp. 242-73.

[35]For example, their creation account speaks of "the Great Manitu" existing while "the earth was an extended fog" (one thinks of Gen 1:2), "lost in space, everywhere." Then Manitu made the land and sky, the sun, moon and stars, and then made dry land appear with a strong wind. After this he spoke "to beings, mortals, souls, and all, and ever he was a manitu to men, and he was their grandfather." See W. Schmidt, *High Gods in North America* (Oxford: Clarendon, 1933), p. 74.

[36]I. Lissner, *Man, God and Magic*, trans. J. M. Brownjohn (New York: Putnam's, 1961), pp. 118-19.

[37]W. Koppers, *Primitive Man and His World Picture*, trans. E. Raybould (New York: Sheed & Ward, 1952), pp. 147-65.

[38]Ibid., pp. 75-94.

[39]Another possibility is to argue, following Brandewie, that the powers of reason naturally lead to monotheism. See Brandewie, *Idea of God*, p. 77. Yet, as Koppers replied, many cultures with a far more developed intellectual life became far less monotheistic. See Koppers, *Primitive Man*, p. 182. The debate is reviewed in Rooney, "First Religion," pp. 216-18.

[40]Rooney, "First Religion," p. 213. In this sense, the widespread common conceptions of one supreme deity could be seen as paralleling the commonalities amid the widespread stories about the creation, the origin of evil, the flood, arrogantly built towers to heaven, the sexual union between humans and gods, giants roaming the earth, etc. See references in chapter three, note 35.

[41]Schmidt postulates a primal revelation to account for this shared stock of knowledge. See his *Primitive Revelation*, trans. J. Baierl (New York: Herder, 1939). As Schmidt himself recognized, the postulation is conjectural, and the primal monotheism position could survive without it.

[42]Snaith, "Advent," pp. 107-8.

[43]On the supreme being as female, or at least as explicitly embodying female qualities, see Smith, ed., *African Ideas of God*, pp. 215ff.

[44]Snaith plausibly speculates that it is the very silence and consequent irrelevance of these high gods that accounts for why they are sometimes missed by outside documenters. See "Advent," pp. 108-9. On the notion of the high God "going away," see J. Mbiti, *African Religions and Philosophy* (Garden City, N.Y.: Doubleday, 1970), pp. 125-29; Smith, ed., *African Ideas of God*, p. 7; Smart, *Religious Experience*, p. 34.

[45]Thus Lang argued concerning the *deus otiosus:* "if the idea of a universal Father and Maker came last in evolution . . . then, of course, it ought to be the newest, and

therefore the most fashionable and potent" (*Making of Religion*, p. 224). Just the opposite is the case, however. An alternative explanation was offered by Nathan Söderblom, who argued that the "high god" was not really a "god," but an *Urheber*, a power that brings things forth. See the discussion in J. de Vries, *Perspectives in the History of Religions*, trans. K. W. Bolle [Berkeley: University of California Press, 1977], p. 116, note 19). In my estimation, this reading presupposes too much philosophical sophistication on the part of the people under consideration.

[46]Much of Father Schmidt's research was conducted by colleagues at the Society of the Divine Word, and in the eyes of some this rendered his work suspect. Several of the more noteworthy attempts to discredit the evidence procured by Schmidt or other defenders of the primal monotheism theory were P. Radin, *Primitive Religion: Its Nature and Origin* (New York: Viking, 1937), pp. 254-67; R. Lowie, *Primitive Religion* (New York: Boni and Liveright, 1924), pp. 124-33.

[47]See the review in de Vries, *Perspectives*, pp. 110-20; Rooney, "First Religion," pp. 210-11.

[48]Snaith, "Advent," p. 108. Almost all the cases Father Schmidt believes illustrate original monotheism have to be qualified by him, argues Snaith. "It may be said that by the time Father Schmidt has mentioned all the modifications and has thus included a great company of 'other supreme beings,' the original Supreme Being in all his pristine excellence . . . exists more in his [Schmidt's] own head than among any primitive people" (p. 105). As Snaith sees it, Schmidt "has demonstrated the existence everywhere of a Supreme Being, but not a primary monotheism. He has not proved a Primary Monotheism existing before all 'low gods.' " But then again, "he has shown that the existence of 'low gods' is not prior to the belief in a Supreme Being" (pp. 105-6). Similarly, illustrating how slippery terminology can be in this debate, Radin argues against the original monotheism thesis on the basis that we never find only a supreme God, but a supreme God surrounded by lesser gods. "Monotheism is extremely rare. What we have is monolatry, and this is essentially merely a form of polytheism" (*Primitive Religion*, p. 266). This is precisely the position I am presently espousing, except I see no reason not to call this monotheism if the supreme God is discerned to be the Creator of the lesser gods. If, as Hayman has argued, monotheists have hardly ever held to the form of exclusivistic monotheism Radin is talking about, then it seems odd, confusing and unnecessary to call this belief monolatry.

[49]On the basis of commonalities between some modern "bear festival" practices among certain primitive tribes (e.g., Gilyaks of Siberia and Ainu of Hokkaido) and similar practices among prehistoric people, Ivar Lissner has argued that we are generally justified in reading the worldviews and behaviors of primitive tribes today as evidence for what prehistoric people generally believed, and that prehistoric humanity likely believed in a single, all-good, invisible Supreme Being. For the "bear festival" of primitive tribes today surrounds just such a conception of a high God, though there are lesser deities to contend with as well. See Lissner, *Man, God and Magic*, pp. 120-94. Cf. H. Kohn, "The Problem of Primitive Monotheism," in *Selections II*, ed. C. Hastings and D. Nicholl (London: Sheed & Ward, 1954), pp. 67-68.

[50]So argue W. Sanford LaSor, D. A. Hubbard and F. W. Bush in *Old Testament Survey: The Message, Form and Background of the Old Testament* (Grand Rapids, Mich.: Eerdmans, 1982), p. 181.

[51]I have seen this idea attributed to Augustine in print but have not been able to locate it in his writings. The concept, in any event, was prevalent in the early church

and goes back at least as far as Philo. Both the historical and theological issues surrounding the issue shall be discussed in my forthcoming *Satan and the Problem of Evil.*

[52]For a general discussion, see W. Wink, *Unmasking the Powers: The Invisible Forces That Determine Human Existence* (Philadelphia: Fortress, 1986), pp. 87-107.

[53]This development becomes more plausible still if we have reason to think that some of these lesser gods were themselves fallen, and were, as such, encouraging humans to err in this direction. As we shall see (chapter six), many authors from the intertestamental period on held to just this view, often basing it on the account of the fall of the "sons of God" in Genesis 6. It was certainly the dominant view of the early church. Many of those who espouse the primal monotheistic position, however, argue that polytheism results from the hypostatization of God's attributes. For the most thorough statement, see H. Ringgren, *Word and Wisdom: Studies in the Hypostatization of Divine Qualities and Functions in the Ancient Near East* (Lund: Hakan Ohlssons, 1947). See also Custance, "Monotheism to Polytheism." I cannot deny that this hypostatization sometimes occurs, but see no grounds for taking it to be the primary basis for a belief in many lesser gods.

[54]G. Parrinder, *Africa's Three Religions*, 2d ed. (London: Sheldon, 1976), p. 47.

[55]Gerald Cooke has demonstrated that the concept of a divine council is found throughout all of Israel's early history. See "The Sons of (the) God(s)," *ZAW* 76 [1964]: 22-47. As with the concept of heavenly councils in Mesopotamian and Ugaritic cultures, for the Hebrews "the essential business of the council is discussion leading to a decision." Often "the high god calls for some god to volunteer to resolve a crisis" (as in 1 Kings 22:19-22). See S. B. Parker, "Council," *DDD*, pp. 392-98.

[56]This raises the issue of why an omniscient and all-wise Creator would invite input from lesser beings, an issue that is essentially no different from the issue of why God would invite us to influence him in prayer. Also important here is the issue of what it means for an omniscient being to change his mind, and what divine sovereignty means if God is literally open to the input of other creatures. Each of these issues shall be addressed in *Satan and the Problem of Evil.* Presently, however, we are simply concerned with observing what Scripture says, not with trying to make it intellectually palatable.

[57]Surprisingly enough, the NIV interprets rather than translates the phrase "LORD of hosts" when they render it "the LORD Almighty" (285 times). The supplied rationale is that the phrase was taken by the interpreters to be "a general reference to the sovereignty of God over all powers in the universe." See note on 1 Samuel 1:3, *The NIV Study Bible*, ed. K. Barker (Grand Rapids, Mich.: Zondervan, 1985), p. 375. This translation thereby turns all these references to the heavenly council in the Old Testament into an attribute of God! Consequently, and unfortunately, the impression of the prevalence of the concept of the society of the gods (the "hosts") in the Old Testament is lessened significantly. On the Old Testament's conception of the "council of Yahweh" in relation to that of other Near Eastern peoples, see E. T. Mullen Jr., *The Assembly of the Gods: The Divine Council in Canaanite and Early Hebrew Literature*, HSM 24 (Chico, Calif.: Scholars Press, 1980); Cross, *Canaanite Myth*, pp. 186-90; idem, "The Council of Yahweh in Second Isaiah," *JNES* 12 (1953): 274-77; G. E Wright, *The Old Testament Against Its Environment*, SBT 1/2 (London: SCM, 1954), pp. 30-41; H. W. Robinson, "The Council of Yahweh," *JTS* 45 (1944): 151-57; P. D. Miller Jr., "The Divine

Council and the Prophetic Call to War," *VT* 18 (1968): 100-107; J. Morgenstern, "The Mythical Background of Psalm 82," *HUCA* 14 (1939): 29-126; Parker, "Council," *DDD,* pp. 392-97; M. Tsevat, "God and the Gods in Assembly," *HUCA* 40/41 (1969-70): 123-37; and especially L. K. Handy, *Among the Host of Heaven: The Syro-Palestinian Pantheon as Bureaucracy* (Winona Lake, Ind.: Eisenbrauns, 1994). See W. H. McClellan, "Donimus Deus Sabaoth," *CBQ* 2 (1940): 300-307, who argues that the phrase "LORD of hosts" refers first and foremost not to an angelic military force but rather to an "unending and ordered servitude which is their lot by nature" (p. 307).

[58]Miller, *Divine Warrior,* pp. 66-70. Modern Western people operate with a worldview that posits a radical bifurcation between the "natural" and the "spiritual" (if the "spiritual" is even acknowledged) that ancient people did not share. We are thus inclined to see the many references to the stars as participants in Yahweh's council as mere poetry. But in the context of the Near Eastern worldview in which they wrote, the biblical authors undoubtedly understood this much more literally. Later Jewish thought, as well as early Christian thinkers, would interpret the Old Testament view that objects and phenomena of nature were part of Yahweh's council to mean that he had entrusted various angels in charge of these objects or phenomena, a point to be further discussed in chapter six. Such an outlook may have implications for our understanding of "natural evil," a point I will discuss in *Satan and the Problem of Evil.*

[59]The undisputed consensus is that *bʿnê hā-ʾĕlōhîm* in the prologue of Job refers to angelic beings. For other passages the question is somewhat more disputed. P. A. H. de Boer concludes that wherever the phrase is found, it refers to one "who belongs to the circle in which the god exercises fatherly authority and for which he manifests fatherly concern." See his "The Son of God in the Old Testament," in *Syntax and Meaning: Studies in Hebrew Syntax and Biblical Exegesis,* OTS 18, ed. A. S. van der Woude (Leiden: Brill, 1973), p. 205. See also J. L. McKenzie, "The Divine Sonship of the Angels," *CBQ* 5 (1943): 293-300.

[60]See R. P. Gordon, "From Mari to Moses: Prophecy at Mari and in Ancient Israel," in *Of Prophets' Visions and the Wisdom of Sages,* ed. H. A. McKay and D. J. A. Clines, JSOTSup 162 (Sheffield: JSOT Press, 1993), pp. 71-74; M. E. Polley, "Hebrew Prophecy Within the Council of Yahweh, Examined in Its Ancient Near Eastern Setting," in *Scripture in Context: Essays on the Comparative Method,* ed. C. D. Evans et al. (Pittsburgh, Penn.: Pickwick, 1980), pp. 141-56.

[61]Against this common approach, P. Joüon has demonstrated that the biblical Hebrew plural of majesty occurs with nouns but never with verbs or pronouns, as in this passage. See *Grammaire de l'hébreu biblique* (Rome: Pontifical Biblical Institute, 1947), §136d-e.

[62]Upon discussing the six possible interpretations of the use of the plural in Genesis 1:26, G. J. Wenham (*Genesis 1—15,* WBC 1 [Waco, Tex.: Word, 1987], pp. 27-28) concludes that the plural most likely constitutes a reference to the angelic heavenly court. See also Cooke, "Sons of (the) God(s)," pp. 22-23. If correct, this implies, as George Foot Moore has noted, that we are made not only in the image of God but in the image of the gods. See *Judaism,* 2 vols. (Cambridge: Harvard University Press, rpt. 1962), 1:447.

[63]See Wenham, *Genesis 1—15,* p. 241; Cooke, "Sons of (the) God(s)," pp. 22-23. The judgment of humankind at Babel may be connected to Deuteronomy 32:8-9, in which Moses says (in the original text) that the Lord divided up the nations

according to the number of the sons of God, a point which may incidentally confirm the reading of the plural of <u>Genesis 11:7</u> as referring to an angelic host. This fascinating passage will be discussed further below.

[64]On Psalm 68:17 Miller comments, "Here the march of Yahweh and his hosts into battle is unmistakably present" (*Divine Warrior,* p. 109).

[65]Ibid., p. 139. See also Muilenburg, *IB,* 5:442. Miller argues that Deuteronomy 33:2 is also to be taken as a reference to Yahweh's army, though this is debatable. See *Divine Warrior,* pp. 75-84.

[66]W. Wink, *Naming the Powers: The Language of Powers in the New Testament* (Philadelphia: Fortress, 1984), p. 131.

[67]F. Garcia Martinez, ed., IQM 1.10-11, 12.8-9; in *The Dead Sea Scrolls Translated: The Qumran Texts in English,* trans. W. G. E. Watson, 2d ed. (Grand Rapids, Mich.: Eerdmans, 1996), pp. 95, 106; see also IQM 7.6, 13.10, 17.6-7. On this view in the Old Testament see T. Longman III and D. G. Reid, *God Is a Warrior* (Grand Rapids, Mich.: Zondervan, 1995), pp. 72-82; P. D. Miller, "The Divine Council and the Prophetic Call to War," *VT* 18 (1968) pp. 100-107; idem, "God the Warrior: A Problem in Biblical Interpretation and Apologetics," *Interpretation* 19 (1965), pp. 40-41; M. Weinfeld, "Divine Intervention in War in Ancient Israel and in the Ancient Near East," in *History, Historiography and Interpretation: Studies in Biblical and Cuneiform Literatures,* ed. H. Tadmor and M. Winfeld (Jerusalem: Magnes, 1984), pp. 124-31. Significantly, the notion that the physical realm is a microcosm of the larger spiritual world, and that the former parallels the latter, is a motif that "appears to be almost universal," according to Wink (*Naming the Powers,* p. 131). For example, the Native American Black Elk speaks of "the nation above" the nations of the world, referring to a heavenly council. See J. G. Neihardt, *Black Elk Speaks* (rpt. New York: Pocket Books, 1972), p. 33. See also M. Eliade, *Cosmos and History: The Myth of the Eternal Return* (New York: Harper & Row, 1959), pp. 6ff.

[68]In the interest of space this study must forgo a review of the various interpretations of Israel's holy war tradition with the various issues they address. For concise introductions to these issues, see G. H. Jones, "The Concept of Holy War," in *The World of Ancient Israel: Sociological, Anthropological and Political Perspectives: Essays by Members of the Society for Old Testament Study,* ed. R. E. Clements (Cambridge: Cambridge University Press, 1989), pp. 299-321; N. K. Gottwald, "War, Holy," in *Interpreter's Dictionary of the Bible, Supplement,* ed. Keith Crim et. al. (Nashville: Abingdon, 1976), pp. 942-44; B. C. Ollenburger, "Gerhard von Rad's Theory of Holy War," introduction to Gerhard von Rad, *Holy War in Ancient Israel,* ed. and trans. M. J. Dawn (Grand Rapids, Mich.: Eerdmans, 1991), pp. 1-33.

[69]On Yahweh's wars against unfaithful Israel see Longman and Reid, *God Is a Warrior,* 48-60; J. A. Soggin, "The Prophets on Holy War as Judgement against Israel," in his *Old Testament and Oriental Studies,* Biblica et Orientalia 29 (Rome: Pontifical Biblical Institute, 1975), pp. 67-81. On Old Testament warfare viewed within the framework of God's battle with Chaos see B. C. Ollenburger, "Peace and God's Action Against Chaos in the Old Testament," in *The Church's Peace Witness,* ed. M. E. Miller and B. N. Gingerich (Grand Rapids, Mich.: Eerdmans, 1994), pp. 70-88. Closely related to this, P. D. Hanson has forcefully argued that the opposite of Old Testament shalom (peace) is not war but chaos, against which Yahweh fights; see "War and Peace in the Hebrew Bible," *Interpretation* 38 (1984): 341-62; see also idem, "War, Peace and Justice in Early Israel," *Bible Review* 3 (1987): 32-45.

[70]M. C. Lind, *Yahweh Is a Warrior: The Theology of Warfare in Ancient Israel* (Scottdale, Penn.: Herald, 1980), pp. 169, 170. See also E. W. Conrad, *Fear Not Warrior: A Study of the 'al tira' Pericopes in the Hebrew Scriptures,* BJS 75 (Chico, Calif.: Scholars Press, 1985), who argues that a central strand of Israelite war theology, rooted in the Davidic tradition and paradigmatically exemplified by Abraham, called the king and the people to passivity in war, allowing Yahweh to fight alone on their behalf.

[71]Miller, "God the Warrior," p. 40. For other such considerations see L. Barrett, *The Way God Fights: War and Peace in the Old Testament* (Scottdale, Penn.: Herald, 1987); P. C. Craigie, *The Problem of War in the Old Testament* (Grand Rapids, Mich.: Eerdmans, 1978); T. R. Hobbs, *A Time for War: A Study of Warfare in the Old Testament* (Wilmington, Del.: Glazier, 1989), pp. 208-33; R. Nysse, "Yahweh Is a Warrior," *Word and World* 7 (1987): 192-201; Ollenburger, "Peace and God's Action Against Chaos"; C. Sherlock, *The God Who Fights: The War Tradition in Holy Scripture,* RSCT 6 (Edinburgh: Rutherford House; Lewiston, N.Y.: Mellen, 1993), pp. 97-105; G. E. Wright, "God the Warrior," in his *The Old Testament and Theology* (New York: Harper & Row, 1969), pp. 121-50.

[72]See L. C. L. Brenton, trans., *The Septuagint with Apocrypha: Greek and English* (rpt. Grand Rapids, Mich.: Zondervan, 1980), p. 277. The NIV, like most English translations, opts for the easier reading "sons of Israel" found in the Masoretic text. A growing majority of scholars, however, argue that the Septuagint (LXX) reading, "angels of God," reflects the original. As early as 1944 H. W. Robinson ("Council of Yahweh," p. 155) could write that the LXX version was "probably original." Since that time, fragments of Deuteronomy 32 found at Qumran have effectively settled the issue. In 1954 P. W. Skehan ("A Fragment of the 'Song of Moses' [Deut 32] from Qumran," *BASOR* 136 [Dec. 1954]: 12-15) discovered a fragment of an ancient Hebrew manuscript that offered the *bᵉnê 'ēl* reading. See also Skehan, "Qumran and the Present State of Old Testament Text Studies: The Masoretic Text," *JBL* 78 (1959): 21. For corroboration and further discussion, see Tsevat, "God and the Gods," pp. 132-33; de Boer, "Sons of God," p. 190; and especially R. S. Hendel, "When the Sons of God Cavorted with the Daughters of Men," in *Understanding the Dead Sea Scrolls: A Reader from the Biblical Archaeology Review,* ed. H. Shanks (New York: Random House, 1992), pp. 168-72.

[73]D. S. Russell, *The Method and Message of Jewish Apocalyptic,* OTL (Philadelphia: Westminster, 1964), p. 248; cf. p. 168.

[74]Ibid., pp. 244-49.

[75]On the ancient Near Eastern idea that particular "gods" are intimately connected to specific territories, see especially D. I. Block, *The Gods of the Nations: Studies in Ancient Near Eastern National Theology,* ETSMS 2 (Jackson, Miss.: Evangelical Theological Society, 1988). Block notes that "Jeremiah's words in 2:11 seem to reflect a theological axiom common to all of the nations of the ancient Near East: 'Has a nation ever changed its gods (even though they are not gods)? But my people have exchanged my glory for "The Useless One." ' " Block adds, "Specific deities tended to be identified with particular nations" (p. 72). For a detailed discussion of the sometimes complex relations among deity, land and nation in the ancient Near East, see also idem, "The Foundations of National Identity: A Study in Ancient Northwest Semitic Perceptions" (Ph.D. diss., University of Liverpool, 1982), pp. 397-492. See also W. Eichrodt, *Theology of the Old Testament,* trans. J. A. Baker, 2 vols., OTL (Philadelphia: Westminster, 1961-1967), 2:199-200.

[76]Some take Deuteronomy 4:19 and Micah 4:5 to entail that "the appointment of gods over the nations is . . . a permanent aspect of the divine economy" (Wink, *Unmasking the Powers,* p. 201, note 12). These verses are taken to legitimize the worship of other gods among the people over whom they are assigned. Such a view would directly contradict the central teaching of Scripture as well as church tradition on the idolatry of worshiping gods other than Yahweh. In any case, the passages can as easily be read in a different light. Deuteronomy 4:19 need only imply that Yahweh has given to all people the sun, moon and stars (and thus they should not be worshiped by any particular nation), and Micah 4:5 need only mean that however other nations may walk (viz., "in the name of their gods"), committed Israelites will follow the Lord.

[77]Russell, *Method and Message,* p. 244. Both the terminology of "gods" and Yahweh's threat that these gods would die like mere mortals if they disobey seem to render it certain that angelic (not human) beings are being referred to here. Some, however, have argued that humans are referred to here on the strength of Jesus' use of this psalm in John 10:34-35. See the discussions in A. Hanson, "John's Citation of Psalm LXXXII Reconsidered," *NTS* 13 (1966-1967): 363-67; J. H. Neyrey, " 'I Said You Are Gods': Psalm 82:6 and John 19," *JBL* 108 (1989): 647-63. It is not certain, however, that Jesus (or John) had only, or even primarily, human beings in mind in his use of this psalm. Even if Jesus did have human beings in mind, it does not follow that this should decide our interpretation of what the original author intended. In any event, most Jewish commentators at the time clearly assumed that the psalm referred to angels (or gods). See J. A. Emerton's thorough research in "The Interpretation of Psalm LXXXII in John X," *JTS* 11 (1960): 329-34; idem, "Melchizedek and the Gods: Fresh Evidence for the Jewish Background of John X. 34-36," *JTS* 17 (1966): 399-401. Also helpful here is G. R. Beasley-Murray, *John,* WBC 36 (Waco, Tex.: Word, 1987), pp. 175-80.

[78]See Wink, *Unmasking the Powers,* p. 111. So too König argues that here Yahweh, taking over the Canaanite god El, "sacks the gods after he has found them guilty of mismanagement" (*Here Am I,* p. 11). Tsevat argues along similar lines, adding that Psalm 58 contains a similar motif, in "God and the Gods," pp. 134-37. See also Morgenstern, "Mythological Background"; J. Ackerman, "An Exegetical Study of Psalm 82" (Th.D. diss., Harvard University, 1966); B. J. Bamberger, *Fallen Angels* (Philadelphia: Jewish Publication Society of America, 1952), pp. 10-11; R. T. O'Callaghan, "A Note on the Canaanite Background of Psalm 82," *CBQ* 15 (1953): 311-14; Robinson, "Council of Yahweh," p. 155; R. Driver, "Notes on the Psalms, I. 1-72," *JTS* 43 (1942): 157.

[79]See, e.g., J. E. Goldingay, *Daniel,* WBC 30 (Dallas: Word, 1989), pp. 291-92, 312-14 (who betrays an influence of Wink's modern reading); G. L. Archer, "Daniel," in *EBC,* 7:124-25; J. J. Collins, *Daniel,* Hermeneia (Minneapolis: Fortress, 1993), pp. 374-76; L. F. Hartman and A. A. Di Lella, *The Book of Daniel,* AB 23 (Garden City, N.Y.: Doubleday, 1978), pp. 282-84; A. Jeffery, "The Book of Daniel," *IB,* 6:506-7; N. W. Porteous, *Daniel,* OTL (Philadelphia: Westminster, 1965), pp. 152-54.

[80]See Wink, *Unmasking the Powers,* pp. 88-94. Here, as often in his work, Wink's biblical exegesis of the "powers" is insightful. But his conclusions are tainted by his denial that the "powers" or "angels" over nations have any autonomous objective existence. They are, in his view, symbols for the national spirit as a whole. In his view the only "mind of its own" that any national god has is the mind of the

collective whole of the people that form that nation. Such a view not only does injustice to the biblical texts but virtually undermines any advantage the Bible's warfare worldview has for understanding evil in the cosmos.

[81]On the "prince of Greece," see Collins, *Daniel,* p. 376.

[82]Wink, *Unmasking the Powers,* p. 91. So observes Goldingay, *Daniel,* p. 313; and Archer, "Daniel," p. 125, who goes so far as to argue that the prince of Persia was "apparently the *satanic agent* assigned to the sponsorship and control of the Persian realm."

[83]Josephus identifies the "sons of God" with angels, and the Nephilim with the twenty-four violent and lecherous giants of Greek tradition who were said to be born of Mother Earth at Phlegra in Thrace. See the discussion in R. Graves and R. Patai, *Hebrew Myths: The Book of Genesis* (New York: McGraw-Hill, 1966), p. 104. On the rather obscure etymology of the term Nephilim, see Wenham, *Genesis 1—15,* 142-43. Concerning the (most likely) related term *gibbôrîm* ("warriors," "giants") in this verse, see E. G. Kraeling, "The Significance and Origin of Gen. 6:1-4," *JNES* 6 (1947): 196-99.

[84]One of the central controversies surrounding this passage has involved the question of whether this story was originally a Canaanite story of the fall of certain gods that was then softened by a Jewish redactor into a story of the fall of certain angels so as to avoid polytheism and render it compatible with Jewish monotheism. So argues, for example, C. Westermann, *Genesis 1—11,* trans. J. J. Scullion, Continental Commentary (Minneapolis: Augsburg, 1984), pp. 371-73; E. van Wolde, "The Sons of God and the Daughters of Men in Genesis 6:1-4," in her *Words Become Worlds: Semantic Studies of Genesis 1—11,* BIS 6 (Leiden: Brill, 1994), pp. 65-66; M. Oduyoye, *The Sons of the Gods and the Daughters of Men: An Afro-Asiatic Interpretation of Genesis 1—11* (Maryknoll, N.Y.: Orbis, 1984), pp. 30-34. From my perspective, far too much is being made of the distinction between gods and angels, owing to the arbitrary assumption that monotheism is incompatible with affirming the existence of other gods and that monotheism evolved out of polytheism. If these two assumptions are not granted (see above), then the issue of whether "gods" or "angels" are being spoken of in this passage becomes merely semantics. As argued earlier, biblical monotheists on the whole reflect no uneasiness with acknowledging the existence of other gods. This observation does not, however, address the issue of whether this passage constitutes a reworked Canaanite story. It only specifies that the issue of whether the "sons of God" were originally understood to be "gods" or "angels" is irrelevant to deciding this issue.

[85]Examples of this tradition in early Christian writings include Justin Martyr *Second Apology* 5 (though cf. his *First Apology* 5, where he seems to equate demons with fallen angels); Athenagoras *Plea for Christians* 24-26; Tertullian *Apology* 22; Lactantius *Divine Institutes* 2.15ff.; 4.27.

[86]Both 2 Peter 2:4 and Jude 6 (following *1 Enoch* and *Jubilees*) may provide support for the angelic interpretation (unless they are referring to a precreation fall). Some have also found possible allusions to this interpretation in 1 Corinthians 11:10, 1 Timothy 2:9, 1 Peter 3:19-20 and even Matthew 22:30. It is then found in Justin Martyr (*Second Apology* 2.5); Irenaeus (*Against Heresies* 4.16.2, 36.4); Clement of Alexandria (*Miscellanies* 5.1.10); Tertullian (*On Idolatry* 9; *Against Marcion* 5.18); Lactantius (*Divine Institutes* 2.15); Clementine (*Homilies* 7.11-15); and Comodianus (*Instructions* 3). On the use of Genesis 6 in the early church, see L. R. Wickham, "The Sons of God and the Daughters of Men: Genesis vi 2 in Early

Christian Exegesis," in *Language and Meaning: Studies in Hebrew Language and Biblical Exegesis,* OTS 19 (Leiden: Brill, 1974), pp. 135-47. Among other things, Wickham argues that the divine beings interpretation of *b'nê 'elohîm* in Genesis 6 was later generally rejected because of the use made of the "sons of God" texts by Arians in fourth-century christological debates (see esp. 144-47). See the discussions in P. S. Alexander, "The Targumim and Early Exegesis of the 'Sons of God' in Genesis 6," *JJS* 23 (1972): 68 (who argues that a Jewish polemic accounts for the dismissal of the divine beings interpretation of Gen 6); R. C. Newman, "Ancient Exegesis of Genesis 6:2, 4," *Grace Theological Journal* 5 (1984): 21-31; Bamberger, *Fallen Angels,* pp. 74-78; Wenham, *Genesis 1—15,* p. 139.

[87]So far as I can discern, Philo was the first to suggest that "sons of God" may refer to humans, though he does not mention the Sethite line per se. Julius Africanus (*Chronography* 2) argues the Sethian interpretation, as does Augustine (*City of God* 15.17). Cyril of Jerusalem (*Glaphyraa* 2) offers a novel twist when he identifies the "sons of God" with the descendants of Enoch. For several modern interpreters who argue along these lines, see J. E. Coleran, "The Sons of God in Gen. 6:2," *Theological Studies* 2 (1941): 488-509; P. Joüon, "Les unions entre les 'fils de Dieu' et les 'filles des hommes' (Gen. 6:1-4)," *RSR* 29 (1939): 108-12; McKenzie, "Divine Sonship of the Angels," pp. 294-95. L. Eslinger takes this general approach but reverses the identifications. In his view "sons of God" are the Cainites while the "daughters of men" are the Sethites ("A Contextual Identification of the *bene ha'elohim* and *benoth ha'adam* in Genesis 6:1-4," *JSOT* 13 [1979]: 65-73).

[88]This view became popular among Jewish exegetes beginning in the mid-second century A.D. See Alexander, "Targumim and Early Exegesis," pp. 61-71; Newman, "Ancient Exegesis," pp. 23-27. Modern proponents include F. Dexinger, *Sturz der Göttersöhne oder Engel vor der Sintlfut?* (Vienna: Herder, 1966); M. Kline, "Divine Kingship and Genesis 6:1-4," *WTJ* 24 (1962): 187-204. D. J. A. Clines takes a both/and approach and argues that the author meant to identify both divine beings and antediluvian rulers with his phrase "sons of God." See his "The Significance of the 'Sons of God' Episode (Genesis 6:1-4) in the Context of the 'Primeval History' (Genesis 1—11)," *JSOT* 13 (1979): 33-46.

[89]Hence the vast majority of contemporary interpreters have been persuaded by the divine being interpretation. See, e.g., de Boer, "Sons of God," pp. 190-01; U. Cassuto, "The Episode of the Sons of God and the Daughters of Man," in *Biblical and Oriental Studies,* vol. 1, *Bible,* trans. I. Abrahams (Jerusalem: Magnes, 1973), pp. 17-28; Cooke, "Sons of (the) God(s)," pp. 23-24; T. E. Fretheim, "The Book of Genesis," in *New Interpreter's Bible,* ed. L. E. Keck et al. (Nashville: Abingdon, 1994), 1:382-83; R. S. Hendel, "Of Demigods and the Deluge: Toward an Interpretation of Genesis 6:1-4," *JBL* 106 (1987): 13-26; Wenham, *Genesis 1—15,* pp. 139-41; V. P. Hamilton, *The Book of Genesis: Chapters 1—17,* NICOT (Grand Rapids, Mich.: Eerdmans, 1990), pp. 262-65.

[90]See, e.g., C. F. Keil and F. Delitzsch, *Biblical Commentary on the Old Testament: The Pentateuch* (Grand Rapids, Mich.: Eerdmans, rpt. 1950), 1:131; J. Murray, *Principles of Conduct* (Grand Rapids, Mich.: Eerdmans, 1957), p. 246; H. G. Stigers, *A Commentary on Genesis* (Grand Rapids, Mich.: Zondervan, 1976), p. 97.

[91]So argues W. A. Van Gemeren, "The Sons of God in Genesis 6:1-4 (An Example of Evangelical Demythologization?)" *WTJ* 43 (1981): 320-48; Newman, "Ancient Exegesis," p. 36; Wenham, *Genesis 1—15,* p. 140.

[92]P. G. Hiebert, "The Flaw of the Excluded Middle," *Missiology* 10, no. 1 (1982):

35-47. See also C. Kraft, *Christianity and Culture* (Maryknoll, N.Y.: Orbis, 1979); idem, "The Problem of 'What We Think We Know,' " *Faith & Renewal*, 16 (Sept.-Oct. 1991): 10-16; idem, *Christianity with Power: Your Worldview and Your Experience of the Supernatural* (Ann Arbor, Mich.: Vine, 1989); Pinnock, *Wideness in God's Mercy*, pp. 122-24. The phrase "the world in between" is taken from the splendid book by Emmanuel Milingo, former archbishop in Zambia. See *The World in Between: Christian Healing and the Struggle for Spiritual Survival* (Maryknoll, N.Y.: Orbis, 1984). As noted in chapter one, it is increasingly evident that our culture as a whole is now moving toward a more Third World perspective on "the world in between." One unmistakable sign of this is the present explosion of interest in angels. For contemporary popular observations, see N. Gibbs, "Angels Among Us," *Time*, Dec. 27, 1993, pp. 56-65; K. L. Woodward et al., "Angels," *Newsweek*, Dec. 27, 1993, pp. 52-57; E. Stone, "Are There Angels Among Us?" *New Age Journal*, Mar.-Apr. 1994, pp. 88-93, 148-51.

[93]As shall be argued extensively in *Satan and the Problem of Evil*, chapters 3—7.

[94]Quoted from the *Timaeus* in C. Hartshorne and W. L. Reese, eds., *Philosophers Speak of God* (Chicago: University of Chicago Press, rpt. 1973), p. 54.

Chapter 5: Rebuking the Adversary

[1]The Hebrew term *śāṭān* means "adversary" or "one who opposes." For discussions, see *New Brown-Driver-Briggs-Gesenius Hebrew-English Lexicon* (Peabody, Mass.: Hendrickson, 1979), p. 966; J. B. Payne, "*śāṭān*," *TWOT*, 2:874-75; E. Pagels, *The Origin of Satan* (New York: Random House, 1995), p. 39; and esp. P. L. Day, *An Adversary in Heaven: śāṭān in the Hebrew Bible*, HSM 43 (Atlanta: Scholars Press, 1988). The verb form *śāṭān* ("to oppose as an adversary") occurs 6 times in the Old Testament (Ps 38:20; 71:13; 109:4, 20, 29; Zech 3:1). The noun form occurs 27 times, 7 of which clearly refer to a human adversary (1 Sam 29:4; 2 Sam 19:23; 1 Kings 5:4; 11:14, 23, 25; Ps 109:6). Twice the "angel of Yahweh" is referred to as a *śāṭān* (Num 22:22, 32). The remaining 18 occurrences of the noun are found in only three passages, all of which will be discussed in this chapter (1 Chron 21:1; Job 1—2; Zech 3:1-2). With the exception of 1 Chronicles 21:1, the noun in these cases is used with the definite article and hence probably cannot be taken as a proper name. I shall italicize *(satan)* when I am referring to the original Hebrew noun and capitalize (Satan) when I am referring to the proper name of this being.

[2]See, e.g., N. Forsyth, *The Old Enemy: Satan and the Combat Myth* (Princeton: Princeton University Press, 1987), p. 110; E. Schwarz, *Evil: A Historical and Theological Perspective*, trans. M. W. Worthing (Minneapolis: Fortress, 1995), pp. 60-63; W. Wink, *Unmasking the Powers: The Invisible Forces That Determine Human Existence* (Philadelphia: Fortress, 1986), p. 14. Elaine Pagels describes *satan* in Job as a "roving intelligence agent," sometimes called in the ancient world "the king's eye" (*Origin of Satan*, pp. 41-42). J. B. Russell argues that Satan "is not yet the principle of evil, which remains with the God. He is still one of the heavenly court and does nothing without God's consent and will" (*The Devil: Perceptions of Evil from Antiquity to Primitive Christianity* [Ithaca: Cornell University Press, 1977], pp. 199-200). See also P. Carus, *The History of the Devil and the Idea of Evil* (New York: Bell, rpt. 1969), p. 71; J. Kallas, *The Real Satan: From Biblical Times to the Present* (Minneapolis: Augsburg, 1975), pp. 22-26; P. J. Nel, "The Conception of Evil and Satan in Jewish Traditions in the Pre-Christian Period," in *Like a Roaring*

Lion . . . : Essays on the Bible, the Church and Demonic Powers, ed. P. G. R. de Villiers (Pretoria: University of South Africa, 1987), pp. 6-7; M. E. Tate, "Satan in the Old Testament," *Review and Expositor* 89 (Fall 1992): 462; W. Tremmel, *Dark Side: The Satan Story* (St. Louis: CBP, 1987). As in Zechariah 4, *satan* is here used with a definite article, thus showing that it is being used not as a proper name but as a title. Hence I do not capitalize it. See Day, *Adversary,* pp. 5, 15 and passim, who argues that none of the uses of *satan* in the Old Testament refers to a particular being.

[3]See esp. P. Volz, *Das Dämonische in Jahwe,* Sammlung gemeinverstandlicher Vortrage und Schritten aus dem Gebiet der Theologie und Religionsgeschichte 110 (Tübingen: Mohr, 1924). Thus R. S. Kluger (*Satan in the Old Testament,* trans. H. Nagel, Studies in Jungian Thought 7 [Evanston, Ill.: Northwestern University Press, 1967], p. 10) writes of "the essential conclusion, fully supported by the biblical texts, that Yahweh was originally a demonic god." See also Carus, *History of the Devil,* p. 70; Tremmel, *Dark Side,* p. 9. For a recent critique of Voltz's theory with regard to the vengeance of God (which Volz understands to evolve gradually into a view of the devil), see H. G. L. Peels, "Appendix A: God's Vengeance and the 'Demonic' (P. Voltz)," in his *Vengeance of God: The Meaning of the Root NQM and the Function of the NQM-Texts in Context of Divine Revelation in the Old Testament,* OTS 31 (Leiden: Brill, 1995), pp. 298-301. For two attempts to wrestle with this issue with specific regard to the book of Job, see C. Duquoc, "Demonism and the Unexpectedness of God," in *Job and the Silence of God,* ed. C. Duquoc and C. Floristan, Concilium 169 (Edinburgh: T & T Clark; New York: Seabury, 1983), pp. 81-87; D. Kinet, "The Ambiguity of the Concepts of God and Satan in the Book of Job," trans. M. Kohl, in ibid., pp. 30-35.

[4]Russell, *Devil,* p. 174. See also Schwarz, *Evil,* pp. 55-56.

[5]Forsyth, *Old Enemy,* p. 109.

[6]Russell, *Devil,* p. 200.

[7]For Jung's own application of this theory, see his *Answer to Job,* trans. R. F. C. Hull (Cleveland, Ohio: World, 1960). For various expositions of or responses to Jung's approach to evil, see H. L. Philip, *Jung and the Problem of Evil* (London: Rockcliff, 1958); J. A. Sandford, *Evil: The Shadow Side of Reality* (New York: Crossroad, 1981); R. A. Segal, "A Jungian View of Evil," *Zygon* 20 (1985): 83-89. Kluger (*Satan,* pp. 79ff.) argues that the figure of Satan was a stage in the development of "the divine personality" in the thinking of the Israelites. Kluger's study was originally published as "Die Gestalt des Satans im Alten Testament," part 3 of Jung's *Symbolik des Geistes* (Zurich: Rascher, 1948). Similarly, D. Wolfers argues that the *satan* in Job is "the projection of doubt and skepticism within the complex mind of the Deity itself." In good Jungian fashion he concludes that this "points to the identity of the Satan as but a facet of God's personality." See his *Deep Things Out of Darkness: The Book of Job—Essays and a New English Translation* (Grand Rapids, Mich.: Eerdmans, 1995), p. 202.

[8]For the most extensive critical overview and refutation of this position to date, see F. Lindström, *God and the Origin of Evil: A Contextual Analysis of Alleged Monistic Evidence in the Old Testament,* trans. F. H. Cryer, ConBOT 21 (Lund: Gleerup, 1983). Lindström initially embarked on this work to further refine the customary view that among Old Testament authors "the Deity was held to be the direct author of all evils affecting man" (p. 7). But his meticulous research brought him to the opposite conclusion.

[9]For several fine, strongly conservative works that provide a defense of the inspiration or infallibility of Scripture from a number of different fronts, see B. B. Warfield, *The Inspiration and Authority of the Bible*, ed. S. G. Craig (Philadelphia: Presbyterian & Reformed, 1970); H. N. Ridderbos, *Studies in Scripture and Its Authority* (Grand Rapids, Mich.: Eerdmans, 1978); idem, *The Authority of the New Testament Scriptures* (Philadelphia: Presbyterian & Reformed, 1963); J. W. Montgomery, ed., *God's Inerrant Word: An International Symposium on the Trustworthiness of Scripture* (Minneapolis: Bethany, 1974); E. J. Young, *Thy Word Is Truth* (Grand Rapids, Mich.: Eerdmans, 1957); C. Pinnock, *Biblical Revelation: The Foundation of Christian Theology* (Chicago: Moody Press, 1971); G. Boyd, *Letters from a Skeptic* (Wheaton, Ill.: Victor, 1994), pp. 77-137. Also informative, and from a slightly more centrist perspective, is I. H. Marshall, *Biblical Inspiration* (Grand Rapids, Mich.: Eerdmans, 1983); B. Vawter, *Biblical Inspiration* (Philadelphia: Westminster, 1972); and P. Achtemeier, *The Inspiration of Scripture: Problems and Proposals* (Philadelphia: Westminster, 1980). My own contention is that the rationality of belief in the divine inspiration and infallibility of Scripture is ultimately connected inextricably with the rationality of belief in the deity of Christ on historical grounds and with the rationality of the Christian worldview considered as a whole. Taken as a whole, my contention would be that this entire belief system—when thought through consistently—constitutes the most rational and existentially fulfilling belief system judged by logical, historical, existential, empirical and phenomenological criteria.

[10]The claim that the Old Testament's understanding of evil as something that God unambiguously opposes and that the conception of Satan as a evil figure set against God arose strictly out of Zoroastrian influence shall be critiqued in the next chapter.

[11]On the centrality and antiquity of the divine warrior material, see T. Longman III and D. Reid, *God Is a Warrior* (Grand Rapids, Mich.: Zondervan, 1995), pp. 31-32; P. D. Miller, "God the Warrior," *Int* 19 (1965): 39-40; idem, "El the Warrior," *HTR* 60 (1967), esp. 428-31; idem, *The Divine Warrior in Early Israel*, HSM 5 (Cambridge: Harvard University Press, 1973); W. Eichrodt, *Theology of the Old Testament*, trans. J. A. Baker, 2 vols., OTL (Philadelphia: Westminster, 1961-1967), 1:228-29.

[12]Lindström, *God and the Origin of Evil*, p. 118. Gordon Lewis ("Response" to Kinlaw, pp. 36-40) raises a similar objection to D. Kinlaw's treatment of Old Testament demonology ("The Demythologization of the Demonic in the Old Testament," pp. 29-35) in *Demon Possession*, ed. J. W. Montgomery (Minneapolis: Bethany, 1976), p. 38. This is, I believe, the most telling question to be posed not only to "demonic in Yahweh" theorists but to conservative Calvinist theorists as well.

[13]Day, *Adversary*, p. 81. So argues Lindström, "the satan is not an enemy of Job in this context, but God's opponent" (*God and the Origin of Evil*, p. 142).

[14]J. Morgenstern, "Satan," *The Universal Jewish Encyclopedia*, 10 vols., ed. I. Landman (New York: Universal Jewish Encyclopedia Co., 1943), 9:380.

[15]E. Langton, *The Essentials of Demonology: A Study of the Jewish and Christian Doctrine, Its Origin and Development* (London: Epworth, 1949), p. 54. See also E. Pagels, "The Social History of Satan, the 'Intimate Enemy': A Preliminary Sketch," *HTR* 84 (1991): 112.

[16]Though both Job and his friends are incorrect, it is also clear that Yahweh is far

more angry with Job's friends, who abused him with their self-protecting theologies and theodicies, than he is with Job himself, who was simply crying out in pain (Job 42:7-9).

[17]According to most commentators today, and much of the early Jewish tradition as well, the intended genre of the prologue of Job is that of a folktale employed to set the stage for an epic, poetic drama. See Day, *Adversary*, pp. 70ff.; Robert Gordis, *The Book of Job* (New York: Jewish Theological Seminary, 1978), p. 2; Samuel Terrien, *Job: Poet of Existence* (New York: Bobbs-Merrill, 1957), p. 30. We must, then, be very cautious about drawing any inferences about God's relationship to Satan, or about God's character, on the basis of the details of their portrayals and mutual dialogue in this work. For example, are we really to suppose that God did not know where Satan was? Was God intimidated into a bet? Does Satan have to ask permission from God every time he acts? Do they have a semicordial relationship such as this prologue suggests? Questions of these sorts are wholly inappropriate to the type of literature we are here considering. One can no more infer doctrine from this portion of Scripture than one can deduce doctrine from incidental features of Jesus' parables. The purpose of these features is merely to serve as the backdrop for the main point being made.

[18]P. D. Miller ("God and the Gods," *Affirmation* 1, no. 5 [1973]: 54-55) has noted the manner in which Jewish theology eventually develops to where the "problem of theodicy . . . begins to be dealt with in terms of conflict in the divine realm" (p. 55). This theme, we shall see, becomes solidified in the New Testament.

[19]See Lindström, *God and the Origin of Evil*, passim, for more extensive treatments of these passages, as well as a refutation of other passages sometimes used in support of the "demonic in Yahweh" theory. Also helpful in this regard is Peels, "God's Vengeance."

[20]C. Westermann, *Isaiah 40—66*, trans. D. M. G. Stalker, OTL (Philadelphia: Westminster, 1969), p. 162.

[21]Lindström, *God and the Origin of Evil*, p. 192. See the entire discussion from pp. 178-99. A. König argues along the same lines. He finally concludes, quite correctly, that the theology which makes "God . . . responsible for all things . . . describes a demon rather than the God of Israel" (*New and Greater Things: Re-evaluating the Biblical Message on Creation* [Pretoria: University of South Africa, 1988], p. 63; cf. pp. 19, 60-62). C. Stuhlmüller refutes this interpretation of Isaiah 45:7 as well in *Creative Redemption in Deutero-Isaiah*, AnBib 43 (Rome: Biblical Institute Press, 1970), pp. 197ff.

[22]See Lindström, *God and the Origin of Evil*, pp. 214-36.

[23]Five verses prior to this statement Jeremiah had expressly stated that Yahweh "does not willingly afflict or grieve anyone" (v. 33).

[24]For a more in-depth discussion, see Lindström, *God and the Origin of Evil*, pp. 199-214. Likewise, both Peels ("God's Vengeance") and Eichrodt (*Theology*, 1:262-66) demonstrate that those instances of the vengeance and "wrath" of God in the Old Testament do not support anything like the "demonic-in-Yahweh" theory. Rather, as Eichrodt argues, "unlike holiness or righteousness, *wrath never forms one of the permanent attributes of the God of Israel*; it can only be understood as, so to speak, a footnote to the will to fellowship of the covenant God" (p. 262). Hence "in the case of God *there can never be any question of despotic caprice striking out in blind rage*" (p. 265).

[25]In Exodus 4:11 Yahweh says, "Who gives speech to mortals? Who makes them mute

or deaf, seeing or blind? Is it not I, the LORD?" Not surprisingly, this verse has frequently been cited in defense of the "demonic-in-Yahweh" theorists (and, predictably, in defense of Calvinism). However we interpret this verse, it should not be used to overturn the general teaching of Scripture, and especially the unambiguous example of Christ's ministry, which instructs us that God is against evil and suffering, not the cause of it. The passage certainly teaches that Yahweh is sovereign over speech and hearing impairments; this is just the point Yahweh is making to the stuttering Moses! The verse makes this point by appealing to the divine agency involved in the creation of all human beings. But, as Fretheim notes, it is significant that the verse does not suggest that this divine activity is "*individually applied,* as if God entered into the womb of every pregnant woman and determined whether and how a child would have disabilities. This is a general statement that the world is so created by God that such things will happen" (T. E. Fretheim, *Exodus,* Interpretation [Louisville, Ky.: John Knox, 1991], p. 72). It is also significant to note, as Fretheim further observes, that the verse does not suggest that "God is the *sole* cause of all such developments" (ibid.). Other causes are perhaps not mentioned only because the point of the verse is to stress that God accepts responsibility for everything in the world (though not the guilt of being the cause of everything), and thus God is not at a loss as to how to use them effectively when necessary. Other passages of Scripture clearly stress human agency and responsibility alongside God on such matters. See also Fretheim's marvelous study *The Suffering of God: An Old Testament Perspective,* OBT (Philadelphia: Fortress, 1984), pp. 71-78. New Testament passages sometimes used to argue that God exercises unilateral meticulous control over all the affairs of history (e.g., Rom 9, 11; Eph 1:3-11) shall be discussed in *Satan and the Problem of Evil.*

[26]See, e.g., Revelation 12:9; 20:2; *Life of Adam and Eve* 16:4. For discussion regarding the identification of Satan with Leviathan/the dragon in Judaism and Christianity, see T. Fawcett, "The Satanic Serpent," in his *Hebrew Myth and Christian Gospel* (London: SCM, 1973), pp. 96-109; C. H. Gordon, "Leviathan: Symbol of Evil," in *Biblical Motifs: Origins and Transformations,* ed. A. Altmann, Studies and Texts 3 (Cambridge: Harvard University Press, 1966), pp. 1-89; as well as J. Day, *God's Conflict with the Dragon and the Sea: Echoes of a Canaanite Myth in the Old Testament,* UCOP 35 (Cambridge: Cambridge University Press, 1985), p. 189.

[27]One could consider Numbers 22:22-35 as well in the light of the fact that the angel of the Lord is here said to have stood in the road as Balaam's "adversary" (*satan*) (v. 22). Although the role of a *satan* is here referred to, the fact that it is the Lord himself who is playing this role, not a different divine being who is playing the role *over against* the Lord as in the other passages, sets this passage apart from the others.

[28]"Satan" is here, as in Job, used with a definite article and thus should not be taken as a proper name. The text should probably read, "and the *satan* [adversary] standing at his right side."

[29]Pagels, however, attempts to argue that the *satan* here (and in 1 Chron 21) represents divisions within Israel. He is on his way to becoming the symbol for "the intimate enemy" (*Origin of Satan,* pp. 44-45).

[30]See Adolphe Lods, "Les origine de la figure de satan, ses fonctions à la cour céleste," in *Mélanges syriens offerts à Monsieur René Dussaud,* 2 vols. (Paris: Geuthner, 1939), 2:649-60. Even Kluger (*Satan,* p. 144) and Forsyth (*Old Enemy,* p. 115), who otherwise stress the servanthood of the *satan* amidst Yahweh's council, see the

beginnings of overt opposition between God and the *satan* in this passage. See also Pagels, "Social History of Satan," p. 113.

[31]The majority of scholars argue that the absence of a definite article suggests *satan* is here a proper name. See, e.g., Eichrodt, *Theology*, 2:206; H. Haag, *Teufelsglaube* (Tübingen: Katzmann, 1974), p. 214; J. B. Payne, "I Chronicles," in *EBC*, 4:406-7; G. von Rad, "The OT View of Satan," *TDNT*, 2:74. It has, however, been challenged by Day (*Adversary*, pp. 127-45).

[32]Cf. Exodus 30:11-16, which reveals that undertaking a census was, within Israel, always a precarious affair.

[33]See, e.g., S. Japhet, *I & II Chronicles*, OTL (Louisville, Ky.: Westminster John Knox, 1993), pp. 373-74; R. Braun, *1 Chronicles*, WBC 14 (Waco, Tex.: Word, 1986), pp. 216-17.

[34]For a discussion of the three main distinctive approaches to the issue of 2 Samuel 24:1 versus 1 Chronicles 21:1—the harmonistic, redactional and exegetical—see J. H. Sailhamer, "I Chronicles 21:1—A Study in Inter-biblical Interpretation," *TJ* 10 (1989): 33-48. Here I offer one version of the harmonistic approach. This is not to deny important aspects of the exegetical approach as delineated by Sailhamer, just as he acknowledges important aspects of the harmonistic approach (pp. 39-40). See also G. L. Archer's harmonistic argument in his *Encyclopedia of Bible Difficulties* (Grand Rapids, Mich.: Zondervan, 1982), pp. 221-22.

[35]See, e.g., G. von Rad, *Genesis*, trans. J. H. Marks, rev. ed., OTL (Philadelphia: Westminster, 1972), pp. 92-93; C. Westermann, *Genesis 1—11*, trans. J. J. Scullion, Continental Commentary (Minneapolis: Augsburg, 1984), pp. 258-61. For several studies that take issue with this conclusion, see U. Cassuto, *A Commentary on the Book of Genesis, Part I: From Adam to Noah, Genesis I—VI 8*, trans. I. Abrahams (Jerusalem: Magnes, 1961), pp. 139-43; V. P. Hamilton, *Book of Genesis: Chapters 1—17*, NICOT (Grand Rapids, Mich.: Eerdmans, 1990), pp. 196-97; M. L. Holert, "Extrinsic Evil Powers in the Old Testament" (Th.M. thesis, Fuller Theological Seminary, 1985), pp. 51-53; I. Hunt, "Fall of Man," *New Catholic Encyclopedia*, ed. W. McDonald, 15 vols. (New York: McGraw-Hill, 1967), 5:816; R. W. L. Moberly, "Did the Serpent Get It Right?" *JTS* 39 (1988): 1-27; G. J. Wenham, *Genesis 1—15*, WBC 1 (Waco, Tex.: Word, 1987), p. 80.

[36]See the various references in L. Jung, *Fallen Angels in Jewish, Christian and Mohammedan Literature* (New York: KTAV, 1974), pp. 68-72.

[37]See, e.g., T. C. Vriezen, *Onderzoek naar de Paradijs-Voorstelling bij de oude Semietische volken* (Wageningen: Veenman & Zonen, 1937), who sees the serpent as a magical animal; F. A. Sayer, "The Image of God, the Wisdom of Serpents and the Knowledge of Good and Evil," in *A Walk in the Garden: Biblical, Iconographical and Literary Images of Eden*, ed. P. Morris and D. Sawyer, JSOTSup 136 (Sheffield: Sheffield Academic Press, 1992), pp. 66-68; H. N. Wallace, *The Eden Narrative*, HSM 32 (Atlanta: Scholars Press, 1985), pp. 159-61; E. van Wolde, "The Serpent in Genesis 2—3," in her *Words Become Worlds: Semantic Studies of Genesis 1—11*, BIS 6 (Leiden: Brill, 1994), pp. 3-12.

[38]For a summary see P. S. Alexander, "The Fall into Knowledge: The Garden of Eden/Paradise in Gnostic Literature," in *Walk in the Garden*, pp. 91-104.

[39]I am intentionally bypassing (because irrelevant) the thorny issue of how much of this passage is to be taken literally and how much allegorically. A plurality of views about this issue has characterized the church from the postapostolic period, but this plurality has gone largely unappreciated by fundamentalists and strongly conserva-

tive evangelicals today. For a balanced overview from an evangelical perspective, see J. J. Davis, "Genesis, Inerrancy and the Antiquity of Man," in *Inerrancy and Common Sense,* ed. R. R. Nicole and J. R. Michaels (Grand Rapids, Mich.: Baker, 1980), pp. 137-59. For a still unsurpassed overview of the traditional positions, see J. Feldmann, *Paradies und Sündenfall* (Münster: Aschendorff, 1913), pp. 501-605.

[40]R. S. Hendel, "Serpent," *DDD,* pp. 1405-6. See also Langton, *Essentials,* pp. 7, 37-38. Langton argues that Numbers 21:6-8, Deuteronomy 8:15 and Isaiah 30:6, as well as Genesis 3:1 refer to demonic creatures. See also E. Williams-Forte, "The Snake and the Tree in the Iconography and Texts of Syria during the Bronze Age," in *Ancient Seals and the Bible,* ed. L. Gorelick and E. Williams-Forte (Malibu: Undena, 1983), pp. 18-43; T. Fawcett, "The Satanic Serpent," in his *Hebrew Myth and Christian Gospel* (London: SCM, 1973), pp. 96-100; M. J. Gruenthaner, "The Demonology of the Old Testament," *CBQ* 6 (1944): 7-15.

[41]K. J. Joines, *Serpent Symbolism in the Old Testament: A Linguistic, Archaeological and Literary Study* (Haddonfield, N.J.: Haddonfield, 1974), esp. pp. 26-31; F. Landy, *Paradoxes of Paradise: Identity and Difference in the Song of Songs,* Bible and Literature 7 (Sheffield: Almond, 1983) pp. 229-42; E. D. Van Buren, "The Dragon in Ancient Mesopotamia," *Or* 15 (1946): 21.

[42]Joines, *Serpent Symbolism,* p. 30. So too Landy concludes that "the venomous formlessness of the serpent is a metaphor for seditious chaos" (*Paradoxes of Paradise,* pp. 229-45), while Van Buren concludes that it represents "the embodiment of evil" ("Dragon in Ancient Mesopotamia," p. 21). See also H. S. May, "The Daimonic in Jewish History [or, The Garden of Eden Revisited]," *Zeitschrift für Religions- und Geistesgeschichte* 23 (1971): 205-19, who concludes that the serpent is "symbolic of the power of evil" and could be used as "a concretization of covenant breaking" (p. 208).

[43]F. Hvidberg, "The Canaanite Background of Gen. I-III," *VT* 10 (1960): 288-89.

[44]One may object that the author of Genesis 1 is different from the author of Genesis 3, and thus one would not expect consistency between the two accounts. While we cannot enter into this tangled issue here, I may simply note that even if the accounts were compiled by a later redactor to read like a continuous narrative, one would still expect consistency. Why think that later redactors had less of an eye for consistency than original authors? If *we* think we pick up an inconsistency that (per hypothesis) slipped by a (hypothetical) redactor, it may very well be that the slip is on our part in thinking there is a genuine inconsistency in the first place. Hence my argument that seeing the serpent as different from natural animals on the basis of Genesis 1:24-25 stands.

[45]Several ancient Jewish works reveal a connection between the Isaianic figure and Satan (*Life of Adam and Eve* 15:3; *2 Enoch* 29:4-5). It may be alluded to also in Luke 10:15, 18 and Revelation 12:7-12. The vast majority of early Christian interpreters made this identification, including Tertullian, Origen, Athanasius, Ambrose, Gregory of Nyssa, Gregory Nazianzus, Jerome, John Cassian, Augustine and Gregory the Great. Henceforth it became the almost (but not totally) unanimous opinion of the church until modern times. On the history of the interpretation of this passage, see G. L. Keown, "A History of the Interpretation of Isaiah 14:12-15" (Ph.D. diss., Southern Baptist Theological Seminary, 1979); J. M. Bertoluci, "The Son of the Morning and the Guardian Cherub in the Context of the Controversy Between Good and Evil" (Th.D. thesis, Andrews University, 1985), pp. 4-36. Today, however, a straightforward identification with Satan is

largely limited to popular conservative works. See, e.g., M. Green, *I Believe in Satan's Downfall* (Grand Rapids, Mich.: Eerdmans, 1981), pp. 39-42; S. D. Swihart, *Angels in Heaven and Earth* (Plainfield, N.J.: Logos International, 1979), pp. 77-80. The scholarly consensus slightly favors viewing this passage as referring exclusively to a purely historical figure, though some concede that it perhaps makes use of a mythic tradition of a cosmic rebellion in the process. Chrysostom, Luther and Calvin offer some historical precedent for this interpretation. For contemporary examples, see R. L. Allen, "Lucifer, Who or What?" *JETS* 11 (1968): 35-39; S. Erlandson, *The Burden of Babylon: A Study of Isaiah 13:2—14:23,* ConBOT 4 (Lund: Gleerup, 1970), pp. 123-25; Keown, "History of the Interpretation"; J. N. Oswalt, *The Book of Isaiah, Chapters 1—39,* NICOT (Grand Rapids, Mich.: Eerdmans, 1986), pp. 320-25; J. D. W. Watts, *Isaiah 1—33,* WBC 24 (Waco, Tex.: Word, 1985), pp. 204-12. For a comprehensive overview of various historical-critical positions, see H. R. Page Jr., *The Myth of Cosmic Rebellion: A Study of Its Reflexes in Ugaritic and Biblical Literature* (Leiden: Brill, 1996), pp. 9-34.

[46]See R. J. Clifford, *The Cosmic Mountain in Canaan and the Old Testament,* HSM 4 (Cambridge: Harvard University Press, 1972), pp. 164-65. The entire text is found in *Corpus des tablettes en cunéiformes alphabétiques,* 3 vols., ed. A. Herdner (Paris: Geuthner, 1963), 1:55-65. Some take *ba-arṣi* in this account to refer to the underworld, not the earth. Hence Athtar is seen as becoming the prince of the underworld. See the discussion in J. W. McKay, "Helel and the Dawn-Goddess," *VT* 20 (1970): 461; P. D. Hanson, *The Dawn of Apocalyptic* (Philadelphia: Fortress, 1977), p. 206. The most comprehensive analysis to date that argues for reading Isaiah 14 as one of the many stories of cosmic rebellion is Page, *Myth of Cosmic Rebellion.* For a discussion of the connection between the Isaiah account and the Athtar myth, see ibid., pp. 51-109.

[47]Forsyth, *Old Enemy,* p. 135.

[48]See G. R. Driver, *Canaanite Myths and Legends,* 3d ed., ed. J. C. L. Gibson (Edinburgh: T & T Clark, 1978 [1956]), pp. 37-45.

[49]See Forsyth, *Old Enemy,* pp. 132-33; Page, *Myth of Cosmic Rebellion,* passim. On related Canaanite and Greek myths, see P. C. Craigie, "Helel, Athtar and Phaethon (Jes 14:12-15)," *ZAW* 85 (1973): 223-25; S. A. Hirsch, "Isaiah 14:12, Helel ben Shahar," *JQR* 11 (1920-21): 197-99; S. H. Langdon, "The Star Helel, Jupiter? (Is 14:12)," *ExpTim* 42 (1930-31): 172-74; J. Morgenstern, "Mythological Background of Psalm 82," *HUCA* 14 (1939): 29-126. Bertoluci ("Son of the Morning") argues that there is no Mesopotamian, Hittite, Greek or Ugaritic myth of Helel ben Shahar that "reflects the Isaian account in its totality" (p. 109). For his analysis of extrabiblical literature, see esp. pp. 57-98. See also Keown's analysis of nine parallel myths (Kumarbi, Seth-Horus-Osiris, *Enuma Elish,* Baal-Yamm-El, Athtar, Shahar and Shalim, South Arabic Athtar, and Phaeton) in "History of the Interpretation," pp. 119-36. For other cultural variations on these myths, see K. Luomala, *Oceanic, American Indian and African Myths of Snaring the Sun* (Honolulu: Bishop Museum, 1940).

[50]On Zaphon as the mountain upon which the divine assembly met, see M. H. Pope, *Job,* 3d ed. (Garden City, N.Y.: Doubleday, 1973), p. 183. On the Canaanite background to Elyon, see Day, *God's Conflict,* pp. 129-38.

[51]Forsyth, *Old Enemy,* p. 138.

[52]Bertoluci, "Son of the Morning," pp. 301-2.

[53]K. L. Schmidt, "Lucifer als gefallene Engelmacht," *TZ* 7 (1951): 161-79, translated

by Bertoluci, "Son of the Morning," p. 303. Even Eichrodt (*Theology*, 2:207) concedes that in this passage, as well as in Genesis 3 and 6:1-4, "there are glimmerings of the idea of a superhuman being hostile to God."

[54]The phrase may also be a question, as the NIV indicates: "Are you wiser than Daniel? Is no secret hidden from you?"

[55]See Forsyth, *Old Enemy*, pp. 140-41; Page, *Myth of Cosmic Rebellion*, pp. 148-58.

[56]On the parallels with the Eden account in Genesis 2—3, see W. Eichrodt, *Ezekiel: A Commentary*, trans. C. Quin, OTL (Philadelphia: Westminster, 1970), pp. 392-93; N. C. Habel, "Ezekiel 28 and the Fall of the First Man," *Concordia Theological Monthly* 38 (1967): 516-24; J. L. McKenzie, "Mythical Allusions in Ezek. 28:12-18," *JBL* 75 (1956): 322-27; H. G. May, "The King in the Garden of Eden: A Study of Ezekiel 28:12-19," in *Israel's Prophetic Heritage: Essays in Honor of James Muilenburg*, ed. B. W. Anderson and W. Harrelson (New York: Harper, 1962), pp. 166-76; A. J. Williams, "The Mythological Background of Ezekiel 28:12-19," *BTB* 6 (1976): 49-61. The Masoretic text's equation of the king and the cherub is now generally rejected. See L. C. Allen, *Ezekiel 20—48*, WBC 29 (Dallas: Word, 1990), p. 95; W. Zimmerli, *Ezekiel II*, trans. J. D. Martin, Hermeneia (Philadelphia: Fortress, 1983), p. 90.

[57]For several cited parallels, see Day, *God's Conflict*, pp. 93-95.

[58]J. Levenson, *Creation and the Persistence of Evil* (San Francisco: Harper & Row, 1988), pp. 18-19.

[59]For an exhaustive overview of angels in the world's religious literature, see G. Davidson, *A Dictionary of Angels, Including the Fallen Angels* (New York: Free Press, 1967).

[60]Calvinists have frequently taken Romans 9:18-21 to be an example of God doing what I here deny God is doing: telling human questioners to be stoically silent in the face of radical evil—indeed, in the face of the prospect of their own *divinely preordained eternal damnation*. On the Calvinist reading, God simply exercises his "right" to choose some people for eternal salvation and "passes over" others, leaving them to eternal damnation. No one can (or had better) question his character in doing so! To an increasing number of modern exegetes, this way of reading Romans 9 is rooted in a myopic, decontextualized and anachronistic understanding of Paul's purpose in the book of Romans as a whole. See, e.g., the excellent discussion by J. D. G. Dunn in *Romans 9—16*, WBC 38B (Dallas: Word, 1988), pp. 521-76. See also J. D. Strauss, "God's Promise and Universal History: The Theology of Romans 9," in *Grace Unlimited*, ed. C. H. Pinnock (Minneapolis: Bethany, 1975), pp. 190-208.

[61]Such shall be my task in the forthcoming *Satan and the Problem of Evil*.

Chapter 6: Tying up the Strong Man

[1]Some works that develop and defend aspects of the thesis I here espouse and that I have found to be most helpful (though not necessarily agreeable) are W. Wink, *Naming the Powers: The Language of Power in the New Testament* (Philadelphia: Fortress, 1984); C. E. Arnold, *Powers of Darkness: Principalities and Powers in Paul's Letters* (Downers Grove, Ill.: InterVarsity Press, 1992); J. Kallas, *Jesus and the Power of Satan* (Philadelphia: Westminster, 1968); idem, *The Significance of the Synoptic Miracles* (Greenwich, Conn.: Seabury, 1961); G. Wingren, *The Living Word: A Theological Study of Preaching and the Church*, trans. V. C. Pogue, (Philadelphia: Muhlenberg, 1960 [1949]); N. Forsyth, *The Old Enemy: Satan and the Combat*

Myth (Princeton: Princeton University Press, 1987), esp. pp. 248-306; J. B. Russell, *The Devil: Perceptions of Evil from Antiquity to Primitive Christianity* (Ithaca: Cornell University Press, 1977); T. Longman III and D. G. Reid, *God Is a Warrior* (Grand Rapids, Mich.: Zondervan, 1995); G. B. Caird, *Principalities and Powers: A Study in Pauline Theology* (Oxford: Clarendon, 1956); H. Berkhof, *Christ and the Powers* (Scottdale, Penn.: Herald, 1962); O. Böcher, *Dämonenfurcht und Dämonenabwehr: Ein Beitrag zur Vorgeschichte der christlichen Taufe,* BWANT 5 (Stuttgart: Kohlhammer, 1970); idem, *Das Neue Testament und die dämonischen Mächte* (Stuttgart: Katholisches Bibelwerk, 1972); idem, *Christus Exorcista* (Stuttgart: Kohlhammer, 1972); T. Ling, *The Significance of Satan: New Testament Demonology and Its Contemporary Significance* (London: SPCK, 1961); H. Schlier, *Principalities and Powers in the New Testament* (New York: Herder and Herder, 1961); J. M. Robinson, *The Problem of History in Mark, and Other Marcan Studies* (Philadelphia: Fortress, 1982), esp. pp. 69-115.

[2]On the covenantal theology that lies behind this conception, see G. W. Buchanan, *The Consequences of the Covenant,* NovTSup 20 (Leiden: Brill, 1970), pp. 123-31; as well as D. R. Hillers, *Covenant: The History of a Biblical Idea* (Baltimore: Johns Hopkins University Press, 1969), pp. 120-42.

[3]For several important collections of essays that serve to chronicle the history of the discussion of apocalyptic in the twentieth century, see R. W. Funk, ed., *Apocalypticism,* JTC 6 (New York: Herder and Herder, 1969); K. Koch and J. M. Schmidt, eds., *Apokalyptik* (Darmstadt: Wissenschaftliche Buchgeselllschaft, 1982); P. D. Hanson, ed., *Visionaries and Their Apocalypses,* IRT (Philadelphia: Fortress, 1983); D. Hellholm, ed., *Apocalypticism in the Mediterranean World and the Near East: Proceedings of the International Colloquium on Apocalypticism, Uppsala, August 12-17, 1979* (Tübingen: Mohr, 1983); J. J. Collins and J. H. Charlesworth, eds., *Mysteries and Revelations: Apocalyptic Studies Since the Uppsala Colloquium,* JSPSup 9 (Sheffield: JSOT Press, 1991). For an excellent up-to-date survey of the issues and bibliography, see F. J. Murphy, "Apocalypses and Apocalypticism: The State of the Question," *Currents in Research: Biblical Studies* 2 (1994): 147-79. For the following material on the origin and nature of apocalyptic thought I am heavily indebted to the research and insight of my colleague and friend Paul Eddy.

[4]On the problem of definition, see T. F. Glasson, "What Is Apocalyptic?" *NTS* 27 (1980): 98-105; R. E. Sturm, "Defining the Word 'Apocalyptic': A Problem in Biblical Criticism," in *Apocalyptic and the New Testament: Essays in Honor of J. Louis Martyn,* ed. J. Marcus and M. L. Soards, JSNTSup 24 (Sheffield: JSOT Press, 1989), pp. 17-48. The 1979 colloquium on apocalyptic failed to reach an agreed-upon definition. See D. Hellholm, "Introduction," in *Apocalypticism in the Mediterranean World,* p. 2.

[5]The distinction goes back to P. D. Hanson, "Apocalypticism," *IDBSup,* pp. 28-31.

[6]G. Boccaccini, "Jewish Apocalyptic Tradition: The Contribution of Italian Scholarship," in *Mysteries and Revelations,* pp. 36-37.

[7]For helpful introductions to Zoroastrianism, see M. Boyce, *Zoroastrians: Their Religious Beliefs and Practices* (London: Routledge and Kegan Paul, 1979); and especially S. A. Nigosian, *The Zoroastrian Faith: Tradition and Modern Research* (Montreal: McGill-Queen's University Press, 1993). For excerpts of some Zoroastrian texts commonly associated with Jewish apocalyptic themes, see M. Boyce, ed. and trans., *Textual Sources for the Study of Zoroastrianism* (Chicago: University of Chicago Press, 1990), pp. 80-94.

[8]So it is portrayed, for example, in W. Bousset, *Die Religion des Judentums im späthellenischtischen Zeitalter,* ed. H. Gressmann, 3d ed. (Tübingen: Mohr/Siebeck, 1926); as well as H. Mills, *Zarathustra, Philo, the Achaemenids and Israel* (New York: AMS, rpt. 1977); idem, *Avesta Eschatology Compared with the Books of Daniel and Revelation* (Chicago: Open Court, 1908). Versions of this view still run strong among post-Bultmannian New Testament scholars. See, e.g., H. D. Betz, "On the Problem of the Religio-historical Understanding of Apocalypticism," in *Apocalypticism,* ed. Funk, pp. 134-56. On the fallaciousness of construing an exclusivistic monotheism as being "purer" than a form of monotheism that allows for the existence of other lesser good or evil gods, see chapter four above.

[9]See G. von Rad, *Old Testament Theology,* trans. D. M. G. Stalker, 2 vols. (New York: Harper & Row, 1962-1965), 2:301-15; idem, *Wisdom in Israel,* trans. J. D. Martin (Nashville: Abingdon, 1972), esp. pp. 263-83. The thesis is also defended by J. Gammie, "Spatial and Ethical Dualism in Jewish Wisdom and Apocalyptic Literature," *JBL* 93 (1974): 356-85.

[10]H. H. Rowley, *The Relevance of Apocalyptic: A Study of Jewish and Christian Apocalypse from Daniel to the Revelation,* rev. ed. (New York: Association, 1963); F. M. Cross, "New Directions in the Study of Apocalyptic," in *Apocalypticism,* ed. Funk, pp. 157-65; P. D. Hanson, *The Dawn of Apocalyptic: The Historical and Sociological Roots of Jewish Apocalyptic Eschatology* (Philadelphia: Fortress, 1975); idem, "Old Testament Apocalyptic Reexamined," *Int* 25 (1971): 454-79.

[11]In addition to Rowley, Cross and Hanson cited above, see L. C. Allen, "Some Prophetic Antecedents of Apocalyptic Eschatology and Their Hermeneutical Value," *Ex Auditu* 6 (1990): 15-28; Forsyth, *Old Enemy,* pp. 142-46; D. S. Russell, *The Method and Message of Jewish Apocalyptic,* OTL (Philadelphia: Westminster, 1964), pp. 92-95; D. G. Johnson, *From Chaos to Restoration: An Integrative Analysis of Isaiah 24—27,* JSOTSup 61 (Sheffield: Sheffield Academic Press, 1988). For a recent study of the connection between Old Testament "proto-apocalyptic" material and the earliest Jewish apocalyptic writings, see E. J. C. Tigchelaar, *Prophets of Old and the Day of the End: Zechariah, the Book of Watchers and Apocalyptic,* OTS 35 (Leiden: Brill, 1996). An increasing number of scholars have been attempting to combine this thesis with elements from the earlier syncretistic view. See, e.g., J. H. Charlesworth, "Folk Traditions in Jewish Apocalyptic Literature," in *Mysteries and Revelations,* pp. 91-113; J. J. Collins, "Jewish Apocalyptic Against Its Hellenistic Near Eastern Environment," *BASOR* 220 (Dec. 1975): 27-36; R. Bauckham, "The Rise of Apocalyptic," *Themelios* 3, no. 2 (1978): 10-23; H. S. Kvanvig, *Roots of Apocalyptic: The Mesopotamian Background of the Enoch Figure and the Son of Man,* WMANT 61 (Neukirchen-Vluyn: Neukirchener, 1988); D. Winston, "The Iranian Component in the Bible, Apocrypha and Qumran: A Review of the Evidence," *History of Religions* 5, no. 2 (1966): 192-94.

[12]See, e.g., S. Shaked, "Iranian Influence on Judaism: First Century B.C.E. to Second Century C.E.," in *The Cambridge History of Judaism,* vol. 1, *Introduction: The Persian Period,* ed. W. D. Davies and L. Finkelstein (Cambridge: Cambridge University Press, 1984), pp. 308-25; and J. R. Hinnells, "Zoroastrian Influence on the Judeo-Christian Tradition," *Journal of the K. R. Cama Oriental Institute* 45 (1976): 1-23. With some justification, Hinnells elsewhere points out that many of the earlier assessments were affected by an anti-Christian prejudice that saw in the Zoroastrian influence theory an opportunity to undermine the uniqueness of Christianity. See "Iranian Influence upon the New Testament," in *Commémoration*

Cyrus, hommage universel, ed. A. Pagliaro et al., Acta Iranica 2 (Leiden: Brill, 1974), 2:272.

[13]E. Yamauchi, *Persia and the Bible* (Grand Rapids, Mich.: Baker, 1990), pp. 458-66. See also J. Barr, "The Question of Religious Influence: The Case of Zoroastrianism, Judaism and Christianity," *JAAR* 53 [1985]: 201-35, who argues that the parallels are superficial at best. Some have argued that this is true even of the "two spirits motif," though this has long been considered the most obvious example of Zoroastrian influence. This influential motif is found in the Qumran *Manual of Discipline* (1QS) and the *War Scroll* (1QM) and throughout the early Christian tradition. See H. G. May, "Cosmological Reference in the Qumran Doctrine of the Two Spirits and in Old Testament Imagery," *JBL* 82 (1963): 1-14; G. W. E. Nickelsburg, *Resurrection, Immortality and Eternal Life in Intertestamental Judaism* (Cambridge: Harvard University Press, 1972).

[14]Indeed, according to Yamauchi (*Persia and the Bible,* pp. 464-66), many of the important Zoroastrian texts are dated as late as the fifth to the ninth century. For a recent thorough discussion, see J. G. Griffiths, *The Divine Verdict: A Study of Divine Judgment in the Ancient Religions,* SHR 52 (Leiden: Brill, 1991), pp. 250-53.

[15]D. Wolfer, *Deep Things out of Darkness: The Book of Job* (Grand Rapids, Mich.: Eerdmans, 1995), pp. 51-54, argues for a date in the early seventh century B.C., as does J. E. Hartley, *The Book of Job,* NICOT (Grand Rapids, Mich.: Eerdmans, 1988), pp. 17-20. Similarly, M. H. Pope concludes that the most likely date for the Dialogue is the seventh century B.C. (*Job,* 3d ed., AB 15 [Garden City, N.Y.: Doubleday, 1973], p. xl). N. M. Sarna ("Epic Substratum in the Prose of Job," *JBL* 76 [1957]: 13-25) concludes that the apparent patriarchal setting "must be regarded as genuine and as belonging to the original saga. In brief, the considerable amount of epic substratum indicates that our present narrative framework is directly derived from an ancient "epic of Job" (p. 25). Even G. von Rad minimizes the extent of Persian influence on Job on the basis of the antiquity of the *satan* material found in the prologue. See his "OT View of Satan," *TDNT,* 2:74.

[16]Later Zoroastrianism (viz., that of the Pahlavi texts of the Sassanian period, third to seventh century A.D.) is clearly dualistic, but it is debated to what extent this can be read back into original Zoroastrianism. For a complete discussion, see J. W. Boyd and D. A. Crosby, "Is Zoroastrianism Dualistic or Monotheistic?" *JAAR* 47 (1979): 557-88.

[17]Yamauchi, *Persia and the Bible,* p. 460. So R. S. Kluger, *Satan in the Old Testament,* trans. H. Nagel, Studies in Jungian Thought 7 (Evanston, Ill.: Northwestern University Press, 1967), p. 156, who agrees that "if one looks at the two figures— that of the Old Testament Satan and of the Angra Mainyu of the Persian religion— not as separate entities but as embedded in the whole religious pattern, a fundamental difference is apparent."

[18]So Kvanvig writes: "the apocalyptic universe emerged in a moment when evil was experienced as a power transgressing human limits. It was the experience of non-human evil. . . . As a result, a new kind of hope arose in Jewish society, by which the transcendental impact of evil was confronted with a transcendental power of justice" (*Roots of Apocalyptic,* p. 613). See also D. Russell, *Method and Message,* pp. 237-38; idem, "Demonology and the Problem of Evil," in his *From Early Judaism to Early Church* (Philadelphia: Fortress, 1986), pp. 85-98; Kallas, *Synoptic Miracles,* pp. 52-53; E. Langton, *Essentials of Demonology: A Study of the Jewish and*

Christian Doctrine, Its Origin and Development (London: Epworth, 1949), p. 57; J. Russell, *Devil,* pp. 185-86.

[19]On the development of Jewish angelology and demonology during this time, see G. A. Barton, "The Origin of the Names of the Angels and Demons in the Extra-canonical Apocalyptic Literature to 100 A.D.," *JBL* 31 (1912): 156-57; A. Piñero, "Angels and Demons in the Greek *Life of Adam and Eve,*" *JSJ* 24 (1993): 191-214; M. J. Davidson, *Angels at Qumran: A Comparative Study of 1 Enoch 1—36, 72—108 and Sectarian Writings from Qumran,* JSPSup 11 (Sheffield: JSOT Press, 1992); H. B. Kuhn, "The Angelology of the Non-canonical Jewish Apocalypses," *JBL* 67 (1948): 217-32.

[20]I am here following the majority view that the Genesis accounts precede the account in *1 Enoch,* though the position is not without its detractors. For discussions see P. S. Alexander and P. Hanson, "Rebellion in Heaven, Azazel, and Euhemeristic Heroes in *1 Enoch 6—11,*" *JBL* 96 (1977): 195-233; G. W. E. Nickelsburg, "Apocalyptic and Myth in *1 Enoch 6—11,*" *JBL* 96 (1977): 383-405; P. S. Alexander, "The Targumim and Early Exegesis of the 'Sons of God' in Genesis 6," *JJS* 23 (1972): 60-71. *First Enoch* 1—36 (commonly referred to as "The Book of the Watchers") provides the fullest account of the Watcher Angels, but they are also found in *Jubilees, Testament of the Twelve Patriarchs, Life of Adam and Eve* and *2 Enoch,* with hints found elsewhere. For discussions see J. Russell, *Devil,* pp. 186ff.; Forsyth, *Old Enemy,* pp. 160-91; F. Gokey, *The Terminology for the Devil and Evil Spirits in the Apostolic Fathers,* Patristic Studies 93 (Washington, D.C.: Catholic University of America, 1961), pp. 10-13; J. J. Collins, *The Apocalyptic Imagination: An Introduction to the Jewish Matrix of Christianity* (New York: Crossroad, 1987), pp. 36-46; S. Kvanvig, "The Book of Watchers," in his *Roots of Apocalyptic,* pp. 85-104; M. E. Mills, "Enoch and the Watchers," in her *Human Agents of Cosmic Power in Hellenistic Judaism and the Synoptic Tradition,* JSPSup 41 (Sheffield: Sheffield Academic Press, 1990), pp. 63-77.

[21]See esp. *Jubilees* 4:15ff. R. Murray has argued that the angelic "watcher" concept can be linguistically traced back to the ancient notion of "guardian gods" who watch over their respective nations/peoples ("The Origin of Aramaic *'ir,* Angel,' " *Or* 53 [1984]: 303-17).

[22]This account of the origin of evil spirits is found in *1 Enoch* 15:8; *Jubilees* 5:2; *2 Enoch* 18:2-5. On demons in intertestamental literature, see E. Ferguson, *Demonology of the Early Christian World* (New York: Mellen, 1980), pp. 74-78.

[23]The same is true of other apocalyptic accounts of the Fall. So *2 Enoch* 29:4-5 (though it also recites the Watcher tradition in chap. 18). So too the *Life of Adam* 12—17, which attributes Satan's fall to jealousy over Adam, a story that was eventually to override the Watcher tradition in the early church.

[24]*Jubilees* 2:2. See *Apocrypha and Pseudepigrapha of the Old Testament,* 2 vols., ed. R. H. Charles (Oxford: Clarendon, 1912), 1:13-14.

[25]*Testament of Adam* 4:2. See *OTP,* 2:995.

[26]For example, *1 Enoch* refers to "spirits" of thunder, sea, frost, snow, mist, dew, wind and rain (60:15-22; 61:10; 66:2; 69:22), as well as angels in charge of seasons (87:7-20). *Second Enoch* refers to angels of fire, hail, wind, lightning, whirlwinds, snow, rain, day and night, sun, moon, planets and constellations (19:1-6; cf. 15:1). And 4 Ezra speaks of angels of wind, fire and the firmament (6:21; 8:21). On this see J. Daniélou, *The Theology of Jewish Christianity,* trans. and ed. J. A. Baker (Philadelphia: Westminster, 1964), pp. 181-84; L. Osborn, "Entertaining Angels:

Their Place in Contemporary Theology," *TynBul* 45 (1994): 286-87.

[27]Wink, *Unmasking the Powers*, p. 157. Philo identifies each angel of a species with a Platonic form in *De Confusione Linguarum* 171-75 and *De Cherubim* 51. For a discussion of similar views in the rabbinic literature, see P. Schäfer, *Rivalität zwischen Engeln und Menschen: Untersuchungen zur rabbinischen Engelvorstellung* (Berlin: de Gruyter, 1975), pp. 56-59; and in early church history, see J. Daniélou, *The Angels and Their Mission*, trans. D. Heimann (Westminster, Md.: Newman, 1953) pp. 68-82. The New Testament clearly shared the first-century apocalyptic belief in the importance of angels (see, e.g., Mk 1:13; Mt 4:6, 11; 13:39-49; Jn 1:51; Acts 7:53; Rom 8:38; 1 Cor 4:9; 11:10; 13:1; 2 Cor 11:14; Gal 1:8; 3:19; 1 Thess 4:16; 2 Thess 1:7; Heb 13:2). Jesus affirmed the existence of guardian angels (Mt 18:10; 26:53) as does the author of Hebrews (1:14). But on the whole the New Testament does not follow the apocalyptic tradition in linking particular angels with particular natural phenomena (though see Rev 7:1; 16:5; 19:17; Heb 1:7? and the Jn 5:4 insertion).

[28]On the free will strand, see, e.g., Sirach 15:14-16, which states that the Lord "created humankind in the beginning, and he left them in the power of their own free choice. If you choose, you can keep the commandments, and to act faithfully is a matter of your own choice. He has placed before you fire and water; stretch out your hand for whichever you choose." Cf., e.g., also 1 Maccabees 9:30; 12:1; 2 Maccabees 4:38; 5:9; 15:32-33; Wisdom of Solomon 7:7-10; Judith 5:17; *Psalms of Solomon* 9. Even within apocalyptic texts (e.g., *Testament of Simeon* 5:2; *Testament of Levi* 19:1; *2 Apocalypse of Baruch* 19:1-3; 54:15, 19; *2 Enoch* 7:3) and at Qumran we find strong statements affirming human choice and responsibility (e.g., 1QH 4.6, 24; 5.9; 13.16; 14.26; 16.10). On the deterministic strand, however, see, e.g., *Jubilees* 10:6, which speaks of evil beings being "created to destroy," while 15:31 adds that over each nation God has "caused spirits to rule so that they might lead them to stray." See *OTP*, 2:76, 87. For discussions on predestination and election in the Qumran scrolls, see E. H. Merrill, *Qumran and Predestination: A Theological Study of the Thanksgiving Hymns*, STDJ 8 (Leiden: Brill, 1975); D. Dimant, "Qumran Sectarian Literature," in *The Literature of the Jewish People in the Period of the Second Temple and the Talmud*, vol. 2, *Jewish Writings of the Second Temple Period*, ed. M. E. Stone, CRINT 2 (Philadelphia: Fortress, 1984), pp. 536-38.

[29]See A. E. Sekki, *The Meaning of Rua at Qumran*, SBLDS 110 (Atlanta: Scholars Press, 1989). Sekki argues in meticulous fashion that there is a crucial difference intended between when *rûah* is spoken of in the feminine and in the masculine case. When the masculine is used it refers to an angel or demon; when the feminine is used it refers to a human disposition. In more deterministic texts (e.g., 1QS 3-4) the feminine is used. On the basis of parallels with 4Q186, this usage suggests an astrological determinism for humans (see J. M. Allegro, "An Astrological Cryptic Document from Qumran," *JTS* 9 [1964]: 291-94), but it does not imply general cosmic determinism.

[30]See Merrill, *Qumran and Predestination*, pp. 45-58; J. J. Collins, "The Origin of Evil in Apocalyptic Literature and the Dead Sea Scrolls," in *Congress Volume, Paris 1992*, ed. J. A. Emerton, VTSup 61 (Leiden: Brill, 1995), pp. 25-38; D. A. Carson, *Divine Sovereignty and Human Responsibility* (Atlanta: John Knox, 1981), pp. 45-83; and esp. G. Maier, *Mensch und freier Wille: Nach den jüdischen Religionsparteien zwischen Ben Sira und Paulus*, WUNT 12 (Tübingen: Mohr/Siebeck, 1971), who attempts to trace the two strands back to two biblical anthropological

motifs, one (Gen 1:26-27) "optimistic" and the other (Gen 2:7) "pessimistic." I argue that rarely did the "pessimistic" motif work itself out into full-blown determinism. Where we do find full-blown determinism, we have grounds for suspecting that it had more to do with astrological assumptions than biblical teachings. See Allegro, "Astrological Cryptic Document."

[31]Kallas, *Synoptic Miracles*, p. 54.

[32]W. F. Albright, *From the Stone Age to Christianity: Monotheism and the Historical Process*, 2d ed. (Baltimore: Johns Hopkins University Press, 1957), p. 362.

[33]The identification of this "highest mediating agent" differs between (and even within) apocalyptic texts. For example, *1 Enoch* identifies Azazel and Semjaza as leaders of the rebel angels but also speaks of a group of fallen angels called *satans* (adversaries) headed up by Satan. *Jubilees* speaks of Mastema but also speaks of the fallen angels being under Satan. Tobit speaks of Asmodeus (who purportedly was in love with a young woman and killed all prospective husbands, 3:8; 6:13-14), a name that also appears in the rabbinic literature. *Second Enoch* speaks of Satanail, whereas the *Martyrdom of Isaiah* refers to Sammael along with Beliar and Satan. On this, see esp. Barton, "Origin of the Names," as well as Ling, *Significance of Satan*, p. 9; Ferguson, *Demonology*, pp. 76-78; Langton, *Essentials*, pp. 119-38; H. Gaylord, "How Satanel Lost His 'El,' " *JJS* 33 (1982): 303-9; W. Foerster, "The Later Jewish View of Satan," in "διάβολος," *TDNT*, 2:75-79; J. Russell, *Devil*, pp. 188-89; S. V. McCasland, "The Black One," in *Early Christian Origins: Studies in Honor of Harold R. Willoughby*, ed. A. Wikgren (Chicago: Quadrangle, 1961), pp. 77-80; C. Molenberg, "A Study of the Roles of Shemihaza and Asael in *1 Enoch* 6—11," *JJS* 35 (1984): 136-46.

[34]Though the members of the infamous Jesus Seminar claim that one of the seven "pillars of scholarly wisdom" is the view that the historical Jesus' thought world was noneschatological (see R. W. Funk, R. W. Hover and the Jesus Seminar, *The Five Gospels: The Search for the Authentic Words of Jesus* [New York: Macmillan, 1993], p. 4), J. H. Charlesworth is certainly correct in affirming that "one of the strongest consensuses in New Testament research" involves the conviction that Jesus' teaching was fundamentally apocalyptic. See his "Jesus Research Expands with Chaotic Creativity," in *Images of Jesus Today*, ed. J. H. Charlesworth and W. P. Weaver (Valley Forge, Penn.: Trinity, 1994), p. 10. For a critique of the post-Bultmannian view of Jesus as noneschatological, see my *Cynic, Sage or Son of God? Recovering the Real Jesus in an Age of Revisionist Replies* (Wheaton, Ill.: Bridgepoint, 1995), pp. 55-56, 145-50; as well as P. R. Eddy, "Jesus as Diogenes? Reflections of the Cynic Jesus Thesis," *JBL* 115 (1996): 449-69; and L. Johnson, *The Misguided Quest for the Historical Jesus and the Truth of the Traditional Gospels* (San Francisco: HarperSanFrancisco, 1995). For several good arguments for an apocalyptic Jesus, see B. F. Meyer, *Christus Faber: The Master-Builder and the House of God* (Allison Park, Penn.: Pickwick, 1992), pp. 41-80; E. P. Sanders, *Jesus and Judaism* (Philadelphia: Fortress, 1985), pp. 222-41, 319-40; B. Witherington, *Jesus, Paul and the End of the World: A Comparative Study in New Testament Eschatology* (Downers Grove, Ill.: InterVarsity Press, 1992), pp. 59-74, 170-80.

[35]Arnold, *Powers of Darkness*, p. 81. The phrase is used of *Beliar* in *Martyrdom of Isaiah* 2:4 (an early first-century apocalyptic work). See J. H. Charlesworth, "A Critical Comparison of the Dualism in IQS 3:13—4:26 and the 'Dualism' Contained in the Gospel of John," in *John and the Dead Sea Scrolls*, ed. Charlesworth (New York: Crossroad, 1990), pp. 76-106. Charlesworth's attempt to demonstrate

that John represents a move away from a "hypostatic" personal view of the devil strikes me as forced.

[36]See H. Bietenhard, *Die himmlische Welt im Urchristentum und Spätjudentum*, WUNT 2 (Tübingen: Mohr, 1951), pp. 114-15; Kallas, *Synoptic Miracles*, p. 62.

[37]The frequent apocalyptic notion that a particular angel was given charge over all creation may be behind the Synoptics' concept of the world being "given" to Satan. See Daniélou, *Jewish Christianity*, pp. 188-89; Gokey, *Terminology*, p. 50. Many in the early postapostolic church held this view. See Daniélou, *Angels and Their Mission*, pp. 45-46. In this case, Satan must be seen as telling the truth when he says that all the kingdoms of the world were given to him. In other words, he did not steal the world, as Kallas maintains (*Synoptic Miracles*, p. 54), and in this sense his power over the world cannot in and of itself be said to be "illegitimate," as I claimed above. Nevertheless, Satan's evil tyranny over the world can be seen as illegitimate even if his God-given authority itself is not.

[38]Beelzebul (and its forms Beezebul, Beelzebub) was a frequent name for the ruler of the demonic kingdom in the Talmud, as well as in the *Testament of Solomon*. There has been much discussion and little agreement as to the etymology of this term and its forms. For several summary discussions with various suggested solutions, see T. J. Lewis, "Beelzebul," *ABD*, 1:638-40; W. E. M. Aitken, "Beelzebul," *JBL* 31 (1912): 34-53; W. Foerster, "βεελζεβούλ," *TDNT*, 1:605-06; L. Gaston, "Beelzebul," *TZ* 18 (1962): 247-55; P. L. Day, *An Adversary in Heaven: Satan in the Hebrew Bible*, HSM 43 (Atlanta: Scholars Press, 1988), pp. 151-59; E. C. B. MacLaurin, "Beelzebul," *NovT* 20 (April 1978): 156-60; S. J. Wright, "Satan, Beelzebul, Devil, Exorcism," *NIDNTT*, 3:468-76. For a superb argument that this Q pericope essentially goes back to the historical Jesus, see J. D. G. Dunn, "Matthew 12:28/Luke 11:20—A Word of Jesus?" in *Eschatology and the New Testament: Essays in Honor of George Raymond Beasley-Murray*, ed. W. H. Gloer (Peabody, Mass.: Hendrickson, 1988), pp. 29-49. The accusation that Jesus was possessed by Satan or a demon is repeated in John 7:20; 8:48, 52; and 10:20. It should be noted that the response to the charge in 10:21, "Can a demon open the eyes of the blind?" recalls Mark 3:24 and is predicated on the assumption that blindness is itself a demonic work.

[39]Arnold sees this verse as the key to understanding Christ's ministry. "Christ has come to engage this 'strong man' and plunder his house: that is, to release the captives in Satan's kingdom" (*Powers of Darkness*, p. 79). See also J. Ramsey Michaels, "Jesus and the Unclean Spirits," in *Demon Possession*, ed. J. W. Montgomery (Minneapolis: Bethany, 1976), p. 53. E. Ferguson sums up well the picture of the world and of Jesus' ministry assumed in this passage when he notes that this world is "enemy-occupied territory; Satan as its ruler has a fortress to protect his ill-gotten possessions. But there comes one stronger than he. The conqueror liberates the fortress, takes away Satan's power, and takes over his possessions for his own use" (*Demonology of the Early Christian World*, pp. 22-23). See also E. Pagels, *The Origin of Satan* (New York: Random House, 1995), p. 20.

[40]J. Newport, response to Michaels in *Demon Possession*, p. 90. Forsyth argues that demons are portrayed in the Gospels as "a sort of loosely organized army under their general, Satan" (*Old Enemy*, p. 293; cf. p. 295). See also J. Russell, *Devil*, p. 237; Gokey, *Terminology*, p. 50; Kallas, *Synoptic Miracles*, pp. 67-68. Ling argues that the Gospels differ from previous apocalyptic literature precisely in the intensity with which they affirm that the kingdom of evil is a unified kingdom and focus most

of their attention on the head of this kingdom, Satan (*Significance of Satan*, pp. 12-22). Roy Yates also sees this as one of the main contributions of the Gospels. For Jesus, "exorcisms are no longer to be seen as isolated victories over a series of autonomous demons. . . . Jesus does not have an atomistic view of the world of evil, but sees it as a unity under Satan, whose power is beginning to crumble" ("The Powers of Evil in the New Testament," *EvQ* 52, no. 2 [1980]: 99).

[41]See Ferguson, *Demonology*, p. 12.

[42]The passage likely means that the success of the disciples' exorcism ministry was evidence that Satan's kingdom was on its way down. So argues G. E. Ladd, *Jesus and the Kingdom* (New York: Harper & Row, 1964), pp. 145ff.; and Forsyth, *Old Enemy*, pp. 294-95. Ling argues that Jesus was here drawing the disciples' attention away from their ability to cast out individual demons to "the fact that the kingdom of evil in its entirety was being conquered in the exercise of the authority which was theirs in his name" (*Significance of Satan*, p. 18). Julian Hills, however, argues in the opposite direction. Jesus was, in effect, saying that the disciples were successful in their exorcisms because the demons saw that their leader was already being dethroned by Jesus' exorcist ministry. See J. V. Hills, "Luke 10:18—Who Saw Satan Fall?" *JSNT* 46 (1992): 25-40. This verse, incidentally, is the only reference to the fall of Satan in the Gospels, and it is clearly not about his original fall. This absence of speculation sets the Gospels apart from the apocalyptic literature of their time. That Satan was a fallen angel, however, seems to be taken for granted by the Gospel authors and is made more explicit in other New Testament literature (1 Tim 3:6; Jude 6, 8-10; 2 Pet 2:4; Eph 2:2; 2 Cor 11:13-14).

[43]So Ferguson correctly notes in commenting on this passage, "Evil may have varied manifestations, but ultimately there is only one principle of evil. Instead of a world dominated by many warring demons (a pagan and polytheistic conception), Jesus saw one kingdom of Satan. . . . Jesus saw his work as demonstrating that the whole dominion of evil was being conquered. The demons functioned as part of a larger whole, the dominion of the devil" (*Demonology*, p. 20).

[44]Later rabbinical tradition had it that demons "surround us like the ridge round a field . . . every one among us has 1,000 on his left hand and 10,000 on his right hand." Moreover, all manner of evil is attributed to them, everything from weakening in the knees to clothes wearing out to sore feet. See Babylonian Talmud *Berakot* 6a, cited in Ferguson, *Demonology*, p. 89. It is unlikely that something of this tradition does not extend back to the first century.

[45]Langton, *Essentials*, p. 147.

[46]Some take John 9:1-5 to be an exception to this. I argue against this interpretation in chapter seven. But even if this passage does presuppose a divine purpose for this particular person's blindness, this only slightly qualifies the point being made here.

[47]For several informative discussions on the connection between sickness and Satanic/demonic activity in the New Testament, see R. Brown, "The Gospel Miracles," in his *New Testament Essays* (Garden City, N.Y.: Doubleday, 1968), pp. 222-28; E. Yamauchi, "Magic or Miracle? Diseases, Demons and Exorcisms," in *The Miracles of Jesus*, ed. D. Wenham and C. Blomberg, GP 6 (Sheffield: JSOT Press, 1986), pp. 92-93; D. S. Russell, *From Early Judaism to Early Church*, (Philadelphia: Fortress, 1986), pp. 90-93; and esp. P. H. Davids, "Sickness and Suffering in the New Testament," in *Wrestling with Dark Angels: Toward a Deeper Understanding of the Supernatural Forces in Spiritual Warfare*, ed. C. P. Wagner and F. D. Pennoyer (Ventura, Calif.: Regal, 1990), pp. 215-37. There is now strong

evidence that first-century Jews (hence perhaps Jesus himself) were assisted in their inclination to think of sickness and disease as demonically induced by the "Solomon/Son of David as exorcist and healer" tradition. J. H. Charlesworth has noted: "We possess traditions that may well derive from the first century C.E. in which Solomon is hailed as an exorcist who controls demons and the sickness, including blindness, they cause" ("The Son of David: Solomon and Jesus [Mark 10:47]," unpublished paper presented to the Jesus Seminar, Rutgers University, New Brunswick, N.J., Oct. 1992, p. 12). See also D. C. Duling, "Solomon, Exorcism and the Son of David," *HTR* 68 (1975): 235-52. Thus it may be that Jesus' title as the "Son of David" is linked with his reputation as a healer/exorcist. See L. Fisher, "Can This Be the Son of David?" in *Jesus and the Historian: Written in Honor of Ernest Cadman Colwell*, ed. F. T. Trotter (Philadelphia: Westminster, 1968), pp. 82-87. For evidence of the prevalence within rabbinic Judaism of the view that much sickness was the result of demonic activity, see H. L. Strack and P. Billerbeck, *Kommentar zum Neuen Testament aus Talmud und Midrasch*, 5 vols. (Munich: Beck, 1922-61), 4:501-35.

[48]Kallas, *Synoptic Miracles*, p. 63.
[49]"Gospel Miracles," p. 224.
[50]Ibid. Cf. Kallas, *Synoptic Miracles*, p. 79.
[51]For references, see BAGD, p. 495.
[52]My translation. The NIV translates *mastix* as "flogging" in Acts 22:24 and Hebrews 11:36, and the verbs *mastizō* and *mastigoō* as "to flog" in Matthew 10:17; 20:19; 23:34; Mark 10:34; 15:15; Luke 18:32; John 19:1; Acts 22:24-25; and as "to punish" in Hebrews 12:6. But it translates *mastix* as "suffering," "disease" and "sicknesses" in the Gospels (Mk 3:10; 5:29, 34; Lk 7:21). Such a translation loses the unique force of this rather unusual usage of this word.
[53]See also Mark 9:29 (parallel Mt 17:21), where Jesus assumes there are different "kinds" of demons.
[54]J. Ramsey Michaels argues on the basis of redaction criticism that possessions became a category of disease, and exorcism a category of healing, by the time Matthew and Luke appropriated Mark's Gospel. Hence too he argues that Paul does not mention exorcism as one of the gifts of the Spirit because by this time it was subsumed under the category of healing (1 Cor 12:9-10, 38-39). See "Jesus and the Unclean Spirits," p. 50. If one accepts Markan priority, his case perhaps has some merit. For example, Mark 1:32-34 mentions the "sick or possessed with demons," whereas the parallels in Matthew and Luke mention only those "possessed with demons" (Mt 8:16-17; Lk 4:40-41; cf. Mk 1:39; Mt 4:23; Lk 4:44; and Mk 3:7-12; Mt 4:24-25; Lk 6:17-19).
[55]Against Böcher, neither this passage nor the evidence in the Synoptics as a whole necessarily implies that all sicknesses and diseases were seen as being the direct result of Satanic activity (though some obviously were; cf. Lk 13:16; 2 Cor 12:7). See O. Böcher, *Dämonenfurcht und Dämonenabwehr* (Stuttgart: Kohlhammer, 1970), pp. 316-17; idem, *Christus Exorcista* (Stuttgart: Katholisches Bibelwerk, 1972), pp. 16, 70. But it does entail that all disorders were seen as being at least the indirect result of Satan's having taken the world hostage. Hence in coming against them (by healing), Jesus was coming against one crucial aspect of Satan's reign. For two critical and balanced reviews of Böcher's argument, see L. Sabourin, "The Miracles of Jesus II: Jesus and the Evil Powers," *BTB* 4, no. 2 (1974): 115-75, and Yamauchi, "Magic or Miracle?" pp. 92-93. On the distinction between demonization and

physical illness, see Ferguson, *Demonology*, pp. 4-5.
[56]Kallas, *Synoptic Miracles*, p. 66.
[57]Wingren, *Living Word*, p. 53; cf. p. 167.
[58]The centrality of Satan and the cosmic/spiritual warfare motif in the New Testament received an unprecedented amount of attention just prior to, during and after World War II. The classic statement of this position is Gustaf Aulen's *Christus Victor*, trans. A. Hebert (New York: Macmillan, 1961). See also from this period R. Leivestad, *Christ the Conqueror: Ideas of Conflict and Victory in the New Testament* (London: SPCK, 1954); J. S. Stewart, "On a Neglected Emphasis in New Testament Theology," *SJT* 4 (1951): 292-301; E. Fascher, *Jesus und der Satan*, Hallische Monographien 11 (Halle: Max Niemeyer, 1949); Schlier, *Principalities and Powers*; Wingren, *Living Word*. This view has received increasing attention in recent scholarship. For strong contemporary representative statements or arguments on the centrality of Satan and of the warfare motif in general for the New Testament, see R. Hiers, "Satan, Demons and the Kingdom of God," *SJT* 27 (1974): 35-47; R. Yates, "Jesus and the Demonic in the Synoptic Gospels," *Irish Theological Quarterly* 44 (1977): 39-57; J. D. G. Dunn and G. H. Twelftree, "Demon-Possession and Exorcism in the New Testament," *Churchman* 94, no. 3 (1980): 211-15; S. R. Garrett, *The Demise of the Devil: Magic and the Demonic in Luke's Writings* (Minneapolis: Fortress, 1989); H. Kruse, "Das Reich Satans," *Bib* 58 (1977): 29-61; Ling, *Significance of Satan*; P. W. Hollenbach, "Help for Interpreting Jesus' Exorcism," SBLSP, 1993, ed. E. H. Lovering Jr. (Atlanta, Ga.: Scholars Press, 1993), pp. 124-26; M. Kelsey, *Encounter with God: A Theology of Christian Experience* (Minneapolis: Bethany Fellowship, 1972), pp. 242-45; J. Russell, *Devil*, pp. 222, 227, 234-39; Forsyth, *Old Enemy*, pp. 249, 286, 295-96; Langton, *Essentials*, p. 156; Yamauchi, "Magic or Miracle?" pp. 124-25; Kallas, *Jesus and the Power of Satan*; idem, *Synoptic Miracles*; idem, *The Satanward View* (Philadelphia: Westminster, 1966); W. Kirchschläger, *Jesu exorzistisches Wirken aus der Sicht des Lukas: Ein Beitrag zur lukanischen Redaktion*, Österreichische Biblische Studien 3 (Klosterneuburg: Österreichisches Katholisches Bibelwerk, 1981); W. G. Kümmel, "Liberation from the Spiritual Powers," in his *Theology of the New Testament*, trans. J. E. Steely (Nashville: Abingdon, 1973), pp. 186ff.; J. J. Rousseau, "Jesus, an Exorcist of a Kind," in SBLSP, 1993, pp. 129-53; Böcher, *Christus Exorcista*.
[59]See J. Jeremias's observation in "The Lord's Prayer in the Light of Recent Research," in his *Prayers of Jesus*, trans. J. Bowden et al., SBT 2/6 (Naperville, Ill.: Allenson, 1967), p. 99. G. E. Ladd (*A Theology of the New Testament* [Grand Rapids: Eerdmans, 1974], pp. 45-56) also draws a strong connection between the coming of the future kingdom and the vanquishing of the evil forces that presently control the world.
[60]In the light of the fact that "the satanic and demonic is a dominant theme of the New Testament," Newport argues, we must see the New Testament as constituting "at least a limited dualism" ("Satan and Demons: A Theological Perspective," in *Demon Possession*, p. 331). Similarly, Kvanvig distinguishes this type of Jewish dualism from the cosmic dualism of Zoroastrianism by casting it as a temporary, eschatological and moral dualism rather than a metaphysical dualism. See *Roots of Apocalyptic*, pp. 610-11. See also C. S. Lewis's strong case for a form of biblical dualism in "God and Evil," in *God in the Dock: Essays in Theology and Ethics*, ed. W. Hooper (Grand Rapids, Mich.: Eerdmans, 1970), pp. 21-24. For an argument along similar lines but cast in relationship to Greek philosophical forms of dualism,

see A. H. Armstrong, "Dualism: Platonic, Gnostic and Christian," in *Neoplatonism and Gnosticism*, ed. R. T. Wallis and J. Bregman (Albany: SUNY Press, 1992), pp. 33-54. For similar assessments of the apocalyptic or New Testament dualism, see J. G. Gammie, "Spatial and Ethical Dualism in Jewish Wisdom and Apocalyptic Literature," *JBL* 93 (1974): 356-59; J. H. Charlesworth, "A Critical Comparison of the Dualism in 1QS 3:13—4:26 and the 'Dualism' in the Gospel of John," *NTS* 15 (1968-69): 389-418; Aulen's classic *Christus Victor*, pp. 4-5, 10-11, 76, 89, 108, 148-49.

[61]Garrett, *Demise of the Devil*, p. 55.

[62]Kallas, *Synoptic Miracles*, p. 78. See also pp. 55, 66. See E. Stauffer: "The Kingdom of God is present where the dominion of the adversary has been overthrown" (*New Testament Theology*, 5th ed., trans. J. Marsh [New York: Macmillan, 1955], p. 124). Similarly, Elaine Pagels notes that for the Gospel authors, "Jesus has come to heal the world and reclaim it for God; in order to accomplish this, he must overcome the evil powers who have usurped authority over the world, and who now oppress human beings" (*Origin of Satan*, p. 36). See also J. Robinson, "The Exorcism Narratives," in *The Problem of History in Mark, and Other Essays* (Philadelphia: Fortress, 1982), pp. 83ff.; Arnold, *Powers of Darkness*, p. 80; Dunn and Twelftree, "Demon-Possession and Exorcism," pp. 219-23; Rousseau, "Jesus, an Exorcist," pp. 150-51. In his recent superb study, Graham Twelftree concludes that "Jesus was the first to make the connection between exorcism and eschatology. For him, his exorcisms were the first or preliminary binding of Satan who would finally be destroyed in the eschaton" (*Jesus the Exorcist*, pp. 217-24).

[63]So Brown writes, "The miracle was not primarily an external guarantee of the coming of the kingdom; it was one of the means by which the kingdom came. In particular, Jesus' miracles were the weapons He used to overcome Satan" ("Gospel Miracles," p. 222). See also Yates, "Powers of Evil," pp. 106-7.

[64]Against this, Robert Guelich has argued: "We find no hint of any cosmic or ethical dualism in Jesus' ministry as portrayed in the Synoptics. The Kingdom of God is never juxtaposed to a 'kingdom of Satan' " ("Spiritual Warfare: Jesus, Paul and Peretti," *Pneuma* 13, no. 1 [1991]: 41). He thus regards Scripture's warfare motif as strictly metaphorical (p. 34). Interestingly enough, however, Guelich does seem to accept that the coming of the kingdom of God is (literally?) simultaneous with the binding of the strong man and the plundering of his house (pp. 38-39). One of the main reasons Guelich argues against the centrality of the warfare motif in the Gospels' portrayal of Jesus' ministry concerns what he regards as the absence of any struggle or theme of conquest against Satan in this portrayal (pp. 40-42). "In every case," he writes, "Jesus is clearly in control of the situation. There is simply no contest" (p. 40). Against this four points can briefly be made: (1) That Jesus (like Yahweh in the Old Testament) at least had to rebuke Satan and demons shows that they are genuine foes who must be conquered. God is (through Jesus) in control, to be sure, but this control has genuine opposition, and it must therefore be established by "a rebuke." (2) If the Gospel accounts of Jesus' temptation don't represent a genuine struggle with Satan, what would? The meaning of Guelich's observation that "Jesus was vulnerable to Satan's 'temptation' but not to Satan personally" is not clear to me (p. 40). (3) It is, we shall see, possible that in at least one Gospel account Jesus' exorcistic command did not issue in an immediate exorcism (Mk 5:6-10; see the discussion in chapter seven), and it is certain that the disciples' exorcisms were not always immediate (Mt 9:17-18). Indeed, one of Jesus'

healings was not instantaneous (Mt 8:24), and Mark implies that on at least one occasion Jesus could not do certain miracles because of people's lack of faith (Mk 6:5). Hence it seems fair to characterize the ministry of both Jesus and certainly his disciples as a struggle against the enemy. (4) It is clear from the Epistles that followers of Jesus understood themselves to be part of an ongoing cosmic battle and thus to be under constant attack from the enemy (see chapters seven to ten below).

[65]Ferguson speculates that "the use of these titles of Jesus was an effort by the demon to claim power over him," since knowing someone's name and office was seen as a form of power (*Demonology*, p. 7). Hence Jesus sometimes inquires into the name of the demon(s) he is confronting (Lk 8:30).

[66]Forsyth captures the theme well: "the teaching is somehow presented by the event [viz., the exorcism] the people have witnessed—a new teaching: power over the spirits" (*Old Enemy*, p. 286).

[67]If Pagels is correct, even the interlude discussion about sabbath propriety is not irrelevant to Mark's warfare perspective, for here (Mk 2:23-26) "Jesus dares claim as precedent for his disciples' apparently casual action [of picking corn] on the Sabbath, the prerogative of King David himself, who, with his men, broke the sacred food laws during a wartime emergency" (*Origin of Satan*, p. 18).

[68]Forsyth notes that this is the same apocalyptic cosmic battle motif, but "the battle scheme has now shifted to Christ's life" (*Old Enemy*, p. 289). See also Longman and Reid, *God Is a Warrior*, pp. 91-118. For a fascinating study that draws the literary connections between this portrayal of Satan and Old Testament and apocalyptic warfare motifs, see H. A. Kelly, "The Devil in the Desert," *CBQ* 26 (1964): 190-220. Adrio König sees in the temptation narratives a reversal of Adam's succumbing to temptation, and hence the beginning of a new creation in Jesus' ministry (*New and Greater Things: Re-evaluating the Biblical Message on Creation* [Pretoria: University of South Africa, 1988], pp. 106-7). E. Best goes so far as to argue that Mark locates the central confrontation between Jesus and the devil in the temptation narrative (*The Temptation and the Passion: The Markan Soteriology*, 2d ed., SNTSMS 2 [Cambridge: Cambridge University Press, 1990]).

[69]Arnold, *Powers of Darkness*, p. 78.

[70]One remarkable aspect of historical Jesus research since the late 1980s is the almost unanimous consensus that has been reached among even the most critical (viz., skeptical) New Testament scholars that the historical Jesus was indeed recognized as an exorcist and a healer by his contemporaries (even when their worldview presuppositions will not allow them to admit the possibility that he actually was so). For example, J. D. Crossan acknowledges that "Jesus was both an exorcist and a healer. . . . His vision of the Kingdom was but an ecstatic dream without immediate social repercussions were it not for those exorcisms and healings" (*The Historical Jesus: The Life of a Mediterranean Jewish Peasant* [San Francisco: HarperSanFrancisco, 1991], p. 332). See also S. Davies, *Jesus the Healer: Possession, Trance and the Origins of Christianity* (New York: Continuum, 1995); P. W. Hollenbach, "Jesus, Demoniacs and Public Authorities: A Socio-historical Study," *JAAR* 49 (1981): 567-88; and esp. Twelftree, *Jesus the Exorcist*.

[71]So argues Newport, "Satan and Demons," p. 59.

[72]Kallas drives home the point when he asks concerning this passage, "What kind of a missionary voyage was this? What were they preaching? Why no summary of their words?" (*Synoptic Miracles*, p. 60). Their healings and exorcisms, clearly, were their

message that "the kingdom of God has come near to you."

[73]Essentially the same point is made even if Julian Hills ("Luke 10:18—Who Saw Satan Fall?") is correct in arguing that Jesus is here referring to *demons* (not he or his disciples) seeing Satan (their captain) being dethroned.

[74]As noted earlier, this is not to say that those critical scholars today who acknowledge that Jesus was perceived to be an exorcist or a healer have necessarily dissociated themselves from an antisupernatural worldview. Many times they have simply expanded a naturalistic worldview and thus account for the supposed exorcisms and healings by psychosomatic and sociological explanations. See, e.g., R. Funk, "Demon: Identity and Worldview," *The Fourth R* 5, no. 3 (1992): 15; Hollenbach, "Jesus, Demoniacs," p. 567; Crossan, *Historical Jesus,* pp. 310-32; Davies, *Jesus the Healer.*

Chapter 7: War of the Worlds

[1]Some conservative scholars have argued that Jesus' deliverance ministry was so distinctive in comparison to the many exorcists of his day that he should not even be classified as an exorcist. See, e.g., A. Konya, *Demons: A Biblically Based Perspective* (Schaumburg, Ill.: Regular Baptist Press, 1990), pp. 36-37; W. W. Everts, "Jesus Christ, No Exorcist," *BSac* 81 (1924): 355-62. While the uniqueness of Christ is a point I shall myself be intent on driving home, the term "exorcism" yet seems to describe best what Jesus did even if it does not capture the uniqueness of how and why he did it. Hence I shall continue to use it.

[2]Matthew, quite typically, notes that there was another demonized person besides the one all three Synoptic narratives center on (Mt 8:28-29). Also, there is in the manuscript tradition disagreement about whether this event took place in Gadara, Gerasa or Gergesa. According to the strongest readings, Mark and Luke have Jesus going to Gerasa, while Matthew has him going to Gadara. Gerasa lies 30 miles off the coast of the sea of Galilee, and Gadara 5 miles, making both difficult to square with the narratives. The most likely solution to the problem seems to be to see the actual town in which the exorcism took place as being Khersa, which is located squarely on the eastern shore. This could be easily spelled Gerasa in Greek (as in Mark and Luke) and could also be included under the territory of Gadara. We can then suppose that Matthew (again, typically) tried to avoid the ambiguity and thus referred only to the larger and much better known region of Gadara. Later scribes, unfamiliar with the territory, then tried to "correct" Matthew's "solution" and change this to Gerasa, hence the geographical problems as well as the ambiguity in the manuscript traditions. For discussions, see W. H. Mare, "Gadara," *The New International Dictionary of Biblical Archaeology,* ed. E. M. Blaiklock et al. (Grand Rapids, Mich.: Zondervan, 1983), p. 201; C. Blomberg, *The Historical Reliability of the Gospels* (Downers Grove, Ill.: InterVarsity Press, 1987), pp. 149-50; E. J. Vardaman, "Gadara," *Wycliffe Bible Encyclopedia,* 2 vols., ed. C. F. Pfeiffer et al. (Chicago: Moody Press, 1975), 1:643; S. Holm-Nielsen et al., "Gadarenes," *ABD,* 2:866-68. For two helpful discussions of this episode, see G. H. Twelftree, *Jesus the Exorcist: A Contribution to the Study of the Historical Jesus,* WUNT 2/54 (Tübingen: Mohr, 1993), pp. 72-87; H. van der Loos, *The Miracles of Jesus,* NovTSup 8 (Leiden: Brill, 1965), pp. 382-97.

[3]On the definition of "demonized," see chapter one, note 42.

[4]So too, as mentioned earlier (chapter six, note 64) Mark suggests that Jesus' prayer for healing did not always immediately effect a complete healing (Mk 8:22-26).

Indeed, he states explicitly that in at least one instance people's unbelief prevented Jesus from doing many miracles (Mk 6:5). As God-become-man, Jesus was sinless, he exercised ideal faith, and he was perfectly open to the omnipotent Father working through him (Jn 5:19-32; 6:38; 8:28-29). But, as I shall argue more extensively in *Satan and the Problem of Evil,* God's power and Jesus' character are not the only variables in bringing about healings and exorcisms. Other factors such as the strength of faith, the persistence of prayer, and the strength and number of opposing spiritual forces have to be factored in.

[5]This observation stands over against R. Guelich ("Spiritual Warfare: Jesus, Paul and Peretti," *Pneuma* 13, no. 1 [1991]: 40-41), who minimizes the warfare dimension of the Gospels largely on the basis of the supposed absence of conflict between Jesus and Satan and demons. "We find no hint of a struggle in these encounters" (p. 40). Not only the failure of Jesus' command here but the acquisition of a name (see note 6 below) and the common rebukes of Jesus during exorcism, as well as the temptation narratives (to say nothing of his explicit teachings; see chapter eight), suggest that Jesus was in fact engaged in a genuine struggle. The temptation narratives in the Gospels alone should be enough to tell us this much (cf. Heb 4:15-16; 5:7-10).

[6]In the ancient Near Eastern world, names were generally viewed as inherently reflecting the realities to which they were attached. Thus to know someone's name was to know the person, and invoking this name could either capture the power of that person's presence, as when Jesus' name is used in exorcism (Lk 10:17; Mk 9:38; Acts 19:13), or give one power over that person, as when the name of demons is used in exorcism. Interestingly, Jesus, in contrast to other exorcists of his day, did not rely upon the power of names in his deliverance ministry. See Twelftree, *Jesus the Exorcist,* p. 164. For the invocation of names in exorcisms and magic in the first century, see D. E. Aune, "Magic in Early Christianity," in *ANRW* (1980), 2/23.2:1545; J. G. Gager, ed., *Curse Tablets and Binding Spells from the Ancient World* (Oxford: Oxford University Press, 1992), pp. 3-14.

[7]See van der Loos, *Miracles of Jesus,* p. 388.

[8]As in Matthew 12:45, however, the number seven here may be symbolic of "fullness." In other words, Mary had a plethora of demons within her. So argues E. Langton, *Essentials of Demonology: A Study of the Jewish and Christian Doctrine, Its Origin and Development* (London: Epworth, 1949), p. 50, who sees it as a synonym for a large group. See also F. X. Gokey, *The Terminology for the Devil and Evil Spirits in the Apostolic Fathers,* Patristic Studies 93 (Washington, D.C.: Catholic University of America Press, 1961), p. 49.

[9]Langton, *Essentials,* p. 147.

[10]J. D. Crossan, who mostly denies the historicity of the Gospel exorcism accounts (though he admits the historical Jesus was something of an exorcist), argues that Roman imperialism is here being symbolized as demonic possession. See *Jesus: A Revolutionary Biography* (San Francisco: HarperSanFrancisco, 1994), pp. 90-91. While his ahistorical, overly symbolic reading of this (and other) passages is unwarranted, he seems correct in making the point that the Jesus of Mark's Gospel was here seeing the demonic "Legion" as being at least analogous to the legions of Roman guards who occupied and oppressed the territory. As Roman imperialism illegitimately rules over and oppresses Israel, so Satanic imperialism illegitimately rules over and oppresses this man, and ultimately the entire world. For a critique of Crossan's exegetical methods, see my *Cynic, Sage or Son of God? Recovering the*

Real Jesus in an Age of Revisionist Replies (Wheaton, Ill.: Bridgepoint, 1995), pp. 77-87.

[11]So, e.g., 4 Maccabees 18:8 speaks of a "seducer of the desert." Cf. *1 Enoch* 10:4-5. On this see E. Ferguson, *Demonology of the Early Christian World* (New York: Mellen, 1980), p. 2.

[12]This again raises the issue of "territorial spirits" discussed in the introduction. See references in introduction, note 3.

[13]Alongside humans and animals, demons were believed sometimes to inhabit such haunts as the desert, water (seas and wells), the wind, fire, trees, caves, graves and garbage heaps. See van der Loos, *Miracles of Jesus*, p. 346.

[14]Like "the disease germs of modern medicine," H. A. Kelly argues, demons in the New Testament are "definitely parasitic in nature" (*The Devil at Baptism: Ritual, Theology and Drama* [Ithaca: Cornell University Press, 1985], 18).

[15]J. Ramsey Michaels, "Jesus and the Unclean Spirits," in *Demon Possession*, ed. J. W. Montgomery (Minneapolis: Bethany, 1976), pp. 53-54.

[16]See Revelation 16:13, which speaks of "three evil spirits" that deceive nations and lead them into war. So too Revelation 20:3, 8, 10 portray Satan (and the legions of demons under him?) as one who "deceives the nations." Something similar may be implied by Paul's use of "principalities" and "powers," as we shall see (chapter ten). The Old Testament conception of "the gods of the nations," discussed in chapter two, lies behind all this. These gods, we saw, sometimes carry out their national duties well; sometimes they do not. When they do not, they become demonic (e.g., Ps 82; Dan 10). T. Ling takes Matthew 12:45 to mean that Jesus saw his own generation as being possessed by Satan. Hence Jesus is here saying that "although an individual member of this generation be exorcised of an evil spirit by some contemporary exorcist, the power of evil in the common life is such that he will almost certainly become re-possessed, and now more desperately than before" (*The Significance of Satan: New Testament Demonology and Its Contemporary Significance* [London: SPCK, 1961], p. 21).

[17]For a contemporary discussion surrounding purported cases of "collective possession," see F. D. Pennoyer, "In Dark Dungeons of Collective Captivity," in *Wrestling with Dark Angels: Toward a Deeper Understanding of the Supernatural Forces in Spiritual Warfare*, ed. C. P. Wagner and F. D. Pennoyer (Ventura, Calif.: Regal, 1990), pp. 249-70.

[18]For discussions see Twelftree, *Jesus the Exorcist*, pp. 91-97; van der Loos, *Miracles of Jesus*, pp. 397-405.

[19]Some manuscripts add "and fasting" to Mark 9:29, and some add "But this kind does not go out except by prayer and fasting" to Matthew 17:20.

[20]Langton, for example, argues, "It cannot be too strongly emphasized that the instances [of demonization] mentioned in the Gospels do not stand alone. They have their exact parallels among many peoples in different parts of the world" (*Essentials*, p. 153). Cf. also idem, *Good and Evil Spirits: A Study of the Jewish Christian Doctrine, Its Origin and Development* (New York: Macmillan, 1942), pp. 54ff. For similar accounts from a crosscultural and historical perspective, see F. D. Goodman, *How About Demons? Possession and Exorcism in the Modern World* (Bloomington: Indiana University Press, 1988); I. M. Lewis, *Ecstatic Religion: An Anthropological Study of Spirit Possession and Shamanism* (Baltimore: Penguin, 1971); M. Ebon, *Exorcism Past and Present* (London: Cassell, 1974); B. P. Levack, *Witchcraft, Magic and Demonology*, vol. 9, *Possession and Exorcism* (Hamden,

Conn.: Garland, 1992); T. K. Oesterreich, *Possession, Demoniacal and Other, Among Primitive Races, in Antiquity, the Middle Ages and Modern Times* (New Hyde Park, N.Y.: University Books, 1966); G. Twelftree, *Christ Triumphant: Exorcism Then and Now* (London: Hodder & Stoughton, 1985). It should be noted, however, that similar accounts are increasingly reported today within contemporary Western culture. Perhaps the most credible recent discussions are M. S. Peck's *People of the Lie* (New York: Simon & Schuster, 1983), pp. 182-253; K. E. Koch, *Demonology, Past and Present* (Grand Rapids, Mich.: Kregel, 1973); V. Stacey, "Christ Cleanses Buildings and Delivers People: Four Case Studies," *ERT* 16, no. 4 (1992): 342-52. Other accounts (from widely varying perspectives) can be found in M. Martin's fascinating report *Hostage to the Devil* (New York: Bantam, 1977); C. F. Dickason, *Demon Possession and the Christian* (Westchester, Ill.: Crossway Books, 1987), pp. 169-213; R. Mayer, *Satan's Children: Case Studies in MPD* (New York: Putnam's, 1991); E. Fiore, *The Unquiet Dead: A Psychologist Treats Spirit Possession—Detecting and Removing Earthbound Spirits* (Garden City, N.Y.: Doubleday, 1987); J. Richards, *But Deliver Us from Evil* (New York: Seabury, 1974); D. R. Petitpierre, *Exorcising Devils* (London: Robert Hale, 1976). My own observation of phenomena similar to this has led me, along with many others, to conclude that it is impossible to explain the sometimes supernatural features of such phenomena on a strictly naturalistic basis.

[21]See, e.g., J. B. Cortes and F. M. Gatti, "The Demon-Possessed Epileptic," in their *The Case Against Possession and Exorcism: A Historical, Biblical and Psychological Analysis of Demons, Devils and Demoniacs* (New York: Vantage, 1975), pp. 173-86. See also J. Wilkinson, "The Case of the Epileptic Boy," *ExpTim* 79 (1967-68): 39-42; van der Loos, *Miracles of Jesus*, pp. 401-6. See esp. p. 401, note 5 for a list of others who adopt a position similar to this.

[22]On the reliability of this account, see G. E. Sterling, "Jesus as Exorcist: An Analysis of Matthew 17:14-20; Mark 9:14-29; Luke 9:37-43a," *CBQ* 55 (1993): 467-93. On the reliability of the exorcist accounts in general, see L. Sabourin, "The Miracles of Jesus (II): Jesus and the Evil Powers," *BTB* 4, no. 2 (1974): 115-75; and esp. Twelftree, *Jesus the Exorcist*, pp. 53-113.

[23]In keeping with general apocalyptic thought, "Christ acknowledges that there are different classes of demons, some of whom had more powers than others" (Gokey, *Terminology*, p. 49). But he never speculates beyond this point, as the apocalyptic thinkers frequently did.

[24]So argues Kallas, *Synoptic Miracles*, p. 63; Langton, *Essentials*, pp. 152-53.

[25]R. Brown, "Gospel Miracles," in his *New Testament Essays* (Garden City, N.Y.: Doubleday, 1967), p. 223.

[26]Langton, *Essentials*, pp. 171-72.

[27]This assumption is formalized into something of a theological principle in all modernist and postmodernist accounts that understand evil beings to be projections of our own inner evil impulses. If the ontological "otherness" of the demonic is not affirmed, then obviously there can be no genuine victims of the demonic. See, e.g., W. Woods, *A History of the Devil* (London: W. H. Allen, 1973), who argues that "both gods and devils, are of course [sic] simply different facets of man, made as large as our imaginations can make them" (p. 12). So with Nels F. S. Ferré, *Evil and the Christian Faith* (New York: Harper & Brothers, 1947), p. 33; H. Pendley, "Views of the Demonic in Recent Religious Thought" (Ph.D. diss., Southern Baptist Theological Seminary, 1976), who (despite holding open the possibility of

the demonic realm as an objective reality) argues that "human demonization occurs when egocentricity becomes the norm for one's existence" (p. 220). This unbiblical assumption gets formalized in otherwise biblically centered theologies as well, however. For example, despite Emil Brunner's many insights concerning the demonic realm, he insists that demonization cannot occur without human complicity. See *The Christian Doctrine of Creation and Redemption*, trans. O. Wyon (Philadelphia: Westminster, 1952), pp. 140-41. While the New Testament generally rejects anything like the excuse that "the devil made me do it"—it assumes people are morally responsible for their actions—it nevertheless depicts radically demonized people in just this fashion. They are casualties of war. See C. Moeller, "Introduction," in *Satan*, ed. B. de Jésus-Marie (New York: Sheed & Ward, 1952), p. xix. I shall address the thorny issue of the relationship between demonic influence and human responsibility in *Satan and the Problem of Evil.*

[28]John Richards drives home the issue poignantly as it concerns demonic possession when he notes: "If there has been *one,* just one *real* case of demonic possession in history, then the theologian must have an understanding of God's world in which such a thing is possible" (*But Deliver Us from Evil*, p. 51). The point is, if the world 's exhaustively controlled by God, such a phenomenon would not be possible. For an excellent exposition of a biblical model of God's providence which makes the cross its hermenuetical center, see E. F. Tupper, *A Scandalous Providence: The Jesus Story of the Compassion of God* (Macon, Ga.: Mercer University Press, 1995).

[29]See J. Geller, *Forerunners to UDUG-HUL: Sumerian Exorcistic Incantations,* FAS 12 (Stuttgart: Franz Steiner, 1985); H. D. Betz, ed., *The Greek Magical Papyri in Translation Including the Demonic Spells* (Chicago: University of Chicago Press, 1986); E. Yamauchi, "Magic in the Biblical World," *TynBul* 34 (1983): 169-200.

[30]John Rousseau, "Jesus, an Exorcist of a Kind," in SBLSP, ed. E. H. Lovering Jr. (Atlanta: Scholars Press, 1993), pp. 148-49. See also E. Yamauchi, "Magic or Miracle? Diseases, Demons and Exorcisms," in *The Miracles of Jesus,* ed. D. Wenham and C. Blomberg, GP 6 (Sheffield: JSOT Press, 1986), pp. 131-42; G. H. Twelftree, "Demon-Possession and Exorcism in the New Testament," *Churchman* 94, no. 3 (1980): 214-15; S. Davies, "Whom Jesus Healed and How," *The Fourth R* 6 (Mar.-Apr. 1993): 1; O. Böcher, *Das Neue Testament und die dämonischen Mächte,* SBS 58 (Stuttgart: Katholisches Bibelwerk, 1972), pp. 35-42; E. Ferguson, "Jesus and the Demons," in his *Demonology of the Early Christian World* (New York: Mellen, 1984), pp. 9-11.

[31]The view that prayer changes only us, not God, goes back at least to the time of Arnobius (*Against the Heathen* 1.27), who logically drew out the consequences of conceptualizing God as altogether impassible. He was refuted by Lactantius, who argued that such a view makes God dead and prayer inconsequential. See the discussion in J. K. Mozley, *The Impassibility of God* (New York: Cambridge University Press, 1926), pp. 48-52. At least by scriptural standards, Lactantius was certainly correct. There is, in any event, an increasing awareness in our time concerning the power of prayer to change things. For several accounts, see J. Deere, *Surprised by the Power of the Spirit* (Grand Rapids, Mich.: Eerdmans, 1993); J. Wimber and K. Springer, *Power Healing* (San Francisco: Harper & Row, 1987); K. Springer, ed., *Power Encounters Among Christians in the Western World* (San Francisco: Harper & Row, 1988).

[32]The understanding that God's activity, and therefore the flow of history, is genuinely conditioned by prayer is increasingly being accepted and emphasized, especially by

those within the spiritual warfare movement. One of the earliest, most radical, most insightful and most neglected works on the subject is P. Billheimer's *Destined for the Throne* (Minneapolis: Bethany, 1975), esp. pp. 43-56. See also C. H. Kraft's excellent book *Christianity with Power: Your Worldview and Your Experience of the Supernatural* (Ann Arbor, Mich.: Servant, 1989), pp. 117-32. I shall attempt to work out a theology of prayer that is rooted in this understanding in *Satan and the Problem of Evil.*

[33]Exegetes have largely ignored this line of argumentation, which is surprising given the growing appreciation of the influence of apocalyptic thought on Jesus and his disciples. Kallas has made more use of this line of thinking than anyone. He sees *all* the miracles of Jesus as being "primarily an attack upon the enemies of God" (*Synoptic Miracles*, p. 33). See also A. König, *The Eclipse of Christ in Eschatology: Toward a Christ-Centered Approach* (Grand Rapids, Mich.: Eerdmans, 1989), pp. 110-27; R. Brown, "Gospel Miracles," pp. 226-27.

[34]Kallas, *Synoptic Miracles*, p. 65. J. Ramsey Michaels argues along the same lines in "Jesus and the Unclean Spirits," in *Demon Possession*, p. 47.

[35]Forsyth argues the "rebuke" here is part and parcel of "the explicit war language of the apocalyptic writings themselves" and ultimately goes back to the Old Testament tradition of Yahweh "rebuking" his cosmic foes (*Old Enemy*, pp. 286-87). See also König, *New and Greater Things*, pp. 140-41.

[36]See Forsyth, *Old Enemy*, pp. 286-87; König, *New and Greater Things*, pp. 50, 107. See also B. L. Blackburn ("Miracles and Miracle Stories," *DJG*, p. 559), who rightly emphasizes the "eschatological/apocalyptic background for the so-called nature miracles," and therefore observes, "The two rescue miracles, Jesus' calming of and walking on the sea, are meaningful against the horizon of Yahweh's assertion of his sovereignty over the sea in creation (Job 26:12-13; Ps 74:12-15), the Exodus (Ps 77:16-20), and the eschaton (Is 27:1; cf. Rev 21:1)." In short, the Gospel authors had something like Leviathan or Yamm in mind when they portrayed Jesus as rebuking and treading on the sea. See also R. Brown, "Gospel Miracles," pp. 226-27; and W. O. E. Oesterley (*The Evolution of the Messianic Idea: A Study in Comparative Religion* [London: Pitman, 1908], p. 175ff.), who has posited a direct line of development from the Old Testament *thôm* (Tiamat) to the New Testament view of Satan. See also König, *Eclipse of Christ,* pp. 115-17; T. Fawcett, "The Satanic Serpent," in his *Hebrew Myth and Christian Gospel* (London: SCM, 1973), pp. 98-101; H. Hendrickx, *The Miracle Stories of the Synoptic Gospels* (San Francisco: Harper & Row, 1987), pp. 184-85; R. Latourelle, *The Miracles of Jesus and the Theology of Miracles,* trans. M. J. O'Connell (New York: Paulist, 1988), pp. 108-9; and G. E. Smith's classic *The Evolution of the Dragon* (Manchester: Manchester University Press, 1919), pp. 137-38.

[37]A slightly different reading of this episode is to see Jesus as the perfect man restoring to humanity the dominion over the sea that we were created to enjoy but then lost in the Fall. This reading is not necessarily incompatible with the reading here offered, for, as D. G. McCartney sees ("*Ecce Homo*: The Coming of the Kingdom as the Restoration of Human Vicegerency," *WTJ* 56 [1994]: 1-21), the Bible consistently associates the rule of God with the rule of the viceroy he established. If humanity has been dethroned, God has, in effect, been dethroned. From this perspective, then, Jesus is seeking to restore both the rulership of humanity and the rule of God, for they are one and the same. Indeed, one could easily draw an intrinsic connection between this insight and the truth

that Jesus was fully God and fully human.

[38]Kallas, *Synoptic Miracles,* p. 65.

[39]See, e.g., J. P. Meier, *A Marginal Jew: Rethinking the Historical Jesus,* vol. 2, *Mentor, Message and Miracle* (New York: Doubleday, 1994), pp. 884-96; van der Loos, *Miracles of Jesus,* pp. 688-98. Both scholars doubt the story's historicity but locate its symbolic meaning to a divine judgment of the temple and the nation of Israel. See also the detailed redactional-critical study of W. R. Telford, *The Barren Temple and the Withered Tree,* JSNTSup 1 (Sheffield: JSOT Press, 1980).

[40]The theme of cosmic restoration arises even in the Old Testament, a restoration that, among other things, includes nature becoming harmonious and bountiful once again as it was originally created to be. See, e.g., Isaiah 11:6-9; 65:17-25; Amos 9:13-15.

[41]See W. D. Davies, *Paul and Rabbinic Judaism* (Philadelphia: Fortress, rpt. 1980), p. 39; König, *Eclipse of Christ,* pp. 114-15; Kallas, *Synoptic Miracles,* p. 95.

[42]See R. H. Hiers, "Not the Season for Figs," *JBL* 87 (1968): 394-400; J. D. M. Derrett, "Figtrees in the New Testament," *HeyJ* 14 (1973): 249-65.

[43]It is interesting that Mark explicitly connects the inability of the disciples to grasp Jesus' power in rebuking the demonic sea with their inability to grasp his power to multiply bread (Mk 6:52). In both instances, Christ was victorious over nature when nature was not doing what it was created to do. See König, *Eclipse of Christ,* pp. 117-21. Not a few scholars have noted the eschatological import of the "gift miracles" (i.e., the feeding of the five thousand, the wine at the Cana wedding feast). These miracles "actualize and foreshadow the messianic feast . . . characterized by an abundance of bread—the eschatological equivalent of the manna miracle . . . and wine" (Blackburn, "Miracles," *DJG,* p. 559).

[44]This is not necessarily to say that physical existence would never have ceased had we not fallen. Theologically speaking, it may be the case that the sort of physical existence we experience now was never meant to be eternal but merely probational. This form of existence was perhaps always meant to metamorphosize into the sort of physical-spiritual existence Jesus enjoyed after his resurrection (and which we shall enjoy after ours). Had we not fallen (viz., failed the Edenic probation) this metamorphosis would not be experienced as "death" as we now experience it. This painful experience of death—this "sting," as Paul puts it (1 Cor 15:55)—was never intended to be part of God's creation. For believers, death need no longer have this sting, for in Christ the original transitional nature of death has been reestablished.

[45]T. W. Manson notes that in the passion, "the *exousia* of Jesus the Messiah comes to last moral grips with the *exousia* of the demonic world" ("Principalities and Powers: The Spiritual Background for the Work of Jesus in the Synoptic Gospels," *NTS* 3 [1952]: 14). See also Wingren, *Living Word,* pp. 50-51, 62, 173.

[46]Emil Brunner is surely correct to see in the horror of the crucified Son of God the clearest evidence of Satan's existence and diabolical work. See *The Christian Doctrine of Creation and Redemption,* trans. O. Wyon (Philadelphia: Westminster, 1952), p. 145. Pagels argues that inasmuch as Luke sees all opposing forces as under Satan's power, Luke 13:32 should be read as a challenge to Satan (*Origin of Satan,* p. 92).

[47]See Kallas, *Significance of Synoptic Miracles,* pp. 85-86. Similarly, concerning the Gospel of Luke, S. R. Garrett argues that "Luke regarded the death, resurrection, and ascension as an 'exodus' because *in these events Jesus, 'the one who is stronger,' led the people out of bondage to Satan*" ("Exodus from Bondage: Luke 9:31 and Acts

12:1-24," *CBQ* 52 [1990]: 659).

[48]Very helpful on this theme is Martinus C. de Boer's study on Paul's understanding of death in the light of his apocalyptic eschatology: *The Defeat of Death: Apocalyptic Eschatology in I Corinthians 15 and Romans 5,* JSNTSup 22 (Sheffield: JSOT Press, 1988). Here de Boer writes: "Paul understands the anthropological reality of death in accordance with the traditions of Jewish cosmological apocalyptic eschatology as an inimical, murderous, quasi-angelic power that has held all Adamic humanity in subjection and enslavement. Death is hypostasized as a power external to human beings, which nevertheless exerts and manifests its hegemony over and among human beings, most particularly in their 'moral' or 'natural' bodies" (p. 183). See also A. G. van Aarde, "Demonology in New Testament Times," in *Like a Roaring Lion . . . : Essays on the Bible, the Church and Demonic Powers,* ed. P. G. R. de Villiers (Pretoria: University of South Africa, 1987), pp. 33-34. Wingren, however, surely goes too far in virtually identifying sin, death and Satan throughout his *Living Word.*

[49]We should perhaps include here Matthew's record that a number of "saints" were resurrected when Jesus died on the cross (Mt 27:52-53). Van der Loos captures the motif well: "the resurrections are signs in which the conquering power of the Messianic Kingdom is manifest and by which it is proclaimed to the world that God is a living God, in whose name the son testifies and acts." See "Miracles of Jesus," p. 566. J. P. Meier (*Mentor, Message and Miracle,* pp. 773-873) argues for the basic historicity of the accounts on a historical-critical basis and concludes that they centrally manifest what Jesus was about (see esp. p. 837).

[50]In the second volume of his monumental study of the historical Jesus, John Meier has concluded that Jesus' eschatology is best described as reflecting "an 'already/not yet' tension." See *Mentor, Message and Miracle,* p. 451. For several helpful discussions, see G. E. Ladd, *The Presence of the Future: The Eschatology of Biblical Realism* (Grand Rapids, Mich.: Eerdmans, 1974); G. Glorovsky, "The Patristic Age on Eschatology: An Introduction," in his *Collected Works,* vol. 4, *Aspects of Church History* (Belmont, Mass.: Nordland, 1975), pp. 63-78; R. H. Stein, *The Method and Message of Jesus' Teachings* (Philadelphia: Westminster, 1978), pp. 68-79; and B. Witherington III, *Jesus, Paul and the End of the World: A Comparative Study in New Testament Eschatology* (Downers Grove, Ill.: InterVarsity Press, 1992).

[51]Several scholars have noted that Jesus was unique in bringing together the phenomenon of exorcism as both a present deliverance and an eschatological event. See, e.g., G. Theissen, *The Miracle Stories of the Early Christian Tradition,* ed. J. Riches, trans. F. McDonagh (Philadelphia: Fortress, 1983), p. 278; Twelftree, *Jesus the Exorcist,* pp. 217-24.

[52]Wingren, *Living Word,* p. 62. Cf. p. 164. It is perhaps worth noting here that Scripture does not generally envisage the eschatological kingdom as "above" the earth so much as it envisages it as "on" the earth. All who overcome will "reign *on earth*" (Rev 5:10). Just as our bodies will be transformed but will still be our bodies (1 Cor 15:35-54), so too the earth will be transformed, but it will nevertheless be our earth (see 2 Pet 3:13; Rev 20:8; 21:1, 24).

Chapter 8: Storming the Gates of Hell

[1]For an overview of this motif, see T. Longman III and D. G. Reid, *God Is a Warrior* (Grand Rapids, Mich.: Zondervan, 1995), pp. 91-118.

[2]In my estimation, Elaine Pagels overestimates the extent to which the Gospel

authors "demonize" their opponents because she reads too much into their portrayal of their opponents as demonically inspired. True, Jesus saw his conflict with Jewish religious leaders and others as a conflict with the devil. But the same could be said of Jesus' conflict with Peter. See her *Origin of Satan* (New York: Random House, 1995), pp. 82-88, and passim.

[3]On the intimate connection between Jesus' use of "Hades" here and Satan, see R. H. Hiers's excellent article " 'Binding' and 'Loosing': The Matthean Authorizations," *JBL* 104 (1985): 242-43, as well as his *Kingdom of God in the Synoptic Tradition* (Gainesville: University of Florida Press, 1970), p. 47. In fact, no less an authority than W. Manson (*Jesus and the Christian* [Grand Rapids: Eerdmans, 1967], p. 83) renders "gates of hades" in this passage as "Satan-Hades." A number of ancient Jewish and early Christian writings set a precedent for the intimate linkage of Satan and Hades. See, e.g., *Testament of Reuben* 4:6-7; 1 Corinthians 15:24-27; Revelation 20:7-10, 13-14. A. Lefevre has also provided strong evidence to suggest that Belial, like Death, was originally a personified monster of the underworld, i.e., Hades personified. See "Angel or Monster? The Power of Evil in the Old Testament," in *Satan: Essays Collected and Translated from "Etudes Carmelitaines,"* ed. B. de Jésus-Marie, trans. M. Carroll et al. (New York: Sheed & Ward, 1951), pp. 55-56. R. Bauckham still attempts to dichotomize "powers of evil" and "the power of Hades" in "Hades, Hell," *ABD*, 3:15. Similarly, C. Brown argues against a connection between the gates of Hades and the powers of Satan; for Brown, Jesus is here ironically referring to his impending entry into Jerusalem. Though this novel thesis is worthy of attention, it seems both cryptic and speculative. It also does not square as well with the apocalyptic context in which Jesus is speaking as does the warfare reading. For Brown's case, see "The Gates of Hell and the Church," in *Church, Word and Spirit: Historical and Theological Essays in Honor of Geoffrey W. Bromiley,* ed. J. E. Bradley and R. A. Muller (Grand Rapids, Mich.: Eerdmans, 1987), pp. 15-43. See also idem, "The Gates of Hell: An Alternative Approach," in SBLSP, 1987, ed. K. H. Richards (Atlanta: Scholars Press, 1987), pp. 357-67.

[4]G. E. Ladd, *The Presence of the Future: The Eschatology of Biblical Realism* (Grand Rapids, Mich.: Eerdmans, 1974), p. 161.

[5]The perfect participle of *deō* (bind) and *lyō* (loose) can be translated "will have been bound" and "will have been loosed."

[6]For a summary of the various interpretations of the two "binding" and "loosing" passages in Matthew (16:19; 18:18), see Hiers, "Binding and Loosing," pp. 233-35; D. C. Duling, "Binding and Loosing: Matthew 16:19; Matthew 18:18; John 20:23," *Foundations and Facets Forum* 3, no. 4 (1987): 3-26. Duling's conclusion that these passages do not go back to the historical Jesus is less than convincing.

[7]Hiers, "Binding and Loosing," p. 235. Hiers makes his solid case largely on the basis of intertestamental parallels.

[8]This popular title, one should note, is quite inappropriate since the whole passage constitutes instruction given by Jesus to his disciples as to how *they* should pray. Hence the prayer is spoken in the first-person plural and is intended to be a communal prayer.

[9]J. Jeremias argues convincingly that "the Lucan version [of the Lord's Prayer] has preserved the oldest form with respect to length, but the Matthaean text is more original with regard to wording" ("The Lord's Prayer in the Light of Recent Research," in *The Prayers of Jesus,* trans. J. Bowden et al., SBT 2/6 [Naperville, Ill.:

Allenson, 1967], p. 93). As the wording of the prayer is what interests us presently, I shall follow the Matthean version.

[10]Meier, *Mentor, Message and Miracles,* p. 299. See also Stein, *Method and Message of Jesus' Teachings,* pp. 72-73.

[11]Jeremias, "Lord's Prayer," p. 99.

[12]See ibid., pp. 82-107; R. E. Brown, "The Pater Noster as an Eschatological Prayer," in his *New Testament Essays* (Garden City, N.Y.: Doubleday, 1968), pp. 270-320; W. D. Davies and D. C. Allison, *A Critical and Exegetical Commentary on the Gospel According to Saint Matthew,* 3 vols., ICC (Edinburgh: T & T Clark, 1988ff.), 1:593-94, 599-615; Meier, *Mentor, Message and Miracles,* pp. 291-302; P. Bonnard, J. Dupont and F. Refoulé, *Notre Père qui es aux cieux,* Cahiers de la Traduction Oecuménique de la Bible 3 (Paris: Cerf/Les bergers et les Mages, 1968); D. A. Hagner, *Matthew 1—13,* WBC 33A (Dallas: Word, 1993), pp. 143-52.

[13]See, e.g., Jeremias, "Lord's Prayer," pp. 100-101; Brown, "Pater Noster"; Meier, *Mentor, Message and Miracles,* pp. 301, 364-65; Davies and Allison, *Matthew,* 1:607-10.

[14]Jeremias argues that this interpretation does not exclude, but rather includes, the petition for "daily bread" ("Lord's Prayer," pp. 101-2).

[15]Ibid., p. 103. Cf. pp. 92-93. So argues, on different grounds, Brown, "Pater Noster," pp. 312-13.

[16]Jeremias, "Lord's Prayer," pp. 102-3.

[17]See Brown, "Pater Noster," pp. 310-12.

[18]Ibid., p. 311. Again, since there is no ultimate bifurcation between this age and the age to come, the request for final pardon includes, rather than excludes, requests for present forgiveness.

[19]B. Gerhardsson, *The Testing of God's Son: An Analysis of an Early Christian Midrash* (Lund: Gleerup, 1966), p. 26.

[20]See the foundational study of J. S. Korn, *PEIRASMOS: Die Versuchung des Gläubigen in der griechischen Bibel,* BWANT 4/20 (Stuttgart: Kohlhammer, 1937). For a helpful review of Korn's work, see M. E. Andrews, "Peirasmos," *Anglican Theological Review* 24 (1942): 229-44. See also H. A. Kelly, "The Devil in the Desert," *CBQ* 26 (1964): 196-202, 212, 216. On *peirasmos* as referring to the final "Satanic trial," as Brown calls it, see Brown, "Pater Noster," p. 319.

[21]Kuhn is certainly correct in pointing out that these two foci are not mutually exclusive. "When Jesus teaches us to pray: 'Lead us not into *peirasmos,*' no distinction can be made between the Now of the believer in the world and the Then of the final battle to come. Both belong together as one act" (K. G. Kuhn, "New Light on Temptation, Sin and Flesh in the New Testament," in *The Scrolls and the New Testament,* ed. K. Stendahl [New York: Harper, 1957], p. 111).

[22]*First Enoch* 69:15 also brings together the activity of "the evil one" with oath taking. On whether *ponēros* in this passage refers to evil in general or to "the evil one" (Satan), see T. Ling, *The Significance of Satan: New Testament Demonology and Its Contemporary Significance* (London: SPCK, 1961), pp. 22-24. Scholars generally favor the second, but either way, no sharp distinction can be made between them. For, as Ling also argues, the evil in the world was, for Jesus, there ultimately because of "the evil one" (p. 24). See also Hagner, *Matthew 1—13,* p. 128.

[23]A possible parallel is found in *Jubilees* 11, where Mastema (a Satan figure) sends birds to devour seed as it is sown.

[24]G. R. Beasley-Murray, *Jesus and the Kingdom of God* (Grand Rapids, Mich.:

Eerdmans, 1986), p. 133.

[25]See Kallas, *Synoptic Miracles,* p. 72. Cf. Brown, "Pater Noster," p. 319.

[26]G. Schrenk's article "βιάζομαι," *TDNT,* 1:609-13, is frequently cited as offering the most substantial defense of the passive-voice reading. For a summary of the arguments, see Hagner, *Matthew 1—13,* pp. 306-7.

[27]P. S. Cameron, *Violence and the Kingdom: The Interpretation of Matthew 11:12,* Arbeiten zum Neuen Testament und Judentum 5 (Frankfurt: Lang, 1984), p. 2, which also includes a list of other suggestions.

[28]This view has been gaining acceptance among scholars. For several noteworthy defenses, in roughly chronological order, see M. Dibelius, *Die urchristliche Über-lieferung von Johannes dem Täufer* (Göttingen: Vandenhoeck & Ruprecht, 1911); A. Fridrichsen, "The Conflict of Jesus with the Unclean Spirits," *Theology* 22 (1931): 128; A. Wilder, *Eschatology and Ethics in the Teaching of Jesus* (New York: Harper & Bros., rpt. 1950), pp. 84, 149, 182; C. H. Kraeling, *John the Baptist* (New York: Scribner's, 1951), p. 156; Kallas, *Synoptic Miracles,* p. 72; W. Kümmel, *Promise and Fulfillment: The Eschatological Message of Jesus,* trans. D. M. Barton, 3d ed., SBT 1/23 (Naperville, Ill.: Allenson, 1956), pp. 121-24; N. Perrin, *The Kingdom of God in the Teaching of Jesus* (Philadelphia: Fortress, 1963), pp. 171-74; idem, *Jesus and the Language of the Kingdom* (Philadelphia: Fortress, 1976), p. 46; D. C. Allison, *The End of the Age Has Come: An Early Interpretation of the Passion and Resurrection of Jesus* (Philadelphia: Fortress, 1985), pp. 120-24.

[29]An alternative interpretation, yet taking the "violent ones" to refer to the forces of Satan's kingdom, is to take the phrase "until now" as implying that the period of violence is going to come to a close with the victory of Jesus over the powers on the cross. "The overthrow of the rule of Satan is assigned to the development of the situation after John, to the phase centering in the ministry of Jesus. . . . Jesus came to see the necessity of his Passion as the finally effective means for the overthrow of the evil powers" (Wilder, *Eschatology and Ethics,* p. 192).

[30]Thus both Luke and John depict Judas as betraying Jesus under the influence of Satan (Jn 6:70; 13:27; Lk 22:3). Perrin takes this "temporary victory" to be the point of Matthew 11:12 (*Kingdom of God,* p. 173).

[31]Beasley-Murray, *Jesus and the Kingdom of God,* p. 326.

[32]Forsyth, *Old Enemy,* p. 250. R. H. Gundry combines an astronomical and a cosmic interpretation: "The falling of the stars refers to a shower of meteorites, and the shaking of the heavenly powers to God's displacing 'the spiritual forces of wicked-ness in the heavenly places' (Eph 6:12)" (*Matthew: A Commentary on His Literary and Theological Art* [Grand Rapids, Mich.: Eerdmans, 1982], p. 487). See also idem, *Mark: A Commentary on His Apology for the Cross* (Grand Rapids, Mich.: Eerdmans, 1993), pp. 782-83; F. W. Beare, *The Gospel According to Matthew* (San Francisco: Harper & Row, 1981), p. 471.

[33]Unlike depictions of demonization in the Synoptics, this case of demonization is by Satan, not demons, and it is portrayed as a moral issue. That is, Judas, unlike other demonized people, is portrayed as being himself evil (Jn 17:12). Also unlike other cases of demonization, this case of Satanic possession leads to no abnormal animal-like behavior: it simply leads to evil action. The "prince of demons," it seems, is far more sophisticated than the demons he rules over, which perhaps also explains why Jesus engages in a prolonged intelligent conversation with Satan in the Gospels (Mt 4:1-11; Lk 4:1-13), while his conversations with demons are only to get information and to then command them to leave. On this see J. Ramsey Michaels,

"Jesus and the Unclean Spirits," in *Demon Possession*, ed. J. W. Montgomery (Minneapolis: Bethany, 1976), p. 56. On Judas as a proto-antichrist figure in John, see W. E. Sproston, "Satan in the Fourth Gospel," in *Studia Biblica 1978*, vol. 2, *Papers on the Gospels*, ed. E. A. Livingstone, JSNTSup 2 (Sheffield: University of Sheffield Press, 1979), pp. 307-11.

[34]Ling is likely correct when he argues that John omits all exorcisms because he wishes to direct "the reader's attention away from . . . the diverse activities of demons, away from what may be called the local subsidiary manifestations of evil in disease or madness or epilepsy. . . . to the real source of such evils, the Devil" (*Significance of Satan*, p. 31). John is certainly not unaware of demonization, for he records Jesus' opponents as accusing Jesus of being demonized (Jn 7:20; 8:48-52; 10:20-21). His understanding of demonization, so far as is discernible, is parallel to that of the Synoptics. So argues J. C. Coetzee, "Christ and the Prince of this World in the Gospel and the Epistles of St. John," in *The Christ of John: Essays on the Christology of the Fourth Gospel*, ed. A. B. du Toit, Neotestamentica 2 (Potchefstroom, South Africa: SASSNT, 1971), pp. 104-21.

[35]J. L. Kovacs, " 'Now Shall the Ruler of This World Be Driven Out': Death as Cosmic Battle in John 12:20-36," *JBL* 114 (1995): 233. The dualism of John, and even much of his terminology, is strongly reminiscent of (but not identical with) the Qumran community. See J. H. Charlesworth, "A Critical Comparison of the Dualism in IQS 3:13-4:26 and the 'Dualism' in the Gospel of John," *NTS* 15 (1968-69): 389-418, reprinted in *John and the Dead Sea Scrolls*, ed. Charlesworth (New York: Crossroad, 1990), pp. 76-106; R. E. Brown, "The Qumran Scrolls and the Johannine Gospel and Epistles," in *The Scrolls and the New Testament*, ed. K. Stendahl (New York: Harper, 1957), pp. 183-207.

[36]Coetzee, "Christ and the Prince," p. 106. For a recent excellent exposition on the centrality of the cosmic warfare motif in John's Gospel, particularly with regard to the understanding of Jesus' death, see Kovacs, "Now Shall the Ruler," pp. 227-47.

[37]As is universally conceded, we have in John much more of a paraphrase of Jesus' teachings than we have in the Synoptics. Hence it is not always clear where Jesus' teachings end and John's commentary on Jesus' teaching begins. Since for the purposes of this work I am operating from the presupposition of canonical authority, this relative difference has no theological import. In other words, since I regard John's portrait of Jesus to be divinely inspired, I have no theological interest in attempting to get behind this portrait to discover the "actual words" of Jesus. I am, then, content to speak of John's portrayal of Jesus.

[38]With the discovery of the Dead Sea Scrolls came the realization that such apparently "dualistic" language would have been quite at home within the context of first-century Jewish monotheism. It does not (pace Bultmann et al.) reflect a Gnostic influence, as Kovacs effectively argues ("Now Shall the Ruler," pp. 235-46). On the significance of the Dead Sea Scrolls for undermining the previous overly Hellenistic estimation of John, see J. C. VanderKam, "The Dead Sea Scrolls and Christianity," in *Understanding the Dead Sea Scrolls: A Reader from the Biblical Archaeology Review*, ed. H. Shanks (New York: Random House, 1992), p. 200. On the use of the "light/darkness" contrast and other expressions of a cosmic-ethical dualism in the Scrolls and John's Gospel, see J. L. Price, "Light from Qumran upon Some Aspects of Johannine Theology," in *John and the Dead Sea Scrolls*, ed. Charlesworth, pp. 18-25; Charlesworth, "Critical Comparison of Dualism"; idem, "Qumran, John and the Odes of Solomon," in *John and the Dead Sea Scrolls*, pp.

107-36; Brown, "Qumran Scrolls and the Johannine Gospel," pp. 184-95. For several discussions concerning the important issues surrounding the variety of "dualism" and the specific forms that existed in ancient Judaism as a background for contextualizing John's Gospel, see J. Gammie, "Spatial and Ethical Dualism in Jewish Wisdom and Apocalyptic Literature," *JBL* 93 (1974): 356-85; B. Otzen, "Old Testament Wisdom Literature and Dualistic Thinking in Late Judaism," *Congress Volume*, Edinburgh 1974, ed. J. A. Emerton, VTSup 28 (Leiden: Brill, 1975), pp. 146-57. With A. T. Hanson, I would argue that the principal influence on John's worldview is the Old Testament. See his *Prophetic Gospel: A Study of John and the Old Testament* (Edinburgh: Clark, 1991), though Hanson's negative assessments of John's historicity are not necessary to his thesis, nor (I would argue) are they implied by the available evidence.

[39] See J. B. Russell, *The Devil: Perceptions of Evil from Antiquity to Primitive Christianity* (Ithaca: Cornell University Press, 1977), p. 236; Pagels, *Origin of Satan*, p. 99. Raymond Brown is certainly correct in seeing the whole of Jesus' ministry in John as a struggle with Satan that culminates in the crucifixion. See his *Gospel According to John*, 2 vols., AB 29-29A (Garden City, N.Y.: Doubleday, 1966-1970), 1:364-76. Kovacs ("Now Shall the Ruler") makes a plausible suggestion when she argues that 1:5 refers both to the general cosmic struggle and, more specifically, to the cross, where "the forces of darkness" attempt to "extinguish the light" in a more particular, and climactic, manner (p. 231).

The nature of the warfare thematically introduced with this verse is significantly qualified and compromised, however, if *katalambanō* is translated "understood" (as in the NIV) as opposed to "overcome." The former suggests a cognitive difficulty on the part of humans confronting Jesus, whereas the latter taps more profoundly into the comprehensive cosmic warfare tradition of Scripture. There are at least five arguments against this translation of *katalambanō* in this context that can be briefly mentioned.

First, the root meaning of the word is to "grasp," "seize," "overcome" or "overtake." While one application of the word can be to express an intellectual grasping (viz. "understanding"), there is nothing in the context to recommend limiting the word to this application here. Second, parallels with the Dead Sea Scrolls suggest that John has in mind a more encompassing warfare conflict with his contrast between light and darkness than the word "understands" allows for. As James VanderKam has convincingly argued, in the light of the Dead Sea Scrolls, *katalambanō* should be translated "overcome" ("Dead Sea Scrolls and Christianity," p. 200). Parallels with other extracanonical literature (e.g., *Odes of Solomon* 18:6; Wisdom of Solomon 7:29-30) suggest the same.

Third, translating *katalambanō* as "overtakes" or "overcomes" is the meaning most strongly supported by the early fathers. Fourth, though verse 10 notes that the world "did not know him," nothing in the text itself supports restricting the verb *katalambanō* in verse 5 to the meaning of the verb *ginōskō* in verse 10 (against, e.g., G. R. Beasley-Murray, *John*, WBC 36 [Waco, Tex.: Word, 1987], p. 11). Verse 10 perhaps describes one illustration of how darkness seeks to encompass the light in verse 5, but there is no grounds for thinking that it exhausts the meaning of this conflict.

And fifth, the NIV itself translates *katalambanō* as "overtakes" in a verse that reads almost like a commentary on John 1:5. In John 12:35 (NIV) Jesus tells his disciples, "You are going to have the light [Jesus himself] just a little while longer. Walk while you have the light, before darkness overtakes you." Now, it is virtually impossible to intelligibly give *katalambanō* the meaning of "understand" in this verse. But this forces the question of why it should be translated in its narrower meaning in 1:5.

For these and other reasons, many scholars argue that verse 5 should be understood to be referring to the attempt of demonic forces of darkness to extinguish ("overtake") the light of God. Among those who concur with this reading are Brown, *John*, 1:7-8; L. Morris, *The Gospel of John*, rev. ed., NICNT (Grand Rapids, Mich.: Eerdmans, 1995), pp. 75-77; M. C. Tenney, "The Gospel of John," in *EBC*, 9:29-30.

[40]See König's insightful exposition on the light/darkness conflict that draws heavily on passages rooting in Genesis 1 (*New and Greater Things*, pp. 92-94). John 1:5 provides "a brief resume of the conflict as well as the victory of light over darkness, a conflict that rages from creation until the advent of the new earth" (p. 94).

[41]John 9:4-5, which speaks of the night overtaking the day in reference to Jesus' coming crucifixion, is also relevant here. The issue, again, is not one of understanding but of overcoming. Darkness overcomes the light of day when Jesus is crucified (cf. 12:34-36). Until then, light overcomes the darkness; hence John has Jesus heal a blind man in the three verses preceding this teaching (9:1-3). Read as a conflict résumé of Jesus' ministry, John 1:5 functions as a commentary on the Synoptics as well, as König argues. For here, as in John (but with different terminology), "Jesus expels the evil powers from creation, from nature, and from human beings, in order to set creation free from their menace" (König, *New and Greater Things*, p. 94).

[42]Coetzee, "Christ and the Prince," p. 106; C. Arnold, *Powers of Darkness: Principalities and Powers in Paul's Letters* (Downers Grove, Ill.: InterVarsity Press, 1992), pp. 80-81. See G. Delling, "ἄρχων," *TDNT*, 1:488-89. For an overview of the concept of "the prince of the world" in Judaism (where it is a positive figure) and Christianity (where it is a negative figure), see A. F. Segal, "Ruler of This World: Attitudes about Mediator Figures and the Importance of Sociology for Self-Definition," in *Jewish and Christian Self-Definition*, vol. 2, *Aspects of Judaism in the Greco-Roman Period*, ed. E. P. Sanders, A. I. Baumgarten and A. Mendelson (Philadelphia: Fortress, 1981), pp. 245-68. Like Pagels (*Origin of Satan*), Segal argues that the Christian identification of "the prince of the world" with Satan arose out of their polemic against the Jews whom they identified as children of the devil.

[43]On the harmony of John's view of Satan and the views espoused throughout the remainder of the New Testament, see Coetzee, "Christ and the Prince," pp. 105-6, 109-10.

[44]Kovacs, "Now Shall the Ruler," p. 231 and passim.

[45]Ibid., p. 233. See R. Bultmann's seminal article "Die Bedeutung der neuerscholossenen mandäischen und manischäischen Quellen für das Verständnis des Johannesevangeliums," *ZNW* 24 (1925): 100-146. For a list and discussion of other works that lean heavily on the Gnostic influence theory, see D. Moody Smith, "Johannine Studies," in *The New Testament and Its Modern Interpreters*, ed. E. Epp and G. MacRae (Atlanta: Scholars Press, 1989), p. 278. Pagels has demonstrated that the influence flowed from John to Gnostics more than the other way around. See her *Johannine Gospel in Gnostic Exegesis* (Nashville: Abingdon, 1973).

[46]Note that while the Word was with God "*in* the beginning," the devil has been a murderer "*from* the beginning" (Jn 1:1; 8:44). Coetzee is on the mark in empha-

sizing this distinction ("Christ and the Prince," p. 111). When exactly this "beginning" of evil occurs we are not told. But the only view that is consistent with the rest of the New Testament, as well as with the intrinsic logic of monotheism, is to understand it as referring to Satan's original fall.

[47]Ling argues that Jesus' perfect obedience to the Father is in principle the dethronement of the devil (*Significance of Satan*, pp. 35-36).

[48]On John's view of Christ's death as the means of defeating the devil, see Beasley-Murray, *John*, pp. 218-19; and Brown, *John*, 1:477-78. Kovacs ("Now Shall the Ruler") makes a strong case that the driving out of the devil (not substitutionary sacrifice) was the central meaning of Christ's death for John. As such, John (as well as Paul) is a predecessor to the Christus Victor motif of the early church (see chapter nine below). R. Recker has attempted to do away with the "already/not yet" tension of Satan's dethronement, and thereby to argue that Satan is no longer prince of this world. See his "Satan: In Power or Dethroned?" *CTJ* 6 (1971): 133-55. As we shall see, however, all the disciples and the early postapostolic church work with the ongoing assumption that the victory that Christ has indeed won has yet to be manifested throughout the world. The war has been won, but there are battles yet to fight.

[49]Delling, "ἄρχων," *TDNT*, 1:489. Delling says that John stretches the tension between the Father and Satan "to the point of almost a transitory dualism." Noting that the dualism is "transitory" is, in my estimation, sufficient qualification.

[50]The cross, says Kovacs, is "the locus of a cosmic battle, in which Jesus achieves a decisive victory over Satan" ("Now Shall the Ruler," p. 246).

[51]On the importance and meaning of the "from above/from below" contrast in John and its transitory dualistic implications, see Charlesworth, "Critical Comparison of Dualism," pp. 89-90; Price, "Light from Qumran," p. 19. This contrast in John has been likened to the more typical contrast in Jewish eschatology between "this present evil age" and "the age to come," a motif mentioned by Paul (Gal 1:4). Conceptually speaking, either John has substituted the more common linear contrast for a vertical/spatial one, or he has merely combined them.

[52]This use of *kosmos* occurs elsewhere in the New Testament (e.g., Mt 18:7; 1 Cor 1:20; 3:19; 2 Pet 2:20) and is close to Paul's concept of "the present evil age" (Gal 1:4; 2 Cor 4:4; cf. 1 Cor 2:6, 8; 3:18). Its contrast with the common Hellenistic philosophical use of *kosmos* to denote order and beauty should be noted. For references, see BAGD, pp. 445-47. The pejorative use of *kosmos* should perhaps be better translated "domination system," as suggested by W. Wink, *Engaging the Powers: Discernment and Resistance in an Age of Domination* (Minneapolis: Fortress, 1992), pp. 51-52, as well as by J. Porffirio *Miranda, Being and the Messiah* (Maryknoll, N.Y.: Orbis, 1977), pp. 101-2. Ling argues that this use of "the world" in John is closely correlated with the devil himself, to the point where "the devil is . . . the world's corporate personality" (*Significance of Satan*, p. 34). Hence John parallels "the world" and "the devil" (ibid., pp. 32-34). On the semidualistic implications of this pejorative use of *kosmos*, see Charlesworth, "Critical Comparison of Dualism," pp. 89-92; Price, "Light from Qumran," pp. 18-23.

[53]Arnold captures the striking limited dualism of John well when he states that for John, "there are only two masters—God and Satan" (*Powers of Darkness*, p. 81). He finds the same sort of thought behind Matthew 13:24-30, 36-43. Wingren captures the connection between faith and unbelief on the one hand and being from God or from the devil on the other when he writes concerning the act of preaching:

"The Word is a decisive act of war, an onslaught on the demonic powers in the world of men, an onslaught against our old man himself. . . . Faith is man when he breaks free from the control of what is alien to him. . . . Unbelief is the Satanic act of war, an onslaught against the work of release, a diabolical attempt to hold man within the prison camps" (*Living Word,* p. 117).

[54]D. A. Carson, *The Gospel of John* (Grand Rapids, Mich.: Eerdmans, 1991), p. 362.

[55]J. Calvin, *The Gospel According to St. John,* trans. T. H. L. Parker, 2 vols. (Grand Rapids, Mich.: Eerdmans, 1959), 1:239.

[56]J. M. Boice, *The Gospel of John: An Expositional Commentary, John 9:1—12:50* (Grand Rapids, Mich.: Zondervan, 1977), pp. 25-26.

[57]On Exodus 4:11, which is also frequently used to ground an omni-causal view of God, see chapter five, note 25.

[58]If we are speaking about an omnicontrolling God who insures that his purposes are meticulously carried out, as the classical-philosophical tradition has held, the distinction between "created" and "allowed" amounts to very little.

[59]Among the other passages that likely use *hina* in this sense are Mark 12:15-19; 14:49; John 13:34; 1 Corinthians 5:2; 14:1; 16:15; 2 Corinthians 13:17; Colossians 2:4; Titus 3:13; Revelation 14:13. See M. Zerwick, *Biblical Greek,* trans. J. Smith (Rome: Pontificio Instituto Biblico, 1963), pp. 141-42, for a discussion favoring this translation. See also C. F. D. Moule, *An Idiom-Book of New Testament Greek,* 2d ed. (Cambridge: Cambridge University Press, 1975), pp. 144-45; and esp. N. Turner's comments in *Grammatical Insights into the New Testament* (Edinburgh: T & T Clark, 1965), pp. 145ff. Carson argues that taking *hina* as an imperative clause here is "just barely possible" and "rendered highly unlikely by the parallel in 11:4" (*Gospel of John,* p. 362). Carson does not spell out his grammatical grounds for judging this reading as "barely possible." But in any case his argument from the parallel in 11:4 is not strong. For one thing, Jesus explicitly states in 11:4 that Lazarus's death was "for God's glory," and only then does he add, "so that God's Son may be glorified" (using *hina* with the aorist passive *doxasthē*). The preceding statement requires that *hina* be taken in a purposive (not imperative) sense. But just this is lacking in 9:3. Exegetes who take *hina* here as a purpose or result clause must assume that Jesus meant simply to modify (not reject altogether) the disciples' misleading question, and hence (as in NIV) must assume that "this happened so that" is implied in *hina.* They must assume, in other words, that Jesus thought the disciples were *right* in looking for a purpose but simply wrong in the purpose they found. But the text certainly does not require this reading. Another relevant point is that in 11:4 Jesus is explaining why he is not going to respond immediately to Lazarus's sickness and the request of his sisters for him to come (11:6; cf. 21). He is not talking about death as such, only about why he allowed Lazarus to die when he could have prevented it. We cannot, therefore, draw conclusions from this passage about Jesus' general view of how death figures into God's providence, and we certainly cannot use it to draw conclusions about Jesus' general view of how blindness figures into God's providence on the basis of how this passage (supposedly) parallels 9:3.

[60]Turner, *Grammatical Insights,* p. 145. As Turner notes (pp. 147-48), this reading also frees us from seeing Judas as fatalistically damned "in order to" fulfill Scripture in John 13:18.

[61]The fact that God can, and sometimes does, use diseases, persecutions and natural disasters to chastise people is assumed throughout the Bible (e.g., the plagues, Ex

7—12; cf. Acts 8:1ff.; Rom 8:28; 2 Cor 12:7-10), and thus we have every reason to assume that Jesus would have believed such. But the force of his teaching here, combined with his general attitude toward evil reflected throughout the Gospels, is to say that one cannot generalize this point into a universal explanation for evil. Most traditional theodicies, unfortunately, are fundamentally rooted in just this misguided generalization.

⁶²That John here speaks of a man being delivered from physical darkness is hardly coincidental in the light of this teaching. As we have seen, Jesus' whole ministry, for John, was about delivering people from darkness. The healing of this man's physical blindness thus functions as a symbol of Jesus' vanquishing of darkness in general. It illustrates the truth of John 1:4-5; 3:19-21; 8:12; 12:35, 46; cf. 11:9-10. See Brown, *John*, 1:379.

⁶³K. Heim, *Jesus the World's Perfecter*, trans. D. H. van Daalen (Edinburgh: Oliver & Boyd, 1959), p. 38.

⁶⁴H. Pendley, "Views of the Demonic in Recent Religious Thought" (Ph.D. diss., Southern Baptist Theological Seminary, 1976), p. 38.

⁶⁵This is certainly not to suggest that God cannot, at times, use Satan's evil intentions, as he clearly does in the crucifixion (1 Cor 2:8) and as he shall in bringing judgment upon the world in the last days (see 2 Thess 3, "delusional spirit"; Rev 9). This follows the pattern of God using evil beings to his own end in the Old Testament (1 Sam 16:14, 22; 18:10-11; 19:9-10; 1 Kings 22:21-23). But to say that God can occasionally use Satan and demons to his own end is very different from saying that God ordains the activity of Satan and demons as a means to his own end. The Bible affirms the former, but never the latter.

Chapter 9: Christus Victor
¹For the classic representative statement of the substitutionary view of the atonement—viz., Anselm's "satisfaction" theory—see *Cur Deus Homo* 22.1. Reformed Protestant thought eventually developed the "penal substitutionary" version of this general approach. For more recent statements in this vein, see L. Morris, *The Apostolic Preaching of the Cross* (Grand Rapids, Mich.: Eerdmans, 1956); idem, *The Atonement: Its Meaning and Significance* (Downers Grove, Ill.: InterVarsity Press, 1983); M. J. Erickson, "The Central Theme of Atonement," in his *Christian Theology*, 3 vols. (Grand Rapids, Mich.: Baker, 1983-1985), 2:802-23; P. Patterson, "Reflections on the Atonement," *Criswell Theological Review* 3 (1989): 307-20; and, in my estimation the best expression of this perspective to date, J. R. W. Stott, *The Cross of Christ* (Downers Grove, Ill.: InterVarsity Press, 1986).

²I am speaking here of a logical priority and emphasis, not a chronological one. In dethroning Satan as ruler of this world, Jesus—the faithful, fully human Son of God—was, at the very same time, saving humanity and reinstating it to its original position as ruler-steward over the earth.

³MacGregor, "Principalities and Powers: The Cosmic Background of Paul's Thought," *NTS* 1 (1954): 23. Similarly, J. Y. Lee demonstrates that in Paul's cosmology, "Jesus was depicted as the Redeemer who came from heaven and died on the cross to rescue not only men but the whole cosmos from thraldom to demonic powers" ("Interpreting the Demonic Powers in Pauline Thought," *NovT* 12, no. 1 [1970]: 67).

⁴As I shall argue in *Satan and the Problem of Evil*, this "Christus Victor" motif encapsulates what was the ruling paradigm for understanding the atoning work of

Jesus throughout the first millennium of church history. It has been recovered in our century primarily through the impetus of the landmark work of G. Aulen, *Christus Victor: A Historical Study of the Three Main Types of the Idea of Atonement*, trans. A. G. Hebert (New York: Macmillan, 1969). Other scholars who have emphasized this approach to the atonement include S. Cave, *The Doctrine of the Work of Christ* (Nashville: Cokesbury, 1937); Karl Heim, *Jesus the Lord* (London: Oliver & Boyd, 1959); idem, *Jesus the World's Perfecter: The Atonement and the Renewal of the World*, trans. D. H. Van Daalen (Edinburgh: Oliver & Boyd, 1959); N. Micklem, *The Doctrine of Our Redemption* (London: Eyre and Spottiswoode, 1943); R. Leivestad, *Christ the Conqueror: Ideas of Conflict and Victory in the New Testament* (New York: Macmillan, 1954); J. S. Whale, *Victor and Victim* (Cambridge: Cambridge University Press, 1960); T. Finger, *Christian Theology: An Eschatological Approach*, 2 vols. (Nashville: Nelson, 1985), 1:303-48; J. Macquarrie, "Demonology and the Classical Idea of the Atonement," *ExpTim* 68 (1956): 3-6, 60-63; D. G. Reid, "The Christus Victor Motif in Paul's Theology" (Ph.D. diss., Fuller Theological Seminary, 1982). The original centrality and later decline of the "Christ the victor" theme in the early church has been recently traced by R. A. Greer, "Christ the Victor and the Victim," *Concordia Theological Quarterly* 59, nos. 1-2 (1995): 1-30. It should be noted that the Christus Victor understanding of the atonement has been gaining in acceptance in recent times and has been emphasized even by those who understand the cross primarily in substitutionary terms. See, e.g., A. McGrath, *Understanding Jesus: Who Jesus Christ Is and Why He Matters* (Grand Rapids, Mich.: Zondervan, 1987), pp. 151-60; Stott, *Cross of Christ*, pp. 227-81. R. E. Webber can thus speak of a "new theological consensus" involving the restoration of the Christus Victor motif that amounts to "a rediscovered emphasis of the lordship of Christ, of His reign over the powers, over the whole of creation, and over history" (*The Church in the World: Opposition, Tension or Transformation?* [Grand Rapids, Mich.: Zondervan, 1986], p. 267).

[5]On the LXX, see R. A. Martin, "The Earliest Messianic Interpretation of Genesis 3:15," *JBL* 84 (1965): 425-27. On rabbinic use of the passage, see M. McNamara, *The New Testament and the Palestinian Targum to the Pentateuch*, AnBib 27 (Rome: Pontifical Biblical Institute, 1966), pp. 217-22; G. J. Wenham, *Genesis 1—15*, WBC 1 (Waco, Tex.: Word, 1987), p. 80.

[6]See Wenham, *Genesis 1—15*, pp. 80-81; T. Gallus, *Die "Frau" in Gen. 3:15* (Klagenfurt: Carinthia, 1979). For recent defenses of the messianic interpretation of Genesis 3:15, against the traditional historical-critical view that we are dealing here merely with an etiological tale (see chapter four above), see G. Van Groningen, *Messianic Revelation in the Old Testament* (Grand Rapids, Mich.: Baker, 1990), pp. 106-15; W. Kaiser, *The Messiah in the Old Testament* (Grand Rapids, Mich.: Zondervan, 1996), pp. 36-42.

[7]Writing from within the "already/not yet" tension of the New Testament, Paul could apply this verse to the victory believers will ultimately have in our battle with Satan as well. Hence he tells the Roman Christians: "The God of peace will soon crush Satan under your feet" (Rom 16:20). What has in principle already occurred on Calvary will in fact occur in our experience: God will crush Satan, and as we stand "in Christ" this crushing will be underneath *our* feet (Eph 1:19-22).

[8]See Matthew 22:41-45; Mark 12:35-37; Luke 20:41-44; Acts 2:34-36; Hebrews 1:13; 5:6, 10; 6:20; 7:11, 15, 17, 21. Other passages that show varying degrees of influence from Psalm 110 include Matthew 26:64; Mark 14:62; [16:19]; Luke 22:69; Acts 5:31;

7:55-56; Romans 8:34; 1 Corinthians 15:25; Ephesians 1:20; Colossians 3:1; Hebrews 1:3; 8:1; 10:12-13; 1 Peter 3:22; Revelation 3:21. It is also prevalent among early extracanonical writings as well, such as *1 Clement* 36:5 and *Barnabas* 12:10.

[9]Whereas the "enemies" originally referred to in Psalm 110:1 were undoubtedly human political opponents, there is evidence of a very early (pre-Pauline) tradition that applied Psalm 110 to Christ's victory over his foes, among whom are counted Satan and the demons, "angelic" powers, as well as wicked humans. For an unsurpassed, comprehensive and insightful exposition on the use of this verse in the New Testament, see D. M. Hay, *Glory at the Right Hand: Psalm 110 in Early Christianity* (Nashville: Abingdon, 1973), esp. pp. 122-29. Other helpful works include W. R. G. Loader, "Christ at the Right Hand—Ps. 110:1 in the New Testament," *NTS* 24 (1978): 208-13; O. Cullmann, *The Christology of the New Testament*, trans. S. C. Guthrie and C. A. M. Hall, rev. ed. (Philadelphia: Fortress, 1963), pp. 222-24. B. A. Stevens argues, with some force, that the Old Testament's divine warrior motif holds the key to understanding Jesus' messianic self-consciousness (see "Jesus as the Divine Warrior," *ExpTim* 94 [1982-1983]: 326-29). On the broader messianic use of Psalm 110:1 in early Christianity, see D. E. Aune, "Christian Prophecy and the Messianic Status of Jesus," in *The Messiah: Developments in Earliest Judaism and Christianity*, ed. J. H. Charlesworth et al. (Minneapolis: Fortress, 1992), pp. 404-22; D. Juel, "Christ at the Right Hand: The Use of Psalm 110 in the New Testament," in his *Messianic Exegesis: Christological Interpretation of the Old Testament in Early Christianity* (Philadelphia: Fortress, 1988), pp. 135-50; Van Groningen, *Messianic Revelation*, pp. 390-97.

[10]Hay, *Glory at the Right Hand*, p. 124.

[11]Note that Paul says the hostile powers will be "destroyed" (*katargeō*). Partly owing to his pacifistic convictions, partly to his denial that "the powers" have an autonomous existence and can autonomously will over and against human beings and social groups, Wink holds that all the powers will ultimately be redeemed. See his *Engaging the Powers: Discernment and Resistance in a World of Domination* (Minneapolis: Fortress, 1992). This position, I shall later argue, is not supported in Scripture.

[12]O. Cullmann, *Christ and Time*, rev. ed., trans. F. V. Wilson (London: SCM, 1962), p. 193.

[13]Hence, speaking eschatologically, Susan Garrett writes: "When Jesus ascends to take his seat at the right hand of God—the place traditionally occupied by Satan [see Zech 3:1]—Satan will fall to earth. . . . Jesus will receive the worship that Satan had wrongfully requested [Lk 4:7; 24:52]. It will only be a matter of time until God will put all things in subjection under Jesus' feet" ("Exodus from Bondage: Luke 9:31 and Acts 12:1-24," *CBQ* 52 [1990]: 669).

[14]Paul's closing reference to "any other creature" clearly entails that he was referring to some sort of demonic beings even with his reference to "height and depth." A solid case can be made that he was referring to well-known astrological deities whom Paul saw as demonic. On this see J. D. G. Dunn, *Romans 1—8*, WBC 38A (Waco, Tex.: Word, 1988), p. 513.

[15]Indeed, Jesus is throughout the New Testament called "Lord" for just this reason. He is Lord over all things, including his enemies, "the powers." All who freely accept his lordship are therefore themselves freed from the tyranny of these powers. Though he does not explicitly refer to Psalm 110, Wingren forcefully expresses the

same conviction: "The New Testament *kerygma* is news of victory in the conflict that is the theme of the Bible as a whole. To say that Christ is Lord of all the Biblical writings is just another way of saying that he is victor in the war that the different writings describe in various ways" (*The Living Word: A Theological Study of Preaching and the Church,* trans. V. Prague [Philadelphia: Muhlenberg, 1960 (1949)], pp. 50-51).

[16]The issues surrounding this controversial passage shall be discussed below.

[17]Heim, *Jesus the World's Perfecter,* p. 70.

[18]Since J. D. G. Dunn's work *Christology in the Making: A New Testament Inquiry into the Origins of the Doctrine of the Incarnation* (Philadelphia: Westminster, 1980), some scholars have questioned the traditional understanding of Philippians 2:5-11 as reflecting a pre-Pauline belief in Jesus' preexistence. N. T. Wright has effectively demonstrated, however, that even for one who grants an Adam Christology, this passage nonetheless entails a concept of Christ's preexistence and a strong claim in regard to his divinity. See his "Adam in Pauline Christology," SBLSP, 1983, ed. K. H. Richards (Chico, Calif.: Scholars Press, 1983), pp. 359-89; idem, "Jesus Christ Is Lord: Philippians 2:5-11," in his *Climax of the Covenant: Christ and the Law in Pauline Theology* (Edinburgh: T & T Clark, 1991), pp. 56-98. But a number of scholars dispute the claim of an Adam Christology in this passage. See, e.g., I. H. Marshall's review of Dunn's book in *TJ* 2, no. 2 (1981): 241-45; T. F. Glasson, "Two Notes on the Philippians Hymn (2:6-11)," *NTS* 21, no. 1 (1974): 137-39; M. Erickson, *The Word Became Flesh: A Contemporary Incarnational Christology* (Grand Rapids, Mich.: Baker, 1991), pp. 475-79; and, on a popular level, my *Oneness Pentecostals and the Trinity* (Grand Rapids, Mich.: Baker, 1992), pp. 106-8.

[19]The case against a universalistic reading of the New Testament is quite solid, to the point where the majority of New Testament scholars regard the issue as closed. See W. V. Crockett, "Universalism and the Theology of Paul" (Ph.D. diss., University of Glasgow, 1986); idem, "Will God Save Everyone in the End?" in *Through No Fault of Their Own: The Fate of Those Who Have Never Heard,* ed. W. V. Crockett and J. G. Sigountos (Grand Rapids, Mich.: Baker, 1991), pp. 159-66; J. Sanders, *No Other Name: An Investigation into the Destiny of the Unevangelized* (Grand Rapids: Eerdmans, 1992), pp. 81-128; N. T. Wright, "Towards a Biblical View of Universalism," *Themelios* 4 (1979): 54-58.

[20]R. P. Roth, "Christ and the Powers of Darkness: Lessons from Colossians," *Word and World* 6, no. 3 (1986): 341.

[21]Heim, *Jesus the World's Perfecter,* p. 72.

[22]On Paul's concept of "the heavenlies," see A. T. Lincoln, "A Re-examination of 'the Heavenlies' in Ephesians," *NTS* 19 (1973): 468-83. For a helpful study that highlights the cosmic/heavenly dimension of Paul's understanding of salvation, see A. T. Lincoln, *Paradise Now and Not Yet: Studies in the Role of the Heavenly Dimension in Paul's Thought with Special Reference to His Eschatology,* SNTSMS 43 (Cambridge: Cambridge University Press, 1981).

[23]Donald Guthrie explains the warfare significance of this verse well when he notes that the "old" and the "new" here refer to "the death of the old creation dominated by adverse spiritual forces, and the emergence of the new creation in which everything is Christ-centered" (*New Testament Theology* [Downers Grove, Ill.: InterVarsity Press, 1981], p. 648).

[24]Commenting on this verse from a contemporary African context (a context of which talk of demonic powers is part and parcel), B. Abijole writes, "For Paul,

Christ's ministry of reconciliation is not confined in its scope to humanity, it is cosmic. . . . By the death of Christ the powers lost all the control they ever had on man" ("St. Paul's Concept of Principalities and Powers in African Context," *Africa Theological Journal* 17, no. 2 [1988]: 125-26).

[25]Wink takes Ephesians 3:10 to be a mandate to preach to the powers, which he takes to be the "interiority" of human institutions. For example, on the basis of this text he says: "It is part of the church's task to remind corporations and businesses that profit is not the 'bottom line,' that as 'creatures' of God they have as their divine vocation the achievement of human benefaction" (Eph 3:10) (*Engaging the Powers: Discernment and Resistance in a World of Domination* [Minneapolis: Fortress, 1992], p. 68). In response, there is no precedent in the New Testament or, with the exception of Origen, in the early church for the notion that the church is to preach to the powers. Nor is it easy to understand how making known the manifold wisdom of God can be interpreted as trying to get the powers (businesses!) to change.

[26]Among the minority who argue that *archontōn* is most probably referring only to human "rulers" are W. A. Carr, "The Rulers of This Age—I Corinthians 2:6-8," *NTS* 23 (1976): 20-35; G. D. Fee, *New Testament Exegesis,* rev. ed. (Louisville, Ky.: Westminster John Knox, 1993), pp. 104-12; T. Ling, "A Note on I Corinthians ii.8," *ExpTim* 68, no. 1 (1956): 26; G. Miller, "*archontōn tou aiōnos toutou*—A New Look at I Corinthians 2:6-8," *JBL* 91 (1972): 522-28; S. H. T. Page, *Powers of Evil: A Biblical Study of Satan and Demons* (Grand Rapids, Mich.: Baker, 1995), pp. 261-62.

[27]Among those who present strong refutations of the "merely human" interpretation of this passage, see Abijole, "St. Paul's Concept of Principalities," p. 120; C. Arnold, *Ephesians, Power and Magic: The Concept of Power in Ephesians in Light of Its Historical Setting,* SNTSMS 63 (Cambridge: Cambridge University Press, 1989), pp. 63-64; idem, *Powers of Darkness: Principalities and Powers in Paul's Letters* (Downers Grove, Ill.: InterVarsity Press, 1992), pp. 101-4; F. L. Arrington, *Paul's Aeon Theology in I Corinthians* (Washington, D.C.: University Press of America, 1978), p. 136, note 51; C. K. Barrett, *The First Epistle to the Corinthians,* 2d ed. (London: Black, 1971); P. Benoit, "Pauline Angelology and Demonology: Reflections on the Designations of the Heavenly Powers and on the Origin of Angelic Evil According to Paul," *Religious Studies Bulletin* 3, no. 1 (1983): 11-12; F. F. Bruce, "Paul and 'the Powers that Be,' " *BJRL* 66, no. 2 (1984): 85; G. B. Caird, *Principalities and Powers: A Study in Pauline Theology* (Oxford: Clarendon, 1956), pp. 16-17; O. Cullmann, *The State in the New Testament* (New York: Scribner's, 1956), p. 64; M. Dibelius, *Die Geisterwelt im Glauben des Paulus* (Göttingen: Vandenhoeck & Ruprecht, 1909), p. 90; J. J. Gunther, *St. Paul's Opponents and Their Background: A Study of Apocalyptic and Jewish Sectarian Teachings,* NovTSup 35 (Leiden: Brill, 1973), p. 181; A. J. Hultgren, *Christ and His Benefits: Christology and Redemption in the New Testament* (Philadelphia: Fortress, 1987), pp. 93-94; W. G. Kümmel, *The Theology of the New Testament,* trans. J. E. Steely (Nashville: Abingdon, 1973), p. 187; Lee, "Interpreting the Demonic Powers," p. 58; MacGregor, "Principalities and Powers," pp. 22-23; Webber, *Church in the World,* pp. 287, 306, note 6; W. Wink, *Naming the Powers* (Philadelphia: Fortress, 1984), pp. 40-45.

[28]Ignatius, Tertullian, Origen and Theodore of Mopsuestia are among those who illustrate this usage. See Benoit, "Pauline Angelology and Demonology," pp. 8-11;

T. Longman III and D. G. Reid, *God Is a Warrior* (Grand Rapids, Mich.: Zondervan, 1995), pp. 152-53.

[29]For example, Lee argues, "To interpret 'the rulers of this age' as angelic powers which stand behind the state is truly Judaic apocalyptic expression of the cosmic powers" ("Interpreting the Demonic Powers," p. 58).

[30]H. Conzelmann, *I Corinthians*, trans. J. W. Leitch, Hermeneia (Philadelphia: Fortress, 1975), p. 61. See also D. G. Reid, "Principalities and Powers," *Dictionary of Paul and His Letters*, ed. G. F. Hawthorne, R. P. Martin and D. G. Reid (Downers Grove, Ill.: InterVarsity Press, 1993), p. 748.

[31]H. Thielicke expresses the point well: "*we* are not the fighters" in the war for our salvation. Rather, "we are the battlefield rather than the heroes in the army. The fight is for us" (Thielicke, *Man in God's World*, trans. J. W. Doberstein [New York: Harper & Row, 1963], p. 176). This much-neglected work expresses a good deal of insight on the warfare situation of humanity on the earth. On the centrality of the cosmic battle against Satan in John's understanding of Jesus' death, see J. L. Kovacs, " 'Now Shall the Ruler of This World Be Driven Out': Jesus' Death as Cosmic Battle in John 12:20-36," *JBL* 114 (1995): 227-47. See also Longman and Reid, *God Is a Warrior*, p. 135.

[32]In arguing against the spiritual warfare movement, R. Guelich attempts to make much of the fact that the metaphor used in this passage (see also 1 Pet 5:8) is that of hunting, not warfare ("Spiritual Warfare: Jesus, Paul and Peretti," *Pneuma* 13, no. 1 (1991): 51. Hence he asks why we don't now have a movement of spiritual hunting. One could respond by noting that the warfare depiction of our ongoing struggle with Satan and his kingdom is (as we have seen) much more frequent and fundamental throughout the New Testament than is the hunting depiction. But even more fundamentally, one wonders how the point being made is relevant to the criticism Guelich intends toward the spiritual warfare movement. What would be substantially changed within the spiritual warfare movement if it were (somewhat oddly) rather called the spiritual hunting movement?

[33]Hence R. C. Tannehill argues rightly that for Paul, "everything depends on the reality of release from the powers of the old world and incorporation in a new world" (Tannehill, *Dying and Rising with Christ: A Study in Pauline Theology*, BZNW 32 [Berlin: Töpelmann, 1967], p. 71).

[34]*Sōzō* here implies that "the believer has now been saved from entrapment in the kingdom of the prince of the authority of the air," spoken of in 2:2-3 (Arnold, *Ephesians*, p. 149). See also A. T. Lincoln, "Ephesians 2:8-10: A Summary of Paul's Gospel?" *CBQ* 45 (1983): 617-30.

[35]Stott, *Cross of Christ*, p. 233. See also P. T. O'Brien, *Colossians, Philemon*, WBC 44 (Waco, Tex.: Word, 1982), pp. 124-26.

[36]J. Jeremias, *The Central Message of the New Testament* (New York: Scribner's, 1965), pp. 36-37; O'Brien, *Colossians, Philemon*, p. 126.

[37]Some have argued that Christ here strips off from himself the principalities and powers that clung to him as a factor of his taking on human flesh. See, e.g., MacGregor, "Principalities and Powers," p. 23; Lee, "Interpreting the Demonic Powers," p. 64. The warfare motif is no less forceful in this view, but it seems to me far more likely that it is the principalities and powers that are being "stripped," that God in Christ is, as O'Brien says, "utterly divesting them of their dignity and might" (*Colossians, Philemon*, p. 127). Among other things, there is simply no evidence for the notion that Christ was ever "clothed" with "the powers." For an

insightful discussion, see ibid., pp. 126-28.

[38]For a thorough discussion of the custom, see H. S. Versnel, *Triumphus: An Inquiry into the Origin, Development and Meaning of the Roman Triumph* (Leiden: Brill, 1970), esp. pp. 56-115. So too O'Brien argues that *thriambeuō* here implies "to lead as a conquered enemy in a victory parade," rather than "to triumph over them," as NRSV and NIV translate it (*Colossians, Philemon*, pp. 128-29). For a similar argument, see L. Williamson, "Led in Triumph: Paul's Use of *Thriambeuō*," *Int* 22 (1968): 317-32. Such studies conclusively refute two alternative interpretations entertained today. On the one hand, R. B. Egan argues that *thriambeuō* basically means "to reveal" ("Lexical Evidence on Two Pauline Passages," *NovT* 19 [1977]: 34-62). On the other, W. Carr argues that the powers being referred to here are not hostile powers but simply angels (*Angels and Principalities: The Background, Meaning and Development of the Pauline Phrase "hai archai kai hai exousiai,"* SNTSMS 42 [Cambridge: Cambridge University Press, 1981], pp. 61-66). So too R. Yates takes *thriambeuō* to mean that Christ "boldly made an open display of the angelic powers; leading them in triumphal (festal) procession on the cross" ("Colossians 2:15: Christ Triumphant," *NTS* 37 [1991]: 573-91, esp. 591). In my estimation, both of these alternative readings are highly improbable.

[39]This, argues Arnold, is the force of Paul's correlating the Colossians' possession of divine "fullness" with Christ's supremacy to the demonic powers (*Powers of Darkness*, p. 116).

[40]For a thorough sketch of the history of the interpretation of this passage, see C. Skrade, "The Descent of the Servant: A Study of I Peter 3:13—4:6" (Th.D. diss., Union Theological Seminary, 1966), pp. 1-144. My categorization of the differing interpretations follows somewhat that of P. H. Davids, *The First Epistle of Peter*, NICNT (Grand Rapids, Mich.: Eerdmans, 1990), pp. 138ff. A number of differently nuanced views are possible within each of these three categories (especially the third), while a number of other views combine elements of these three views.

[41]J. Calvin, *The Epistle of Paul the Apostle to the Hebrews, and the First and Second Epistles of St. Peter*, trans. W. B. Johnston, Calvin's Commentaries (Grand Rapids, Mich.: Eerdmans, 1963), pp. 292-95.

[42]See, e.g., L. Goppelt, *A Commentary on I Peter*, ed. F. Hahn, trans. J. E. Alsup (Grand Rapids, Mich.: Eerdmans, 1993), pp. 258-60. W. Grudem offers a variation on this interpretation by suggesting that the verse refers to Christ's preaching to human beings before the flood through Noah (*The First Epistle of Peter*, Tyndale New Testament Commentaries [Grand Rapids: Eerdmans, 1988], pp. 157-61, 203-39).

[43]The position has a number of variations. See W. J. Dalton, *Christ's Proclamation to the Spirits*, AnBib 23 (Rome: Pontifical Biblical Institute, 1965); J. R. Michaels, *1 Peter*, WBC 49 (Waco, Tex.: Word, 1988), pp. 194-222; idem, *Word Biblical Themes: 1 Peter* (Dallas: Word, 1989), pp. 70-77; B. Reicke, *The Disobedient Spirits and Christian Baptism: A Study of 1 Peter 3:19 and Its Context* (Copenhagen: Ejnar Munksgaard, 1946), who suggests that both human and evil angelic spirits associated with the Noachian judgment are intended; Skrade, "Descent of the Servant," pp. 261-65.

[44]Davids, *First Peter*, pp. 139-40.

[45]*First Enoch* 21:6, 10. See Davids, *First Peter*, p. 140. E. J. Goodspeed ("Some Greek Notes," *JBL* 73 [1954]: 91-92) goes so far as to suggest that the original version of this passage had Enoch carrying out the descent.

[46]I shall explore the point fully in *Satan and the Problem of Evil.*

[47]Because I see the "spirits" as nonhuman, and because I understand *kēryssō* to be proclamation instead of evangelization, I'm inclined not to agree with those who would want to find in this verse an apologetic for "postmortem evangelization." See, e.g., G. Fackre, "Divine Perseverance," in *What About Those Who Have Never Heard? Three Views on the Destiny of the Unevangelized,* ed. J. Sanders (Downers Grove, Ill.: InterVarsity Press, 1995), pp. 81-86.

[48]Even many scholars who argue against seeing Christ's descent here as a descent into "the underworld" (e.g., Hades) nevertheless find the Christus Victor theme to be the central driving force of the passage. M. Barth, *Ephesians 4—6,* AB 34A (Garden City, N.Y.: Doubleday, 1974), p. 432, is a case in point. So too F. F. Bruce emphasizes the "victory ode" form of this passage (*The Epistles to the Colossians, to Philemon and to the Ephesians,* NICNT [Grand Rapids: Eerdmans, 1984], p. 341).

[49]On the lively history of the interpretation of this passage, see W. H. Harris, "The Descent of Christ in Ephesians 4:7-11: An Exegetical Investigation with Special Reference to the Influence of Traditions About Moses Associated with Psalm 68:19" (Ph.D. diss., University of Sheffield, 1988), pp. 4-48.

[50]Versions of this position are espoused by M. Barth, *Ephesians 4—6,* pp. 433-34; Bruce, *Colossians, Philemon, Ephesians,* p. 343; R. Schnackenburg, *The Epistle to the Ephesians: A Commentary,* trans. H. Heron (Edinburgh: T & T Clark, 1991), pp. 178-79.

[51]See, e.g., G. B. Caird, "The Descent of Christ in Ephesians 4:7-11," *Studia Evangelica* 2, ed. F. L. Cross, TU 87 (Berlin: Akademie, 1964), pp. 535-45; Harris, "Descent of Christ," pp. 235-65; C. H. Porter, "The Descent of Christ: An Exegetical Study of Eph 4:7-11," in *One Faith,* ed. R. L. Simpson (Tulsa, Okla.: Phillips University Press, 1966), pp. 45-55.

[52]This interpretation is embraced by Tertullian, Irenaeus, Chrysostom, Theodoret, Victorinus, Jerome and Aquinas, and is enshrined as doctrine in the Apostles' Creed. For some contemporary defenders (of some version of this position), see H. Odeberg's excellent little study *The View of the Universe in the Epistle to the Ephesians,* LUÅ 29/6 (Lund: Gleerup, 1934), pp. 17-19; R. C. H. Lenski, *The Interpretation of St. Paul's Epistles ot the Galatians, to the Ephesians and to the Philippians* (Minneapolis: Augsburg, rpt. 1961), pp. 521-22; Reicke, *Disobedient Spirits,* p. 233; J. Schneider, "μερόω," *TDNT,* 4:597-98; Dunn, *Christology in the Making,* pp. 186-87; F. W. Beare, "The Epistle to the Ephesians," in *IB,* 10:688-90.

[53]See Arnold, *Ephesians,* pp. 56-58. The concept of a descent to the underworld may also lie behind Revelation 1:18, which portrays Christ as holding "the keys of death and Hades." See Arnold, *Powers of Darkness,* pp. 108-9. Paul's reference to beings "under the earth" in Philippians 2:11 may also be relevant here.

[54]Yet Andrew Lincoln is surely justified in wondering why the superlative of *katōtera* is not then used, especially since it is used in the LXX of Psalm 62:10 and 138:15, which speak of the underworld. See A. T. Lincoln, *Ephesians,* WBC 42 (Dallas: Word, 1990), p. 245. The objection is strong, but not decisive in overturning the rest of the evidence favoring reading this passage as referring to the underworld.

[55]Dunn, *Christology in the Making,* p. 187. Taking this instead as a genitive of apposition, Dunn argues, is difficult.

[56]Ibid.

[57]So argues M. Barth: "Who are the ones caught? . . . According to Eph 4:8 those made prisoners are probably the principalities, powers, aeons" (*Ephesians 4—6,* p.

432. So J. L. Houlden, *Paul's Letters from Prison,* (Philadelphia: Westminster, 1970), p. 311; Beare, *Ephesians,* pp. 688-89.

[58]Odeberg, *View of the Universe,* p. 19.

[59]This frequently missed dimension of the concept of redemption is captured well by Ethelbert Stauffer in his *New Testament Theology,* 5th ed., trans. J. Marsh (New York: Macmillan, 1955), pp. 146ff.

[60]Stott, *Cross of Christ,* p. 176. See the excellent discussion of Leon Morris in *The Atonement: Its Meaning and Significance* (Downers Grove, Ill.: InterVarsity Press, 1983), chap. 5, pp. 106-31. On *lytron* and related terms, see O. Procksch, "λύω," *TDNT,* 4:328-35; C. Brown, "Redemption," *NIDNTT,* 3:189-200.

[61]This concept of redemption was anticipated in the *Testament of Zebulon,* which speaks of God redeeming "every captive of the sons of men from Beliar" (9:8).

[62]See my forthcoming *Satan and the Problem of Evil.*

[63]J. Kallas, *The Satanward View: A Study in Pauline Theology* (Philadelphia: Westminster, 1966), p. 74.

[64]Ibid., note 2.

Chapter 10: Engaging the Powers

[1]The frequently used (because insightful) analogy of the victory of the cross with D-day in World War II goes back to Oscar Cullmann, *Christ and Time,* trans. F. V. Filson (Philadelphia: Westminster, 1949), pp. 139-43. E. Ferguson offers another appropriate analogy when he likens Satan's defeated state, while he yet rules over the world, to the ending term of office for a "lame-duck" president. "He will not last much longer. But during that time he has all the authority of the office. . . . The devil is the 'lame-duck' ruler of this world" (Ferguson, *Demonology of the Early Christian World* [New York: Mellen, 1984], p. 162).

[2]Most scholars agree that the primary background to the terminology for the angelic and demonic realm in the New Testament is Jewish pseudepigraphal literature. G. H. C. MacGregor, however, has argued for the primacy of astrological beliefs in the first century. See his "Principalities and Powers: The Cosmic Background of Paul's Thought," *NTS* 1 (1954-55): 17-28, a view anticipated by W. L. Knox, *St. Paul and the Church of the Gentiles* (Cambridge: Cambridge University Press, 1939), esp. pp. 104-7, 220. While this approach clearly sheds the best light on some of Paul's terminology (e.g., "height and depth," Rom 8:38), most scholars reject it as the principal source of Paul's talk about principalities and powers. By contrast, Pierre Benoit has concluded that none of this evidence—the apocalyptic texts, the seemingly parallel references in Qumran, nor the available evidence of astrological beliefs—sufficiently accounts for Paul's terminology. See his "Pauline Angelology and Demonology: Reflexions on the Designations of the Heavenly Powers and on the Origin of Angelic Evil," *Religious Studies Bulletin* 3 (1983): 1-18.

[3]Satan is explicitly named in Acts 5:3; 26:18; Romans 16:20; 1 Corinthians 5:5; 7:5; 2 Corinthians 2:11; 11:14; 12:7; 1 Thessalonians 2:18; 2 Thessalonians 2:9; 1 Timothy 1:20; 5:15; Revelation 2:9, 13, 24; 3:9; 12:9; 20:2, 7.

[4]On the rare term *kosmokratores,* see C. Arnold, *Ephesians, Power and Magic: The Concept of Power in Ephesians in Light of Its Historical Setting,* SNTSMS 63 (Cambridge: Cambridge University Press, 1989), pp. 65-66. The issue whether *exousia* in Romans 13:1 refers to angelic authorities, human authorities or both is hotly contested. One of the foremost defenders of the "double-reference" thesis— the notion that *exousia* refers here both to human rulers and to spiritual rulers that

empower them—has been Cullmann. See his *Christ and Time,* pp. 191-210; idem, *The State in the New Testament* (New York: Scribner's, 1956), pp. 95-114. M. Dibelius (*Die Geisterwelt im Glauben des Paulus* [Göttingen: Vandenhoeck & Ruprecht, 1909], pp. 189, 193ff.) had preceded Cullmann in this interpretation, and it is in varying degrees supported by Cullmann's student C. D. Morrison, *The Powers That Be: Earthly Rulers and Demonic Powers in Romans 13:1-7,* SBT 2/29 [Naperville, Ill.: Allenson, 1960]), as well as by Benoit, "Pauline Angelology and Demonology," p. 12; MacGregor, "Principalities and Powers," pp. 24-25; B. Reicke, "The Law and the World According to Paul: Some Thoughts Concerning Gal. 4:1-11," *JBL* 70 (1951): 269. Others have rather argued that Paul has only human rulers in mind here. See, e.g., Arnold, *Ephesians,* pp. 44-45; F. F. Bruce, "Paul and the Powers That Be," *BJRL* 66 (1984): 88-90; W. A. Carr, *Angels and Principalities: The Background, Meaning and Development of the Pauline Phrase "hai archai kai hai exousiai,"* SNTSMS 42 (Cambridge: Cambridge University Press, 1981); and most recently, T. Page, *Powers of Evil: A Biblical Study of Satan and Demons* (Grand Rapids, Mich.: Baker, 1995), pp. 262-63.

[5]So translates NRSV; cf. "elemental spirits of the world" (NEB, RSV). The question of the meaning of the phrase *stoicheia tou kosmou* in Paul's writings is vigorously debated. W. Wink ("The 'Elements of the Universe' in Biblical and Scientific Perspective," *Zygon* 13, no. 3 [1978]: 225-48) has noted no fewer than seven different interpretations (p. 227). Generally speaking, however, scholars today roughly divide into three camps. (1) Following the Reformation tradition, some take *stoicheia* here to refer to the Old Testament law. See, e.g., A. J. Bandstra, *The Law and the Elements of the World: An Exegetical Study in Aspects of Paul's Teaching* (Kampen: Kok, 1964). (2) Some scholars take the term to refer to the material components of the cosmos. See, e.g., E. Schweizer, "Slaves of the Elements and Worshipers of Angels: Gal 4:3, 9 and Col 2:8, 18, 20," *JBL* 107 (1988): 455-68. (3) Other scholars take the term to refer to personal beings, typically recognized as "astral spirits." See, e.g., Arnold, *Ephesians,* pp. 131, 168; Benoit, "Pauline Angelology and Demonology," p. 13; J. J. Gunther, *St. Paul's Opponents and Their Background: A Study of Apocalyptic and Jewish Sectarian Teachings,* NovTSup 35 (Leiden: Brill, 1973), pp. 172ff.; Reicke, "The Law and the World"; and esp. C. J. Kurapti, "Spiritual Bondage and Christian Freedom According to Paul" (Ph.D. diss., Princeton Theological Seminary, 1976). Although it is clear that there is no unambiguous usage of *stoicheia* as referring to angelic or astral spirits until after Paul (e.g., *Testament of Solomon* 8:1-4; 18:1-4), it can perhaps be located as early as the late first century (see Kurapati, "Spiritual Bondage," pp. 56-57, 72-74). When one further considers just how enamored intertestamental Judaism was with angelic beings (including their relation to the physical world; see, e.g., *Jubilees* 2:2; *1 Enoch* 60:12-21) and how well taking *stoicheia* as referring to angelic/astral spirits fits in the Galatian context, the third interpretation of *stoicheia* seems most probable. For a recent argument in this direction, see C. E. Arnold, "Returning to the Domain of the Powers: *Stoicheia* as Evil Spirits in Galatians 4:3, 9," *NovT* 38 (1996): 55-76. Arnold has recently made a similar argument regarding *stoicheia* in Colossians; see *The Colossian Syncretism: The Interface Between Christianity and Folk Belief at Colossae* (Grand Rapids, Mich.: Baker, 1996), pp. 158-94.

[6]R. Leivestad only slightly overstates the case when he argues that "Paul has no particular interest in angelology. He pays no attention to their interrelations, and applies the titles indiscriminately" (*Christ the Conqueror: Ideas of Conflict and*

Victory in the New Testament [New York: Macmillan; 1954], p. 93). T. Ling, however, certainly goes too far in arguing that Paul is taking "various contemporary conceptions of spirit powers which were thought of as ruling over the religio-cultural life of men, and is compressing them into one single conception" (*The Significance of Satan: New Testament Demonology and Its Contemporary Significance* [London: SPCK, 1961], p. 65).

[7]F. I. Andersen, in *OTP,* 1:134.

[8]E. Issac, in *OTP,* 1:42.

[9]Arnold, *Ephesians,* 51-69. Hence the relevance of Greek magical texts for understanding Paul's concepts cannot be minimized. See W. Grundmann, *Der Begriff der Kraft in der Neutestamentlichen Gedankenwelt,* BWANT 8 (Stuttgart: Kohlhammer, 1932), esp. pp. 32-55. MacGregor ("Principalities and Powers") attempts to make the case that the Gentile astrological beliefs and writings are the primary source of Paul's terminology for the spiritual realm. Relevant here as well is T. B. Cargal, "Seated in the Heavenlies: Cosmic Mediators in the Mysteries of Mithras and the Letter to the Ephesians," *SBLSP,* 1994, ed. E. H. Lovering (Atlanta: Scholars Press, 1994), pp. 804-21.

[10]So concludes P. O'Brien in his excellent article "Principalities and Powers: Opponents of the Church," *ERT* 16, no. 4 (1992): 353-84, esp. 378.

[11]H. Schlier, *Principalities and Powers in the New Testament* (Freiburg: Herder and Herder, 1961); H. Berkhof, *Christ and the Powers,* trans. J. H. Yoder (Scottdale, Penn.: Herald, 1962). So too argues G. B. Caird in his highly influential *Principalities and Powers: A Study in Pauline Theology* (Oxford: Clarendon, 1956). On the history of this discussion through the twentieth century, see O'Brien, "Principalities and Powers"; T. H. McAlpine, *Facing the Powers: What Are the Options?* (Monrovia, Calif.: MARC, 1991).

[12]Wesley Carr argues against this, maintaining that the various "powers" are all angelic, not demonic, at least in Colossians and Ephesians. See his *Angels and Principalities.* A host of exegetical problems attend this thesis. To cite two examples: (1) Carr must argue that *apekdyomai* ("disarming" or "stripping off") in Colossians 2:15 does not refer to Christ stripping away the weapons of diabolical powers but (as later Gnostics would contend) to Christ laying aside "his battle-dress (his flesh)" (p. 65). Hence too he must argue that the "public spectacle" of this verse is a positive display (not mockery) and that the triumph here is not over these powers but with these powers. This exegesis is exceedingly stretched. (2) Carr must maintain, on entirely circumstantial grounds, that Ephesians 6:12 is a later Christian interpolation (pp. 104-10). On the integrity of this passage in Ephesians, see C. Arnold, "The 'Exorcism' of Ephesians 6:12 in Recent Research: A Critique of Wesley Carr's View of Evil Powers in First Century AD Belief," JSNT 30 (1987): 71-87. For other critical reviews of Carr's unusual thesis, see M. D. Hooker, review of *Angels and Principalities* by W. Carr, *JTS* 34 (1983): 606-9; O'Brien, "Principalities and Powers," pp. 369-72; W. W. Wink, Union Seminary Quarterly Review 39 (1984): 146-50.

[13]See, e.g., V. Eller, *Christian Anarchy: Jesus' Primacy over the Powers* (Grand Rapids, Mich.: Eerdmans, 1987); A. H. van den Heuvel, *Those Rebellious Powers* (New York: Friendship, 1965); R. Sider, *Christ and Violence* (Scottdale, Penn.: Herald, 1979), who takes Ephesians 3:10 to be a mandate of the church to preach against the "powers" (p. 51), as does Wink, *Naming the Powers,* p. 89.

[14]Many who argue along these lines contend that the fallen "powers" are held in place by violence and hence can be overthrown only through pacifism. Indeed, according

to Wink, C. Myers and others, the pacifistic overthrow of these powers is precisely what Christ in principle accomplished on the cross. See Wink, *Engaging the Powers*, esp. pp. 173-92, 319-24; C. Myers, *Binding the Strong Man: A Political Reading of Mark's Story of Jesus* (Maryknoll, N.Y.: Orbis, 1988), pp. 452-53.

[15]Berkhof, *Christ and the Powers*, p. 23. Both Schlier and Berkhof, however, stop short of completely reducing the "powers" to social structures, though Berkhof argues that even if Paul did hold that the powers were transcendent to these structures, its significance is so marginal as to be negligible (p. 24). G. B. Caird opts for this interpretation in *Principalities and Powers*, though two decades later he seems to admit the powers are personal beings. See *Paul's Letters from Prison* (Oxford: Oxford University Press, 1976), p. 96. Also arguing that Paul "demythologized" apocalyptic concepts is J. C. Beker, *Paul the Apostle* (Philadelphia: Fortress, 1980), pp. 189-92.

[16]Wink, *Naming the Powers: The Language of Power in the New Testament* (Philadelphia: Fortress, 1984), p. 62.

[17]Ibid., pp. 65-66.

[18]Ibid, p. 104.

[19]Ibid., p. 105.

[20]Schlier, *Principalities*, pp. 30-32; Wink, *Naming the Powers*, p. 83.

[21]Arnold, *Ephesians*, p. 60.

[22]Cited in Arnold, *Powers of Darkness*, p. 197; cf. idem, *Ephesians*, pp. 60-62. Arnold especially faults Wink for paying insufficient attention to this evidence. See *Ephesians*, pp. 50-51.

[23]See, e.g., *Ascension of Isaiah* 2:2-4, which speaks of Beliar leading Jerusalem astray.

[24]So argues Arnold against Beker, *Ephesians*, p. 131. Wink, however, understands even Satan, demons and angels along the same lines as the cosmic powers; they are transcendent but not personal or autonomous realities.

[25]The NIV unfortunately interprets rather than translates *sarx* (lit. "flesh") as "sinful nature," making it sound as if even regenerate Christians who are "new creations" in Christ (2 Cor 5:17) still have a sinful nature. In my estimation, a better way of understanding "flesh" is to see it as a way of living, apart from God, rather than something inherent even in the nature of believers.

[26]See E. Schweizer, "σάρξ κτλ.," *TDNT*, 7:133.

[27]Beker argues in the opposite direction. Because such categories as sin, death and the flesh are frequent in Paul's thought, and they are not portrayed as independent agents, we should take his apocalyptic terminology in a demythologized fashion. See his *Paul the Apostle*, pp. 189-92. For a cogent refutation, see Arnold, *Ephesians*, pp. 129-32. For a helpful book that takes seriously the "structural" aspect of the "powers" without thereby reductionistically denying their personalistic dimensions, see R. E. Webber, *The Church in the World: Opposition, Tension or Transformation?* (Grand Rapids, Mich.: Zondervan, 1986).

[28]Arnold, *Powers of Darkness*, pp. 104-7.

[29]R. Recker raises the question of whether we should say that Satan is "still" the "prince of this world"; see "Satan: In Power or Dethroned?" *CTJ* 6 (1971): 133-55. While Christ's accomplished victory must always be emphasized, as it is in the New Testament, it nevertheless remains true that all the verses cited above concerning the rule of Satan are composed after the resurrection. Recker resolves the "already/not yet" tension of the New Testament and thereby loses the eschatological dimension of the dethroning of Satan.

[30]See the discussion in Ling, *Significance of Satan,* p. 40.

[31]I cite this only as another example of the general view that the demonic kingdom can cause physical afflictions. But it must be noted that the theme of diabolical destruction in the book of Revelation differs significantly from the rest of the New Testament. For while Jesus did not come "to condemn the world" (Jn 3:18), the book of Revelation speaks of a time when this period of grace has come to an end. Here, at the end of time as we know it, Jesus and the Father are no longer fighting for the world to set up their kingdom, but against what remains of the world after it has rejected their kingdom. Hence as the Lord did against the Egyptians when freeing the children of Israel, the Lord here takes the radical measure of sending "woes" upon the earth, and sometimes using the vengeance of demons to do it (e.g., Rev 6:7-8, 12-17; 9:1-20; 20:7-9). Unlike the rest of the New Testament, in which God fights against demonic powers, then, here the demonic powers are for a time specially allowed by God to work their destruction. It is a mistake, however, to adopt this apocalyptic perspective—when God will judge a hopelessly demonic world—when we are trying to understand evil in the gracious interval between the cross and the eschaton—viz., when God is yet working to save the world from the demonic kingdom. In the forthcoming *Satan and the Problem of Evil* I shall argue that one of the fundamental errors Augustine made was that he adopted just this erroneous perspective. In doing so, he altered the motif of the world as a battlefield to the world as a penal colony. So notes R. Brown, "Sorcery, Demons and the Rise of Christianity: From Late Antiquity into the Middle Ages," in his *Religion and Society in the Age of Augustine* (New York: Harper & Row, 1972), pp. 119-42. As a result, the church has by and large seen evil as punishment for sin, and the devil and demons as God's instruments for bringing this punishment about. This is the perspective of Revelation, but it is difficult to imagine anything further from Jesus' perspective on the demonic kingdom, and on evil in the world, as he fought (and still fights through the church) to set up his kingdom in this world. For an excellent discussion of the theme of the final victory of the saints through the onslaught of demonic forces in the book of Revelation, see S. L. Homey, " 'To Him Who Overcomes': A Fresh Look at What 'Victory' Means for the Believer According to the Book of Revelation," *JETS* 38 (1995): 193-201.

[32]So Ling notes, *Significance of Satan,* p. 40.

[33]W. Sanday and A. C. Headlam, *The Epistle to the Romans,* 5th ed., ICC (Edinburgh: T & T Clark, 1902), p. 431.

[34]On this, see E. Langton, *The Essentials of Demonology* (London: Epworth, 1949), p. 190.

[35]Pace, e.g., R. Guelich, "Spiritual Warfare: Jesus, Paul and Peretti," *Pneuma* 13, no. 1 (1991): 33-64. Guelich's argument is interesting because he clearly wants to accept a literal devil as a literal evil leader of a literal multitude of demons who are literally against Christians, yet he wants to argue that the warfare motif in Scripture is a metaphor. Indeed, he is concerned that the "metaphor" of military engagement has been taken with excessive literalness by the modern spiritual warfare movement: "What began as a metaphor for the Christian life has become a movement whose expression is found above all in Frank Peretti's novel, *This Present Darkness*" (p. 34). While the portrayal of warfare in Peretti's novel certainly far outruns anything we find in Scripture (it is, after all, a novel), it does not follow from this that Scripture's own talk of warfare is not literal.

[36]The traditional ending of Mark has Jesus list "driving out demons" as the first "sign"

of those who believe (Mk 16:17). While the text is certainly not Mark's, it just as certainly reflects an early postapostolic awareness that exorcism was to be a standard part of the church's ministry. I shall provide a comprehensive review of the role of exorcism in the early church in my forthcoming *Satan and the Problem of Evil*.

[37]"Spirit of python" could refer to an ability to predict the future. We know that the divinizing prophetess at Delphi was called "pythia" because it was believed she was inspired by the god Apollo, who, legend had it, defeated a dragon named python. Or it may refer to a "spirit of ventriloquism"—the demon spoke through her—since we know from Plutarch that ventriloquists were sometimes called "pythons." See E. Langton, *God and Evil Spirits: A Study of the Jewish and Christian Doctrine, Its Origin and Development* (New York: Macmillan, 1942), p. 159. On the ancient python myth in general, see J. Fontenrose, *Python: A Study of the Delphic Myth and Its Origins* (Berkeley: University of California Press, 1959).

[38]This account seems to stand in tension with Mark 9:38-40 and Luke 9:49-50, where Jesus affirms (against his disciples) the validity of an exorcist who was not following him but who used Jesus' name in successful exorcisms. Perhaps the Gospel accounts differ from the Acts account in that the solo exorcist in the Gospels seems to have been working, however unknowingly, in league with Jesus. Though not a full-fledged disciple, he was glorifying Jesus. This does not seem to have been the motivation of the seven sons of Sceva. Cf. Matthew 7:21-23.

[39]See the introduction above, note 16.

[40]The success of Christian exorcism, as opposed to the spotty success of their contemporaries, was one of the strongest selling points of Christianity in the ancient world. As Adolf von Harnack observed: "It was as exorcisers that Christians went out into the great world, and exorcism formed one very powerful method of their mission and propaganda. It was a question not simply of exorcising and vanquishing the demons that dwelt in individuals, but also of purifying all public life from them" (*The Mission and Expansion of Christianity in the First Three Centuries*, trans. and ed. J. Moffatt [New York: Putnam's, 1908], 1.131). Also significant is that neither Jesus nor his disciples used any of the common techniques for exorcism, e.g., various magical names, formula, potions, charms. See D. E. Aune, "Magic in Early Christianity," in *ANRW* (1980), 2/23.2:1545; G. Twelftree, *Jesus the Exorcist: A Contribution to the Study of the Historical Jesus*, WUNT 2/54 (Tübingen: Mohr/Siebeck, 1993), p. 164; G. Boyd, *Jesus Under Siege* (Wheaton, Ill.: Victor, 1995), pp. 43-62; E. Ferguson, *Demonology of the Early Christian World* (New York: Mellen, 1980), p. 9. The uniqueness of the Christian approach to exorcism, as opposed to all magical techniques, was a point of contention in the early postapostolic church as well. On this see H. Remus, *Pagan-Christian Conflict over Miracle in the Second Century* (Cambridge, Mass.: Philadelphia Patristic Foundation, 1983), pp. 48-72; idem, " 'Magic or Miracle?' Some Second-Century Instances," *The Second Century* 2 (1982): 127-56; E. R. Dodds, *Pagan and Christian in an Age of Anxiety* (Cambridge: Cambridge University Press, 1965), pp. 124ff.; E. V. Gallagher, *Divine Man or Magician: Celsus and Origen on Jesus* (Chico, Calif.: Scholars Press, 1982).

[41]As Leivestad argues, there is no reason to take these "arrows" as referring only to spiritual temptations. He contends that they refer to physical tribulations brought on by persecution from the devil or from the hostile earthly people he governs. See *Christ the Conqueror*, p. 163. For several helpful studies on Ephesians 6:10-12, see Arnold, "The 'Exorcism' of Ephesians 6:12 in Recent Research"; A. T. Lincoln,

" 'Stand, Therefore . . .': Ephesians 6:10-20 as *Peroratio*," *Biblical Interpretation* 3, no. 1 (1995): 99-114 (which, interestingly enough, makes the case that this warfare passage sums up the central theme of the whole epistle); R. A. Wild, "The Warrior and the Prisoner: Some Reflections on Ephesians 6:10-20," *CBQ* 46 (1984): 284-98.

[42]Ling, *Significance of Satan*, p. 45, quoting T. K. Abbott. One is reminded of James 4:7: "Resist the devil, and he will flee from you."

[43]Guelich argues that the author of this passage "abandons the military imagery of 6:10-17 and calls for the believers to remain alert" with verse 18 ("Spiritual Warfare," p. 50). It is true that prayer and alertness are not part of the armor of the Christian, but it is difficult to agree for this reason that the author has discontinued the military imagery. For whom is the Christian to remain "alert" if not for the "devil," the "rulers," the "authorities," the "powers of this dark world" and the "spiritual forces of evil" just mentioned five verses earlier?

[44]Beliar or Belial is frequently mentioned in Jewish literature as an alternative name of Satan. The root meaning of the word seems to be "worthlessness." See H. H. Rowley, *The Relevance of Apocalyptic: A Study of Jewish and Christian Apocalypses from Daniel to the Revelation*, rev. ed. (New York: Association, 1963), p. 72. A number of scholars argue that these passages may echo an early Christian prebaptism catechism that involved renouncing Satan, such as we find practiced throughout the early postapostolic church. On Ephesians 5:14-16 see H. A. Kelly, *The Devil at Baptism: Ritual, Theology and Drama* (Ithaca: Cornell University Press, 1985), p. 26; D. Mollat, "Baptismal Symbolism in St. Paul," in *Baptism in the New Testament*, ed. A. Grail, trans. D. Askew (Baltimore: Helicon, 1968), pp. 81-83. On Romans 13:12 see M. E. Boismard, "I Renounce Satan, His Pomps and His Works," in *Baptism in the New Testament*, pp. 107-112. On the Qumran background of 1 Corinthians 6:14-15, see Kelly, *Devil at Baptism*, pp. 39-40.

[45]On various aspects and perspectives regarding Qumran dualism, especially as portrayed in the "light versus darkness" motif, see K. M. T. Atkinson, "The Historical Setting of the 'War of the Sons of Light and the Sons of Darkness,' " *BJRL* 40 (1958): 272-97; R. E. Brown, "The Qumran Scrolls and the Johannine Gospel and Epistles," *CBQ* 17 (1955): 183-207; J. J. Collins, "The Mythology of the Holy War in Daniel and the Qumran War Scroll: A Point of Transition in Jewish Apocalyptic," *VT* 25 (1975): 596-612.

[46]In the light of all these passages, it is in my view remarkable that Guelich concludes that the warfare motif in Paul and the whole of the New Testament is rare ("Spiritual Warfare," p. 51). It is, he thinks, surprising "how relatively little Paul has to say about Satan and the 'rulers and authorities' and especially how little he actually makes of military metaphors when speaking of Satan and the forces of evil in the light of his consistent portrait of them as adversaries" (ibid). While I can certainly appreciate Guelich's concern to avoid an overly literal acceptance of "Peretti's portrait of the demonic" (p. 54)—the central concern of this essay—and thus I can appreciate his emphasis on how reserved Paul (and Jesus) is in terms of his speculations about the unseen enemy, I simply cannot agree with his minimalist reading of the warfare motif in either Paul or the Gospels.

[47]For several helpful discussions on ancient Jewish perspectives, see B. J. Bamberger, *Fallen Angels* (Philadelphia: Jewish Publication Society of America, 1952); S. Revard, *The War in Heaven: Paradise Lost and the Tradition of Satan's Rebellion* (Ithaca: Cornell University Press, 1980).

[48]I shall argue in *Satan and the Problem of Evil* that freedom is a "metaphysical given"

and is, as such, incapable of further analysis. It thus constitutes a justifiable ultimate principle of explanation.

[49]Whether the connection between Satan and Lucifer in Isaiah 14 had been made at the time of Paul's writing is a matter of dispute, largely hinging on the dating of the longer recension of the *Book of the Secrets of Enoch* that clearly makes this connection (29:4-5). This work had been generally dated in the first century, but some recent scholars have argued that it was actually composed much later. See Kelley, *Devil at Baptism,* p. 18; idem, "The Devil in the Desert," *CBQ* 26 (1964): 203-4.

[50]A point to be developed in part three of the forthcoming *Satan and the Problem of Evil.*

[51]On Gehenna see D. F. Watson, "Gehenna," in *ABD* 2:926-28; L. Bailey, "Gehenna: The Topography of Hell," in *BA* 49 (1986): 187-91; C. Milikowsky, "Which Gehenna? Retribution and Eschatology in the Synoptic Gospels and in Early Jewish Texts," *NTS* 34 (1988): 238-49.

[52]This biblical motif grounds the annihilationist doctrine of hell that is gaining notoriety today. In this view, the damned are eventually (or immediately) annihilated. Eternal punishment, like eternal redemption, is eternal in *consequence,* not in experiential *duration.* The most comprehensive and, in my estimation, the most compelling work defending annihilationism is E. W. Fudge's *The Fire That Consumes: The Biblical Case for Conditional Immortality,* rev. ed. (Carlisle, U.K.: Paternoster, 1994). See also D. Edwards and J. R. W. Stott, *Evangelical Essentials: A Liberal-Evangelical Dialogue* (Downers Grove, Ill.: InterVarsity Press, 1988), pp. 312-20; J. Wenham, *The Goodness of God* (London: InterVarsity Press, 1974), pp. 27-41; idem, "The Case for Conditional Immortality," in *Universalism and the Doctrine of Hell,* ed. N. M. de. S. Cameron (Grand Rapids, Mich.: Baker, 1992), pp. 161-91; P. Hughes, *The True Image* (Grand Rapids, Mich.: Eerdmans, 1989), pp. 398ff.; C. Pinnock, "The Conditional View," in *Four Views on Hell,* ed. W. Crockett (Grand Rapids, Mich.: Zondervan, 1992), pp. 135-66.

[53]The apocalyptic literature that forms the background to the New Testament sometimes speaks of the devil and fallen angels being tormented eternally while other times as being utterly annihilated. *First* and *Second Enoch* as well as 4 Maccabees clearly depict both the devil and his angels, along with all human sinners, suffering endless conscious punishment. Most of the Qumran writings, the *Sibylline Oracles, Psalms of Solomon* and 4 Ezra are quite clear in depicting total annihilation as the fate of the angelic and human rebellion. A host of other documents are either unclear or seem to teach both doctrines. See Fudge, *Fire That Consumes,* pp. 78-92. For a discussion on how annihilationists handle these verses, see ibid., pp. 93-198.

[54]"If we see the work of Jesus as the defeat of Satan and the destruction of Satan's grip on this world," argues Kallas, "then suddenly the life, work, death, and resurrection of Jesus assume an impressive unity. . . . The life of Jesus thus seen is a cohesive, closely knit, ascending battle which reaches its climax in the resurrection" (*The Significance of the Synoptic Miracles* [Greenwich, Conn.: Seabury, 1961], p. 86).

[55]G. Wingren, *The Living Word: A Theological Study of Preaching and the Church* (Philadelphia: Muhlenberg, 1949), p. 181.

Selected Bibliography

Adler, Mortimer J. *The Angels and Us.* New York: Macmillan, 1982.

Arnold, Clinton E. *Ephesians, Power and Magic: The Concept of Power in Ephesians in Light of Its Historical Setting.* Society for New Testament Studies Monograph Series 63. Cambridge: Cambridge University Press, 1989

———. *Powers of Darkness: Principalities and Powers in Paul's Letters.* Downers Grove, Ill.: InterVarsity Press, 1992.

———. "Returning to the Domain of the Powers: *Stoicheia* as Evil Spirits in Galatians 4:3, 9." *Novum Testamentum* 38/1 (1996).

Aulén, Gustaf. *Christus Victor : A Historical Study of the Three Main Types of the Idea of Atonement.* Translated by A. G. Hebert. 1931. Reprint, New York: Macmillan, 1969.

Barnhouse, Donald Grey. "The Great Interval." In *The Invisible War,* 9-20. Grand Rapids, Mich.: Zondervan, 1965.

Basinger, David. "Can an Evangelical Christian Justifiably Deny God's Exhaustive Knowledge of the Future." *Christian Scholars Review* 25/2 (1995): 133-45.

Battu, B. F. "The Covenant of Peace: A Neglected Ancient Near Eastern Motif." *Catholic Biblical Quarterly* 49 (1987): 187-211.

Berkhof, H. *Christ and the Powers.* Translated by John Howard Yoder. 1962. Reprint, Scottdale, Penn.: Herald Press, 1967.

Böcher, Otto. *Christus Exorcista.* Stuttgart, Germany: Kohlhammer, 1972.

———. *Dämonenfurcht und Dämonenabwehr: Ein Beitrag zur Vorgeschichte der christlichen Taufe.* Beiträge zur Wissenschaft vom Alten und Neuen Testament 5. Stuttgart, Germany: Kohlhammer, 1970.

———. *Das Neue Testament und die dämonischen Mächte.* Stuttgart, Germany: Katholisches Bibelwerk, 1972.

Boyd, Gregory A. *Trinity and Process: A Critical Evaluation and Appropriation of Hartshorne's Di-Polar Theism Towards a Trinitarian Metaphysics.* New York: Peter Lang, 1992.

Breuninger, C. "Where Angels Fear to Tread: Appraising the Current Fascination with Spiritual Warfare." *Covenant Quarterly* 53 (May 1995): 37-43.

Caird, G. B. *Principalities and Powers: A Study in Pauline Theology.* Oxford: Clarendon, 1956.

Calvert, B. "Dualism and the Problem of Evil." *Sophia* 22/3 (1983): 15-28.

Carr, Wesley. *Angels and Principalities: The Background, Meaning and Development of the Pauline Phrase hai archai kai hai exousiai.* Society for New Testament Studies Monograph Series 42. Cambridge: Cambridge University Press, 1981.

Clifford, Richard J. *The Cosmic Mountain in Canaan and the Old Testament.* Cambridge: Harvard University Press, 1972.

Collins, Adela Yarbro. *The Combat Myth in the Book of Revelation.* Harvard Dissertations in Religion 9. Missoula, Mont.: Scholars Press, 1976.

Cooke, Gerald. "The Sons of (the) God(s)." *Zeitschrift für die alttestamentliche*

Wissenschaft 76 (1964): 22-47.

Crenshaw, James L. "The Shift from Theodicy to Anthropodicy." *Theodicy in the Old Testament.* Edited by James L. Crenshaw. Philadelphia: Fortress, 1983.

Cross, Frank Moore. *Canaanite Myth and Hebrew Epic: Essays in the History of the Religion of Israel.* Cambridge: Harvard University Press, 1973.

Custance, Arthur C. "Analysis of Genesis 1:1." *Time and Eternity and Other Biblical Studies.* Doorway Papers 6. Grand Rapids, Mich.: Zondervan, 1977.

———. *Without Form and Void.* Brockville, Ont.: Arthur Custance, 1970.

Daniélou, Jean. *The Angels and Their Mission, According to the Fathers of the Church.* Translated by David Heimann. 1953. Reprint, Westminster, Md.: Newman, 1957.

Davids, Peter H. "Sickness and Suffering in the New Testament." In *Wrestling with Dark Angels: Toward a Deeper Understanding of the Supernatural Forces in Spiritual Warfare,* 215-37. Edited by C. Peter Wagner and F. D. Pennoyer. Ventura, Calif.: Regal, 1990.

Davies, Stevan L. *Jesus the Healer: Possession, Trance and the Origins of Christianity.* New York: Continuum, 1995.

Davies, Thomas Witton. *Magic, Divination and Demonology Among the Hebrews and Their Neighbors.* 1898. Reprint, New York: KTAV, 1969.

Davis, Stephen T. *Logic and the Nature of God.* Grand Rapids, Mich.: Eerdmans, 1983.

Day, John. *God's Conflict with the Dragon and the Sea: Echoes of a Canaanite Myth in the Old Testament.* University of Cambridge Oriental Publications 35. Cambridge: Cambridge University Press, 1985.

Day, Peggy Lynne. *An Adversary in Heaven: Satan in the Hebrew Bible.* Harvard Semitic Monographs 43. Atlanta: Scholars Press, 1988.

Driver, G. R. "Mythical Monsters in the Old Testament." In *Studi Orientalistici in onore di Giorgio Levi Della Vida,* 1:234-49. 2 vols. Rome: Instituto per l'Oriente, 1956.

Dunn, J. D. G., and Graham H. Twelftree. "Demon-Possession and Exorcism in the New Testament." *Churchman* 94/3 (1980): 211-15.

Eller, Vernard. *Christian Anarchy: Jesus' Primacy over the Powers.* Grand Rapids, Mich.: Eerdmans, 1987.

Fascher, Erich. Jesus und der Satan: Eine Studie zur Auslegung der Versuchungsgeschichte. Hallische Monographien 11. Halle, Germany: Max Niemeyer, 1949.

Ferguson, Everett. *Demonology of the Early Christian World.* New York: Mellen, 1984.

Fields, Weston W. *Unformed and Unfilled: A Critique of the Gap Theory of Genesis 1:1, 2.* Winona Lake, Ind.: Light and Life Press, 1973.

Forsyth, Neil. *The Old Enemy: Satan and the Combat Myth.* Princeton: Princeton University Press, 1987.

Fretheim, Terence E. *The Suffering of God: An Old Testament Perspective.* Overtures to Biblical Theology 14. Philadelphia: Fortress, 1984.

Garrett, Susan R. *The Demise of the Devil: Magic and the Demonic in Luke's Writings.* Minneapolis: Fortress, 1989.

Gokey, Francis X. *The Terminology for the Devil and Evil Spirits in the Apostolic Fathers.* Patristic Studies 93. Washington, D.C.: Catholic University of America Press, 1961.

Goodman, Felicitas D. *How About Demons? Possession and Exorcism in the Modern World.* Bloomington: Indiana University Press, 1988.

Gordon, C. H. "Leviathan: Symbol of Evil." In *Biblical Motifs: Origins and Transformations,* 1-89. Edited by Alexander Altmann. Lown Institute of Advanced Judaic

Studies 3. Cambridge: Harvard University Press, 1966.

Grønbæk, Jakob H. "Baal's Battle with Yam—A Canaanite Creation Fight." *Journal for the Study of the Old Testament* 33 (1985): 27-44.

Guelich, Robert A. "Spiritual Warfare: Jesus, Paul and Peretti." *Pneuma* 13 (Spring 1991): 33-64.

Gunkel, Hermann. *Schöpfung und Chaos in Urzeit und Endzeit: Eine religions-geschichtliche Untersuchung über Gen 1 und Ap Joh 12.* Göttingen: Vandenhoeck and Ruprecht, 1895.

Handy, Lowell K. *Among the Host of Heaven: The Syro-Palestinian Pantheon as Bureaucracy.* Winona Lake, Ind.: Eisenbrauns, 1994.

Hayman, P. "Monotheism—A Misused Word in Jewish Studies?" *Journal of Jewish Studies* 42 (1991): 1-15.

Heidel, Alexander. *The Babylonian Genesis: The Story of the Creation.* 2nd ed. Chicago: University of Chicago Press, 1951.

Henninger, J. "The Adversary of God in Primitive Religions." In *Satan: Essays Collected and Translated from "Etudes Carmelitaines,"* 105-20. Edited by Bruno de Jésus-Marie. 1948. Translated by Malachy Carroll et al. New York: Sheed & Ward, 1951.

Heuvel, Albert H. van den. *These Rebellious Powers.* New York: Friendship Press, 1965.

Hick, John. *Evil and the God of Love.* 1966. Reprint, London: Fontana, 1968.

———. "The Problem of Evil in the First and Last Things." *Journal of Theological Studies* 19 (1968): 592.

Hiebert, Paul G. *Anthropological Insights for Missionaries.* Grand Rapids, Mich.: Baker Book House, 1985.

———. "The Flaw of the Excluded Middle." *Missiology* 10/1 (1982): 35-47.

Hiers, Richard H. " 'Binding' and 'Loosing': The Matthean Authorizations." *Journal of Biblical Literature* 104/2 (1985): 242-43.

———. "Satan, Demons and the Kingdom of God." *Scottish Journal of Theology* 27 (1974): 35-47.

Hodgson, Leonard. *For Faith and Freedom.* Gifford Lectures, 1955-1957. 2 vols. Oxford: Blackwell, 1956.

Hollenbach, Paul W. "Help for Interpreting Jesus' Exorcism." In *Society of Biblical Literature Seminar Papers* 1993, 124-26. Edited by E. H. Lovering Jr. Atlanta: Scholars Press, 1993.

———. "Jesus, Demoniacs and Public Authorities: A Socio-historical Study." *Journal of the American Academy of Religion* 49 (1981): 584.

Ice, Thomas, and Robert Dean Jr. *Overrun with Demons: The Church's New Preoccupation with the Demonic.* Eugene, Ore.: Harvest House, 1990.

Jensen, S. S. *Dualism and Demonology: The Function of Demonology in Pythagorean and Platonic Thought.* Copenhagen: Munksgaard, 1966.

Jung, C. G. *Answer to Job.* Cleveland, 1960.

Kallas, James G. *Jesus and the Power of Satan.* Philadelphia: Westminster, 1968.

———. *The Satanward View: A Study in Pauline Theology.* Philadelphia: Westminster, 1966.

———. *The Significance of the Synoptic Miracles.* Greenwich, Conn.: Seabury Press, 1961.

Kelly, Henry Ansgar. *The Devil at Baptism: Ritual, Theology and Drama.* Ithaca, N.Y.: Cornell University Press, 1985.

———. *The Devil, Demonology and Witchcraft: The Development of Christian Beliefs in Evil Spirits.* 1968. 2nd ed. Garden City, N.Y.: Doubleday, 1974.

Kelsey, Morton T. *Discernment: A Study in Ecstasy and Evil.* New York: Paulist Press, 1978.

Kloos, Carola. *YHWH's Combat with the Sea: A Canaanite Tradition in the Religion of Ancient Israel.* Leiden: E. J. Brill, 1986.

Kluger, Riukah Schärf. *Satan in the Old Testament.* 1948. Translated by Hildegard Nagel. Studies in Jungian Thought 7. Evanston, Ill.: Northwestern University Press, 1967.

Koch, K. "Is There a Doctrine of Retribution in the Old Testament?" In *Theodicy in the Old Testament,* 57-87. Edited by James L. Crenshaw. Philadelphia: Fortress, 1983.

König, Adrio. *New and Greater Things: Re-evaluating the Biblical Message on Creation.* Pretoria: University of South Africa, 1988.

Kovacs, Judith L. " 'Now Shall the Ruler of This World Be Driven Out': Jesus' Death as Cosmic Battle in John 12:20-36." *Journal of Biblical Literature* 114 (1995): 227-47.

Kraft, Charles H. *Christianity with Power: Your Worldview and Your Experience of the Supernatural.* Ann Arbor, Mich.: Servant Publications, 1989.

————, and M. White, eds. *Behind Enemy Lines: An Advanced Guide to Spiritual Warfare.* Ann Arbor, Mich.: Servant Books, 1994.

Kraft, Marguerite G. *Understanding Spiritual Power: A Forgotten Dimension of Cross-Cultural Mission and Ministry.* Maryknoll, N.Y.: Orbis, 1995.

Kuemmerlin-McLean, J. K. "Demons: Old Testament." In *The Anchor Bible Dictionary,* 2: 138-40. Edited by David Noel Freedman. 6 vols. New York: Doubleday, 1992.

Langton, Edward. *The Essentials of Demonology: A Study of Jewish and Christian Doctrine, Its Origin and Development.* London: Epworth, 1949.

————. *Supernatural: The Doctrine of Spirits, Angels and Demons, from the Middle Ages to the Present Time.* London: Rider, 1934.

Leeper, Elizabeth Ann. "Exorcism in Early Christianity, " Ph.D. diss., Duke University, 1991.

Lefevre, A. "Angel or Monster? The Power of Evil in the Old Testament." In *Satan: Essays Collected and Translated from "Etudes Carmelitaines,"* 55-56. Edited by Bruno de Jésus-Marie. 1948. Translated by Malachy Carroll et al. New York: Sheed & Ward, 1951.

Leivestad, Ragnar. *Christ the Conqueror: Ideas of Conflict and Victory in the New Testament.* New York: Macmillan, 1954.

Levenson, Jon. *Creation and the Persistence of Evil: The Jewish Drama of Divine Omnipotence.* San Francisco: Harper & Row, 1988.

Lewis, C. S. *The Problem of Pain.* New York: Macmillan, 1945.

Lewis, Edwin. *The Creator and the Adversary.* New York: Abingdon-Cokesbury, 1948.

Lindstöm, Fredrik. *God and the Origin of Evil: A Contextual Analysis of Alleged Monistic Evidence in the Old Testament.* Translated by Frederick H. Cryer. Lund, Sweden: Gleerup, 1983.

————. *Suffering and Sin: Interpretations of Illness in the Individual Complaint Psalms.* Translated by M. McLamb. Coniectanea Biblica Old Testament Series 37. Stockholm: Almqvist & Wiksell, 1994.

Ling, Trevor Oswald. *The Significance of Satan: New Testament Demonology and Its*

Contemporary Significance. London: SPCK, 1961.

Longman, Tremper, III, and Daniel G. Reid. *God Is a Warrior.* Grand Rapids, Mich.: Zondervan, 1995.

Lust, J. "Devils and Angels in the Old Testament." *Louvain Studies* 5 (1974): 115-20.

Martin, Malachi. *Hostage to the Devil: The Possession and Exorcism of Five Living Americans.* New York: Reader's Digest Press, 1976.

Mascall, E. L. *Christian Theology and Natural Science: Some Questions on Their Relations.* London: Longmans, Green, 1956.

Mbiti, John S. *African Religions and Philosophy.* New York: Praeger, 1969.

McCabe, L. D. *Divine Nescience of Future Contingencies a Necessity.* New York: Phillips and Hunt, 1882.

———. *The Foreknowledge of God.* Cincinnati: Granston and Stowe, 1887.

Milingo, Emmanuel. *The World in Between: Christian Healing and the Struggle for Spiritual Survival.* Maryknoll, N.Y.: Orbis, 1984.

Miller, Patrick D. "The Divine Council and the Prophetic Call to War." *Vetus Testamentum* 18 (1968): 100-107.

———. "El the Warrior." *Harvard Theological Review* 60 (1967): 428-31.

———. "God the Warrior." *Interpretation* 19 (1965): 39-40.

———. *The Divine Warrior in Early Israel.* Harvard Semitic Monographs 5. Cambridge: Harvard University Press, 1973.

Mills, Mary E. *Human Agents of Cosmic Power in Hellenistic Judaism and the Synoptic Tradition.* Journal for the Study of the New Testament Supplement Series 41. Sheffield: JSOT Press, 1990.

Montgomery, John Warwick, ed. *Demon Possession: A Medical, Historical, Anthropological and Theological Symposium.* Minneapolis: Bethany House, 1976.

Morgenstern, J. "The Mythical Background of Psalm 82." *Hebrew Union College Annual* 14 (1939): 29-126.

Mullen, E. Theodore. *The Assembly of the Gods: The Divine Council in Canaanite and Early Hebrew Literature.* Harvard Semitic Monographs 24. Chico, Calif.: Scholars Press, 1980.

Murray, R. *Cosmic Covenant: Biblical Themes of Justice, Peace and the Integrity of Creation.* Great Britain: Sheed & Ward, 1992.

Nel, P. J. "The Conception of Evil and Satan in Jewish Traditions in the Pre-Christian Period." In *Like a Roaring Lion—Essays on the Bible, the Church and Demonic Powers,* 6-7. Edited by Pieter G. R. de Villiers. Pretoria: University of South Africa, 1987.

Nigosian, Solomon Alexander. *Occultism in the Old Testament.* Philadelphia: Dorrance, 1978.

O'Brien, P. "Principalities and Powers: Opponents of the Church." *Evangelical Review of Theology* 16 (October 1992): 353-84.

Osterreich, Traugott Konstantin. *Possession and Exorcism: Among Primitive Races, in Antiquity, the Middle Ages and Modern Times.* 1921. Reprint, New York: Causeway, 1974.

Page, Hugh R. The Myth of Cosmic Rebellion: A Study of Its Reflexes in Ugaritic and Biblical Literature. Supplements to *Vetus Testamentum* 65. Leiden: E. J. Brill, 1996.

Page, Sydney H. T. *Powers of Evil: A Biblical Study of Satan and Demons.* Grand Rapids, Mich.: Baker Book House, 1995.

Pagels, Elaine. *The Origin of Satan.* New York: Random House, 1995.

————. "The Social History of Satan, the 'Intimate Enemy': A Preliminary Sketch." *Harvard Theological Review* 84/2 (1991): 112.

Peck, M. Scott. *People of the Lie.* New York: Simon & Schuster, 1983.

Peels, H. G. L. *The Vengeance of God: The Meaning of the Root NQM and the Function of the NQM-Texts in Context of Divine Revelation in the Old Testament.* Oudtestamentische Studiën 31. Leiden: E. J. Brill, 1995.

Penelhum, Terence. *Religion and Rationality: An Introduction to the Philosophy of Religion.* New York: Random House, 1971.

Peretti, Frank. *Piercing the Darkness.* Wheaton, Ill.: Crossway, 1989.

————. *This Present Darkness.* Wheaton, Ill.: Crossway, 1986.

Pinnock, Clark, et al. *The Openness of God.* Downers Grove, Ill.: InterVarsity Press; Carlisle, U.K.: Paternoster Press, 1994.

Placher, William C. *The Domestication of Transcendence: How Modern Thinking About God Went Wrong.* Louisville, Ky.: Westminster/John Knox Press, 1996.

Plantinga, Alvin. *God, Freedom and Evil.* New York: Harper & Row, 1974.

————. *The Nature of Necessity.* Oxford: Clarendon, 1974.

Rice, Richard. *God's Foreknowledge and Man's Free Will.* Minneapolis: Bethany House, 1985.

Robinson, H. Wheeler. "The Council of Yahweh." *Journal of Theological Studies* 45 (1944): 151-57.

Rodewyk, Adolf. *Possessed by Satan.* 1963. Translated by Martin Ebon. Garden City, N.Y.: Doubleday, 1975.

Russell, Jeffrey Burton. *The Devil: Perceptions of Evil From Antiquity to Primitive Christianity.* Ithaca, N.Y.: Cornell University Press, 1977.

————. *The Prince of Darkness.* Ithaca, N.Y.: Cornell University Press, 1988.

————. *Satan: The Early Christian Tradition.* Ithaca, N.Y.: Cornell University Press, 1981.

Sauer, E. *The King of the Earth.* 1959. Reprint, Palm Springs, Calif.: Ronald N. Hayes, 1981.

Schäfer, Peter. *Rivalität Zwischen Engeln und Menschen: Untersuchungen zur rabbinischen Engelvorstellung.* Berlin: Walter de Gruyter, 1975.

Schlier, Heinrich. *Principalities and Powers in the New Testament.* New York: Herder and Herder, 1961.

Schmidt, Wilhelm. *Der Ursprung der Gottesidee: Eine historisch-kristische und positive Studie.* 12 vols. Münster in Westfalen: Aschendorffsche Verlagsbuchhandlung, 1926-1955.

Scott, M. "The Morality of Theodicies." *Religious Studies* 32/1 (1996): 1-13.

Sider, Ronald J. *Christ and Violence.* Scottdale, Penn.: Herald Press, 1979.

Smith, Jonathan Z. "Towards Interpreting Demonic Powers in Hellenistic and Roman Antiquity." *Aufstieg und Niedergang der römischen Welt (1978): 2.16.1, 425-39.*

Snaith, N. A. "The Advent of Monotheism in Israel." *The Annual of Leeds University Oriental Society* 5 (1963-65): 100-13.

Stewart, J. S. "On a Neglected Emphasis in New Testament Theology." *Scottish Journal of Theology* 4 (1951): 292-301.

Surin, Kenneth. *Theology and the Problem of Evil.* Oxford: Blackwell, 1986.

Tate, M. E. "Satan in the Old Testament." *Review and Expositor* 89 (Fall 1992): 462.

Thompson, R. Campbell. *The Devils and Evil Spirits of Babylonia.* London: Luzac, 1903-1904.

Tilley, Terrence W. *The Evils of Theodicy.* Washington, D.C.: Georgetown University

Press, 1991.

Tremmel, William C. *Dark Side: The Satan Story.* St. Louis: CBP, 1987.

Tsevat, Matitiahu. "God and the Gods in Assembly." *Hebrew Union College Annual* 40/41 (1969-1970): 123-37.

Turner, Edith L. B. *Experiencing Ritual: A New Interpretation of African Healing.* Philadelphia: University of Pennsylvania Press, 1992.

———. "The Reality of Spirits." *ReVision* 15/1 (1992): 28-32.

Unger, Merrill Frederick. "Rethinking the Genesis Account of Creation." *Bibliotheca Sacra* 115 (January-March 1958): 27-35.

Wakeman, Mary. *God's Battle with the Monster: A Study in Biblical Imagery.* Leiden: E. J. Brill, 1973.

Waltke, Bruce K. "The Creation Account in Genesis 1:1-3: Part I: Introduction to Biblical Cosmology." *Bibliotheca Sacra* 121 (October-December 1975): 25-36.

———. "The Creation Account in Genesis 1:1-3: Part II: The Restitution Theory." *Biblotheca Sacra* 122 (July-September, 1975): 136-44.

Webb, Clement C. J. *Problems in the Relations of God and Man.* London: Nisbet, 1941.

Webber, Robert E. *The Church in the World: Opposition, Tension or Transformation?* Grand Rapids, Mich.: Academie/Zondervan, 1986.

Wingren, Gustaf. *The Living Word: A Theological Study of Preaching and the Church.* 1949. Translated by T. V. Pague. Philadelphia: Muhlenberg, 1960.

Wink, Walter. *Engaging the Powers: Discernment and Resistance in a World of Domination.* Minneapolis: Fortress, 1992.

———. *Naming the Powers: The Language of Power in the New Testament.* Philadelphia: Fortress, 1984.

———. *Unmasking the Powers: The Invisible Forces That Determine Human Existence.* Philadelphia: Fortress, 1986.

Worsely, Richard. *Human Freedom and the Logic of Evil: Prolegomenon to a Christian Theology of Evil.* London: Macmillan; New York: St. Martin's, 1996.

Wright, R. K. McGregor. *No Place for Sovereignty: What's Wrong with Freewill Theism.* Downers Grove, Ill.: InterVarsity Press, 1996.

Yamauchi, Edwin. "Magic or Miracle? Diseases, Demons and Exorcisms." In *The Miracles of Jesus,* 89-183. Gospel Perspectives 6. Edited by David Wenham and Craig Blomberg. 6 vols. Sheffield, U.K.: JSOT, 1986.

Yates, R. "Jesus and the Demonic in the Synoptic Gospels." *Irish Theological Quarterly* 44 (1977): 39-57.

———. "The Powers of Evil in the New Testament." *The Evangelical Quarterly* 52/2 (1980): 99.

Author/Subject Index